Saving America's Countryside

Saving America's Countryside

A GUIDE TO RURAL CONSERVATION

SECOND EDITION

Samuel N. Stokes, A. Elizabeth Watson & Shelley S. Mastran

with contributions by Genevieve P. Keller & J. Timothy Keller

FOR THE NATIONAL TRUST FOR HISTORIC PRESERVATION

The Johns Hopkins University Press / Baltimore and London

Published in cooperation
with the Center for American Places, Harrisonburg, Virginia

Both editions of this book were brought to publication with the
generous assistance of the Laurence Hall Fowler Fund. The first edition
was supported in part by grants from the Cecil Howard Charitable
Trust, the Eva Gebhard-Gourgaud Foundation, the Richard King Mellon
Foundation, and the National Endowment for the Arts.

The Johns Hopkins University Press
2715 North Charles Street, Baltimore, Maryland 21218-4319
The Johns Hopkins Press Ltd., London

ISBN 0-8018-5547-0, ISBN 0-8018-5548-9 (pbk.)

Library of Congress Cataloging-in-Publication Date will be found at the
end of this book.

A catalog record for this book is available from the British Library.

Title page illustration:
Ranch at foot of the Grand Tetons, Jackson Hole, Wyoming

Contents

Case Studies

MN

Proposed
Ice Age Trail •

WI

Madison ○

Dubuque County •

IA   Des Moines ○

Bonaparte •

MI

Lansing •

Eaton Co. •

Chicago ○

IL

IN

OH

MO

Louisville •   KY

Middlesboro •

Rugby •   Knoxville ○

TN

Horsepasture
River •

AR

MS

Jackson ○

Claiborne Co. •

LA

AL

GA

FL

ME

Portland ○

NY   VT   NH   Wells •

Brattleboro •   Vernon •

Syracuse ○   MA   Boston ○

Cazenovia •

Appalachian Trail •   CT   RI

New Haven ○   Guilford •

PA   Oley •   NJ   New York

Reading ○   Bucks Co. •

Philadelphia ○

Carroll Co. •   Baltimore

MD   Waterford

Snickersville   DE

Turnpike

Washington, DC

WV

VA

Tyrrell Co. •

Jonesborough •   Raleigh ○

NC

Union •

Columbia ○

SC

Sidebars

Preface to the Second Edition

Since the publication of the first edition of *Saving America's Countryside,* there has been substantial progress in developing more and better organizations and refining available techniques for rural conservation, and in the actual saving of our vanishing countryside. New rural conservation organizations, land trusts, and local government programs devoted to rural conservation—incorporating both natural and historic resources—have proliferated. Cooperation between local governments and nonprofits has become more common. Conservationists are more willing to work with those concerned with economic development and vice versa. Promising approaches to conservation that were experimental a decade ago have now become widespread. One is greenways, linking population centers to natural areas and natural areas to each other, for the benefit of both wildlife and people. Another is heritage areas—a concept that incorporates both conservation and economic development. Finally, the idea of sustainable development has gained widespread credence and promises a new foundation for future development and conservation in rural communities, enlisting new partners and encouraging new alliances.

There have also been disquieting developments. Suburban sprawl is worse than ever; federal laws that are behind much successful rural conservation are threatened; and the so-called "property rights" movement has slowed the pace of conservation in many communities. Finally, in this time of federal and state government downsizing, there is a growing realization that if conservation is going to happen, it is going to happen because local government and local nonprofit organizations are going to make it happen.

Why a new edition? We certainly wanted to report on these trends. We have added a chapter on how economic development can be made compatible with rural conservation and new ideas in the other chapters. We also wanted to bring you fresh stories of successful rural conservation at the community level. We have added case studies, dropped a few, and brought others up to date. A glance at the bibliography for this edition will attest to the wealth of new conservation publications available, many of them written to guide community leaders. We have written about new organizations that can help; added an appendix on using this book to teach rural conservation; and provided information on recent techniques, such as GIS and computer simulation, which were in their infancy when the first edition was in preparation.

We would like to reiterate our thanks to all of those who made the first edition possible, listed in the preface to that edition. Their contribution was and remains invaluable. It is they and their colleagues who make rural conservation happen.

There is a wealth of inspiration, innovation, and experience in America, and for the second edition we feel privileged to have talked with the following leaders working for local and state conservation organizations and units of government. We wish to thank DeWayne Anderson (Landmark Asset Services, North Carolina), Marjorie Atkins (Alliance for the Chesapeake Bay, Maryland), Brenda Barrett (Pennsylvania Historical and Museum Commission), Fred Belk (Downtown Union Revitalization Association, South Carolina), Robert Berner (Marin Agricultural Land Trust, California), Kathy Bero (Ice Age Park and Trail Foundation, Wisconsin), Teresa Biddick (Collin County, Texas), Betty Ann Bierele (Community Heritage Consultants, Wyoming), Tim Bishop (Baker City, Oregon), J. D. Brickhouse (Tyrrell County, North Carolina), Reeves Brown (Colorado Cattlemen's Association), Michele Byers (New Jersey Conservation Foundation), Richard Cawthon (Mississippi Department of Archives and History), Doug Cheever (Heritage Trail, Dubuque, Iowa), Marlene Conaway (Carroll County Planning Department, Maryland), Thomas L. Daniels (Agricultural Preserve Board, Lancaster County, Pennsylvania), Dawn Darbey (Nantucket Land Bank Commission, Massachusetts), Jim Davis (Tracks Across Wyoming), John Dorff (Eckerd Family Youth Alternatives, Inc., Tyrrell County, North Carolina), Tom Duffus (Adirondack Land Trust), Karen Edgecombe, Esq. (Dunkirk, Maryland), Hilda S. Fisher (Oley Valley Heritage Association, Pennsylvania), Chris Ford (Colorado Heritage Area Partnership Program), Rupert Friday (Maryland Office of Planning), Tom Gallaher (Silos & Smokestacks, Waterloo, Iowa), Shirley Girioni (Guilford Preservation Alliance, Connecticut), Thom Guzman (Main Street Iowa), Lanny Haldy (Amana Heritage Society, Iowa), Rhonda G. Henderson (Rockingham County, Virginia), Lisbeth Henning (Utah Heritage Foundation), Mavis Hill (Tyrrell County Community Development Corporation, North Carolina), Phoebe B. Hopkins (Berks County Conservancy, Pennsylvania), Steve Humphrey (Hugh Moore Park, Pennsylvania), Kat Imhoff (Piedmont Environmental Council, Virginia), Bruce Jensen (Texas Historical Commission), Stephen T. Johnson (Sudbury Valley Trustees, Massachusetts), Tom Kerr (Wildlands Conservancy, Pennsylvania), Faith Knapp (Cazenovia Advisory Conservation Commission, New York), Zad Leavy (Big Sur Land Trust), Tina Lewis (Park City, Utah), Nancy Lindroth (McCormick County Chamber of Commerce, South Carolina), G. Sage Lyons (Coastal Land Trust, Mobile, Alabama), Peggy Maio (Piedmont Environmental Council, Virginia), Jeff Marshall (Heritage Conservancy, Pennsylvania), Linda Mead (Heritage Conservancy, Pennsylvania), Constance Meek (City of Bonaparte, Iowa), James E. Miller (Claiborne County, Mississippi), Mary W. Miller (Historic Natchez Foundation, Mississippi), Kathy Mitchell (Snickersville Turnpike Association, Virginia), Susan Moerschel (Delaware Department of Natural Resources and Environmental Control), Ann Orth (Berks County Conservancy, Pennsylvania), Robin Pearson (Michigan Department of Natural Resources), Jim Pepper (Blackstone River Valley National Heritage Corridor, Massachusetts and Rhode Island), Feather Phillips (Pocosin Arts, Columbia, North Carolina), Raymond C. Pickering (Pennsylvania Department of Agriculture), Bill Powel (Carroll County, Maryland), Robert Quinn (New York State Tug Hill Commission), Tom Quinn (Wisconsin Farmland Conservancy), Myles Rademan (Park City, Utah), Dorothy Reister (Cazenovia Preservation Foundation, New York), Harold W. Roller (Virginia Cooperative Extension Service), Mikki Sager (Conservation Trust for North Carolina), Tom Saunders (Maryland Environmental Trust), Wendy Scott (Wisconsin Farmland Conservancy), Kimberly Sells (Town of Jonesborough, Tennessee), Sidney H. Shearin (Pettigrew State Park, North Carolina), Barbara Stagg (Historic Rugby, Tennessee), Sherry Staples (Vermont Land Trust), Brian Steen (Big Sur Land Trust, California), Bill Steiner (South Carolina Downtown Development Association), Clare C. Swanger (Taos Land Trust, New Mexico), Jack Thomas (Blackfoot Challenge, Missoula, Montana), Susan Van Wagoner (Snickersville Turnpike Association, Virginia), Doris Voltin (Westphalia Historical Society, Texas), Lynn Werner (Housatonic Valley Association, Connecticut), Nick Williams (Maryland Environmental Trust), Mark Wolfe (City of Deadwood, South Dakota), and Leonard Ziokowski (Economic Development Council of Northeastern Pennsylvania).

Many other conservation and preservation leaders freely contributed ideas and suggestions. In particular, we would like to thank Kathy Barton (Land Trust Alliance), Neal A. Brown, Esq. (New York City), Michael Clarke (Natural Lands Trust), Kevin Coyle (River Network), Page Crutcher (The Conservation Fund), Susan Doran (Land Trust Alliance), Frances A. Dubrowski, Esq. (Washington, D.C.), Cheryl Fischer (Montpelier, Vermont), Michele Frome (Institute for Conservation Leadership), Jennie Gerard (Trust for Public Land), Richard Hawks (SUNY Syracuse), John Linn Hopkins (Hopkins and Associates, Memphis, Tennessee), John C. Keene (Coughlin and Keene Associates, Philadelphia), Judith LaBelle (The Countryside Institute and Glynwood Center), Jessica Landman (Natural Resources Defense Council), Roy Mann (Roy Mann Associates, Austin, Texas), Robbin Marks (Natural Resources Defense Council), Ian McHarg (University of Pennsylvania), Marya Morris (American Planning Association), Elizabeth Morton (Massachusetts Institute of Technology), Phyllis Myers (State Resource Strategies), Terri Myers (Hardy, Heck, Moore and Associates, Austin, Texas), Marsha Oats (Hopkins and Associates, Memphis, Tennessee), Daniel P. (Pat) O'Connell (Evergreen Capital Advisors, Inc., Harvey Cedars, New Jersey), Sally Oldham (Scenic America), Debi Lee Osborne (Trust for Public Land), Teresa Opheim (Environmental Law Institute), Anne Pearson (Alliance for Sustainable Communities), Luther Propst (Sonoran Institute), Dianne Russell (Institute for Conservation Leadership), Donovan Rypkema (The Real Estate Services Group, Washington, D.C.), Matt Sexton (The Conservation Fund), Mark Shaffer (The Nature Conservancy), Stephen J. Small, Esq. (Boston, Massachusetts), Jimmy Neil Smith (National Storytelling Association), Susan M. Smith (University of Tennessee-Knoxville), Sandra Tassel (Trust for Public Land), Edward Thompson, Jr. (American Farmland Trust), Gary Werner (Partnership for the National Trails System), French Wetmore (French and Associates), Marilyn Wood (The Nature Conservancy), Lisa Wormser (Two Heads Communications, Washington, D.C.), and Marty Zeller (Conservation Partners, Denver, Colorado).

Federal officials again took the time to explain their programs and review drafts of what we wrote. In particular we would like to thank Calvin Beale (Economic Research Service, USDA), Bill Cobb (Consolidated Farm Service Agency), Bob Cox (Federal Emergency Management Agency), Craig Faanes (U.S. Fish and Wildlife Service), John Fay (U.S. Fish and Wildlife Service), Noel Gallehon (Economic Research Service), Jack Harris (Economic Research Service), William Kramer (U.S. Fish and Wildlife Service), Linda McClelland (National Park Service), Ben Mieremet (National Oceanic and Atmospheric Administration), Craig Schafer (National Park Service), Stuart Tuller (Environmental Protection Agency), and Lloyd Wright (Natural Resources Conservation Service).

A number of staff at the National Trust provided support and guidance, notably Constance Beaumont, Daniel Carey, Paul Edmondson, Cheryl Hargrove, Mary Humstone, Susan Kidd, Dan Marriott, and Amy Jordan Webb. A special contribution was made by Clare Novak, who worked on the bibliography and sources of assistance. Rebecca Brown and John Meisel each contributed substantively to research for all chapters of the book, including case studies and sidebars. Dan Marriott drew the illustrations of rural design guidelines in Chapter 4.

We wish to thank Genevieve P. Keller, Principal, Land and Community Associates, and J. Timothy Keller, Chair, Department of Landscape Architecture, Iowa State University, for their valuable insights on rural communities and many contributions to the first edition.

This second edition would not have been written without the strong support of the National Trust. Many thanks to Henry Jordan, Richard Moe, and Peter Brink for their endorsement of the project.

We are especially grateful to the Claneil Foundation, without whose support of the National Trust's Rural Heritage Program this edition could not have been prepared.

We are once again most grateful to George F. Thompson, president of the Center for American Places, our editor, Anne Whitmore, and their colleagues at the Johns Hopkins University Press for their guidance, patience, and encouragement. They have been a pleasure to work with.

We each contributed to all chapters of the second edition. Samuel N.

Stokes, principal author of the first edition, was the editor of this edition and wrote the new appendix on educational programs. A. Elizabeth Watson was once again the primary author of chapters 2, 4, and 5 and of the conclusion. Shelley S. Mastran was the primary author of chapter 6, revised chapters 1, 3, 7, and 8, and coordinated the overall effort.

Finally, we wish to thank our families, friends, and colleagues for encouraging us to undertake this second edition and bearing with us while we worked to bring this book to press.

Samuel N. Stokes
A. Elizabeth Watson
Shelley S. Mastran

Preface to the First Edition

Our love of America's countryside motivated us to write this book. We find many attractions in rural America: certainly they include streams to canoe, mountains to hike, productive farmland to behold, and historic small towns to explore. But more important, rural America has been home for significant periods of our lives, and it is where many of our relatives and friends reside. We feel privileged to have been able to work for its conservation.

As have many Americans, we have become increasingly concerned about the many threats to the rural environment we cherish and have puzzled over how to protect it. There are excellent publications on land trusts, zoning, historic preservation, and farmland conservation, but none gives an overview of all the techniques that can be used to protect the rural environment, particularly if one is concerned not about just one resource, but about all the resources that make a rural community unique. It was out of this concern that this book was born.

It was out of this same concern that one of the authors, Samuel N. Stokes, urged the National Trust for Historic Preservation to establish its Rural Program in 1979. The program has focused national attention on the importance of America's diverse rural historic resources, including the environments of which they are a part, and forged new alliances among organizations concerned with the protection of historic, natural, and agricultural resources. The program staff, which for several years consisted primarily of Samuel N. Stokes and A. Elizabeth Watson, advised rural communities, wrote publications, and led workshops on the techniques for protecting rural areas. The program started in the Trust's Mid-Atlantic Region and is now a national program, coordinated from the organization's headquarters.

Two major components of the Rural Program were demonstration projects in Cazenovia, New York (Case Study 6), and Oley, Pennsylvania (Case Study 1), designed to show how rural communities could protect their natural, historic, and agricultural resources by working through both local government and nonprofit organizations. The two communities, chosen competitively, had outstanding resources and, most important, a strong local commitment to protect what they had. In collaboration with the College of Environmental Science and Forestry of the State University of New York at Syracuse (in the case of Cazenovia) and the Berks County Conservancy (in the case of Oley), the Rural Program staff worked with these communities intensively from 1980 to 1984, advising them on the range of techniques described in this book. Although the National Trust and other outside advisors were much involved in these protection efforts, the leadership for the projects was always at the local level and the Trust benefited from the collaboration at least as much as did the communities.

This book would not have been possible without the assistance of numerous individuals. First, we would like to thank the residents and leaders of Cazenovia and Oley who allowed the National Trust to work in their communities. Without this first-hand experience and the insights they provided, we could never have written this book. In Cazenovia, we are particularly indebted to Don R. Callahan, Andrew F. Diefendorf, Faith T. Knapp, Terry R. LeVeque, James D. Mietz, and Dorothy W. Riester; in Oley, to E. Garrett Brinton, Dennis G. Collins, Hilda S. Fisher, Andy Glick, Phoebe L. Hopkins, Jane Levan, Duane E. Pysher, and Donald Shelley. In addition to these individuals, volunteers too numerous to name devoted many hours to filling out inventory forms, taking photographs, preparing maps, checking well gauges, and performing many other essential tasks.

Much of the inspiration for this book has come from the leaders of local and state conservation organizations and from local and state officials across the country. They patiently described protection programs in their communities, and the case studies are the result of their contributions. In particular we would like to thank the following leaders of nonprofit organizations: Mark C. Ackelson (Iowa Natural Heritage Foundation), Thomas C. Bailey (Little Traverse Conservancy, Michigan), Richard W. Carbin (Vermont Land Trust), Constance K. Chamberlin (Waterford Foundation, Virginia), Doug Cheever (Heritage Trail, Iowa), Caroline Evans (Guilford Land Trust, Connecticut), Joseph M. Getty (Historical Society of Carroll County, Maryland), Hank Goetz (Lubrecht Forest, Montana), Ralph H. Goodno, Jr. (Housatonic Valley Association, Connecticut), Samuel M. Hamill, Jr. (Middlesex-Somerset-Mercer Regional Study Council, New Jersey), Robert J. Hammerslag (Essex Community Heritage Organization, New York), Jean W. Hocker Jackson Hole Land Trust, Wyoming), Robert J. Kiesling (Nature Conservancy, Montana), Randi S. Lemmon (Housatonic Valley Association, Connecticut), Fredric L. McLaughlin (Citizens Concerned about I-69), Morton K. Mather (Laudholm Trust, Maine), Richard M. Monahon, Jr. (Historic

Harrisville, New Hampshire), Robert Myhr (San Juan Preservation Trust, Washington), William H. Schmidt (Vermont Land Trust), Marc Smiley (Yakima River Greenway Foundation, Washington), Barbara Stagg (Historic Rugby, Tennessee), Brian L. Steen (Big Sur Land Trust, California), Bill Thomas (Friends of the Horsepasture, North Carolina), Gary Werner (Ice Age Trail Council, Wisconsin), Frank A. Wright (Cranbury Housing Associates, New Jersey), and Martin E. Zeller (Colorado Open Lands).

We are also most grateful to the following local and state officials: Stephen E. Aradas (McHenry County, Illinois), Catherine W. Bishir (North Carolina State Historic Preservation Office), K. Marlene Dorsey Conaway (Carroll County, Maryland), Daniel R. Cowee (Teton County, Wyoming), Arthur A. Davis (Pennsylvania Department of Environmental Resources), Dennis A. Gordon (Hardin County, Kentucky), and Charles E. Roe (North Carolina Heritage Program).

We have been assisted by many other conservationists and preservationists who inspired us and freely contributed ideas and suggestions. In particular, we would like to thank Joe Belden (Housing Assistance Council), Norman A. Berg (American Farmland Trust), Kathleen A. Blaha (Trust for Public Land), Christopher N. Brown (American Rivers), David Cottingham (Washington, D.C.), G. Ken Creighton (Nature Conservancy), Janet Diehl (Trust for Public Land), Ben Drake (Highlander Center), Benjamin R. Emory (Land Trust Exchange), Lynne Espy (North Yarmouth, Maine), Robert J. Gray (American Farmland Trust), Richard Hawks (State University of New York at Syracuse), Robert G. Healy (Conservation Foundation), John Jakle (University of Illinois), Mark B. Lapping (Kansas State University), Stanford M. Lembeck (Cooperative Extension Service, Pennsylvania), Stephen U. Lester (Citizen's Clearinghouse for Hazardous Wastes), Chester H. Liebs (University of Vermont), Richard A. Liroff (Conservation Foundation), Jim Lyon (Environmental Policy Institute), Edward T. McMahon (Coalition for Scenic Beauty), Margaret S. Maizel (American Farmland Trust), Robert Z. Melnick (University of Oregon), Erik J. Meyers (Environmental Law Institute), James F. Palmer (State University of New York at Syracuse), Caroline Pryor (Land Trust Exchange), Thomas W. Richards (Arlington, Virginia), Nobby Riedy (Wilderness Society), Frederick Steiner (University of Colorado, Denver), Robert E. Stipe (Chapel Hill, North Carolina), Isaac N. P. Stokes (Jericho, Vermont), Thomas E. Waddell (Conservation Foundation), and Warren Zitzmann (Falls Church, Virginia).

Numerous federal officials took time to explain their programs and review drafts of what we wrote. In particular we would like to thank Ty Berry (U.S. Fish and Wildlife Service), Gary R. Evans (U.S. Department of Agriculture), John J. Fay (U.S. Fish and Wildlife Service), Cathy A. Gilbert (National Park Service), Robert A. Hoppe (U.S. Department of Agriculture), Alan Jabbour (American Folklife Center), Robert J. Karotko (National Park Service), Don L. Klima (Advisory Council on Historic Preservation), Linda F. McClelland (National Park Service), Donald E. McCormack (U.S. Soil Conservation Service), Hugh C. Miller (National Park Service), Carol D. Shull (National Park Service), William S. Sipple (Environmental Protection Agency), LaVerne Smith (U.S. Fish and Wildlife Service), and Richard C. Spicer (National Park Service).

The book would not have been possible without a great deal of assistance and understanding from several staff members at the National Trust (both past and present), notably Greg Coble, Bonnie Cohen, Paul W. Edmondson, Marilyn Fedelchak, William B. Hart, Peter Hawley, Mary M. Humstone, Russell V. Keune, Mary C. Means, Elizabeth S. Merritt, Stefan Nagel, Charles F. Rotchford, and J. Jackson Walter. Douglas R. Horne designed the demonstration programs in Cazenovia and Oley; Susan Kidd did extensive research for Chapter 6; and Diane Maddex, director of the Preservation Press, provided guidance and assistance from the beginning and arranged for the book's publication. Monica B. Rotchford, the Rural Program secretary from its inception, typed and retyped the manuscript, made numerous suggestions to improve it, and cheerfully put in long hours on its final production.

Many others too numerous to mention helped us immeasurably in providing information, reviewing drafts, and obtaining illustrations.

We are also most grateful to George F. Thompson and his colleagues at the Johns Hopkins University Press, and Carolyn I. Moser, our copyeditor. They made numerous helpful suggestions to improve the text and illustrations.

We are particularly grateful to the Cecil Howard Charitable Trust, the Eva Gebhard-Gourgaud Foundation, the Fowler Fund, the Richard King Mellon Foundation, and the National Endowment for the Arts for their generous support of this book. We also wish to thank the Geraldine R. Dodge Foundation and the J. M. Kaplan Fund for their generous assistance in helping establish the Rural Program.

Many of the drawings were prepared especially for this book. For the maps in Chapter 3, we gratefully acknowledge the contributions of the volunteers and staff of the Cazenovia Community Resources Project, the students and faculty of the State University of New York at Syracuse, and Land and Community Associates of Charlottesville, Virginia. Special thanks are due to Frederick Schneider, AIA, Shaun Eyring, and W. Thomas Ward of Land and Community Associates, who, under the direction of J. Timothy Keller, prepared many of the drawings.

Each author has worked in rural conservation and contributed ideas to the entire manuscript. Samuel N. Stokes developed the concept of the book and was its editor and principal author. He was the primary author of Chapters 1, 3, 6, and 7 and wrote portions of the other chapters. A. Elizabeth Watson was the primary author of Chapters 2, 4, and 5 and the Conclusion. Genevieve P. Keller wrote portions of Chapters 1, 2, 3, and 7. J. Timothy Keller contributed to the sections on scenic areas and design guidelines and Case Studies 7, 14, and 24.

Finally, we wish to thank our families and friends for their inspiration, encouragement, patience, and support over the years it has taken to make this book a reality.

Samuel N. Stokes
A. Elizabeth Watson
Genevieve P. Keller
J. Timothy Keller

Saving America's Countryside

Introduction: Rural Conservation, a Strategy for Sustainability

Rural Americans protect their communities for a variety of reasons. Some begin their endeavors because of a burning issue—a proposed highway next to a scenic river, a shopping mall planned for prime farmland, or the imminent demolition of the last one-room schoolhouse in the county. Others become involved because they sense a general threat—often increased or unplanned development—and believe that existing efforts are inadequate to counteract it. Some are interested in protecting natural areas; others want to save farmland or historic buildings; growing numbers have a concern for the total environment and its sustainability. They may be elected officials, members of a community group, old-timers, or newcomers. Their livelihoods may be farming or ranching, or they may work in a local business or in the nearest town. If you are one of these people, whatever your interests, whoever you are, this book is intended for you, the concerned citizen who wants to take action locally to protect and conserve the heritage and resources of a rural community.

If you are already part of a group, so much the better. Although it is true that one person can make a difference, group action (which in this context includes government action) is more effective than one person working alone. Organizing to protect the countryside often follows a typical process: a small group of people get together, outline the problems they see, conduct research on the needs of the community, define a mission, develop a strategy and program, and begin the long, hard haul to make it all work. From holding meetings to buying land, group action can help you accomplish dozens of tasks. You need people, knowledge, money, and access to the media and public officials—frequently all at once and in a hurry. This book helps you to divide the process of organizing and taking action into manageable steps.

Before going further, let us discuss definitions. Few people, whether scholars, citizens, or public officials, agree on what, precisely, is "rural." In this book, the definition is up to the reader to decide. Generally, we expect the place in question to be a relatively sparsely populated area that lies beyond the city and its suburbs; it is a place where natural resources are the basis for at least some of the residents' livelihoods—farming, ranching, fishing, timbering, mining, or outdoor recreation, among others.

What we mean by "rural conservation" is more important. The word "conservation" means, in the traditional sense imparted by Gifford Pinchot, the turn-of-the-century founder of the U.S. Forest Service, the wise use and management of natural resources to achieve the greatest good for the greatest number of people for the longest period of time. Conservation as Pinchot knew it was a rather utilitarian attitude; he had little use for the concern of his contemporary, John Muir, for places of wild beauty. Today, however, the idea of wilderness preservation is regarded by conservationists as one kind of "use" or "management." Our own, expanded concept of conservation not only acknowledges this more modern attitude but also embraces the idea of the *community* as a resource, from individual farms or landholdings, to social institutions, to the local economy and sustainability of the community as a whole. The rural communities that people have managed to build over the years, using both the natural resources at hand and their own talents and traditions, represent a substantial investment. That investment deserves our respect and creativity as we protect it and build upon it. Rural conservation, then, includes protecting natural and scenic resources, preserving buildings and places of cultural significance, and enhancing the local economy and social institutions.

Rural America has never been static. We recognize the inevitability, and desirability, of change. Rural conservation calls for the foresight to manage change: to minimize its negative effects and to use it to improve the community's economic vitality, employment and educational opportunities, municipal services, and civic amenities. We believe that change need not preclude respect for natural areas, retention of agriculture, and preserving diverse cultural and historic resources. Indeed, rural communities should demand no less.

Many forces work against rural conservation, though often with the best of intentions, and these forces are frequently outside your community's control. Contaminated wells may lead local authorities to extend water and sewer lines, to meet residents' health needs, but water and sewer lines characteristically lead to development pressures that threaten farmland or create denser population growth than existing roads or schools can handle. An example of well-intended actions outside a community's direct control may be the decisions of the state highway department: rural communities traditionally have needed better roads to get their goods to market; now, however, improved roads may bring increased development. Similarly, changes in federal farm or tax policy may have an enormous effect on a farmer's decisions about what and how much to plant, or whether to plant at all, or may affect a real estate developer's expectation that an office building at the new highway interchange miles outside the city limits will be a success.

Still other obstacles to rural conservation lie within the community. Many property owners are reluctant to accept even well-thought-out regulation of changes to their properties. Likewise, many developers do not wish to incorporate into their designs desirable but unprofitable features, like those to counteract noise, traffic problems, storm-water runoff, or other unhappy impacts of new development. Convincing both owners and developers to act in the interests of the community at large, for the common good, is a difficult challenge. Simply stating that well-planned development enhances everyone's property values is hardly enough when the benefits of conservation are long term but the profits of development are short term. Even those who are anxious to pursue rural conservation may find problems within their ranks. Too frequently, those working to protect various rural resources have pursued separate strategies. Moreover, rural communities frequently lack the funds and knowledge necessary to deal firmly with development pressures or to approach creatively the problems of declining population. In the latter situation, a community may feel compelled to welcome any kind of development that offers taxes and employment, no matter what the trade-offs. This book suggests ways for you to help your community develop a rural conservation program in spite of the obstacles. Although the issues and the solutions can differ greatly from community to community, we believe the following principles are common to most successful rural conservation programs.

Rural conservation should integrate natural resource conservation, farmland retention, historic preservation, and scenic protection. Rural conservation offers an opportunity for people with a broad range of concerns to work together to protect and improve their communities. While there may be good reasons in some instances for those concerned with protecting wildlife habitat, for example, to organize separately from those concerned with preserving farmland or historic buildings, joining forces often makes more sense. Seemingly different concerns are often in fact closely linked. The windbreak that is designed to prevent soil erosion also provides habitat for wildlife and is a scenic element in the landscape. The historic farmhouses and barns prized by the local historical society are far more interesting if they are still used by farm families and surrounded by actively farmed land. In addition, most of the techniques designed to protect these resources are the same. If a new zoning ordinance or easement program is proposed for a community, it will be more effective—and easier to marshal public support for—if it addresses all of a community's threatened resources, not just one or two.

A successful rural conservation program is linked to the social and economic needs of the community. A program that does not take into account social and economic needs is unlikely to gain wide community support. Direct action on such concerns as inadequate low-income housing, joblessness, or the problems of minorities and single-parent families may be beyond our agenda as conservationists, but we should at least make sure that our programs do not create problems for those attempting to address those concerns. Moreover, there may indeed be opportunities to combine rural conservation with the advancement of other community interests toward achieving sustainability: Conserved resources can attract tourists and new employment opportunities, and historic houses can be rehabilitated for low-income housing, to mention but two examples. By the same token, social service organizations should not ignore conservation issues. Rural conservation is important to everyone, whatever their circumstances.

Rural conservation programs will be more sustainable if local governments and private nonprofit organizations cooperate. Local governments and private nonprofit organizations each have strengths and weaknesses. Working together makes it possible for each to do what it does best while making up for other's disadvantages. Some activities, such as environmental inventories, can be undertaken cooperatively. Other projects are best handled by one or the other, but preferably in complementary ways. For instance, local government can regulate the use of private land in a way that a nonprofit organization obviously cannot. Involvement of local government may confer legitimacy on a rural conservation program, in many people's eyes. On the other hand, a nonprofit organization can undertake more controversial projects, can deal with landowners who may not trust government, is less bound by rules, and generally can act faster. If a key parcel of lakefront property, the ideal site for a much-needed county park, suddenly comes on the market, a nonprofit organization may be able to buy it quickly. The local government, on the other hand, may be required to get approval from the voters, by which time the property may have been sold to another party or become too expensive to acquire. Yet, the private nonprofit organization can subsequently sell the lakefront site to the local government, which may have the long-term resources to develop and maintain the park. In many communities, environmental organizations have histories of adversarial relationships with local government. This may be inevitable in some communities; we believe, however, that in many more there are great opportunities for each to help advance the rural conservation agenda of the other.

Rural conservation programs will be more effective if they rely on more than one technique. If successful rural conservation calls for the cooperation of local government and nonprofit organizations and an integrated approach to protecting multiple resources, it follows that a strategy of using multiple techniques to protect the character of rural communities is also desirable. For example, you can seek to protect wetlands by simultaneously educating the public about their importance, regulating their exploitation through ordinances, and acquiring them by donation.

The public should be involved at all stages. The more you engage people in your community in planning a rural conservation program, the more ownership they will have in it and the better will be your chances for success. You cannot alienate or exclude any group—farmers, newcomers, public officials, or the press—and expect to succeed. For rural conservation to succeed, public involvement has to be more than keeping the public informed or seeking their opinions. Communities with effective public involvement strategies develop specific plans and improve their lines of communication for all decision making, and they make use of a wide variety of techniques to stimulate public participation well before entrenched positions are expressed in public hearings.

Sustainable rural conservation requires a long-term commitment. Although you may solve an immediate crisis—say, a water pollution threat or the proposed demolition of a historic bridge—other threats undoubtedly will occur in the future. If conservation programs are in place, the community will be better able to deal with future challenges. It takes time to reveal to a community the benefits of protecting its farmland, its wetlands, or its historic architecture. It also takes time to persuade landowners that implementing soil conservation plans or donating easements can be wise economically as well as environmentally.

No one book can cover all the conservation issues facing rural communities or describe all of the available protection techniques. *Saving America's Countryside* introduces you to the basic techniques necessary for a comprehensive rural conservation program, concentrating on those issues and techniques that apply at the local level to a large number of communities. This is not to say that action at the state and national levels is not very important as well; such action, however, is beyond the scope of this book. *Saving America's Countryside* is a how-to manual designed to be read in its entirety, but not everyone will use it that way. It also works as a reference book of ideas, information, and encouragement. You will find additional information, both on subjects that are covered and on related topics, in References and Suggested Reading, at the back, which is divided into sections for each chapter.

In a capsule, here is what this book is about: Chapter 1, which covers most of the conservation issues faced by rural communities, should be helpful both in deciding what issues you wish to address and in marshaling arguments to use in discussing the importance of protecting your community's resources. Chapter 2 describes the basic principles of organizing a rural conservation effort through local government and nonprofit organizations. Chapter 3 shows you how to gather and evaluate information about significant resources. Chapters 4 and 5 outline the specific tools that local governments and nonprofit organizations can use to protect a community's resources. Chapter 6 gives you ideas for combining economic development with rural conservation. Chapter 7 explains how to obtain help from the many national and state agencies and organizations that are prepared to assist communities. Chapter 8 discusses educating your community about the importance of its resources and of implementing protection programs and seeking support for these programs. Although the order of the chapters suggests a logical progression, working to protect special resources and achieve sustainability is never this neat. You will no doubt find that you are undertaking several of these activities simultaneously.

Although we will give you an overview of many rural conservation techniques, you will need to decide which ones will work in your community. Some techniques may be politically unacceptable, cost too much, or lack the necessary enabling state legislation. Addressing the issues in your community requires you to understand what is unique about your community and to develop a strategy that best fits it. This book suggests how you can build that understanding, what processes might work as you take action, and which ideas you should consider in tailoring programs to your own community. Regretfully we remind you of a platitude that is all too true here: there are no easy answers. While uncomplicated boosterism sometimes goes a surprisingly long way—any place looks better without litter, or with trees planted along the village sidewalks, or with a welcome sign at the entrance to the community—other more challenging programs will be needed as well. While the strategies of other communities that have tried rural conservation can provide some of the answers, ideas that work in one place generally need adaptation to be grafted onto another. Our concept of rural conservation calls on you to provide not only motivation and determination but also creativity and a "can-do" attitude. We hope that you will take the ideas in this book and make them work in your situation, or even develop new means of conserving resources.

Do not allow yourself to be overwhelmed by the magnitude of your conservation task and be paralyzed into inaction. You can start small and look for short-term successes. Perhaps all your group can do for now is develop a plan to educate fellow citizens about the value of the community's resources, or change one particularly troubling section of the zoning code, or work for the protection of a single significant property. So be it. While more comprehensive programs do have a better chance in the long run, you have to start somewhere.

Along the way, you are likely to encounter frustration or delay, opposition, or just plain stubbornness. It is not easy to gain the political cooperation or foster the team spirit so necessary to long-term success. If citizens in your community do not agree with your characterization of the issues, or are opposed to the solutions you propose, try to discover what their real concerns are. Their doubts may not be accurately revealed in their rhetoric. For instance, opposition to zoning as a way of protecting open space may in essence be opposition to government regulation, not to protecting open space per se. There may be other avenues to protecting open space—through an easement program, for example, as was the case along the Blackfoot River in Montana (see Case Study 5.2), or through a voluntary registry program, as the Heritage Conservancy has done in eastern Pennsylvania (see Case Study 5.1). Agreeing on a vision for your community before proposing solutions will certainly help, as we discuss in Chapter 2.

Also along the way, we expect, you will gain personal satisfaction from organizing a rural conservation program. Perhaps that satisfaction will come from associating with fellow residents and sharing information about and hopes for your community. Or perhaps that satisfaction will come from implementing a new program and seeing it gain widespread support within the community. At the very least, you will know that the things you value in your community stand a better chance of being enjoyed by future generations because you cared enough to advocate for and participate in a conservation program. The dividends are well worth the effort it will take.

Rural Concerns

1

INTRODUCTION

What makes your community special? Clean water? Rich farmland? A dramatic coast? Historic sites? Opportunities to hike and fish? The willingness of neighbors to help one another? No doubt there are many resources and less tangible values that have made you decide your community is a place worth protecting. No doubt you also have a number of concerns about the future of your community. Is the groundwater being polluted? Are farmers being forced out of business by mounting debts or encroaching development? Are vacation homes cluttering the waterfront? Is a new super-discount store being constructed on the edge of town, threatening the survival of downtown businesses? Are historic farmsteads falling into ruin? Are "no trespassing" signs blocking access to a favorite trail? Do you no longer know your neighbors? Perhaps your worries about the future have to do with what is happening to a nearby community. Or perhaps your concerns are more with the loss of a traditional way of life.

Identifying community values and concerns is a good way to start the rural conservation process; it can be enjoyable, too. For instance, the arts council of Harrison County, Iowa, located in the Loess Hills along the Missouri River, sponsored a day-long bus trip around the county. Participants observed, sketched, and mapped the natural and built environment and ended the day with a group discussion on the county's problems and potentials. The day's activity resulted in an increased commitment to improving the appearance of the towns and enacting conservation measures to protect the fragile bluffs overlooking the river.

1.1 Questions for a Rural Conservationist

Alan Gussow, artist, author, and speaker on environmental matters, suggests that rural conservation leaders start by asking themselves the following questions:

1. If you took a visitor around your community, what places would you be certain to include?

2. Where would you get out of the car and walk around? Why those places?

3. What are the recurring events, both natural and human, in your environment? Are they marked or observed? How?

4. Small towns and their surrounding countryside interact with each other. What indicators, if any, do you find in your town that reveal the beneficial effects of being in a rural setting? Can you think of any good qualities in the countryside that result from the nearness to a town?

5. What part of the environment in which you live is most likely to change? Is this change for the better? If not, why not, and what could you do to prevent or lessen the impact of this change?

6. If you could change one thing about your community, what would it be? Most importantly, what would be the first step to take in order to work toward that change?

(See Notes to Sidebars)

Identifying values and concerns is a first step toward developing a community vision: an idea of what citizens want the community to be in the future, say in fifteen to twenty years. Community change is inevitable, but with a clear vision, citizen groups can guide change; with a vision, communities can take positive action instead of reacting to outside forces.

While we can describe national trends, you have to decide what applies to your community. Obviously, each county and town has its own particular character and needs. A community in the West may have a water shortage and controversy over its allocation, while a community in the Midwest may have an abundant water supply but worry about its being polluted; a county in the Rockies may consist primarily of public land managed by the U.S. Forest Service and be particularly concerned about federal land-management policy, while a county in the South may be more concerned about the actions of private landowners. The needs of communities that are losing population or watching their economies decline, as is the case in much of the Great Plains, are very different from those of communities with rising populations and booming economies.

Fortunately you can protect many resources—such as wetlands, fertile soils, and cultural resources—at the community level. Other resources are more difficult to protect locally or are best addressed at the regional, state, national, or even international level. Watersheds, for instance, typically cross political boundaries. While a community can do much to protect the quality of its water, it probably will need to cooperate with neighboring jurisdictions as well. Although you can do a great deal to promote farmland retention, escalating land values in the region or declining commodity prices may force farmers out of business nonetheless. A problem such as acid rain requires not only federal action but also international cooperation. In this chapter we concentrate on those rural conservation issues that can be addressed, at least in part, at the local level. We will give you national data, arguments for conservation, and a context into which you can fit your own community's program. You will find in this chapter many references to federal laws and programs, which are discussed in the comparable sections of Chapter 7.

ECONOMIC, DEMOGRAPHIC, AND SOCIAL ISSUES

Inseparable from issues concerning the protection of the environment—broadly defined to include natural, agricultural, scenic, and historic resources—are economic and social issues relating to the growth and decline of communities and the livelihood of individuals. Although the causes and the symptoms may differ, both communities that are growing and those that are declining face environmental degradation.

Rural Communities That Are Growing

WHERE GROWTH IS OCCURRING

All Americans are familiar with the sprawl that has grown up around American cities and towns since World War II. As better roads, and particularly the interstate highway system, have made it easier for people to

1.1
This house in Purcellville, Virginia, was photographed just before giving way to a shopping center. The loss of familiar landmarks and landscapes prompts the start of many rural conservation programs.

1.2
Between 1990 and 1994, population increased in most rural areas, although certain counties, notably in the Plains states, experienced population decline. Most counties with increasing population are losing farmland and natural areas to new construction; counties with declining population often face severe economic problems.

Nonmetro Population Change, 1990-94

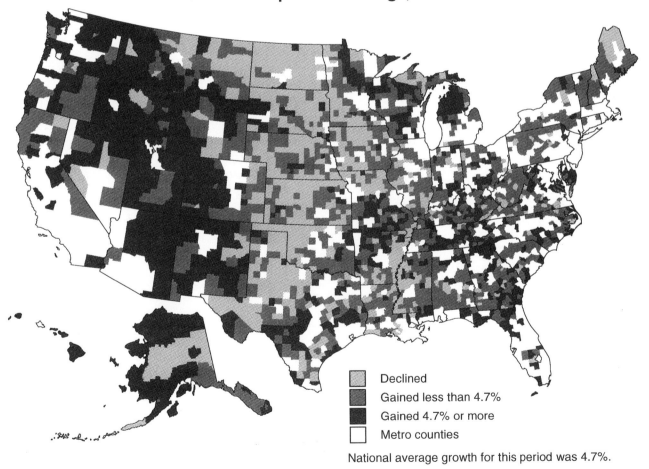

Declined
Gained less than 4.7%
Gained 4.7% or more
Metro counties

National average growth for this period was 4.7%.

commute longer distances to jobs, development has been pushed to the point that corridors of almost uninterrupted development now link many cities, such as Boston and Washington, D.C., on the East Coast, and Los Angeles and San Diego on the West Coast. Open space is fast disappearing across many regions of the United States. According to the National Growth Management Leadership Project, during the past twenty years, for example, Seattle's population grew by 38 percent, but the size of the urban area grew by 87 percent. During the same period, the New York metropolitan area grew by 8 percent, but the urbanized area as a whole grew by 65 percent.[1] In many parts of the country, a driver leaving a city is hard pressed to say where the city ends and the country begins. Shopping centers and complexes of office buildings have been built well outside urban downtowns, allowing commuters to live even farther out in the country. Piecemeal strip development of houses, stores, service stations, and fast-food restaurants along country roads accounts for the loss of much farmland and gives many rural areas a cluttered appearance. The term "exurban"—suggesting suburban development far from the city—applies to much of rural America. A 1995 report on California, for example, sponsored by Bank of America, the California Resources Agency, Greenbelt Alliance, and the Low Income Housing Fund, found that fifty years of sprawling development has destroyed wetlands, ecosystems, and agricultural land, polluted the air, caused a serious depletion of groundwater, and threatened one of the most essential assets of California—the beauty and drama of its landscape.[2]

In addition to the areas adjacent to towns and cities, many more remote rural areas are gaining in population. During the 1980s, although rural areas as a whole lost population, selected ones grew rapidly, and between 1990 and 1994, the majority of rural counties gained population. Most of the gains were in counties near metropolitan areas in the West, the upper Great Lakes region, parts of the South, the Northeast, and the Ozarks.

There are many reasons for growth in selected rural areas. Some people believe that rural areas are healthier, more pleasant places to live and work. For others the motivation to move there stems from a desire for less expensive housing and lower taxes. For corporations locating new plants in rural communities, the impetus is often cheaper land or labor, which in turn can lead to greater residential growth nearby. The areas that have grown fastest, however, are destinations for retirees and vacationers, such as northern Arizona, the Ozarks, and the Outer Banks of North Carolina.[3]

THE EFFECTS OF GROWTH

Whether rural growth is the result of urban sprawl or is taking place in more remote rural areas, it is having a profound influence on the environment. Some of the changes that accompany increased population are clearly beneficial: increased employment opportunities, and more services, such as better schools, health care, and roads. Unfortunately, growth usually brings problems as well. Some of the more general problems created by development are described below.

1.3 Templeton, Iowa. The farms and natural areas that traditionally surrounded towns created sharp edges between town and country and enhanced appreciation of both. The sight of a town's lights from a nearby field or glimpses of planted fields through a village street not only provide visual links between town and country but also reinforce the strong social, cultural, and economic ties between a rural settlement and its outlying area.

1.4 Change has always been a part of rural America. Here a farmer in New Lenox, Illinois, describes to a Natural Resources Conservation Service district conservationist how this round barn used to house fifty-six cows.

1.2 The Costs and Revenues of Development

Since the seminal 1974 study The Costs of Sprawl, *which showed that clustered development is more cost-effective than conventional single-family subdivision development, numerous studies have documented the costs and revenues of different types of development and different developmental patterns.*

For example, the American Farmland Trust studied residential development in Loudoun County, Virginia, and concluded that for all densities (from 1 unit per 5 acres to 4.5 units per acre), public costs exceed revenues and that this excess is greater with lower densities (American Farmland Trust 1986). A study conducted in Culpeper County, Virginia, found that residential development costs $1,242 more per unit in public services per year than it generates in revenue. Examining industrial, commercial, residential, open-space, and agricultural land use in three Massachusetts towns, the American Farmland Trust concluded that residential development costs more in services than it earns in tax revenues; industrial and commercial development brings in more tax revenue than it costs in services; and that open space and farmland, although bringing in little in taxes, cost even less in services and, therefore, are a

Inability of local governments to cope. Many rural governments are run largely by unpaid officials and part-time staff. They often are ill-equipped to deal with the increasing complexity of governing a larger population. Rural governments frequently do not have professional planners to help them manage growth and ensure that new development does not harm the environment.

Increased cost of services. Many rural community leaders believe that, because more development will increase the real estate tax base, it will help them balance municipal budgets. While additional tax revenues certainly are generated, the cost of the additional services needed by new residents almost always outstrips the new revenues. This is particularly true in communities where new businesses attract families with school-age children, as the cost of building schools exceeds all other municipal service costs by a wide margin. New residents may also demand improvements that natives found unnecessary, such as paving of roads, addition of special school programs, and an increase in police protection. In order to offset the cost of residential development, some communities try to attract commercial development, which contributes more in tax revenue than the cost of services it requires. Yet commercial development can detract even more from the rural character of a place and may, in turn, attract even more residential development.

Increased social tensions. Many rural communities have a close-knit character, and new residents may never be accepted totally by natives. The newcomers may have social, cultural, or educational backgrounds different from those of the existing population. They may have more money and different tastes. The immigration of wealthy outsiders (sometimes referred to as "gentrification") stimulates the local economy and may result in the preservation of the properties they purchase, but it may substantially alter the traditional social and cultural character of the community. The gentrification of a rural town may affect the agricultural economy if agricultural businesses are displaced by antique shops and boutiques, for example.

Nimbyism. The not-in-my-backyard (NIMBY) mentality often appears when communities feel threatened with intense development. Ironically, many owners of new homes in rural areas are among the most vocal in arguing for curbs on further development. People who have come to rural areas from more urban places usually have a strong appreciation for rural character: the beauty, open space, slower pace of life, and peacefulness they may have sought in moving. When new development is proposed—no matter how well it is planned—they are likely to object, often adding to tensions the longer-term residents may already feel about them.

Changes in land values. As new residents buy homes or build new ones, property values are likely to rise. This will certainly be welcome news for many landowners. For others, however, it will cause problems, particularly for young families who may find they can no longer afford to buy places of their own. The problem can be particularly acute in agricultural areas, where the price of land for farming or grazing may become prohibitive because of its value for development. This has happened in Jackson Hole, Wyoming, as it has in other parts of the West. In

Jackson Hole, the average price of a single-family home increased 38 percent per year between 1989 and 1994, by which time it was more than $550,000. In Jackson Hole and similar resort communities, the school teachers, firefighters, and waiters who earn their living in the service sector have a difficult time finding affordable homes, and many must now live in mobile homes or small cabins or commute long distances to work.[4]

ACCOMMODATION OF GROWTH

The amount of new growth that rural communities can accommodate varies. In some instances, where finite resources are at stake, almost any growth may cause problems. The community's water supply may already be stretched to the limit, or it may be that new construction can take place only on a dwindling supply of prime farmland, threatening the future viability of agriculture in the community.

Fortunately, in most cases growth can be accommodated, and, as described in subsequent chapters, a community can do much to ensure that the negative impacts of any new development are minimized. Development can be channeled into those sections of the community that are best equipped to deal with it—for instance, areas that are adjacent to existing towns or villages; areas that are not environmentally, historically, or visually significant; or areas where utilities and other community services can be offered at a reasonable cost. Rural communities should also ensure that, insofar as possible, developers pay for the costs added by the development. For instance, they can be asked to pay for environmental studies of the proposed building sites, for road improvements, for landscaping, and so forth. Finally, rural communities should, where appropriate, encourage developers to employ site planning and architectural styles that are compatible with existing buildings in the community and with the natural setting (for information on rural design guidelines, see Sidebar 4.12). If done well, new construction can enhance a rural community rather than detract from it.

TOURISM AND RESORTS

Developments associated with tourism and recreation are increasingly common throughout the country. Some, such as Steamboat Springs, a ski resort in Colorado, or Sea Pines, a tennis and golfing resort on the coast of South Carolina, are large-scale operations that create whole new communities consisting largely of second homes.

Attracting visitors is a high priority for many rural communities. Tourism and resort development can stimulate the local economy and provide new jobs without creating some of the obvious environmental problems that a polluting industry might. Moreover, visitors do not require expensive public schools for their children, and so local governments are likely to collect more revenue than they spend for added services.

There are problems with tourism, however. On Tangier Island in the Chesapeake Bay, for example, watermen rolling wheelbarrows full of crab pots at the end of a workday often find the community's narrow streets choked with day-trippers who come by ferry for an afternoon visit. Residents of the Amana Colonies, Iowa's leading visitor attraction,

tax surplus to local government (American Farmland Trust 1992).

Local communities can conduct their own cost-of-community-services (COCS) study without a professional economist—but experience with a computer spreadsheet is helpful, and persistence and familiarity with your community's budget and political processes are pluses. A handbook on how to conduct a COCS study, leading the reader through the basic steps, is available from the American Farmland Trust.

(See Notes to Sidebars.)

1.5
Tourism and recreation generate visitor dollars, but they can also lead to excessive development. Telluride, Colorado, is a former mining town and a National Historic Landmark. The adjacent ski resort has brought in economic revival, but new development has overwhelmed some of the community's historic and scenic qualities.

complain that visitors pick their apples, peek in their windows, and block their driveways. Scenic Napa Valley, California, and its famous wineries receive more than four million visitors each year—an eight-fold increase in the past ten years. The visitors were initially welcomed because they brought in additional income and helped to publicize the wines. Now, however, the boom in tourist-related development threatens the valley's primary functions of growing grapes and making wine.

Ironically, visitor-oriented businesses and developments often destroy the cultural, scenic, and natural qualities that attracted visitors in the first place. Many tourist sites are noted for their adjacent long stretches of fast-food restaurants, motels, campgrounds, gift shops, and gas stations. Too many visitors create crowded conditions, excessive traffic, noise, and pollution, especially on rural roads. Parking can become scarce, and pressure may be placed on existing infrastructure and services, such as police and fire protection. Too many visitors can harm the resources they've come to enjoy. A Civil War battlefield, for example, may become overrun with visitors to the extent that earthworks and other structures may be threatened. Many rural communities that become popular tourist destinations, such as Park City, Utah, also experience second-home, and even permanent home, development (see Case Study 6.3). Visitors may turn into long-term residents.

Resorts can create environmental problems, particularly when they are built in fragile ecosystems such as barrier islands or the steep slopes of mountains. Several towns in Vermont, for instance, are concerned about water pollution resulting from condominium development at ski resorts, where septic systems on the steep mountain slopes cannot adequately handle the waste water generated.

Since it is often the aesthetically pleasing environment that attracts visitors, it is in the self-interest of most communities with resorts and visitor attractions not to kill the goose that lays the golden eggs. It makes good economic sense to plan for tourism and to regulate development

in order to assure that the environment remains attractive. While some individual property owners may be able to make more money in an unregulated community, the population as a whole should benefit economically from reasonable environmental controls.

Rural Communities in Decline

While many rural communities are dealing with the problems of growth, many others are struggling to escape the grip of economic stagnation and decline. The decline may be resulting from local problems, such as the bankruptcy of a major business, the closing of a rail line, or a new highway's bypassing rather than including the community, or from national or international economic trends, such as a drop in commodity prices.

Many declining rural communities have relied for decades on agriculture or on the extraction or harvesting of a single natural resource, such as minerals, lumber, or shellfish. With improvements in the technology of resource extraction, agricultural economies of scale, competition from foreign suppliers, costs of pollution abatement, and resource depletion, employment in natural resource–based, extractive industries has seriously declined. In northern California, for example, between 1987 and 1993, some 3,800 sawmill jobs were lost, as timber companies found it less expensive to ship logs to mills closer to their markets than to process the lumber in mills near the forests. Del Norte County, with no railroad and no interstate access, was particularly hard hit by this restructuring and in 1995 had an unemployment rate of nearly 16 percent.[5] Cambria County, Pennsylvania, in the bituminous coal area of the state, saw five coal companies close in the past decade, with a loss of more than 15,000 jobs.[6] In such communities, residents must find new sources of employment and often desperately and sometimes recklessly pursue rural development strategies.

Also hard hit in the 1980s and 1990s have been communities in the

1.7
Many small towns, including Hillsboro, Texas, are working to enhance their downtown businesses, to compete with regional shopping malls and to stem sprawl. Here, an architect working with the Texas Main Street Center points out possible facade improvements to a store owner.

1.3 Boom and Bust

Some communities, particularly those near large-scale mining or construction projects, go through periodic cycles of boom and bust. Many new workers may be needed today because the price of the ore being extracted is high, but once the price of the ore goes down, or the vein runs out, there may be little need for those miners. Towns such as Crested Butte, Colorado, have been through several cycles of boom and bust. Often, boom towns have to absorb large numbers of workers quickly, without time to plan adequately or to provide for new housing and community services.

Local governments sometimes support mining and energy development, despite the potential problems, because of expectations of new jobs and economic development. Although initial construction projects employ local rural workers, many mining and energy development operations bring in specialized workers instead of hiring local people.

Great Plains, where rising interest rates for farmers, lower commodity prices, mechanization, and consolidation have led to a drop in population. During the 1980s, the nonmetropolitan counties of the Great Plains lost 4.9 percent of their population.[7] As farmers go out of business, so do the businesses they patronize. Vacant stores, abandoned gas stations, and gaping holes where buildings once stood are visual evidence of the major impact that economic decline has had.

While there are many possible solutions for communities that wish to manage growth, finding solutions for communities that are losing population poses a greater challenge. Some have managed to create new jobs by attracting new businesses. Winner, South Dakota (pop. 3,316) has become home to a nationwide hotel reservation service employing about fifty local workers. Communities blessed with attractive scenery, like Choteau, Montana (pop. 1,729), have been able to promote tourism. Clearly, more needs to be done to help rural communities diversify their economies and find new sources of income. Some rural organizations concerned with historic preservation have assisted in the revitalization of declining communities by promoting new uses for old buildings or by actually rehabilitating old buildings. In Bonaparte, Iowa (see Case Study 6.1), they have found that they have a particular opportunity to help provide better housing and promote economic development, since much substandard housing and many unused commercial properties are also of historic interest.

Revitalizing Small Towns

Small towns are the economic, cultural, social, and political centers in much of rural America. For centuries, the rural town has been the meeting place, where stores, schools, doctors, farm equipment dealers, and grain buyers have most often located. A rural town may also be the county seat, the home of a college, or the location of an industry.

Some rural settlements are hamlets consisting of fewer than a dozen structures. Often such settlements are located at a crossroads or near a boat landing or railroad depot. They may be dominated by a church, school, post office, diner, grain elevator, general store, gas station, or other local institution.

Few rural towns and hamlets are the diverse, largely self-sufficient communities they were when settled, or even twenty-five years ago. Rural Americans are increasingly making their purchases at regional "superstores" like Wal-Mart, in regional shopping malls, or in larger towns. Since the early 1960s, regional shopping centers and shopping centers located along highways ("strip" centers) have proliferated. In 1994 there were more than 2,100 Wal-Marts across the United States, and some 110 were added annually during the early 1990s. More recently, large discount department stores and other retail chain stores that specialize in one product line have proliferated. These superstores, many more than 100,000 square feet in size and accompanied by enormous parking lots, not only consume farmland and natural areas but often attract other businesses out of downtown to locate close by, thus contributing to sprawl.

As a result, many smaller towns and crossroad communities have suf-

1.8
Large discount retailers like this Wal-Mart outside State College, Pennsylvania, present serious competition for small town merchants. Typically located on the edge of town, such establishments consume acres of land for sprawling stores and enormous parking lots.

fered. Not only have businesses gone under, but also key social institutions, such as the local school, church, or post office, have often become the victims of consolidation in the name of cost-effectiveness. With the loss of their stores, schools, post offices, cafés, and gas stations, many villages survive as little more than a collection of houses, alone and out of context.

Many towns are now working to enhance their downtown businesses to compete with the malls by taking advantage of attractive historic store fronts, finding new uses for vacant and underutilized buildings, providing better parking, and assuring a full range of stores and services. These efforts often go hand-in-hand with land conservation efforts; rehabilitation and new construction downtown not only enhance the town but also protect the countryside. When Wal-Mart proposed a major new store outside of Greenfield, Massachusetts—originally on a ridge overlooking the Connecticut River—environmentalists allied themselves with businesses in the downtown to fight the proposal, and they won. The community leaders voted not to rezone the land, and the Wal-Mart was never built.

While towns and cities have developed successful strategies to promote their downtown businesses, the smaller crossroad settlements have received less attention and an increasing number of their merchants are going out of business (see Chapter 6).

The Residents of a Rural Community

A rural community's people are its most important asset. As each community was settled and developed, its residents gave it a unique character based on their ethnic, religious, and occupational backgrounds. Human commitment and energy created rural communities; their vitality today still relies on people. Some rural conservation organizations will decide that it goes beyond their scope to address social and economic concerns directly. Others may find that they have an opportunity not only to pro-

1.9
Preservationists have played constructive roles in the economic revitalization of small rural communities such as Harrisville, New Hampshire. When the company that owned the village mills went bankrupt in 1970, community leaders interested in protecting the village's historic buildings and revitalizing its economy established Historic Harrisville. With funds raised locally and nationally, the nonprofit organization purchased six commercial buildings in the village core and rented them to a variety of new tenants, including a manufacturer of wooden looms, an engineering firm, and a day-care center. This venture into real estate not only saved historic buildings but created jobs for residents.

tect the environment but also to improve the economic well-being of their community's residents.

There are social and economic problems that cannot be ignored in rural America. Rural poverty rates are consistently higher than poverty rates for urban areas, but rural poverty receives less attention. The signs of urban poverty—dilapidated tenements, scattered trash, and the homeless—are often more visible than those of rural poverty, which may be hidden from view on little-traveled back roads. A natural setting may make the scene of an unpainted farmhouse, outdoor privy, and gullied fields appear picturesque.

While rural poverty knows no boundaries, much is concentrated in certain areas such as Appalachia, the Ozarks, and the Mississippi delta region. In fact, more than one-half of the nation's rural poor live in the South. Rural poverty, like its urban counterpart, is more prevalent among blacks, Hispanics, American Indians, and migrant farmworkers. Inadequate housing is a particularly serious problem for these groups. Some rural poor live in large houses with no insulation and exorbitant heating costs, while others are crowded into rented shacks with no plumbing. A relatively high proportion of people living in rural areas are elderly, and many of them exist principally on Social Security payments.

Local governments in rural areas usually provide fewer services,

whether they be police, fire protection, public transportation, municipal water, or social services. In some cases there may be less need for these services than in cities. In others, it may be prohibitively expensive to offer them to widely scattered rural residents. While most communities provide public education, rural school children often have long bus rides and may have fewer opportunities to participate in remedial programs, advanced classes, and extracurricular activities. Many businesses also offer fewer services to their rural communities: bus service to rural communities is declining, and rural electric companies sometimes charge high installation fees to customers in remote locations. Rural water supplies are more likely to be contaminated, and health care, when available at all, may be inadequate and far away.

Each year many rural Americans move to town. Some may be forced to move because of increasing age, poverty, unemployment, or the lack of services. For others, there may be the lure of greater opportunities in

1.12
In many hamlets, such as Waterford, Virginia, the post office is one of the few remaining local services. In addition to providing an important function, it is a place where neighbors exchange greetings and news.

the city. Those who are leaving the countryside—whether dairy farmers in Wisconsin or ranchers in Montana—may be replaced by newcomers, but in the process, much of what makes Wisconsin Wisconsin and Montana Montana is lost. Saving land, water, wildlife, and historic buildings is indeed important, but if these resources are preserved while the existing population leaves, the success may be a hollow one. Conservationists should help make it possible for those who have traditionally lived in rural communities to continue to do so if they wish.

The Property Rights Movement

Prominent in recent years is a resentment of governmental controls, particularly over the use of land. In part a legacy of the Sagebrush Rebellion of the early 1980s, when western interests sought a return of federal land to state and local authorities, the property rights movement has members and spokespersons in all regions of the country. Property rights advocates resist zoning and other ordinances, federal landownership, federal regulation of wetlands and other resources, designations to the National Wild and Scenic Rivers System, and even listings in the National Register of Historic Places.

One of the chief arguments of the property rights movement is that land use ordinances, regulation, and designations constitute a "taking" of the value of private property and that just compensation is required by the Fifth Amendment to the Constitution as a remedy (see Sidebar 4.5). By 1995, eighteen states had passed some form of takings legislation, and takings legislation had been introduced in all other states except Connecticut. Takings bills have also been introduced in both the U.S. House and the Senate. Typically, takings legislation requires either that local governments conduct studies to predetermine how their programs might affect property owners or that government payments be made to those who can prove that the value of their property has been reduced by certain laws. Only three of the eighteen states with takings laws require such payments, known as "owner compensation."

Conservation leaders face a tough challenge in countering the arguments of property rights advocates. In many cases, the arguments are based on a belief in the supremacy of the rights of individuals over the common good. For example, a property owner wanting to build a marina along his shoreline might construe regulations establishing a 100-foot buffer against development along the shore—for the common good of preventing erosion and flood damage—as a taking. In such cases, even with excellent legal arguments on their side, conservationists often find themselves on the defensive, as property rights advocates press home their concerns about the ability of property owners to make an adequate return on their land and investments.

In fact, in the example of the 100-foot buffer zone, as long as the property owner is still able to achieve economic use of the land, such regulations are not a taking. Although the use of individual properties may be limited by regulation, with appropriate regulations overall community values can be enhanced, more than making up for the inconvenience, in both monetary and nonmonetary terms.

Property ownership and use do not exist in a vacuum. The public is often called upon to take action to ameliorate the negative impacts of careless or improper land use. As another example, poor timbering practices can silt up streams, reduce fish populations, and cause downstream flooding—all problems that other property owners or the public at large must pay to address when the owners of the land being lumbered do not pay for on-site prevention of these problems. Indeed, land values are often enhanced because of a property's proximity to such public improvements as water or sewer service or a major highway. Since there can also be beneficial impacts from land and natural resource development, the task of the community is to determine whether the benefits outweigh the costs and to minimize those costs with the least amount of government intrusion.

We now move on to specific environmental concerns, concerns which are in most cases closely related to the economic, demographic, and social issues already discussed. While we examine environmental resources individually, it is important to remember their interconnections. Water pollution may result not only in unsafe drinking water but also in declining fish population and species diversity. Removing trees along streams may lead not only to increased soil erosion on farmland but also to stream siltation, degradation of wildlife habitat, and loss of scenic quality.

WATER AND RELATED RESOURCES

Sufficient water of high quality for domestic consumption, agriculture, industry, recreation, and wildlife is among a community's most important assets. Water supply directly affects the economic value of land, and as anyone who has tried to buy waterfront property can attest, water has both scenic and economic value. Water-based recreation, including boating, fishing, and swimming, is the most popular form of outdoor recreation in the United States.

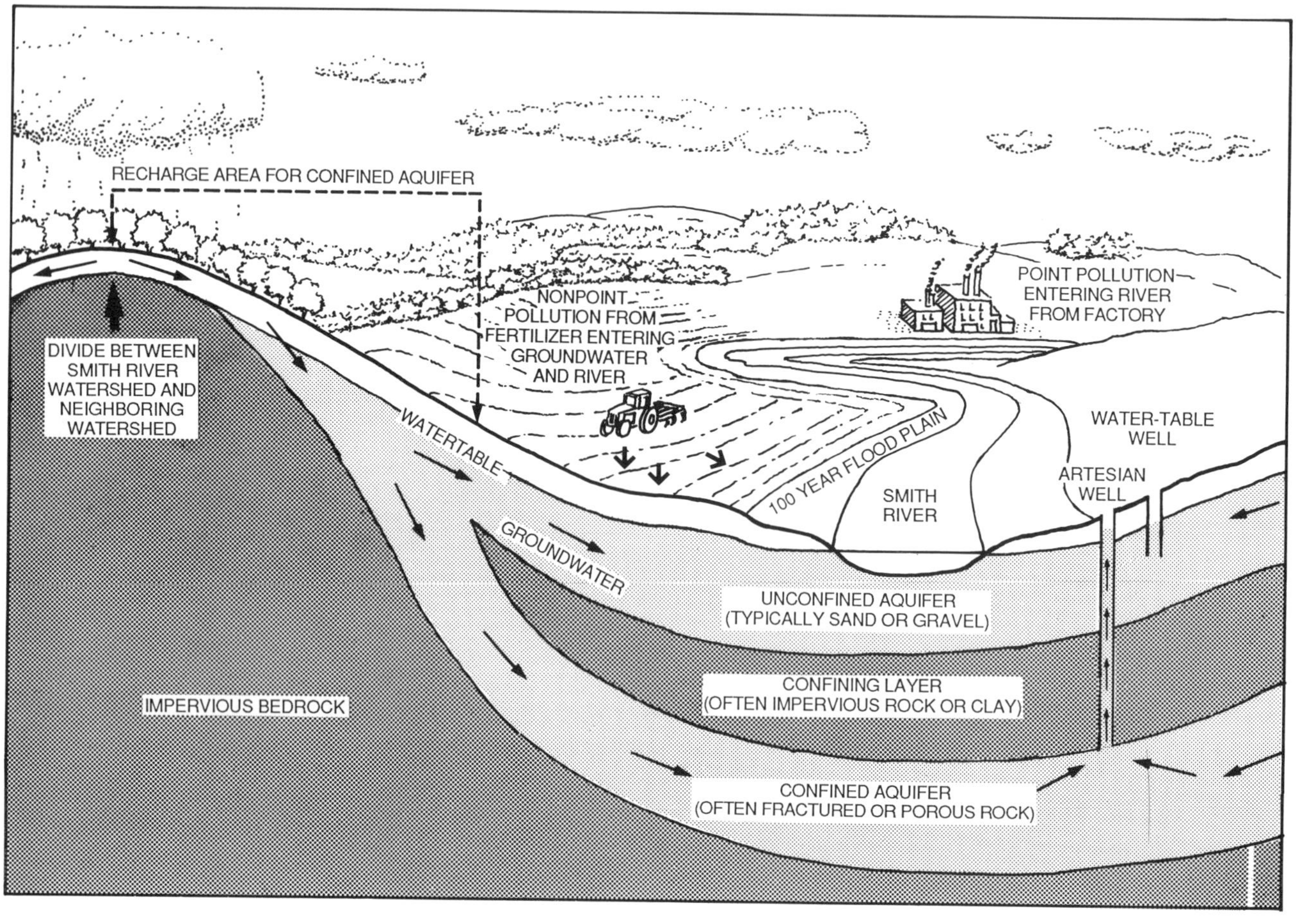
RECHARGE AREA FOR CONFINED AQUIFER
DIVIDE BETWEEN SMITH RIVER WATERSHED AND NEIGHBORING WATERSHED
NONPOINT POLLUTION FROM FERTILIZER ENTERING GROUNDWATER AND RIVER
POINT POLLUTION ENTERING RIVER FROM FACTORY
WATERTABLE
100 YEAR FLOOD PLAIN
SMITH RIVER
WATER-TABLE WELL
ARTESIAN WELL
GROUNDWATER
UNCONFINED AQUIFER (TYPICALLY SAND OR GRAVEL)
CONFINING LAYER (OFTEN IMPERVIOUS ROCK OR CLAY)
IMPERVIOUS BEDROCK
CONFINED AQUIFER (OFTEN FRACTURED OR POROUS ROCK)

1.13
The flow of water. This drawing is a simplified illustration of watersheds, water tables, groundwater, aquifers, aquifer recharge areas, floodplains, point source pollution, and nonpoint source pollution. The arrows indicate the direction of water movement. Rain and pollutants flow into surface water and groundwater. Pollution of groundwater, particularly in confined aquifers, is very difficult to correct.

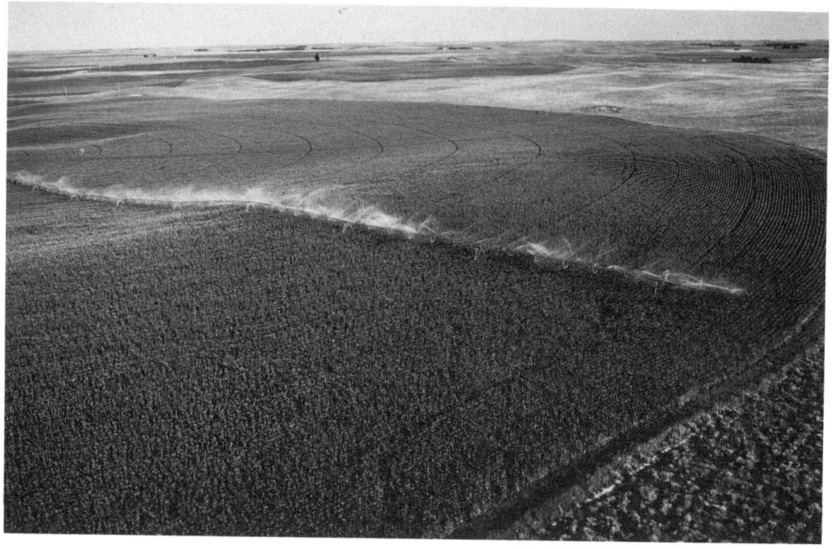

1.14
Center-pivot irrigation has become a familiar landscape feature—particularly to air travelers crossing the Plains. This system covers 40 acres of a Nebraska cornfield. Although irrigation allows greater crop production, underground aquifers are being depleted by it.

Water Supply and Quality

Surface water—streams, rivers, lakes—is the major source of water used in this country. It is replenished by rainfall and drainage from the surrounding watershed (the land area draining into a stream or other body of water). Groundwater is the other important source of water. Most rural Americans depend on groundwater for drinking, and about 37 percent of irrigation water is from the ground.[8] Although some groundwater is renewed by rain or melted snow that is absorbed into the soil, most groundwater has accumulated over centuries and cannot be replenished easily. Geologic formations called aquifers store groundwater, while the area of land that contributes water to an aquifer is called its recharge area. A recharge area may be quite distant from the place where the water is withdrawn.

Water use in the United States increases each year. Many communities allow more construction of homes, industries, and irrigation systems than their water supplies can support. They may eventually be forced to purchase water from other areas at considerable expense. Farmers are the biggest users of water, with irrigation accounting for 40 percent of all water withdrawals.[9] Most irrigation is in the West, particularly in California, Idaho, Colorado, and Montana, where per capita water consumption is many times greater than that of eastern states.

Many parts of the United States have abundant rainfall to replenish water supplies; those with little rainfall find water in short supply the year round. In the arid areas of the Southwest some rivers have had so much water removed that the flow is inadequate for boating, generating electricity, and the survival of aquatic life. The Colorado River, for in-

1.15
A Natural Resources Conservation Service district conservationist examines the soil in an irrigated field of the Imperial Valley in California. Here, salt buildup, caused by long-term irrigation, restricts crop growth and poses a major problem in much of the West.

1.16
Feedlots are a source of water pollution in many rural areas. The owner of this Arkansas farm has dealt with the problem by building a "debris basin" with help from the Natural Resources Conservation Service. Solids remain in the basin while liquids are strained out and used to fertilize fields.

1.4 Water Contaminants in Rural Areas

Sediments. Sediments released into surface waters through erosion result in cloudy water that threatens both plant and animal life by reducing the amount of light, and hence photosynthesis, in the water. Once they settle, sediments can smother life on the bottom and decrease the capacity of reservoirs. Sedimentation is a particular problem near plowed fields and construction sites.

Nutrients and oxygen-reducing wastes. Elevated concentrations of nutrients such as phosphates and nitrates from waste water and fertilizers promote the growth of algae and seaweed, which take the place of other aquatic plants that fish and wildlife prefer for food. Decomposing aquatic plants, sewage, and animal manure use up oxygen as they decay, depriving fish and other animals of the oxygen they need to survive. The excessive decay speeds up eutrophication in lakes (the natural enrichment process that, over geologic time, causes lakes to fill in). The discolored, eutrophic water has an unpleasant odor that reduces its appeal for recreation.

Salts. Water salinity is a major problem in irrigated areas of the West. For example, the soils of the upper Colorado River Basin naturally contain a high concentration of salt. Water taken out of the Colorado for irrigation in this area is returned with such high salinity levels that it hampers downstream agriculture in the southwestern United States and northern Mexico. Also, groundwater overdrafts in coastal areas can cause

stance, is usually dry by the time it reaches the Gulf of California. Although the most severe water shortages are in the Southwest, periodic shortages occur in most regions.

The response to lack of rainfall in many areas has been to irrigate. Modern technology allows farmers to bring water from farther away and deeper under the surface than used to be possible. Much of the prairie is underlain by huge aquifers containing water trapped since the Ice Age. Today's powerful pumps can bring this water to the surface and distribute it on fields by center-pivot irrigation systems. But irrigation is usually a short-term solution, since the aquifers generally cannot be replenished.

Depletion of groundwater is particularly serious in some areas. As water is withdrawn, the land often subsides, diminishing its storage capacity. In some areas along the Texas coast as much as 77 percent of the water removed is not replenished. As groundwater reserves are depleted, irrigation users dig deeper, more expensive wells.

There is much that rural communities can do to assure an adequate supply of water. Besides the obvious and important step of encouraging conservation, communities can identify the locations of their watersheds and aquifers on maps, establish a system to monitor water quantity, and limit development if it will endanger the supply of water. Measuring water availability was an important aspect of the Oley Resource Conservation Project in Pennsylvania (see Case Study 2.1). Also, communities can limit the location, density, and type of development through zoning, to assure that the community's water capacity is not exceeded.

A community's water quality depends largely on land use and waste disposal practices. Water quality can also be affected by air pollutants. In some communities industry is the major source of pollution; in others it is the acid drainage from mining; while in others agriculture or runoff from urban areas may be the major contributor. Sources of water pollution may include inadequate septic systems, animal waste, seepage from landfills, leaking underground storage tanks, and runoff from roads and parking lots. Since rivers may carry pollutants long distances, the source of the problem may be in a neighboring community or even another state.

Water pollution sources are frequently categorized as "point" or "nonpoint," depending on whether the pollution comes from a specific source or point, such as a storm sewer or industry, or a land area, such as runoff from farmland or grazing areas. Most pollution abatement programs have focused on point source pollution. As a consequence, nonpoint source pollution is now more serious but is generally more difficult to identify and regulate.

Although pollution of any water source is serious, groundwater contamination is particularly difficult and costly to correct. Pollutants tend to degrade more slowly in subsurface environments where there is no sunlight and microbiologic activity. In addition, water often moves so slowly through an aquifer that contaminants can remain long after the source of pollution has been eliminated. Determining the extent of groundwater pollution may be difficult, since one area may be polluted while another nearby may not be.

Major improvement in water quality has been made since the early 1970s, when increasing concern over pollution prompted the passage of the federal Clean Water Act and subsequently the Safe Drinking Water

Act. There is still a great deal of contaminated water; however, deterioration in much of the nation's water supply has been checked. Although federal programs have been established to control nonpoint source pollution, there has been more progress on checking point pollution, and more has been done to protect surface water than groundwater.

Zoning ordinances can limit the use of septic systems in poorly percolating soils, over aquifers that supply the community's water, or in watersheds draining into reservoirs. Zoning can also be used to prohibit or restrict agricultural practices that may contribute to water quality problems—feedlots or destruction of vegetation along streams, for instance. Finally, communities can acquire easements on land that is important for the maintenance of water quality, as described in Chapter 5.

Rivers

Free-flowing streams and rivers have obvious aesthetic, recreational, and ecological values. They are pathways for wildlife, linking habitats and critical natural areas. They provide low-cost flood protection and maintain water quality. They offer scenic beauty and help maintain the rural landscape. In addition, their recreational value contributes substantially to the economies of watershed communities as increasing numbers of Americans enjoy rivers for fishing, rafting, canoeing, kayaking, and the like.

Unfortunately, dams, water diversion, and stream channelization (moving, deepening, and straightening stream beds) have frequently destroyed these values. Also, entire human settlements have been submerged under reservoirs. Moreover, dams, diversion, and channelization generally result in changes in water depth, velocity, and temperature that in turn cause marked and undesirable changes in flora and fauna. In addition to flood control, power generation, and water supply, the recreational benefits of reservoirs are often touted by dam builders. While reservoirs do allow for increased use by lake fishermen and the owners of large boats, they remove recreational opportunities for whitewater boaters, river fishermen, and those who simply find a free-flowing river aesthetically pleasing.

In past decades, many large-scale projects were financed by the federal government; many smaller projects, such as small-scale hydroelectric power dams, were financed by individual investors. Although hydropower dam building has virtually stopped in the United States, hundreds of potential dam sites have been identified and, should the market for hydropower change, building on these sites could threaten numerous rivers.

Stream channelization, while protecting adjacent land from flooding and erosion, often creates more problems than it solves. During floods, downstream velocity rises, increasing the flood's destructiveness; also, more silt and pollutants are carried down to lakes and estuaries where they cause additional problems. Channelization also results in the loss of riparian habitat for wildlife. Unfortunately, stream channelization is usually undertaken by individual landowners; thus, it is more difficult to monitor and regulate, and its effects are cumulative.

The principal federal legislation protecting scenic rivers is the Wild

seawater to enter an aquifer. In southeastern Georgia, for example, several aquifers have such high concentrations of salt that they are no longer dependable for fresh water. Salts used to treat icy winter roads may also enter water supplies through runoff.

Disease-producing contaminants. *Contaminated water spreads disease when the bacteria, viruses, and parasites found in sewage, animal manure, and food-processing waste find their way into water supplies. In the Southeast, where many rural residents obtain their drinking water from shallow wells too close to septic systems and privies, water-borne disease is a particular problem.*

Toxic chemicals. *Many chemicals used in industry and agriculture are toxic to humans or wildlife. Pesticides and nitrates from fertilizer frequently find their way into rural water supplies. Some industrial chemicals are toxic at levels of one part per billion, the equivalent of four drops in a large swimming pool. Seepage into groundwater from landfills, impoundments for industrial wastes, and leaking underground gasoline tanks is particularly dangerous, since many of the chemicals are not filtered out by soil and rock and are not biodegradable. According to the Environmental Protection Agency, in 1995 more than 285,000 underground storage tanks leaked gasoline or other chemicals. Since no one monitors most underground storage tanks and chemical dump sites, citizens are often unaware that chemical concentrations in their drinking water have reached hazardous levels.*

(See Notes to Sidebars.)

and Scenic Rivers Act of 1968, although the act protects designated segments of rivers, not whole watersheds. Many communities have formed partnerships with other communities within the same watershed to heighten awareness of, and to protect, their shared resource. In the Zuni River watershed of New Mexico, for example, private landowners and the Zuni and Navajo tribes are working together, as well as with state and federal agencies, to plan for the management and protection of the natural and cultural resources of the watershed.

Communities can protect rivers through zoning and subdivision controls restricting inappropriate uses on adjacent land and through land acquisition or easements along the banks.

Wetlands

Wetlands are transitional areas between terrestrial and aquatic environments where the water table (the level of groundwater) is at or near the ground surface or the land is covered by shallow water. About 5 percent of the land area of the continental United States today consists of wetlands. Wetlands are a diverse lot, ranging from tidal flats, salt-hay marshes, and mangrove swamps on the coast, to prairie potholes, peat bogs, and cypress swamps inland, to name just a few.

Wetlands are areas of high biological diversity, providing habitat for numerous fish, waterfowl, and other wildlife, many of which have economic value. Some animal species spend their entire lives in wetlands, while others use them primarily for breeding and raising young. Many salt- and fresh-water fish depend on wetlands for at least a part of their life cycles. Numerous reptiles and amphibians depend on wetlands, as do many mammals, including mink and muskrat. Just in terms of the great variety of species that depend on wetlands directly or indirectly, there are few ecosystems that are more important.

In some communities wetlands are the primary recharge or water-

1.17
Federal law requires that when developments destroy wetlands, new wetlands—called "mitigated wetlands"—be created nearby. Here, a biologist explains a mitigated wetland within the South Slough National Estuarine Reserve in Oregon.

supply areas for aquifers. Wetlands also help to purify the water passing through them, by filtering out silt and nutrients. Additionally, wetlands absorb floodwaters and then release them slowly, attenuating flooding of downstream communities. Along coasts, they act as barriers to damaging storm waves. Finally, wetlands have high recreational value for hunters, fishermen, boaters, and many others who enjoy observing the scenery and wildlife.

The importance of wetlands was poorly understood until recently, and more than half of the wetlands in the continental United States have been destroyed since the arrival of Europeans. Historically, drainage to create more land for agriculture has been the greatest cause of destruction. Destruction for farming continues in such areas as the Southeast, where forested bottomlands are being clearcut and drained for soybean production. Other causes of destruction include dredging to aid navigation, reservoir construction, pollution, waste disposal, and adding fill to create sites for housing, industry, and highways. Since the mid-1980s, however, wetland losses have been slowing, largely as a result of programs established by the 1985 Food Security Act.

Floodplains

Water, in the form of floods, can cause tremendous damage, as the country witnessed during the acute Mississippi River floods in 1993. Floodplains—land that is subject to periodic flooding—serve a vital function by reducing the height and speed of spreading flood waters. Floodplain vegetation slows flood water and allows some of it to be absorbed by the soil. Floodplains also serve as areas of groundwater recharge and wildlife habitat. Approximately 10 percent of the United States is within a one-hundred-year-flood plain (land that has at least a 1 percent chance of flooding in any given year).[10]

Floodplains have frequently been used for settlement, industry, and agriculture, despite their vulnerability. The soil is often excellent for agriculture, since floods periodically deposit soil washed off lands upstream. Floodplains are relatively flat, a characteristic that facilitates construction of roads and railroads; and they have good access to water for irrigation, industry, and transportation. Because of these advantages, people are willing to live and work in floodplains while risking the probability of floods.

Construction on floodplains not only endangers life and property but also increases the severity of floods by reducing the land's ability to store and buffer flood waters. Removing vegetation and paving over permeable soils in floodplains destroys wildlife habitat, increases runoff, and results in intensified flooding downstream. While these consequences are problems in all watersheds, floodplains and wetlands are especially important to the natural flow of water.

Floodplains can be used in limited ways. They are often quite appropriate for agriculture and recreational facilities, such as playing fields that suffer little or no damage from a flood. Most floodplains have been mapped and, if not, can easily be identified, so local governments can zone them to prevent inappropriate development. There is also assistance

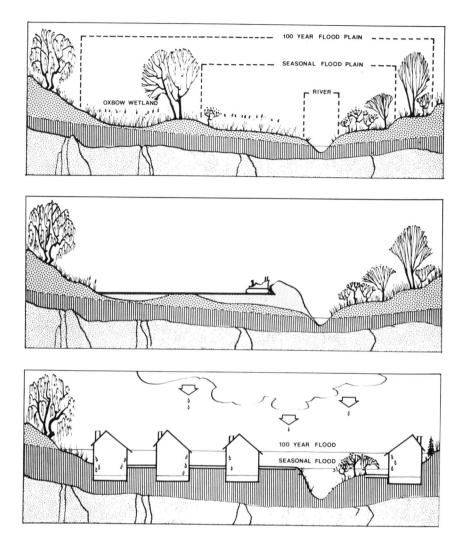

1.18
The impact of development in floodplains.

available from the federal government in the form of floodplain identification and federal flood insurance for property owners in communities with appropriate controls on floodplain development.

Coasts

Coasts are among America's most spectacular scenic and recreational resources. They also have great biological diversity and productivity. Coastal wetlands and estuaries are vital habitats for many fish and shellfish of commercial value. Since most of America's population is concentrated along coasts, many are under considerable development pressure and have suffered environmental degradation. Bay and ocean waters are threatened by pollution from municipal sewage, dumping, oil spills, and pollutants coming down the rivers that empty into them. Estuaries (partially enclosed water bodies, like the Chesapeake Bay, where fresh water mixes with sea water) and their associated wetlands are particularly vulnerable to pollution.

The barrier islands of the Atlantic and Gulf coasts are among the least stable of environments, being formed and destroyed by waves, tides, and ocean currents at relatively rapid rates. The cities and vacation homes built on them are particularly vulnerable. Unfortunately, more than 40 percent of America's 2,700 linear miles of barrier islands have already been developed.[11]

The principal federal laws protecting coasts are the 1972 Coastal Zone Management Act and the 1982 Coastal Barrier Resources Act. Local controls and land acquisition can also help.

THE LAND

Soils

Composed of disintegrated rock, water, air, decaying organic matter, and microorganisms, soil is the critical link between rocks and plants. Soils vary greatly in their composition, and different soils best support different types of vegetation. Deep, well-aerated soils that retain sufficient water, contain a high percentage of nitrogen and organic matter, and are not too acidic are generally the most suitable for agriculture. The ability of soils to support building foundations, septic systems, roads, and structures also varies greatly. Most soils with a high clay content, for example, drain poorly, causing problems for septic systems. Such soils also frequently swell when wet, causing building foundations to crack.

The major threat to soils is erosion, a process that occurs naturally but can be greatly accelerated through human activity. Most soils in their natural state are protected from wind and rain by vegetation, which may range from grasses to dense forests. When vegetation is removed, fertile topsoil, which may be only a few inches thick, is the first to erode. Topsoil generally has more capacity than the subsoil to hold the moisture necessary for plant growth, supplies more nutrients, and more readily allows plants to establish root systems.

Topsoil erodes quickly if land is farmed without conservation measures. The result over time is less favorable growing conditions, reduced crop yields, and decreased livestock productivity. Fall plowing, a common practice that allows harsh winter winds and rains to move the bare topsoil, exacerbates the problem. Soil on farmland is eroding far faster than it is being replaced. It can take one thousand years to form one inch of topsoil, yet it takes thirty-three years to lose an inch at an erosion rate of five tons of soil per acre per year—a rate the Natural Resources Conservation Service generally considers to be tolerable. Erosion occurs in all regions, but it is a much greater problem in certain parts of the country, such as the Corn Belt of the Midwest and the Palouse area of eastern Washington and northern Idaho. Average erosion rates have been declining over the past decade. In 1982, average erosion rates on cropland were 4.1 tons per acre per year; whereas, by 1992, average rates were down to 3.1 tons per acre per year.[12]

Erosion problems are not limited to farmland. Construction, mining, logging, and other activities destroy protective vegetation. The rates of erosion from such operations may be even more dramatic than those resulting from agriculture. Landslides caused by disturbing the vegeta-

1.19
Topsoil erodes quickly if land is farmed without conservation measures. Erosion is particularly severe in the wheat fields of the Palouse area of eastern Washington State and northern Idaho.

1.20
Wind erosion became a national crisis during the Dust Bowl years of the 1930s and remains a problem where farmers do not practice proper soil conservation. Here a field in Cascade County, Montana, is literally blowing away.

tion on steep slopes result in the destruction of numerous homes, highways, and other structures every year.

Although the actual losses of topsoil and the impacts on agricultural production are alarming in themselves, the damage caused by washing, blowing, or dumping soil into other places is also a concern. Wind-blown soil can choke crops, suffocate livestock, and sandblast buildings. Moreover, water running off exposed soils carries silt, fertilizer, pesticides, and herbicides, polluting water supplies and threatening aquatic life.

Fortunately, a great deal has been learned about the soils of the United States since the Dust Bowl years of the 1930s. The Natural Resources Conservation Service (NRCS), formerly the Soil Conservation Service,

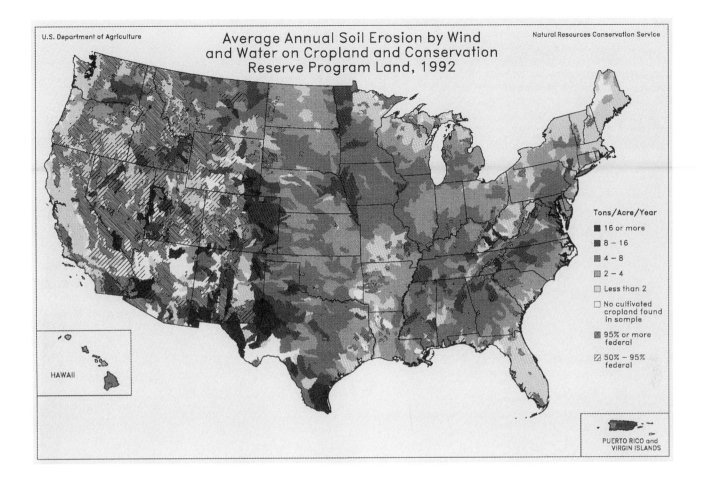

U.S. Department of Agriculture

Natural Resources Conservation Service

Average Annual Soil Erosion by Wind
and Water on Cropland and Conservation
Reserve Program Land, 1992

Tons/Acre/Year

- ■ 16 or more
- ■ 8 – 16
- ■ 4 – 8
- ▦ 2 – 4
- □ Less than 2
- □ No cultivated cropland found in sample
- ▨ 95% or more federal
- ▨ 50% – 95% federal

HAWAII

PUERTO RICO and
VIRGIN ISLANDS

which was formed in response to those problems, has established a number of programs to protect soil.

Good methods have been developed to control erosion both on the farm and off. Leaving vegetation along streams, contour plowing (plowing across the slope), and terracing (building terraces on slopes) decrease the speed of runoff and allow more water to soak into the soil. More recently, many farmers have adopted "conservation tillage" and "no till" farming methods. In the former, some or all of the residue of the previous crop is roughly plowed into the soil. In the latter, new seeds are planted in a slit in the midst of the last crop's stubble with little or no plowing. These techniques, while very effective in combating erosion, depend on herbicides to control weeds, which can cause water pollution and health problems. Off the farm, runoff from construction sites can be controlled by such measures as temporary dams and reseeding; in logging operations, erosion can be controlled by assuring that heavy equipment does not make ruts that water can readily follow. Streambanks, slopes, gullies, roadcuts, and other erodible surfaces can also be stabilized through biotechnical erosion control (BEC), which uses dormant tree cuttings to create living structures under and along the surface of the soil. BEC is more effective and more attractive than other stabilization methods, such as

1.21
Erosion rates depend on soil conditions, climate, and the type of agriculture practiced.

1.22
No-till farming is becoming increasingly popular because it requires less labor and decreases erosion. Unfortunately, it requires more use of herbicides, which raises pollution and health concerns. Here in Montgomery County, Kansas, soybeans have been planted in wheat stubble.

1.23
These grass backslope terraces, which decrease erosion, were the first to be installed in southwestern Iowa.

riprap, a fill of large pieces of stone arranged to reduce the velocity of the water.

While these techniques unquestionably conserve soil, they can be expensive and thus reduce short-term financial returns for farmers, builders, and loggers. In many areas contour plowing and terracing are being dropped because the width of the big new farm machinery makes it difficult to plow on the contour or over the terraces. This heavy equipment also causes soil compaction that results in less water being absorbed— and hence, more runoff and erosion. Many farmers engage in poor conservation practices when they need a quick return on their investment to pay off debts. Leased farmland is more likely to be abused, since the farmer has less long-term incentive to practice conservation on someone else's land. The NRCS's Conservation Reserve Program, which encourages farmers to plant grass or trees on highly erodible or environmentally sensitive cropland, has contributed greatly to reducing overall soil erosion.

In addition to what individual farmers, builders, and loggers can do, local governments can protect soils by regulating construction sites and prohibiting agricultural and forestry practices that lead to excessive erosion. The Natural Resources Conservation Service's soil surveys should be of great assistance to communities interested in developing appropriate regulations to protect soils (p. 128).

Farming and Farmland

America's farms are diverse: Iowa corn and soybean farms, Washington apple orchards, North Dakota wheat farms, cranberry bogs in Massachusetts, Wisconsin dairy farms, poultry operations in Maryland, citrus groves in Florida, and California vineyards are all part of American agriculture. The owners and operators of these farms are as varied as the types of farms. There are full-time and part-time farmers, family-owned and -operated farms and those owned by absentee landlords or international corporations. For some, farming is a livelihood; for others it is a hobby or a tax shelter. Americans engaged in agriculture may be fifth-generation farmers living on the land of their ancestors, back-to-the-land counterculture farmers, affluent gentlemen-farmers, or subsistence "dirt farmers." Some farm thousands of acres, while others make a living intensively cultivating ten acres.

American agriculture produces food and fiber for this country and for much of the world. In 1994, agricultural products accounted for 9 percent of all American exports.[13] Although only 2.5 percent of the American work force is directly engaged in agriculture, many other industries and businesses, including the manufacturers of farm equipment and the distributors and processors of food products, are based on agriculture.[14]

Farmland has an inherent aesthetic appeal for many people. The seasonal changes of growing crops, the colors and textures of fields, and livestock grazing in pastures provide visual enjoyment. Farms also provide incidental recreational opportunities. Many farm owners allow access to their noncultivated land for hunting and other recreational activities. Agriculture has also been associated with a particular way of life that has contributed to American folk traditions, literature, music, dance,

1.24
An abandoned farmstead makes way for more wheat in North Dakota. With increased mechanization, there are fewer farmers on the land, and many farm structures are abandoned or demolished.

and other arts. Technology and economics, however, are radically reshaping life in farming areas.

The population growth in rural areas over the past decade does not indicate an increase in the number of farmers; in fact, both the number and the proportion of farmers in American society are smaller than ever before. In 1991 only 1.9 percent of Americans lived on farms, as compared to 44 percent in 1880.[15] There are also fewer farms today, but the ones that remain are larger. The average farm in 1995 was 469 acres, more than three times larger than the average farm in 1880.[16]

Farming methods and farms have changed dramatically since World War II. Until the 1950s most farmers, in addition to raising a variety of cash crops, engaged in general farming to meet family and community needs. They planted vegetable gardens and orchards and raised animals to produce milk, eggs, and meat. Although this aspect of family farming continues on small farms, many modern farming practices require increased acreage, and most of America's food is produced by large-scale farms. In order to compete economically, farmers often feel forced to buy or lease more land, plow marginal soil, or pull down obsolete structures on land that can be cultivated.

The startling visual impacts of farm modernization indicate the profound changes in the way crops and livestock are produced. Agriculture has become increasingly mechanized and less diversified in crops and livestock. Bigger and different machinery and the obsolescence of draft animals have resulted in a need for larger yet simpler outbuildings and an abundance of obsolete farm structures on most farms.

Monoculture (the exclusive planting of one crop) is the rule on many farms today. Although monoculture may be more efficient, it makes a farmer more vulnerable to such problems as pests and declining prices that might affect a single crop. Consequently, Cooperative Extension agents are increasingly advising farmers to diversify. Farmers close to urban markets, where the demand for local produce has increased, are finding diversified agriculture profitable, particularly when they can sell their produce directly to consumers through farmers' markets.

Many American farms have multimillion-dollar capital investments in land, buildings, equipment, and livestock. On paper, these farmers may be wealthy, but their assets are usually tied up in the land and equipment they need to make a living. Moreover, the risks of farming are high: crops can be destroyed by drought, floods, or pests, or their value may plummet because of fluctuations in commodity prices. In the 1980s many farmers were forced to quit farming or lost their land to foreclosure because of high interest payments on mortgages taken out when land values and agricultural commodity prices were higher. As farmers fail, their farms are usually consolidated with other holdings, bringing about a reduction in the number of family-owned farms.

It is often the medium-sized farms that have suffered the most. They do not have large enough operations to justify much of the efficient but expensive new machinery, and smaller farms have fared better because their owners often have the option of working a second job off the farm.

One-third of agricultural production occurs in metropolitan counties near large cities, and another one-fourth in counties adjacent to those.[17] Between 1982 and 1992, an average of 1.4 million acres of crop, pasture, and rangeland were converted to development each year.[18] Much of this land is considered prime farmland—land that has the best combination of physical and chemical characteristics, growing seasons, and moisture supply needed to produce sustained high yields with proper management. Unfortunately, prime farmland is often very desirable for development, since it tends to be flat and well drained. Although development on prime farmland occurs in every section of the country, most of the concern has been in the Northeast, in the Sunbelt, and along the West Coast.

The various causes of the loss of farmland—whether to development, mineral exploitation, or destructive farming practices—can usually be traced to a single factor: farmland is an economic asset. Farmers' land is not only their primary asset but also their life insurance and retirement fund. A disproportionately high percentage of American farmers are approaching retirement: in 1987, the average age of American farmers was 52 and climbing.[19] Their land is the final cash crop they can sell at retirement to buy a house in town, a condominium in the Sunbelt, or a place in a retirement community. Few younger farmers (most are not fortunate enough to inherit a farm) can afford to purchase the land and equipment necessary to get started.

Farms adjacent to towns and cities are the ones most likely to become victims to creeping urbanization. Strip development along roads in agricultural areas diminishes the viability of remaining interior properties by reducing farm acreage, fragmenting farms into noncontiguous parcels, and creating nonagricultural neighbors. Suburban living and farming usually do not mix well; the combination often results in tensions between farmers and nonfarming neighbors. Thoughtless trespassers frequently trample crops, damage fences, litter, and allow their dogs to chase livestock.

Farmers often lose political control of local government as population changes occur. Local governments dominated by nonfarmers sometimes

1.25
This nearly abandoned crossroads in Owen County, Indiana, reflects population and job loss in an area once dependent on strip mining.

1.26
An auction marks the close of another family farm. Increasingly, farmers are being forced out of business by declining prices and rising debt.

enact ordinances that discourage farming operations—for example, by prohibiting the driving of slow farm machinery on highways, the operation of agricultural machinery at night, or the use of manure as fertilizer.

Urbanization in rural areas discourages agricultural activity even before the bulldozers arrive. As development moves closer, farmers may be unwilling to make improvements to their land and buildings. This attitude sets an "impermanence syndrome" in motion: Farmers cease to invest in new equipment; this reduces the level of farm business for distributors of agricultural supplies and equipment. As these suppliers go out of business, there are fewer nearby places for farmers to buy farm implements and have them repaired, to purchase fertilizers, pesticides, and seed, and to obtain veterinary and other services. This further discourages the remaining farmers, who must travel great distances to obtain the goods and services they need.

A related development is the "farmette" or "ranchette." In many rural areas exurbanites are purchasing tracts of farmland that are bigger than typical suburban lots but smaller than the minimum size for a farm that could support a family. The new hobby-farmers may be protecting some farmland but are generally not a part of the agricultural economy.

The increase in value of land, the departure of lifelong friends, and the proximity of new neighbors with suburban lifestyles all hasten the selling-out process. Farmland conversion feeds on itself: each lost farm not only brings new houses with nonfarm families but also stimulates more farmers to develop their land.

Ironically, although farmland loss is tied to economic factors, keeping land in agriculture actually benefits a community financially. Even if agricultural land is taxed at a lower rate, farming generates more in taxes than it costs in services. On the other hand, converting agricultural land to residential subdivisions costs local government more in services than the new houses generate in property taxes (American Farmland Trust 1992).

The need to protect farmland has been a national concern since the

late 1970s, when the federal government established the National Agricultural Lands Study. Although subsequently enacted federal laws provide a small measure of protection, most of the burden to preserve farmland rests on state and local governments. Increasingly, local governments—using their powers to regulate subdivisions, enact zoning ordinances, offer real estate tax relief, and purchase development rights—are attempting to protect farmland. The record, unfortunately, is spotty.

Forests

Forests cover approximately one-third of the total American landscape. Lumbering has been a major industry since the earliest colonial times. The first settlers quickly saw the great profits that could be made by shipping lumber—particularly white pine for ships' masts—back to England, where wood was in short supply. Extensive precolonial forests fell as the demand for cleared farmland and wood for construction grew. Actually, much of the land that was cleared for agriculture in the East has since reverted to forests, as anyone who has come across stone walls while walking in New England woods can observe. The descendants of the original settlers learned that the soils of the Midwest were generally better for agriculture and they moved west, leaving their old farms to grow up in trees.

The greatest period of American forest exploitation was during the second half of the nineteenth century, when population growth and industrialization created many demands for wood. During this period, most lumbering was done without concern for environmental consequences. There was little effort to protect forest soil from erosion, and forest fires and flooding were common. It was largely Theodore Roosevelt's concern for the rapidly diminishing American forest that led to the establishment of the U.S. Forest Service in 1905.

Aside from their economic importance, forests provide habitat for many wildlife species. The importance of forests in protecting watersheds has long been recognized: by slowing runoff, they allow rainwater to soak into the ground, recharging aquifers, and reducing the potential for floods. Finally, forests are a source of enjoyment for many. The giant redwoods of the West and the fall foliage in the Upper Midwest, Appalachian Mountains, and New England draw visitors from afar. Throughout the nation, forests have high recreational value as a setting for hiking, skiing, camping, nature study, hunting, and other outdoor pursuits.

Approximately 27 percent of productive forest land is publicly owned,[20] principally by the Forest Service and the Bureau of Land Management (BLM). The balance is owned by individuals and corporations. How privately owned woodland is treated varies greatly. Many small lots are left alone, their owners being primarily interested in their aesthetic, wildlife, and recreational values. Other small lots are harvested haphazardly, with the owners cutting firewood as needed or removing saw logs when lumber prices are high. Most lumber companies and an increasing number of individual owners now manage their forests for long-term sustained yields. The Forest Service and other agencies are prepared to advise private owners and conservation organizations on wise forest management.

Although environmentally sensitive management of private forests is much more common than it once was, abuses still occur. Small-scale owners are not always careful to design the skid roads needed to get logs out of forests in ways that prevent erosion. Trees along streams that shelter wildlife and provide shade for trout are sometimes removed. Large-scale owners often rely on spraying pesticides from the air, a practice that may harm wildlife and water quality. Monoculture has taken over commercial forests as it has cropland in some areas. In parts of the South, acres of fast-growing loblolly pine have replaced diversified stands dominated by oak and other pine. In addition to being aesthetically less pleasing to most people, monoculture provides less diverse habitat for wildlife and invites pests that can multiply more rapidly on a single species.

Rangeland

Rangeland is land on which the vegetation is predominantly native grasses, non-grass herbaceous plants (forbs), or shrubs. Chiefly valued for the forage it produces for livestock and wildlife, it covers more than one-third of the nation. Most rangeland is located in the West, with states such as Wyoming and Nevada being composed of more than three-fourths range. To many people the range is synonymous with cowboys and the wide open spaces, "where the deer and the antelope play." While this image does apply in some instances, rangeland also includes alpine meadows and fenced pastures that are carefully managed for maximal production of grasses. What constitutes rangeland is difficult to estimate precisely, since there is often no sharp line between range and forest or range and cropland. In addition to supporting cattle and wildlife, rangeland often contains large aquifer recharge areas and has many recreational uses.

Rangeland or prairie once extended much farther east than it does today, including much of the midwestern farmbelt. As settlers moved west, they settled the tall-grass prairie of the eastern plains first. The ag-

Here in Nevada, overgrazing, which makes it difficult for beneficial grass species to regenerate, has damaged the rangeland to the right of the fence, making it less attractive to both the livestock and wildlife.

ricultural potential of these soils was and remains tremendous. However, as settlers moved farther west, into the more arid short-grass prairie (roughly west of the 100th meridian, which runs from central North Dakota to central Texas) where average rainfall is typically under 20 inches a year, they found themselves in areas where agriculture was increasingly marginal. In good years, when rainfall was abundant, crops did well. But in bad years, when rainfall was less than 20 inches—generally the minimum required for agriculture—crops failed. To make matters worse, when the crops failed, wind carried off much of the topsoil. This process culminated in the infamous Dust Bowl of the 1930s.

Much of the West, particularly the more arid regions, is devoted to livestock rather than crop production. Overgrazing, however, principally by cattle, has been a major problem. When too many cattle are allowed to graze, they tend to graze favored species to the point where those species cannot easily regenerate. Non-native plants and shrubs, like sagebrush, creosote bush, and mesquite, that have little value for cattle then take their place. Overgrazing often results in soil compaction and erosion, which further reduce range productivity. Also, cattle frequently compete directly with wildlife for forage. The Natural Resources Conservation Service estimates that more than 60 percent of American rangeland is in poor or fair condition.[21] The Bureau of Land Management, which manages 40 percent of the rangeland in the United States, has been criticized for permitting too much grazing.

Concern about overgrazing began in the late nineteenth century. The Forest Service set limits on grazing in national forests shortly after its establishment. The Taylor Grazing Act of 1934 gave the federal government the authority to control grazing on the public domain, and since that date, rangeland conditions have improved. Today the Forest Service and BLM control range use on public land, while NRCS advises private owners on range conservation.

Overgrazing is not the only threat to rangeland; it can also be overused for recreation. Use of off-road vehicles and trail bikes on rangeland has resulted in soil compaction, elimination of native grasses, threats to wildlife, and erosion.

WILDLIFE AND ENDANGERED SPECIES

It is a rare rural community that does not value its wildlife—at least some of it. Farmers may consider deer pests if they trample corn crops; gardeners may object to groundhogs nibbling away in vegetable patches; and ranchers may wish to exterminate coyote that kill sheep. Yet hunting, trapping, fishing, and observing wildlife are major recreational activities for large numbers of rural residents, and these pursuits provide supplementary food and income for others. Moreover, the economies of many communities are heavily dependent on income from visiting hunters and fishermen. In a 1991 survey, the U.S. Fish and Wildlife Service found that 57 percent of Americans fished, hunted, or observed and photographed wildlife.[22]

Fortunately, Americans are becoming increasingly aware of both the value and the interconnectedness of wildlife and plants. We now realize that protecting habitat is the key to the survival of most endangered species. The habitat needs of wildlife vary tremendously. Some, such as the grizzly bear, require large areas of undisturbed land. Others require much less space or are more adaptable to human activities. Deer, for instance, thrive on a combination of second-growth forest and adjacent fields, a condition that is far more prevalent today than it was before European settlement. Consequently their numbers have increased markedly.

Many rural property owners place a high premium on making appropriate habitat for wildlife available, through such activities as leaving dead trees favored by woodpeckers and eagles, creating wetlands, and encouraging the growth of shrubbery that shelters and provides food for small mammals and game birds. Unfortunately, other rural property owners destroy wildlife or their habitat by such activities as poisoning prairie dogs, draining wetlands to create more cropland, and removing hedgerows, which are excellent wildlife habitat but get in the way of efficient crop production.

Concerns about protecting wildlife started with game hunters, who became alarmed in the late nineteenth century at the disappearance of such species as the buffalo and the passenger pigeon. Traditionally, most efforts to protect wildlife, particularly by state fish and game departments, were focused on species that were hunted and fished. Great progress has been made in their protection. Hunters who realize the importance of protecting breeding grounds and other habitats are often active conservationists.

Since the 1960s there has been growing interest in the protection of nongame and endangered species as well. More than one hundred species of vertebrate animals alone have become extinct in the continental United States since the arrival of Europeans. Even more invertebrates and plants have become extinct, but an exact number cannot be determined, since

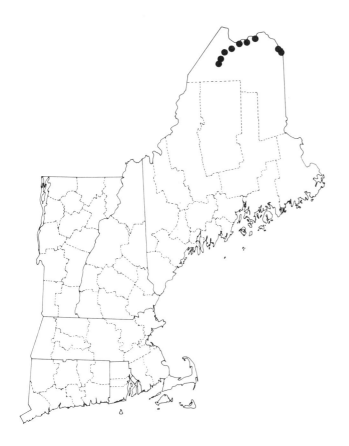

1.29 & 1.30
The furbish lousewort, *Pedicularis furbishiae,* is found only in northern Maine and New Brunswick. Much of its habitat—to say nothing of a spectacular free-flowing river—would have been destroyed had the Dickey-Lincoln Dam been built on the St. John River in the 1970s. The project was canceled in part because of concern for this endangered species.

there is only incomplete information on what existed before. Relatively little is known about the habitat requirements of many species that might be endangered, particularly amphibians, invertebrates, reptiles, and plants.

The U.S. Fish and Wildlife Service is the principal federal agency responsible for wildlife protection; a number of nonprofit organizations are involved in the endeavor as well. The Endangered Species Act of 1973, which the service helps to administer, is one of the strongest environmental laws. Many states have passed wildlife protection laws modeled on the federal Endangered Species Act.

SPECIAL RESOURCES

Historic and Cultural Resources

Rural America has a wealth of historic resources—not only outstanding landmarks, like Thomas Jefferson's Monticello, but everyday places as well, buildings and land that have been in use for many years and help give a community its identity. Rural historic resources are varied; while farmsteads, mills, one-room schoolhouses, covered bridges, and rural churches are important, there are many other structures and sites that should not be ignored, including general stores, Grange halls, the trails used by pioneers, early gas stations, and diners.

Each rural area has groups of buildings and landscapes that its residents consider important because they are pleasant to look at, because they have been an integral part of a rural way of life, or because they evoke familiar and comforting associations of family and community. Protecting these buildings and landscapes conserves tangible and visible links with a community's past, preserves places that are important parts of a community's identity, and retains important resources that may provide historical information about how an area was settled, developed, or declined.

The agricultural landscape is particularly rich. Historic resources on American farms may include houses, barns, springhouses, smokehouses, root cellars, corn cribs, silos, windmills, and family burial plots. In addition, knowing how farmers laid out their fields and manipulated the land through terracing, contour plowing, and drainage systems not only adds interest to the landscape but also provides tangible evidence of a community's agricultural history. So does farmers' choice of fencing materials, which can be as varied as split-rails or Osage orange hedgerows or barbed wire. The agricultural landscape is constantly evolving, as it reflects changes in the economy as well as in the needs, aspirations, and traditions of generations of farm families. It is not simply the individual farm building, but the grouping of buildings on the land and the repetition of farmstead after farmstead that give significance to an agricultural landscape. The farm complex takes on a significance that any one building alone lacks; viewed as a group, these buildings tell the changing story of agricultural life. The juxtaposition of building shapes and forms, the mix of architectural styles and building materials, and the color and texture of the land itself give diversity to the rural landscape.

Frequently in rural communities the harmonious relationship of build-

1.31
Rural adobe mission churches have been religious and social centers and are important Hispanic contributions to American architecture. Traditionally, the earthen plaster was periodically renewed by the community, but many churches are falling into disrepair. The New Mexico Community Foundation is assisting communities in preserving historic churches like San Rafael, pictured here. The church is located within the La Cueva National Register district in Mora County.

1.32
A Polish Catholic roadside shrine in Portage County, Wisconsin. Each region has characteristic landmarks that help make it special; more than forty ethnic groups have left their mark on the rural Wisconsin landscape.

ings and their natural or agricultural settings is of special appeal to residents and visitors alike. But a beautiful barn in the midst of a subdivision or a covered bridge adjacent to an interstate overpass loses much of its integrity and appeal. The particular arrangement of buildings on the land makes each community unique. Historic communities such as Cranbury, New Jersey; Bishop Hill, Illinois; and Lodi, California, remain distinctive, and their preservation is very important to their residents. On the other hand, modern subdivisions or shopping centers in New Jersey, Illinois, and California may have little to distinguish them from each other.

1.33
Historic resources take many forms. Wagons traveling the Oregon Trail left deep ruts in the sandstone like these near Guernsey, Wyoming. Trail remnants, many of which are on public lands, present a major preservation opportunity in the West.

Battlefields are a special kind of historic resource, and in recent years they have received increasing attention and interest from conservationists. Some battlefields bear little tangible evidence that they were the site of key military events; others may exhibit fortifications, trenches, graveyards, and other signs of war. Ranging in size from less than several hundred acres to thousands of acres, many battlefields of the Revolutionary and Civil War, as well as wars between Native Americans and white settlers, have been protected through federal, state, or local government ownership, and some battlefields are also protected through easements. However, dozens of battlefields in private ownership are threatened with development (see Sidebar 7.3).

Not all historic resources are visible above ground. Many communities also possess significant archeological resources that contain evidence about the way the land was used previously and about the lives and occupations of earlier residents. Archeological resources may be either historic—from the period since European settlement—or prehistoric—from earlier Indian and Eskimo settlements. Many archeological resources are located in riparian areas, as these were early avenues of transportation and places of settlement. Because most archeological resources are not above ground, landowners are often unaware or unappreciative of them. Yet many archeological sites are revered by the descendants of the people who occupied them, and their protection from souvenir hunters as well as developers is of great importance. Indeed, because of the threat of looting, the exact location of archeological resources is sometimes not made public.

Folklife traditions are as important to protect as more tangible reminders of our past. Because of the great ethnic diversity of Americans, we have a tremendous wealth of traditions, folk tales, arts, and crafts. Culturally distinct rural areas usually have had unique ways of building,

1.34
Hedgerows, such as these in Mecklenberg, New York, tell us much about how fields were laid out and how land was divided. In addition, they curb erosion, add visual interest to the landscape, and provide habitat for wildlife.

laying out farms, and creating furnishings and foods. With the passing of rural life styles and older and no longer cost-effective ways of doing things, the varied legacy of cultural traditions is in danger of extinction in all regions of the country.

There are fewer people each year who have the skills and time for traditional crafts or can remember old place names and customs, identify historic photographs, and tell and retell the folk tales of rural communities. The older residents of most rural communities—the people who have this knowledge and these skills—are untapped cultural resources. They are often pleased to be interviewed and pass on craft techniques to young people who wish to keep a tradition alive.

Historic buildings and structures often fall victim to abandonment or obsolescence. A vast number of rural buildings stand vacant or are used only marginally. Since few farmers engage in general farming in the 1990s, chicken coops, sheep sheds, and small granaries are useless on many large farms today. The slatted corncribs that stored feed corn on the cob, for example, are obsolete on most farms, because modern equipment harvests corn by the individual kernel and modern dryers assure proper humidity levels for storage. The result is the obsolescence of the corncrib—once a traditional element on American farms. Such historic resources have been lost almost universally and without much notice.

Surplus barns are a preservation problem in every region of the country. The condition of many barns today contrasts sharply with that of the general farming era, when a well-kept barn was the symbol of successful farming. Our magnificent barns were often built to house machinery, animals, and hay; but today's combines do not fit through the barn doors, livestock live in feedlots, and hay stays outside in compact one-ton bales.

There are other threats to historic resources. Development, of course, is a major cause of destruction. Individual buildings may survive—as in

1.35
The bald cypress trees lining this road in Washington County, North Carolina, were planted by settlers before the Civil War.

1.36
Archeological resources may be dramatic, like the cliff dwellings at Mesa Verde National Park in Colorado, but more often they look like this cellar hole, which is all that remains of a late-seventeenth-century house at the Jefferson Patterson Park in Maryland. However, such archeological sites can tell us much about Native American and early European settlement.

1.37
Stacking hay with a beaver slide is a
fast-disappearing tradition in Montana, and the skill is as important to
preserve as is the artifact. The American Folklife Center of the Library of
Congress has documented this and
many other rural traditions.

the case of a barn in the midst of a subdivision—but stripped of their
natural or agricultural context. Road-widening projects all too frequently may destroy historic bridges and the stone walls and ancient trees
that line scenic roads. Also, as farms consolidate, farmers frequently
remove fences and hedgerows that are no longer useful as boundary
markers and make the efficient use of large machinery more difficult.
The result is an expansive landscape with fewer subdivided fields and
diminished historical associations and wildlife habitat.

Declining farm populations have resulted in consolidations that leave
unused church and school buildings in the countryside. Although many
are historically and architecturally significant, they may be left to deteriorate or be demolished. Population decline also threatens the preservation
of buildings in small towns that traditionally served the needs of farmers.

Another handicap to preservation of historic resources in rural areas
comes from the commonly held belief that "old" means poor, while
"new" means prosperous. Farm families—especially those who may have
had to make do at times with outdated farm equipment, antiquated
household appliances, second-hand trucks, and hand-me-down clothes
because of the demanding economic conditions of farming—are not always sympathetic to historic preservation.

1.38
The Emminger round barn near Watertown, South Dakota, was built in 1910 and is listed in the National Register of Historic Places. Its current owner renovated it for continued use in his dairy operation.

1.39
Hillsboro, Virginia. Owners of rural buildings of architectural or historic interest are showing increased interest in rehabilitation.

The many farmers who would like to preserve their historic buildings and structures face frustrations and expenses. Maintenance and energy costs may be prohibitive or the necessary restoration skills unavailable. Not many people today, for example, are experienced at building stone walls or split-rail fences. Also, real estate taxes and liability insurance on unused or underused buildings may be too high for some property owners to justify keeping them. Fortunately, for income-producing properties listed in the National Register, investment tax credits of 20 percent are available for restoration (for information about investment tax credits, see p. 327).

There has long been an interest in protecting outstanding monuments important in American history, such as Mount Vernon and the Alamo. The National Park Service, state park agencies, and numerous nonprofit organizations own thousands of historic buildings throughout the United States. Widespread interest in the protection of nonmuseum buildings for their architectural or scenic qualities is more recent, dating from the late 1960s. More recent still has been the growth of interest in protecting whole districts. Preservationists have established Main Street projects to enhance older deteriorating commercial areas, and neighborhood conservation efforts have brought new life to numerous declining residential areas.

Historic preservation in rural areas, however, has often lagged behind such work in cities. Rural historic preservation programs have tended to focus on the protection of individual buildings, often as museums. Much more needs to be done to protect rural historic structures that are still lived in and worked in. New uses can often be found for buildings of historic or architectural interest if they are no longer needed for their original uses. Farm buildings can often be repaired or adapted to store new equipment and different crops. Throughout the country, mills, schools, and other rural structures have been adapted for a variety of uses, including residences and stores. Fortunately an increasing number of local governments and nonprofit organizations are working to protect historic buildings that are still in use.

Scenic Areas

No matter how important such resources as prime agricultural soil, clean water, and wildlife habitat may be, they rarely have the emotional appeal of a beautiful countryside setting. A love for scenic beauty often provides the common bond among people who work for the protection of such resources as wetlands, historic houses, air quality, and farmland. A community leader may strive to protect the economic well-being of local farmers, realizing that this is the key to farmland retention, but may be motivated—consciously or not—by the pleasure of observing scenic farmland and farming activity.

Many people appreciate and enjoy the countryside for its natural beauty. A 1995 survey showed that driving for pleasure is the second most popular recreational activity (after walking).[23] The high automobile counts on scenic highways such as the Blue Ridge Parkway in North Carolina and Virginia attest to the popularity of visiting beautiful areas. Scenic beauty not only gives people pleasure but also promotes mental health. Researchers have learned that drivers subjected to the landscape of sprawl—strip development, uncoordinated signage, and haphazard design—experience a higher level of stress than drivers who travel through more natural or parklike environments.[24] The National Scenic Byways Program and state scenic byways programs designate special routes that provide drivers with scenic beauty, unusual natural areas, historic and cultural resources, and special recreational opportunities.

Most natural and cultural resources have scenic value. Clear and unpolluted water, a pheasant poised in a meadow at the edge of a country road, field patterns accentuated by fences and hedgerows, a well-kept farmstead, a hardwood forest ablaze in fall colors—all are visual delights. Resource misuse has serious visual implications. Cloudy and stagnant water, channelized streams that no longer meander, bare fields scarred by erosion, mountains left pocked by strip mining, straight lines of look-alike houses, and muddy feedlots in the half-shadow of a tumbled-down barn are visual symbols of a threatened rural landscape. In addition, there are problems that are primarily visual, such as billboards and automobile graveyards.

Of course, not everyone agrees on what constitutes scenic beauty. We have all heard that "beauty is in the eye of the beholder." Nor is there universal agreement that strip development, billboards, and automobile graveyards are blights that should be removed from the rural landscape. Some observers find such landscape elements interesting to observe for what they teach us about ourselves and our society (Jackson 1984). Moreover, visual preferences change with time. Wetlands would not have been considered beautiful a generation ago, and in the colonial era wilderness was more an object of fear than of beauty. Nevertheless, there is more agreement on how people rate scenery than is commonly thought. Reports planner Frederick Steiner, "In a visual assessment study we did of the Verde Valley [in central Arizona], we found strong consensus on what was visually preferred—beauty—and that which isn't. I'm convinced many people do agree on what's beautiful, so it isn't merely in the beholder's eye." [25] Researchers have found that preferences for some views—of grasslands, water, and distant mountains, for example—occur even cross-culturally (Hiss 1990, pp. 36–40; Smardon, Palmer, and Felleman 1986, p. 107).

The first step in protecting scenic resources is to establish community consensus on which scenery should be protected. Communities can then use the results to designate areas to be protected through local controls and voluntary agreements. Specific visual blight problems such as billboards and junkyards can be regulated through ordinances.

Greenways

Since the 1980s, greenways—linear corridors of open space that provide recreation opportunities as well as wildlife habitat—have been growing in popularity. Greenways can be both rural and urban, and often form a linkage between the two. Frequently greenways follow waterways and ridges, but they may also be road or railroad corridors, or may even follow utility lines—or all of these. Greenways usually include a trail for bicyclists and pedestrians. One advantage of greenways is that, because of their linearity, they have more edge area than other types of parks; thus, they can provide recreational access to relatively more people and a greater amount of habitat for certain kinds of wildlife. Greenways also provide migration routes for wildlife. As natural corridors, they help maintain a high level of biological diversity and protect water quality and the health of aquatic communities. Numerous studies have shown that people will pay a premium to live close to a greenway and that the value of land along a greenway appreciates significantly more than land farther away (Rivers, Trails, and Conservation Assistance 1995).

Outdoor Recreation

Interest in outdoor recreation has increased greatly during the twentieth century, particularly since 1960. Although some outdoor activities, such as hunting, fishing, walking, ice skating, and boating, were popular in the last century, others, such as skiing and white-water boating for sport, were practically unheard of. Increased leisure time and disposable income have stimulated interest in recreation. Furthermore, improved transportation has made it possible for most Americans to travel to a wide variety of places for recreation.

Americans participate in outdoor recreation for enjoyment and health. According to a 1995 survey, some of the most popular outdoor recreational activities, and the estimated percentage of American adults who participated in them, were walking for pleasure (67%), visiting a beach (62%), picnicking (49%), visiting a nature center (46%), visiting a historic site (44%), swimming (44%), wildlife viewing (31%), and boating (30%).[26]

Demands for outdoor recreation have been the impetus for protecting many environmental resources. In addition to land that is set aside for parks, land originally intended for other purposes is now used for recreation. For instance, many national forests are now used more for recreation than for logging. Much of the effort to clean up water supplies has been a result of pressure from water-sports enthusiasts and fishermen. But outdoor recreation can also result in environmental degradation when too many people visit a park, use a campground, or paddle a river. For certain recreational areas it has become necessary to limit visitation. Environmental problems also result from inappropriate use—for instance, when trail bikers crush fragile desert vegetation or when boaters discard plastic waste that snares mammals or is eaten by fish.

Providing outdoor recreation opportunities for profit and pleasure is

1.40
Outdoor recreation can cause problems when it becomes too concentrated or damages fragile resources. Here, trail-bike riders have formed gullies on Idaho rangeland, destroying vegetation and encouraging erosion.

a concern for many rural communities, particularly those that are far from publicly owned land. Traditionally much recreational activity has taken place on private land, either one's own or a neighbor's. In many communities it is traditional to permit people from the community to use private land for recreation if they do no harm. "No trespassing" signs are becoming more common, however, as demands for outdoor recreation increase and as more people leave the city looking for recreational opportunities. Many landowners are becoming concerned about vandalism, about the number of people using their land, and about potential liability for injuries.

Rural conservation leaders can play a role not only in protecting land for the enjoyment of community residents but also in working out agreements with property owners for responsible use by area residents. Trail clubs in particular, such as the Ice Age Park and Trail Foundation in Wisconsin (see Case Study 7.4), have been active in working out such agreements.

Public Lands

Virtually all communities contain government-owned land, if it is only the land around schools and municipal buildings and along road rights-of-way. Particularly in the West, a large proportion of the land in some communities is owned by the federal government or, to a lesser extent, by state or local governments. The biggest federal land managers are the Bureau of Land Management, the Forest Service, the National Park Service, the Fish and Wildlife Service, and the Department of Defense. The land may be directly managed by the federal government or leased to individuals or corporations.

BLM is the largest of the federal land managers, overseeing many types of public land, including rangeland, forests, watersheds, wilderness areas, wildlife habitats, recreation areas, and historic sites. All told, it is responsible for nearly 270 million acres of public lands. BLM rangelands are often permitted or leased to ranchers for ten-year periods, while lands containing fossil fuel and mineral reserves are leased to private corporations for resource development.

There are many issues related to the appropriate uses of federally owned land. Logging companies, mining companies, ranchers, outfitters, and other businesses often lobby for more intensive use of these lands, while conservationists decry overuse. BLM and the Forest Service are committed by law to the concepts of "multiple use" and "sustained yield" (ensuring that the timber, grasses, and other resources on their land will be available for generations to come). Many conservationists argue, however, that BLM allows overgrazing and does not charge enough for its forage. (Many ranchers, on the other hand, resist raising the federal grazing fees, viewing such an increase as a threat to their traditional lifestyles; and a few ranchers resist all federal ownership of grazing lands.) Conservation groups also seek reform of the 1872 Mining Law, which governs hardrock (gold, silver, and lead, for example) prospecting and mining on federal lands. Under this law, miners have an automatic right to mine, pay no royalty for their ore removal, and are not required to restore the land to premining condition. Conservationists also argue that the Forest Service builds too many roads and allows too much cutting in areas that should be designated for wilderness and that the income received from timber sales does not equal the expense to the government of building the roads and administering the cutting program. Conflicts in the Pacific Northwest, in particular, over timbering versus protecting old-growth forests and endangered species like the spotted owl have been heated.

Communities with significant public lands within or along their boundaries need to deal with the responsible officials in their conservation efforts. Activities on public lands will have a major impact on adjacent communities and vice versa. For instance, development adjacent to Yellowstone National Park makes it difficult to protect the grizzly bear, whose range includes land outside the park. Conversely, the popularity of the park means there is great pressure to develop land in communities near the park. Such pressure in Jackson Hole, Wyoming, for instance, makes it difficult for conservationists there to protect that community's scenic ranch land.

Vast areas of the Midwest and West contain Native American reservations, where tribes have sovereignty over their members and their territory. Although these are not public lands but tribal lands, they are subject to federal government regulation. For example, federal law dictates the conditions under which gambling casinos can be developed on tribal land. Many residents of reservations live in poverty, and economic development is a high priority for most tribes. Many Native American tribes are promoting tourism on reservation lands as an economic development strategy.

POTENTIAL PROBLEMS AND OPPORTUNITIES

Highways

Highway construction is an issue that frequently pits neighbor against neighbor and community against community. "Yes, we need the road, but not through my back yard," goes the familiar refrain. Highway construction, especially the widening of existing highways or the creation of bypasses, is closely related to rural growth issues. Clearly, construction provides jobs and roads lure new business. Unfortunately, employment projections often do not consider the lost jobs of farmers and others whose livelihood depends on a rural environment. Furthermore, cost-benefit analyses can never adequately put a price tag on such aesthetic values as a historic farmstead or a valley without development.

Although good roads are undoubtedly needed in many areas, they have sometimes been built where the need for them is questionable or along alignments that destroyed more resources than necessary. In particular, bypasses constructed around towns are often very destructive to the vitality of downtown businesses. And, although roads are often built to relieve congestion or facilitate the movement of traffic, they lead, almost invariably, to new development. Road construction is thus responsible for much of the sprawl that covers the rural landscape. Highway construction is an issue that can unite rural conservationists and urban preservationists.

1.41
Roadbuilding in conjunction with increased housing development threatens pastoral Hardin County, Kentucky.

New highway construction and improvements to existing roads continue to be a leading cause of lost farmland, historic sites, wetlands, wildlife habitat, scenic areas, and many of the other resources that rural communities care about. In addition, because roads are usually built and maintained according to engineering standards contained in the "Green Book" published by the American Association of State Highway and Transportation Officials,[27] road "improvements" may destroy the scenic and historic character of country roads. But there is hope. Especially since the passage of the Intermodal Surface Transportation Efficiency Act of 1991 (ISTEA), the process of deciding which highway projects are to be funded is more open to the voicing of community concerns than it once was, and alternative solutions, such as improved public transportation and linkages among modes of transportation through bicycle trails, and alternative road design standards are more likely to be explored today than in the past.

Mining

The mining of coal, iron, uranium, gold, gravel and sand, and other minerals is important to the economies of many rural communities. It is also one of the most challenging and potentially devastating environmental problems. Not only does it scar the landscape, but it also can destroy people's homes and livelihoods. Some of the most serious problems are in the coal-mining areas of Appalachia, where farmers sold their mineral rights to absentee mining companies, little realizing the ultimate impact. When the companies eventually exercised their rights, they were able to do pretty much as they pleased with the land, regardless of the impact on the surface. By dumping mine tailings down mountain sides as they stripped off the coal, miners in the past created enormous problems downstream. Sulfuric acid draining from early coal mining sites continues to kill aquatic plants and fish, and acid drainage remains a threat even from modern coal operations. Tailings washing into streams have raised stream beds and flooded communities. In communities such as Oley, Pennsylvania, limestone quarrying resulted in the draining of an aquifer on which farmers depended (see Case Study 2.1). Hardrock mining has created devastating damage in areas of the West, and acid mine drainage, which occurs when iron pyrite is exposed to water and air through mining activity, threatens communities downstream.

Responsible mining practices followed by reclamation are possible (see Figure 7.20). Some communities have made good use of reclaimed land. Such land may even support rare plant species, as is the case for reclaimed limestone tailings in Michigan.[28] All told, however, the record on reclamation has not been good, and mining operations have left a legacy that will cost a great deal to correct. The Office of Surface Mining estimates that some 170,000 acres of coal-mined land alone is in need of reclamation.[29] Until the passage of the 1977 Surface Mining Control and Reclamation Act, there were few controls on coal mine owners and few requirements that they restore the land after they cease to mine it. There is no federal law that regulates hardrock mining.

Hazardous Waste

In the past, hazardous waste dumps, like the one along Love Canal in Niagara Falls, New York, captured headlines. Many others, however, are much less publicized. Toxic chemicals pose obvious health hazards when they are indiscriminately dumped onto the land or flushed into municipal sewer systems ill-equipped to deal with them, as was the case in Middlesboro, Kentucky (see Case Study 7.1). They pose even greater problems when they are dumped in unknown locations. Even homeowners may unwittingly add to the problem: many household chemicals—such as rodent baits, drain cleaners, and spot removers—are toxic and should not be sent to a landfill with other trash (see Sidebar 4.16). Older municipal dumps may contain significant concentrations of toxic wastes that can seep into aquifers supplying drinking water.

The Environmental Protection Agency (EPA) estimates that some 250 million tons of hazardous waste are generated in the United States annually, or more than one ton per citizen.[30] In 1995, the EPA identified over 14,000 hazardous waste sites across the country which were awaiting cleanup under the Superfund program.[31]

Major industries have improved their handling of hazardous wastes in recent years. Furthermore, the technology for dealing with hazardous waste has greatly improved. In many cases waste can be incinerated, treated to reduce its toxicity, reduced to smaller quantities, or recycled into useful products. The EPA now regulates dumping, but enormous problems remain from past unregulated dumping practices and are still being caused by smaller, less scrupulous or knowledgeable manufacturers.

Solid Waste

According to the EPA, Americans generate more than 195 million tons of garbage a year—a number that is expected to increase. The problem of where to dispose of this solid waste is becoming more serious, as many older landfills are reaching capacity. Siting a new landfill is almost always a controversial issue, since no one wants it "in my back yard." Many cities, with inadequate space for new landfills, turn to rural areas to receive their garbage; and rural areas—in search of new revenues—are sometimes willing to accept it. Charles City County, Virginia—so rural that it has only two grocery stores and no stoplight—opened a landfill to receive the solid waste of the cities of Richmond, Virginia Beach, Norfolk, and Hampton. Although there was concern that the landfill was not an ideal new industry for the county, citizens are grateful for the income, which allowed them to fund new schools and recreation facilities and to lower real estate taxes.

Recycling programs, required in many communities, ameliorate the solid-waste accumulation problem. The federal government regulates the location, design, and operation of landfills, and state governments are required to develop solid waste disposal programs (p. 343).

Air Pollution

Addressing air pollution is frustrating for those rural communities that suffer from this problem, since the major sources of air pollution are not generally within the jurisdiction of the local government. Given the ease with which airborne pollutants travel great distances, controls usually need to be imposed at the regional, national, and international levels to be effective.

Air pollution certainly causes health problems, and its role in respiratory ailments, heart disease, and cancer is well-documented. Air pollution can also have long-term adverse impacts on the environment. Sulfur dioxide and nitrogen dioxide, emitted primarily from coal- and oil-burning power plants and industries, combine with water in the atmosphere to create acid rain, which has a potentially devastating effect on water bodies and forests. As acidity has increased, fish and some tree species are dying. There may be adverse effects on human health as well. Acid rain is also causing damage to stone buildings and monuments. Particularly affected are many rural areas in the East, downwind from midwestern industrial areas. Air pollution can also diminish the appeal of rural areas by eliminating clean air and the ability to see great distances.

As a result of the 1970 Clean Air Act, air quality does seem to be improving in most parts of the country for most pollutants. However, some problems, such as acid rain, are getting worse, since the effects of many pollutants are cumulative. Along with relying on federal and state air pollution laws, communities can regulate some causes of air pollution locally, particularly the burning of trash (see Sidebar 4.16).

RESOURCE STEWARDSHIP

It is one thing for a community to initiate zoning to protect farmland, or for a forest owner to donate an easement along a stream, or for a preservation organization to buy a historic building through a revolving fund—all techniques that will be covered in subsequent chapters. It is another matter to make sure that the topsoil on that farmland is carefully maintained and that the farm's unplowed wet soils or steep slopes provide top-quality wildlife habitat, or that a timbering operation has a minimal impact on songbird nesting sites and the stream's water quality and that the stream itself is clear of trash, or that the historic building is rehabilitated to a condition that is a credit to its residents and its neighborhood.

The kind of intensive care implied in such endeavors is known as stewardship, and it goes beyond the protection offered by local government and conservation organizations. To many, the word may be more familiar in association with church finances—and the implication is the same. Stewardship requires giving and never-ending management, a deep commitment to building a long-term relationship with a special place. While whole communities can exercise stewardship over resources enjoyed in common, such as roads or rivers, the stewardship of most historic and natural resources has long been in the hands of individual owners. These owners may regard the condition of these resources as a credit to their name and thus invest in picture-perfect maintenance—or they may lack the time, funds, knowledge, skills, or strength to maintain them. Creating conditions within the community to enable good stewards to continue their work and to encourage more people to undertake such stewardship is more than simply a matter of establishing a growth management system or starting a land trust or historic preservation organization—although these steps can often help.

Assessment of the condition of resources during an inventory (see Chapter 3) may suggest the need for specific community-based approaches to supplement the efforts of owners—a revolving fund, a grant and loan fund, a volunteer corps to assist elderly owners, a streamwatch group that can undertake the week-to-week projects involved in restoring the bed and banks of a creek, or design assistance for store owners on Main Street. Where resources are shared, as in trails, rivers, roads, or greenways, it is often appropriate for local governments to lend engineering or other technical assistance or equipment, while labor is offered by volunteers and community groups. Communities frequently lend trash-hauling equipment and pay landfill tipping fees when volunteers clean roadsides—an increasingly visible stewardship activity across the country. When the Blackstone River Valley National Heritage Corridor in Massachusetts and Rhode Island was designated, with a plan encouraging independent action by a wide variety of supporting interests, a group of canoeists and others banded together to clean the river on a continuing basis. The group's first grant request to the heritage corridor commission was for funds to buy heavy-duty work gloves.

Residents of Boggsville, in eastern Colorado, joining forces through the Bent County Pioneer Historical Society, restored a group of abandoned historic adobe buildings, constructed by early settlers in 1862. A preservation architect helped them assess the buildings' significance and structural condition and plan steps toward restoration. With the help of funds raised from within and outside the community—but mostly with hard work and determination—the residents were successful in their restoration efforts. The buildings of Boggsville were named Colorado's first official site on the Santa Fe Trail, and the community is building a heritage tourism program around them.

In some cases, government agencies, such as the Natural Resources

Conservation Service and the Forest Service, are already set up to assist property owners, in these cases most notably farmers and forest owners, with management of their resources. Issues that have joined the environmental agenda more recently, such as stream cleanups and restoration, control of nonpoint source pollution of the nation's waterways, and heritage areas, tend to be addressed by a variety of public and private groups and individuals, guided by a variety of leaders. The Blackfoot Challenge (see Case Study 5.2) has as a part of its agenda the restoration of the premier trout habitat on the Blackfoot River in Montana and the control of invasive weeds on adjoining rangelands. The Register of Significant Natural Areas, run by the Heritage Conservancy in eastern Pennsylvania (see Case Study 5.1), allows that organization to provide property owners with needed information for the proper management of significant wildlife habitat and other kinds of special natural resources. In all cases, one important goal is to assure that new knowledge about the science and technology needed in the maintenance and restoration of special resources is shared with their owners and managers.

CONCLUSION

There may be many existing or potential problems in your community. However, you should not feel discouraged. There is much that rural leaders can do to deal with these problems, as we describe in the chapters that follow. We hope this chapter has begun to make you aware of underappreciated assets in your community, assets that can be used in developing a rural conservation program.

Change is a common thread in many of the concerns we have discussed. Rural America has always experienced change, but the scale and pace of the change are accelerating. Large residential subdivisions, shopping centers, superhighways, resort complexes, and mining operations are increasingly common in many areas. In others, farmers are leaving the land, and merchants the small towns, in increasing numbers.

Opinions on whether change is good, bad, or a mixed blessing are sure to vary in your community. The conflict over change is often between rich and poor, native and newcomer, young and old, but not always. Rising land values may mean profit for the retiring farmer who wants to sell land to a developer but may spell bankruptcy for a neighboring farmer in need of increased acreage to make a living. Locating a manufacturing plant in a rural county may provide employment opportunities for some but ruin the countryside for others. Building a consensus for your rural conservation program on what change is needed and how it should be managed will no doubt be one of your greatest, and potentially most rewarding, challenges.

2 Organizing a Rural Conservation Program

INTRODUCTION

Why organize? Although you as an individual can accomplish much, your efforts can be far more effective when you are part of an organized group. An emotional appeal for support may be successful in initiating an ad hoc conservation effort during a crisis; it is rarely enough to develop a coherent vision for the future and sustain the long-term effort to make that vision a reality.

An organized group can solicit funds, influence legislation, and support legal action. By spreading responsibilities and providing appropriate outlets for different talents, an organized group is able to take greatest advantage of individual talents, creating better ideas and results than an individual could. Moreover, a group can grow and change over the long term, by taking on new members, new leaders, new issues, and new programs, further expanding its influence. There are other important reasons to organize: to help you to gain credibility and clout in the community and to allow you to meet legal requirements for raising funds and owning property.

Rural residents often have a tradition of organizing, to benefit their community and to help their neighbors. This barn-raising spirit is a definite advantage in getting things accomplished. Moreover, in stable communities with a number of long-time residents, most people already know their community and their neighbors well, which will make it easier for you to tap the best sources of support and knowledge.

Many rural citizens are active in local government and such private organizations as service groups, churches, and youth clubs, and thus can

2.1 & 2.2
Rural Americans have long cooperated to build their communities and carry out seasonal activities such as haying. In Figure 2.1, neighbors help a farm family near Millerstown, Pennsylvania, rebuild their dairy barn after a fire. With inadequate insurance to cover the loss, the family would have quit farming without such encouragement from the community. In 2.2, ranchers and neighbors work to brand, castrate, ear mark, dehorn, and vaccinate calves at the Circle A Ranch near Paradise Valley, Nevada.

choose to work through either governmental or private action, or both. Sometimes people assume that government is not responsive and that private action is the only route to follow. While this may be true in some communities, in others local government may support or even initiate rural conservation efforts.

The phrase "rural conservation efforts" can cover a wide variety of

2.1 Steps for Dealing with a Crisis

Preservation Pennsylvania suggests the following guidance for dealing with an environmental crisis:

1. Know the resource that is threatened—Determine its significance, owner, zoning, physical condition, value, and accessibility to the public.
2. Identify the threat—Demolition? Neglect? Incompatible project or use?
3. Determine the reality of the situation—Understand public opinion and availability of support from various groups; time limits; process for project approvals if any.
4. Know your goals—Be clear regarding the specific case, the community, and your own organization.
5. Explore alternatives—Prepare thoroughly to negotiate.
6. Question further action—How far should you go if you lose? Can you afford to lose? How will conflict affect your community?
7. Prepare for conflict—Secure necessary resources and allies; appoint a small committee and a coordinator.
8. Plan to win—Develop your case, know your facts, seek media coverage, involve the public.

(See Notes to Sidebars.)

ambitions. Some endeavors address many issues; others may focus on a single concern. Sharing the load among several new and existing organizations, both governmental and nonprofit—and sharing information as you go—may be a useful way to think about pursuing rural conservation in your community.

In organizing, timing is key. If there is no sense of urgency or widespread feeling that new issues need addressing, even a well-conceived proposal may fail. A crisis is perhaps the best spur to action, despite the high potential for failure in acting when a threat is already on the doorstep. The need for action may not be evident to many people. Threats may be less immediate: perhaps a past crisis was resolved unsatisfactorily, perhaps it is time to fine-tune previous policies, or perhaps little things are adding up to major change, even if only a few people are doing the arithmetic. If most area residents do not see the need for action, education of the community may be your first task. When the potential impact of seemingly minor changes or past problems and decisions is clarified, they can become the kinds of issues that will inspire action.

Although approaching rural conservation in a spirit of collaboration is usually best, you may find it necessary to confront governmental or corporate entities, either within or outside your community. When all else fails, it may be time to fight—as the farmers in Eaton County, Michigan, learned in opposing a highway through their lands (see Case Study 2.4). On the other hand, in many rural communities it may be more important to avoid certain conflicts in order to assure widespread public support and preserve valuable working relationships toward achieving more vital goals.

The order of the ideas presented in this chapter is somewhat arbitrary—organizing is more a "do, learn, and plan, and do it again" process than a linear, plot-it-all-from-the-beginning, fill-in-the-blanks kind of exercise. While we have chosen first to outline your options for a studied organizational approach, some of the initial issues you might face as you are getting started may call for you to skip right to the section on dealing with a crisis, or even to check out sections in Chapter 8 on fund raising, public relations, or community education projects. At some point along your path to effective community action, however, you will probably take all of the steps discussed in this chapter.

Whether you are assessing community needs, creating a vision, or developing a plan of action for your organization or your community, the process is much the same. Although we are writing largely from the point of view of a nonprofit effort, most of the techniques described in this chapter apply to both local governments and nonprofit organizations—as do many of the techniques described in Chapter 8. More on community planning—which can be undertaken by nonprofits as well as local governments—can be found in Chapter 4.

Unfortunately, many people drawn into rural conservation find themselves focusing on the technical aspects of the issues they face, and they neglect building the skills and attitudes that will make them more effective in the long run. Fortunately, there are many organizations that can help build the effectiveness of leaders and groups, offering publications, technical assistance, training, and conferences. Some are mentioned in this chapter; others are suggested in the appendix entitled "Sources of Assistance."

Oley, Pennsylvania: Organizing for the Long Haul

Communities build local consensus and take action for rural conservation in a variety of ways. Activities in Oley Township, Pennsylvania (pop. 3,362), where residents concerned about their community's heritage have worked through both local government and nonprofit organizations, illustrate several of these ways. Work in Oley began with a demonstration project in 1981 involving the National Trust for Historic Preservation and the township government, and more than a decade after that project ended, the effort is still going strong through both governmental and private action.

Oley's experience shows that rural conservation goes well beyond zoning and agricultural preservation—although these are a large part of Oley's story, as is communitywide concern about balancing individual and community rights and responsibilities. But Oley's citizens have also faced problems related to many other matters: a landfill, quarrying, a variety of concerns about water, truck traffic, preservation of a covered bridge, regional impacts of neighboring local governments' decisions, and the relationship of state government decisions to local options. Step by step, over time, they have sought expert information and advice, gained experience, built relationships, and seen the rewards of hard work and determination as they have dealt with each challenge to their special rural community.

The heart of a larger prosperous farming area known as the Oley Valley, some 10 miles from Reading, Oley has always cherished its heritage. Most of the township's 24 square miles are rich, rolling grain fields outlined by mature hedgerows, dotted with eighteenth-century stone farm buildings. Agrarian traditions based on the Pennsylvania German culture are still strong, and the valley is home to dozens of farm families whose roots reach back to Oley's first European settlers, who arrived in the early eighteenth century. The oldest family farm in Pennsylvania, farmed by the same Hoch family for eleven generations, is located in the township.

On the whole, Oley is remarkable for farms and villages that strongly evoke the eighteenth and nineteenth centuries, when they were built. Outbuildings on many farmsteads retain distinctive handmade tile roofs dating from the eighteenth century; one covered bridge is still in use and a second is scheduled for restoration; and several of Oley's eight mills still retain their machinery, intact, awaiting a day when a patient owner might test the passage of time. Although many newer homes have been built throughout the twentieth century, until very recently most had vegetable gardens, woodsheds, even the occasional small flock of chickens, and other signs of owners with rural roots and occupations.

Oley's residents rely on local government for basic services—roads, schools, and policing (not yet round-the-clock), plus water and sewer lines in some areas. Fire protection is still all-volunteer. Zoning and subdivision regulation at the time the demonstration project began were similar to those found in many

2.3
A side view of the house, stone barns, and other outbuildings of the Kaufman homestead in Oley, Pennsylvania. The locust trees surrounding the large barn at right are common to hedgerows and woodlots throughout the area.

2.4
Cemeteries can yield a wealth of historical information. The Hoch family cemetery is one of many to be found in Oley. It is on Pennsylvania's oldest family farm, now in its eleventh generation. Note the roofed stone wall and Germanic inscription, both familiar sights in Pennsylvania German areas.

rural communities, with a presumption toward uniform residential development everywhere. Many months into the project, a lengthy comprehensive plan dating from the 1960s was unearthed in the municipal building's attic—telling evidence of a long-ago failure to connect the idea of planning with the township's real needs. A seven-page "policy statement" adopted as the township's comprehensive plan in 1971 stated an intent to retain the "rural-like identity" of Oley. Nowhere, however, was this goal equated with preserving agriculture and historic sites, the two central elements of that identity.

Oley Township's proximity to Reading (and to Philadelphia for more determined commuters) plus its attractive environment had encouraged some residential construction. Over the years, such development had been gradual, often one lot at a time. Starting in the late 1970s, though, suburban-style "bedroom communities" began to sprout on township farms, and some residents began to view residential development as a threat.

Until that time, Oley's most bitter experience with land use conflicts had come not from housing developments but from quarries. Oley's prime agricultural land is underlain in part by high-calcium limestone, much in demand for

2.5
Designed in 1972, the logo of the
Oley Valley Community Fair com-
memorates the valley's cultural heritage and its agricultural productivity.

cement and crushed stone. The first large-scale quarry in the area opened in the
1950s; two more quarries were opened by another company soon thereafter. Together, the two quarry companies own more than 1,200 acres in the township—
not much in terms of land area, but plenty in terms of impact. For years residents endured in silence the blasting, the heavy truck traffic, the visual blight of
mountains of wastes, and the companies' neglect and destruction of historic
buildings on the properties they bought. But in 1978, the suspicious coincidence
of the opening of a new quarry hole and the disappearance of a stream and several springs in the vicinity provoked an outcry from neighboring farmers, one of
whom had relied on the stream to water his dairy herd. When the landowners
were given no assurance by quarry representatives or the state agency that governed quarry permits that anything could be done about this, they formed a concerned citizens group. The group later urged the township government to create
the Oley Resource Conservation Project.

In early 1979, the director of the Berks County Conservancy—a nonprofit organization concerned with protecting the county's farmland, natural areas, and
historic sites—encouraged Oley to apply to become a demonstration community
for the National Trust for Historic Preservation. When the trust accepted the
township's application later that year, the township's supervisors appointed a
four-member subcommittee of the planning commission. With the help of representatives from the trust, the subcommittee designed a three-year work program
calling for resource identification, resource analysis, including research into protection methods, and resource protection. The subcommittee was chaired by
Hilda Fisher, a farmwife and retired schoolteacher from a widely respected family descended from the valley's original settlers. Other members over the life of
the project included a social worker, a retired museum administrator, a farmer,
a banker, and a realtor.

Each member of the subcommittee became responsible for a group of volunteers. Three took responsibility for the three main areas of the inventory (histori-

cal, land use, and agricultural), and the fourth produced a newsletter. Like many rural communities, Oley has a variety of news sources, but none covers the entire township, making a uniform news source about the project a necessity. Moreover, publishing a newsletter was a concrete, short-term accomplishment that helped volunteers see quick results for their efforts.

After an initial period when it seemed as though there were too many things to do all at once, the subcommittee settled down into a routine of monthly meetings held a week in advance of the planning commission's scheduled date. Volunteer activities tended to revolve around producing results in time for the subcommittee meeting. In turn, the subcommittee's monthly reports to the planning commission assured commissioners and the township's elected supervisors that their many activities indeed were part of a larger picture. The workload for the subcommittee soon became enough that it saw the need for a part-time coordinator. After advertising the position nationally, the subcommittee members chose one of their cohorts, Phoebe Hopkins.

Resource identification took the greatest amount of time during the first two years of the project and required assembling a long list of outside advisors. For example, given the township's continuing concern about the effect quarrying was having on its groundwater and a growing concern about the potential impact on the Manatawny (Oley's major but small stream) by a small landfill in the ridge just to the east of Oley in Earl Township, the subcommittee persuaded the U.S. Geological Survey (USGS) to cooperate on an eighteen-month "water budget" study. (A water budget measures how much water goes in and out of an area and by what means.) Fortunately, the fact that the township's political boundaries closely correspond to the watershed made it feasible to conduct the study largely within a single jurisdiction. The USGS agreed to use volunteers to read the stream and the rain gauges placed around the township, and to count the value of the volunteers' time toward the township's half of the costs. The township also received a federal Community Development Block Grant toward its participation. The study yielded valuable data for both water quantity and water quality, providing a basis for comparison with data that would be collected in the future. And while the study did not directly provide an answer to why the stream and springs had dried up, USGS geologists theorized that an impervious layer of rock supporting a high, or "perched," water table was irreparably cracked during blasting for the new quarry.

Analysis of the resources, research into protection methods, and establishment of some protection took place as the inventory progressed. For historic resources, this happened quickly. In 1983, the National Register of Historic Places accepted Oley Township in its entirety as a historic district, one of the largest ever listed. A consultant experienced in architectural history and the National Register process helped the subcommittee to submit the application. With her guidance, volunteers organized records, completed historical research on the land and its settlement, and assessed the relative historical and architectural merit of the township's many rural structures.

In the meantime, an agricultural survey, revealing that the average age of Oley's ninety farmers was well over the national average, had raised fears that widespread turnover in farm ownership was imminent and that key parcels of framland might fall prey to development. An immediate step open to the township and cooperating farmers was the designation of an "agricultural security area," or an agricultural district. Thus, only a few months after designation of the National Register district, a second major step toward protection of the township's resources was completed: designation of more than 8,000 acres of farmland as a security area. Today the area includes 9,886 acres and 190 farmers.

As Phoebe Hopkins recalls, "the maps and data generated by the project proved invaluable in facilitating planning activities. Without the information,

2.6
The mountainous tailings of high-calcium limestone quarrying exist side by side with cornfields and historic buildings in Oley. Concern about quarrying prompted rural conservation efforts in the township. The highest tailings pile shown is taller than state regulations now allow; new piles are much lower, and thus less visible, but they cover more prime farmland.

the initiatives, and the community education that the project fostered, Oley Township would be easy prey for inappropriate development." But it is now equally clear that even after three intensive years, the project was merely a beginning. In 1984, toward the end of the National Trust's involvement, the subcommittee disbanded, with members going on to participate in both a new township-formed task force and a new nonprofit organization, the Oley Valley Heritage Association. Phoebe Hopkins joined the Berks County Conservancy as director of its historic preservation program, and in 1991 became its executive director.

One of subcommittee's recommendations was that any efforts to change the township's planning and land use regulation needed broader official representation. In response, the township appointed twenty township residents to a committee to conduct a planning study. The appointees included representatives of the board of supervisors, the planning commission, the water and sewer authority, and the new heritage association. The committee was asked to update the comprehensive plan, articulate a clear commitment to the township's agriculture and historic character in all township policies, and decide how best to deal with demands for development. To provide technical guidance to the committee, the township engaged the Brandywine Conservancy, a nonprofit land conservation organization that offers extensive advisory service to municipal governments in Pennsylvania.

The planning study would require substantial funding. At that time, residents were deciding that the National Register listing, a source of community pride, deserved a celebration. Thus was born, in 1984, the Oley Valley Heritage Association. Its first activity was a "heritage festival," complete with a ceremony celebrating the Register listing attended by Pennsylvania's secretary of agriculture. The festival raised seven thousand dollars toward the planning study. The association, which has remained an all-volunteer organization, has continued to conduct a variety of educational activities to persuade township residents to provide special care for the area's historic character (see p. 375). An equally important role, however, may be the opportunity its regular and special meetings provide to members and residents to associate with one another, exchanging information and building relationships over time that allow them to move swiftly and effectively in other forums.

For eighteen months in 1984 and 1985 the planning study committee wrestled with ways to address the community's most important concerns. What emerged were recommendations for new policy initiatives, including agricultural

2.7
The handmade orange-red tiles on the roofs of many stone outbuildings are a distinctive characteristic of the Oley Valley.

zoning, new subdivision controls, regulations to minimize damage to the limestone bedrock found in much of the township, and an ordinance delaying any demolition of historic buildings.

The political commitment necessary to convert these ideas to township policy, however, took several more years to build. Moreover, a state-mandated revision of the sewage plan (completed in early 1987), a major effort that involved assessing future development, occupied township attention for a time. Not until late 1987, nearly three years after the planning study, did the township supervisors adopt a comprehensive plan based on committee recommendations.

Agricultural zoning has been at the center of continuing controversy over land use regulation in Oley. From the moment it was set as a top priority of the planning committee, efforts to enact sliding-scale agricultural zoning in a portion of the agricultural security area met with considerable landowner opposition and were rebuffed repeatedly by the supervisors. Development interests both inside and outside the community even obtained the signatures of fifty-five landowners in the township on a petition opposing the ordinance. Not until 1991, when conservation-minded voters achieved a majority of two on the board of three supervisors (see p. 78), was it passed. Exit polls supporting agricultural protection proved an excellent tool for informing the supervisors about the opinions of the voters at large (see also p. 161).

Unfortunately, just as the township was in the process of passing sliding-scale zoning, five neighboring farmers in the southern end of the district (close to the major highway leading to Philadelphia) filed applications for subdivision. When the township balked, attempting to impose the new ordinance, the owners took Oley to court; they won their case in 1995, allowing them to develop under the old ordinance.

Among the specific measures proposed by the planning committee, only the delay-of-demolition measure has yet to be passed, but in 1988 the township did establish and appoint a five-member historic district commission, with Phoebe Hopkins as chairman. In 1991, following groundwork by the commission, the supervisors passed an ordinance allowing designation of historic districts. At that time, they designated approximately 150 acres in and around Spangsville, once a busy village associated with one of the valley's earliest iron forges, the remains of which are still in evidence nearby. Residents there were unanimous in asking for the designation, which includes both village and surrounding farms, down to the Manatawny, a key element of the village scene. The area is also protected by an agricultural district and agricultural zoning.

Other portions of the township, however, equally eligible, await historic designation. "We're thinking about changing the ordinance," commented Phoebe Hopkins, "but we need something user-friendly. Given the controversy over any regulation here, historic district regulations are a little too formal and often misunderstood. We need something that encourages everyone to talk before they make decisions." Voluntary design guidelines may be a part of this new thinking, as the commission faces a growing concern about the impact of new suburban-style residential construction on the historic landscape.

The best preservation story in Oley to date, however, may be the fate of the covered bridge south of Pleasantville (see Fig. 2.5), rated among the state's top bridges for its unusual construction. In 1992, weakened by flooding and neglect of maintenance (although still in use), the bridge lost part of an abutment and was put out of commission. It was the last covered bridge in the county which was being maintained by the state, and the state highway department, PennDOT, saw the situation as an opportunity to eliminate its special maintenance responsibilities for the bridge. "Even before the wing wall collapsed, PennDOT was planning to build a bypass and discontinue use of the bridge," recalls Phoebe Hopkins. "The bypass was going to go through a couple of farms to the east of the bridge, passing close to a historic house, but the agricultural security area prevented it. In fact [a township supervisor] signed up two additional farmers who were not included in the security area," when he learned of the bridge's endangerment and the possible bypass. The Pennsylvania Historical and Museum Commission also weighed in, thanks to Oley's National Register status. The happy ending: the state will restore the bridge, with a stronger foundation to carry a heavier load and special barriers to safeguard it from too-large trucks, and the county has agreed to take over its maintenance.

As the covered bridge's fate illustrates, not every major issue in Oley has revolved strictly around local planning and zoning. Nor has Oley been master of its own fate—no single community ever is. The quarries and later the covered bridge have involved state agencies, and two other controversies involved both the state and neighboring townships, even a neighboring county: the expansion of a landfill in Earl Township by its new owner, Delaware County, Pennsylvania, and a proposal by a Philadelphia water bottling company to extract groundwater from a former trout hatchery site just over the Oley line in Pike Township. In such situations, in addition to working with supportive township officials—supervisors, planning commission, historic district commission—and the heritage association and Berks County Conservancy, Oley residents have also joined with citizens outside their township to influence state agencies, the county, and officials in neighboring communities.

The landfill was an especially contentious issue. Many garbage trucks from Delaware County took shortcuts through Oley until the community prevailed on the state to impose limits on the trucks' routes and established teams of volunteer "surveyors" who assured strict enforcement. Earl and Oley community representatives together petitioned state officials to deny the application for expansion of the landfill, to no avail. Ultimately, the community's deep unhappiness over the landfill affected the outcome of the 1989 election of township supervisors in Oley, as the township sewer authority was entertaining the idea of expanding the sewage treatment plant to accommodate the landfill's leachate (liquid that drains from beneath a landfill). Fred Eyrich, a farmer and member of the Oley Valley Heritage Association, decided to run in protest, and he won (see p. 78); shortly thereafter the sewer authority refused to accommodate the landfill. Finally, Delaware County, after years of having to truck away its leachate and of being blocked by the township's agricultural security area and National Register status from discharging its treated leachate at the point it originally proposed on the Manatawny, obtained a permit to discharge the waste several miles away, just south of the township line.

Oley's citizens are not averse to forming new groups when needed. For the current water-bottling controversy, for example, residents of the three townships most affected have formed the Pike-Oley-District Preservation Coalition, reinforcing and adding to the voice of the Pine Creek Watershed Association, which had long guarded the condition of the small watershed that would be affected by the groundwater withdrawal.

Although Oley's historic and natural resources may be quite special, its problems are not unique, nor are its solutions. Oley's is a story of doing ordinary things very well, through multiple civic and official bodies and community leaders involved in various issues, and its willingness to seek out the best possible information and advice. Most of all, it is clear that eternal vigilance is the price of rural conservation in Oley. Hilda Fisher recently commented that she and other original Oley Resource Conservation Project leaders still attend all township meetings, reluctant to relax their watchfulness even with a full complement of elected officials strongly supportive of rural conservation initiatives. "It never ends," she says. In addition, she worries that "the young don't have time for what we do," a reference to the busyness of the younger members of the Oley Valley Heritage Association. Will Oley's heritage survive? Through both strong local government and strong volunteer organizations, it still has a fighting chance, but residents there know they must be involved for the long haul.

DEVELOPING A PROGRAM

Even if an organization begins as a way of confronting a crisis, it is useful to consider long-term questions as soon as possible. What are the community's needs? If a new organization is necessary, what "clients" would it serve? Where should it concentrate its efforts, and what should those efforts be? Although the answers to these questions can be simply stated, the steps taken to arrive at them may not be so simple and may require careful thought and a specific process that often includes "visioning," to elicit the underlying values and assumptions held by the organizers. During the process of visioning, it is also possible to develop enough detailed ideas to guide the action of dozens, perhaps hundreds of volunteers and supporters for the mission ahead—whether that mission belongs to a committee within an existing organization, a local government agency, a board or citizens' advisory group, or a new organization entirely.

A crucial step in developing a program is the organizers' commitment to the time and teamwork needed. What is sometimes called strategic planning can be a creative, even fun way to develop team spirit and an appreciation of each others' ideas and values. Ideally, strategic planning will make all the difference between a plodding group going through the motions and a spirited team making real headway in achieving public support and taking action. Regular assessment of where the team is headed should become a natural part of its meetings and activities, to help create a "learning organization."

Assessing Community Needs

Along with a resources inventory (described in detail in Chapter 3), a survey of a community's needs can be invaluable in building local support and in setting goals and objectives. Kim McAdams, director of the Brazoria County Park Commission in Angleton, Texas, says that assessing a community's needs can "eliminate the unknowns and get a true picture of the public you're serving. . . . The effectiveness of a needs assessment is well worth the time investment. You'll learn things about your public you don't know, and be able to justify project proposals and funding requests." [1]

In Brazoria County, a telephone survey, designed with the help of staff at a local university and conducted by volunteers, was made of randomly selected residents over a two-month period. The survey revealed that, contrary to popular belief, the beach was more popular than athletic fields and sports complexes; that water-oriented recreation was preferred over other types of recreation; and that residents were often unaware of what recreational opportunities were available. The county used its new knowledge to create a plan for a countywide park system to be developed through user fees and bonds and to sponsor the formation of the Cradle of Texas Conservancy, a private nonprofit organization designed to work with the county in the acquisition of the "unique areas with wide open spaces" valued by the survey's respondents. [2]

On the other hand, a show of modest support for rural conservation issues should not discourage organizers. Says a nonprofit organization director, "There does not have to be unanimous agreement within a community for conservation to take place. There are always going to be some people who are not in favor of it." [3]

Just two years after it began work in 1990, the Taos Land Trust in New Mexico decided it needed to explore how landowners felt about land use, conservation, and development, and how much they were aware of conservation techniques and estate tax issues. With support from the World Wildlife Fund's Innovation Grants Program, staff and board members developed a series of open-ended questions and interviewed thirty-three community residents, spending from half an hour to more than two hours with each person. "The goal was to gain as broad and balanced a range of contacts and opinions as possible, and to use the results to design an outreach strategy. We were specifically not promoting the land trust, but rather were listening to the opinions of those we surveyed," says Clare C. Swanger, the land trust's executive director. She adds, "Basically, we expected to hear much of what we did. But there are benefits to having that validated. We don't have to say 'we think we know'—we can say, 'the survey showed.' " The survey afforded the land trust easier access to selected community residents, helped it to understand the particular issues facing different areas in the community, and reinforced continuing efforts to reach out to community leaders and landowners about the purposes and activities of the land trust.[4]

The planning department in Thomas County, Georgia, used a similar technique, in which residents selected at random were asked to discuss their concerns about social issues, jobs, governmental relations, and land use. Open-ended questions were used to elicit a wide range of opinion. The information from the survey was then collated and presented to teams of outside consultants, who were asked to assess the options open to the county in each of those four areas of concern.

Setting priorities is a vital part of needs assessment. One helpful exercise for identifying issues and setting priorities is a brainstorming session, in which a group leader guides a discussion focusing on issues the group might address. Using a flip chart, someone records ideas as they are raised. Each participant then ranks each issue, assigning points as to its level of importance; a handy and fun way to "vote" is to offer each participant several self-adhesive, brightly colored paper dots to place on the chart next to the issues they care most about. At the end of this exercise, it is easy to see where consensus lies, literally at a glance.

The process of assessing community needs should include an identification of potential threats to or changes in the community. Sometimes, the community survey can provide some clues: Are many of the property owners retirees? Are many farmers nearing retirement? Is the community heavily reliant on a single industry for its economic base? Are jobs available for young residents entering the job market? Is housing readily available for all segments of the population? Are property owners deeply concerned about taxes and regulation? A check of public investment plans should also be organized, beginning with the community's capital investment planning and proceeding to the plans of state and federal agencies.

Creating a Vision, Developing a Mission

Sometimes organizers are so anxious to get on with a program or plan that they are reluctant to spend much time developing a clearly articulated *vision*—a statement of the future they imagine and are willing to work toward. It is all too easy to proceed to the immediate work at hand on the assumption that everyone involved shares the same values and dreams. Yet, the investment of a group's or community's time and energy in melding individual visions and philosophy into a workable whole can result in more consensus in the initial stages, and more efficiency over the long term as an organization's program or a community's plan is being carried out.

One reason that visioning is so effective for communities and organizations is that it creates a powerful framework for both individuals and the whole to make decisions and undertake cooperative action in the face of new opportunities or changing conditions. A shared vision helps to refine the "gut reaction" that individuals may have to a particular proposal, and may suggest possible responses, which individuals and teams may then undertake as required by the situation. With the vision clearly in mind, these actors have more room to maneuver and may be more creative in carrying out their tasks.

Visioning is a way of acknowledging that nearly everyone has a mental version of the future that guides his or her choices. To make these ideas and dreams explicit, a selected (or self-selected) group from the community or the organization imagines how the community or region will appear five, ten, or even twenty years into the future. A facilitator—someone experienced in leading such a group exercise in a neutral but energetic way—may be useful in assuring that everyone in the group is heard and in moving the discussion along. Group exercises to identify ideas, resources, or issues include asking people to imagine they are Rip Van Winkle waking up twenty years hence; taking walking tours—maps, notebooks, and cameras in hand to record impressions to discuss later; and creating and discussing a "favorite photo gallery," to enable them to see the community through each others' eyes (Bredouw and McClelland 1991b, p. 8).

Many hopes for a community's future might be just what one would expect—good schools, jobs for young people, uncongested highways, a clean river, or trails and open space threaded throughout the community. The usefulness of the visioning exercise will depend on how detailed the discussion becomes, about the assets of that particular place and the way change could occur. Typically, such a discussion should "throw out the rules"—the limits posed by laws, funding, and community politics that make some ideas seem impossible. Reality will have a way of asserting itself, anyway—visioning is about dreaming, and asking, "Why not?"

A final version of the vision should be framed in present tense, as brief, eloquent, and memorable as the group can make it: "In the year 2010, Prairieville is a tranquil community with . . ." To inspire participants in the exercise, it is helpful to imagine the vision stated in a beautiful color brochure, with photos and artwork to inspire the reader. Or to imagine burying a copy in the cornerstone of the new municipal or bank building for future generations to find—how much of that vision will they know as reality? To achieve a concise product, it might be helpful also to create a single paragraph that can appear on the group's stationery or in every press release. The more such inspirational uses that can be found for the vision, the better—it should become commonplace, what "everyone knows."

In 1995, the communities along the eastern Indiana stretch of the National Road (U.S. 40) created a vision for the management of the road corridor as a scenic byway, balancing preservation and tourism development. The vision statement, which guides the goals and objectives of the corridor management plan, is a simple and straightforward statement of what the communities hope the National Road corridor will be in ten to fifteen years:

> The National Road in Indiana is known for the quality of its historic architecture and for the unique pleasure offered by the rhythm of passing through historic pike towns and countryside as one travels the route. The interpretation of the road's cultural heritage, along with accessible and available visitor services attract tourists from a wide geographic area. Responsible economic development maintains a stable economic base, ensuring a high quality of life for the people of the region.[5]

2.2 A Sample Mission Statement

While every organization is unique, one organization's description of its mission—and what further information it chooses to enlarge upon it—can provide a model in some way for others. Here is what the Rincon Institute of Arizona published on the first page of the Rincon Institute Newsletter *in autumn 1992:*

Mission: *The Rincon Institute was created in November 1990 to protect the ecological integrity of Saguaro National Monument by ensuring that development occurring adjacent to the Monument adheres to the highest ecological standards. This goal is being accomplished through ecological research, conservation, and environmental education activities in the Rincon Valley, and through development of cooperative approaches to resolving community conflicts in land use planning and decision making.*

Developing a *mission* statement may be part of developing the vision, or it may come after a process like that which produces the vision statement. When communities in southern Wyoming formed Tracks Across Wyoming to promote the transportation heritage of the region, they developed a vision and mission statement simultaneously (see Case Study 6.5). Both require creative thought, but the mission is a more boiled-down, straightforward statement that implies action. The basic question a mission statement should answer is, What is the business we mean to undertake? A nonprofit organization's mission is closely attuned to the purpose it declares when it files incorporation papers.

Developing Goals, Objectives, and a Work Program

Creating a vision or a mission is not enough. Putting a program in place to make that vision into reality is equally important. Identifying the issues and the steps—the components that make up the whole—begins the problem-solving portion of the planning process. It is one thing to dream; it is another job altogether to make that dream into reality. Both are vital to making a community or an organization effective.

Goals link the vision or mission of an organization with its activities or program. Goals are expressed as general statements of what to work toward, in essence breaking down the vision into briefly stated principles or issues, such as "protecting the recreational opportunities that make our community special," "preserving our historic architecture and cultural identity," "making attractive, affordable housing available to all our residents," "assuring a future for agriculture in our community," or "assuring a safe water supply."

Objectives are the specific outcomes that together will meet a group's goals. For a group engaged in long-term change, as many rural conservation organizations will be, isolating objectives can help to create more satisfaction along the way, for they are more readily achievable than goals or missions.

Objectives should be realistic and precise and help a group to measure its effectiveness in meeting its goals. They are usually stated in such terms as "to establish twenty-five miles of public hiking trails in this decade," "to conduct three educational tours of our historic areas each year," "to make thirty units of low-income housing available within five years," "to develop and enact an agricultural zoning ordinance within three years," or "to establish a monitoring system for wells in all parts of our community over the next year." Classifying the objectives as urgent, necessary, or desirable will help an organization to establish its priorities.

After defining goals and objectives, an organization needs to plan the *work program* that will achieve its objectives. This step is often undertaken by committees made responsible for different activities or issues. Planning a work program will suggest the staff hours needed and define the organization's financial needs, which in turn can lead to preparing a budget (see Sidebar 2.3) and a fund-raising plan (see p. 367). In a work program, each objective is broken down into a reasonable number of tasks that can be accomplished according to a specific timetable. For example, a new organization whose highest priority in its first six months is recruiting members must identify and assign all of the tasks associated

with recruitment: designing and printing brochures; developing a list of potential members and contacting them; collecting, recording, and depositing dues; setting up membership records; and acknowledging the new members.

The development of goals, objectives, and a work program are akin to the process a local government uses in developing a comprehensive plan (see p. 161). In either case, it is important to maintain flexibility. While staying focused on its vision, which may change little over the years, an organization or government should be willing to change its objectives and work program to become more effective in achieving its goals. It may even need to change the emphasis among its goals in response to community needs.

Defining Boundaries

Determining a geographic area of concern is part of developing a program—indeed, there is a chicken-and-egg quality to the question of which comes first, the program or the area? You may have to wait until after an immediate crisis is addressed, but then you can step back and look at the region that makes most sense for long-term focus.

Often, the area can be defined by political boundaries—township or county lines, for example. If the organizers are concerned about a natural resource, such as their water supply, they might designate the watershed as their area of concern. The Waterford Foundation in Virginia used visual criteria to define its boundaries, including all of the land that was visible from the village (see Case Study 8.3). Such other factors as property ownership, cultural characteristics, and economic conditions can also influence decisions about boundaries. The resources inventory and the community needs assessment may be ways of testing assumptions about boundaries, and they can be used to define the boundaries at a later stage in the organization's development.

2.3 Preparing a Budget

Even an organization with very modest needs should prepare an annual budget that shows estimated expenditures by category and revenues by source. Making a realistic budget forces an organization to establish its priorities, provides a financial planning tool that reduces the meeting time devoted to money, and establishes fiscal accountability for all of the organization's decisions.

A budget can include the following categories:

> *Staff (salaries and fringe benefits)*
> *Consultants*
> *Office space (including rent and utilities)*
> *Equipment (e.g., furniture, computer, camera)*
> *Telephone*
> *Supplies (e.g., stationery, film)*
> *Printing and photocopying*
> *Postage*
> *Publications (books and periodicals)*
> *Travel (local and out-of-town)*
> *Insurance*
> *Special projects*
> *Contingency (to meet unexpected needs)*

2.9 & 2.10

The boundaries of the Waterford National Historic Landmark in Virginia include much of the land visible from the village, as illustrated by this topographic map. The boundaries also describe the primary area of concern for the Waterford Foundation (see Case Study 8.3). The delineation was intended to protect not only the village but also its pastoral setting, shown from the air in Figure 2.10 (opposite). As development around Washington, D.C., spreads farther into the countryside, the open land around the village has come under increasing development pressure. In 1986 a developer proposed a major subdivision in the fields to the east of the village (arrow), which could have jeopardized the integrity of the rural landmark. The developer eventually agreed to limit construction to the least visible areas of his parcel.

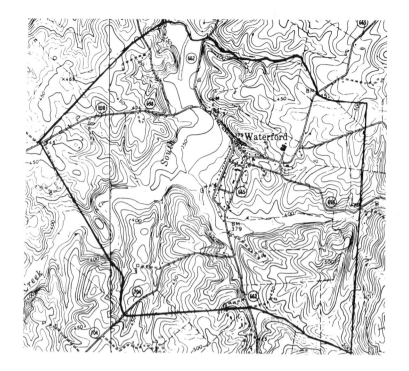

For some kinds of endeavors, drawing lines on maps can lead to controversy—whether the lines determine the area a new organization will serve, or plot a trail or greenway. Property owners in a given region or community may be suspicious of what, however mistakenly, they perceive as attempts to control their land management decisions—and thus, often, their financial security. Boundaries, in such a situation, can be a two-edged sword: they tell people with certainty who is "in" and who is "out." Suspicion can be ameliorated with information. If all people know about a project is a new line on the map and not the vision of what could take place within the defined area, many may reject the project out of hand. This may be especially true if real estate transactions are to be involved. Knowing the mission being pursued may make them less fearful. Organizers also should consider whether it is necessary or to their advantage to create a new boundary. Would existing municipal boundaries or some other well-understood geographic area do as well?

DETERMINING AN ORGANIZATIONAL APPROACH

Should a rural conservation effort be sponsored by the local government or by a private, nonprofit organization? Should a formal organization be incorporated, or is an informal group sufficient? Over time, should the form of the group change? Is some middle ground or cooperative approach possible, such as working with an established nonprofit organization, or a collaboration among nonprofit and government entities? While government involvement may confer resources and credibility on an effort, private action may prove more flexible; a formal organization has more institutional staying power than an informal committee, but it takes extra work and resources to initiate. Collaboration can com-

bine the strengths of multiple parties but require the ability to compromise and extra attention to leadership issues if different entities are to act as a whole. This section explores these options and their implications.

Dubuque County, Iowa:
Capitalizing on a Window of Opportunity for the Heritage Trail

Not every urgent reason to organize needs to be a threat. In the case of the Heritage Trail in Dubuque County, Iowa, the Dubuque County Conservation Board and a nonprofit, all-volunteer organization, Heritage Trail, Inc. (HTI), capitalized on a unique opportunity to acquire a 26-mile railroad right-of-way in the rugged and picturesque Mississippi River valley.

In 1973, a county plan had recommended the acquisition of the railroad right-of-way, should the opportunity ever arise. Rich with "human history, geological interests, and botanical delights . . . delicate prairie [and] rugged woodlands," as HTI's publicity has described it, the right-of-way offered a cross-county conservation corridor in an area with very little land in public ownership. But in 1979, when plans for the abandonment of the rail line became known, the county government faced financial limitations because of a depressed local economy and could not assure funds for both acquisition and development of a public recreational trail. Just as the 'window of opportunity' seemed to be closing, HTI arose to lead a seven-year effort to acquire and build the trail.

Key to the success of the fledgling organization was breaking down a seemingly overwhelming task into discrete, achievable projects. "We got started by asking people we thought might be interested in the trail to give us five hours a week for six months to get us off the ground," recalls Doug Cheever, HTI's president and one of the organization's founders. Step by step, with an eye on successful projects elsewhere in the Midwest and the help of the Iowa Natural Heritage Foundation (a statewide nonprofit land trust), HTI obtained the necessary approvals and opened sections of the trail to public use.

As the trail grew, public awareness and support from trail users mounted. A few owners of adjacent land actively opposed the trail, however, fearful of the adverse impacts of public use—vandalism, for example. The HTI was "a buffer for the conservation board and handled most of the confrontation," comments Cheever. These anxious owners were far outnumbered by supporters of the trail. By the time the trail was completed in 1987, local businesses and more than 1,200 individuals had paid for more than half its cost—$235,000 for acquisition by the conservation board and approximately $5,500 per mile for fencing and surfacing, supervised by HTI volunteers. The volunteers donated an estimated 45,000 hours of work toward trail improvements and promotional activities over the five years it took to create the trail.

2.11
Norma Cade, a founding board member of Heritage Trail, Inc., is shown with a trail neighbor crossing a newly rebuilt railroad trestle. The bridge, one of more than thirty along the trail, was decked by volunteers just two months after title to the corridor was secured from the railroad. Visitors flocked to the trail from the beginning, even though only a few miles at a time could be opened, because burned bridges needed repair and title questions had yet to be resolved.

Today, an estimated 100,000 visitors use the trail each year, primarily for biking and hiking—double the number of users ten years ago—offering a significant boost to the local economy. Little did the organizers know it at the time, but efforts in Dubuque ignited a statewide movement. Today Iowa has more rail-trail miles than any other state, and the state has become a mecca for bicyclists nationwide. HTI no longer runs the trail; having turned over operation of the program to the county after the trail's completion, the group now serves as "friends" of the trail.

Working through Local Government

By getting involved in local government, rural conservation leaders may be able to affect legislation and influence appointments to boards that can help their cause. It is often necessary to work with more than one local government body. For example, government services involving local roads may be a function of county government, while other government activities, such as zoning, may be a function of the municipality. Independent authorities often control water or sewer service, the provision of which can greatly influence rural development.

Local government involvement is useful, because attention from elected officials adds credibility to rural conservation activities. Moreover, governments can appropriate funds and pass bond issues to support programs or acquire property. And, of course, decisions by local government have the force of law.

Citizens may participate in local government in both informal and formal ways. Establishing an informal dialogue with local officials is the first step in educating them about rural conservation. Visiting, telephoning, and writing letters to local officials keep them aware that rural conservation issues are important to constituents. In both Cazenovia, New York, and Yakima, Washington, informal meetings with local officials were the first step toward full-fledged programs (see Case Studies 3.1 and 8.1). Such governmental staff members as planning directors, zoning administrators, or building inspectors can become valuable allies if they sympathize with rural conservation concerns—or formidable foes if they do not.

Individuals can also work more formally with local government as members of commissions or by becoming elected officers. Citizens wishing to be appointed to such established local government bodies as environmental commissions, planning boards, and historic district commissions should express an interest to their elected officials or attend meetings and express opinions. Rural communities sometimes have a shortage of people interested in government service; consequently, those who attend meetings and offer good ideas are likely to be considered when a vacancy on a committee occurs. Establishing a temporary task force appointed by elected officials to deal with rural conservation concerns—the approach used in both Cazenovia, New York, and Oley, Pennsylvania—is another effective way to work through government.

Getting elected to a government position is a different story altogether, but again, participation in the public life of the community is often the first step along this path and provides individuals with a sense of the

2.4 Nuts and Bolts

Meetings. Meetings should have a specific purpose and agenda, which are communicated ahead of time to participants. It may be helpful in moving the meeting along to assign time limits to specific agenda items. The person chairing the meeting should keep the discussion on the subject, solicit questions and opinions from all participants, and clarify decisions that are made or deferred for further discussion. Participants should leave knowing what tasks they need to accomplish before the next meeting. A regular meeting time is useful so that participants can plan ahead.

Scheduling. A group's schedule of activities should be compatible with the rhythm of the community. In farming communities, winter may be the time for holding meetings or scheduling intensive projects. Expect to take a break during planting and harvest. "We sell a lot of cucumbers to pickle companies, so everything else stops when we have to get the cucumbers out in June," reports a North Carolina county historic preservation leader. Beware of local pitfalls: only three people showed up in an Iowa community for a talk on rural conservation that was scheduled for the same night the local basketball team played its arch rival.

Work space. Buy, rent, share, or borrow space at the town hall, a schoolroom, a restaurant, a church basement. Remember that an office is more than simply a place to meet and work: it is a symbol of the organization. Committee meetings may appropriately be held in private homes for the sake of convenience, but public meetings should take place in public spaces where no one would feel uneasy about attending.

Equipment and supplies. An organization's needs may be as modest as

issues, likely supporters and opponents, and an idea of whether they have the will to engage in political life. In Oley, Fred Eyrich, a farmer and a member of the Oley Valley Heritage Association, decided to run as a candidate for township supervisor (one of three) in 1989 when controversy involving a nearby landfill reached fever pitch. His many friends and supporters in the community swung into action behind his decision, and the local political landscape was altered when he was elected with a solid majority. During the next two elections, two other candidates agreeing with rural conservation goals in the township successfully ran for the other two seats. Eyrich's reelection to his second term in 1995 is part of a regional trend, as communities across Berks County struggle with rural conservation issues. "Right now, political is the way to go," comments Phoebe Hopkins, an Oley community leader and executive director of the Berks County Conservancy. "Almost all of the candidates in the region have come out of concerned citizens' groups. There's much more active participation in government" than was apparent when the township-sponsored, citizen-based Oley Resource Conservation Project began.

Informal Private Groups

Most local rural conservation efforts originate as small, informal groups that arise out of concern for one or more community issues. Although incorporated nonprofit organizations or officially sanctioned governmental committees are often more effective, especially over the long term, informal groups may work quite well, as was demonstrated in the case of the Eaton County, Michigan, highway fight (see Case Study 2.4). Organizers may decide they want to remain an informal group that meets to discuss issues from time to time, influences local policy, and mobilizes support in times of crisis. This may be an especially useful way of organizing leaders of several community-based groups who want to share information and strategies from time to time. They may not wish for yet another organization to incorporate or fund, and may not have the time to keep official records or meet on a regular basis. Community leaders in Guilford, Connecticut, have found this a particularly effective rural conservation strategy (see p. 212).

Establishing a Nonprofit Rural Conservation Organization

An incorporated nonprofit organization established especially for rural conservation is another way to focus community attention on the issues. It has certain advantages over an informal group, especially in representing the prospect of a long-term commitment to the community and thus lending weight to the conservation agenda. Moreover, the corporate entity in itself provides certain protections for the organization's volunteers and staff from liability and can help the organization obtain financing for real estate transactions.

A nonprofit organization has certain advantages over a governmental program. First, nonprofit organizations can act more quickly and with less red tape than government can. This is true especially in real estate transactions, where private organizations may be more trusted by property owners who dislike government's taxes, land use controls, and bureaucratic procedures. Second, while nonprofit organizations operate in the public interest, they need not obtain widespread voter approval, as government officials must do in creating rural conservation programs. Third, in most communities a nonprofit organization can obtain donations more easily than can local government.

Deciding on the purposes of the organization and its membership policy are particularly important steps in establishing a nonprofit organization. Many nonprofit organizations state their purposes broadly so that they may expand their activities in the future, even if they are being organized to deal with a single issue. The purposes of the organization also suggest what powers should be specifically mentioned in its articles of incorporation. For instance, if an organization might some day acquire property, the right to engage in such activity should be stated in its powers clause.

The issue of whether to seek members from the general public is a major one for a new organization. A large membership base may mean more income and volunteers and will create within the community a knowledgeable core of people committed to rural conservation issues. Organizations with large memberships may be able to convince elected officials to pay more attention to their concerns, since their members potentially could influence the outcome of an election. If members are needed primarily to show community support, keeping dues nominal will encourage more people to join.

A large membership base can, however, be a disadvantage. Most organizations feel some responsibility to provide services for members—a newsletter, advice on land stewardship, discounts on items offered for sale, for instance—and providing such benefits can divert resources from an organization's mission. Moreover, organizations with only a board of directors involved in decision making can move more swiftly than organizations in which the members at large must be consulted before action is taken.

Although most nonprofit rural conservation organizations invite members of the public to join, such effective organizations as Delaware Wild Lands and Alabama's Coastal Land Trust do not. In other instances, membership organizations are closely affiliated with nonprofit entities without a general membership that is empowered to carry out land transactions.

Organizations that decide not to have a general membership may still have subscribers, donors, friends, or other categories of supporters who make donations and receive newsletters or other benefits but who do not vote on the organization's decisions or policies. Tug Hill Tomorrow (THT), for example, is a land trust founded in 1991 through the auspices of the Tug Hill Commission, a quasi-governmental regional organization serving a unique area of New York between Lake Ontario and the Adirondacks. THT has an independent board of directors working with part-time staff who are paid and provided office space by the commission. The land trust has no voting members, but more than 200 individuals have donated $25 to become Friends of Tug Hill and receive a THT newsletter.

stationery and stamps. In most rural conservation organizations, a computer for word processing and a camera are used regularly, but even these often can be borrowed. More sophisticated equipment such as photocopiers, computers for using geographic information systems, or projection equipment for slide shows, films, or videotapes may come in handy. Consider buying used equipment or, better yet, obtaining donations of equipment from local businesses.

Transportation. Members can use their own cars to conduct inventories, attend conferences, and visit other communities, and for this they may receive tax deductions. Check out using a vehicle owned by local government. Soon after it was established, the Big Sur Land Trust in California accepted the donation of a good used car for its staff to use on organization business.

Tyrrell County, North Carolina: A Community Takes Advantage of the Unexpected

"Seize the day" is a good rule in organizing. The ability to recognize and then respond creatively to new opportunities can be crucial, and it does not always come naturally. In Tyrrell County (pop. 3,856), in eastern North Carolina, however, community leaders have at several important junctures proven able to capitalize on unexpected events: a failed "smokestack" chase, a new state program to encourage tourism where few tourists had been known to go, an agribusiness's bankruptcy, a national conservation organization's intervention to create a national wildlife refuge and its involvement in forming a community development corporation, and, most recently, a former art teacher's gamble on regional arts and crafts.

Is this a story about insiders who were savvy enough, and open enough, to enlist the outsiders in their plans? Or is it a story about outsiders bringing new resources and ideas to help the community address critical needs in a new way? Whatever the emphasis, central to the story is a pattern of listening, learning, organizing, and empowerment that has led to widening opportunities for both economic development and conservation in Tyrrell County and in Columbia, the county seat.

The region in which Tyrrell County lies, a peninsula lying between the Albemarle and Pamlico sounds, is known to most North Carolinians as the interminable wooded swamps and pocosins (shrubby peat bogs found on higher ground) through which they must pass on U.S. Route 64 to reach the beaches at Nags Head and the Outer Banks; but, after the Chesapeake Bay, it encompasses the nation's most productive estuarine system. In 1987, this least populated of North Carolina's 100 counties was poised to become the site of a major manufacturing facility on some of the last high ground in this primarily wetland region. The county's careful preparations with the manufacturer lacked only issuance of county-backed industrial revenue bonds when federal tax law changes caused the county's bond underwriter to pull out at the last moment. Along with many county residents, more than 2,000 others were to be disappointed, former residents and relatives who had spontaneously written to the county to inquire about rumors of the new jobs. It was an indication of the close family ties maintained with many people beyond the region—the sign of a special community, rich in heritage but unable to provide jobs for all who wanted to stay.

J. D. Brickhouse, the county manager, was among the most disappointed. A

2.12
The first meeting of the Tyrrell County Community Development Corporation.

native of the county, he knew only too well how important the new plant would have been to expanding the county's limited economic base, reliant primarily on farming, forestry, and fishing. Shortly afterward, in what may have seemed like a consolation prize, the county applied for and was accepted into the state's recently developed Coastal Initiative program to stimulate tourism in coastal communities. A local committee was formed, focusing on planning for tourism development in Columbia. A charming but struggling small town with a two-block downtown and one of the state's oldest county courthouses, Columbia sits on the banks of a lovely waterway, the Scuppernong River. Now, on the face of it, tourism might appear to be an economic development strategy worthy of exploration for Tyrrell County and Columbia, especially since the growing state and federal protection of wetlands has made it unlikely that the county could sustain growth in manufacturing or even corporate agriculture. To anyone acquainted with the region, however, the notion that any number of the thousands of tourists intent on reaching North Carolina's world-famous beaches might be persuaded to stop for a while to explore the unglamorous inland seemed, well, unexpected.

Yet, the signs that this approach might work were seen by the imaginative: the growing appreciation for environmental education in general and wetlands in particular; that tremendous acreage in the region was already under federal ownership and management as wildlife refuges; the success of nearby Somerset, a restored former rice plantation, renowned for its interpretation of slave life and its annual homecoming for descendants of its slaves; a native plant nursery being developed by a state park superintendent; and enhancement of historic waterfronts by other communities on the peninsula. Even the chance of glimpsing one of the recently reintroduced red wolves or the eastern black bear now making a comeback, or exploring the region's untapped archeological riches, might be exciting to some. If only a small portion of the tourists passing through could be persuaded to stop, to visit and shop, it could mean a significant difference to the local economy. The logic of the plan, completed in 1988, in retrospect seems impeccable; it called for retaining the special character of the community for the benefit of its residents while attracting visitors with a boardwalk, a visitor's center, a walking tour, and parking—all of which are now complete.

At this point, however, the story takes several more unexpected turns. One of the peninsula's corporate farmers went bankrupt, and a national organization, the Conservation Fund (TCF), stepped in to purchase 104,000 acres on behalf of the Richard King Mellon Foundation's American Land Conservation Program. The acreage soon became Pocosin Lakes National Wildlife Refuge, the sixth refuge within less than a three-hour drive of Columbia.

Seemingly far from good news, the removal of some 50,000 acres, or 20 percent of Tyrrell County's land base from the county's already overburdened tax rolls, might have caused a public outcry. But when TCF's regional director called Brickhouse in 1989 to ask for the county's support, Brickhouse and other county leaders elected to treat the unexpected transaction as an opportunity to advance the tourism plan. Instead of sharing the unhappiness of the other counties affected by the transaction, Tyrrell's leaders embraced the idea of a new refuge, and asked for help in securing the visitor center in Columbia that was central to their plan. Both the U.S. Fish and Wildlife Service and TCF agreed, linking Tyrrell's ambition to a critical lack in the region: not one of the refuges has a visitor's center. TCF also offered to help the community in developing a greenway along the Scuppernong River to enlarge its focus on the eco-tourism angle. Moreover, TCF's interest soon expanded to helping to raise funds for a community foundation that would support development in the county.

When Mikki Sager and Page Crutcher, TCF's project staff, began working in Tyrrell County in 1991, they found almost no tourism-related infrastructure

2.5 Establishing a Nonprofit Organization

Laws governing the establishment of nonprofit organizations vary from state to state. The advice of an attorney is important to assure that all steps are followed correctly. Here are the basic requirements:

• *Decide on the purposes and the powers of the organization.*
• *Decide whether to invite members of the general public to join and, if so, what privileges they should have, such as electing the board.*
• *Draft and file with the appropriate state office articles of incorporation, the document that sets forth the decisions regarding how the organization will be run.*
• *Draft and adopt bylaws, which include the number and types of officers and committees.*
• *Authorize officers to sign checks and make contracts.*

2.6 Tax Exemption

Qualifying for gifts that can be deducted from federal income taxes is essential for most nonprofit organizations. (If, however, a substantial portion of an organization's activity, as defined by the Internal Revenue Service, will consist of lobbying, it cannot qualify for tax exemption.) Many individuals and most foundations and corporations will give only to an entity that is considered a publicly supported, tax-exempt organization. In order for the IRS to recognize an organization as tax exempt—frequently a 501(c)(3) organization, as described in the Internal Revenue Code, although there are other, similar categories—the organization must file an application with the IRS and undergo a test phase of several years, after which the organization's sources of income are analyzed to assure that its support is indeed "public." If it has an income greater than a certain level ($25,000 in 1995), the organization must also file an annual report on its sources of income, called a Form 990, even though the organization pays no federal taxes on this income. A similar designation from the state government may provide for exemption from state income and sales taxes, or local property taxes. Like incorporation, obtaining tax-exempt designation calls for an attorney's assistance.

(See Notes to Sidebars.)

(lodging, restaurants, and other amenities), and no private, community-based organization working to ensure that development would benefit those most in need, community residents. They also realized that the region was too impoverished to let even a penny be invested in anything so passive as a community foundation's bank account. With funds and advice from a foundation with a record of assisting communities statewide, TCF and Tyrrell County set out to explore the option of a community development corporation (CDC). And because it was such a small community, says Sager, "all segments of the population needed to be invested in a community-based organization and it needed to have a holistic approach to addressing the county's problems, so that there would be no duplication of effort. The proposed visitor center site bordered on a predominantly African American neighborhood, so it was critical that the black community be fully involved." Crutcher and Sager identified two interested black residents, who had left the county in their youth and recently returned to retire, and asked for their help in reaching out to the black community—more than 40 percent of the population—as the project was initiated.

The project was two-fold: Sager worked on the CDC idea and Crutcher, a landscape architect, concentrated on the greenway. Both were aided by an economic development study that built on the 1988 plan, supported by a small grant from the U.S. Forest Service. Completed in 1993 by a team from the University of North Carolina's graduate program in city and regional planning and its Institute for Economic Development, the new plan supported the idea of a greenway as "green infrastructure" for tourism-related small businesses—canoe liveries, bed-and-breakfasts, fishing and nature tours, and so on.

TCF's work in Tyrrell County involved months of meetings, private discussions, and community outreach. "While we were holding the public meetings, which were very well-attended, we were also going to the Rotary Club, to 4–H hog shows, and to churches to talk with people and answer the questions they might have on a one-to-one basis," Sager recalls. Many of the public meetings involved visits from CDC administrators from other North Carolina communities. The CDC in the nearby small town of Wilson, for example, had accomplished much in the way of low-cost housing, the predominant activity of CDCs nationwide. But participants in Tyrrell's meetings identified two other needs: "one, jobs, and two, something for the young people," as Sager puts it. Crutcher notes that there was not a great deal of discussion about the environment during these meetings, but, she says, "there was a large number of folks who truly appreciated the natural, cultural, and historic resources of the community."

By the last few meetings, almost 150 people, both black and white, had become regular participants and had developed a consensus that a CDC would be a good idea for the county as a whole. During one discussion on how the CDC board should be structured, Sager and Crutcher proposed having a board that reflected the cultural make-up of the county population: 40 percent black, 60 percent white. One of the black residents stood up and said, in effect, "No, this is not right. If you're in the minority, you'll always be in the minority. It needs to be fifty-fifty." There was heated discussion both during and after the meeting, and it was obvious that this was an issue of concern to all residents. But by this time, the habit of listening to one another, developed through so much public and private discussion, was firmly in place, and it was agreed to try out the fifty-fifty idea, at least temporarily. "It was critical to have both public and private support if the CDC was to be successful, so we made sure that, ultimately, everyone would be comfortable with a board that was half black and half white. At the next meeting, there was a unanimous vote for equal representation," recalls Sager. It was a "temporary" decision that soon became a custom.

A fifteen-member board was selected through an application process. Mavis

Hill, a black resident from a neighboring town in Washington County, was asked to serve on the carefully structured selection committee of nine members. "I thought about it," she says, "but then I realized I wanted to be part of the real action, and I turned in an application, instead." She was one of those chosen from the thirty applicants for the board—all of whom were required to have participated in the early meetings. Incorporated in October 1992, the board wound up with seven black and seven white members, who also represented the smaller communities or neighborhoods scattered throughout the county and a variety of ages, socioeconomic groups, and public and private interests. As the representative of TCF, which administered the foundation grant to establish the program, Sager, who is white, was appointed the fifteenth member.

Crutcher downplays TCF's role in this story. "When you get right down to it, Tyrrell was ready to work on this," she says. "There was a lot more agreement than there was disagreement about what should happen in the community." For example, the plan developed under the Coastal Initiative, in place before TCF's appearance on the scene, speaks compassionately of the need for "productive and fulfilling jobs," and notes that local government must deal with a "very serious perception" among many residents, expressed by "one youth [who] said, 'there ain't nothing in it [the waterfront development] for us. The rich farmers run this county and don't care about us.'" When the CDC first surfaced as an idea, it was apparent to many that it offered a new way to work constructively on more economic opportunities for everyone in the county, to overcome old patterns yet to build on the basic strengths of the community.

This was not as simple as it sounds, however. As with any start-up organization, the CDC had its challenges early on, in part because some of the board members had been fully involved in the Coastal Initiative planning while other members had not been involved at all. Some were interested in promoting tourism while others wanted to develop programs that focused on human development and quality of life. Some of these differences did occur along racial lines, but ultimately the group worked together to recognize all points of view and accommodate them. In keeping with the issues identified in the public meetings, the board settled on a strategy of human development as a means of developing eco-tourism. In collaboration with the Cooperative Extension Service, the board arranged for the nearest community college to offer small business development courses for adults, and began to solicit funds for a youth corps. The group also agreed to publish a brochure promoting the Scuppernong greenway created with Crutcher's help, and several board members organized a March for Parks walkathon that looped through Columbia in April 1993, raising $1,300 for Pettigrew State Park.

Initiated as a pilot project in the summer of 1993, the CDC's youth corps provided training and part-time jobs for twenty-four economically disadvantaged youth. For many, it was the only employment income for their household. (The idea originally had been to serve twelve youths full time, but when fifty applied, the board decided to select twenty-four for half-time employment.) The first summer was a solid success, boosting the board's confidence and the public's trust; but, as board member Hill notes, it was an enormous amount of work for the all-volunteer board.

By the following year, TCF had helped the board to find an experienced non-profit contractor to undertake coordination of the program. The CDC now has a year-round program aiming to serve up to twenty youths each year. Also in 1994, the board decided it was feasible to hire an executive director—whose primary requirement would be an enthusiasm for continual fund raising—and Hill was chosen for the job. Her experience included having organized a Jerry's Kids fund raiser when she managed a convenience store and regional community out-

2.13
This sketch of the Scuppernong River waterfront in Columbia, North Carolina, was drawn in 1993 by Page Crutcher to illustrate ideas for eco-tourism development. The proposed visitor center and nature trail have been constructed, and the site of the Center for the Sounds, a regional exhibit facility for six U.S. Fish and Wildlife refuges, has been acquired.

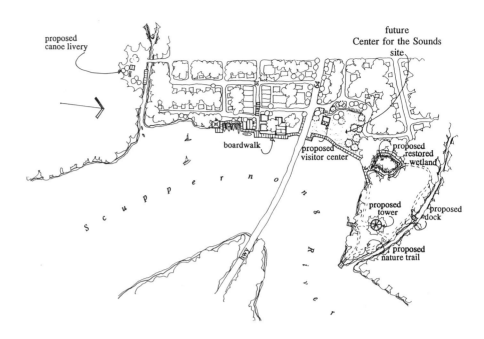

reach as a radio station employee. The long-term plan is for the corps to become self-sustaining through payment for construction, wetlands mitigation, and other labor-intensive work they do for various public agencies—not to rely on job-training funding—but the CDC will always need to raise funds for investment in its programs.

The first project for the corps in its first full year of operation was to lengthen the boardwalk that had been begun several years earlier in Columbia. Crutcher had designed, and the corps constructed a half-mile loop through forested wetlands south of town, manually pounding in every piling to support the boardwalk. They also installed interpretive signs explaining such features as cypress knees, spring wildflowers, and a nineteenth-century drainage canal. On a nice day, townspeople can be seen meeting over lunch on the deck at the end of the loop, which is visible from the U.S. Route 64 bridge, beckoning visitor and resident alike. The boardwalk has had the advantage of being neutral space—associated with neither the black nor the white community—and children from both bring their parents there to enjoy educational programs and the river.

The state department of transportation recently completed a new rest area and visitor center beside the boardwalk. This attractive facility is designed to resemble an eastern North Carolina farmhouse, complete with porches and rocking chairs for anyone lingering over the lovely view of the Scuppernong. Until the U.S. Fish and Wildlife Service's regional visitor center can be built on a site next door, it functions as the gateway for visitors to the region. The rising number of visitors attracted to the boardwalk and visitor center—20,000 in its first six weeks—confirms that Tyrrell County can "make money off the natural resources without messing them up," as one community resident puts it.

The CDC is now working both to expand the youth corps to nearby counties and to develop programs that will train corps members for environmental jobs. Plans include wetland restoration projects for road construction mitigation, expansion of the native plant nursery at Pettigrew State Park for use in wetland projects and for retail sales, and helping graduates gain internships at several state agencies with environmental responsibilities. The CDC is also setting up a regional "enterprise center," complete with office services and small-business

2.14
The boardwalk extended by the Tyrrell County Community Development Corporation's youth corps incorporates numerous interpretive signs. This sign offers information about bald cypress trees, a southern species that grows in standing water. The bridge crossing the Scuppernong River in the background was built in 1959.

training to help county residents become part of the planned eco-tourism industry. So many residents are already working in their homes, using such skills as quilting, fine needlework, and woodworking, says Hill, that she is confident many will benefit from the CDC's small-business emphasis.

Meanwhile, it seems as though one good thing has led to another—not all of them planned. In 1995, Feather Phillips, a local art teacher, realized her dream of creating Pocosin Arts, a nonprofit educational organization. With the aim of "connecting the dots between people and place, culture and environment," as Phillips puts it, the organization's programs include workshops and field tours, plus an art gallery to display the work of regional artists. From a spectacular loft space on the second floor of one of the buildings on Main Street she makes studio space available to local artists and students—those who can pay tuition and those who cannot—and through the gallery and workshops hopes to make it possible for some of these artists to gain the skills, recognition, and financial stability they need to work full time on their art. An auto mechanic, for example, exhibits African art–inspired walking sticks and powerful, intriguing sculptures of crated figures in chains reflecting another side of his heritage. An exhibit at the gallery shows how he seeks specially shaped branches from the swamps for his walking sticks—one of the ways that Phillips hopes to celebrate the local environment through the gallery. Pocosin Arts also works with the CDC's youth corps, several members of which visit weekly to serve as interns and learn weaving; those who have not graduated from high school are helped to earn their high school equivalency. In addition to its educational mission, the gallery represents considerable potential as a destination for a growing clientele of folk art lovers. Such economic success is undoubtedly reliant in some measure on symbiosis with the place it serves—Columbia provides the setting that reflects the homegrown roots of the artists whose works are on display.

J. D. Brickhouse, moreover, having been involved in the realization of so many ideas begun with the Coastal Initiative, is now dealing with another unexpected opportunity, the acquisition of the abandoned 1930s theater on Main Street that seems ideal for a cultural heritage center. More remains to be done for tourism development as well: seeking investors for the next economic development project—a thirty-bed, independent inn reflecting the simple hospitality of a North Carolina village—and dealing with development planning along U.S.

POCOSIN WILDLIFE
"Sweetgum and Black Bear"

2.15
Self-taught artist Max Liverman, employed for years by Tyrrell Hardware in Columbia's downtown, has drawn for friends and family all his life. He donated the use of some of his favorite images to Pocosin Arts, which published and sold note cards bearing the images to raise funds for, and community awareness of, the environment and the arts of Tyrrell County.

Route 64 to preserve the rural character of the corridor and the entrance to town.

As for the future in Tyrrell County, Sager notes, "Not everything is perfect, but people are making real strides. From the environmental perspective, one of the real issues was protecting natural resources. Because jobs are now more closely tied to the environment, natural resources have become more important to people there." She likes to tell the story of the minister who told her early in the project, "We need jobs, and if a chemical plant came in here tomorrow proposing to dump in the river, I would vote yes. We'll deal with it if there are environmental problems." Two years later, when he encountered Sager one day on the boardwalk, he commented, "Our kids were having to be out there working in that river. Do you know what we can do to clean it up?"

Like families, each community and its story are unique, stamped by the personalities involved. Tyrrell's is the story of a place where intervention from the outside worked especially well, providing crucial reminders of the community's long-term goals and shared values despite individual differences of race and economic status. And it is also the story of a community that understood both the strengths and the weaknesses of its natural and cultural heritage and tapped its innate strength and imagination to look to the future in a new way.

Working through an Existing Nonprofit Organization

Sometimes, the individual initial organizers of a rural conservation effort already belong to one existing organization, perhaps a nature club, historical society, garden club, or Grange. In such a case, that organization might lead the effort, on either a permanent or a temporary basis. For example, the Amana Heritage Society, an established nonprofit organization in Amana, Iowa, created a temporary landmark committee that coordinated local conservation activities and directed the preparation of the community's historic preservation plan. The landmark committee took advantage of the society's ability to accept a state grant and deductible donations to fund its work. Later, the committee formed the nucleus of the board of directors of a new organization, the Amana Preservation Foundation.

Some rural communities already have a number of nonprofit organizations. There is usually considerable overlap of officers and members. A new organization might be the last thing anyone wants, since many people already have too many meetings to attend. Michele Byers, assistant director of the New Jersey Conservation Foundation, comments that while her statewide nonprofit land trust has been encouraging new organizations for the past several years, "We have reached a saturation point. Most new initiatives are coming from rural areas, but there's just not the base, the resources to go around. We have been saying, 'Look at piggybacking, merging, chapters, try modifying the agendas of existing institutions.' I find it surprising, since local initiatives often do result in the formation of new land trusts, but people are agreeing with this strategy despite differing egos or agendas."[6]

A pitfall to working with an existing organization, however, is that it already may have a long agenda. Making rural conservation a high priority may require so much time and effort that starting a new organization will be more efficient. Plus, adds one specialist in organizational development, collaboration "might not give your goals enough of an identity or focus—your great idea could be dismissed as 'just some of the garden club members' pet issue.' "[7]

The Amana Preservation Foundation, mentioned above as a spinoff from the Amana Heritage Society, returned to the society in 1993, becoming its standing Landmark Preservation Committee. Lanny Haldy, executive director of the society, comments that the consequence is that "historic preservation in our community is improved in the reorganization. The society's umbrella has given historic preservation new life and it is easier to share resources. . . . In 1979, the society was not in a good position to take on the task of historic preservation. That would have been too much, so the foundation was formed to do that work. Now the society has grown and circumstances have changed, so it is beneficial to have the standing committee." Moreover, the needs of the community have changed, he adds: "These days we don't need to preach historic preservation as much as give practical help in accomplishing it." The Preservation Foundation donated volunteer time to fixing up various buildings, reconstructing historic fences and lanterns along one village street, planting an orchard, and enhancing the community's lily lake. Today, the Heritage Society's committee performs a less direct, more supportive role, providing technical support to business owners seeking to take advantage of federal tax incentives, organizing workshops for homeowners and contractors, and working with local banks to establish low interest-rate loans for historic preservation projects.[8]

GETTING PEOPLE TO DO THE WORK

Part of creating a rural conservation organization is organizing people to get a host of jobs done. Once initial organizers have taken the first, most immediate steps, they should establish an institutional basis for advancing the work, even if they personally do not continue to be involved. Even small organizations need to decide who will do what and pass the jobs around: who will determine policy, type the minutes, collect the mail, speak to the press, and notify members about meetings. Long-term leadership is an especially important issue to address from the beginning, but leaders are only one resource for getting the work done. Each supporter brings certain skills, talents, and interests to the organization; the trick is to use them well. Establishing committees is an effective way to delegate authority and to divide the work. Recruiting outside advisors from government agencies, staffed nonprofit organizations, or academic institutions can add expertise and clout to an organization's knowledge and strategy. Volunteers can do much of the long-term work required, but sometimes the most efficient means of getting things done is to hire someone to do the work, either as a consultant or by paying one or more people to run the organization day to day. Each of these options has its strengths and weaknesses, as discussed below.

Initial Organizers

The initial nucleus of people interested in organizing for rural conservation may be small and informal—perhaps only a few neighbors concerned about protecting the area where they live. In other communities, the initial impetus may come from government officials; two or three members of the planning board, for instance, may be concerned about community problems and want to enlist citizen support.

A small group of dedicated individuals can be particularly effective in the initial stages of organizing. In a group of five to fifteen, everyone has a high level of participation. Members of a small group are likely to enjoy a personal sense of accomplishment when tasks are completed, strong group loyalty, and a sense of belonging. Such feelings are essential to sustaining the group's momentum.

Early organizers are most effective if they draw allies from a cross-section of the community. It is natural for organizers to call on friends and neighbors for help. The danger of a small informal group is that it may be regarded as a social or political clique that does not represent the entire community. The failure of a rural conservation organizing attempt in a New Jersey township was largely the result of not including a broad enough cross-section of residents. Some of the more vocal farmers were not invited to the initial meetings for fear they would object to such an initiative. Once they learned about the proposed program, they lobbied energetically and successfully against it. Some of these same farmers later became leaders of a countywide effort to protect farmland, using many of the same techniques they had earlier opposed. The difference was that in the countywide effort they were invited to participate from the beginning.

Including both old and new residents may result in a group with a variety of backgrounds and skills helpful to a rural conservation effort. In some communities, the initial organizers may be newcomers who moved to the community because of its rural character. They may be first to realize the need to organize because they have experienced the results of poorly planned change in other communities where they have lived.

Successful organizers enlist people who reflect the different occupational, economic, educational, ethnic, religious, and age groups found in the community. After all, the intention of the group is to foster communitywide involvement in determining the future of that community. In many rural areas, older residents own much of the land and are politically influential. Members of a prominent family, the school principal, or the president of a local company may be useful allies as well; less well known members of the community may have much to contribute—the Sunday school teacher or the girls' soccer coach, for example, might provide insights in involving children. Often, the person who makes the request or issues the invitation to new supporters determines the success of an endeavor. Successful community organizers look for individuals who are willing to work together across segments of the community and have the standing to invite their cohorts to participate.

Leadership

Any successful organization needs leaders. Different organizations need different kinds of leaders, and often more than just one. Congenial mediator or articulate spokesperson, able coordinator or idealistic visionary, such individuals are the "sparkplugs," as one community organizer has put it. "Without able, dedicated, competent mobilizers," she says, "it's not likely that things will coalesce."[9]

In many groups, the work always falls on the same shoulders (as an old saying goes, "If you want to get something done, find a busy person"). All the same, it is wise to pass positions around, in order to develop the leadership skills of members and to encourage informal leaders to take on formal responsibilities. Many organizations have been left floundering when a key individual resigned, moved away, or died. One staff member of a local nonprofit organization observes, "We have a 10 to 20 percent annual turnover in our trustees that needs to be planned for. We strive to have qualified replacements trained and waiting."[10]

An advisor to community groups, Dianne Russell, emphasizes the need for an organization's bylaws to limit terms for officers and board members, basically mandating "shared leadership. There's a great danger in one leader—this is common in early organizers—taking on too much of the load," she comments. "The attitude of 'doing it all myself because no one else will' sets up a dangerous dynamic of the 'Super Leader.' This person sets standards so high that everyone else thinks they can never do as well—and they never take on leadership. Another name for the problem among organizational development specialists is 'founder's disease,' because we see it so frequently in troubled institutions."[11]

Anyone with vision, tact, time, and commitment is potentially a leader, but he or she may need opportunities to gain community respect and to develop or refine skills such as public speaking. Presidents and board members need not possess professional experience in business, real estate, banking, or law. Hilda Fisher, for example, taught in the elementary school and became a leader in her church and a volunteer for the annual Oley Fair. These experiences made her a well-known and respected person in the community with a number of skills to bring to a leadership position in Oley's rural conservation project.

Volunteers

Every organization needs volunteers; at the very least the board members are usually volunteers. The extent to which a nonprofit organization or local government is able to enlist volunteers with various skills and backgrounds has considerable impact on its effectiveness and reputation. Quite apart from the service they perform, volunteers strengthen an organization by learning more about its vision and operations from their work. If members feel their involvement is vital to an effort, they are more likely to retain interest over a longer period of time and have a stronger sense of commitment to the organization and its goals. They may also have a significant impact on public opinion. Just from numbers alone, it is easy to see that in Oley, Pennsylvania, volunteers have strengthened rural conservation's long-term credibility in the community. Of a population of 3,000, 7 percent, or more than 200 voting-age residents, were involved in the early Oley Resource Conservation Project.

Volunteers can perform routine tasks, such as making telephone calls or stuffing envelopes, but they may also be able to perform skilled tasks such as making maps, tracing deeds, or conducting tours. Occasionally, an organization's supporters donate professional services: a local attor-

2.16
Service organizations and youth clubs can often assist rural conservation programs. In Washington, the Yakima Valley Council of Camp Fire Girls has adopted the Yakima River Greenway Foundation (Case Study 8.1) as one of its projects. These girls earned badges by planting and maintaining trees in one of the Greenway parks.

ney might be willing to draft articles of incorporation and bylaws; an accountant may audit financial records or administer grant funds; an art student might design a poster; a retired newspaper reporter might be willing to write press releases. Many rural areas have a number of retirees with a lifetime of experience to apply and enough leisure time to donate their services. Retired people who have moved to a new community often see volunteer work as a good way to become acquainted with new neighbors while making a contribution to their chosen community.

A Virginia group, the Friends of Staunton River, found that one of its members had worked as a nuclear power specialist for more than twenty years and could "run circles around" the local power company at public hearings by challenging their projections on demand for power generation. The Cazenovia Community Resources Project in New York was fortunate to have among its residents a professional geologist, who volunteered to map geological and water resources. Such informed volunteers provide a local group with invaluable assistance that is normally available only from paid consultants.

The Wildlands Conservancy of Pennsylvania started its revolving fund, the Wildlands Trust Fund, for the acquisition of wildlife habitat and other special lands at the inspiration of volunteer Charlie Nehf. A retired school administrator and field-sports writer for Allentown's daily newspaper, Nehf had stepped in as a board member of the conservancy to negotiate the purchase of a 40-acre parcel of land in the Lehigh Valley on behalf of the Pennsylvania Game Commission. The commission had recently decided that land purchases in the region were too expensive; Nehf volunteered to raise funds to close the gap between what the commission was legally able to pay and what the seller needed. When he wound up with a little money in the bank after closing the deal, he went in search of more such deals. While not every nonprofit organization will be as fortunate as the Wildlands Conservancy in finding a Charlie Nehf ("actually, he found us," says Tom Kerr, the conservancy's executive director), the conservancy's success in keeping Nehf as a volunteer—from 1980 to 1996—offers a key lesson in volunteer management: Find support for the volunteer's work, either from other volunteers or, if necessary, paid staff. As Nehf became more and more involved in this work, he generated more projects than one person could handle. The conservancy provided him with paid staff—a full-time assistant who could help with negotiations and keep track of multiple projects over time, and a part-time clerk to help with paperwork.[12] (For further description of how this revolving fund operates, see p. 248.)

Keeping a file of members' or residents' skills and of who is willing to do what prepares an organization to use volunteers effectively. Some organizations distribute questionnaires asking members to volunteer for a variety of services. The actual request for each volunteer's help, however, is usually made in person once the volunteer coordinator or committee chair has verified that the volunteer is equipped to do the job. One of the most ticklish situations in coordinating volunteers is turning down a volunteer who is not capable of performing the task at hand. It may be useful in such a situation to be ready to suggest a different task more suited to the volunteer's skills, or to provide that individual with an opportunity to receive training.

Most volunteers appreciate being given a choice of tasks. People volunteer for a variety of reasons; knowing their motivations and using this information to assign them appropriate work is essential. Someone who volunteers in order to keep busy may enjoy an ongoing task such as compiling the group's scrapbook or heading the telephone tree. A new resident who sees community service as a way of becoming integrated into the community might be happiest working on a large committee with an assignment that will allow contact with a number of people.

Whatever the tasks, most volunteers appreciate the opportunity to experience team spirit through socializing—perhaps over food, or after the conclusion of specific events. Providing specific orientation to the organization and training for tasks at hand—including linking the tasks, no matter how small, to the organization's goals and objectives—are also important ways of building volunteers' skills and commitment. David Startzell, executive director of the Appalachian Trail Conference, which is highly reliant on volunteer labor, says that work in teams "sustains volunteer motivation and participation. It encourages a sense of community by making the volunteer feel that he or she is not alone in dealing with the challenges and frustrations of trail work. Even when the work may seem like anything but fun, a sense of association can help sustain commitment to the project. In addition, volunteers learn new techniques and problem-solving approaches from one another."[13]

Although volunteers are not paid, their work is important and they should be accountable for their actions. Volunteers who collect information or write reports need to be just as accurate as paid professionals. Volunteers who meet the public are official representatives of the organization; their behavior and ability to explain the organization's mission and accomplishments reflect on the organization's reputation. To provide regular guidance of volunteers' activities, an organization can create one or more volunteer "captains," form volunteer teams that relate to specific committees or board members, or provide a staff member whose job it is to work closely with volunteers.

A group's leaders and staff should regularly and frequently acknowl-

2.7 Looking a Gift Horse in the Mouth

While many local groups have benefited from aid offered by other non-profit organizations, whenever a non-profit organization offers services that may be helpful, it is a good idea also to consider its motivation. Universities, for example, provide excellent research, but it may be more extensive than necessary, tangential to the community's real concerns, and more academic than practical. Professors may be hoping for a stimulating educational experience for their students or may need to conduct field work for a research paper. In either case, while they no doubt also have the interest of the community at heart, and the community may indeed benefit, the project design may be dictated more by the academic calendar or by preconceived research considerations than by the community's specific needs. As another example, if a national organization offers its assistance in litigation, its interest may be in setting a national legal precedent, whereas the local interest may be better served by settling out of court and preserving the ability of opposing parties to work together in the future.

2.8 Interns and Youth Corps

An intern—either paid or volunteer—can often fulfill some of the functions of a consultant or a staff member. Some schools and professions require internships for degrees and licensure. Interns can be used most effectively in the following circumstances:

• when their work is supervised by a professional who is qualified to advise in the subject;
• when they work on a specific, well-defined project;
• when they have sufficient time to devote to a project to assure its completion; and
• when the project is straightforward. Controversial or sensitive projects are probably beyond students' capabilities.

In addition to universities and colleges, interns may also be available through nonprofit organizations. Among organizations working on environmental issues with intern programs are the Environmental Careers Organization and the Student Conservation Association. Such service organizations as the Lutheran Volunteer Corps and Public Allies are also good sources of interns.

Many states have agencies that help to coordinate placement of teams of young volunteers or job trainees (often called "youth corps" or "conservation corps") to work in communities on specific assignments, ranging from building trails to repairing older buildings. The communities may have to provide some support, but the cost is often much lower than obtaining such labor directly. The Silos and Smokestacks heritage area, encompassing the Cedar River Valley and based in Waterloo, Iowa, hosted teams of five volunteers in

edge and thank all volunteers for their efforts. Publicizing the extent of volunteer services in a newsletter, recognizing volunteers at the annual meeting, or holding a reception in their honor are good ways to let volunteers know they are important.

Local Groups and Agencies

It is important to work with other local organizations to develop cooperative approaches to local problems and to avoid duplicating efforts. Even the smallest rural community can call on a number of agencies and organizations for assistance. Local organizations such as the Rotary, Ruritans, Lions, or Home Demonstration clubs may be valuable sources of labor in rural conservation programs.

There may be several local governmental agencies whose help can be enlisted. The sewer authority, for instance, may employ an engineer who can identify sources of groundwater pollution. The county planner may be able to identify areas where development pressures are anticipated. In addition, there may be local representatives of agencies who can be of assistance. In Oley, Pennsylvania, for example, the Soil and Water Conservation District's district conservationist trained volunteers to use the Natural Resource Conservation Service's soils inventory to produce drafts of the natural resource maps that the Oley Resource Conservation Project needed. Universities, along with their allied research institutes or Cooperative Extension Service offices, frequently offer their services to communities, sometimes at low rates or for out-of-pocket costs. The State University of New York, for example, provided invaluable assistance to the Cazenovia Community Resources Project. The University of North Carolina at Chapel Hill, through its Department of City and Regional Planning and its Institute of Economic Development, created an economic development plan for eco-tourism in Tyrrell County that won a state chapter award from the American Planning Association (see p. 82).

Outside Experts

Outside experts can provide information on a variety of matters, ranging from fund raising to zoning. A planning professor from a nearby university can be invited to show slides at a public meeting to illustrate the impact of uncontrolled growth, in order to help citizens envision the future consequences of continuing unrestricted growth in their community. Agricultural preservation proponents in Brattleboro, Vermont, for example, asked speakers from other places to visit and discuss successful projects. While outside professionals can supplement local efforts with information or guidance and can provide credibility (the word of an outsider often carries more weight) they cannot make up for a lack of local interest or leadership.

A number of state, regional, and national organizations and agencies have professional staffs who are available to give lectures, help groups brainstorm, and offer advice (see Chapter 7 and Appendix 2 for sources of assistance). For example, when Amana, Iowa, first became interested in preparing a historic preservation plan, it sought the assistance of the

Iowa State Historic Preservation Office in developing a scope of services and in identifying prospective consultants. The agency not only supplied half of the funding for the project but also advised the steering committee on questions to ask prospective consultants and helped to evaluate those who were interviewed.

Outside experts are sometimes mistrusted. Local leaders should therefore choose the outside professional with the most appropriate credentials and the most empathy for the particular community and should consider carefully who introduces the visitor to the community. For instance, farmers may listen with more interest to a visiting landscape architect who is introduced by a banker or county official rather than by the president of a civic group.

Paid Consultants

What is said above of outside experts also applies to paid consultants. If the amount of work to be done is limited, it is usually simpler to contract with a consultant than to hire an employee who would require not only a salary but also benefits, office space, and assurances of continued employment. Hiring a consultant also encourages a group to accomplish its work within a set amount of time.

Before a group decides to hire a consultant, it should know what specific tasks it wants the consultant to perform. Establishing a steering committee is an effective way to begin the process of hiring a consultant, as well as supervising the work once the choice is made. This committee sets the project's goals and objectives and develops a detailed work program or outlines the scope of the needed services. The steering committee may find it helpful to investigate similar projects in other areas to develop a list of potential consultants, determine the going rate for such work, and set a realistic calendar in which to complete the project.

If the project is relatively large, then the committee may decide to issue a request for proposals (often called an RFP), inviting prospective consultants to bid for a contract by outlining their approach and specifying their cost of services. For a small job, the committee may wish to retain the services of a consultant already known to the group, without going through the more time-consuming RFP process.

An interview gives the steering committee and the prospective consultant an opportunity to get acquainted. Three is usually a good number of consultants to interview. An effective way to start is to ask consultants to explain their approaches and relevant experiences. Interviewers should ask consultants to talk about similar projects; note how well they seem to understand other communities. It is often helpful to ask why a consultant wants to do the work and which aspects of the project would be most stimulating or challenging. The prospective consultant's attitude, understanding of the community, and ability to communicate ideas are important things to consider. A good consultant will use the interview to ask questions about the community and the work desired.

The interview, the quality of the proposal (if any), recommendations from previous clients or other professionals, and the price should form the basis for choosing a consultant. It is not always a bargain to accept the lowest bid; if a higher one comes from a more qualified candidate

1995 and three in 1996 under the federal AmeriCorps program, with full support from the U.S. Department of Agriculture. One outstanding volunteer developed an auto tour for the program. Silos and Smokestacks applied to the state's coordinating agency for the AmeriCorps positions and then interviewed a list of applicants supplied by the agency, as they would interview any prospective employee. The volunteers each received $12,500 and a $4,200 credit toward college tuition after 2,500 hours of service. The National Association of Service and Conservation Corps can provide more information on AmeriCorps and other youth corps programs.

(See Notes to Sidebars.)

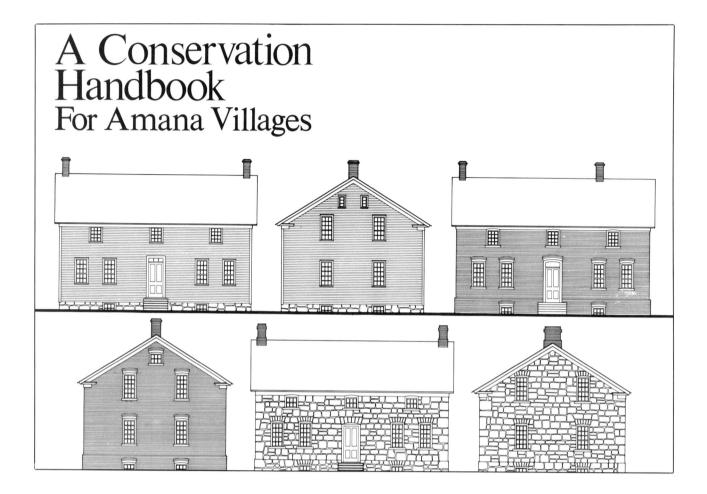

A Conservation Handbook
For Amana Villages

2.17
Cover of the handbook prepared for
residents of the Amana villages in
Iowa to advise them on appropriate
techniques for the restoration and
maintenance of their buildings and
land.

and is still within the group's financial means, it could be a good idea to
accept it.

Once the consultant is chosen, the organization and the consultant
should develop a contract or letter of agreement. The contract should be
as specific as possible, covering the work to be done, responsibilities of
the organization, due dates, payment schedule, and provisions for
amending or terminating the contract.

Consultants can be paid either a fixed fee for portions of the work as
they are completed or by the hour through the duration of the contract.
A fixed-fee contract reduces the chance of unpleasant surprises—if, for
example, the work takes longer to complete than expected. On the other
hand, an hourly fee may work best if it is difficult to estimate how long
a project will take or to know at the beginning what all of the tasks may
be. If a consultant is paid by the hour, then it is wise to agree beforehand
on a maximum number of hours. Breaking the job into several phases
allows for a periodic review of the work, promotes regular communication, and helps to assure that the project stays within budget.

The organization is ultimately responsible for the work produced on
its behalf and has the right to question the consultant's work and recommendations until all is understood. Likewise, the group should be suffi-

ciently flexible to revise its contract if conditions change or the services are too complex to complete in the time allowed.

Paid Staff

Common complaints about consultants are that too often they do a great deal of learning on the job and, moreover, obtain their best ideas from people in the community—complaints that, from a consultant's point of view, may be an indication of a fruitful level of collaboration. Once the job is over, however, the community's investment in that collaboration is lost. Hiring staff instead of consultants is a way of capitalizing on the learning anyone must do to serve a particular organization or community well; over time, the relationships that staff members build with the community, supporters, other organizations, and government agencies can be invaluable.

Making the decision to hire staff is a big step for nonprofit organizations and for many local governments. Accordingly, many start small. When volunteers can no longer do the job, a part-time secretary may be the most efficient use of scarce funds, since managing a growing amount of correspondence, memberships, and contributions on a timely basis can be a burden for volunteers. Much of what applies to retaining consultants applies to hiring staff. A written job description ensures that the applicant, the group's board, and any existing staff know what is expected.

In searching for staff members, organizations should not overlook candidates within the community. Just as there are many skilled volunteers in rural communities, there may be residents who can apply a variety of work and life experiences to a new career in rural conservation. Phoebe Hopkins, for example, started out as a steering committee member for the Oley Resource Conservation Project before she became the project's single paid staff member. Her knowledge of the community as well as her background in environmental education made her a good choice for a staff position. Even if residents have less professional experience than outsiders, they may more than make up for it in commitment and firsthand knowledge of the community. Mavis Hill, the first executive director of the community development corporation created in Tyrrell County, North Carolina, was first a board member who had also gained experience in community outreach through her work in a convenience store's community fund-raising program, and in developing a membership program for a local radio station.

DEALING WITH CONFLICT

Rural conservation is not without controversy, certainly. While many rural organizations work solely in support of their own projects, some groups may decide that part of their work is to take a concerted stand against others' proposals as well. Besides confrontation, lobbying, and litigating, dispute resolution and enlarging a community's commitment to public involvement may help in dealing with conflict and solving problems.

2.9 Orienting Professional Visitors

The following suggestions should help make the visits by consultants and advisors from outside your community more productive:

• *Before the visit, provide visitors with previous reports, such as the comprehensive plan or a summary of goals and objectives, plus copies of the local newspaper and the organization's newsletter, so that visitors can gain a sense of the community before arriving.*

• *Be honest about any opposition to an outsider's involvement in the program. Warn a speaker if a challenge is anticipated at a public gathering.*

• *Be candid about community problems. If certain controversial issues are not discussed publicly in the community, say so.*

• *Let visitors know what to expect. Will boots be needed for a visit to a dairy farm, or will a warm jacket and hat make a day's outing more comfortable?*

• *Provide visitors with a map and a tour of the entire community. Don't focus only on what is unique and overlook the everyday, characteristic nature of the area.*

• *Introduce visitors to a cross-section of the community—including farmers, nonfarmers, and business people.*

• *Visit places where local people go to shop or eat. Suggest morning coffee with farmers at the local diner— don't just go to the chic new restaurant for out-of-towners.*

• *Invite visitors to attend such community events as fairs, church services, and public meetings, and make them feel welcome. Participating in local events will give outsiders an opportunity to know the community better.*

Eaton County, Michigan: Fighting a Highway—and Winning

Sometimes an informal unincorporated group works best, and sometimes organizing around a single issue rather than rural resources in general works best. Citizens Concerned about I-69 is a case in point on both counts. This is also the story of a group that went beyond efforts to persuade and decided to lobby and litigate as well. Despite the age of this story—the fight happened a generation ago—it stands the test of time as one of the great victories of grassroots common sense. Even with "modern" highway planning under the Intermodal Surface Transportation Efficiency Act of 1991, threats to farmland from highway construction continue to arise today, and the tactics here are just as useful as they were then.

Eaton County, Michigan, is largely agricultural, with much of it prime farmland. Farmers make their living from dairy products, livestock, corn, and wheat. Since the 1960s, the growth of nearby Lansing and other suburban growth, plus the construction of highways in the county, has put considerable pressure on the agricultural sector.

When, in the early 1970s, the Michigan Department of Transportation (MDOT) proposed connecting Charlotte and Lansing by a new 16–mile section of Interstate 69 that would sweep through much of the remaining agricultural land and encourage increased sprawl from Lansing, many of the county's farmers objected. The Eaton County Planning Commission and several township boards expressed concern as well. The proponents of farmland preservation recommended that the new interstate be placed alongside U.S. Route 27, an alignment that would use much less agricultural land. However, MDOT argued that the Route 27 alignment would destroy more wetlands (which proved not to be the case) and that the dogleg alignment (see Fig. 2.18) would serve anticipated development to the west of Lansing. In 1976, MDOT approved an environmental impact statement (EIS) for the dogleg alignment.

In May 1976, Fred McLaughlin, a Lansing architect, read about the controversy in a local paper. McLaughlin, who was raised in rural Eaton County, sympathized with the farmers and decided to investigate. After studying the EIS and meeting with MDOT officials, he became convinced that the new interstate was not needed, or at least that the dogleg was not justified. With the support of several farmers in the area, McLaughlin set out to see what could be done.

In January 1977, McLaughlin met with several aides to the governor. "Their reaction," he reports, was " 'You are right; we've got to call the chairman of the state transportation commission and tell him to put a hold on this project until we can look into it.' Well, my jaw fell. I could not believe I was getting that kind of reaction." The aides asked the Michigan Environmental Review Board to investigate. In April, however, the board concluded in a report to the governor that proper procedures had been followed and that there was no justification for changing the alignment. The governor concurred. Although McLaughlin and his colleagues lost this round, they learned an important lesson: they could make top officials pay attention to their concerns, but they were also going to need grassroots political support for their cause.

In early 1977 McLaughlin and a half-dozen farmers established Citizens Concerned about I-69 (CCAI) as an ad hoc, unincorporated group. They purposely chose a name that did not express a point of view, so as to generate broad support in the affected communities. The group never had regular meetings or

2.18
Opposite: This page out of the environmental impact statement for re-routing Interstate 69 in Eaton County, Michigan, shows why the dogleg "approved alignment" of 1977 stirred such opposition. Ultimately, opponents to the alignment, who had coalesced around a concern for the impact on farms in the area, were successful in obtaining approval for an alternative alignment along an existing route. (Note the grid settlement pattern of secondary roads, which is commonplace in the Midwest. Each section is one square mile.)

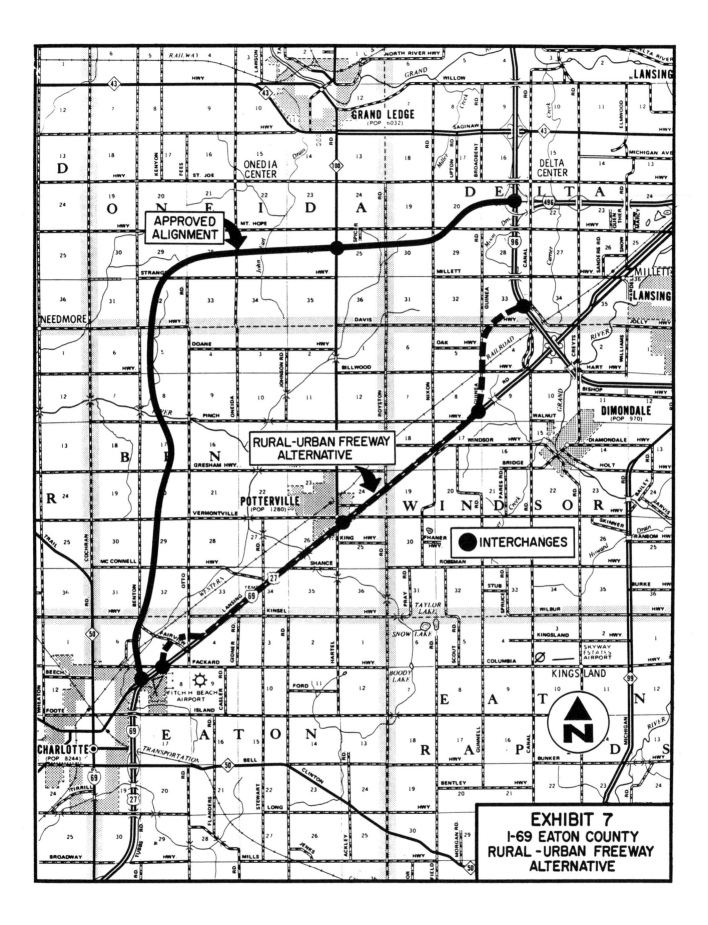

APPROVED ALIGNMENT

RURAL-URBAN FREEWAY ALTERNATIVE

● **INTERCHANGES**

EXHIBIT 7
I-69 EATON COUNTY
RURAL-URBAN FREEWAY
ALTERNATIVE

2.10 How to Negotiate

Preservation Pennsylvania suggests that negotiators work to

• *distinguish people from the problem;*
• *listen to other parties' interests, treat others' concerns with respect;*
• *avoid emotional outbursts, and don't react to those of others;*
• *establish a flexible position: focus on a desired goal, not a bargaining position;*
• *recognize each party's multiple interests, identify shared interests;*
• *avoid debate, seek dialogue;*
• *propose realistic options for mutual benefit;*
• *don't be a victim: question phony "facts," offer alternatives to biased "experts," and beware less than full disclosure.*

(See Notes to Sidebars.)

launched a formal membership campaign. However, it developed a highly effective informal network with which to get timely information to the people who needed it, by telephone and newsletters. According to McLaughlin, the group did not need a high degree of organization. The meetings they had were usually held in someone's home and started with coffee and doughnuts and talk about crops and weather.

CCAI prepared a resolution calling for rerouting I-69 out of prime farmland. They avoided questioning the need for I-69 and avoided the obvious recommendation that it should parallel Route 27. CCAI had a reason for being vague: they did not want to appear to be telling MDOT where or how to build a highway, because that would give MDOT the opportunity to marshal specific arguments against the resolution.

In 1978, CCAI took the resolution to most of the township and municipal boards in the county. The group planned each meeting carefully, deciding which members would make the best impression. According to McLaughlin, "We were fortunate in having people in our group who were very well regarded in the area—through family and business ties. We made a real effort to be credible and we handled ourselves responsibly. Even MDOT staff said privately that we had been very fair in our dealings with them."

The boards of twelve of the sixteen townships in the county supported the resolution, as did key municipal councils, planning commissions, and the Eaton County Farm Bureau. This led to a turnaround vote of support for the resolution by the Eaton County Board of Commissioners, which had earlier agreed with MDOT's proposed alignment.

In addition, the press was supportive. Several editorials in the Detroit Free Press supporting CCAI's position, written after CCAI members met with the editor, were particularly helpful.

The group's members also contacted their congressman and senators. Howard Wolpe, who ran Senator Donald Riegle's Lansing office, listened sympathetically and gave them much good advice on strategy, occasionally assisting in making key contacts in the federal bureaucracy. Wolpe was himself elected to Congress in 1978 and continued to help.

In 1979 the group filed suit against MDOT, seeking an injunction against further development of the road, claiming that EIS procedures had not been followed and that inadequate attention had been given to farmland retention. Although the court dismissed the suit in August 1980, the litigation further delayed MDOT.

Disappointment over the lawsuit was overshadowed by great news from Washington. Wolpe's office called to say that a rider could be placed on the 1981 U.S. Department of Transportation and Related Agencies Appropriations Act to halt all work on I-69 for ninety days to allow for federal review and a new public hearing. A few weeks later several CCAI members drove to Washington for a meeting, chaired by Wolpe, with several top U.S. Department of Transportation (USDOT) officials. A number of issues were discussed, but the meeting did not seem to be getting anywhere until one of the Eaton County farmers made an emotional appeal for immediate action. He predicted that if the road went through, it would spell the end of agriculture in the I-69 area within twenty years. According to McLaughlin, he told the officials to get serious and act, or he might as well head home to get on with his farming and watch Eaton County agriculture dwindle quickly to nothing. That simple statement seemed to have a greater impact on them than all the reports and figures. Later that day, USDOT staff called Wolpe to say that they favored reopening the issue. The rider on the appropriations bill passed the Congress.

The USDOT public hearing was held in November 1980. Most of the testimony and most of the witnesses, including CCAI's own highway and environmental consultants, supported the Route 27 alignment. In December, the U.S. Secretary of Transportation recommended that the highway alignment be moved to Route 27 in order to conserve farmland. Bowing to the pressure, MDOT reluctantly reopened the EIS process and finally, in December 1981, approved the Route 27 alignment.

Although CCAI no longer exists, it has left an important legacy. In addition to having achieved their goal, the former members now know they can have a say in their community's future. More tangibly, several were appointed or elected to positions of civic authority in the county.

Confronting (and Avoiding) a Crisis

One of the most frequent motivations for organizing is the eleventh-hour protest in a time of crisis. A rezoning controversy or a school closing are common examples. Angry and concerned, citizens band together to take action. Such a crisis can quickly mobilize many people, including those who might not otherwise become involved.

Though it may be easy to mobilize opposition in a crisis, it may be more difficult to quickly reach a consensus on a course of action. As one organizer has put it, "You get a group of people in a room: some want to sue; some want to form a citizens' group; some want to hire their wife's nephew who is a planner to do an impact statement to refute the existing impact statement. How is a group going to sift through all of these ideas and figure out what's going to work?" [14]

Whether a group has two weeks, two months, or two years to deal with a crisis, the odds of success are better if the group approaches the problem systematically. When a crisis develops or a potential problem is forecast, it is important for the group to meet with the concerned parties to explore all of the options and to seek possible solutions. Conflict management techniques, described below, may offer alternatives to outright confrontation.

There are many reasons why last-minute efforts often fail. Frequently, the sponsor is already organized and has a paid staff to combat any opposition; in some cases, a political deal has already been struck before plans were made known to the public. To fight such opponents may require either going to court or the classic last-ditch demonstration in front of the bulldozer.

Win or lose, a crisis may stimulate a community's awareness and not only prompt action on related issues but also provide a basis for organizing a long-range effort. In Cazenovia, New York, for example, an unsuccessful attempt to prevent construction of a subdivision on a wetland was later helpful in gaining support for improved protection for other areas. Once a crisis is over, it is important to evaluate the effort to determine what went right or wrong and why, to thank supporters and contributors, and to assess the group's strengths and talents to learn from the experience. Reflecting on her experience as part of the successful effort to stop the damming of the New River on the North Carolina–Virginia border, one organizer says:

> After you win, keep working. Old dams never go away; old water projects never go away. They're going to come back at you a couple

2.11 The Difference between Public Relations and Public Involvement

Lucy Moore, a facilitator in natural resource–related mediation, wonders if public involvement is "being used to distract or flatter the public while business goes on as usual," or whether it is "a genuine and democratic effort to involve people in making decisions that affect them." She has expressed the following thoughts on this question:

> *People are right to be skeptical. More and more agencies and companies are realizing that public involvement helps public relations and that good facilitation can insulate them from hostile citizens. Some are motivated only by a legal obligation to solicit public input and merely go through the motions of doing so.*
>
> *Others, however, recognize the real value of public involvement—its ability to tap the insights, energy and ideas of the citizenry and to build support for implementing decisions that are ultimately made. Plus, as one state environmental worker told me, public involvement helps the public understand the complexity of issues. "It takes part of the burden off," he said, "When people understand the spot I'm in."*
>
> *To distinguish between public*

of years later, or some other issue is bound to affect you. While you have power, while you've got people geared up, get them to keep going and do something positive to permanently protect it. It also makes you look better. Otherwise, you're just obstructionists or you're just anti-progress. Instead, get your group to be for something. Start saying "We don't just want to stop things; we want people to know that our area is a special place."[15]

Another valuable result of fighting a crisis is learning how to avoid other crises in the first place. Once organized, a group should develop an early warning system to head off crises—to discover potential problems before project proponents have successfully made their way through the various stages of approval that usually are required. Monitoring the public notice section of local newspapers and attending governmental public meetings are generally useful steps. Most states have "sunshine" laws that prevent closed door meetings of elected officials where decisions will be made, and citizen participation in the form of public hearings and comment periods for proposals often is mandated.

Land development projects in particular often require multiple permits, from both local and state agencies, so it may pay to investigate the routines followed by each relevant agency for public participation in their decision making. Many local, regional, and state agencies require public notice and comment in the process of reviewing permit applications for public or private projects. Public highway projects can enter the planning process as much as twelve years before funds are committed to construction; other kind of projects usually involve much less lead time.

Agencies whose routines should be investigated include more than just such obvious ones as the local planning or zoning office, if any, and the state agencies responsible for wetlands and wastewater permits or highway construction. It may pay to check out the state's waste management agency (for landfills or trash transfer stations, for example, or special facilities treating hazardous wastes) or state agencies that may have a role in decisions about where large trucks may go or where communications towers, cross-country gas lines, or electrical transmission lines may be sited. Oley, Pennsylvania, and neighboring communities discovered only after the fact that both regional and state agencies regulating groundwater withdrawals had granted permits to a water bottling company to extract spring water from a source along their common boundary. Such a business could be expected to bring high numbers of tanker trucks to narrow township roads and to affect water levels in the local watershed, which includes a stream protected as an outstanding national resource water under the federal Clean Water Act and a wetland containing several threatened species of plants and the bog turtle, a candidate for national listing as an endangered species.

Particular vigilance in monitoring changes to roads serving a community may be required, since several agencies may be involved at the state, regional, and local levels. The state highway department (which regulates new access points along state highways, for example), a regional organization under federal law governing planning for federal expenditures, known generically as the "metropolitan planning organization" (which can include outlying rural communities), and the local roads department will all have some say in what road alteration and construction will take place in a rural community.

While it can be time-consuming to become directly involved in such activities as citizens' advisory councils to state or regional agencies, it may be useful to get to know those who are involved, or to join organizations that make it their business to monitor state and regional agencies and publicize their findings through newsletters and alerts.

Resolving Disputes

Implementing cooperative approaches to problem-solving and to resolving disputes can make a rural conservation organization more effective in dealing with an immediate crisis. Cooperative approaches also inspire creativity in resolving the conflicting priorities inherent in land use and resource protection, in both critical and long-term situations.

The process termed dispute resolution, or conflict resolution, is a voluntary procedure focused on identifying the interests of all parties rather than attempting to meet negotiation terms. A citizens group's *position* might be "We want zoning," but the *interest* that underlies this position might be "We are concerned about the pace and scale of development in our community." Dispute resolution involves a series of steps: (1) mutual education of the interested parties, (2) creation of a jointly acceptable description of the issue and its potential impact, (3) generation of options for resolution, (4) bargaining over the acceptability of the options, and finally (5) agreement. A continuing relationship among the parties, to implement the agreement, may also result.[16] In mediation, one form of dispute resolution, someone without a stake in the issue assists those with conflicting interests in exploring their differences and discovering where they agree. A negotiated settlement that meets each party's most critical objectives is sought by making accommodations on lesser concerns, the mediator's objective being to identify an outcome in which each party can declare a partial victory. Dispute resolution, unlike binding arbitration or litigation, allows all parties to remain in control while reaching any terms or settlement.

Dispute resolution can be used when the parties involved are the ones that will decide the outcome, and when each has the power to affect the outcome for the others. Without some amount of urgency and some room for bargaining, dispute resolution may not work. Using dispute resolution techniques without some sophistication in negotiation and some ability on the part of the negotiator to assert the organization's interest, or without the guidance that a mediator or facilitator can provide, can endanger the organization's effectiveness and public support. On the other hand, these techniques can markedly enlarge an organization's options beyond lobbying and litigating. To governmental agencies, dispute resolution can offer approaches for accomplishing community goals without more regulation.

In 1995, the board of supervisors for Rockingham County, Virginia—one of the most productive agricultural counties in the nation—together with the board of the Shenandoah Valley Soil and Water Conservation District, created a voluntary program to investigate pollution complaints

relations and genuine public involvement, the facilitator and the citizen need to ask several questions:

1. Is the decision already made, or is the process still truly open?
2. How will this decision-making process work? What are the points of influence?
3. How will I know that my concern is taken seriously?
4. Who is designing and running the public involvement process: Are they professional? Experienced? Neutral? Are they open to new ideas about the process itself?

Even if all answers are satisfactory, the citizen still has to ask, "Do I have the energy for this or will I just get facilitated to death?"

The choice is rarely easy, but then again, democracy is usually a long, sloppy and difficult process. Moreover, if democracy requires an informed citizenry, then the challenge to educate and be educated increases daily. Public participation programs, well planned and facilitated, become an opportunity for that education, and a vehicle for democratic expression.

As a facilitator, I insist that citizens and bureaucrats listen to each other, learn from each other, and recognize that, since the problems before them are shared, the solutions must be mutual.

(See Notes to Sidebars.)

against farmers. Other partners in the effort include the Cooperative Extension Service and representatives of the dairy, beef, and poultry industries. Part of the motivation was a fear that greater regulation would fall across-the-board on the farming community from state or federal agencies, especially regulations concerning water pollution, when it seemed simpler to deal with specific problems one by one, educating the farming community in the process. Under the program, complaints go to the county planning department, which refers them to the appropriate partner or partners, who attempt to resolve the problem; a mediation committee is the next step, which works with the offending farmer to develop a voluntary correction plan. The Virginia attorney general's office will handle any problems the voluntary program cannot resolve.[17]

CASE STUDY 2.5

Appalachian Trail, Connecticut: The Housatonic Valley Association Becomes Part of the Protection Solution

Sometimes a local organization may be able to provide a key role in resolving an impasse by adding its own thoughts to the dialogue or by committing itself to becoming part of the solution, or both. In 1983 the Housatonic Valley Association, a watershed conservation organization, ventured into a standoff among a landowner, the federal government, and local residents to help provide information, ideas, and finally a local commitment to protecting a portion of the land in dispute.

The issue involved protecting a 5–mile segment of the Appalachian Trail that runs through a tract of more than 2,000 acres in the northwestern hills of Connecticut. The corporate owner insisted on selling all or none of the tract to the National Park Service, which had authorization only to acquire a 1,000–foot-wide corridor, or some 300 acres. Even if it were to obtain congressional authorization to acquire the whole tract, the Park Service quickly learned, local sentiment in the three affected towns was adamantly opposed to such extensive federal ownership.

With approval from the three towns, the Housatonic Valley Association enlisted a state-sponsored environmental review team advising western Connecticut towns on the effects of proposed land use changes. For this project, the team was composed of representatives from federal, state, and local agencies and the association, plus representatives from the Appalachian Trail Club and the Appalachian Mountain Club, voluntary groups responsible for trail management. Both the team and the association embarked on studies of the tract, the team to provide baseline information and preliminary maps and the association to refine the team's studies and inject ideas for resolution.

Federal ownership was of special concern to area residents. Farmers took a dim view of abandonment of prime farmland; wildlife and forestry managers worried that nuisance species would get out of hand with prohibition of timbering and hunting; and residents in the affected area feared recreational overuse and increased traffic. Moreover, one town's landfill and sand and gravel pit were located on the tract, which the Park Service stated should be closed. The same town opposed removal from its tax rolls of hundreds of acres of land ripe for development.

With study and accommodation, a reconciliation of these competing and conflicting interests began to emerge. First, land visible along the trail was defined as a visual buffer area for permanent protection by the Park Service and the towns, leaving the way open for negotiation on exactly what that protection might entail. The company relented on its all-or-nothing stance.

The solution involved the acquisition by the Park Service of only scenic easements in much of the area under dispute, allowing continuation of forestry, farming, hunting, and even the landfill and sand and gravel operations (under strict screening and reclamation requirements). The corporate owner, working in conjunction with the association, will complete the master plan developed through the project by undertaking limited residential development on 200 acres and conveying more than 20 acres to expand a popular nearby state park. The association continues to work closely with the Park Service, the volunteer trail management agencies, the towns, and the current landowner by compiling information on the important natural features of the property and sharing conservation land planning expertise and strategies as the development plan is updated.

Public Participation

There are various ways of bringing members of the public into decision-making processes. Public hearings and requests for written comments from the public on proposed policies or decisions are now standard governmental fare, usually required by law. How well such steps allow a governmental agency to gauge and respond to public opinion can vary and often depends on the agency's commitment to public participation and to the ideas that might result.

Unfortunately, for many projects, both public and private, plans are often far advanced when "the public" is brought into the picture. It is quite typical for managers responsible for such projects to wish to limit the number of "cooks stirring the broth" and attempt to avoid conflict by keeping plans quiet. It takes wisdom and a certain amount of courage to keep options open while seeking public opinion that may bring conflict. Yet, conflict is not always to be feared: "Conflict can create opportunities for individuals and groups to clarify their own values, goals, and objectives; to expose each other to new information and points of view; and to balance competing interests," observes one team of dispute resolution specialists.[18]

Besides public hearings and written public comments, there are more creative methods for bringing members of the public and representatives of various interests together to address a problem or develop a policy before decisions are proposed. Visioning, for example, includes a high level of public participation when done to initiate an open-ended public planning process—a point when it is easiest to consider a wide range of ideas and community concerns and develop consensus. Another idea is compatibility assessment, a process in which neighbors are asked to meet with a developer to comment on a proposal for development at the earliest stage of public review.[19] Such a process may help to reduce such site-specific negative impacts as increased traffic, creation of unsightly views, noise, lighting problems, loss of privacy, and increased need for public services. One inherent problem in such an exercise—common to all public participation in development planning—is that those who stand to profit from development are often represented by experts (planners, lawyers, landscape architects), whereas neighbors often cannot afford expert representation. This imbalance of power can be ameliorated if the local government is committed to broad public participation and development of consensus or if a community-based group develops enough strength to support the individual concerns of its members and residents.

In some cases, it may be difficult to tell where public participation leaves off and dispute resolution begins. In fact, if brought in early enough, specialists in dispute resolution can help to design public participation processes that aim to improve the quality and extent of participation and reduce the level of conflict in public decision making. A community's commitment to public involvement can also be enhanced by establishing specific policies and procedures in a public involvement plan (Creighton, 1992).

Besides acting as watchdog and advocate, a rural conservation organization can perform the equally important role of assuring that all voices within the community are heard and respected. This is easier said than done, for often, governmental decision-making processes can reinforce the values of certain groups and not others. Miscommunication, either with outside public agencies or corporations or among varying local groups, is not uncommon in rural communities. The possibility of miscommunication and discord within the community may especially be overlooked when ethnic or racial variation is not a factor. Even in communities where most if not all residents share a common ancestry, people may possess not only diverse values, but different ways of communicating.[20]

The Taos Land Trust serves the spectacular northern New Mexico region, which has a tricultural heritage of Native Americans, Hispanic families tracing their ancestry back to 1600s Spanish royal and Mexican colonial land grants, and "Anglos" whose families settled there in the 1800s. In 1992, the board and staff of the trust set out to interview members of the community about their attitudes toward land preservation and development and their knowledge of land conservation techniques. Working in teams "constructed for maximum potential comfort for the person to be interviewed," of varying numbers and mixed in terms of both gender and ethnicity, interviewers quickly discerned differences in the rhythms of their communications. "Breaking the ice" with Hispanic landowners before digging into a discussion about land—a sensitive issue in this cash-poor, land-rich community facing significant growth pressure—involved talking about family, "such as genealogy, what the children and relatives are doing, and who knew whom," and about irrigating, "such as what ditch they are on, how the water supply has been this year, and who the ditch commissioner is," recalls Clare C. Swanger, the land trust's executive director. "With the Anglo landowners, initial conversation about what brought them to Taos inevitably led into their feelings and attitudes about the area, and the entire range of topics we wanted to discuss."[21]

Information Sharing

Simple information sharing, as opposed to an activist stance, may be a useful way to begin breaking down barriers to communication. Among other benefits, it can provide an opportunity to get to know people on a personal level, rather than identifying them as part of an impersonal interest group, making communication more effective and enjoyable. The Colorado Cattlemen's Association was involved in the formation of the Colorado Riparian Association (CRA), which addresses problems of streambanks resulting from, among other causes, intensive cattle grazing. Reeves Brown, a member of the Cattlemen's Association, says:

> I think our association's initial interest in becoming involved stemmed as much from concern about what might be done to us if we weren't at the table as it did from what we might be able to do if we were at the table. . . . Over the course of the last few years, the CRA has provided a welcome stage for our association, the livestock industry, and private landowners in general to communicate with land management agencies, conservation organizations, and resource academia concerning riparian and watershed resource management. In my opinion, the key to the CRA's effectiveness has been adherence to the original mission of serving as an information clearinghouse for such matters rather than being a bureaucratic think tank or eco-policeman. Two rules of conduct at each CRA board meeting have helped maintain this integrity: (1) no one points any finger at or places blame for resource damage on anyone else, and (2) all order-in pizza is dutch treat. (The latter rule probably has less significant long-term impact on Colorado's riparian resources than the former, but nonetheless helps preserve the CRA leadership's cohesiveness.)[22]

A commitment to empowering every voice within a community through shared information and on-going dialogue may go a long way toward strengthening the community's ability to deal with longstanding conflict. Such sharing may also strengthen long-term civic ties among groups and individuals which will further enable them to undertake needed community projects.[23]

One example of a rural conservation organization created specifically to share information and improve cooperation among various stakeholders is Montana's Blackfoot Challenge, created in 1993 after two years of deliberations among a wide variety of public and nonprofit organizations, corporations, and individuals. Although for years the Blackfoot Valley has enjoyed the protection of a highly effective conservation easement program (see Case Study 5.2), the Blackfoot Challenge is devoted to protecting "the rural lifestyle and economic health of the Blackfoot Valley." Through tours, public meetings, informational workshops, development of educational materials, and teaching consensus-building techniques, the Blackfoot Challenge strives to keep a large number of public and private cooperators in touch with each other and aware of useful research.

Although it employs a holistic approach that incorporates the entire watershed, the groundwork for the new organization rested on "the people side of resource management," says Jack Thomas, the group's executive director.[24] The Blackfoot Challenge is a nonprofit coalition; the group invites anyone to join their "charter" who can support its mission statement, hammered out with the participation of more than 200 people. A series of committees is in charge of the group's work, which includes exchanging information and fostering communication, examining the cumulative effects of land management decisions toward lessening their adverse impacts, and helping to resolve issues and avoid confrontation. As a result of its efforts, a much broader cross-section of area residents now feels a part of the conservation process in the valley, and collaborating organizations are making greater headway—stretching dollars and bending agendas to lend each other a hand—in addressing the water pollution and habitat issues intertwined with land use and land stewardship in the valley.

COOPERATION AMONG COMMUNITIES

Special resources are frequently shared by multiple jurisdictions—a town and the county in which it is located, or several townships, or several counties or states for that matter. Rivers, trails, greenways, cultural landscapes, mountain ridges, canals, railroads, scenic roads, wildlife corridors—the list grows quite long when one stops to consider such resources. Not only do strict community boundaries often fail to match the ecological realities or the history and development of the region; they also do not necessarily correlate with the community interests of businesses or with the leadership and other assets that can be brought to bear on particular problems and needs.

Accordingly, any rural conservation program, no matter how locally focused, should ask, "How can we develop a cooperative relationship with our neighboring communities?" While it may not make sense in the earliest months or years of organizing to put resources toward the answer or answers to this question, ultimately, reaching out beyond one's boundaries may pay dividends.

Traditional areas of cooperation among multiple rural jurisdictions include schools, landfills, and transportation, to mention three of the most common examples. These have often been driven as much by economies of scale and the funding and regulations of state and federal agencies as by local interest. Regional approaches to economic development, tourism promotion, recreation, environmental improvement, and heritage conservation are adding positive notes to this collaborative menu. These approaches are sometimes driven by local governments and sometimes by nonprofit organizations.

The challenges are considerable in overcoming regional rivalries, identifying new boundaries, and developing appropriate institutional support for efforts to collaborate among local governments or organizations. One telling point, sure to draw knowing chuckles in any discussion of regional cooperation, is that high school students learn that the towns down the road are their rivals in football or other sports. As trivial as it may seem on its face, this can be powerful conditioning that acts as a barrier to multicommunity collaboration. Plus, states one observer, "regional agencies or governments are always recommended as solutions for problems that overwhelm local jurisdictions or set off competition among local governments. Advocates of regional conservation planning have not really grappled with the fear that regional management will undermine local control or accountability. Most coalitions behind regional conservation planning are therefore politically fragile."[25]

Still, nothing ventured, nothing gained. It is well worth trying to join with one's neighbors to address common problems and explore common opportunities. James R. Pepper, former executive director of the Blackstone River Valley National Heritage Corridor, which follows the river in both Massachusetts and Rhode Island, has this advice for regional organizers: "You need two main things to start with: one, a regional vision which can captivate and inspire people, and two, a broad-based 'umbrella' coalition. As you work in communities, develop simple themes and reinforce them; focus your programs around the themes. Have something going in every community—people seem to need to 'connect the dots' mentally to understand the concept of region. Finally, do projects that help create a regional identity—for example, for a historic theme, it could be roadway signs."[26]

In some cases, governments have led the way in experimenting with regional collaboration, through regional councils of governments or other means of organizing. In many cases, nonprofit organizations create the best cooperative mechanisms. Wisconsin's Ice Age Trail (see Case Study 7.4), protection of California's Big Sur coastline (see Case Study 5.7), and the celebration of southern Wyoming's heritage in Tracks Across Wyoming (see Case Study 6.5) are examples of regional stewardship led by nonprofits. Montana's Blackfoot Challenge is an example of regional collaboration among a mix of public and private stakeholders, as was creation of the Blackstone heritage corridor.

Business groups are another means of achieving regional collaboration, typically but not necessarily among businesses reliant on tourism. For example, the Economic Development Council of Northeastern Pennsylvania is a long-time player in industrial, commercial, and tourism development in seven counties in Pennsylvania. It has participated in regional conversations on protecting the Delaware and Lehigh Canal National Heritage Corridor, preserving the Pocono Mountains, and promoting tourism in the northern Delaware River region, working along the way with such conservation groups as the Nature Conservancy and the Heritage Conservancy, as well as with the region's business leaders.[27]

EVALUATION

Every organization, no matter how successful, needs periodically to take stock of its activities, ponder the future, and consider possible changes in its structure, approach, and outlook. Evaluation can help an organization to face new circumstances, whether they be a dramatic increase in members or a failure to achieve an important objective. Each year, the board, other leaders, and staff of an organization should reserve time to reflect on their efforts. This questioning process may prompt a group to end programs that have achieved their primary objectives and to consider new programs.

2.12 Recovering from Failure

Rural conservation organizations do suffer setbacks. Such setbacks may not be all bad. As one experienced nonprofit director, Dennis Collins, says: "The most important thing about a failure is, you never fall back to square one. It's never a total failure because you've changed the perceptions of people whether you got what you wanted or not." Even so, dealing with discouragement and a loss of income following a poorly attended event, or a defeat on an important zoning issue, is difficult. To make an effective comeback, the group needs leaders determined to accomplish the group's goals in spite of the setback.

An organization can learn from what went wrong by asking: Where did our strategy fail? Did we need more resources—more money, people, information? Did we fall short on publicity? Were we too dependent on one or two individuals who did not help as we had expected? Was communication weak among our members? Do we need more programs in order to be of real service to the community?

Once a group knows what its problems are, it can begin to solve them. One nonprofit management consultant has this advice for organizations facing difficulties: "Emphasize that the purpose of looking at problems is to find ways to make the organization better. It is not to cast blame or wallow in guilt. The Greek philosopher Heraclitus said, 'You can't step in the same stream twice.' . . . Learn from your mistakes, but do not dwell on them. . . . The secret is to keep trying."

(See Notes to Sidebars.)

2.19
Hilda Fisher (*third from left*) and other members of the Oley Resource Conservation Project's steering committee meet to plan activities and evaluate progress. Meetings around her kitchen table often ended with a glass of mint tea and home-baked desserts, and time to chat.

Those who are deeply involved with a group may not see strengths and weaknesses in their own program. Bringing in an outside evaluator may be useful in gaining a fresh perspective. The Delaware Coastal Heritage Greenway Council, for example, brought in a consultant experienced in the environmental and cultural heritage issues that the council addresses; the consultant spent a day helping council members reflect on the group's accomplishments. The exercise helped the council's staff to realize that visitors and residents did not always appreciate the region's overall identity. This led to a new emphasis on such regionwide projects as expansion of an award-winning auto tour along the entire coast and recognition of the region's primary route, State Route 9, as a scenic byway. The council also collaborated with the state's lieutenant governor and legislature in expanding its mission and became the statewide Delaware Greenways and Trails Council, acknowledging the rising demand for help coming from community groups outside the coastal greenway.

Some groups find that getting away from home helps the evaluation process. Isolation from everyday concerns and a change of environment, plus recreation and socializing, can promote a more creative and objective examination of the organization. Participants usually return from such retreats with renewed interest and enthusiasm.

Consultants in organizational development and specific kinds of work, such as greenways or community planning, are available to work with groups developing goals and evaluating programs. Some consulting services are available from nonprofit or governmental organizations. The regional offices of the National Trust for Historic Preservation offer such assistance to groups, as do the Institute for Conservation Leadership, River Network, community development agents of the Cooperative Extension Service, and field staff of the National Park Service's Rivers, Trails, and Conservation Assistance program. State community development agencies or other state services may also provide assistance.

CONCLUSION

Effective organizing is more art than science, but it is hardly a mysterious art. The skills you bring to initiating and managing your rural conservation efforts are the same skills you use at home, on the job, and in your leisure-time activities. Many of these are "people skills": learning to judge people and situations and to apply the right amount of persuasion and incentive to bring about the best possible outcomes. Still other skills are managerial: determining how you can best organize your time and resources (including people) to get the work done. Like any art, however, learning to organize well takes practice: to learn and improve on the skills you need to be successful in rural conservation, you need to plunge in. And remember that forming a group and keeping it going is well worth all of your hard work—it is no accident that many cultures have such adages as "many hands make light work."

3

Analyzing the Rural Community

INTRODUCTION

L earning about your community is an important and enjoyable part of a rural conservation program. To implement a rural conservation program and persuade fellow residents of the need for protection, you need both general information about your community and specific data about natural, historic, and agricultural resources: what they are, where they are located, and how they are threatened or can be enhanced. This detailed information is called a resources inventory (or an environmental or natural resources inventory).

A resources inventory usually consists of a set of maps locating the important features and problem areas of a community. These maps are typically supplemented with a report describing the resources, how they were identified, why they are important, what threats they face, and how they can be protected. An inventory may also include drawings, photographs, lists of species, statistics, oral histories, and the like.

The last step in an inventory, the analysis of the data, is probably the most important. The analysis should provide both local governments and nonprofit organizations with an objective basis for selecting the most important issues to address.

Unfortunately, once completed, many inventories sit on the shelf, particularly if they are done by outsiders with little community involvement. You can guard against this result by considering from the start how the inventory will be used and organizing the data for easy accessibility by your community's decision makers. Knowing what information you need

3.1
Stow Witwer reminisces about ranch life. His barn is virtually a museum of Weld County, Colorado, history. Older residents can provide a community with invaluable information for an environmental inventory.

and how it will be used will help you guard against the twin dangers of collecting too little or too much data. Too little data makes it difficult to reach wise decisions about land use, decisions that will be accepted in the community and which, if necessary, will stand up in court. On the other hand, collecting too much data, in addition to wasting time, can result in not seeing the forest for the trees.

Your community's resources inventory should provide the information necessary for making sound decisions on land use. It should be the major source of information used by local government in land use planning and in designing ordinances to guide development. Using the inventory, planning boards can steer development away from such important resources as wetlands, prime farmland, easily erodible slopes, scenic vistas, and historic sites, or they can require appropriate adjustments to developments that will affect these resources. Property owners, too, can use the inventories, to determine the appropriateness of their land for specific uses.

An inventory also establishes baseline data, allowing a community to monitor the effects of future changes on clean water, wildlife, prime farmland, and other quantifiable resources. For instance, a major aspect of the inventory in Oley, Pennsylvania, was the mapping of groundwater and measuring stream flow. As a result of the inventory, Oley can monitor the effects of future limestone quarrying on the water table and hold the quarries' owners accountable for changes (see Case Study 2.1).

Finally, a resources inventory has educational value: it can be used to inform fellow citizens about the community and to build consensus for a protection program.

Having touted the advantages of inventories, we should warn you of the danger of letting inventorying become an end in itself. For some communities, gathering information may be easier than implementing protection measures for resources the community cares about. On the one hand, you need good information before making decisions; on the other,

3.1 Collecting General Information in a Community

Community leaders embarking on a rural conservation program should be able to answer basic questions like the following:

• *What is the history of our community? When did most of the settlement take place and why? How have land uses and the local economy changed over the years?*
• *What level of local government most directly affects decisions about rural resources in our community? The county? The township?*
• *Are there other local government entities, such as water or school authorities, that influence the fate of our community's resources?*
• *Who are the key officials in our community? What are their names, titles, and responsibilities? Are they elected? Appointed? Salaried? Full-time? Does their influence go beyond their official responsibilities? Where does their support come from in the community? Who are the unofficial leaders? How do they exert their influence?*
• *What does the latest census reveal about our community? What are the statistics on population, age, sex, race, education, housing, occupation, and income? Have there been major changes since the last census? Is the population growing or declining? Getting richer or poorer?*
• *What are the principal businesses in our community? How many people do they employ? To what extent are residents employed in the community?*
• *Is there an official comprehensive or master plan for our community? How helpful is it? Is it used as the basis for decision making? Does it take rural conservation issues into account?*

you do not want to spend so much time gathering data that you miss protection opportunities. Inventorying can be an ongoing process that continues while a conservation program is being implemented.

We will use the resources inventory conducted by the Cazenovia Community Resources Project (CCRP) in New York to illustrate the inventory process throughout this chapter. Cazenovia's inventory convinced many Cazenovians that their town was a very special place that should be protected from uncontrolled development. It has also resulted in effective new ways to guide the community's future.

PREPARING AN INVENTORY

The biggest challenge to rural conservation leaders is often how to achieve community consensus on the need to protect resources. A number of citizens should be involved from the beginning in shaping the purposes and methods of the inventory. Various local boards and commissions will need to consider the findings of the resources inventory and hold public meetings to discuss them and build consensus. In the Sautee-Nacoochee Valley of Georgia, for example, a resources inventory conducted in the early 1980s led to a protection plan that specified treatments for agricultural lands, steep slopes, historic structures, and special views, as well as to a nomination to, and subsequent listing in, the National Register.

What Information to Include

The information included in a resources inventory depends upon the type and number of resources present and the threats to them. Almost all communities need to know about such basic resources as soils, water, wildlife habitat, and significant historic buildings. Most communities also have more specialized needs. A county in Nebraska, for instance, might identify the location of segments of the Oregon Trail that should be protected, while a Michigan county might map abandoned railroad rights-of-way as potential recreation trails and sanctuaries for native grasses. A county in California may have an urgent need to identify hillsides prone to mud slides, and a county in South Carolina might wish to pinpoint the nesting sites of bald eagles.

Ideally, an inventory will be comprehensive and identify all of the community's significant resources. The more comprehensive the inventory is, the more likely it is that a community will discover potential problems or opportunities. For instance, a community may already know that a proposed dam will flood prime farmland, but a comprehensive inventory might show that the impoundment will also destroy habitat for valued game and a prehistoric Native American burial ground.

A community should guard against collecting and mapping too much data, however; potential users may become overwhelmed by the detail and fail to take into account the most important findings. The inventory need only contain sufficient information to raise the necessary questions about proposed changes to the environment. Maps showing data on soil types, for instance, do not have to be accurate to the foot, but they should delineate general areas where different soils are located. If a subdivision is proposed in an area where clay soils might cause foundations to crack and prevent adequate percolation from septic systems, the planning board can insist that the developer pay for a more detailed, site-specific study, to demonstrate that the actual building and septic system sites are not on such soils.

Although a comprehensive inventory may at first seem expensive, it is usually more cost-effective to conduct an inventory all at once than to inventory separate categories over a long period of time. Much of the information collected for one aspect of the inventory is necessary for others. However, some communities do not have the financial resources, personnel, or governmental commitment needed to undertake a comprehensive inventory, and others may urgently need information about a particular resource. In situations like these, communities may concentrate on one or more resources of immediate concern, such as wetlands, historic sites, or prime farmland. The inventory may then be expanded as changing circumstances demand or as additional time and money become available.

Before making final decisions on how comprehensive the inventory will be, there should be discussions with all appropriate community leaders and an opportunity for public comment. Some members of the community may be suspicious or object to having features of their property inventoried. Citizens should understand up front what data are to be collected, how the data will be made public, and to what uses the data will be put.

• What ordinances and regulations affect private property? Is there a zoning ordinance? A subdivision ordinance? How effective are they? What state laws affect private property?

• What state and federal regulations directly affect our community? For example, are there properties in the National Register of Historic Places? Are there wetlands or coastal zones regulated by state law? What land is owned by the federal or state government?

How to Record Data

There is a variety of ways to record inventory information. Methods typically involve the use of forms, maps, and photographs. Inventories for certain resources should follow standard formats. For instance, most states use a particular format for historic building inventories. For other resources, where there may be no standard formats, the community must decide how to organize the information it collects.

Even if some resources require special formats, the community should ensure compatibility of the different parts of its inventory so that various types of information can be compared and analyzed. For example, maps should generally be prepared at the same scale. All maps, photographs, and other documentation should also be labeled and numbered in such a way that they can be used and stored in a systematic manner. Investigators should always note the source and date of any information. The community should establish a single place to file all recorded information and should assemble a library of the reports and reference books used in compiling the inventory.

Geographic Information Systems

Some communities may have, or desire to obtain, the capability of recording inventory data in a geographic information system (GIS). A GIS is a computerized system for entering, storing, analyzing, and displaying spatial or mapped data. A GIS allows a much more comprehensive organization of data and analysis of the relationships among variables than is possible without the system. The advantage of a GIS is that environmental, land use, and demographic information can be stored as individual, superimposable map layers, which can be turned on and off to suit the user's needs. For example, if the user wants to show the relationship between the location of a proposed road and its proximity to wetlands, the GIS allows the road layer to be superimposed on the wetlands layer to create a map showing the relationship. GIS uses the same principle as overlay maps, as illustrated on page 155.

Any variable that can be located spatially—by latitude, longitude, elevation, ZIP code—can be entered into a GIS. Spatial information is entered into a GIS through a process known as digitizing. Through digitizing, a special table, or tablet is used in conjunction with a hand-held point-and-click device (similar to a personal computer's mouse) to convert locations on a map or aerial photograph to locations on a computer image or map. A scanner can also be used to convert map information into GIS form.

Through a GIS, communities can analyze complex relationships among spatial variables. For example, the relationship between wetlands and population density or between mining activity and surface runoff can be analyzed over time to make predictions about the results of future human activity. The relationships may be illustrated through different types of maps, depending on the nature of the data. Three-dimensional perspectives can be created to reveal patterns not discernible from two-dimensional maps.

More and more communities are choosing to store and map data through a geographic information system. The hardware and software costs of a GIS are increasingly affordable. There are numerous GIS software packages, and the field is expanding, with new products being added all the time. Most are easy for the layperson to use. The Brandywine Conservancy in Pennsylvania is using a GIS to estimate the effects of development on groundwater recharge in the Delaware River Basin. GISs are also gaining popularity because many federal and state agencies provide mapped data in digital form. Among the most common sources of digital data are the U.S. Geological Survey Digital Elevation Models (the digital version of the 7.5 minute quadrangles) and the TIGER (Topologically Integrated Geographic Encoding and Referencing) files of the Bureau of the Census, which contain digital data for all 1990 census map features, geographic units, political units, and census areas. In addition, some states, counties, and regional planning agencies have integrated map systems that can provide local communities with the maps needed to start up a GIS.

For help in accessing or setting up a GIS, communities may contact a local university's department of planning, landscape architecture, or environmental studies. Many state and regional planning agencies have GIS systems that local communities can use.

The kind of resources inventory and analysis that most rural communities undertake does not require computerization, and GIS does have drawbacks. It costs more than a manually assembled data base, will be more difficult for some volunteers to use, and may be less participatory for the community. Nevertheless, many communities will find a GIS to be of great assistance.

When to Conduct an Inventory

Conducting an inventory at the beginning of a rural conservation effort provides a sound basis for decision making and is an effective way to ensure that proponents can back up their positions. Early publication of the inventory findings can build support for a newly organized rural conservation program. Since properly conducted resources inventories are usually not controversial, they are good initial projects. Other logical times to conduct an inventory are prior to developing or amending a community's plan or land use ordinance.

Cazenovia, New York: Using an Inventory to Build Consensus for Rural Conservation

Cazenovia is typical of rural communities just beyond the fringe of metropolitan areas—but more beautiful than many, and therein lies the problem. Its rolling farmland, historic village, wooded ridges, large lake, and clean streams attract

3.2
Residents in most communities can identify views that make their hometowns distinctive. For residents of Cazenovia, New York, its dairy farms and wooded ridges make the community a special place, worth protecting.

3.3
This lithograph provides a bird's-eye view of Cazenovia in 1890. Today, most of the structures are still standing, although the railroad no longer exists and most of the elms have succumbed to Dutch elm disease. Old views are of great assistance in tracing architectural and landscape history.

many who would like to settle there. Cazenovia, with a population of 3,137 and an area of 50 square miles, has a full range of retail services and recreational opportunities, a library, a newspaper, a small college, and good schools—with the added benefit of having Syracuse just down the road providing city conveniences. Until the 1970s, the community was far enough from Syracuse—a 20-mile drive—to have preserved a distinct sense of place and to have escaped the suburbanization that was the fate of towns nearer Syracuse.

But as thoughtful town residents watched homes on 1–, 2–, and 3–acre lots sprout up around the village and the lake they asked, How many more and how long before Cazenovia becomes just another Syracuse suburb? They knew that Cazenovia's historic character, lake, and farmland might not survive the growth such assets attract. When the National Trust for Historic Preservation announced its demonstration program for rural communities in 1979, Cazenovians saw a possible fit with their needs.

The township's history of successful conservation efforts appealed to the National Trust: an informal citizens group, incorporated in 1969 as the Cazenovia Preservation Foundation, had been working since the early 1960s to document and protect historic buildings in the village. As a result of the group's successful campaign to revitalize Albany Street, Cazenovia's main street, a number of downtown businesses had voluntarily restored their storefronts and replaced unattractive signs. The foundation had also protected the banks of Chittenango Creek within the village and established a trail along it. Furthermore, the Cazen-

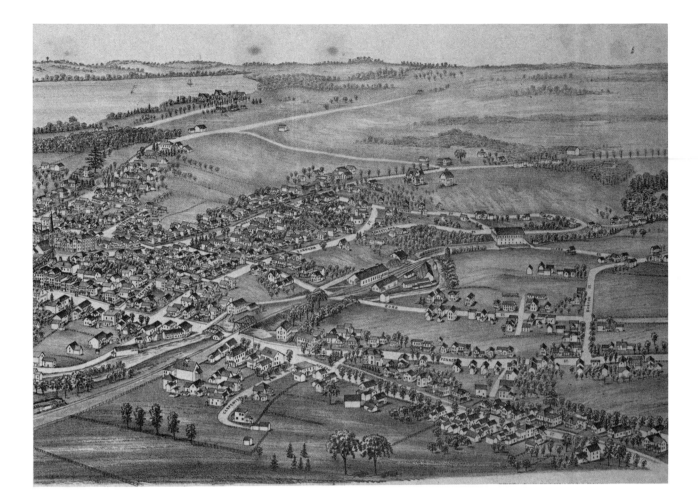

ovia Advisory Conservation Commission, established by the town board in 1974 to advise the township on environmental protection, had identified the township's significant wetlands and was ready to take on new responsibilities. Above all, a number of Cazenovians were concerned about their community, had conservation experience, and were willing to devote time to the protection of their town.

While there had been efforts to protect historic buildings, wetlands, and the creek, less had been done to protect other resources, particularly farmland and the lake. Although dairying is still a major occupation in Cazenovia, farmland is threatened by development. Subdivisions of the large estates surrounding the lake not only mar the scenic views of the lake but also threaten water quality, as increased quantities of lawn fertilizer and effluent from septic systems find their way into it.

A lawsuit over drainage problems made many township leaders realize that the town needed to pay closer attention to conservation. In 1967 the state district health officer gave approval for septic systems for twenty units to be built on fill over a wetland at the northern end of the lake. As one might expect, problems soon developed with the septic systems. The residents of the subdivision sued the developer, the state, and the township. By approving the subdivision, they argued, the state and township were partly responsible for the problem. The township eventually agreed to put in a drainage system, and the state put a moratorium on further development in the area. The suit forced township lead-

3.4
The village of Cazenovia was laid out in 1794. In the 1960s, conservation leaders initiated a successful program to help businesses on Albany Street preserve their historic storefronts. This experience helped prepare conservationists for the broader goal of protecting environmental resources throughout the township.

ers to realize that inappropriate development threatened not only their environment but municipal coffers as well. The town passed a new subdivision ordinance that addressed the worst problems, but many residents believed that they also needed a more comprehensive approach to environmental protection.

In 1980, the National Trust selected Cazenovia as a demonstration community, and Don Callahan, the town supervisor—the elected chief administrator of the town—appointed representatives of key municipal and service organizations to a committee to oversee what became known as the Cazenovia Community Resources Project (CCRP). Callahan asked Dorothy Riester, a noted artist and leader of the Cazenovia Preservation Foundation, to chair the committee. The town board, the planning board, and the conservation commission were all represented. There were also representatives of the separately incorporated village of Cazenovia, the unincorporated hamlet of New Woodstock, the farmers, and the business community.

The Faculty of Landscape Architecture at the State University of New York (SUNY) in Syracuse was a major source of technical advice throughout the project. Richard Hawks, an associate professor of landscape architecture at SUNY, specializing in communitywide environmental planning, provided guidance to the steering committee from the outset. Hawks saw an opportunity to put into practice mapping techniques and to provide experience to his landscape architecture students.

Hiring a part-time staff to supplement and coordinate the work of the community volunteers was essential to the success of CCRP. Terry LeVeque, a landscape architecture graduate student at SUNY, was hired as a graduate assistant in the summer of 1980 to help with the environmental inventory. She later became project director, working under the supervision of the steering committee.

The CCRP steering committee decided to follow a four-step process:

1. define the assets of Cazenovia to be protected and learn about threats to them;
2. study techniques that could be used to protect those assets;
3. recommend specific actions for the town, village, and private groups to undertake; and
4. assist in the implementation of the recommendations.

3.5
Cazenovia conservationists were particularly concerned about the protection of their lake and wetlands. A connecting portion of these wetlands (not visible here) was filled in and built upon in the 1960s. The resulting drainage problems inspired community commitment to environmental protection. These wetlands are also visible in the aerial photograph on p. 133.

The steering committee then established six task groups to focus on Cazenovia's agricultural, historic, environmental, municipal, recreational, and visual resources. The committee invited additional volunteers with appropriate skills and backgrounds to join the task groups.

The task groups, whose activities are described throughout this chapter, set out to inventory community resources. The volunteers and LeVeque collected information in a variety of ways: studying maps and other documents in town, village, and county offices; asking farmers to fill out questionnaires; interviewing hunters about wildlife habitat, and hikers and cross-country skiers about recreation trails; and documenting every pre-1930 building in the town. Volunteers also sought information on population trends, the agricultural economy, the needs of small businesses, and potential threats, such as sewer lines planned by the Madison County Sewer District. Most of the volunteers regarded the inventory as an exciting opportunity to learn about their community. Some commented that they traveled back roads they had not known existed.

LeVeque and the volunteers recorded much of the information they collected on maps. These maps became the basis for analyzing both resources and problems and were used in CCRP's public presentations (see Sidebar 3.2). The conservation commission still uses the maps for its review of subdivision requests.

Education was an important ingredient of the project. In December 1980, each task group made a report at a major public meeting in the village hall. As a result of the meeting, Cazenovians became more aware of just how special their community was, and more people began to volunteer their services. LeVeque periodically prepared press releases on CCRP, and the weekly *Cazenovia Republican* covered many of the project's activities. In the summer of 1982 the paper ran a popular series of articles on the township's assets (see Fig. 8.3). Each article was written by a CCRP volunteer and highlighted a different resource. Moreover, information from the inventory was used to prepare pamphlets for owners of historic houses on how to preserve them and for residents of the lake watershed on how to protect its water quality.

When the inventory was completed in the winter of 1981, the CCRP steering committee started the second step in the process, namely, analyzing the community's resources in relation to the techniques that could be used to protect them. To conduct this analysis, SUNY students supervised by Hawks prepared a series of overlay maps that made possible the comparison of resources (see Fig. 3.23). CCRP also recommended to the town board that it establish an ad hoc planning commission that could receive the recommendations of CCRP and consider new ordinances. Although the town already had a planning board, that body had enough to do reviewing applications for subdivisions. The planning commission was able to spend its entire time considering new ordinances without other pressures.

The final major CCRP activity was the preparation of its *Land Use Guide* (Town of Cazenovia, N.Y. 1984), which summarized the CCRP's work and presented its recommendations. The guide makes recommendations for the protection of each natural resource, cultural resource, and "character zone." (The report divides Cazenovia's landscape into six character zones—areas, such as the lake watershed and the farmland, that have similar physical and cultural characteristics.) To assure implementation of its recommendations, the guide assigns responsibility for follow-up to specified governmental groups and nonprofit organizations. In 1987, both the town and the village boards adopted the guide as their official plans. In 1995, the guide was still Cazenovia's official planning document, equivalent to a master plan.

The conservation commission uses the list of critical and sensitive resources identified in the guide for environmental reviews of proposed developments prior to making recommendations to the town and village planning boards. The identification of these resources has helped to provide an objective basis for the commission's work and strengthened its role.

The Cazenovia Preservation Foundation has used the environmental inventory to identify important properties that should be protected through easements and acquisition. In 1990, with the help of the *Land Use Guide,* CPF developed an evaluation and priority system to facilitate the organization's easement program. Weighing a property's location (whether in greenbelt areas, corridors, viewsheds, or critical environmental areas), land use, size, and development barriers, as well as an urgency factor reflecting market conditions and the owner's attitude toward sale, CPF identified and scored ten zones containing fifty-seven properties for potential easement acquisition. The scores range from 38 in zone 1 (high priority) to 18 in zone 10 (lower priority).

CPF has taken action in each of the zones and by 1995 had acquired easements on ten properties and owned another nine properties outright. For example, CPF acquired the 93-acre Meadows Farm south of Cazenovia Lake and offered it for sale subject to protective covenants that run with the land. A similar technique was used to protect the 700-acre Rose Farm. The Reisters donated their own home and the 75 acres surrounding it to establish an art park for the community.

Cazenovia's community leaders, all volunteers, believe they are well equipped to make wise decisions about land use. The data they have collected and the skills they have developed have made it possible for them to better evaluate proposed developments and to take proactive steps to protect the areas they value. According to Reister, the *Land Use Guide* maps, resource inventory, character zones, and recommendations have been invaluable. Faith Knapp adds that the guide has been a timeless reminder that Cazenovia's character zones and resources warrant nurturing and respect.

Who Conducts the Inventory

Resources inventories are usually sponsored by local governments, which need the information for preparing plans and land use ordinances. Although some rural counties and townships have staff planners who can conduct inventories, most rely on consultants. Volunteers from the community are frequently overlooked as sources of assistance. Using a combination of local government staff, consultants, and volunteers, designating one person as the inventory coordinator, usually produces the best results. The coordinator can assure that the work gets done, that the format for data is consistent, and that the information collected is accurate and unbiased. The coordinator should have training and experience in ecologically based planning. Many graduates of university programs in landscape architecture, planning, geography, and environmental science receive this kind of training.

STAFF

Many counties have full-time planners, although few rural counties or townships can afford them. A county planner may be able to prepare a county inventory and plan, or contract for its preparation, and may be able to assist townships in preparing theirs. In many states, counties are not broken down into townships (Virginia, for instance), or, if they are, planning may not be a function of township government (as in Illinois, for instance). Regardless of the availability, dedication, and skills of staff planners, they seldom have all of the skills necessary to complete a comprehensive resources inventory unaided. In New York the Cazenovia Community Resources Project received considerable advice from Madison County's planner. Since he was the only planner for the county, the amount of time he could devote to Cazenovia, one of sixteen towns in the county, was necessarily limited.

CONSULTANTS

A community can either retain a consulting firm to undertake the entire resources inventory or contract with individual consultants who have skills unavailable within the community to supplement local efforts. If the community foresees a possible lawsuit—perhaps by a developer whose subdivision application may be denied on the basis of data collected for the inventory—it is a good investment to retain a consultant with unimpeachable credentials to conduct the inventory, or at least to review and endorse its findings. The consultant may do the work alone or supervise and coordinate the work of volunteers. CCRP retained a consultant to help design the scenic resources portion of the inventory.

Assigning a member of the staff or a volunteer resident to work closely with any consultant is essential. A consultant working without community involvement can easily miss features that residents can point out.

VOLUNTEERS

An inventory done with volunteer labor is usually less expensive and more sensitive to the community's needs than the typical inventory con-

---

3.2 Resources Inventoried and Mapped in Cazenovia

Geological Resources
  Surficial geology
  Sand and gravel deposits
  Unique geological areas
Soil Resources
  Soil type
  Slope
  Depth of bedrock
  Depth to seasonal high water table
  Permeability
  Soil erosion potential
Water Resources
  Groundwater resources
  Aquifer recharge areas
  Surface water
  Wetlands
  Flood hazard areas
  Cazenovia Lake watershed
  Surface water drainage
Habitat
  Woodlots
  Deer winter shelter areas
  Fish spawning areas
Agricultural Resources
  Prime agricultural land
  Farmer-owned and -leased land
  Agricultural districts
Architectural and Historic Resources
  Historic buildings survey
  National Register nominations
Recreation Resources
  Recreation areas
  Recreation activities
Visual Resources
  Visual inventory
  Viewsheds
Composite Analysis Maps
  Critical resources
  Sensitive resources
  Residential suitability
  Industrial or commercial suitability
  Critical farmlands analysis

(See Notes to Sidebars.)

ducted solely by staff or consultants. A major advantage of volunteer involvement is that in the process citizens become more knowledgeable about inventory techniques and their own community; this knowledge stays in the community long after the inventory is completed. Few communities, however, can rely entirely on volunteers, since they will probably lack essential skills and sufficient time to complete all the tasks required.

A staff coordinator or consultant may be able to give volunteers on-the-job training. Also, some universities, nonprofit organizations, and state agencies offer short courses on techniques for inventorying certain resources. Cazenovia's inventory was accomplished by a combination of volunteer and staff work. CCRP was fortunate to have the volunteer talents of such residents as Andy Diefendorf, a professional geologist, who mapped the geology and groundwater, and Faith Knapp, a landscape architect, who gathered information on wetlands, wildlife habitat, and woodlots. Both were also leaders in the conservation commission. In all, some two hundred volunteers were involved in the inventory. In addition to providing a valuable service, the volunteers became more committed to conservation because they had a personal stake in assuring that the information they collected was reliable and used.

Work can be divided in many ways, depending on the scope of the task, the budget, the schedule, and the skills, knowledge, and interests of the citizen volunteers. Having separate task groups for each resource worked well in Cazenovia. In some communities, volunteers are able to make maps, type reports, take photographs, or accomplish other necessary tasks. In other communities, volunteers may have the time only to serve as advisors and informants to consultants.

OTHER ASSISTANCE

Communities conducting resources inventories can also get free assistance from a number of sources. District conservationists of the Natural Resources Conservation Service (NRCS) can provide invaluable assistance. The NRCS district conservationist for Madison County gave extensive help to CCRP in mapping soils and wetlands. He also helped the agricultural task group to survey farmers' needs for land.

High schools, colleges, and universities can assist in inventory projects and, in the process, enrich the curriculum for students in biology, geography, geology, history, landscape architecture, architectural history, planning, wildlife ecology, or other courses.

Maps

Maps are the principal means of storing and presenting much of the data collected during a resources inventory. They are the most effective medium for showing the locations of community resources at a single glance. A reproducible base map includes the standard information that the surveyors wish to have appear on all of the individual resource maps, such as contour lines, surface water, roads, and buildings. If data are recorded through a GIS, computerized maps can be produced.

For the Cazenovia Community Resources Project, a State University of New York (SUNY) landscape architecture student prepared a base

3.6
Opposite: The Cazenovia Community Resources Project (CCRP) spliced together four U.S. Geological Survey topographic maps to prepare its base map. The scale was large enough for people to see details but kept the maps to a manageable size. The CCRP added larger-scale inset maps of the villages of Cazenovia and New Woodstock to accommodate the greater number of roads and structures that needed to be represented there.

CAZENOVIA
LAKE

0   1500

VILLAGE OF CAZENOVIA

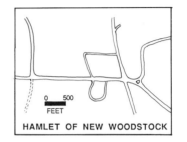

0   500
FEET

HAMLET OF NEW WOODSTOCK

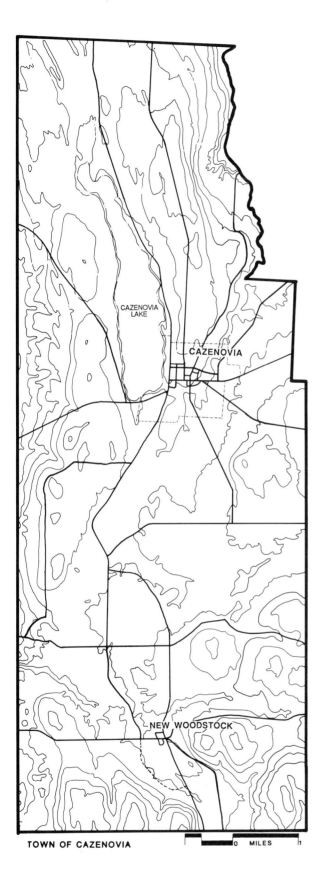

CAZENOVIA
LAKE

CAZENOVIA

NEW WOODSTOCK

TOWN OF CAZENOVIA   0   MILES   1

CAZENOVIA
COMMUNITY
RESOURCES
PROJECT

3.3 *Preparing a Base Map*

Base maps for rural areas are usually made from U.S. Geological Survey (USGS) topographic maps, which are available for the entire country. In addition to topography, the maps show the location of surface water, major wetlands, roads, buildings, and other features. The most detailed topographic maps measure 7.5 minutes of latitude and longitude on a side. These quadrangles (or "quads") cover fifty to seventy square miles at a scale of 1:24,000— that is, one inch on the map equals 24,000 inches (2,000 feet) on the ground. Topographic maps in the 7.5-minute series are available for most of the United States and are the ones most frequently used for base maps. For areas not covered by the 7.5-minute series, less detailed smaller-scale topographic maps are available.

You will probably need to use several USGS maps. The relevant portions can be pieced together and the resulting collage photographically reproduced on Mylar to make a base

map by splicing together U.S. Geological Survey (USGS) 7.5–minute quadrangle maps. Project volunteers used aerial photographs and their own observations to update the map. Volunteers were especially interested in locating their homes and learning about resources present on their properties. Working on inexpensive paper maps was a valuable learning experience for Cazenovia's citizen volunteers. They did not worry excessively about mistakes, knowing they could make more-finished copies later.

The appearance of maps can affect the acceptance of the inventory. Even if a community group conducts its own inventory and makes its own maps, its final maps should be of professional quality. A cartographer, drafting teacher, landscape architect, engineer, geologist, or planner may volunteer to prepare the maps or can offer advice on graphics and format and then review the maps for accuracy and appearance.

Sources of Data

After creating a base map, a community should decide which individual resources to inventory, and then collect the data. Data can be collected from a number of sources. Much of the information should be readily available in previous studies done by local, state, or federal agencies and nonprofit organizations, but it is wise to make sure those studies are reliable. In Cazenovia, project workers found that NRCS had completed the county soil survey and had studied the lake's watershed; the Cazenovia Preservation Foundation had inventoried historic buildings in the village; and the conservation commission had surveyed the township's wetlands. The CCRP needed only to update the data and ad-

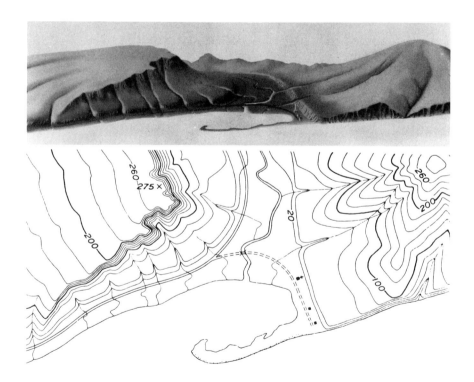

3.7
The relationship between topography (*top*) and contour lines (*bottom*).

just the scale of existing maps to make them consistent with the new ones.

Each community needs to decide how many maps to prepare. Some, like Cazenovia, prepare a large number, but others might combine several features and produce far fewer maps. A minimum number of maps might be three: one that shows land use, a second that shows the most important resources (such as historic sites, prime farmland, and wetlands) and constraints (for example, steep slopes and high water table), and a third that shows the suitability of land for development.

EXISTING SURVEYS AND MAPS

Soil surveys prepared by NRCS are often the single most useful source of information for a resources inventory. The survey maps and explanatory text contain information on much more than agricultural potential; they indicate slope, wetness, depth to bedrock, and other valuable information. The NRCS district conservationist can provide great assistance in understanding soil survey data.

The U.S. Geological Survey has maps, publications, and services that can be helpful to many aspects of the inventory, including topography, geology, and water resources. Maps can be ordered from USGS or, in many areas, purchased at local stores.

In addition to USGS and NRCS maps, many other maps may prove useful. Some states, such as Iowa and Massachusetts, have general-purpose maps showing a variety of environmental information. Tax maps usually show property lines and are available for most communities. Cazenovia used tax maps to record information about the ownership of individual farms. Of course, the scale of these maps might not be the same as the community's base map, and so they might require enlargement or reduction, but many printing and engineering firms have the specialized photographic equipment to accomplish this. If a GIS is being used, maps of different scales and projections can be manipulated so that they are compatible for analysis.

AERIAL PHOTOGRAPHS

All rural communities have been photographed from the air by USGS and by other federal and state agencies. These photographs are available to communities and are valuable in developing resource maps. They can be used to identify such features as land use, new construction, drainage patterns, types of vegetation, wetlands, landslides, and forgotten historic ruins. Older aerial photographs can be particularly useful in identifying past land uses and historic sites.

With the aid of an inexpensive stereoscope, overlapping aerial photographs, used in pairs, can create dramatic three-dimensional images similar to that made by the commercially produced photographic pairs our great-grandparents enjoyed on their hand-held stereoscopes. Stereo pairs can be helpful in identifying such features as stone walls, steep slopes, rock outcroppings, and buildings, as well as problems such as erosion. An inventory team studying historic resources in remote parts of the U.S. Virgin Islands used stereo pairs to locate sugar-plantation ruins lost in tropical forests.

map. Mylar, the trade name for the most commonly used material for making high-quality, durable maps, is a transparent plastic sheet that can have information transferred to it photographically or by pen, stencils, and ready-made transfer letters that stick on. Photographic techniques may also be used to expand or reduce the size of the preliminary base map.

You can add the following to the base map:

- *Buildings and roads constructed since the USGS maps were made*
- *Up-to-date municipal boundaries*
- *Some adjacent areas, since some resources in need of protection, such as aquifers, may extend beyond the community's boundaries*
- *Title block with the name of the community and state, the name of the inventory project or plan of which the map is a part, the name of the group that made the map, the date it was made, a legend that defines symbols, indication of scale, and a north-pointing arrow*

Once all the desired information is on the Mylar base map, you can reproduce as many inexpensive paper copies as you need.

3.4 Assuring a Good Reception for Field Workers

To assure that field surveyors are received well as they move about the community, the sponsoring organization may find the following steps advisable.

• Arrange for introductions from friends and neighbors where possible.
• Make appointments in advance to visit at times convenient for the property owner.
• Publish a notice of the inventory with the names and photographs of the recorders in the local newspapers or send notices to property owners.
• Supply surveyors with a letter of introduction verifying the project, on the letterhead of the local sponsor.
• Supply the police or sheriff with the names of surveyors, the license numbers of the automobiles they are using, and the field work schedule, in case residents complain about suspicious people taking notes and photographs or driving slowly past their homes.

For some areas of the United States, USGS makes available "orthophotoquads," which are aerial photographs that correspond to the topographic quadrangles.

Also available from USGS are color and infrared photographs for the entire country. Infrared photography, which uses special film and filters, highlights certain features, such as water, wetlands, vegetation patterns, and environmental pollution. The Earth Observation Satellite Company (or EOSAT) also sells satellite images, which are particularly helpful when large areas are being surveyed. However, the Landsat images it is currently providing do not have sufficiently high resolution to be useful for most local resources inventories.

OTHER SOURCES

State natural resources departments, regional planning commissions, and numerous other agencies and organizations can also help with community resources surveys. State transportation departments often have detailed environmental information and aerial photographs prepared as part of the highway planning process. Universities may have valuable reference materials, as well as personnel who can provide assistance. Communities in special settings may seek out other sources of data; for example, state offices responsible for coastal management are good sources of data for coastal communities. In the late 1970s, most coastal states received grants under the Coastal Zone Management Act to undertake comprehensive inventories. The Federal Emergency Management Agency (FEMA) has prepared maps of floodplains across the United States. Local boards of health, watershed associations, and sewer authorities are other potential sources of information. Previous studies by consultants, universities, government agencies, or nonprofit organizations may also prove helpful. If a federal or state environmental impact statement has been prepared for a nearby project, it may contain useful information about environmental resources and sources of data (for information about environmental impact statements, see Sidebar 7.1).

Local engineering, planning, and landscape architecture firms may have applicable maps or data and be able to recommend other sources. Not all firms, however, are willing to share the information they have collected; others may expect to be paid for their time or at least be reimbursed for such out-of-pocket expenses as map reproduction, telephone calls, and postage.

Residents, too, may have valuable information to contribute to an inventory. A farmer may know a great deal about soil and other resources; local hunters may be able to provide information about wildlife habitat; and an elderly resident, whose family has saved letters, diaries, farm journals, and photographs, may have an attic full of historic materials.

Field Work

Although data can be obtained from maps, aerial photographs, and other reports, there is no substitute for information collected in the field to verify and supplement existing sources. Field checks should always be made before important decisions on sites are made. In many cases, the sharp divisions between different resources or conditions shown by lines on maps do not exist on the ground. Soil types, for example, tend to grade from one to another. If there is not too much snow, winter is often the best time to conduct field work, since the leaves are off deciduous trees and there is less vegetation to hide conditions. A camera, notebook, and map are essential equipment; a tape recorder may be useful. (For information on photographing the countryside, see Sidebar 8.2.)

Field work can be fun, and it provides volunteers with the opportunity to get to know their environment first-hand. There are risks, however: Field surveyors should be informed about any residents (or their animals) who are likely to be unfriendly and about trespassing laws and natural hazards, such as poison ivy, ticks, and snakes. They should also be mindful of seasonal activities like hunting and plan their visits accordingly. To reduce the suspicion that often greets surveyors, the sponsoring organization should publicize the inventory project, make advance arrangements for visits, and keep the authorities informed. If possible, surveyors in rural areas should work in pairs; using a buddy system is safer, more enjoyable, and more efficient. For example, one person can photograph a property while the other records on a map where the photograph was taken; one can drive while the other takes notes.

The following sections describe how to inventory specific features, resources, and problems. Most communities will not need to inventory all of these features; each community will decide on its own priorities.

INVENTORYING NATURAL FEATURES

Relief

Relief is the most basic feature mapped by any community. Since most of the work has already been done by the Geological Survey and the Natural Resources Conservation Service, it is the easiest feature to map. It is important to identify steep slopes, where loose soils held by only light vegetative cover may be prone to erosion or landslides. Slope information, available on topographic and soil maps, is essential in identifying which areas are appropriate for development and which are best left alone. Slope is usually described as a percentage and is usually mapped in ranges, such as 0 to 8 percent, 8 to 15 percent, and so forth (see Figures 3.8 and 3.9). The percentage of slope at which land becomes too great for safe construction depends on soil conditions, climate, bedrock geology, vegetation, and construction technique.

Geology

Geology is the key to understanding why the land is shaped the way it is, why some areas have abundant groundwater and others none, and why some have rich topsoil and others poor. The geological inventory provides information about a community's soil, vegetation, and water resources, and also points to such potential problems as earthquakes, sinkholes, landslides, and aquifer contamination. A study of a community's geology also determines the location of sand, gravel, stone, clay, coal, and other useful minerals.

Although some communities may require a professional geologist to

3.5 Taking to the Air

In need of gaining a bird's-eye view of your community, a river or trail, or a property under easement? One of the more innovative ideas for environmental action is enlisting experienced private and commercial pilots and airplane owners to donate flying time on behalf of the environment. There are two national nonprofit organizations that do this: Lighthawk and the Environmental Air Force (EAF).

In addition to helping with aerial photography and reconnaissance surveys—for which they are much in demand—EAF and Lighthawk take public officials, reporters, and teachers up in the air to help them gain a new perspective on community issues. (They also help transport wildlife.) EAF, for example, has helped the Heritage Conservancy of Bucks County, Pennsylvania (Case Study 5.1), survey the islands of the Delaware River so that landowners there might be contacted about permanent protection of their resources. Lighthawk flew Zuni Nation farmers, ranchers, and tribal council members over newly acquired lands to develop an ecologically sound development plan.

Volunteer pilots can also help with monitoring environmental conditions and easements. Whether through the EAF or Lighthawk, or by direct association with a pilot willing to donate a few hours of flight time, taking to the air can bring such returns as extraordinary photographs, greater interest from government agencies, and added media coverage.

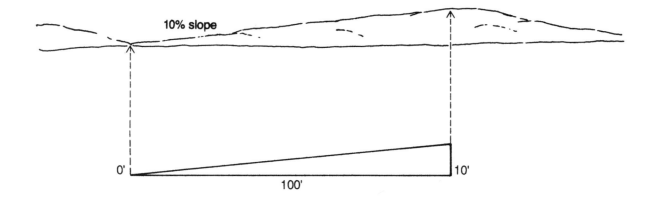

10% slope

0'   100'   10'

3.8
Slope is usually described as a percentage. A 10 percent slope, or a "one in ten slope," means that the ground rises 1 foot in elevation for every 10 feet of horizontal distance. Slope information can be determined from USGS topographic maps using a special ruler that measures the distance between contour lines and gives a reading in percentage of slope. It can also come directly from NRCS maps, where the range of slope percentages is noted for each soil type. Most communities find the slope information from NRCS maps satisfactory for their purposes. An NRCS district conservationist, a landscape architect, or a land-use planner can assist in analyzing slope information.

3.9
Opposite: Maps are the most useful way to record slope information; an accompanying narrative can explain the constraints of each particular slope classification. Cazenovia used the categories on the Natural Resources Conservation Service maps and recommended that slopes greater than 8 percent be used with caution and that slopes greater than 15 percent be left largely undisturbed.

conduct an inventory, most can rely on geological maps prepared by USGS, state geological surveys, universities, and other sources. Unfortunately, USGS geological maps are not as extensive as the topographic maps. Assistance in interpreting information and in mapping data can be sought from the NRCS district conservationist, a high school earth-science teacher, or a geologist at a nearby college. Much information about such geological features as sand and gravel deposits and depth to bedrock can also be obtained from NRCS maps.

Soils

Many people mistakenly assume that soil surveys are useful primarily for agriculture. In fact, they provide vital information on the suitability of soils for construction, recreation, water impoundment, and many other land uses. Because of soil's interrelationship with so many other natural features and processes, soil characteristics often reveal more about an area than data about any other single resource. Many soils with an abundance of clay, for example, drain poorly, shrink, and swell, presenting problems for both agriculture and construction. Other soil characteristics—such as depth of topsoil, susceptibility to flooding, and potential for erosion—can also limit an area's usefulness for particular purposes.

Communities generally do not need to conduct their own soils inventory, because the NRCS surveys cover most of the country. The quality of the surveys varies with their age. The more recent ones are more accurate and thorough and include more information on soil characteristics for land uses other than farming. The NRCS district conservationist can assist citizens in interpreting the soils data and understanding soil properties.

Soil scientists have developed a system for identifying soils and assigning them to "soil series" on the basis of such factors as particle size, mineral composition, organic content, and degree of acidity. More than fifteen thousand soil series have been identified in the United States. Each series has a name, usually derived from the name of the location where it was first identified. A single township may have twenty or more soil series; in Cazenovia there are forty-six. Each series is further subdivided into phases, based on percentage of slope, depth, and other characteristics.

VILLAGE OF CAZENOVIA

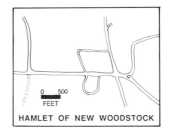

HAMLET OF NEW WOODSTOCK

SLOPE ANALYSIS

0 - 8%

8 - 15%

Greater than 15%

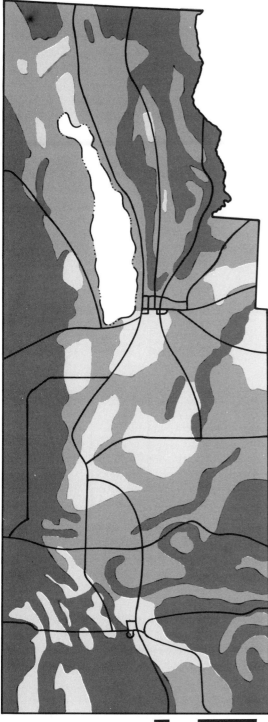

TOWN OF CAZENOVIA

0 MILES 1

CAZENOVIA
COMMUNITY
RESOURCES
PROJECT

3.10
A section of the Madison County soil survey map showing soils found near Cazenovia Lake. The first two letters for each area refer to the soil series and the third letter refers to the slope class. "HnB," for instance, refers to Honeoye silt loam, with a slope class of B (3 to 8 percent). The HnB areas are well-suited for a variety of crops but only moderately well-suited for construction, because the substratum does not drain well. "Ce" refers to the Carlisle muck series. As the name implies, it represents wetland.

A soil survey consists of maps, descriptions of each soil phase, and charts that describe the best uses and limitations of each. A typical survey rates each soil phase for its suitability for different crops, trees, wildlife habitat, construction, septic systems, and water management.

Soil scientists make use of topographic maps, geological maps, and aerial photographs to prepare soil surveys. They also conduct extensive field work, studying vegetation and digging pits to analyze the soil's depth, texture, acidity, and wetness. Their maps, superimposed on aerial photographs, delineate boundaries between soil phases, although in many areas soil phases grade from one to another.

If NRCS has completed its soil survey of the county, the main task is transferring the information from the NRCS maps onto the community map. Although one NRCS map incorporates all of the information about soil for a given area, it may be more useful for the community to record different characteristics on different maps. CCRP, for instance, chose to make separate maps for soil groups (series with related characteristics), slope, depth to bedrock, depth to seasonal high water table, permeability, and soil erosion potential. For a small number of counties, NRCS soil survey data are available in digitized form for GIS use.

In addition to soil surveys, NRCS has prepared maps of important farmland for many counties that are confronting development pressures. These maps show prime farmland (land that has the best combination of

physical and chemical characteristics, growing season, and moisture supply for producing sustained high yields with proper management), unique
farmland (land used for specialty crops, like cherries or cranberries), and
farmland of state and local importance.

Water and Related Resources

A study of water resources is a basic component of any resources inventory. An inventory of water resources can identify locations of both
groundwater (water found underground) and surface water (such as
streams, ponds, and estuaries) and of wetlands, floodplains, and scenic
areas and can document water quantity, current uses and future needs of
water in the area, and existing and potential threats to water quality. The
inventory can also establish baseline data on water quantity and quality
that can be compared with data collected in the future, to measure deterioration or improvement in the community's water resources.

With professional supervision, volunteers can collect and map much
of the data. Since setting up a water study and analyzing the data require
professional expertise usually not available in rural communities, it may
be necessary to seek assistance from a regional, state, or federal agency
or a professional consultant. The NRCS district conservationist can assist
a community in compiling and analyzing water-related data. State agencies responsible for health, natural resources, and geological surveys; regional planning commissions; watershed associations; water and sewer
authorities; and health boards can also provide data, assist in mapping
water resources, and help to monitor water quantity and quality.

Water quantity is determined by estimating the volume of surface water and groundwater reserves, studying stream flow, and surveying yields
from municipal and residential wells. Such studies, which often require
extensive drilling, can be expensive. Sometimes, valuable information is
obtainable from the logs of commercial well drillers.

The USGS *Hydrologic Investigation Atlas* series includes maps of groundwater and surface water for some areas of the country. In addition to identifying water supply, the maps indicate such potential problems as floods, sedimentation in streams, and salinization of aquifers in coastal areas.

SURFACE WATER AND WATERSHEDS

Identifying watersheds lets a community know what runoff water drains into which streams, lakes, wetlands, and reservoirs. Watershed boundaries (see Figure 1.13) are generally defined by the highest points of land between bodies of water. USGS topographic maps help in making these determinations. A community can use watershed maps to keep polluting activities off land draining into reservoirs and other waters that should be kept clean. Twenty-eight states have inventoried river resources with assistance from the National Park Service's Rivers, Trails, and Conservation Assistance program. These statewide assessments help communities identify streams they may wish to protect.

Maintaining the water quality of Cazenovia Lake was a concern of CCRP. For a lake of its size, its watershed is unusually small, resulting in a slow turnover of water and making the lake vulnerable to pollution from septic systems, lawn fertilizers, and sedimentation. CCRP mapped the lake's watershed and recommended stricter land use controls within it.

GROUNDWATER

Groundwater comes from aquifers, geologic formations that yield water in usable quantities. The aquifer can be bedrock or unconsolidated sand and gravel. An aquifer recharge area is the surface area where rainfall or runoff seeps through the ground into the aquifer. Protecting aquifers and their recharge areas from pollutants is especially important for a community dependent on groundwater for human consumption or irrigation. The inventory should indicate the location of aquifers, aquifer recharge areas, and land uses that may contaminate aquifers.

WATER QUALITY

Keeping water supplies free of pollution is essential for every community. Unfortunately, many communities do not realize a problem exists until water quality is monitored. Although there have long been programs that monitor water supplies for waterborne diseases, many communities have not tested for chemical pollutants, such as gasoline leaking from deteriorating underground tanks or high levels of nitrates from agricultural fertilization.

State health or environmental departments routinely test water quality and may be able to do all of the necessary monitoring for a community. In some cases, however, a community may need more intensive monitoring than the state is capable of providing. Water pollution is generally classified as point source pollution (coming from a known source, such as a storm sewer or discharge from a factory) or nonpoint source pollution (coming from a general area, such as farm fields or a subdivision with septic systems). Potential sources of pollution, such as landfills, feedlots, and gas stations, should be mapped.

The water table is the level below which the soil is saturated with water. In some areas, the water table rises during certain times of year. Intermittently high water tables can interfere with the function of and be polluted by septic systems and can cause water to seep into basements. The soil survey can reveal areas with periodically high water tables. CCRP mapped Cazenovia's seasonally high water tables and recommended that areas with water seasonally within two feet of the surface not be built upon.

WETLANDS

A map of wetlands shows a community and property owners the locations of these vital resources. There can be considerable controversy over what areas should be classified as wetlands, since controls on their use are generally quite restrictive. Many can be identified through soil surveys, which indicate poorly drained soils. Vegetation is also a useful indicator: many plants prefer wetlands or exist only on them. Infrared aerial photographs can help to distinguish between wet and dry areas.

3.12
Aerial photographs are invaluable aids to environmental inventories. In addition to showing land use, they make possible the identification of such resources as wetlands, which are important for maintaining a community's water quality and protecting wildlife. This aerial photograph of Cazenovia shows a wetland extending from the north end of the lake to the upper edge of the photograph. The subdivision to the east of the wetland (arrow) was built on fill over what was once part of the wetland.

Wetlands are classified on the basis of hydrologic, geomorphologic, chemical, and biological factors. The U.S. Fish and Wildlife Service is conducting a national wetlands inventory that includes all of the nation's coastal and inland wetlands. About 75 percent of the continental United States, 24 percent of Alaska, and all of Hawaii has now been mapped. Information on the inventory and other assistance is available from wetland coordinators in the regional offices of the service, and maps can be ordered from the Earth Science Information Center of USGS. Many states have conducted their own detailed inventories of wetlands. Finally, communities may want to hire an engineering consultant to delineate wetlands.

FLOODPLAINS

All communities should identify floodplains so that construction on them can be avoided or controlled. The Federal Emergency Management Agency has mapped floodplains for about 18,200 communities. These maps are designed to be used by communities in implementing flood damage prevention ordinances and in other ways reducing the impact of potential floods. Typically, FEMA maps one-hundred-year floodplains, which are areas that have at least a one in one hundred chance of flooding in any given year. Riverine floodplains can be subdivided into floodways—areas designated to carry the peak discharge and where flood waters are generally deepest and fastest—and flood fringe areas outside the floodway.

Other federal agencies—the Army Corps of Engineers, the Bureau of Reclamation, and the NRCS—have also prepared some floodplain maps. Information on precipitation, topography, land use, and past floods is used to prepare floodplain maps. In the absence of engineering studies, data on floods of record or historical data (plus or minus some margin of variability) are useful in delineating floodplains. In addition to floodplain maps, communities should consider the potential depth and velocity of flooding and the amount of warning time available.

The Cazenovia Community Resources Project mapped floodplains and identified them as critical resources that should not be developed in any way that would impair their ability to retain flood waters.

Vegetation

Vegetation, both natural and planted, is a significant resource to include in any comprehensive inventory, yet it is often overlooked or treated only briefly. An inventory of vegetation indicates the presence of such resources as trees for timber and wildlife habitat. Certain plant species are characteristic of wetlands or certain soil types. Others may indicate disturbed areas, loss of topsoil, or the presence of pollutants. Vegetation can reveal past land use: a stand of white pine may mark the place where a farmer's field once lay, and daffodils may indicate a former house site. Since vegetation usually provides a visual amenity, mapping it can help residents to identify some of the special attributes of their community.

Several classification systems can be used in inventorying vegetation. A community should base its choice of system on the nature of its vegetation and the purposes of the inventory.

One basic classification system is the USGS Land-Use and Land-Cover System for use with remote sensing data. This system classifies land cover as agricultural land, rangeland, forest land, wetlands, barren land, tundra, or the like. Another basic classification system is based on structure, or the overall assemblage of plants in an area. William M. Marsh defines the following eight classes: forest, woodland, orchard or plantation, brush, fence rows, wetland, grassland, and field (see Figure 3.13). This classification system is often sufficient. A community that wishes more detail could subdivide these classes. For instance, forests can be classified as deciduous, evergreen, or mixed and wetlands as forested or not forested.

The next level of sophistication is to identify plant "communities" or "associations," which are assemblages of plants typically found together. A forest community in Virginia might be termed oak-hickory or in Idaho, ponderosa pine–douglas fir, indicating which species are dominant (defined as exerting the greatest influence on other plants in the community).

The most sophisticated vegetation inventory lists all of the species found in a given area and notes their relative abundance. Although this degree of detail usually is not necessary, rare species or exceptional occurrences of common ones, such as particularly fine specimens or old-growth timber stands, should be included. (If rare or endangered species are found, it may prove counterproductive to publicize their location beyond those with a need to know, since excessive visitation or destruction could result.)

More specialized inventories may be appropriate in some communities. For example, a county in Utah might wish to study the health of its rangeland, a county in Indiana might note the locations of undisturbed prairie, and a town in North Carolina may want to note the location of shade trees along public rights-of-way. Such information could inspire a program to protect the rangeland from overgrazing, native grasses from herbicides, or street trees from road widenings. It can also be used to advise property owners which plantings are most appropriate in preserving the community's historic appearance.

Personnel needs depend largely on the scale of the inventory. An inventory of plant structure can be carried out largely by knowledgeable volunteers with access to topographic maps and recent aerial photographs. In more intensive surveys volunteers can identify plants and map findings but may require the assistance of someone trained in biology, ecology, forestry, horticulture, or landscape architecture. Among sources of assistance are biology teachers, who may assign a vegetation inventory as a student project; a garden club; scientists working in the area for the U.S. Forest Service, the National Park Service, the Natural Resources Conservation Service, or the Bureau of Land Management; and the Nature Conservancy. Many communities also have nature centers and state or local

3.13
Surveyors studying a community's vegetation can adapt William M. Marsh's structural inventory categories or develop their own.

Level I
(vegetative structure)

Forest
(trees with average height greater than 15 ft with at least 60°₀ canopy cover)

Woodland
(trees with average height greater than 15 ft with 20–60°₀ canopy cover)

Orchard or Plantation
(same as woodland or forest but with regular spacing)

Brush
(trees and shrubs generally less than 15 ft high with high density of stems. but variable canopy cover)

Fencerows
(trees and shrubs of mixed forms along borders such as roads. fields. yards. playgrounds)

Wetland
(generally low. dense plant covers in wet areas)

Grassland
(herbs. with grasses dominant)

Field
(tilled or recently tilled farmland)

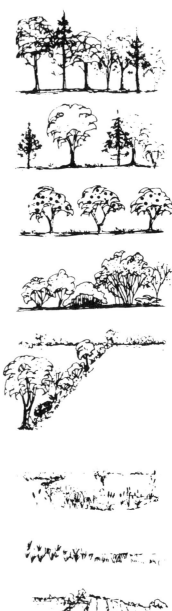

parks with trained naturalists who may be eager to assist with communitywide projects as a way of increasing public interest in their facilities. Nearby parks and public lands may already have species lists that can provide a basis for community surveys.

The Nature Conservancy is working in partnership with natural lands programs in all fifty states to inventory natural resources that are exemplary, rare, or endangered. Most of these programs are within state natural resource agencies. The resources inventoried by the programs can be an endangered plant or animal species, a community of plants and animals, habitat for an endangered species, or other natural features. Data is recorded on each resource's occurrence, number, condition, and degree of endangerment.

There are many useful field identification guides. Some are national in their coverage and others regional or local. A local botanist can advise which are the best for a particular area. Aerial photographs can be used not only to identify structure but also to make finer distinctions. For instance, the texture of the tree tops in the photographs can be used to tell mature stands from younger ones; infrared photographs can help distinguish between coniferous and deciduous trees; and stereo pairs of photographs can indicate relative tree height and hence maturity.

Wildlife

Although relatively few communities inventory their terrestrial and aquatic wildlife or assess the health of wildlife populations, there may be good reasons to do so. Wildlife is a major asset in most rural areas. Many people enjoy observing wildlife. Hunting and fishing may also be important food sources, offer popular forms of recreation, or provide significant occupations in a rural community.

Since many animal species range over a wide area, it can be difficult to count them. Wildlife biologists count some species through the use of aerial photographs, or they tag birds or mammals to monitor their movements. Wildlife biologists frequently estimate wildlife populations by counting individual animals, droppings, burrows, or nests in a sampling area. The degree to which foliage or grasses have been eaten is also a good indication of wildlife populations. Estimates of age and sex distribution indicate whether a population of a particular species is healthy.

The National Biological Survey, conducted by the National Biological Service of the Department of the Interior, is coordinating a gap analysis of biodiversity across the United States. Gap analysis uses a GIS to locate areas rich in vegetation and vertebrate species and to assess their representation in protected areas, such as national parks, national forests, and state parks. Areas that are biologically diverse but unprotected represent gaps in conservation. Communities may wish to consider special protective actions where such gaps exist.

For most communities the best approach to wildlife protection is to identify and protect habitat, including nesting grounds and spawning areas. Fortunately, for many species considerable information exists concerning favorable habitat. Plant species preferred by wildlife can also be noted for protection. For instance, retaining trees that shade streams assures the cool water temperatures that trout require. Consequently, the conservation commission in Cazenovia concluded that the best approach to protecting trout in the township's streams was to monitor and control adjacent land use. The commission also mapped fish spawning areas in the township. Deer in upstate New York require the shelter of forested

3.14
Wildlife is often inventoried by the tracks animals leave behind. These bear paw prints near Miles Lake, Alaska, indicate a recent presence.

3.15

Communities interested in wildlife protection may wish to develop a species-habitat matrix similar to this one, which was developed for Albion, Washington. Matrices can be prepared for other resources as well.

G–GRASS S–SHRUB W–WOODS C–CROP R–RIVER

SPECIES	ANIMAL HABITAT			OCCURRENCE					COMMENTS
	BREED-ING	LIVING	EATING	COMMON	UN-COMMON	RARE	MIGRANT	RESI-DENT	
American Robin *Turdus migratorius*	W	W	G S	●			●		
Barn Owl *Tyto alba*	W	W	W S	●				●	
Mourning Dove *Zenaida macroura*	G S	G S	G S C	●				●	
Red tailed hawk *Buteo jamaicensis*	W	W	G W S C R		●			●	
Porcupine *Erethizon dorsatum*	W	W	W			●		●	
Norway rat *Rattus norvegicus*	G S	G S	G S C	●				●	
Beaver *Castor canadensis*	W R	R	W R		●			●	
White tailed deer *Odocoileus virginianus*	W	W S	W S G C	●				●	

areas to protect them from winter storms, and they prefer southern and western facing slopes, where snows melt earlier. Therefore CCRP mapped areas most favorable as deer habitat.

Depending on the needs and skills available in the community, inventories of wildlife or wildlife habitat can be conducted by either community volunteers or outside professionals. Most communities have a number of amateur bird watchers, naturalists, and hunters who are skilled at animal identification. If they are organized in a club, such as a chapter of the National Audubon Society or a rod and gun club, their group may be willing to take on a wildlife inventory as a project. Local amateur naturalists may already participate in wildlife censuses, such as the Audubon Society's annual Christmas bird count.

Additional information and assistance are available from the same sources as for vegetation inventories. State fish and game agencies can be of assistance for game species, and many now maintain information on all kinds of creatures (sometimes called nongame species) as well, especially if they are endangered or threatened. Biologists working at national wildlife refuges or field offices of the U.S. Fish and Wildlife Service may offer advice. For coastal communities, the service has prepared comprehensive inventories and maps of fish, wildlife, and plant species.

Climate

Data on microclimates—the climates of small, distinct areas—may be particularly important for communities where conditions vary greatly from one part of the community to another, as they frequently do in mountainous and coastal areas. A microclimate, because of its particular exposure, elevation, or vegetation, may have warmer or cooler temperatures than adjacent areas, different average wind velocity, more or less precipitation, or a greater likelihood of fog. Such conditions may affect the suitability of a site for construction or agriculture. For example, the North Fork of Long Island, New York, and the Old Mission Peninsula in Michigan have unusually moist and moderate microclimates, with long frost-free growing seasons. The microclimatic conditions in both of these areas result in highly productive agriculture. Temperature and precipitation records for many communities are available from the National Oceanic and Atmospheric Administration. Additional weather information may be available from the Cooperative Extension Service and the Natural Resources Conservation Service.

INVENTORYING SPECIAL RESOURCES

Historic and Cultural Resources

Conducting a cultural resources inventory helps a community to identify and understand the economic, geographic, environmental, social, and cultural forces that shaped its development. An inventory establishes where and why settlement occurred; traces transportation networks such as roads, canals, and railroads; identifies agricultural patterns and practices; outlines the development of commerce and industry; identifies ethnic and other influences on the community's environment; and documents special places like battlefields and cemeteries. Such information can be used in preparing nominations to state and national registers and in developing a local ordinance to protect resources.

An inventory should record not simply the oldest or the finest examples of architecture, or only the homes and gardens of the rich and famous. It should include a wide range of buildings, landscapes, and archeological sites; to be thorough, the rural inventory should address all of the components of the rural landscape and include land as well as buildings. A farmhouse, for example, should not be considered as an isolated architectural landmark, but rather as part of an agricultural complex that has evolved over time.

The degree of detail for a cultural resources survey will vary with the community's needs. If a nomination to the National Register is contemplated, considerable information will be required. If the purpose is to note the location of potential resources that can be studied later in greater detail should demolition, alteration, or adjacent new construction be proposed, then a less detailed study may be appropriate. Archeological surveys may be a component of the historic and cultural resources inventory, although they are usually undertaken when a construction project threatens known or suspected resources. Archeological surveys can also be done at different levels of intensity, depending on the the number and type of resources in question and the purpose of the survey, but they are generally expensive. The precise location of unprotected archeological sites should be kept confidential to protect them from looters.

Most State Historic Preservation Offices (SHPOs) supply inventory forms for recording data (see Sidebar 7.2). Many state forms have been developed for use in urban areas and may not be well suited for recording landscape features and rural structures. Rural communities may thus find it necessary to develop their own supplemental forms on which to record this information.

When documenting a site, those conducting the cultural resources inventory should take enough black-and-white photographs to record all aspects of a property's character. There should be at least one overall landscape view, showing the property in its environmental context, as

3.6 Evaluation Criteria for the National Register of Historic Places

Once you have completed a historic resources inventory, you may wish to evaluate the significance of the inventoried properties. Here is the National Park Service's description of criteria for nomination to the National Register of Historic Places:

> *The quality of significance in American history, architecture, archeology, and culture is present in districts, sites, buildings, structures, and objects that possess integrity of location, design, setting, materials, workmanship, feeling, and association, and*
>
> **A.** *that are associated with events that have made a significant contribution to the broad patterns of our history; or*
> **B.** *that are associated with the lives of persons significant in our past; or*
> **C.** *that embody the distinctive characteristics of a type, period, or method of construction, or that represent the work of a master, or that possess high artistic values, or that represent a significant and distinguishable entity whose components may lack individual distinction; or*
> **D.** *that have yielded, or may be likely to yield, information important in prehistory or history.*

(See Notes to Sidebars.)

well as photographs of all the associated structures and landscape elements. Late fall, winter, and early spring, when there are few leaves on deciduous trees and few crops in the fields, are usually the best times to take photographs that show landform, extent of the property, and architectural features such as fences and outbuildings (see Sidebar 8.2 for tips on photography).

The final step in conducting the cultural resources inventory is to evaluate significance. The criteria developed by the National Park Service for the National Register should be helpful in this regard.

WHO CONDUCTS THE INVENTORY

To conduct a cultural resources inventory, a community needs persons with a knowledge of archeology, architectural history, and landscape history, an understanding of local history and land use, and experience in doing inventories. Although some skills should be available locally, most communities need professional assistance. Many communities combine the services of a paid consultant with those of local volunteers. The SHPO can often provide names of qualified individuals or firms to conduct historic inventories.

Regardless of who conducts the inventory, it should be done in cooperation with the SHPO. That office can provide useful guidance and possibly some funding. Since important reasons for undertaking an inventory are to augment the statewide survey of historic properties and to nominate properties to state and federal registers, thereby affording them a measure of protection, it is essential that the information be recorded in an approved manner.

Volunteers can trace deeds, read old newspapers, and scan past census reports. A local historical society may be able to help. Local volunteers may be more likely than outside consultants to recognize kinship links and historic place names used in boundary descriptions in deeds.

CASE STUDY 3.2

Westphalia Historic District, Texas: The Cultural Landscape

Although many historic preservation organizations have inventoried historic structures, fewer have surveyed the cultural landscape. Westphalia, a farming community settled by German Catholics in the early 1880s in east central Texas, gained a renewed sense of its identity from surveying approximately five square miles of Falls County.

In 1992, the Westphalia community learned about the proposed construction of a bullet train from Dallas to San Antonio which threatened literally to cut their historic community in half. The Westphalia Historical Society, organized in 1991, had begun the groundwork research for a listing in the National Register of Historic Places. Now, with the train threat, the community decided to pursue National Register designation as a potential protection mechanism. Through its various fund-raising events—a Memorial Day celebration, a fall homecoming, and an annual dinner raffle (for which the tickets cost $100 each and the prize is a $10,000 certificate of deposit)—the historical society raised enough money to hire a consulting firm to help inventory their historic properties. With the advice of the State Historic Preservation Office, the consultant, Terri Myers, decided that Westphalia's agricultural community remained remarkably intact, and she expanded the scope of the inventory to include the cultural landscape.

Ultimately, the plans for the bullet train were dropped. However, the landscape survey gave the Westphalia community a renewed sense of identity, and the survey is used as a public education tool for both adults and children. Doris Voltin, former president of the Westphalia Historical Society and a leader of the fund-raising effort, sees the survey as a means of getting recognition for a group of German immigrants who came to this country to farm and a community that still pursues traditional agriculture; it is to let everyone know that rural America is still alive. The community was listed in the National Register in 1996.

The National Register nomination identifies the eleven landscape features that occur in most cultural landscapes. The features, or characteristics, examples of which are illustrated in Figures 3.16.A–K, are published by the National Park Service (McClelland, Keller, Keller, and Melnick). They can be used to compile a checklist of historic landscape elements to investigate which can be adapted to reflect local conditions and resources. Although most National Register nominations of rural historic districts do not formally itemize each of the eleven landscape features, they at least treat them indirectly.

FOLKLIFE TRADITIONS

Communities concerned with protecting their folklife resources and traditions may wish to conduct a folk arts inventory. Also, traditional ways of siting, constructing, and furnishing buildings are of interest in a historic resources survey. A folk arts inventory can include listings of which people in the community still practice such traditional crafts as building stone walls or split-rail fences. It can identify extant examples in the community of such folk arts as basketmaking or rug weaving and can document the practitioners' techniques and the history of their crafts. It can also include recordings or videos of folk musicians or storytellers relating local folk tales and legends, and identify traditional places where practitioners gathered materials, like clay for pottery or reeds for basketmaking.

Volunteers can conduct much of a folk arts inventory. Such a project is often a good way to involve both senior citizens and schoolchildren. A nearby university or the state government may have a folklife program with a folklorist on staff who can offer assistance in locating a qualified person to help organize the inventory and assist in choosing the appropriate type of documentation. The Heritage and Preservation Division of the National Endowment for the Arts and the American Folklife Center of the Library of Congress may also be able to assist a community.

Scenic Areas

An inventory of scenic resources can be an important component of a resources inventory. The results of a scenic inventory can be used in

A

B

C

D

3.16

The following series of photographs illustrates eleven cultural landscape characteristics with scenes from Westphalia, Texas. (*A*) *Land use.* Farming, mining, ranching, fishing, recreation, industry, and forestry leave their imprint on the land. Raising wheat is a typical land use in Westphalia. (*B*) *Patterns of spatial organization.* Natural boundaries, road systems, and field patterns organize the landscape. In Westphalia, animal and tractor barns are usually located a practical distance from the house, separated by a driveway. Typically, building complexes sit on elevated land, with narrow driveways leading in from county roads. (*C*) *Response to the natural environment.* Mountains, rivers, forests, and other natural resources influence the location of structures and fields and provide building materials. Typically, the stock pond is built at the lowest point in the field, to collect rain runoff for watering the cattle. (*D*) *Cultural traditions.* A group's culture is reflected in land use practices, structures, technology, use of plants, and ethnic or religious institutions. This wood-frame German Catholic church was built in 1894 on the highest point of land in the district. The twin towers dominate the surrounding landscape, a visual reminder of the religious focus of the community. (*E*) *Circulation networks.* Footpaths, livestock trails, roads, railroads, and canals link elements of the landscape. Narrow gravel and packed-dirt roads cross the Westphalia district in a grid pattern. (*F*) *Boundary demarcations.* Streams, ridges, fences, stone walls, or hedgerows may serve this function. In Westphalia, cedar posts with barbed wire fencing separate pastures from cultivated fields and mark property lines. (*G*) *Vegetation as related to land use.* Characteristic vegetation that has been planted or intentionally let stand could include orchards, wood lots, windbreaks, and ornamental plants. Trees often provide shade and protection around clusters of farm buildings. (*H*) *Buildings, structures, and objects.* All structures, including barns, sheds, schoolhouses, canals, windmills, mine shafts, and monuments should be inventoried. The Buckholt farmstead barn, shown here, is a 1920s structure of milled pine, used principally for hay storage. (*I*) *Clusters.* The arrangement of villages, farmsteads, harbors, or ranching complexes reflects social and economic patterns of a culture. In Westphalia, the outbuildings on farmsteads are usually clustered close together. (*J*) *Archeological sites.* Traces of roads and ruins of farmsteads, mills, mines, irrigation systems, and quarries are historic or prehistoric remnants. This ruin of a barn and mound of earth mark the site of the original Roessler farmstead. A bed of bulbs, typically planted along foundations of houses, is one clue to the former land use. (*K*) *Small-scale elements.* Often overlooked are such features as fence posts, abandoned farm machinery, road markers, and foot bridges. The ruins of a privy and a clothesline poles made from cedar posts mark the site of a Westphalian farm.

E

F

G

H

I

J

K

3.17
Each community undertaking a historic inventory needs a data sheet. In some instances, the State Historic Preservation Office issues a standard form. In others, the local organization develops its own to reflect local conditions, building practices, and terminology: for instance, this form, developed for Hanalei, Hawaii, includes references to cultural affiliations that would not be found in most other U.S. communities. Two of the structures inventoried by the Hanalei Project were the Hanalei Bridge and this board and batten farmer's cottage.

HANALEI PROJECT: HISTORIC STRUCTURES DATA SHEET
1000 Friends of Kauai and Land & Community Associates

Tax Lot Number:_____

1. Site name (if applicable or N/A):_____

2. Address or location:_____

3. State zoning:_____County zoning: _____Use permit:_____

4. Field recorder(s):_____

5. Date(s) recorded in field:_____

6. Owner's name:_____

7. Owner's address:_____

8. Use: Original: Agricultural Residential   Non-Agricultural Residential   Store   Mill/Warehouse

       Institutional (specify)_____   Other _____

    Present: Same   Part-time Residential   Vacation Rental   Retail and General

9. Condition: Excellent   Good   Fair   Deteriorated   Ruin

10. Threats to structure: None/ Not Known   Abusive Alterations   Neglect   Road Construction

        Private Development   Government Activity

11. General style groups:_____

12. Height: 1 Story   1 1/2 Story   2 Story   More than 2

13. Facade width: 1 Bay   2 Bay   3 Bay   4 Bay   More than 4 Bay

14. Wings and additions: Rear   Side   Front   (Show location on attached grid sheet)

15. Principal Roof configuration: Gable   Hipped   Shed   Other_____

16. Roof materials: Orignial (if known)_____Existing_____

17. Exterior wall materials: Original (if known):_____

        Existing:_____

18. Principal lanai type: Engaged   Attached   Location: Front   Side   Rear

19. Principal lanai integrity: Original   Screened Enclosed   Other Alteration   Removed   Unknown

20. Foundation treatment: Slab   Elevated   Other_____

21. Foundation materials:_____

22. Other distinguishing features:(Describe)

    Windows:_____

    Porch Details:_____

    Other:_____

23. Outbuildings:_____

                   Commercial Agricultural-related Commercial Other (specify)_____

    (Attach additional form for each pre-1946 outbuilding and show location on attached grid sheets.)

                 Auwai Other

24. Distinguishing site features: Walls Fences Plant Materials Gardens Walkways Ponds

    Describe_____

25. Site integrity: Original   Moved   Distance moved: <1/2 mi 1/2-2 2-4 More than 4

    Original location, if known _____

    Original occupants:_____

26. Cultural/ethnic affiliations:

    Native Hawaiian Chinese Japanese Filipino Causacasion Unknown Other_____

    Cultural/ethnic affiliations of subsequent occupants:_____

27. Persons or events of significance associated with structure (if known):

    Owner/Occupant:_____

    Event:_____

    Architect/Builder:_____

    Date(s):_____

28. Quad map used:_____

29. UTM Data: Zone: _____   Northing:_____   Easting:_____

30. Direction building faces: N S E W NE NW SE SW

31: Comment:_____
_____
_____
_____
_____
_____
_____
_____
_____
_____

3.7 Sources of Information for Historic Inventories

The following are good sources for inventories of historic resources:

- *State Historic Preservation Office*
- *State and local libraries and archives*
- *State and local historical societies and preservation organizations*
- *Census reports and homesteader records*
- *Architectural history and history faculty at area schools*
- *Family letters, papers, and Bibles*
- *School, church, and business records*
- *Books on local history and accounts of travelers*
- *Historic photographs, maps, and engravings*
- *Cemetery inscriptions and burial records*
- *Deeds and wills*
- *Newspaper archives*

In addition, surveyors need to make contact with local-history, genealogy, and architecture buffs as well as with older people who have good memories and have lived in the community a long time. Older citizens often know which buildings are the oldest, who lived in them, and what crops were planted in which fields in the past.

developing comprehensive plans, land use ordinances, and design guidelines, in determining the potential visual impact of a proposed development (see Sidebar 4.13), educating community residents, deciding what properties to acquire or protect through easements, and in determining locations for new developments, roads, trails, or utility lines.

During the past two decades, landscape architects have pioneered a number of methods for assessing visual quality and visual preferences in a community. Some methods rely primarily on experts with skills in landscape architecture, computers, or statistics; others place heavy emphasis on a community's participation. By its very nature, assessing visual impact includes a degree of subjectivity. The approach chosen should depend largely on how the inventory information will be used. For example, if a zoning ordinance is going to be based in part on a survey of citizens' preferences, a statistically sound method of sampling public

3.18
Documenting folklife is an important part of gaining community understanding. Here a member of the Montana Folklife Survey team interviews Agnes Vanderburg on the Flathead Reservation about her method for baking wild camas roots. Vanderburg instructs children about tribal traditions at a summer camp on the reservation.

opinion will be required. On the other hand, if the primary objective is to increase a community's awareness and to demonstrate to community residents that there is much agreement on what is beautiful in the community, a less comprehensive (and less expensive) approach may be appropriate.

An inventory of scenic features should not be limited to what is "beautiful." Scraggly hedgerows or a dilapidated store, while not scenic, may be prominent visual features that serve as major points of identity in a community and should be preserved because of their cultural and social significance. Chesterfield County, Virginia, is an example of a community that conducted a visual resource analysis as part of a comprehensive plan update. The study identifies characteristic areas the community thinks are visually significant and makes recommendations for their protection in light of future development.

Many communities, most states, and some federal land-management agencies have programs to designate and protect scenic roads. The National Scenic Byways Program designates certain roads as a National Scenic Byway or All-American Road. Determining what roads are scenic requires a system for assessing scenic value. Nevada has developed a system in which roads nominated by local communities are rated by a statewide committee, by segment, according to a set of positive and negative features. In the Loess Hills region of Iowa, local residents participated in a visual assessment of alternate roadways to designate a set of scenic routes for tourism development.

A good way to introduce the issue of visual quality in a community is to show photographs of the community—both scenic and not so scenic—to residents and ask them to discuss their impressions of the views, their opinions on what constitutes good design, and their feelings about what resources are important to protect.

WHO CONDUCTS THE INVENTORY

Many landscape architects have specific training in visual assessment and can assist a community in designing a survey to fit its needs. Assistance may also be available from the Natural Resources Conservation Service, the National Park Service, the Bureau of Land Management, or

3.19
The Bureau of Land Management uses specific criteria when conducting scenic quality inventories to identify areas of public land that should be protected.

Scenic Quality Inventory/Evaluation Rating Criteria and Score

Landform	Vegetation	Water	Color	Adjacent Scenery	Scarcity	Cultural Modifications
High vertical relief such as prominent cliffs, spires or massive rock outcrops; **or** severe surface variation or highly eroded formations including major badlands or dune systems; **or** detail features dominant and exceptionally striking and intriguing such as glaciers. **5**	A variety of vegetative types in interesting forms, textures, and patterns **5**	Clear and clean appearing, still, or cascading white water, any of which are a dominant factor in the landscape. **5**	Rich color combinations, variety or vivid color; **or** pleasing contrasts in the soil, rock, vegetation, water or snow fields. **5**	Adjacent scenery greatly enhances visual quality. **5**	One of a kind; **or** unusually memorable; **or** very rare within region. Consistent chance for exceptional wildlife or wildflower viewing. **6**	Free from esthetically undesirable or discordant sights and influences; **or** modifications add favorably to visual variety. **2**
Steep canyons, mesas, buttes, cinder cones and drumlins; **or** interesting erosional patterns or variety in size and shape of landforms; **or** detail features present and interesting though not dominant or exceptional. **3**	Some variety of vegetation. but only one or two types. **3**	Flowing or still, but not dominant in the landscape. **3**	Some intensity or variety in colors and contrast of the soil, rock and vegetation. but not a dominant scenic element. **3**	Adjacent scenery moderately enhances overall visual quality. **3**	Distinctive. though somewhat similar to others within the region. **2**	Scenic quality is somewhat depreciated by inharmonious intrusions. but not so extensively that they are entirely negated; **or** modifications add little or no visual variety to the area. **0**
Low. rolling hills. foothills **or** flat valley bottoms. Interesting. detailed landscape features few or lacking. **1**	Little or no variety or contrast in vegetation. **1**	Absent. or not noticeable. **0**	Subtle color variations. contrast or interest; generally muted tones. **1**	Adjacent scenery has little or no influence on overall visual quality. **0**	Interesting within its setting. but fairly common within the region. **1**	Modifications are so extensive that scenic qualities are mostly nullified or substantially reduced **-4**

the Forest Service, all of which employ landscape architects to assess the visual impacts of proposed development or changes in vegetation on federal lands, or, in the case of NRCS, on lands whose owners receive federal assistance. Each of these agencies has publications available on the visual assessment procedures it uses.

A professional visual analysis is based on the trained eye of a landscape architect who classifies and evaluates landscapes. There is no one set of criteria uniformly used by landscape architects. Many visual analysis studies, including those conducted by the Bureau of Land Management and the Forest Service, use elements of artistic composition—form, line, color, and texture—to evaluate landscapes (see Figure 3.19).

Appraisals using the opinions of citizens have the obvious advantage of reflecting a community's values and attitudes. Although professional assistance is advisable, particularly if the results of the survey will be used as the basis for an ordinance, community volunteers can undertake much of the work. Discussing the scenic qualities they appreciate in their community's landscape gives citizens an opportunity to increase their environmental awareness.

There are many ways to solicit citizens' opinions. One method is for surveyors to take photographs of typical scenes throughout the community and then ask citizens to rate the beauty of each scene on, say, a five-point scale or to rank the photographs in order of scenic preference. The results can be mapped. To insure optimal objectivity, the photographs being compared should be as uniform in quality and lighting conditions as possible.

CASE STUDY 3.3

Cazenovia, New York:
Citizens Participate in a Visual Survey

Terry LeVeque, project director of the Cazenovia Community Resources Project (CCRP), and James Palmer, a research associate at the State University of New York, designed a citizens' scenic preference survey for Cazenovia in 1981. Residents were asked to locate their favorite and least favorite views on a map. LeVeque then entered the combined results on a copy of the community's base map. CCRP asked twelve local organizations, selected to represent the geographical, social, and age diversity of Cazenovia's population, to participate in the survey; they included the Rotary Club, the Garden Club, the Boy Scouts, the League of Women Voters, the Cazenovia Merchants' Association, the New Woodstock Historic Association, the Future Farmers of America, and the Volunteer Fire Department. A total of 170 individuals participated, representing approximately 3 percent of the town's population.

Dorothy Riester, chair of the CCRP, and LeVeque attended meetings of each organization to explain CCRP's purposes and administer the survey. They asked each person at the meetings to identify on a copy of the CCRP base map "up to ten favorite views and scenes" and "up to five least favorite views and scenes."

The exercise took each participant about forty-five minutes to complete. The favorites were Chittenango Falls—a unique natural feature—and views of Cazenovia Lake. There were few negative responses, other than for a shopping plaza on the outskirts of the village, indicating a largely positive regard for the community's visual environment.

The results of the visual survey helped to define the community's character zones and were incorporated into Cazenovia's *Land Use Guide*. CCRP used the results to make recommendations for acquisition of scenic easements for all of the significant views and scenes and to suggest that all of the significant views be incorporated into the Cazenovia Advisory Conservation Commission's environmental review process. The planning boards have been responsive to the value placed by the community on scenic resources. For example, in 1988, on a ridgeline lot overlooking the lake, a builder was required to remove a garage foundation he had poured in an area subject to a restrictive covenant that preserved the scenic view of the property. Not only did the visual survey stimulate community interest in Cazenovia's environment, by allowing residents to realize that by and large they shared perceptions on what was beautiful in their town, but it also helped them ensure that the most beautiful views were preserved.

3.20
Chittenango Falls, protected as part of a state park, was one of the favorite views identified in the Cazenovia visual survey.

Sometimes, particularly when new development is proposed, it is useful to know how visible it will be. Assessing the visual impact of proposed development involves analyzing what currently can be seen around the site, particularly from public rights-of-way. Developers can then be asked to design their projects so as to minimize the visibility or visual impact of the structures.

The simplest way to determine visibility is to go to a "viewpoint"—the place from which a view is visible—and note on a map the "viewshed"—the area that can be seen from the viewpoint. Of course, vegetation must be considered when determining visibility. Viewsheds may be very different in winter than in summer if deciduous trees are present. Also, trees that would hide a development today might be removed in the future.

Alternatively, there are computer programs that can display a theoretical viewshed, using topographic information. (The results need to be checked in the field.) Through a computerized simulation process, elements in the viewshed can be changed, and a series of potential development scenarios, for example, can be evaluated (see Sidebar 4.13).

Outdoor Recreation

Many people choose to live in rural communities because of the potential for outdoor recreation, on both public and private property. It may be helpful to map recreation resources. This may be easy in the case of publicly owned lands but ticklish in the case of private property. Owners who allow hikers, fishermen, hunters, and cross-country skiers to use their land may not wish to have the community advertise the fact through an inventory. Whether recreational uses of private property are mapped or not, the community may wish to survey the demands for recreational use of land and use this information in working out agreements with property owners for public access, easements, or acquisition. In Cazenovia, CCRP mapped recreation areas rather than specific trails and access points to private property. It also identified abandoned railroad rights-of-way. Since there was a demand for more recreational opportunities, CCRP recommended that some of these rights-of-way be acquired for development as trails. The Cazenovia Preservation Foundation later purchased three miles of railroad right-of-way for this purpose.

Sacred Places

A final element a community might wish to inventory is its sacred places, meaning buildings, outdoor spaces, or landscapes that exemplify the true character of the community and are essential to the daily lives of its residents. Often they are places as common as a diner, a ball park, or a post office, but they are integral to the fabric of the local community. They are the places people love, miss when they are away, and identify with home. Sacred places may be as subjective as scenery, and an increasing number of communities are inventorying them as they strive to pro-

3.21
Opposite: This map summarizes the scenic preferences of the Cazenovia citizens who participated in the visual survey. The arrows indicate favorite views. Negative areas, of which there were few, are the least favorite views. Conservation leaders used the results to decide which land to protect. The participants enjoyed doing the survey, and it helped to stimulate the community's interest in conservation.

VILLAGE OF CAZENOVIA

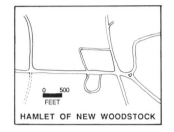

HAMLET OF NEW WOODSTOCK

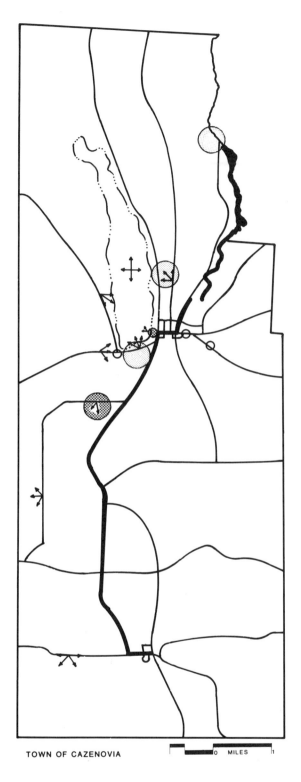

TOWN OF CAZENOVIA

VISUAL RESOURCES

   VERY SIGNIFICANT

   SIGNIFICANT

$<$ VIEW

o   NEGATIVE AREA

CAZENOVIA
COMMUNITY
RESOURCES
PROJECT

Opposite: Cazenovia's agricultural-land ownership survey was conducted by farmers with the aid of aerial photographs. Conservation leaders were surprised to learn how much of Cazenovia's cropland is rented rather than owned by farmers. They concluded that the future of agriculture was more vulnerable than they had realized.

tect the local culture and character of their towns in the face of increased development.

A sacred places inventory brings together people in the community with different interests—historic preservationists and the business community, say. A successful sacred place inventory is impossible without public involvement. The necessary first step is to find out which places in the community residents agree are the most important. This can be done by distributing a questionnaire or by holding a series of public meetings. When questionnaire or meeting responses are tabulated, it will be apparent which places are mentioned most frequently and thus where agreement lies.

Manteo, North Carolina, is an island community that used its Sacred Structures inventory to help promote tourism while preserving the village quality and waterfront intimacy that make the town special to its residents. Similarly, the residents of Wendell, Massachusetts, used a survey they called Places of the Heart to help protect the rural quality of their small town in the face of development pressures.

The following questions are the types of questions on which a useful sacred places inventory could be based.

—What buildings and outdoor spaces, public or private, are most memorable to you?
—What landmarks do you use to direct people to your home?
—What place, area, feature, or symbol most represents (your town) to you?
Name/Location
Description
Why do you go there?
How often do you go there?
—What three wishes or visions would you most like to see come true for (your town)? [1]

INVENTORYING LAND USE AND OWNERSHIP

It is helpful to map how land is used and to compare land use with resources. If, for instance, land with a seasonally high water table is zoned for intensive development, a change in zoning might be warranted. Mapping such general land use categories as residential, commercial, industrial, agricultural, institutional, and forested is probably sufficient. A map showing current zoning at the same scale as the inventory maps allows a community to analyze whether the zoning is appropriate for the resources. If a wetland is identified in the inventory and is zoned for quarter-acre residential lots, there would be sound justification for revising the zoning. In addition, it may be useful to map subdivisions that have been approved by the local planning agency, as well as water and sewer districts. The community may also want to map general ownership information that would show privately owned land and land owned by government agencies and nonprofit organizations. Such a map could include railroad and utility rights-of-way and properties subject to conservation easements.

Cazenovia was particularly concerned about preserving farmland;

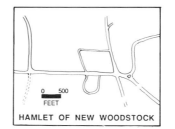

VILLAGE OF CAZENOVIA

HAMLET OF NEW WOODSTOCK

AGRICULTURAL LAND

 FARMER OWNED
CROPLAND

 FARMER OWNED
WOODLAND

LEASED CROPLAND

LEASED WOODLAND

CAZENOVIA
COMMUNITY
RESOURCES
PROJECT

TOWN OF CAZENOVIA   0   MILES   1

consequently, CCRP mapped farmland ownership. The members of the CCRP agriculture task group went to each farm to determine land use, ownership, and other data on the status of farming in the township. Task group members showed aerial photographs to property owners and asked them to identify what land they leased and owned and the agricultural uses of each parcel (see Figure 3.34).

The U.S. Geological Survey has compiled land use and land cover maps and digital map data for all the continental U.S. at the scale of 1:250,000 inches (250,000″ = 3.946 mi.). Maps and digital data are available for only selected areas of Alaska at that scale. Some areas of the continental United States and all of Hawaii have also been mapped at the scale of 1:100,000. A few states, including Alaska and Massachusetts, have mapped land use over the whole state. Existing maps may be a useful point of departure, but the information on them will probably need to be checked in the field and supplemented by the community. Land use and ownership can be surveyed at the community level by volunteers. The tax assessor or the planning office should have information on land ownership, but such information is not always easy to use.

ANALYSIS OF INVENTORY RESULTS

Once the inventory is completed, it is time to put the pieces together and reap the benefits of all the community's hard work. The analysis is the most important part of the inventory process. It is all very well and good to have collected data, but what does it all add up to? How does it fit together?

As surveyors collect data, they may reach preliminary conclusions on what resources are important and should be protected. In some cases, the presence of a single resource—perhaps a wetland, prime farmland, or a historic landmark—might, by some, be deemed sufficient to make a site inappropriate for development. In addition to a resource-by-resource analysis, a community needs to compare resources, weigh their importance, and decide which land areas in the community should be considered for protection. Areas that contain few or no special resources and that are close to roads, sewers, and other development might be recommended as the most appropriate for new development. For instance, the fact that a field is prime habitat for game birds may not in itself be sufficient grounds for disallowing new development. If that field, however, is also located in an area with a seasonally high water table and is the foreground of the principal view of the community's most significant historic site, protection may become a high priority.

In addition to assets that need to be protected, most communities unfortunately have problem areas that should be identified, mapped, and evaluated. These may include dumps that contain hazardous wastes, areas that have become polluted from rusting underground gasoline storage tanks, abandoned quarries, areas underlain with abandoned mine shafts that could cause land to subside, and sites of high-tension lines or microwave towers that mar scenery and may be causing health problems (see Sidebar 4.16).

Composite and Synthesis Maps

Since using many individual maps is cumbersome, to aid in synthesizing the information, many communities prepare composite maps that take into account all of a community's resources and environmental constraints. Each area in the community can be compared with others, areas with similar characteristics can be identified, and areas can be evaluated for their suitability for development and other uses.

Composite maps, made from overlaying translucent maps or by using computer mapping programs generated from a GIS, will be helpful in determining where resources overlap and thus which areas are the most and least appropriate for certain uses. They can illustrate, for example, how close wetlands may be to sources of pollution and whether subdivisions have been planned in areas with a great concentration of wildlife.

The simplest way to compare different resource inventories is to lay the individual resource maps, made to the same scale and reproduced on a transparent or translucent material, over one another on a light table. Overlay maps can be made of inexpensive tracing paper (although it tears easily and features become hard to distinguish when more than three sheets are overlaid) or clear plastic Mylar (more expensive but a better alternative for overlay maps that will receive hard use). Graphic symbols

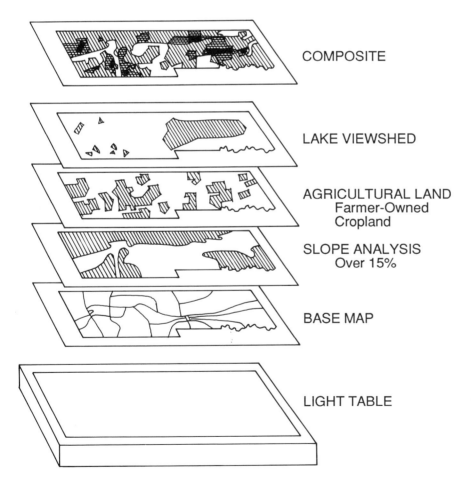

COMPOSITE

LAKE VIEWSHED

AGRICULTURAL LAND
Farmer-Owned
Cropland

SLOPE ANALYSIS
Over 15%

BASE MAP

LIGHT TABLE

3.23
Overlaying translucent maps allows comparison of resources. This simplified depiction of an overlay consists of Cazenovia's base map and elements from three other maps prepared for the project: slope of over 15 percent, farmer-owned cropland, and the lake viewsheds (identified as one of the favorite views in the visual survey). The composite image that results from viewing the four maps simultaneously highlights the areas (the darkest) where all three constraints overlap, which are therefore the most important to protect.

3.8 Land Evaluation and Site Assessment System

Communities wishing to evaluate cropland, forest land, and rangeland can make good use of the Land Evaluation and Site Assessment (LESA) system developed by the Natural Resources Conservation Service (NRCS). LESA incorporates the values and objectives of the communities that make use of the information. The system has two parts: land evaluation, which rates land on the basis of soil quality and agricultural potential, and site assessment, which considers relative location and local development conditions. The LESA criteria are designed to protect farmland with the greatest production potential and farmland located within a viable agricultural area.

A local LESA system is usually designed by a committee of farmers, elected officials, planners, soil scientists, and extension agents with the help of NRCS. Most LESA systems evaluate land on a 300-point scale, with up to 100 points assessing soil characteristics and up to 200 points applied to site assessment. For the latter, a community selects appropriate factors and each factor is assigned a maximum number of points

3.24
Mapping by computer is becoming increasingly popular. Information is entered into the computer for each resource in each area. The computer can then display maps comparing resources and constraints on development. This computer-generated map of aquifers in Elbridge, New York, was prepared by the Faculty of Landscape Architecture, State University of New York, Syracuse.

and colored plastic cutouts can be applied to the Mylar. It is difficult to distinguish individual map features in an overlay of more than five sheets of Mylar.

For its overlay maps, CCRP used Color Key, a transparent plastic material developed by the 3M Company. Richard Hawks from SUNY introduced the 3M process to CCRP because it provided the ability to overlay up to fifteen maps at one time. SUNY students mapped each feature on a separate transparent Color Key sheet, and CCRP volunteers overlaid the maps to do their analyses. CCRP, the conservation commission, and the planning commission have used the maps for public education and for studying the appropriateness of certain areas for development.

With a geographic information system, the possibilities for mapping are almost endless: any combination of variables can be mapped together and their relationship analyzed, much as would be done using Mylar

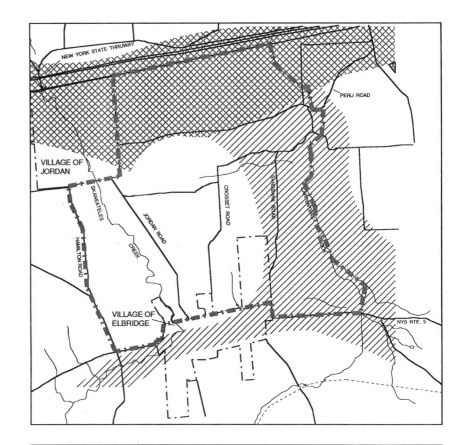

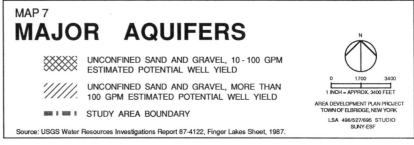

MAP 7
MAJOR AQUIFERS

⌗⌗⌗ UNCONFINED SAND AND GRAVEL, 10 - 100 GPM ESTIMATED POTENTIAL WELL YIELD

/// UNCONFINED SAND AND GRAVEL, MORE THAN 100 GPM ESTIMATED POTENTIAL WELL YIELD

▬ STUDY AREA BOUNDARY

Source: USGS Water Resources Investigations Report 87-4122, Finger Lakes Sheet, 1987.

0   1700   3400
1 INCH = APPROX. 3400 FEET

AREA DEVELOPMENT PLAN PROJECT
TOWN OF ELBRIDGE, NEW YORK

LSA 496/527/695 STUDIO
SUNY-ESF

sheets by hand, laying one map over another to illustrate the relationship among various features. The various data collected can be projected onto a computer screen as well as be printed on paper.

The overlay or GIS process should produce clear patterns of which areas have an abundance of resources and which areas have few. Also, areas with similar characteristics will emerge. Areas with similar physical and cultural features are often called character zones. They reflect common environmental conditions and may also share a cultural heritage and land use patterns. For example, as a result of an inventory process in communities on the north shore of Oneida Lake in upstate New York, residents identified seven distinct character zones: village and hamlet, lake edge, farmland, succession field, forest and stream, wetlands, and highway corridor.[2] In the Hanover area of Adams and York counties, Pennsylvania, residents identified seventeen character areas, including horse farms, small towns and villages, and quarries.[3] Analyzing their community in terms of character zones not only helps residents understand the relationships among its various resources but may also suggest resource protection techniques and development guidelines that would be appropriate. Residents should compare the character zones identified through the mapping process with their own perception of special places in the community.

Some communities develop a numerical scoring system to compare resources and establish which areas should receive the highest degree of protection. A map charting suitabilty for development, taking into account all of a community's resources, might divide the entire community into the following categories for development control: "slight constraint," "moderate constraint," and "severe constraint." Alternatively, a communitywide map might define areas with the labels "developmental opportunity," "constrain development," and "suitable for development."

Reports

An inventory should not consist of maps alone. For some resources—vegetation and historic sites, for instance—maps should be accompanied by lists, inventory forms, and photographs, as appropriate. Also, a written report should accompany the maps and other data to explain how and when the inventory was conducted, who did the work, and how the results can be used. There should be an explanation of each resource map that includes the nature of the resource, the process used in identification and evaluation, sources of information, threats to the resource, potential protection techniques, and the relationship of the resource to others in the community.

The report may include recommendations that can be incorporated into a master plan or ordinance. Recommendations can appear in a distinct section of the report or as a separate document.

CONCLUSION

Although information gathering may be your group's first activity, it should not end when the early stages of a rural conservation program are

to indicate its relative importance to the community. Some of the factors a community may wish to consider are

- *percentage of land in the area in agriculture;*
- *economic viability factors, including the size of a farm, land ownership, and investment in such improvements as barns, equipment, and drainage systems;*
- *impact of any change in use on the natural, agricultural, historic, recreational, and scenic resources of surrounding properties;*
- *compatibility with local or regional plans, zoning, and other programs to protect farmland; and*
- *presence of urban infrastructure, including water and sewer lines, roads, nearby community services, shopping, schools, and jobs.*

By combining the land evaluation points with the site assessment points for a total score ranging from 0 to 300, the community can then compare the relative value of all sites and set its protection policies accordingly. LESA systems are often used to support purchase of development rights programs, for example.

According to a 1991 nationwide survey, 138 local and 8 state governments were using a LESA system. A large proportion of the local systems were in eastern states experiencing strong development pressures.

While LESA was developed to inventory and evaluate agricultural, range, and forestry resources, similar numerical rating systems can be developed for other community resources. However, such systems have their limitations. Perceptions of such resources as scenery are subjective and do not easily lend themselves to numerical ratings. Furthermore, there may not be a consensus within the community on the relative value of resources.

(Steiner, Pease, and Coughlin 1994)

completed. Rather, periodic updating and reassessment of information should continue as new events occur and new data become available.

If your inventory is unbiased and contains the appropriate information, it should be of use to all segments of the community and help to assure rational development and resource protection. Furthermore, the inventory produces more than data; the process of conducting an inventory raises consciousness about the community—its assets and its challenges—and helps to build a sense of identity among community members as well as with the physical environment.

In spite of all the benefits of a resources inventory, for some communities a formal inventory may not be necessary or feasible. They may find that an informal tour works successfully as a way of educating people about their community's resources and gathering information about what people care the most about and, therefore, want most to protect (see the case of Harrison County, Iowa, p. 7). In general, the programs implemented by local governments and nonprofit organizations to protect natural, historic, agricultural, and scenic resources will be much more effective if they make use of a good resources inventory.

Rural Conservation through Local Government

4

INTRODUCTION

To be successful in rural conservation, you need to work with local government. Through local government, you can build official support for rural conservation, influence existing programs, and implement new ones. These programs might include not only ordinances governing land use, but also educational efforts or economic development assistance and such specific projects as a resources inventory, the development of a greenway, or the development of a community museum.

In the first three chapters we discussed the initial steps of rural conservation: identifying the issues, organizing your efforts, and inventorying resources. Once you have accomplished these steps, achieving actual results is next. This chapter and the following three provide information about public and private activities that are possible in conserving special resources, promoting good development, and influencing investment in your community. While this chapter describes the basics of land use management, it cannot stand alone as a resource for your work in rural conservation: no community can achieve rural conservation exclusively through land use planning and regulation.

Let us begin with some general comments about land use management. First, the challenge in using the techniques in this chapter is to tailor them to fit your community's specific needs. The communities we cite here generally followed similar paths and examined well-known techniques in their search to address local needs. In that regard they are no different from many others. What is striking about these communities is that they adapted their chosen techniques and crafted purely local innovations.

4.1 Managing Growth to Foster Land Conservation: How Does Your Community Measure Up?

Michael Clarke and Randall Arendt of the Natural Lands Trust of Media, Pennsylvania, use the following questions to stimulate community discussion and self-diagnosis, in the interest of making a community's land conservation efforts more effective.

1. The Community Resource Inventory. Has the community adequately inventoried its resources, and does the public have a sufficient understanding and appreciation of them?
2. The "Community Audit." Is the community monitoring and assessing its likely future under its current growth management practices, and is it taking steps to change what it does not like?
3. Policies for Conservation and Development. Has the community established appropriate and realistic policies for land conservation and development, and do they produce a clear vision of lands to be conserved?
4. The Regulatory Framework. Do the community's zoning and subdivision regulations reflect and encourage its policies for land conservation and development?
5. Designing Conservation Subdivisions. Does the community know how to work cooperatively and effectively with subdivision applicants?
6. Working Relationships with Landowners. Does the community have a good understanding of working relationships with its major landowners?
7. Stewardship of Conservation Lands. Does the community have in place the arrangements required for successfully owning, managing, and

Second, beware the urban bias of much land use planning, which can frequently favor new residential, industrial, or commercial development over maintenance of traditional land uses like farming, ranching, and forestry. Moreover, in its assumption that development will occur in most parts of a community, urban planning often fails to recognize the natural and scenic values inherent in the more open, less-developed areas of rural communities. Planning for a rural community is different from planning for an urban one, and you should be alert to this distinction as you listen to planners and read the literature.

Third, in many states, there are few rules regarding how extensive your community's written plan should be or how much control should be built into land use ordinances. Common wisdom in urban planning is that a comprehensive plan, with sections on economic development, housing, transportation, land use, and public services, is a prerequisite to good government. For some rural communities, however, a land use plan may be all that is needed. The numerous regulations, extensive procedural requirements, and detailed design standards to be found in urban land use ordinances may not be needed. Complicated land use ordinances are often difficult to administer consistently, and they may increase costs for developers, who either pass the increase on to buyers or renters or pay less to land sellers. It often makes sense to simplify review procedures and design standards in order to streamline the administration of an ordinance, as long as it provides for sufficient control to encourage development that is sensitive to the environment and consistent with requirements for due process. Developers are more likely to demand timely action, fairness, and consistency in the administration of regulations, rather than an absence of regulations altogether.

Also, a word about vocabulary: while this chapter will describe many land use management techniques by a given name, the more important information is not the name of the technique but how it works. The technique known as "clustering," for example, has earned a bad name in some places because it conjures up houses too close together for the tastes of many rural residents; the name "open space subdivision," which describes a nearly identical technique, implies the more positive values of protecting green fields or wildlife habitat.[1] "A rose by any other name . . .": if the name of a particular technique doesn't work for you and your community, invent another. After all, we are already advocating that you adapt the technique itself to your own needs. But planning jargon can be useful when you are giving direction to planning consultants or comparing your use of a given technique with the way others have adapted it.

What local governments are permitted to do is more or less controlled by state laws known as "state enabling legislation." The use of most of the techniques we discuss here depends on the existence of such legislation, which gives local governments the right to pass the necessary ordinances and may prescribe certain standards for those ordinances. For some of the more innovative techniques, such as transfer of development rights, your community may first need to obtain state enabling legislation.

How do you become involved in local government if you are not already? It may be quite simple. Local governments in areas with small populations sometimes find it difficult to find qualified people to fill all of their positions. If you have the time, energy, good ideas, and a willingness to attend meetings, you might readily be appointed or elected to office (see p. 78). It may be equally helpful to conduct public surveys and present the results to local officials or provide information about how other jurisdictions have tackled issues similar to those your community faces.

In Oley, Pennsylvania, volunteers for the Oley Valley Heritage Association have conducted several exit polls after local elections to provide reassurance to township supervisors that despite vocal dissenters to proposed regulations to protect agriculture, much of the community was behind passage of an agricultural zoning ordinance (see Case Study 2.1). Phoebe Hopkins, who in recent years has participated in several exit polls in the Oley community to support township action, adds that as a bonus "it's a real lift to talk to people who live in Oley and love it the way it is. It's really great to talk to people—seventy-five to eighty percent want to preserve the character. That's why people live here." Moreover, people in Oley are still listening and talking to one another. "People stand up for things in Oley. It's not hard to do things right now while you've got the right people in office," says Phoebe, "The township supervisors are out talking to farmers and property owners plenty of the time."

Simply attending meetings and informing those who are already active are not always enough. If, over time, local officials remain steadfast in their opposition to rural conservation, you may need to make your views known more widely, through publicity or by running for local office. Causing an informed and well-argued public outcry has its place.

PLANNING

Planning should be the first step in local community action to address rural conservation. Although planning will not solve every problem that confronts a rural community, it does provide an organized approach to land use and to other areas of governmental regulation and services. Good planning, as long as it is faithfully carried out, is first and foremost a money-saving exercise. It encourages a local government to consider its future and to set its priorities for expenditures. So serious are the ramifications of designating land for new development—siting utility, water, and sewer lines; providing roads and schools—that each rural community should consider planning among its most important tasks.

The best way to start planning is with a strong and well-articulated community understanding, or vision, of what you are trying to accomplish through planning. A simple but powerful planning technique, "visioning" (see p. 70) has come to be viewed as an essential first step in an increasing number of communities undertaking or revamping their planning.

What a Plan Is

A plan is the community's blueprint for the future, specifying what actions the community expects to take in order to achieve its vision. The plan outlines what needs to be done, and how and when to do it in an

using lands set aside for conservation purposes?

8. *Ongoing Education and Communications. How are local officials and the general public maintaining their knowledge of the state of the art in managing growth to conserve land?*

(See Notes to Sidebars.)

4.2 *Planning Defined*

The International City/County Management Association has defined planning as follows:

> *The broad object of planning is to further the welfare of the people in the community by helping to create an increasingly better, more healthful, convenient, efficient, and attractive community environment. The physical as well as the social and economic community is a single organism, all features and activities of which are related and interdependent. These facts must be supplemented by the application of intelligent foresight and planned administrative and legal coordination if balance, harmony, and order are to be insured. It is the task of planning to supply this foresight and this overall coordination. (Smith 1979, p. 27)*

4.3 A Sample Plan's Contents

The table of contents of the plan for Vernon, Vermont (pop. 2,215), adopted by the board of selectmen in 1995, shows how one rural community organized its plan. Vernon's forty-two-page plan covers not only land use and the community's natural, recreational, cultural, and scenic resources, but also housing, transportation, economic development, and public services. Other communities might choose to include more or fewer topics or to organize them differently.

Town of Vernon

organized fashion. It is comparable to an industry's management plan or a nonprofit organization's goals and objectives (see p. 72). Detailed plans may be called a comprehensive plan, master plan, or general plan; rural communities may find shorter versions of written plans—sometimes called summary plans, minor plans, or miniplans—more useful (Daniels, Keller, and Lapping 1995). We are not speaking of the more general goals and plans that all conscientious officials follow in some fashion. The written plan is one result of a continuing planning process. The written plan serves as a public guide to public and private decision making in order to help a community avoid costly mistakes that might occur if no plan existed. In sum, says Warren Zitzmann, a rural planning consultant, a plan "is a realistic program for describing 'where we are, where we want to go, and how we are going to get there.' "[2]

A good plan should respect natural, cultural, and scenic resources, consider the economic activities and needs of the community, and outline a course of action that is compatible with the community's traditions and settlement patterns. The plan should balance environmental protection and rural amenities on the one hand with needed residential, commercial, and industrial growth on the other, and should consider the public facilities and services the community will provide. Growth should be encouraged only in those locations where the land and the community have the capacity to support development.

The plan is usually the foundation for any of the land protection and development regulations a community may enact, although there may not be a specific state legal requirement that land use regulations conform to the plan. Some states require local governments to have an official plan and to update it periodically. For example, in Vermont the local plan expires every five years. In other states, the plan is a legal document that is acceptable in court as evidence that a community's land use controls are based on rational considerations.

A plan should deal with both the near and the long term; some of its proposals should be capable of immediate implementation. A plan should state specific policies or recommended actions to support its lofty statements; otherwise, it will sit on a shelf, leaving the community to muddle along as it did without a plan.

The plan is basically a report, generally in map and narrative form. The report repeats the vision and summarizes other objectives, assumptions, and standards that guided the development of the plan's policies. It usually includes a summary of the resources inventory, which should precede the plan's preparation. Most comprehensive plans include current data, projections, and proposals concerning population size, demography, land use, economic activities, historic preservation, traffic, parks and open space, housing, utilities, and other pertinent aspects of a community's life and resources.

When to Develop a Plan

Ideally, both the vision and the plan should be developed immediately after data gathering and a resources inventory are completed, so that they are based on up-to-date information and can draw on the participation of community residents who were involved in the inventory. Unfortunately, sometimes communities that have never developed a plan or are in the midst of doing one must take immediate action to regulate development. In such instances, a community may need to institute basic zoning or another technique as an interim measure and follow up quickly with a resources inventory and plan. In states where a plan is required before regulations may be implemented, it might be possible to impose a temporary moratorium on development before creating a plan.

The main thing to remember about appropriate timing is that planning does not create a final product but is a process in which inventorying, analysis, visioning, plan writing, and implementation are steps to be done repeatedly. Even when timing is not ideal, some of these steps can always be started. To embark on planning is to commit to continual learning and improvement.

That said, however, enough time for citizen involvement must be built in to the process. The preparation of a responsive plan often takes a year or more. Where opposition arises—from property owners concerned about excessive regulation, for example—the process should allow enough time for "getting to yes," to borrow the title of a popular book on creative ways to mediate differences that arise in negotiations (Fisher, Ury, and Patton 1991). Allowing time for plenty of informational meetings and a full exchange of ideas before finalizing the plan—or ordinances and expenditures to carry out the plan—can pay many dividends by inspiring community support, creative ideas, and actions by property owners and businesses that will reinforce the plan.

Who Prepares the Plan

Effective planning brings citizens and officials together to develop community policies, and citizen involvement should remain a constant throughout the plan's development and final adoption. Involving as many people as possible from a broad cross-section of the community early in the process increases the chances for community understanding and acceptance. A plan perceived to have been imposed on a community, whether by an overzealous planning commission, an outside consultant, or a clique within the community, is doomed from the start. Besides encouraging better implementation of a plan, citizen involvement has other advantages. It will save money if volunteers can assume some of the duties a consultant might otherwise be paid to perform; it will produce a better plan, because the citizens involved will be those who care about the community; and citizens will learn more about their community.

A useful way to coordinate citizen planning efforts can be establishment of a steering committee to assist the planning commission in developing a plan, as community leaders did in Cazenovia, New York. A community's planning commission or board is technically responsible for preparing a plan, but planning commissions are frequently too busy dealing with requests for zoning changes and other routine matters to spend time gathering and analyzing the necessary information. This was the case in Cazenovia (see Case Study 3.1).

Even when government officials and citizens are mutually involved in developing a plan, most rural communities without at least a part-time planning staff need the guidance of a planning consultant or a planner

IV. *Natural Resources Use and Conservation: Specific Policies and Recommendations*
   A. *Agricultural Resources*
   B. *Forest Land*
   C. *Water Resources*
   D. *Wildlife Habitat*
   E. *Fragile Areas*
   F. *Flood Hazard Areas*
   G. *Soils*
   H. *Earth Resources*
V. *Recreational, Cultural, and Scenic Resources: Specific Policies and Recommendations*
   A. *Public Recreational Resources*
   B. *Historic and Architectural Resources*
   C. *Scenic Resources*
VI. *Government Facilities and Public Utilities: Specific Policies and Recommendations*
   A. *Planning for Growth*
   B. *Public Facilities or Services Adjoining Agricultural or Forestry Lands*
   C. *Planning for Transportation and Utility Corridors*
   D. *Planning for Solid Waste Disposal*
   E. *Privately Owned Facilities and Services*
   F. *Fire and Police Protection*
   G. *Education and Libraries*
   H. *Health*
   I. *Town Government Administration*
   J. *Emergency Management*
VII. *Town Plan Maps*
   Locally Protected Land
   Wetlands
   State Protected Lands
   Surface Water and Floodplain
   Structure and Right-of-Way Distribution
   Sensitive Land Use and Culturally Significant Area
   Provisional Depth of Water
   Fire Ponds
   Farm Lands

4.4 Buying Time for Planning

A moratorium (in this case, an across-the-board stoppage of development permits until a certain governmental action is completed) can buy time for a community. For example, when the community is revising its comprehensive plan or land use controls, a moratorium helps avoid a situation in which landowners rush to get permits under the old system so that they are "grandfathered" in or allowed to proceed to develop under the old rules even after the new ones are in place. A moratorium may also be used to limit development temporarily in certain areas until troublesome conditions, such as traffic congestion or limited sewer capacity, are corrected.

A moratorium should not be used to postpone development indefinitely. Indefinite postponement amounts to procrastination, at best, and deliberate foot-dragging at worst—and is likely to expose a community to numerous court challenges.

from a regional or state planning agency. Few citizens have the experience or technical background on the wide variety of subjects that a plan must cover—especially if it is to be a comprehensive plan—or the objectivity to help the community find a balance between competing interests and inevitable personal biases. Even visioning—which does not call for technical expertise on the part of participants—can benefit from an independent advisor who can help identify themes, assure the broadest possible cross-section from the community, coordinate the logistics of meetings, and keep track of results.

Adopting, Implementing, and Revising a Plan

Once a draft plan is acceptable to the steering committee in charge of the process, it should be widely distributed. Some communities have even printed and distributed draft versions of their plans as inserts in the local newspaper—complete with mail-in questionnaires that let readers comment without attending meetings. Public forums allow for discussion and provide the steering committee or planning commission with an opportunity to answer questions and encourage suggestions for revision. Several revisions may be necessary before the plan becomes a document that truly meets the community's needs. Ultimately, the time comes for the planning commission (and the elected body ultimately responsible for community direction) to make its decision, requiring a formal public hearing and a vote. A plan is often controversial, no matter how much citizen involvement is built into the process. Emotional arguments on both sides may well be as persuasive in the court of public opinion as carefully marshalled facts. The plan's supporters must carry out a campaign that both informs the public and assures public officials that the public wants and needs the plan.

After the town or county government has adopted the plan, no decision relating to community growth, land use regulations, or local budgets should be made without reference to the goals and policies outlined in the plan. When unforeseen circumstances require a deviation from the plan, the impact of the change on other components of the plan should be anticipated and evaluated, and an amendment to the plan may be desirable.

Even the most thoughtfully prepared plans need to be revised every few years. When a plan, no matter what its age, is not working as a guide to decision making in the community, it is time to go through the planning process again. Before revising or discarding elements of its plan, a community should determine why the original plan no longer represents the community's current needs. In general, any plan more than five years old should be reviewed to make sure it is still relevant.

Partial Plans

A community may elect to plan for a single area, such as a watershed or highway corridor, or one kind of resource, such as wetlands, farmland, or historic sites, or to address one community issue, such as tourism or community involvement in public decision making, instead of preparing a communitywide or comprehensive plan. This approach is reasonable if the need involves only one resource or a community can afford only the partial plan. Any partial or functional plan should include a section on the effects its implementation may have on other aspects of the community.

A community may find that its existing plan does not address a certain issue that now concerns the community. In this case, a plan dealing with that particular issue could fill in the gaps in an otherwise acceptable community plan. Collin County, Texas, as a first step in spending a $1.5 million bond issue approved in 1983 to acquire open space lands, developed an award-winning open space plan. The plan led to a program addressing three distinctive "sectors"—rural, urban, and the shorelands of Lake Lavon, a large Army Corps of Engineers impoundment with twenty parks and three wildlife areas—with priorities for action in each sector. The bond issue and plan were spurred by growth influenced by the Dallas metropolitan area; the county's population in 1970 was 66,920, rose to 144,576 in 1980, and was 290,873 in 1995. Among other features, the plan called for the preservation of the unspoiled remnants of North Texas Blackland Prairie that are still to be found in parts of the county. Today, the county maintains a 436-acre preserve, Parkhill Prairie, that features 52 acres of the native tallgrass prairie, and is working to establish a residential outdoor education camp on the shores of Lake Lavon and a greenway along a creek linking the county seat, McKinney, and four other towns.[3]

Like planning overall, partial planning can be undertaken by private organizations or coalitions. The Guilford Preservation Alliance, a nonprofit organization in Connecticut, sponsored the development of an "unofficial" plan for preservation and scenic conservation. The plan calls for a wide variety of steps to protect the 49-square-mile town's environment. Steps include the establishment of visual resource overlay districts (see p. 177) and creation of a scenic resources board, the adoption of a public roadway management plan to address scenic concerns in road maintenance and improvements, and the launching of a community land trust program (see Sidebar 5.10). Guilford's Planning and Zoning Commission endorsed ("unofficially adopted") the first plan in 1987, and the town subsequently established a design review board and a tree protection and planting program.[4]

4.1
Public funds can be used to guide planning decisions in rural communities. Woodson County, Kansas, earmarked public funds for the renovation of its courthouse, built in the late nineteenth century in Yates Center and now listed in the National Register of Historic Places.

SPENDING MONEY *IS* PLANNING

A local government is involved in planning every time it drafts next year's budget, decides to pave a road, or authorizes the school board to renovate an old school or build a new one, even if it has no planning commission, planning department, or written plan. What has already been planned in the way of governmental expenditures can affect rural conservation—positively or negatively. Governmental expenditures can have as much or more effect on the successful implementation of a community's plan as land development ordinances. Ideally, such expenditures are not only included in the community's annual budgets but are the subject of a written plan, often called a capital improvement plan, that identifies the public facilities to be provided or expanded by government several years into the future.

Citizens often overlook the impact that such capital improvements as sewer systems, water systems, roads, bridges, fire stations, and schools can have on their community's environment. The presence of good public improvements does more to stimulate development than any community plan ever will; similarly, a lack of these facilities may deter development. Acquiring land for parks and natural areas, purchasing development rights, developing scenic trails, and implementing programs to protect or develop special resources can become part of a community's capital improvements budget as well.

The annual planning and review of the local budget should reveal what capital improvements are planned, what they will cost, how they can be implemented, where they will be located, and what their likely or desired impact will be. It is often necessary for conservationists to scrutinize not only the local government's budget but also the budgets of such separate governmental entities as school boards, water and sewer authorities, regional park agencies, and state highway departments.

Increasingly, communities realize that public expenditures encourage growth, and so they are planning for the timed allocation of public facilities to encourage concentric growth around existing settlements or are identifying urban growth boundaries beyond which public facilities and utilities will not be provided. Such measures concentrate growth where the delivery of services is most efficient. Lexington, Kentucky, has used this method to protect from development the famous Bluegrass Country that surrounds the city.

ZONING AND SUBDIVISION ORDINANCES

Rural communities vary widely in the land use regulations they are likely to have. Some have none, so owners can develop their property with few, if any, local restrictions, although statewide regulations may apply. Others have codes requiring building permits, observance of certain building standards, and inspection when work is completed. Many local governments require a percolation test to determine if the soils are suitable for a septic system. Other rural governments have more or less complex systems of controls that often include zoning and subdivision ordinances.

Zoning

Zoning divides the land under a local government's jurisdiction into districts or zones, each of which may have different requirements, in order to regulate the use of land and the placement, size, density, and use of buildings. Zoning is used to segregate different, sometimes incompatible uses, such as industrial uses in residential areas or nonfarm residences in agricultural areas, and to steer more intensive development into portions of the community where roads, sewer, and other services are available to support it.

To protect environmental resources, a community may use zoning to limit the density of residential development in areas where soils are less suitable for septic systems—protecting groundwater and streams from sewage—or where slopes are too steep—again, protecting streams from

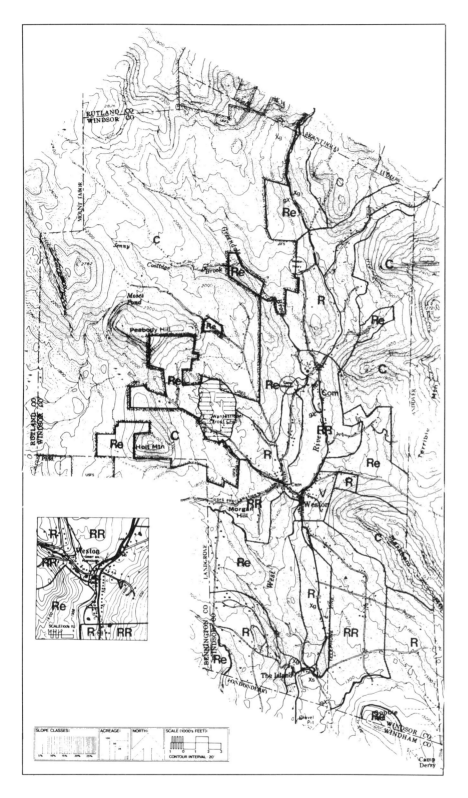

4.2
A zoning map for the town of Weston, Vermont. Weston's zoning ordinance, which was adopted in 1976, includes seven categories (not all shown here): conservation (C), resource (Re), rural low intensity (R), rural residential (RR), village (V), commercial (Com), and industrial (I). In addition, there is an overlay shoreland zone around the pond (horizontal lines), where uses that might pollute the water are prohibited. The most restrictive zone, the conservation category, has a 5-acre minimum lot size and is reserved for areas with "substantial physical limitations to development." Permitted uses include forestry and single-family homes. The least restrictive zone is the industrial category, where there is a 1-acre minimum lot size and permitted uses include quarrying and gasoline stations. The boundaries between zones are based on such factors as property ownership, existing use, and natural features, such as the steepness of the slope.

4.5 The Constitutional Challenge: Is Zoning a "Taking" without Compensation?

In community battles over zoning and other land use regulations, property owners frequently invoke the "takings" clause of the Constitution's Fifth Amendment, which provides that private property shall not "be taken for public use, without just compensation." This amendment, written in the eighteenth century, came about in part to assure that when government takes land physically—to build a road, for example—it would use legal procedures and pay a fair price to the owner.

It was not until the twentieth century that the Fifth Amendment began to be applied to circumstances in which regulations by themselves were challenged as takings. In various cases, the Supreme Court has ruled that the takings clause does not prohibit local governments from imposing reasonable controls on the use of land without providing compensation. Key early cases are Euclid v. Ambler Realty Co. *(1926) and* Penn Central Transportation Co. v. New York City *(1978); permissible public goals for land use and environmental regulations include protection of open space and agricultural land, landmark preservation and design controls, and protection of such environmentally sensitive areas as wetlands and floodplains. The answer to the question posed in the title to this sidebar, then, is a resounding "no."*

Property owners, however, may still be able to argue that a taking has occurred, on the grounds either that a regulation is not reasonably necessary to protect the public health, safety, or welfare (that is, not a valid exercise of the "police power" [see p. 207]) or that its effect is so ex- *treme that it does not permit any economically viable use of land. If successful, a takings challenge may result in the invalidation of a land use regulation. Under the Supreme Court's 1987 decision in* First English Evangelical Lutheran Church v. County of Los Angeles, *a successful challenge can also lead to a financial award to an affected property owner if the regulation is found to be so extreme as to have "taken all use" from the property; if the regulation is subsequently found invalid, the Court suggested, the local government must pay compensation for the "temporary taking." The possibility of such challenges—and the prospective financial consequences of lawyers, court costs, and payments to owners—causes local governments to be cautious in regulating land uses, unfortunately to the point of paralysis in some communities.*

*Other Supreme Court decisions in recent years have invalidated local regulations that attempted to require property owners to dedicate a portion of their properties to public access (*Nollan v. California Coastal Commission *[1987] and* Dolan v. City of Tigard *[Oregon] [1995]) In both cases, the Court reaffirmed a longstanding requirement that conditions imposed on any project be designed to alleviate the problems created by that project—in other words, the owner's proposal cannot be treated as an opportunity for the public to gain more mitigation than is reasonably related to the project.*

The takings issue has become more visible in recent years, as alliances of individual and corporate property owners both large and small, many with interests in such natural resource development as mining, graz- *ing, and timbering, have "gone political" to redress a combination of grievances that only partly includes the constitutional questions concerning local government that are raised here. The impact of federal ownership and management on those reliant on federally owned natural resources, and federal regulation in such environmental concerns as wetlands and endangered species, are issues integral to the furor. "Wise use" proponents call for legislation requiring owner consent in regulatory actions and payment of compensation even for a small diminution of property value that may be caused by regulation. These legislative initiatives are generally at the federal and state levels, but changes in either case can affect local government prerogatives.*

Both the American Planning Association (APA) and the American Resources Information Network (ARIN) have developed guidelines for communities in examining their land use regulations in light of this evolving political climate. Good planning is implicit in their approaches. ARIN recommends six basic steps:

• Establishing a sound basis for land-use and environmental regulations through thorough planning and background studies
• Instituting careful administrative procedures that allow property owners to present evidence of undue economic impact prior to going to court
• Establishing a means of relief for extreme economic hardship
• Preventing subdivisions of land that may result in economically unusable, unbuildable, or substandard parcels (the Achilles heel of any land use management scheme—see Sidebar 4.6)

• Calculating development fees or conditions on a fair and rational basis
• Avoiding government incentives, subsidies, or insurance programs that encourage development in sensitive areas

The APA makes recommendations similar to ARIN's and also counsels flexibility and the consideration of nonregulatory means of accomplishing public purposes.

In addition to taking such steps, local governments must expect to invest in legal counsel, both in establishing sound land use regulations and in defending them from takings challenges—or from a variety of other legal challenges. "You have to budget for it," says the zoning administrator for Bath, Michigan, whose legal costs rose from $500 to $4,000 one year in defending its land use ordinance.

Is there hope that municipalities can continue to create and defend reasonable rules for land management? Of course. None of these cases changes two key ideas: no owner has the right to use property so as to harm public health, safety, or welfare, or interfere with property interests of neighbors or the community; and while a property owner does have a right to a reasonable return on use of the land, the Constitution does not guarantee the most profitable use. Both of these points offer intriguing points of departure for relatively new thinking about the role of government in controlling nuisances and managing land.

Students of "takings law" have pointed out that states may be able to protect the public health and welfare not only under the Constitution

but also through the public trust doctrine. Under this long-established doctrine of American common law (that is, law established over the years by the courts, reaching back for centuries into English traditions), property owners cannot exercise their common law rights in such a way as to injure others—including the state, as trustee for the people. "The unfettered right to despoil the state's trust lands does not exist," declares Virginia state delegate W. Tayloe Murphy, Jr., who chaired the Virginia Commission on Population Growth and Development from 1990 through 1995. Some have interpreted the public trust doctrine to hold that the public is not required to pay the costs of pollution created by a polluter, and that the state is entitled, as Murphy puts the argument, "to place reasonable restrictions on potentially damaging activities without having to defend its action against a claim of being arbitrary and capricious."

Another approach, recommended by law professor John A. Humbach, is to consider the existing use of land in a community. In this line of thinking, a community can limit rural land to its existing uses, without necessarily running afoul of the Constitution. As interpreted by the Supreme Court, the Constitution requires an "economically viable use," but this does not oblige a rural community to provide for future, perhaps more profitable, uses of land. Says Humbach: "The fact is that open land, even land in its natural state, can provide a respectable financial return, provided the owner has not paid too much for it. Typical open space uses for which people pay handsomely include hunting,

fishing, grazing, forestry, buffer, or aesthetic enjoyment. It is only when woodlands or wetlands are sold at building lot prices that these natural uses seem inadequate. It could not, however, follow that a buyer has a constitutional right to use raw land as a building site just because the buyer was willing to pay 'too much.' " "Existing use zoning" addresses the need for stability in rural communities and the speculative problems inherent in the "impermanence syndrome" feared by farmers in a way that standard zoning, with its assumption that land use will change, does not.

(See Notes to Sidebars.)

4.6 Conditional Uses, Special Exceptions, Variances, and Rezoning

Those responsible for the administration of a zoning ordinance sometimes find that flexibility is desirable. An existing parcel may not conform to the size requirements for a proposed use, for example. Also, government officials may have their doubts about certain uses in a given zone, but when presented with a reasonable development plan that takes into account their concerns, they may find those uses acceptable in that location.

Conditional uses, special permits, or special exceptions provide flexibility by permitting an irregular proposed use under conditions that can be prescribed in the ordinance. A variance may be allowed if the owner would experience a hardship—not just inconvenience or fewer profits—in complying with the ordinance. Generally, a variance is limited to dimensional, not use, requirements. Rezoning actually changes the zoning category—preferably for the entire zone rather than just one parcel. The latter is called spot zoning and is frowned upon by the courts.

All of these means of adjustment have one great disadvantage: the danger that their indiscriminate use will erode popular support for the whole zoning ordinance. As one observer notes, "The greatest single cause for the failure of zoning to effectively guide land use development . . . has been the misuse of the variance technique." (Smith 1993, p. 109).

silt that too easily washes off disturbed hillsides (called "mud pollution"). Setbacks from streams or shorelines may be required under zoning, to further reduce the potential for water pollution. Zoning can also be used to help a community absorb new growth efficiently. A community may decide, for instance, to restrict all areas away from major highways to low-density residential or agricultural uses, to avoid the expense of upgrading country roads and to encourage denser growth in areas where services are adequate.

Adjusting or instituting zoning is often the first technique considered by those opposed to the proposed location of a prison, factory, or shopping center. For others, zoning is an infringement of individual rights, a red flag prompting protests of "Nobody's going to tell me what I can do with my land." Both proponents and opponents of zoning are likely to possess misconceptions about what zoning is and how it can be used. While zoning can be an effective means of regulating land development in rural areas, it is not the only technique, nor always the best technique; and used alone it is usually unsuccessful in protecting rural character. Zoning—and most other land use regulations—can prevent the *worst* from happening, but its power to encourage the *best* design or uses is limited.

While zoning predates planning in many rural communities, it is most effective and most defensible if it implements a written plan based on a resources inventory and other up-to-date information about the community. Zoning usually cannot protect people or their property from harm caused by existing uses: the best time to establish zoning is before problems develop.

The Zoning Ordinance

A zoning ordinance usually has two parts: an explanatory text and a map showing the boundaries of each zoning district. The text will include references to appropriate state enabling legislation, legal definitions, provisions for relief in certain cases, and procedures for appeal. It should also include a carefully written statement of purpose for each category of zoning, enumerating both permitted and prohibited uses. Boundaries between zones usually follow such visible borders as roads or easily identifiable natural features, such as floodplains, steep slopes, or wetlands.

A basic zoning ordinance defines residential, commercial, industrial, and agricultural uses and designates specific areas for each use. Uses in each zone can be exclusive or combined. Exclusive-use zones allow only those uses specified by the ordinance; zones that combine uses allow "lesser" uses in addition to the uses named for that zone—for example, a commercial zone might also allow residential uses (residential is almost always considered "lesser" in such a scheme). Some communities may need other special categories: industrial zones to permit mineral extraction, recreational development zones to regulate such uses as marinas or campgrounds, or conservation zones to protect floodplains or other sensitive resources. Most ordinances include a "grandfather clause" that allows existing nonconforming uses to remain where they are or be phased out ("amortized") by a specified date or when the property is sold. Such amortization periods often apply to billboards and junkyards.

Large-Lot Zoning

Some communities have adopted large-lot zoning in the hope of slowing development and preserving open space. Under a large-lot ordinance, a house may be built only if it is located on a lot that is much larger than the 1- to 3-acre minimum sizes typically permitted in rural ordinances—perhaps 10 or 25 acres. Unless the minimum size is larger than that demanded in the local market for the largest rural residential lots, and preferably as large as the minimum size for a viable working farm, large-lot zoning can do more harm than good. Although the intent may be to protect land, large-lot residential zoning may actually waste land and increase environmental problems rather than alleviate them. Low-density development on, say, 10-acre lots often causes development to spread farther into the countryside. It may require improved roads and increased sewer, water, and other services that are costly to establish and maintain. As large-lot zoning spreads development across the countryside, it contributes to loss of the area's scenic qualities, especially if the development occurs in strips along roads. It can also hamper farm operations scattered within such development, by dividing farmland into uneconomical plots or by introducing nonfarm neighbors who don't like the smells and noise of farming or slow machinery on their roads.

Large-lot zoning is frequently regarded with disfavor by the courts, which have sometimes ruled it "exclusionary," since larger lots are expensive and thus tend to prevent low- and middle-income residents from purchasing property. Communities considering large-lot zoning should take care that it actually does protect environmental resources and so can withstand a legal challenge as to its purpose. A reasonable limit may be the minimum lot size that is able to support economically viable agriculture.

Marin County, California: Tackling the Impermanence Syndrome with Large-Lot Zoning

Large-lot zoning for agriculture has proven to be vital to farmland protection in Marin County, California, whose westernmost reaches along the Pacific Ocean are home to dairy and ranching operations despite its proximity to San Francisco. Although Marin is well known as an affluent residential community, more than 40 percent of the county's land remains in agriculture. Marin dairies, in fact, supply 25 percent of the milk purchased in the San Francisco Bay metropolitan region. The annual value of agricultural production in the county is approximately $50 million; the worth of its beautiful working landscape to Marin's image as a good place to live, work, and visit for thousands of nonfarmers may be even greater.

Despite ever-increasing pressures on land values and the agricultural industry, the county has so far succeeded in maintaining its agricultural base, in large part because of firm signals to the farming community that agriculture has a future in the county. "The worst threat facing [Marin's] agriculture is the uncertainty that goes with farming in an urban region," warns a case statement by the Marin Agricultural Land Trust (MALT). "Will new development reach this way? Will neighbors still be in agriculture ten years from now? Will a developer make an offer that can't be refused?" The resulting "impermanence syndrome" can be deadly. Policies encouraging agricultural uses over residential development are vital to stem this negative cycle.

Key among such policies in Marin has been its longstanding support for its agricultural zoning. In a hard-fought battle of the early 1970s, the county mandated a minimum lot size of 60 acres, believing such acreage was far larger than anyone would want to buy for a residence. Sixty acres was known to be too small for modern dairying, the county's chief agricultural industry, but the more realistic size of 200 acres was (and remains) politically impossible as a minimum lot size. Nevertheless, the success of any agricultural preservation program depends on its effectiveness in addressing land speculation among owners of agricultural land, and the 60-acre lot size has helped—even though by the late 1970s, a market existed of people willing to buy such "large backyards." "Because the county established fairly firm policies years ago, and has stuck by them, we haven't had the kind of impermanence syndrome other places have had. Farmers have tended to invest to maintain profitability," says Robert Berner, executive director of MALT.

Instead of attempting to increase the minimum lot size allowed by its agricultural zoning, the county has supplemented it with other approaches, principally the purchase of agricultural conservation easements (see p. 228) and the creation of MALT, formed in 1980 to help with implementation of these and other approaches to agricultural preservation. (A program for transfer of development rights also is on the books, but without planning and political support to create an adequate receiving zone, it is an unreliable approach, having been used only once in Marin County.)

MALT is renowned as the nation's first land trust devoted exclusively to agricultural land, and there are still only a few such organizations, although some 54 percent of the nation's land trusts include farms among types of land they have protected. Today, MALT holds conservation easements on thirty-eight farms, totaling more than 25,000 acres—some 20 percent of the county's privately owned agricultural land. Most of these easements were purchased, largely through a 1988 state bond act that allotted $15 million to the county. Although county officials and members of the farm bureau are among the county residents who sit on MALT's board, MALT is completely independent. To gain access to state funds, MALT executed a cooperative agreement with the county, agreeing to initiate and package easements; for its part, the county agreed to apply for state funds to convey as grants to MALT to conclude the purchases.

The Marin Agricultural Land Trust is also an advocate for public policies supporting farmland conservation and conducts public education programs, believing that the future of Marin's farmland is dependent on an informed and supportive public.

As both the state and the county face increasing political difficulties in raising more funds for purchase of agricultural easements, the county's agricultural preservation supporters are looking hard at every option for continuing to increase the county's base of protected lands. Making the TDR program more workable may be one way—"it's an extremely appealing prospect to make the marketplace pay for resource conservation," says Berner. Another option may be to encourage more donations—MALT's few have come from developers required to protect open space (see Sidebar 5.11) and a community foundation that bought some agricultural land and donated easements over the land. But, comments Berner, "it's very difficult to operate a donation program side by side with an easement purchase program." After all, why should the county's farmers donate easements when one can be paid for the same thing, and they are financially unable to take full advantage of the income tax incentives for donating easements? As many of them take a careful look at estate planning in the coming years, however, seeking ways to assure transfer of the land and the farm operation to the next generation, donated easements are likely to play a greater role in the county than they have heretofore.

Today, the concern is maintaining the county's dairying industry in the face of buyers willing to purchase entire ranches as "mega-ranchettes." Such owners would keep the land open but not operate it as a dairy farm. Says Berner, "Agriculture is a business, an industry. [Conservation] easements don't guarantee its survival. Unlike buying parkland, when you're trying to save farmland, it's a never-ending struggle. I don't think you ever lick the impermanence syndrome. With a metropolitan area of 6 million people [nearby], the pressures aren't going to go away, it's something you contend with constantly."

But Berner is optimistic that MALT, its 2,000 members, and farmland protection supporters among the county's leaders will find a way to continue the progress the agricultural community has made over more than twenty years: "People emotionally have always been fond of farmers and farmland and that lifestyle, but we're beginning to learn more about the fiscal, environmental, community pros and cons for maintaining farmland. The benefits of agricultural preservation start with open space, but there's also the social and cultural diversity and community character, which low-density suburban residential development doesn't bring with it. And then there are the relatively recently recognized realities that . . . residential development consumes more in public services than it pays in taxes. The net result is, everyone's taxes increase when you lose farmland—it's a real lose-lose situation."

Agricultural Zoning

Many agricultural zones permit nonfarm activity to so large an extent that the zoning virtually constitutes a holding category for "vacant" farmland until some kind of development comes along. Such zones do not really protect farmland; it is therefore misleading to call them agricultural zones. True agricultural zoning, which limits nonfarm uses and often mandates very large, farm-sized lots, has as its aim the protection and maintenance of farm operations.

Many agricultural zoning ordinances include "antinuisance" clauses that protect farmers from complaints by residential neighbors about such agricultural activities as spraying herbicides or night plowing (see p. 211). Agricultural zoning often permits additional dwellings when they are necessary for extended families who are living on one farm or for farm laborers. Ordinances linked to preferential tax assessment provide farmers with a degree of property tax relief (see p. 207).

Some communities have experimented with ways to accommodate limited development while protecting agricultural uses. Under some ordinances, farmers are permitted to sell off a small number of residential lots, staying within a certain proportion of the farm's overall acreage. In Peach Bottom Township, Pennsylvania, for example, a sliding scale allows one 1-acre residential lot for the first 7 acres, 2 lots for 7 to 30

4.7 Sliding-Scale Zoning

Clarke County, Virginia, is an example of a community that has implemented sliding-scale zoning. Below is the scale they have established.

Size of Tract of Land (in acres)	Number of Single-Family Detached Dwellings Permitted
0–14.99	1
15–39.99	2
40–79.99	3
80–129.99	4
130–179.99	5
180–229.99	6
230–279.99	7
280–329.99	8
330–399.99	9
400–499.99	10
500–599.99	11
600–729.99	12
730–859.99	13
860–1,029.00	14
1,030 or more	15

Minimum lot size: 1 acre (less if lot is an existing lot of record). Maximum lot size: 2 acres (more if necessary for septic fields).

acres, and another lot for each additional 50 acres up to a maximum of nineteen lots.[5]

Regulating Subdivision

While zoning controls the density and type of land uses at different locations in the community, a subdivision ordinance governs the design of new development that is permitted, along with its traffic circulation, drainage, and the like. A subdivision ordinance, as the name indicates, sets standards for the division of larger parcels of land into smaller ones; it also specifies the shape of lots and the location of streets, open space, utilities, and other improvements.

Used in concert with a zoning ordinance, or even by itself, the subdivision ordinance can be an important technique for rural conservation. Although the word "subdivision" is often used to apply to a housing development, subdivision regulations can apply to any division of land.

Subdivision and subsequent development affect a community's character, its natural resources, and its public services. Good design and engineering standards mandated by a subdivision ordinance can go a long way toward lessening the negative impacts of development, especially its visual effects, even when zoning permits intensive development. For example, regulations can mandate that strips of natural vegetation be retained or added to create buffers between residential areas and agricultural land, or they can require the planting of street trees or other vegeta-

4.3
A development of prefabricated houses in King County, Washington. Although the development is located on prime farmland, an increasingly scarce resource, it takes up less farmland than a large-lot subdivision of the same number of units. King County now has a program to purchase development rights in order to protect the remaining prime farmland.

tion that could eventually help a new development to blend into the rural landscape.

A subdivision ordinance usually contains a set of definitions, procedures for filing applications, approval procedures, design standards, and provisions for general administration. Subdivision of a limited number of lots, usually from two to five, may be exempted from the full approval process, especially if no new streets would be necessitated by the further subdivision. This avoids unnecessary administrative procedures that would burden property owners and governments alike. A community should retain a measure of control, however, over even a minor subdivision, to ensure that certain standards are met, since a number of small changes can add up to major effects, and to guard against the creation of substandard, unbuildable parcels (see Sidebar 4.5 for constitutional reasons to avoid creating unbuildable parcels).

An important part of a subdivision ordinance is its performance guarantees, for instance an escrow account or secured bond, which ensure that development will take place only in the form that was approved. The guarantees permit the community to use designated funds to complete a project in the event of any default by a developer or to correct deviations from the approved plan.

A problem many communities face is platted but unbuilt subdivisions that were created when land use controls were nonexistent or weak. One rural planner in Maryland refers to the numerous unbuilt subdivisions in his county as "ghost subdivisions," a kind of "time bomb set for who-knows-when in the future" that could hurt the county's more recent efforts to improve its development standards. Some newer subdivision ordinances provide for a "sunset" rule, which requires that if sales or construction have not actually occurred within a given period of time, the property owner must reapply for approval.

4.8 Subdivision Checklist

In general, a subdivision ordinance establishes design and engineering standards for

- *General design and layout of lots and buildings*
- *Streets and rights-of-way*
- *Grading*
- *Sidewalks, curbs, and gutters*
- *Drainage and storm-water runoff*
- *Street trees and street lighting*
- *Utilities*
- *Landscaping*
- *Trails and bike paths*
- *Open space and common areas*

(See Notes to Sidebars.)

4.4
Landslides can be a problem on steep slopes where vegetation is removed and inappropriate construction has taken place. As this 1967 photograph of San Anselmo, California, suggests, this is not a new problem. District conservationists from the Natural Resources Conservation Service can advise rural communities of what areas are vulnerable and suggest appropriate development regulations.

4.9 Making Land Use Ordinances Interactive

A growing trend for land development codes has been the inclusion of drawings and photographs to illustrate design requirements. A pioneering project to provide land ordinance information has been completed for Findlay Township, Pennsylvania (a growing rural community near Pittsburgh's new airport), by an interdisciplinary team led by members of the department of landscape architecture at Penn State. Using multimedia computer technology, which can combine two or more kinds of information—text, graphic art such as drawings or maps, photographs, sound, animation, or video—the team created an affordable personal computer–operated "visual interactive code" (VIC) that will allow users to retrieve information via a computerized menu. The program works "in dramatic contrast to paging through a thick regulatory booklet," says Kelleann Foster, a team leader. "Photographs of community attributes can be linked to explanatory text, diagrams, and maps." An additional advantage of such a program is that users can obtain information as and when they need it, cross-referencing with the touch of a button. The VIC will allow access to information by one of three methods: geography (a "maps" button), key words (a "topics" button), or actual text from regulations (an "ordinances" button). Initial reports from users, says Foster, are that the VIC is "very easy— even engaging." At last, a land development code someone might actually want to read.

(See Notes to Sidebars.)

Related to subdivision regulation is the reservation of land for the creation of future roads, trails, and drainage systems at the time development occurs. This is done by designating the reservations on an official map of the subdivision, adopted by the local government well in advance of development. It may also be feasible to designate land for parks, schools, fire stations or other facilities. At the time development occurs, a developer can be required to dedicate or sell such land to the community.

Rural communities increasingly are adopting erosion and sediment controls to combat problems related to water pollution and flooding. Such controls are sometimes enacted as part of a community's subdivision regulations; they may also be enacted separately or as part of the zoning ordinance or building code. Many are developed and enforced in cooperation with the local soil and water conservation district, whose staff can assist with technical knowledge. Such ordinances may address site suitability, the rate and volume of storm-water runoff, the extent and duration of soil exposure during construction, and the design of construction and landscaping to reduce the amount of impervious surface and improve drainage. A typical requirement during construction, for example, is the use of barriers—black "filter fence" is now common—to retain as much soil on site as possible while it is exposed to the elements. Forestry and agricultural practices that can cause excessive erosion may also be regulated (for more on water pollution, see Sidebar 1.4).

Combining Zoning and Subdivision

Since there is little reason to separate zoning and subdivision ordinances, other than that they are usually authorized by different state enabling acts, a few communities (Medford, New Jersey, for example) have consolidated them to create an ordinance that addresses all factors related to land development regardless of whether they involve use, lot size, design, utilities and services, or all of these. Such an ordinance may not only simplify the application and review process for developers and administrators but may also eliminate the possibility of incompatibility between two ordinances developed at different times by different people. Creating a new land development code also may allow for the incorporation of the flexible land use techniques discussed in the following section.

FLEXIBLE LAND USE REGULATIONS

Several major criticisms apply to the use of traditional zoning and subdivision regulations, especially for rural areas. First of all, they may be inflexible. Since it is difficult to write an ordinance that covers all of the variables in development, a community may find that, although it is getting development that is technically acceptable, it is not particularly happy with the results. Developers may be equally unhappy. A subdivision ordinance's prescribed solutions to common design or engineering problems may be more expensive than alternatives more appropriate to the particular site characteristics. For instance, an ordinance may call for paved gutters for drainage. In relatively level areas, however, grassed swales allow for maximum absorption of storm-water runoff on site and may be cheaper and more attractive. Applying for special exceptions, variances, or zoning changes to avoid inflexible standards is frequently cumbersome, and especially inconvenient in small projects, where such maneuvering can be burdensome for local property owners.

Another difficulty with zoning in rural areas is the assumption that different uses should be segregated. This does not always protect a community's character or its natural environment. Moreover, it may often be more convenient to rural lifestyles to permit facilities such as a grocery store or veterinary clinic to locate in an agricultural area or to intersperse some multiple-family housing among single-family houses. In rural areas especially, with development typically scattered over some distance, traditional zoning can create seemingly arbitrary or unnecessary exclusions of uses.

Some of the more pleasing traditional settlement patterns to be found in older villages, neighborhoods, and rural areas today would not be permitted under common zoning and subdivision standards. Many of these standards evolved in response to the need for adequate land for septic systems and wells: Villages, with their narrow, small lots, may be charming today, but because they were built without public water and sewer, they were vulnerable to water-borne disease (a problem recognized only late in the 19th century). From the 1950s onward, even with the increasing availability of water and sewer services to newer developments, more and more communities accepted minutely prescriptive formulas that virtually require standard suburban residential sprawl. Strange as it may seem, even with the evolution of many newer techniques and standards for designing new development, many communities still rely on the legacy of those long-ago formulas. Standards for setbacks, frontages, acreage, off-street parking, and other features in existing ordinances can make it impossible to replicate or complement older settlement patterns in many communities. As designers and developers have realized these limits, they have begun to call for more flexible regulations.

For these reasons, more and more communities today are using ordinances that offer more flexibility and more land protection. Relatively new tools are being used in some communities as alternatives or additives to traditional zoning and subdivision regulations. This section briefly describes a few of the best-known of these techniques, which can be used alone or in combination.

Overlay Zoning

Protecting certain resources found in various locations throughout the community, such as steep hillsides or a scenic river, presents a challenge to standard zoning schemes. "Overlay zoning" or "critical area zoning" does not affect the density or use regulations of existing zoning; rather, it is superimposed (hence "overlay") across a community's various zones, creating an additional set of requirements to be met when the special resources protected by the overlay would be affected by a proposed change. Designation and protection of historic districts and sites is a kind of overlay zoning, as is the creation of a buffer with special restrictions along scenic roads. The protection of shorelines is another example (see Figure 4.2), and the handling of areas experiencing the special difficulties associated with karst topography (where soluble limestone forms sink-

4.10 Conservation Subdivision Design

Randall Arendt, of the Natural Lands Trust of Media, Pennsylvania, suggests the following four-step procedure to arrive at a plan for development that achieves maximum conservation (Arendt 1996). The conventional development approach is illustrated in Figures 4.5–4.7. Arendt's first step is to identify areas to be conserved; areas remaining may be appropriate for development (4.8–4.10). The second step is to locate potential house sites in the developable areas (4.11). Third, streets and trails are laid out (4.12). Finally, the lot lines are drawn accommodating the natural features, not in defiance of them (4.13 and 4.14). While individual developers can adopt this process where community regulations allow, an even better result can be achieved when larger areas are developed in this way, under community guidelines or regulations, affording the potential for networks of trails, greenways, scenic open space, and protected habitat, streamsides, and watershed lands.

(See Notes to Sidebars.)

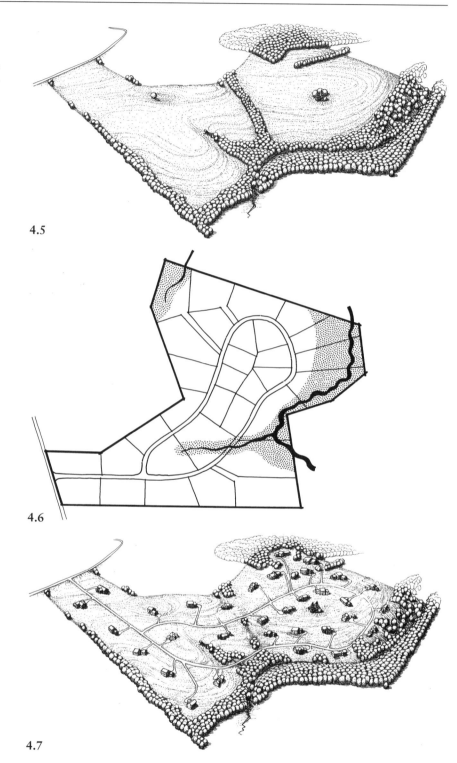

4.5

4.6

Aerial sketch of an 82-acre parcel prior to development, "yield plan" for the parcel, using the typical large-lot layout, and an aerial sketch of the resulting sprawling pattern of development. This demonstrates the maximal legal development potential of the site.

4.7

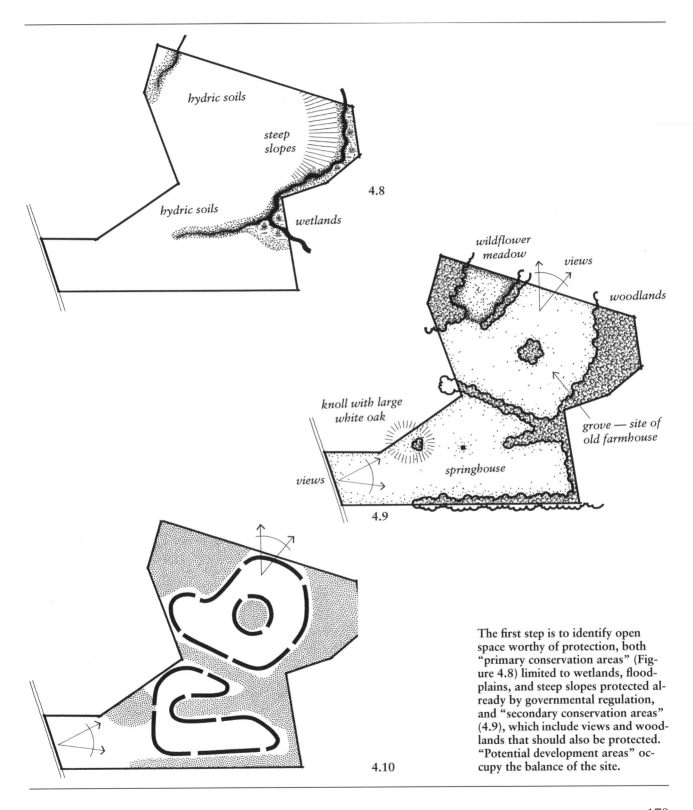

hydric soils

steep
slopes

hydric soils

wetlands

4.8

wildflower
meadow

views

woodlands

knoll with large
white oak

grove — site of
old farmhouse

views

springhouse

4.9

4.10

The first step is to identify open space worthy of protection, both "primary conservation areas" (Figure 4.8) limited to wetlands, floodplains, and steep slopes protected already by governmental regulation, and "secondary conservation areas" (4.9), which include views and woodlands that should also be protected. "Potential development areas" occupy the balance of the site.

Illustrating a full-density scheme, thirty-two house sites—the same number the conventional yield plan provided for—are located on the plan. For marketing and quality-of-life reasons, they are sited at a respectful proximity to the conservation areas and arranged both to take advantage of views across meadows or fields and to back up to hedgerows and wooded areas for privacy.

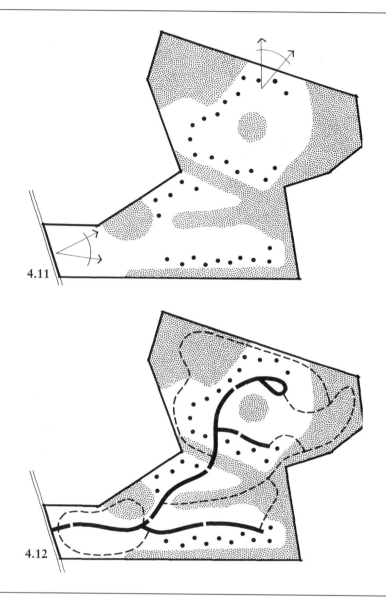

4.11

Logical alignments are then drawn onto the plan to connect the thirty-two homes via streets and informal footpaths.

4.12

holes as subsurface drainage patterns shift) may also employ overlay zoning.

Clustering

One of the major impacts of standard zoning and subdivision ordinances has been the creation of sprawling developments laid out with little regard for natural, agricultural, scenic, and historic resources, with little variety in design and density, and with little open space that is acces-

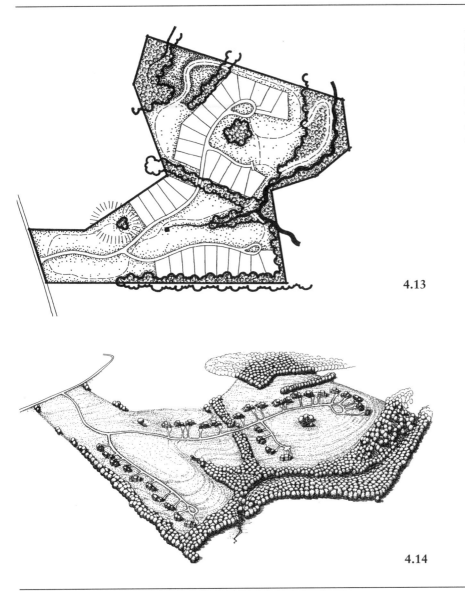

Lot lines are drawn around each site. Sites will sell faster, at higher prices, and appreciate more rapidly over time following this approach than in standard development, not because of the lot size, but because of the attractive parklike setting created by the conservation design for the subdivision.

4.13

4.14

sible to nearby property owners or the public. Subdivision rules that allow the grouping of buildings and lots on a small portion of a tract, away from the most special resources on that tract, can be an effective and flexible way to allow limited amounts of development in rural areas. This may be called "clustering" or "flexible development" or "open space subdivision." Let us say that a 100-acre tract under existing zoning and subdivision rules could be divided into fifty 2-acre residential lots. If the zoning provisions for subdivision layout and density were more flexible, the developer would be able to maintain the same average density of fifty units on 100 acres but could offer smaller lots. The remaining land could be dedicated to agriculture through a lease with a nearby farmer, as a park under local government jurisdiction, or as recreational open space maintained by a homeowners' association. Such development might protect more of the environment and provide a more attractive setting than would a standard subdivision.

The developer's incentive to undertake these desirable things is financial. Greater flexibility in site planning would, for example, allow the developer to avoid building on parts of the site that might present expensive construction problems. Clustering might allow retention of more natural vegetation, resulting in a more attractive development. Clustering also requires fewer streets and shorter utility lines—with the added long-term benefits of reduced maintenance costs for the municipality—and leaves more space for such amenities as trails and wildlife habitat, adding to the appeal of the site and giving the developer an edge in the marketplace.[6] Some communities view clustering as a significant enough improvement over standard subdivision that they offer extra density as a bonus to induce a developer to choose this approach. Other communities simply allow it as an alternative to conventional zoning. A few, such as Calvert County, Maryland, have decided that the benefits so outweigh those of ordinary development that they require clustering.

Communities sometimes distrust clustering, however, because it can appear to be denser than ordinary development, particularly if it is poorly designed. Neighbors may also fear a loss of property values if clustering permits less expensive homes to be built or if the open space is not properly maintained. Moreover, unless effective protections for the open land are established and enforced, through such means as conservation easements, it may not remain permanently open.

Fauquier County, Virginia, revamped its clustering requirements in 1986 to improve its protection for rural resources and to manage growth. A former limit of three new units per tract was frequently exceeded by special exception, apparently because county officials were concerned that the limit was not always reasonable and therefore not legally or politically defensible. A change to a sliding scale increased the maximum number of units permitted per tract, and because county officials were more comfortable with the sliding scale, they granted fewer special exceptions. The net effect, according to Virginia's Piedmont Environmental Council, was to decrease the intensity of development in the agricultural zone by at least 50 percent. Moreover, the county now requires that up to 85 percent of any tract remain open and that conservation easements or deed restrictions be used to protect the reserved lands.[7]

Planned residential development (PRD) and planned unit development (PUD) are variations of flexible site design. While a cluster ordinance allows variety in layout and lot size, a PRD incorporates these provisions and encourages mixed housing types. A PUD allows mixed uses and is generally applied to large-scale developments, typically 100 acres or more. Developers apply for permission to use these approaches when they can meet standards set for such development under the zoning or subdivision ordinance. Such standards are more often found in places where large developers are common—counties that are rapidly suburbanizing or regions where retirement or resort communities are being created. (On gaining support for community projects from large development, see Sidebar 5.8.)

A recent development in community planning is the construction of new communities based on design elements of the past. On a small scale, this can occur when new homes are built adjacent to historic towns using a street pattern and architectural style compatible with local, traditional patterns. On a larger scale, some innovative architects and builders are creating subdivisions or whole new towns reflecting the settlement patterns of communities of the past. Known as neotraditional development or "the new urbanism," this type of development is characterized by a tight grid of streets, small lots, front porches on homes, public squares, sidewalks, and the location of commercial development at the center of the community. The emphasis is on walkable space, which minimizes the use of the automobile and fosters opportunity for social interaction. Although laudable in principle, neotraditional development undoubtedly works best when located adjacent to existing development, where roads and sewer and water lines already exist. A neotraditional new town in a rural setting, miles from another town, may threaten natural resources as much as standard sprawling subdivisions. And, as with any large-scale development in a rural area, there is no guarantee that a neotraditional town would not generate sprawling, incompatible development on its borders.

Carroll County, Maryland: Multiple Means of Protecting Agricultural Lands

Protecting farmland has been a high priority in Carroll County, Maryland, since 1978, when the county commissioners amended the county's zoning ordinance. Farmland preservation is carried out through three interconnected programs: agricultural zoning, voluntary creation of agricultural districts, and purchase of development rights.

A large rural county with substantial amounts of prime farmland, Carroll County is close enough to both Baltimore and Washington, D.C., to be facing considerable development pressure. Between 1970 and 1992, the county's population increased by 104 percent, from 66,230 to 131,030 residents. Despite such growth, agriculture—principally dairy products, livestock, and corn—is still big business there. In 1992, Carroll County farms and businesses supporting farms grossed more than $115 million. Fifty-four percent of the 289,920-acre county is devoted to agriculture, comprising 7.8 percent of the total acreage of cropland in the state.

As of 1994, there were 339 farms, comprising more than 41,780 acres, protected by agricultural districts in the county. Farmers enter agricultural districts voluntarily with approval of the county. Farms must be at least 100 acres and consist of good-quality soils. Land in agricultural districts must remain in agriculture for at least five years and cannot be subdivided, except to provide homes for the owner's children or farm laborers. Farmers in agricultural districts are

4.15
Advertisements like this one on a Carroll County, Maryland, dairying barn add much to the cultural landscape.

4.16
Dairying is still a major business in Carroll County, despite its proximity to Baltimore, Frederick, and Washington, D.C. The county has restricted subdivision within agricultural districts and acquired development rights to preserve farmland. However, much farmland has already given way to development.

protected from nuisance suits related to their agricultural activities and are eligible to sell their development rights to the state upon approval by the county.

The county's agricultural districts and agricultural zoning go hand in hand. The agricultural zone, covering 62 percent of the county, allows only one new dwelling unit per 20 acres, with a minimum lot size of 1 acre. The county planning commission requires that, wherever feasible, developers cluster any development that occurs in the agricultural zone, so that some land on developed parcels remains permanently available for agriculture. Clustering, however, is "not as easy to accomplish as we'd like it to be," says Marlene Conaway, assistant director of planning and development. "It's difficult because many people who move out here want farmettes, especially for horses. But we have been fairly successful." She hopes that, as farm owners see more clustering in use and realize

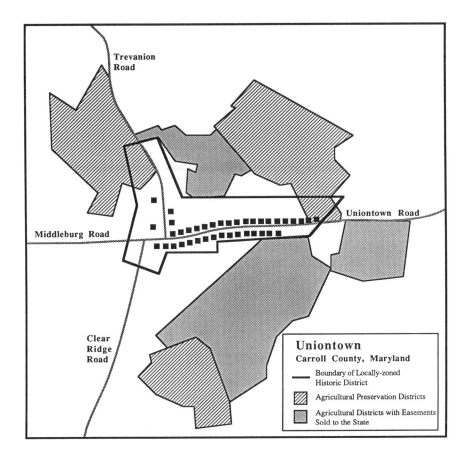

Trevanion
Road

Middleburg Road

Uniontown Road

Clear
Ridge
Road

Uniontown
Carroll County, Maryland

——— Boundary of Locally-zoned
Historic District

Agricultural Preservation Districts

Agricultural Districts with Easements
Sold to the State

4.17
Conservationists in Uniontown, Carroll County, have protected both historic buildings and the surrounding farmland that provides the setting for the village. Uniontown, which dates from 1809, is listed in the National Register of Historic Places and is protected by a county historic preservation ordinance that regulates changes to the buildings, sidewalks, and street trees. Farmers whose land surrounds Uniontown have voluntarily placed their land in agricultural districts. The owners are protected from nuisance suits and are eligible to sell their development rights to the state.

that the county is committed to discouraging sprawl in the agricultural zone, more owners will be encouraged to form agricultural districts.

Passing the agricultural zoning required assurances from the county that farmers would be able to form agricultural districts, thus becoming eligible to sell their development rights, and that the county would participate financially in the state's program for purchase of development rights. Each is necessary for the other to exist, says Conaway: "Zoning covers more farmland, but it's not forever: the political climate could change. If we lose the zoning, then we'd start losing districts when their time is up. The more agricultural easements we get, though, the surer we are of maintaining the zoning." It would make little sense to alter the agricultural zoning in areas where most farms are protected by purchase of their development rights.

In all but two years since 1979, the State of Maryland has appropriated funds for the Maryland Agricultural Land Preservation Foundation to purchase development rights from farmers whose land is in agricultural districts. Counties also contribute. Carroll County has maintained its leadership in the state program (19.2 percent of all the state's easements) by committing an average of about $500,000 each year. Over a fifteen-year period, the program has secured permanent easements which prohibit development on 21,000 acres of farmland.

The foundation uses a bidding system to arrive at a price per acre for development rights. In 1994, Carroll County's average for development rights was $1,774 per acre, just under half the going rate, given that unrestricted farmland in the county sells for around $3,600 per acre. Once a farmer has notified the state of an interest in selling development rights, the foundation appraises the farm to establish its unrestricted market value, and the restricted market value is determined by a formula. The difference between the two values is the appraised value of the development rights. The farmer informs the state of his or her asking price per acre before the appraisal is done. Those with asking prices below appraised value receive first consideration by the state—allowing the state to stretch its limited dollars through below-market-value purchases—and the state cannot pay more than the appraised value.

The program has proven popular with county farmers and their neighbors, who are "happy to see the farms protected and their rural lifestyle maintained," says Conaway. In fact, farmers have offered more easements than the foundation can buy. County officials hope eventually to obtain easements on 100,000 acres. They believe this is the minimum amount of farmland the county must preserve to assure the continued viability of agriculture and local agribusiness. In the meantime, the county has developed the Critical Farms Program for new owners of qualifying farms, as a way of supporting their financial needs during their most vulnerable period of ownership, startup. Through this program the county guarantees 75 percent of the value of easements that the owner wants to sell to the state. The program has enabled the county to guarantee easements on two farms per year since 1992.

County officials note that much of the money farmers are receiving for their development rights is being reinvested in their farms, often to buy more land or equipment. An added bonus of the program to purchase development rights is that owners of the restricted farms become very interested in soil conservation in order to maintain productivity. As evidence that Carroll County's farmers have long been good stewards of the land, approximately 70 percent of all farms in the county with erodible soils have installed soil-saving management practices, such as contour strips and sod waterways. In addition, the foundation requires that all farms in its program implement a conservation plan.

In 1994, Carroll County passed a right-to-farm ordinance stronger than the state's. In addition, the county is considering creating a transfer of development rights program and establishing its own, county-level purchase of development rights program, which would be funded through a 1 percent real estate transfer tax. These would help ensure that Carroll County retains the amount of land needed to preserve agriculture as a viable industry for the future. It is a process, as Conaway says, of "trying to stay ahead of the developer."

Point Systems and Growth Guidance Programs

One way to deal with some of the shortcomings of zoning is to use a point or rating system, the most widely used basis for which is the LESA (land evaluation and site assessment) system (Steiner, Pease, and Coughlin 1994) (see Sidebar 3.8). A point system can help in avoiding "one-size-fits-all" formulas—for example, always basing the number of parking spaces on a commercial site's square footage. The actual environmental or community effects, or performance, of a given development might vary considerably—in the case of parking, the number of spaces actually needed may depend on the type of commercial activity and on whether people will need to park for fifteen minutes or two hours. This emphasis on performance is the basis for one name for this kind of approach, "performance-based regulations" (Ndubisi 1992, p. 45); some ordinances incorporate the terms "growth guidance" or "land use guidance" into their names to imply their purpose and to distinguish them from ordinary zoning regulations.

With a point system, the community can assess projects individually for their impact on wetlands, vegetation, critical slopes, groundwater, lighting, noise, traffic, scenic qualities, and the like. Projects that fail the required rating would have to be redesigned. Points may also address other factors the community considers important—rewarding a residential project for its proximity to public sewers or schools, for example, might encourage more compact growth. Standards can be established that must be met regardless of the overall score. For example, a community concerned about nonpoint source runoff may require that proposed projects meet a certain rating for impact on water quality. One of the best-known point systems has been used in Fort Collins, Colorado since 1979, under an ordinance know as the "land development guidance system." [8] Charles County, Maryland, uses a point system in its development guidance system, established in 1992, to evaluate proposals for larger residential and mixed-use development projects. [9]

In such growth guidance programs, the burden is placed on the developer to reduce objectionable impacts before local permits can be issued for construction. Some growth guidance programs incorporate not only a point system to assess these impacts but also an "informal compatibility meeting" early in the review process, in which neighbors critique the project. If the developer is unable or unwilling to modify the proejct to meet concerns, the proposal is reviewed by public officials, who decide what modifications to require (Hale 1994, p. 7). Hardin County, Kentucky, which originated the idea of having project neighbors contribute to compatibility assessment, ran into trouble with this feature of its program, because it was judged to substitute neighbors' opinions for those of duly elected or appointed officials. [10] Informal reviews by neighbors which lead to voluntary changes by developers, however, may be less problematic, and are increasingly common requirements in many states. [11]

Under a growth guidance program, all current uses are "as of right," and all changes and new uses are scrutinized one by one—if a project is not built, the review process starts over for the next proposal for that site. This process bears some resemblance to the reviews of "conditional uses" that are found in many ordinary zoning ordinances, in which the community provides a list of additional, optional uses it is willing to consider within the zone provided the use meets certain conditions (see Sidebar 4.6). In practice, however, conditional uses tend to receive less scrutiny than is provided under a point system. [12]

Carried to its logical conclusion, a growth guidance system can be used to eliminate some or all zoning boundaries, potentially conferring more development potential on more properties, since it relies more on demand from buyers and developers to determine where development will proceed and less on zones that may not successfully predict or meet the market's need. Hardin County, Kentucky, for example—which first used only a point system based on LESA when it instituted land use regulations in 1984—has only three commercial and four residential zoning categories in which the design of development is given some latitude depending on conditions. Available road frontage and size of the road, for example, determine a residential lot size.

Although growth guidance systems appear to offer great potential for application in rural communities, few models exist—a disadvantage to communities hoping to create such a program, for they would benefit from others' experience in developing ratings and procedures. Thus, the preparation of an ordinance might be more difficult (and thus more costly) than the preparation of standard zoning and subdivision ordinances. Moreover, the necessity of more intensive review of development proposals can be a procedural burden for any community, with or without a trained planner on staff. Bedford County, Virginia, which established its land use guidance system ordinance in 1989, following Hardin County's lead, discovered that initial demands on staff time were greater than anticipated (Ndubisi 1992, p. 49). Balanced against this drawback is the public support Bedford's program has earned for its solicitation of citizen opinion early in the development review process (Hale 1994, p. 1). Other examples of rural communities using growth guidance programs are Burke County, North Carolina, which has followed Bedford County's experience,[13] and Bath Township, Michigan, which combined performance standards with traditional zoning more than ten years ago (Ndubisi 1992, p. 49).

Transfer of Development Rights

Traditional zoning practice assumes that over time all parcels within a given zone will be developed. But what if the zone should not be developed at all? What if it is prime farmland, complete with viable agricultural enterprises? Or valuable forest land or wildlife habitat? Agricultural zoning may be an answer in some communities (see p. 173). For places where the value of the land for residential or commercial development is much higher than its value as open space or farmland or ranchland, another idea might work better: separating the development rights and transferring them to a different area altogether. This technique is usually called "transfer of development rights" (TDR). Basically, a local government allows the right to develop a parcel of land to be separated from the ownership of the land itself; both the land and the development rights remain private property and can be sold separately. The development rights in the protected area, or "sending zone," can be sold and used on a different parcel of land in an area called a "receiving zone," which has been designated as appropriate for development because it has adequate public services available or fewer resources to be protected. TDR increases the amount of development on a receiving parcel of land and eliminates or reduces development on a sending parcel.

The TDR transaction has obvious advantages for the developer in the receiving zone; the advantage to the property owner in the sending zone is being able to cash in on the monetary value of the land's potential for development while protecting a resource or continuing to work the land. For the community, TDR extends the benefits of open space to larger areas of the community, rather than creating it parcel by parcel through clustering—at little or no cost to the public. And like clustering, TDR encourages concentration of development where it is most appropriate, for savings in the cost of providing public services.

For TDR to work, there must be a healthy market for the rights, since property owners hoping to sell development rights yet disappointed by sluggish sales may clamor for a return to zoning-as-usual. To initiate the TDR program in Montgomery County, Maryland, county officials reduced the allowable density for development in the farming area they wanted to protect from one unit per 5 acres to one unit per 25 acres. This "downzoning" would not have been politically feasible if it had not been offset by allowing farm owners to sell their development rights based on the old 5-acre minimum and if the market for these rights had not been healthy. Another problem is the resistance of residents in the receiving zone or zones, who may oppose increased density, as has been the case with Montgomery County's program. Still another problem is that TDR programs can be complicated to administer and are difficult to explain. There are approximately fifty TDR programs in operation across the nation, most of them in cities and small towns;[14] rural TDR programs include those in Monterey County (see Case Study 5.7) and Marin County (see Case Study 4.1), Calfornia, Burlington County, New Jersey (Gottsegen 1992), and Calvert County, Maryland.

ADDRESSING ENVIRONMENTAL PROTECTION, DESIGN QUALITY, AND HISTORIC PRESERVATION

The use of flexible land use regulations answers many of the criticisms of standard zoning and subdivision. Environmental concerns and good design, however, must be incorporated into whatever controls are in place—environmental concerns when development is proposed for a particular site, and design concerns when the development goes onto the drawing board. How is the community to succeed in addressing both of these concerns? The answer is to create a review process with clear guidelines, flexibility, and room for good judgment by a responsible board.

For most rural communities, a modest level of environmental review and design control is administered by a planning commission, generally through subdivision regulations. In some communities, however, one or more separate boards may be responsible for environmental, design, or historic review. The powers of planning commissions and review boards may vary according to state enabling legislation. In some places, a review board must approve a proposal before the developer can proceed to a review by the planning commission or before a building permit is issued. In other communities, the board simply comments on the proposal, sometimes only at the commission's request. One liability of this extra layer of review is that it takes more time to arrive at a decision to permit or deny a development. When handled sensitively, however, review by such boards can assure that local property values and community goals for a good environment are reinforced—a benefit for both property owners and developers. The members of such boards should be a mix of interested citizens with and without expertise in design fields. Members with training or experience can not only help spot flaws in proposals but also suggest revisions that may not have occurred to the developer. Lay members reflect the values and concerns of the community and may be able to explain design concepts to inexperienced applicants without using the jargon of the planning and design profession.

4.11 Transfer of Development Rights

The transfer of development rights process in its simplest form works like this: Farmer Brown lives in an area where the county government wishes to protect and encourage agriculture, a "sending zone" (see Fig. 4.18). He wants to continue farming but needs cash. Developer Smith owns a tract in an area where the county has the resources to accommodate more development, a "receiving zone" (4.19), and he would like to develop the tract at a greater density than allowed by the zoning ordinance. Farmer Brown's development rights are based on the zoning in his area, which allows one residential unit per 5 acres. Since his farm is 110 acres, Farmer Brown has 22 rights (4.20). Smith's development rights are also based on zoning,

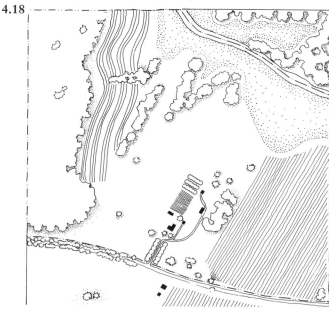

Brown's farm before subdivision

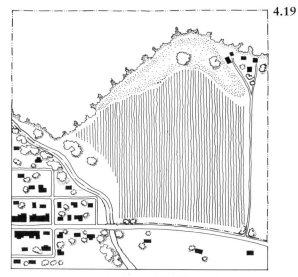

Smith's property before subdivision

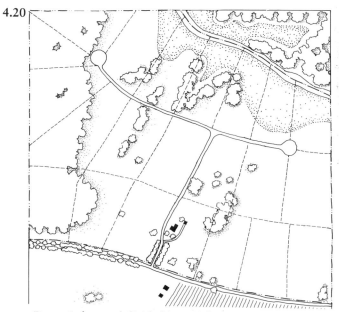

Brown's farm subdivided into 22 lots

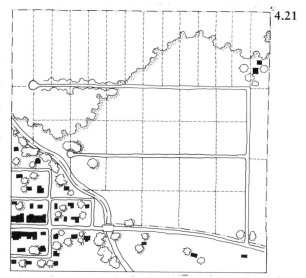

Smith's property subdivided into 38 lots

which in his area allows one residential unit per 2 acres. Since his property is 76 acres, Developer Smith has 38 rights (4.21). Farmer Brown sells 18 of his rights to Developer Smith, reserving 1 right for his own residence and 3 rights in order to give his children land on which to build their own homes (4.22). Developer Smith adds Farmer Brown's 18 rights to the 38 he already owns on his 76-acre parcel, enabling him to develop 56 lots (4.23). The sale of rights is recorded on the deed to Farmer Brown's farm, so he can no longer build more than three new residences (although he can build new farm buildings), nor can he sell his rights again.

4.22

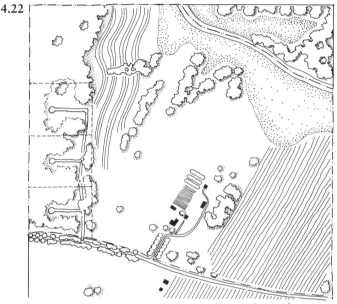

Brown's farm after creating 3 new lots and transferring the rights to 18 lots to Smith

4.23

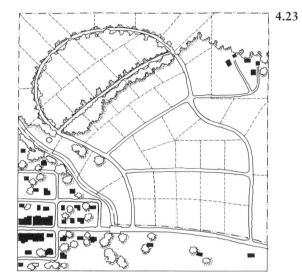

Smith's property has 56 lots after receiving the rights to 18 lots from Brown

Environmental Review

Environmental review can be a first line of defense in protecting natural resources and farmland. A community whose development approval process includes environmental review can require the developer to submit an environmental impact assessment specifying the resources on the site and the impacts of the planned development on those resources. Like federal and state environmental impact statement procedures (see Sidebar 7.1), environmental review does not necessarily mandate the avoidance of detrimental environmental impacts. One helpful tool in such reviews is the land evaluation and site assessment system, used by local and state governments in situations where objective evaluation is needed.

Environmental review generally makes clear the choices involved, provides warning to the community that some harm to the environment will result from the development as it has been proposed, and may point the way toward some on-site mitigation of the worst impacts. In some

4.12 General Design Guidelines for Rural Development

Whether a community simply offers guidelines or requires design review and approval, appropriate development in rural areas should respect certain aspects of design that contribute to the community's "sense of place"—those things that add up to a feeling that a community is a special place, distinct from anywhere else. It is often difficult to identify precisely those things that contribute to sense of place. (The photographs of Westphalia, Texas [pp. 142–43], may be helpful in understanding sense of place.) Concerned citizens may find themselves at a loss for words or concepts in explaining why they find some types of change disturbing. Indeed, communities often do not realize until it is too late that approved developments should not have been built the way they were.

Sometimes it is useful to look at the individual components of a landscape to arrive at community value judgments about the anticipated visual impact of proposed changes and to provide a basis for evaluating those changes. An architect or landscape architect can assist a community in reaching consensus about good design and the key elements and patterns in the current landscape that should be reflected in new development. The following discussion, while not comprehensive, identifies categories of design issues. Although there can be differences of preference on design, most people would feel that in each pair of drawings, below, the one on the right represents better design than the one on the left.

Character of Place. Special features and views contribute to a community's visual character. New development should be avoided in such areas, but if inevitable, it should be designed sensitively, to minimize visual intrusions. Developing designs that protect such features as stream crossings, unique rock outcroppings, significant vegetation, or a distinct village entrance preserves the special character of a community. New development also should not block or mar scenic views, particularly those from roads, rivers, or trails. Development on the tops of ridges may be more intrusive than on side slopes or lower level areas, depending on vegetation, topography, and building and site design.

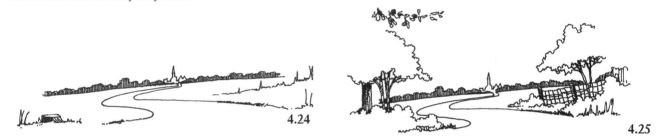

4.24

4.25

Character of place: special features. The destruction of a hedgerow (4.24) eliminates a distinctive entrance to the town (4.25).

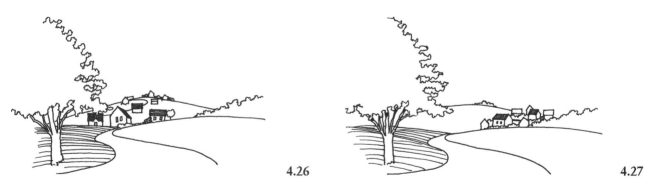

4.26

4.27

Character of place: views. A housing development sited inappropriately on a steep slope also mars a scenic view (4.26). Figure 4.27 shows the housing constructed in a less obtrusive location in the community.

Roads. Many rural roads are narrow and bordered by vegetation, fences, or rock walls. They generally follow old alignments developed in response to the topography and geography of the area. Designs for new roads and alterations to existing roads should keep their physical impact on the natural and historic environment to a minimum. Extensive cutting through wooded areas to provide wide shoulders or planting along road edges in open areas alters the traditional character of a rural road. Roads should be designed to accommodate the anticipated volume of traffic—including pedestrians and bicycles—but should be kept as narrow as safety allows. Narrower roads may encourage drivers to slow down.

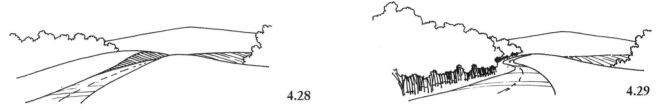

Roads: siting. A road passing through the middle of an open field intrudes in the landscape (4.28); it could be less intrusive if placed along the edge of the field (4.29).

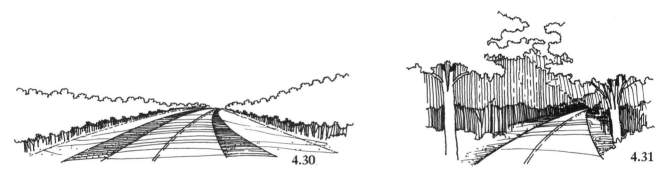

Roads: width. Excessive cutting of trees destroys the wooded character of the land (4.30), while a narrow clearing along the right-of-way preserves it (4.31).

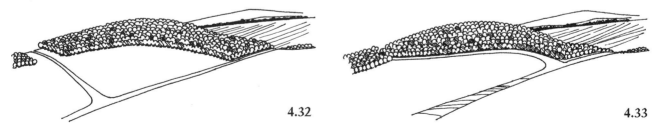

Roads: layout. Instead of crossing hilltops (4.32), roads should curve with the contours of the land (4.33).

Siting of Buildings. In some regions, farm buildings are clustered for weather protection and easy access, while in other regions they are scattered in order to separate diverse or incompatible functions. Where possible, new buildings and outbuildings should be sited in a manner that is in keeping with local traditions, and they should be located so that neither they nor their access roads cause substantial modification to the topography and natural resources.

Building Design. Most communities have characteristic building types that occur more frequently than others. Local building traditions usually originated in response to available building materials, climate, and the ethnic origins and occupations of residents. The one-and-a-half-story wooden cottage, for example, is characteristic of many East Coast fishing communities, while the two-story brick or stone farmhouse predominates in the German-American communities of eastern Pennsylvania, and one-story adobe construction is traditional to the Southwest. New buildings and changes to existing buildings should be compatible with the community's existing buildings,

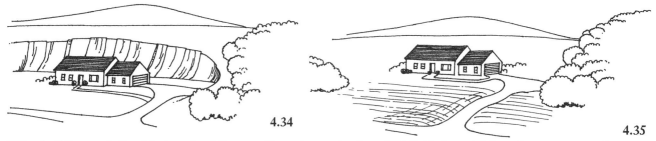

Siting buildings: relationship to natural features. Extensive cutting into the hillside is unsightly and can create erosion (4.34), whereas proper siting avoids substantial modification to a landform (4.35).

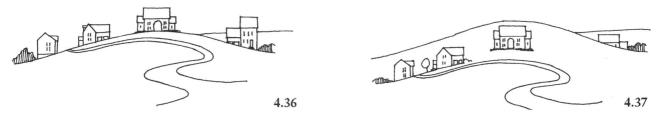

Siting buildings: protection of vistas. Buildings should not be built on ridges (4.36) but, rather, on side slopes or lower levels (4.37).

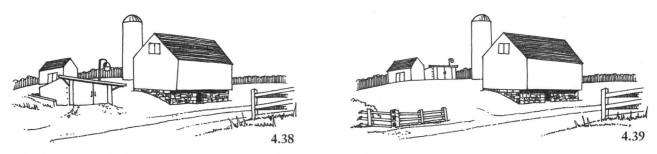

Siting buildings: relationship to other structures. When prefabricated agricultural structures are installed, they should supplement existing buildings, not replace them. Although the new structure (*front left* in 4.38) may be practical, it detracts visually from the existing barn. A new structure can be both practical and part of the total composition of the farm buildings (4.39).

although it is not necessary for new buildings or additions to imitate a particular historic architectural style. In fact, it is usually preferable for new construction to appear as a product of its own time, as long as it is compatible in form, scale, material, and color with existing buildings.

Roof pitches, building height, use of porches and courtyards, and building layout are some of the elements that help define the characteristic building forms of a community. If only gable and shed roofs, for example, are traditional in a community, gambrel, A-frame, or flat roofs may be visually incompatible. The size of

new buildings and the proportion of such design elements as wings, porches, windows, and doors are also important in determining their compatibility with existing buildings and the natural environment. New buildings should not dwarf existing buildings; nor should they overwhelm nearby trees, rise above ridge

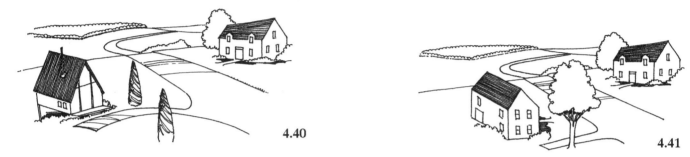

Building design: form. The form and massing of the new building at left in Figure 4.40 does not complement the area's traditional architecture. Roof form, height, and massing can be designed so that a building is compatible with traditional community forms (4.41).

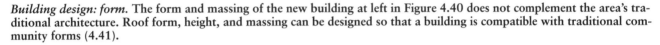

Building design: setbacks and orientation. The new house on the right in Figure 4.42 does not face the road and is set back much farther than the older house. New buildings should be oriented to the road in a way that complements the traditional community pattern (4.43).

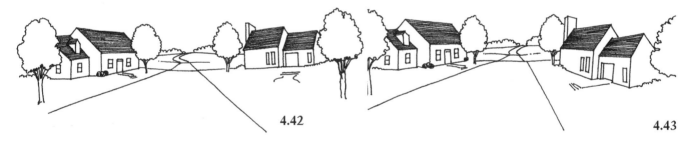

Building design: scale. A building typical of much new development dwarfs traditional building (4.44). A new building can be designed as a cluster of smaller parts to offer a sense of integrity to the landscape (4.45).

lines, or tower above other landscape features. When a facility such as a school or factory needs a new building larger than the norm, it may be preferable to construct a cluster of buildings instead of one large building or to vary the heights of parts of a single building to make it appear less monumental. Elements such as windows and doors also establish a building's proportion and can make a large building appear more compatible in scale to existing buildings if their placement is skillfully designed.

Where possible and appropriate, traditional materials and colors should be used to help new buildings be more compatible with existing buildings or complement the natural environment. Buildings with a natural color stain, for example, may blend into wooded areas more easily than those that are painted in bright colors. Roof colors can make a big difference in the visual impact of new development, with dark colors generally being less obvious.

Vegetation. In addition to native vegetation, most communities have vegetation that has been introduced because of the preferences of its residents or climatic conditions. In addition, most communities have characteristic ways of grouping plants. The evergreen windbreak located north of the farmhouse to provide shelter from harsh winter winds and the hedgerow along fence lines are two examples of this. Traditional plant species and historic planting patterns should be employed wherever possible. New species should harmonize with existing vegetation and planting traditions. Planting species that when mature will obscure significant views should be avoided. Land along streets and roads is especially visible and should be planted in a manner compatible with local practice.

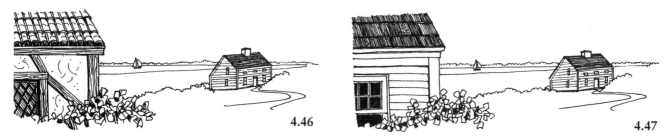

4.46

4.47

Building design: materials and color. The use of a tile roof and half-timbering seems inappropriate when compared to the materials and colors associated with a traditional Cape Cod dwelling (4.46). Complementary materials have been used in the new building shown in Figure 4.47.

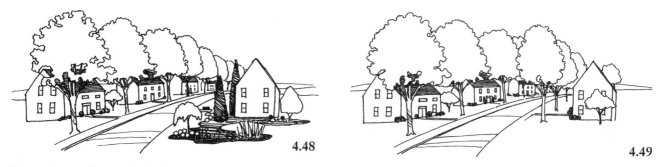

4.48

4.49

Vegetation. A distinct lack of harmony with traditional plant materials and planting patterns appears in Figure 4.48, while traditional plant species and planting patterns are retained in the scene shown in 4.49.

Utilities. Utility lines are often located without regard to their visual impact on scenic and historic resources. Locations of utility lines and their rights-of-way should avoid interfering, either physically or visually, with existing trees or other vegetation, buildings, or significant views. If lines must run above ground, poles should be set either well in front of roadside trees or far enough back to avoid the all-too-common row of half trees—pruned to accommodate the wires—at the edge of the road. Similarly, satellite dishes, radio towers, and other utility structures should be located so that they do not mar views. Whenever possible, such structures should be painted dark colors so that they appear less obvious.

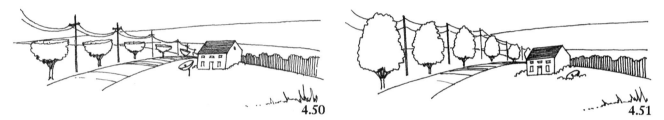

Utilities. Conspicuous utilities and injurious pruning of roadside trees (4.50) compare poorly with utility lines that are set back and screened (4.51).

instances, off-site mitigation may also be considered in the environmental review process—for example, the protection of three acres of wetland elsewhere in exchange for permission to disturb one acre on-site. Another example of off-site mitigation would be a developer's provision of road improvements, such as widening a road or upgrading an intersection, in recognition of the added traffic burdens of the new development.

A good communitywide resources inventory can provide information independent from that provided by the developer. While such an inventory is generally not sufficiently site-specific for an impact review, it can at least help the review board to ask the right questions. In the best of all possible worlds, the developer pays for an independent environmental impact assessment contracted for by the review board. If the developer

4.13 Visual Simulations

If a physical change, such as a new subdivision, a highway widening, or a commercial strip mall is proposed, it is often valuable to simulate what it will look like so that the community can determine its acceptability or whether modifications in the design or siting should be proposed. There are many simulation devices that can be used, including drawings, computer graphics, models, videos, and photographs that have been altered to include the new development. Photographs that have the proposed new development realistically painted in or added by photomontage (combining photos) are effective and inexpensive. The combination of computers and video technology can create an especially realistic view in advance of construction (see Fig. 4.53). Of course, any of these techniques can be manipulated to make a proposal seem better than it is. For further information, see Hiss 1990, Maguire 1993, and Smardon, Palmer, and Felleman 1986.

4.52 & 4.53
Photographic simulation or photomontage can help decision makers and the general public visualize a proposed development or change. A design professional alters a photograph to portray the visual impact of the change realistically, as was done here for Hartwick, in central New York. The simulation was prepared for a citizens' group opposing the development of a large shopping center on open fields.

provides a review directly, there is the possibility that the review will paint a rosier picture than the situation warrants. Although developers may balk at the expense, an independent assessment is worth insisting on, particularly for larger developments.

Design Review

When aesthetic matters are at issue, "Beauty is in the eye of the beholder!" often becomes the battle cry of beleaguered property owners and frustrated developers and designers, accompanied by the groans of officials reluctant to become arbiters of taste. Yet, without some recognition of the desirability of good design, a community may experience a decline in its visual character, and, consequently, a decline in property values and the community's ability to attract commerce and industry, including tourists. Conversely, community standards for good design can encourage investment—when owners in a historic district, for example, are assured by regulations that their investments in their homes will not be undermined by inappropriate changes next door or down the street.

Design guidelines can illustrate what acceptable development in the community should look like, and they can be published by citizens' groups or governmental bodies without the need for state enabling legislation. Such a publication can encourage voluntary efforts to design new buildings and development, or alterations to old buildings, to be compatible with the existing site and surroundings. Whatcom County, Washington, for example, has a set of voluntary design guidelines for incorporating new agricultural structures into the historic dairy complexes and landscape of the Nooksack River valley (Carlson and Durrant 1985). Hanalei, Hawaii, created voluntary design guidelines based on the principles in the Secretary of the Interior's Standards for Rehabilitation (see Sidebar 4.15), as part of a project that also included a cultural landscape survey and a cultural resources management plan. The guidelines influenced the design of compatible replacement structures built after Hurricane Iniki in 1994.[15]

Design controls go a step further, by requiring compliance with design guidelines, and they must be permitted by state enabling legislation. Such controls are generally overseen by design review boards. The historic district commission in Nantucket, Massachusetts, reviews and approves all new construction on the entire island. Its design guidelines, first published in 1978, take into account both historic styles and a sensitivity to the landscape (Lang and Stout 1996).

Developing design guidelines requires sensitivity to economic realities. Where agriculture is a business, guidelines should acknowledge the necessity of new building types and landscape changes. Guidelines should also recognize the desirability of new design, rather than rigid imitations of historic styles, in enhancing the landscape and community character.

It requires skill to create guidelines general enough to cover most circumstances that may arise and yet specific enough to protect the community's special resources and unique character. Guidelines for rural communities should not only address the aesthetics of new buildings or their compatibility within the existing built environment but should also include guidance for site selection and the way a proposed site is to be developed. Other factors to consider include patterns of land use, access, and circulation, location of the building(s) on the parcel, utility placement, vegetation, and open space.

Most communities should seek professional assistance in developing design guidelines, but residents should participate as well. Rather than relying solely on individual opinions—professional or not—it may be best to use the most attractive portions of the community itself as the templates for the guidelines. What would it take in the way of standards to replicate a particularly scenic road or an attractive group of houses? Design professionals can help the community identify the different ele-

4.54 & 4.55
Corporate franchise buildings do not all have to look alike. For example, Burger King is one of a number of fast-food restaurant chains that have adapted building design to conform with local architectural styles or to satisfy local design guidelines. Illustrating this are two new buildings constructed by Burger King, one in Cathedral City, California *(top)* and the other in Chesterfield Courthouse, Virginia *(bottom)*.

ments and underlying patterns that gave such places their current appearance and can provide modern translations that encourage new development that is sensitive to its context.

Claiborne County, Mississippi: Putting Rural Historic Preservation into Practice

South of Vicksburg and north of Natchez—renowned destinations for tourists interested in Civil War history and antebellum traditions—and bordered on the east by the historic Natchez Trace, Claiborne County sits on the high bluffs of the Mississippi River along Mississippi's historic and scenic Highway 61. Just outside Port Gibson, the county seat (pop. 1,800), lies one of the South's most famous icons, the Ruins of Windsor—twenty-three stone columns of one of the largest plantations ever built, which survived the Civil War only to burn at the end of the nineteenth century. The county has begun the process of capitalizing on its historic resources through protection and tourism.

Port Gibson itself is Mississippi's third oldest town. General Grant is said to have called it a "town too beautiful to burn," as he landed his troops there for the siege of Vicksburg. Perhaps thanks to Grant's appreciativeness, a small number of rare antebellum commercial buildings exist along its main street. Most buildings in the town were listed in the National Register in 1979. Today, Port Gibson is home to a Main Street program, begun in 1990 and now combining a core of 180 volunteers, the mayor, and the board of aldermen in an enthusiastic public-private partnership. In its first five years, the program netted five new businesses and thirty-one new jobs and stimulated the renovation of twenty-seven buildings through a low-interest loan and grant program aimed at improving building facades.

The Main Street program also led to the establishment of historic preservation commissions for the county and Port Gibson—to allow them to receive a share of state grants under the federal Certified Local Government (CLG) program. Here is where the story in Claiborne County moves into unfamiliar territory: rural county historic preservation commissions are rare across the nation; in Mississippi, Claiborne's is the only one.

Much of the impetus for creating the Claiborne commission comes from the county's interest in tourism. With one of the highest unemployment rates in Mississippi, the county is intensely interested in economic development. "The question," says county administrator James E. Miller, "was, how could we carve out our little niche to capture all the people traveling down Route 61? In most rural communities, most people have not thought of tourism as economic development. . . . In Claiborne County, we decided to try to preserve some of our unique assets for tourism—our scenic byways, our rich African American heritage, our European heritage, the antebellum history everyone already knows. We want to mesh all these together." The county wanted to create a fresh approach to marketing its heritage.

At about the same time, timbering threatened one of the county's premier historic resources, Shaifer Road, which General Grant's troops are thought to have followed on their way north toward Vicksburg. The narrow road, known regionally as a "sunken trace," lies deep within steep banks and is shadowed by tall trees laden with Spanish moss. "It gives you a very eery kind of feeling if you're there late at night," says Miller. John Hopkins, the county's historic preservation surveyor agrees, adding, "You can tell how old a road is in that region by how deep it is. This one is twenty feet deep, still unpaved—you can't pave a real trace, because the banks will collapse even more—and has to be regraded after every heavy rain. It is awesome to see a tree lying across the road overhead and no one worries about it! You have cliff-swallows in the clay banks, only certain types of vegetation growing in the acidic soil—there's nothing like it anywhere else in the U.S."

Shaifer Road is prized by county residents. So when trees were cut along one

4.56
Shaifer Road, a sunken trace, declared a Mississippi Landmark, loops through western Claiborne County's highly erodible loess soils. The county road maintenance crews and property owners on either side cooperate in maintaining the fragile balance between the roadbed and its steep banks.

stretch by a timber company—endangering the steep banks where tree roots no longer helped to stabilize them—the elected county supervisor from that district led the outcry. Shortly afterward, the board of supervisors passed a resolution and appointed the nine-member Claiborne County Historic Preservation Commission.

Although to qualify under the CLG program the commission by ordinance has project review responsibility, its role has largely been advisory. Members take on special projects—caring for the small abandoned family cemeteries that dot the landscape is one—hold monthly meetings to exchange ideas and information, and act as go-betweens seeking help and contributions from county officials and private supporters. County juvenile offenders have performed their community service clearing some of the graveyards during winter—when snakes and poison ivy are less in evidence.

Resolution of the several threats to Shaifer Road was taken care of through commissioners' conversations with property owners along the road, with the county road crews (to assure that they would not pare back the banks in an effort to reduce the high maintenance the road requires), and with the timber companies, after owners agreed to maintain "no-cut" set-asides. A study of the road by the National Park Service and the Mississippi Department of Archives and History helped to increase the entire community's knowledge of its significance, and in 1996, it was named a Mississippi Landmark.

The commission also applied for funds to update the 1972 county historic resources survey. In the new survey, Hopkins, the surveyor, found that approximately 30 percent of the structures previously surveyed had since been lost to fire or demolition. The county has no zoning ordinance but on the recommendation of the commission has begun to study the possibility of instituting some greater level of project review than is currently afforded by the historic preservation ordinance alone.

In addition to these direct efforts to protect historic resources, the county began working with the state tourism office to develop a message that would boost tourism to Claiborne's benefit, by marketing the African American experience or by capitalizing on eco-tourism through canoe trails and rail-trails. Bicycle tour groups already visit the community, thanks to the Natchez Trace, and Port Gibson has at least two bed-and-breakfasts and a restaurant to serve them. Three rivers and their bayous are navigable by canoes and john-boats. "The bayous are marvelous," says Hopkins. "They have lots of wildlife and waterfowl, and they are very, very different from canoeing down the Battenkill River in Vermont or going out in the marshes in Chesapeake Bay."

Clearly, Claiborne County stands to benefit from tourism; and with its historic preservation commission leading the way, it has begun to put other ideas in place to celebrate and protect the county's heritage. It is still searching for the balance of voluntary preservation and project review suited to its circumstances—a combination that is only improved with the prospect of jobs from tourism and a boost in community pride with the step-by-step accomplishments and celebrations along the way.

Historic District and Historic Site Review

Historic districts and historic site review are well-established techniques that apply elements of design review to protection of significant historic resources. Charleston, South Carolina, passed the first historic district legislation in the United States, in 1931; today there are nearly two thousand cities and counties with locally protected historic districts.

4.14 Certified Local Governments

More than one thousand local governments across the nation now are recognized as "certified local governments" (CLGs), official partners with their State Historic Preservation Officers (SHPOs) and eligible to receive technical assistance, grants, and other benefits.

CLG status is viewed by many historic preservationists and state and federal agencies as recognition of a certain level of achievement in a local preservation program. To receive this recognition under the National Historic Preservation Act and National Park Service regulations, CLGs in all states are required to:

• enact and enforce appropriate ordinances for the designation and protection of historic properties;
• establish and maintain a qualified historic preservation commission;
• maintain a system for identifying historic properties; and

• provide for public participation in the local historic preservation program.

In addition, as agreed with the SHPO, the CLG may perform other delegated functions, such as acting for the SHPO in reviewing federally funded local projects that affect historic properties. Each SHPO has criteria for certifying CLGs, modified from the federal requirements according to the needs of each state, and independently determines grant requirements. Criteria include the kinds of local ordinances that are acceptable and the expertise expected of the members of the local commission. SHPOs are required to provide training to CLGs, which often takes the form of an annual statewide conference.

SHPOs are required to set aside at least 10 percent of their federal allocations for distribution to CLGs.

While in many states this is not a great deal of money, CLGs have been remarkably creative in making these funds go far. CLG grants have provided seed money for historic resources surveys—including cultural landscapes—National Register nominations, design guidelines, restoration and rehabilitation projects, site management plans, low-interest loans for single-family residential rehabilitation, Main Street programs, guidebooks, curriculum development, and much more. For example, the CLG of Torrey, Utah (pop. 122), used a series of small grants to restore its log meetinghouse; and the CLG for Walsh County, North Dakota, supported a multiyear project to identify and preserve early-nineteenth-century ox cart trails made by fur traders.

(See Notes to Sidebars)

A local ordinance protecting a historic district or landmark, unlike the National Register of Historic Places, may require property owners to obtain approval from a review board before taking any action to alter their properties through demolition, exterior alterations, or new construction. For exterior alterations, for example, synthetic sidings or a change in the size of windows may not be permitted in a locally administered district. The federal Secretary of the Interior's Standards for Rehabilitation often form the basis for design review in historic districts (National Park Service et al. 1995, p. 5).

There are historic districts in rural small towns, but few exist in large agricultural areas or unincorporated villages. A good example of one, however, is a historic district in Loudoun County, Virginia. The largest of the county's six districts, the Goose Creek Historic District, includes about ten thousand acres, covering farmland, a village, and many large-lot residences both new and old. A major innovation of the Loudoun County zoning ordinance is that it provides for review of the "relationship of the size, design and siting of any new or reconstructed structure to the landscape of [a] district." The impact of new construction on a historic landscape with substantial open land has not been considered in most such ordinances, perhaps because most are based on urban models.

Another example of a locally designated rural historic district is in

4.15 The Secretary of the Interior's Standards for Rehabilitation

The federal government developed the following standards for evaluating rehabilitation work done on buildings for which owners apply for tax credits (see p. 327). These standards can also be incorporated into local preservation ordinances.

1. The property shall be used for its historic purpose or be placed in a new use that requires minimal change to the defining characteristics of the building and its site and environment.

2. The historic character of a property shall be retained and preserved. The removal of historic materials or alteration of features and spaces that characterize a property shall be avoided.

3. Each property shall be recognized as a physical record of its time, place, and use. Changes that create a false sense of historical development, such as adding conjectural features or architectural elements from other buildings, shall not be undertaken.

4. Most properties change over time; those changes that have acquired historic significance in their own right shall be retained and preserved.

5. Distinctive features, finishes, and construction techniques or examples of craftsmanship that characterize a property shall be preserved.

6. Deteriorated historic features shall be repaired rather than replaced. Where the severity of deterioration requires replacement of a distinctive feature, the new feature shall match the old in design, color, texture, and other visual qualities and, where possible, materials. Replacement of missing features shall be substantiated by documentary, physical, or pictorial evidence.

7. Chemical or physical treatments, such as sandblasting, that cause damage to historic materials shall not be used. The surface cleaning of structures, if appropriate, shall be undertaken using the gentlest means possible.

8. Significant archeological resources affected by a project shall be protected and preserved. If such resources must be disturbed, mitigation measures shall be undertaken.

9. New additions, exterior alterations, or related new construction shall not destroy historic materials that characterize the property. The new work shall be differentiated from the old and shall be compatible with the massing, size, scale, and architectural features to protect the historic integrity of the property and its environment.

10. New additions and adjacent or related new construction shall be undertaken in such a manner that, if removed in the future, the essential form and integrity of the historic property and its environment would be unimpaired.

Birmingham Township, Chester County, Pennsylvania. The district protects the portion of the early-eighteenth-century Birmingham Road that runs through the township and the fields where the Battle of the Brandywine was fought during the Revolutionary War. In addition to the usual historic district review, commercial zoning for the portion of the district covering the village of Dilworthtown is tailored to its historic character. Outside the village, "the rolling open fields along Birmingham Road are as precious to Birmingham Township as the architecture of the district," declares the township's Historic Architectural Review Board. The board's guidelines (technically speaking, design controls, as described earlier), adopted in 1986, state a further focus on site planning, bulk (overall size) of buildings, and landscaping. For example, one landscaping guideline states, "Where existing hedgerows, walls, changes of grade, and overgrowth along road edges presently obscure or screen the view of fields beyond, such screening shall be protected." A certificate of appropriateness is required to remove any tree that "contributes significantly to the character of the landscape."

Birmingham's ordinance includes rough but effective sketches as dos and don'ts for developers and property owners, illustrating road layout, protection of vistas, cluster development, siting of buildings and out-

4.57
This ancient live oak festooned with Spanish moss is found on the Middleton Place plantation, along the Ashley River in South Carolina. The plantation is a National Historic Landmark and is protected by Dorchester County, which requires a special permit for any development which would alter a landmark, or which "by the creation of vibration, air emissions, noise or odor" would adversely affect a landmark, or which would be visible from the landmark up to a distance of 10,000 feet. The ordinance limits development to three stories, or no taller than the top of the surrounding tree canopy (whichever is lower), and regulates removal and planting of trees and other vegetation.

4.58
The historic preservation ordinance for Loudoun County, Virginia, protects not only historic houses but also the farm buildings that have traditionally been a part of the county's landscape.

buildings, and yard edges. Building design guidelines are like those found in many more urban historic districts; they cover building shape, roof design, windows, wall materials, porches, chimneys, and more. For features not expressly covered by the guidelines, the ordinance states a preference for "historical precedents" found first in the district and secondly in Chester County. Buildings built in open fields are encouraged to be low and horizontal "to blend development into the landscape." Subdivision entrance signs are prohibited, to encourage residents to "perceive themselves as residents of the township, not of a particular development."

OTHER TECHNIQUES

It may be helpful at this point to categorize the many powers that local governments can use for rural conservation. So far, we have concentrated on local government regulation of land use for the health, safety, and general welfare (including aesthetic well-being) of the community, a collection of powers often called the "police power." Other powers of local governments can also be used to guide land use. The power to tax, for example, can be used to encourage farmland retention. The power to spend and the power to acquire property are highlighted in the earlier discussion of capital improvements (see p. 165) and are treated in this section as aspects of agricultural districting, a hybrid approach using a variety of governmental powers. A twist to the police power is also discussed: a "hands-off" approach forbidding government hindrance of ordinary farm practices called a "right-to-farm" law.

Taxation

Adjustments in all kinds of taxes can influence the protection of special lands. Real estate taxes are the most obvious kind. Among the oldest of tax policies addressing rural conservation is a real estate tax approach called "preferential taxation." Also known as use-value, restricted-use, deferred or differential taxation, and permitted in various forms in all fifty states, preferential taxation lowers the tax burden on lands that a community wishes to protect from development. Rather than assessing these lands at their full market value, the local government assesses them at "use value." For instance, farmland close to a city might be assessed at the same rate as farmland of comparable quality remote from development pressure, instead of being assessed as land ripe for development. Since high property taxes are among the factors influencing some farmers to sell their land for development, reduction of these taxes may encourage farmers to continue farming or to resist the temptation to sell off portions of their farms. Agriculture, then forestry, are the most frequently designated uses that entitle an owner to preferential tax assessment. Natural, scenic, recreational, and historical resources are named in some states' programs.

In most states, the owner who develops a property that is under preferential assessment must pay a penalty and the back taxes that would have been owed if the preferential assessment had not been in effect. The prospect of paying several thousand dollars in penalties and back taxes is not a significant disincentive to a major development, however. Ironically, preferential assessment lowers the costs of holding land for speculators, who frequently qualify for such programs by arranging for their land to be farmed or otherwise maintained as specified by the program.

Preferential taxation used alone, therefore, is an expensive and inefficient way to achieve open space protection. As part of a package of techniques, however, preferential tax assessment programs can help to preserve undeveloped lands. Some communities have coupled deed restrictions with lower taxation. In California, for example, communities can enter into voluntary restrictive agreements with landowners, who receive lowered taxes in exchange. Perinton, New York, has created a

4.16 Special Purpose Ordinances

Provided the state enabling legislation allows, a local ordinance can be written to protect any resource or deal with almost any problem. Ordinances such as those described here can be passed separately, or they may form subsections of zoning or other ordinances. They may range from very simple, freestanding local regulations aimed at a single problem to sophisticated components of a growth management system. As two observers of rural planning note, "It is not unusual for a small town or rural area to begin with a junk car ordinance, move on to a mobile home ordinance, and end up with a comprehensive plan and zoning ordinance."

Air Pollution. Although air pollution that drifts in from nearby cities or regional industrial areas may be something rural governments can do little about, they can regulate air pollution that originates in the community. Many regulate the burning of trash. A number of communities in Vermont, Colorado, and Montana that are especially susceptible to local pollution because they are in valleys also regulate the use of wood stoves. The Environmental Protection Agency limits allowable air emissions from new stoves.

Forests. Just as locally valued farmland can be protected from nonagricultural development, so can productive forest lands be conserved. Delta County in Michigan's Upper Peninsula, which is more than 80 percent forested, enacted a zoning ordinance in 1976 to protect its timber industry. The ordinance, which implemented a comprehensive plan targeting "forest and related lands," created three forest zones. The prime timber production zone provides for timber growth and harvest almost exclusively. Special permits control

other development, including residences. The other two, less restrictive zones cover general resource production and open space. Maryland and Florida both mandate local ordinances governing the protection of forested lands, primarily for water quality benefits.

Hazardous Wastes. Disposal of locally produced hazardous wastes is an area of potential regulation for the protection of streams, lakes, and underground water supplies. While federal law deals with the worst problems, most households and farms generate small amounts of harmful wastes. Unregulated "small generators" (industries producing about a ton or less of waste annually) and industries that choose onsite disposal of their wastes can also present problems. An ordinance can forbid deposition of hazardous wastes with regularly collected trash, to help prevent contamination of landfills. This regulation can be reinforced by the establishment of special collection days for household hazardous wastes at the local landfill.

An important related area of regulation is the siting and buffering of land uses near operating or closed hazardous waste sites. In California, for example, state law requires a 2,000-foot buffer between a waste site and neighboring land uses. Other communities have regulated truck traffic. The Citizens Clearinghouse for Hazardous Wastes can provide further information.

Mining. For surface mining of coal, sand, gravel, or other mineral substances, state or federal controls on coal mining, blasting, and air quality generally provide some protection to the community (see p. 340), but it is possible to enact further regulations

to deal with the impacts or hazards of such activities. The location of mines, the usefulness of the land after mining, the pace of the mining operations, and the impacts on roads are community concerns that may be addressed, primarily through zoning provisions and enforcement of vehicle codes.

Noise Pollution. Noise pollution is a serious problem in some communities, particularly along major highways and near airports. In some cases it is a mere annoyance; in others, it can cause hearing losses for nearby residents. The level of the problem can be assessed by measuring the noise decibel levels. Data collected in a noise study may provide the basis for controls through a local ordinance, including procedures for predicting the noise impact of new development and requiring appropriate mitigation. Local governments can limit residents' exposure to traffic noise through zoning and subdivision regulations that limit development adjacent to major highways and by requiring vegetative buffers or deep setbacks for any development that does occur. Some communities where the problem has become acute have resorted to the more expensive and sometimes unsightly options of building walls or earthen berms, or requiring that developers install them.

Power Lines and Communications Towers. Some research indicates there may be long-term health risks for people who live in the immediate vicinity of power lines and radio and television transmission towers, which produce nonionizing radiation. Moreover, quite apart from potential health problems, power lines and towers are unattractive. Local governments can limit the impact of these installations by working with utility companies to locate high-voltage power lines away from residential areas and highly visible locations, by controlling the locations of communications towers through planning and zoning, and by steering residential development away from existing installations. Although placing power lines underground can cost several times as much as overhead transmission, some communities, such as Frederick, Maryland, have been successful in requiring utilities to place lines underground. Sometimes utilities can be persuaded to place their lines above railroad or pipeline rights-of-way, thereby reducing their combined impact.

Rivers. In Massachusetts, local river protection bylaws (ordinances) are used to protect fragile riverine areas and to direct development to more appropriate places within communities. These bylaws can mandate no-build zones, or setbacks, together with requirements to maintain vegetated buffer areas within the zone, and can specify allowable uses within the delineated setback. Such local laws can protect streams and rivers from nonpoint source runoff and other pollution problems; if approved by the appropriate state official, the local bylaw's provisions can be the means by which the state's River Protection Act is administered, eliminating duplicative regulations.

Signs. In some communities amending local regulations with language promoting better sign control and fewer billboards may be an inexpensive and simple option for improving the community's appearance, although opposing the politically powerful outdoor advertising industry can be difficult.

Many communities regulate the size, height, number, lighting, and place-ment of signs both on site and off site. Scenic America can provide comprehensive information. More than a thousand local governments now prohibit off-site advertising—commonly known as billboards—and still more control on-site signs. An ordinance may even, after an appropriate period of time called an "amortization period," require the removal of signs that do not meet the regulations but are already in place at the time the ordinance is passed. Hardin County, Kentucky, for example, prohibits all blinking signs, either permanent or temporary, and limits the size of off-site signs to a maximum of three hundred square feet and their overall height to a maximum of twenty-five feet.

Water Pollution. Communities are increasingly addressing the effects of nonpoint source water pollution by mandating erosion controls and, in fewer places, by retaining forest cover or riparian (streamside) vegetation. Few programs, however, have dealt as effectively with the problem of animal wastes as has Rockingham County, Virginia. Rockingham's ordinance, which won a 1991 award from the National Association of Counties, was inspired by both fears of water pollution and growing conflicts over poultry operations between growers and their neighbors. Developed with the participation of the county's growing poultry industry, it established acreage requirements and a range of setbacks, including requirements designed to separate poultry houses from public wells, residential neighborhoods, parks, schools, and churches.

The ordinance is the centerpiece of an aggressive county program to deal with agricultural pollution while supporting agricultural devel-opment; it also has included the creation of more than 700 voluntary nutrient-management plans. (Nutrients in both fertilizer and animal waste cause water pollution; see p. 24.) The plans cover much of the county's farmland and have resulted in a substantial decrease in the amount of fertilizer purchased in the county. The county also warns new homebuyers to understand agriculture in their neighborhood before they buy (the brochure's wry title is "The Sweet Smell of Agriculture") and has established strong agricultural zoning to limit nonagricultural development in the most rural areas of the county. Moreover, in 1995, the county established a voluntary program to investigate pollution complaints against farmers (see p. 101).

Wildlife. Unfortunately, prime wildlife habitat, like prime farmland, is frequently the most desirable land in the community for development, especially in the West, where valued riparian habitat is scarce. Teller County, Colorado, first passed legislation protecting sixteen species of wildlife from the impacts of development in 1984; in 1989, the state's Department of Wildlife created a composite map for the county showing areas where development would have a high, moderate, or low impact on wildlife habitat—to help distinguish the level of review and mitigation that might be required—and produced a guide to habitat protection, "Planning for Wildlife in Teller County." In 1995, the county planning commission initiated legislation to require developers to analyze and plan for the habitat needs of species found in high and moderate impact areas.

(See Notes to Sidebars)

program of voluntary short-term conservation easements tied to a sliding-scale reduction of taxes based on the number of years the easements run. (See agricultural districts, below, for another technique that can be combined with preferential taxation.)

The authority to tax can also serve rural conservation when a high capital gains tax is levied on real estate held for a short term. Vermont has found that a capital gains tax tied to the length of time the land is held helps to protect rural land from short-term speculation. Under Vermont's Land Gains Tax, owners are liable for taxes of up to 80 percent of their profit if they sell property within the first year of ownership. A sliding scale reduces the maximum tax liability to 50 percent the second year and so on downward until there is no penalty after six years of ownership. The law allows long-term farmers to make a profit on their land when they retire but discourages speculators who want to make a quick profit. (A different kind of tax on real estate transactions, the transfer tax, is described on p. 229.)

Wisconsin, Michigan, Minnesota, Oregon, and North Carolina all have versions of state income tax credits for conservation. In Wisconsin, farmers are eligible for a credit on their real property taxes if their land is located in an exclusive farm zone or subject to a land preservation contract. To date, 6.7 million acres are under 7,600 farmland preservation agreements. In Michigan, farmers must grant "farmland development rights agreements" over their land to qualify for the state income tax credit, which applies to property taxes over 7 percent of household income. To date, approximately 4.5 million acres are subject to these agreements. The state will also repay owners for a portion of the property taxes on "designated open space easements" held by the state.[16] In Minnesota, farmers are given a property tax credit of $1.50 per acre for land in exclusive agricultural zones. (The state also reimburses local governments for the portion of their tax receipts reduced because of preferential tax rates for agricultural lands.)[17] In Oregon, property owners who improve fish habitat—for example, by fencing cattle out of streamside lands—receive a state income tax credit for up to 25 percent of the cost of the project, provided the plans are approved by the state.[18] North Carolina offers a state income tax credit of up to 25 percent of the value of donated real property (including easements), capped currently at $25,000.[19]

Agricultural Districts

Sixteen states have enacted provisions for agricultural districts, wherein state and local governments may be limited in their ability to restrict farm practices (as described below), to take farmland by eminent domain or annexation, or to allow the construction of utilities. To participate, farmers sign agreements to keep their land in agriculture for a specific period of years, with the option of renewing. In some states, farmers must be part of an agricultural district to qualify for preferential tax assessment or purchase of development rights (see p. 228 and Case Study 2.1).

The required number of participating farmers, the amount of acreage that must be included, and the duration of time a district will exist vary from state to state. In New York, for example, an owner or owners of at least five hundred acres may apply to form an agricultural district. Public hearings and county and state approval are needed to establish a district. The need for a district is reexamined every eight years. Cooperative Extension Service agents or Natural Resources Conservation Service district conservationists can provide information on a particular state's programs.

Right-to-Farm Laws

Most states have laws addressing the conflicts between farmers and their nonfarm neighbors, generically called right-to-farm laws. In general, these laws seek to protect farmers from nuisance suits by nonfarm neighbors who might object to odors, dust, noise, or other aspects of farming they find unpleasant. The laws also prevent local governments from passing ordinances regulating ordinary farm practices. Not only farms but also food processors and related enterprises may be covered by such laws. Negligent or improper management, water pollution, or impacts on public health and safety generally are excluded from such protections.

DRAFTING AND ADMINISTERING ORDINANCES

In practice, when drafting new regulations, most local governments write variations on ones in place elsewhere. By using existing ordinances as models, a community can avoid the errors and oversights that might result from drafting an original ordinance. "Plagiarism," says one rural planner, "is an asset in planning."[20] Another expert, though, cautions rural communities about this practice: "Do not assume that another community's ordinance is perfect. There are many obsolete and even illegal provisions in existing land use regulations."[21] Moreover, a substantial amount of time may still be needed to eliminate inappropriate provisions and add those that are tailored to a community's own particular circumstances. Both development pressures and environmental conditions vary from place to place (just think of the dry desert of Arizona versus subtropical Florida), and uses that are compatible in one community may be incompatible in another—hog confinements, for example, may or may not have their place.

Since land use regulations have been used in this country for almost eighty years, there are numerous legal precedents. Even so, drafting or amending an ordinance, like creating a written plan, usually requires professional assistance, in this case often from both an attorney experienced in land use law and a member of the planning staff or a planning consultant. The involvement of such professionals helps to ensure that an ordinance will be consistent with the state's enabling legislation and that it will be able to withstand a legal challenge. As is also the case with developing a vision and a plan, the more community involvement there is in writing an ordinance, the more useful and acceptable the product is likely to be. This may be particularly true when a community decides to take greatest advantage of state enabling laws, which few rural communities have done. Cautious elected officials will need information and encouragement from constituents who have learned about the potential for improving local laws.

A common failure among activists who have worked to see a law enacted is to overlook how it is administered. Funds and trained staff or qualified volunteers are needed to assure the benefits of a good law. Conservation leaders should make certain that enforcement is indeed carried out. Since many rural jurisdictions are large and have limited staff, illegal activities may all too easily go unnoticed. In Guilford, Connecticut, seven preservation and conservation organizations—representing approximately 2,500 regular voters—joined forces in 1994 as the Ad Hoc Committee of Seven to see that town regulations and policies were respected by developers and town officials. The committee was formed after two buildings exceeded the size of approved plans and one hundred trees were cut down in a town right-of-way in violation of the town's tree-protection ordinance. The group articulated seven goals and submitted them to the town, asking for a meeting to discuss them. Now the group meets regularly with town officials and employees, and it has enjoyed a series of successes—from amending the building inspection requirement to include certification by a surveyor after the foundation is complete, to rebuilding instead of replacing a 1935 stone bridge. In 1995, the town drew national headlines when it decided to forgo $985,000 in federal and state highway funding to improve a town road leading from the common, because the funding required adherence to standard design requirements that meant clearcutting trees and removing stone walls.[22]

Many ordinances are dependent upon citizen boards, appointed or elected, who review and approve development proposals. These boards include zoning boards, planning commissions, environmental commissions, and design review boards. In most cases, these boards are advisory only; the local governing body must approve their decisions. Obviously, it is important that a community's boards have members who have few vested interests and represent a broad cross-section of the community. Unfortunately, many boards dealing with land use come to be dominated by contractors, real estate agents, large landowners, and others who may profit from development. Rural conservation leaders should select and promote candidates for these boards who will be dedicated in representing the entire community.

Second in importance only to careful selection of board members is their training. Training may be available from the state's community affairs agency, a university, the Cooperative Extension Service, peer groups within the region or state, like the Maryland Citizen Planners Association, or such national organizations as the National Alliance of Preservation Commissions or the Countryside Institute. The American Planning Association also offers education and training sessions, as do its many state and regional chapters, and the Lincoln Institute on Land Policy organizes informative seminars on many topics of interest to citizen planners and local public officials.

CONCLUSION

We have described various techniques that local officials can use to avoid undesirable fiscal, economic, environmental, and social impacts from changes that may loom on your community's horizon and to shape the character and impact of desirable development. Many of these techniques have their limitations, most notably that your next set of elected officials could dismantle them. If your community is like many rural places, however, the problem you face is that of enacting good ordinances in the first place, since few communities currently have more than the bare minimum of land use regulations.

As you embark on the exploration and campaigns ahead, remember that there are no shortcuts. You need plenty of time to build partnerships, enlist residents in public discussion, create approaches unique to your community, and foster additional leaders and followers. And finally, remember that respect for one another's needs and differences, simple listening, and a sense of humor can go a long way in the politics of your community.

5

Voluntary Techniques for
Protecting Property

INTRODUCTION

From governmental action, we turn now to the private sector, where experimentation and creativity have resulted in a healthy ferment of ideas. Private, nonprofit historic preservation organizations have existed in this country since 1853, when the Mount Vernon Ladies' Association was established to save George Washington's home in Virginia. Nonprofit conservancies or land trusts (organizations dedicated to conservation through property ownership and encouragement of private stewardship) have existed since the founding in 1891 of the Trustees of Reservations in Massachusetts. Indeed, in the Trustees of Reservations we have the earliest example of an organization dedicated to both historic preservation and land conservation.

The advent of growth pressures in the decades following World War II, combined with a dawning environmental awareness in the 1960s, spurred growth in the number of local and regional organizations dedicated to protecting special resources. Many were born out of last-minute desperation to save threatened properties—or in a "never again" reaction to irretrievable loss. With that growth came innovations. "Conservation easement," for example, was a term barely known thirty years ago. Now, it is almost a commonplace idea in many urban and rural areas. Bargain sales, limited development, and management agreements are all ideas that have sprung from the kinds of organizations discussed here. And from the handful of nonprofit land trusts that existed prior to 1970 the number has grown to nearly 1,100, having increased at the rate of one per week from 1991 to 1995. As of 1995, these organizations had protected more than 4 million acres of land (Land Trust Alliance 1995, p. vi).

In this chapter we first explore the range of voluntary private techniques for land conservation you can use in working with property owners. One important idea to bear in mind as you read the ideas here is that they all rely on decisions of the property owner, who may have to consider many factors—income, inheritance, taxes, family and business concerns—in making decisions. Satisfying shareholders, in the case of a corporation, or meeting the fiduciary responsibilities of an executor, in the case of an inheritance, may take precedence over conservation considerations. A property owner may wish wholeheartedly to assure that the special qualities of a property are protected forever but may feel unable to do so. Indeed, the reason that a property is worth your interest in the first place is often because a property owner has been a good steward; your task, ultimately, is to help such owners understand all possible options for continuing their stewardship, during their ownership and, if possible, beyond.

Although most of the techniques described in this chapter are more often undertaken by nonprofit organizations, government agencies use them as well. (Therefore, for the sake of convenience, "organization" as it is used in this chapter refers to both private nonprofit organizations and governmental agencies.) Moreover, the techniques described in this chapter can be combined with the local government protection techniques described in Chapter 4. Indeed, the more techniques you can combine—and often, the more partners involved—the more flexible and widely applicable will be your rural conservation program. Cost, permanence, coverage, and the ability to encourage or discourage certain uses are all considerations as you evaluate both governmental regulations and voluntary techniques. While zoning and other land use regulations broadly influence rural conservation, requiring all property owners to adhere to certain standards, they cannot be tailored to specific properties. Private or voluntary agreements with property owners, on the other hand, while allowing you to pay particular attention to the specific resources on any one property and the objectives of the owner, can result in a patchwork approach to land protection, depending on where you find willing owners. Today, government agencies and nonprofit organizations are cooperating more closely than ever to address whole communities, landscapes, watersheds, and ecosystems through comprehensive approaches and combined techniques.

Some techniques described below are on the order of "handshake" agreements; others, such as conservation restrictions, are legally binding. Some are only temporary, while others are perpetual. The costs of implementing and administering these techniques vary considerably. Some involve modest sums of money and little paperwork; others may require you to make substantial expenditures and obtain assistance from accountants and attorneys. The following discussion proceeds from the least binding and most easily implemented techniques to more binding and more complex ones.

5.1 "Bundle of Rights": What a Property Owner Really Owns

The interest in a property held by a property owner is called "fee simple" interest. Land trusts and others working to protect real estate employ techniques deriving from a basic concept in property law: What a property owner really owns is not a single item but a set of interests— like a bundle of sticks. Each stick represents a right associated with the property. Such rights include the rights to farm, to extract minerals, to cut timber, to exclude others, to transfer the property, and to do anything else with the property unless that action is prohibited by law (through zoning or other land use regulations). Like a single stick, an individual right can be separated from the bundle and transferred to another party. For example, an owner can sell to a mining company the right to extract ore or give a neighbor the right to cross a field; easements covering mineral rights and rights-of-way have been used for centuries. In what is commonly called a "conservation easement," an owner can agree not to exercise certain rights, such as the right to build houses on the land, to cut trees along a stream, or to alter the exterior of a historic building.

NOTIFICATION, RECOGNITION, AND NONBINDING AGREEMENTS

The techniques described in this section are often the first steps in protecting special properties. They involve the education of both property owners and—as appropriate—the public about the nature of special resources in the community. Although they lack the financial incentive of a tax deduction, these actions make great sense for conservation-minded owners, who may be interested in having more information about their properties, receiving recognition from the community, or obtaining advice on property management. They may also be the first step in enlisting property owners in voluntarily undertaking other, more binding protection steps.

Notification

Owners who are made aware of important resources on their properties are often willing to protect them once they learn of their existence. A notification program might logically follow a comprehensive resources inventory, but it is separate and distinct from the inventory (described in Chapter 3). The rural conservation organization simply lets the owner of a historic house, natural area, or other property know of its significance and suggests that the resource deserves protection. Notification generally consists of a brief letter describing why the property is significant and a follow-up visit to answer questions. Publicity is not necessary, and indeed may be undesirable. Although entailing no actual agreement, notification can be an important first step in establishing a good relationship with a property owner; this relationship may eventually lead to a permanent commitment to protect a significant resource.

5.1
Evan and Catherine Roberts flank two members of the Fort Collins Historical Society who presented them with a centennial farm award. Originally homesteaded in 1873 by Mr. Roberts's grandfather, the Roberts Ranch now encompasses 20,000 acres.

In some cases there may be a risk that a property owner, upon learning of the existence of a special resource, might seek to destroy it rather than endure the prospect of government regulation; this is a concern especially in the case of endangered species, where destruction of limited habitat or plant populations can spell doom for a species. Archeologists, paleontologists, and geologists are also sometimes cautious about revealing known resources. It is important to consider carefully how, if at all, to approach a property owner who may not be conservation minded. Who should communicate with the property owner, and how, and when? How can the organization anticipate and address the owner's concerns about government regulation, trespass, or other potential impacts? If it is not known how the property owner will react, sharing knowledge about that property, early and personally, may enlist the owner in working to protect the resource—or at the least will forestall complaints about the withholding of information, which can lead to unwelcome controversy. "Why wasn't I told?" is not a quote any conservation organization would want to read in the front page of the local newspaper, since a reputation for not being straightforward can damage relations with other owners and supporters.

Recognition

A recognition program takes notification one step further by announcing publicly that a property is significant. Recognition programs have been used by state and local governments as well as nonprofit organizations. For example, "century farms" programs, established in many states, honor families who have owned and farmed the same property for a hundred years or more.

Recognition programs work because they capitalize on the natural pride of owners, many of whom enjoy being praised publicly for good stewardship of their special properties. Plus, who would want to lose face in the community by harming a resource after having enjoyed such praise? Some organizations present plaques or certificates to owners of recognized properties. The Berks County Conservancy of Pennsylvania sells a hand-painted plaque in the shape of the county, made of cast iron in honor of early iron mining done in the region, to owners of historic buildings designated in the county. The plaque is suitable for affixing to the exterior of a building.

Even though it may not be necessary to ask an owner to agree to list a property in a roster of significant properties that will be publicized, it is wise to do so. Some owners may not want information about their holdings to be publicized; still others may wish to avoid intrusions that such publicity might encourage. Respecting privacy may have greater payoffs in the long run, for both owners and others in the community, than insisting on a complete listing.

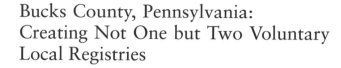

Bucks County, Pennsylvania: Creating Not One but Two Voluntary Local Registries

The nonprofit Heritage Conservancy, headquartered in Doylestown, Pennsylvania, is an example of an organization that is using both a register of historic places and a register of significant natural areas to recognize special resources in Bucks County.

Since 1975, the conservancy has operated a voluntary register of historic places in this predominantly rural county along the Delaware River, with the intention "to identify and promote public awareness of historically or architecturally significant buildings that merit recognition." The conservancy's volunteer Historical Review Board meets quarterly to review applications, which are prepared either by property owners or by the conservancy. Applicants pay a small application fee; about 50 percent are accepted by the program.

Properties in the register are qualified to display an official plaque, sold by the conservancy. Listing in the register can also function as a first step for properties being nominated to the National Register of Historic Places, and it allows them to qualify for county programs under the federal Community Development Block Grant program.

To date, the conservancy's register includes more than 650 houses, barns, bridges, mills, schoolhouses, ruins, and industrial buildings, 100 of which are also listed in the National Register. According to Jeff Marshall, who directs the conservancy's registration program, one of its greatest benefits is that it recognizes buildings that might not be eligible for the National Register and would otherwise go unnoticed. "Our local register is an outstanding way to recognize the preservation efforts for a typical old house. Many have alterations that might not make them appropriate for the National Register, but through this program we can publicly commend people for preserving old structures. In addition, because people have invested time, effort, and money in researching their properties and applying, they take great pride in being accepted into the register."

Despite the success of the historic register program, the conservancy realized a decade after its inception that recognizing historic structures—along with ongoing efforts to protect them through other means—was not enough. Encroaching development also threatened the county's scenic and natural qualities. As a result, in 1988 the conservancy created a register for the county's most important natural areas, called the Register of Significant Natural Areas. To be eligible, an area must meet one or more of the following criteria: it must be an outstanding example of scenic countryside or productive agricultural land, contain significant plant or wildlife habitat, qualify as a critical area for maintaining water quality, or be an important link in the regional greenway system.

Landowners join the natural areas program after being approached by conservancy staff or by contacting the conservancy themselves. Through mailings, the conservancy targets desired properties, such as those that might lie adjacent to a stream that needs protecting. Landowners are also recruited at informal neighborhood gatherings, which are often hosted by register members to help introduce others to the program.

Owners of registered natural properties agree to protect, maintain, and preserve their special features. They also agree to notify the conservancy of outside

5.2
The plaque presented to landowners registering their land with the Heritage Conservancy of Bucks County, Pennsylvania.

threats to the property, such as nearby development, or if they decide to sell the land. In exchange for joining the program, a landowner receives a written report explaining the significance of the property and recommendations for management. In addition, landowners receive a plaque, similar to the historic register's, bearing the owner's name, the name of the natural area, and a photograph of the special feature to be protected (see Fig. 5.2). In order to foster a sense of stewardship and community among the owners of register properties, the conservancy twice a year hosts an awards reception to welcome new register members and to present plaques. All register members are invited to attend the receptions so that they can develop an informal network to deal with future environmental threats to the community.

While owners in the natural areas program are free to cancel their commitment at any time, very few have done so. According to Linda Mead, who directs the program, the only departures have been landowners who have either died or moved out of the area. In most cases, the conservancy has been successful in recruiting the next owners to register.

To date, 120 landowners have taken part in the natural areas register, committing themselves to the stewardship of 4,300 acres of significant natural lands, including eight islands in the Delaware River. The registered parcels range in size from several acres to more than 400 acres.

In registering their properties, landowners take a first step in protecting their land. Those who are interested receive help from the conservancy in moving to the next step: donating a conservation easement. Easements on more than 1,600 acres of land have been donated to the conservancy; many of them started out as listings in the natural areas register.

The conservancy has built its excellent regional reputation through its outreach and services to property owners and partners among both government and nonprofit agencies, evolving in recent years from a county-based effort into an organization that serves the entire Delaware River region. The conservancy also acquires land, conducts environmental education programs, and participates in several regional coalitions addressing quality-of-life issues. In fact, working with other public and private partners and property owners, the conservancy hopes to use the natural areas register as one tool to tackle one of the largest land use challenges in the region, protection of the watershed and improvement of the water quality of the Delaware River.

The historic and natural registers operated by the Heritage Conservancy in Bucks County offer low-cost, low-key, but personalized ways of introducing many property owners and their neighbors to the pleasures and responsibilities of understanding and conserving their properties. That both registers have often led to other forms of protection is an added and very important benefit for both owners and the conservancy.

Nonbinding Agreements

A number of state governments and nonprofit organizations operate nonbinding agreement programs for natural resources, often called registry programs, many in association with recognition programs. Property owners agree in writing to protect specified features of their properties and usually receive in return a plaque or certificate that acknowledges the special nature of the property and the owner's stewardship. The owner's obligation to comply is strictly voluntary; the owner can withdraw from the program at any time with advance notice, typically thirty days. The

5.2 Tax Incentives for Donations of Property

Along with altruism, tax incentives are often a major reason why property owners donate all or part of their property to nonprofit tax-exempt organizations. Federal tax law allows both individuals and corporations to take deductions from their taxable income for gifts of property, including perpetual easements, to certain organizations designated as tax-exempt by the Internal Revenue Service or to a government agency. (The nonprofit organization must be a qualified conservation organization in the case of a gift of an easement—see p. 226.) Individuals may deduct the value of the gift up to a certain percentage of their income and can spread a sizeable deduction over several years. If the gift can be divided into stages, it may be possible to spread deductions over many years. Donating a property can also reduce the value of the donor's estate at the time federal estate taxes must be paid, an increasingly significant factor in recruiting donors, since the average age of large property owners is on the rise. Similar savings may be available in state income and estate taxes.

Consultation with experts is usual for anyone considering seeking a charitable contribution deduction or estate tax reduction for a gift of property, as not every donation of property qualifies. Moreover, the federal government has established specific procedures that donors must follow for appraisals.

Through tax incentives the federal government encourages gifts of property and partial interests in property that are often of significant conservation value to the nation. Since the public forgoes tax receipts it might otherwise collect, the IRS has reasoned that a recipient organization has a responsibility to the nation's taxpayers to assure that the conservation values involved in those gifts will endure.

For a conservation easement to be deductible, it must meet one of several tests for "conservation purpose" (described in section 170[h] of the Internal Revenue Code). Conservation purposes include the preservation of land for outdoor recreation or education, protection of "relatively natural habitat," and preservation of historically significant properties. A conservation purpose is also served if the preservation of open space, including farmland and forest land, creates a "significant public benefit," either for the "scenic enjoyment of the general public" or "pursuant to a clearly delineated federal, state, or local governmental conservation policy." To be deductible for federal income tax purposes, an easement must be perpetual.

agreements are based on mutual trust, pride of ownership, recognition and appreciation of the resource, commitment to conservation, and the feelings of satisfaction that participation brings. The owner receives no financial compensation and no tax benefits. A number of states operate registry programs in association with state natural heritage programs or in collaboration with the Nature Conservancy.

Notification, recognition, and nonbinding agreement programs alone are not enough to insure protection over the long run; but by using these programs initially, a group may enhance its standing in the community, make first contacts with property owners, and enlarge the possibilities for protecting special community assets. As their capability and funds allow, many rural conservation organizations move to more complex, binding agreements with property owners.

TEMPORARY BINDING AGREEMENTS

Temporary binding agreements, which are enforceable, are an approach that falls between nonbinding agreements and acquisition of property or easements. By negotiating contracts with owners which will be in force for a specified period of time, an organization can be confident that certain properties are protected at least for that long. During the period of the contract, the organization has time to work out more permanent protection or raise funds for acquisition.

Management Agreements and Leases

Under a management agreement, a property owner agrees to care for a property in a specified manner for a set period of time, or the owner allows an organization to carry out the management. Sometimes the owner receives compensation for the cost of an activity, such as building a fence to protect an endangered plant or repairing a historic stone wall, that will help protect the property over the long term. Management agreements work well where owners have a tradition of conscientious management or at least a personal commitment to rural conservation. They are also useful in instances where an owner, such as the federal government or a corporation, is unable to lease or sell a property or donate an easement.

Occasionally it may be advantageous to lease a property to protect it from overuse or poor management. Leases entitle the lessee to control the use of a property in return for rent, which may be nominal. An owner may agree in the lease simply to forgo destructive forestry, mining, or other practices that threaten the property, or may agree to allow the lessee actually to use the property for some appropriate purpose.

Agreements Tied to Loans and Grants

Some organizations may wish to provide small sums of money in the form of loans and grants to property owners to encourage conservation activities on their properties. The Amana Preservation Foundation in Iowa, for example, gave a matching grant to the Amana Artists' Guild to reconstruct a historically accurate wooden fence adjacent to its gallery. Other organizations have provided materials for housepainting and other repairs. It may be desirable to ask property owners to agree in writing that any work supported by such means be done in accordance with certain standards and that the property's historical, natural, scenic, or agricultural integrity be maintained for an appropriate length of time.

CASE STUDY 5.2

Blackfoot River, Montana: Protecting a Stream Corridor through Easements

The Blackfoot River in western Montana is one of the state's best trout streams, made even more popular in recent years by the filming of the best-selling 1976 novel by Donald MacLean, *A River Runs through It*. But what many who admire both the book and the stream do not know is that the Blackfoot today en-

5.3
Overuse of the Blackfoot River in Montana by rafters and fishermen, among others, led to a successful cooperative effort by public and private interests to manage recreational access to the river.

joys some of the most complete protection afforded by easements anywhere in the nation. This protection is the result of long-term conservation efforts by far-sighted and dedicated property owners in the valley.

In the late 1960s, landowners became highly conscious of threats to their agricultural and timbering activities as recreational pressures began to mount. The river was beginning to draw not only fishermen but also canoeing and rafting enthusiasts as well, all of whom found their way onto the river despite a lack of public access. "Farmers got tired of getting off their tractors and running down to deal with trespassers," recalls one ranch owner along the river. Fire, vandalism, and livestock harassment were among the problems the owners faced from unwelcome visitors.

Clearly, something had to be done—but proposed federal designation of the river as a Wild and Scenic River and county zoning did not offer satisfactory solutions to the problems of recreational use. Such ideas were also highly controversial among owners accustomed to little regulatory interference with the way

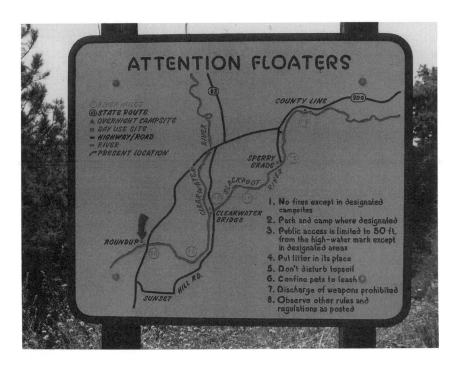

ATTENTION FLOATERS

◎ *RIVER MILES*
⊠ *STATE ROUTE*
▲ *OVERNIGHT CAMPSITE*
▫ *DAY USE SITE*
▬ *HIGHWAY/ROAD*
~ *RIVER*
↗ *PRESENT LOCATION*

COUNTY LINE

SPERRY GRADE

CLEARWATER BRIDGE

ROUNDUP

SUNSET HILL RD.

1. No fires except in designated campsites
2. Park and camp where designated
3. Public access is limited to 50 ft. from the high-water mark except in designated areas
4. Put litter in its place
5. Don't disturb topsoil
6. Confine pets to leash
7. Discharge of weapons prohibited
8. Observe other rules and regulations as posted

5.4
This sign for boaters was installed by the state on privately owned, state-developed access points along Montana's Blackfoot River. The state also provides maintenance and policing.

they used their property. To address the problems along one stretch of the river, the landowners—a combination of ranchers, the state, the University of Montana, and a timber company—banded together with representatives of the county, the state, and recreational groups in a search for answers. The first step was to find technical assistance, which they obtained from Jerry Stokes, a planner in the Denver office of the former federal Bureau of Outdoor Recreation (similar assistance is now available from the Rivers, Trails, and Conservation Assistance Program of the National Park Service). A long-time observer of the project credits his "deft community organizing" with being a key to the success of what now can be called the first phase of work on the Blackfoot.

What ultimately emerged from the discussions was the realization that dealing with the problems of recreational use and achieving long-term protection of the river could be done separately. This understanding is the basis of a model program that, with local adaptations, could protect and enhance the corridors of trails and scenic roads as well as rivers in many other places.

To deal with the pressures of recreational use of the river, the landowners worked with the state to create a recreation management plan based on voluntary short-term agreements. In these agreements, landowners dedicated land along the river for public access points that were developed and maintained by the state. The state also provided a river manager to patrol the area. While the provision of public access and the river manager might have been sufficient to deal with the problems created by recreational use, the state considered that its investment for recreation required long-term assurances that the quality of the river would be maintained—the purpose of the conservation easements.

A number of roadblocks to the use of easements existed, however. First, landowners had to be educated as to what conservation easements were and how they worked. Second, until a concerted effort by interested landowners resulted in passage in 1975 of state legislation permitting use of easements, their legality was open to question. Third, each landowner's decision to contribute an easement was highly individual and likely in some cases to take a long time to complete.

The recreation management plan covered more than 30 miles of the river; however, easements were sought first only for a 10-mile pilot segment. Each easement was tailored to the property in question. Many have special provisions for the land immediately adjacent to the river, such as restrictions on development, to complement the recreational use. Back from the river the restrictions are less stringent (for a related idea, see Sidebar 5.3). Today, virtually all of the first 10-mile segment is under easement, and all but one easement has been donated to the Nature Conservancy. In 1985, the goal was expanded to protecting many more miles of the river, particularly in the Ovando Valley section upstream of the recreational area. Recent biological studies in the valley revealed that unique wetland habitat is present, owing to the glacial geology, and the Fish and Wildlife Service has purchased easements on 45,000 acres there. The relationships generated in the process have also helped create an umbrella group, the Blackfoot Challenge. This group acts as a forum for public and private organizations—local, state, and national—and the valley's private property owners to enhance their cooperation in addressing the land stewardship issues that remain unresolved by the easement program (see p. 105).

ACQUISITION OF CONSERVATION EASEMENTS

A conservation or preservation easement is a voluntary agreement between a property owner and the holder of the easement concerning treatment of the property by current and future owners. Such an agreement allows a property owner to continue owning and using a property while assuring its protection. The property can still be sold, rented, mortgaged, bequeathed, or otherwise transferred.[1] The easement "runs with the land" (that is, continues to affect the title) regardless of ownership.

An easement is an entirely different tool from owning property outright or from such governmental regulation as zoning. From the point of view of a rural conservation organization, ownership might offer greater control and public access, but it imposes considerable management costs. In the case of an easement, such costs generally remain the responsibility of the owner, who continues to enjoy the property. Zoning and most other government regulations cannot be tailored to protect specific aspects of a property, and they are likely to change over time. While it is theoretically possible under certain circumstances to amend an easement to address issues that arise over time, it is generally perpetual, and its protections are not subject to changing political conditions.

Easements can protect land, buildings, or both. Although an easement may be called a scenic, open-space, conservation, agricultural, facade, or historic preservation easement, the name has more to do with the kind of property it protects than the way it works. Easements have been used extensively across the United States, to protect buildings and their settings in rural villages such as Waterford, Virginia (see Case Study 8.3) and Harrisville, New Hampshire (see Figure 1.9); scenic rural areas such as Jackson Hole, Wyoming, the Great River Road in Wisconsin, and the Big Sur coastline in California (see Case Study 5.7); and farmland in such places as King County, Washington, and Carroll County, Maryland (see Case Study 4.2). Easements have also been used to protect such other sensitive environmental resources as watersheds, marshes, unique geological formations, and habitats for endangered species.

As legal instruments, easements date to the dawn of English common law, but their use to protect natural and cultural resources is relatively new. The first conservation easement in the United States was granted late in the nineteenth century. Such easements have become widespread since the early 1960s, when the IRS declared that donors of easements could deduct the value of the gift when calculating their income taxes.

Technically, an easement is a legally enforceable interest created by the transfer of some of the rights in the property and is recorded in local land records. A conservation easement may legally be termed a "conservation restriction" in most states; in casual conversation, it may also be called a deed restriction.[2]

Conservation easements can be either purchased or acquired by donation. In most cases, nonprofit organizations obtain easements as donations and government agencies typically purchase them, although there is nothing that precludes the reverse. Pennsylvania has a grants program for conservation organizations enabling them to purchase easements, and both the Big Sur Land Trust and the Marin Agricultural Land Trust purchase easements (usually with funds from state or local government).

The value of an easement for tax purposes is usually the difference in the value of the property before and after the grant of the easement. The amount of reduction in value caused by an easement depends on the nature of the property involved and the terms in that specific easement. (While easements generally reduce property values, this is not always so; in the case of luxury real estate that includes a residence, an easement may have no effect on the property's value.) In addition to its potential for reducing a donor's federal and state income and estate taxes, depending on the donor's financial situation, a perpetual easement may reduce an owner's local property taxes. This varies from state to state and from one locality to another and can depend on the practice of individual assessors. Where property taxes are already based on less than 100 percent of fair market value, or if the property has not been assessed for some time in an area of rising property values, the savings may not be worth the owner's trouble in pursuing a reduction in property taxes. Local taxation is a sensitive issue, with both local governments and property owners feeling hard pressed. Maryland has a program to compensate local governments for a portion of property tax reductions caused by easements.

Drafting an Easement

An attractive feature of an easement is that it can recognize the special qualities of a single property, as well as the particular needs of an individual property owner and the standards established by the holding organization. Typically, the easement document is jointly produced by the owner and the organization and their respective legal advisors, through negotiation and review; the owner usually pays for such associated costs as surveying, photography, and appraisal, all of which are generally tax deductible.

An easement document usually begins with a statement of purpose and proceeds to state what the owner may not do with the property. Generally speaking anything not prohibited remains among the owner's

5.3 Riparian Easements

The Valley Conservation Council in Virginia's Shenandoah Valley has pioneered the use of conservation easements in combination with management agreements to protect streamside, or riparian, areas. As in most watersheds across the nation, the land along hundreds of miles of streams in the Shenandoah Valley is under private ownership, and this land is key to improving not only water quality but other environmental values in the valley. The advantages of this protective approach are that it targets some of the most sensitive lands on a given property, requires the restriction of only a small portion of most properties, specifies good management practices (more than simply preventing development), and permits owners to receive state and federal income tax deductions.

Working with the Virginia Outdoors Foundation and local soil and water conservation districts, the council encourages property owners to establish either permanent or temporary easements covering riparian areas. Under the easement, the owner delineates and agrees not to harm the buffer zone closest to the stream and develops a management plan in cooperation with the easement holder and other agencies to ensure its protection. Such plans usually include limits on livestock access to the stream and guidelines for establishing and maintaining vegetation in the buffer zone. The Natural Resources Conservation Service and state agencies may also share the costs of such conservation steps as tree planting or developing an alternative water source for livestock.

In Augusta County, working with the Headwaters Soil and Water Conservation District, the owners of a

rights. The document also grants the organization the right to inspect the property to assure observance of the easement's terms. It may also provide for enforcement procedures such as binding arbitration. Litigation to enforce an easement, of course, is always an option. The easement boundaries are usually documented by a survey, after agreement on what historical, visual, natural, political, and other factors will be considered, and then are set forth in the document. All areas to be covered by the easement, and their condition, should be documented in a comprehensive inventory that includes maps and photographs and is "incorporated by reference" into the easement document. Such attachments are legal support for the terms of the easement and may be more easily altered (to account for changes caused by a storm, for example) than the deed of easement itself. This documentation is helpful if disputes arise later.

Conservation easements typically limit earthmoving, dumping, signs, utility lines, subdivision, construction, significant changes to existing structures, and the uses that may be made of the property. Commercial use of a residence may be prohibited, for example. Public access can be specifically granted by the owner, to allow such activities as hiking or fishing, but many owners prefer to maintain their privacy or choose to grant such access by separate agreement. Frequently, an organization will agree to allow an owner to reserve the right to build on a particular site or to sell off a specified portion of the property for development, where such provisions pose little risk to the resources being protected.

Who Holds an Easement

Both nonprofit conservation organizations and government at the local, state, and national levels can hold the kinds of easements discussed here. Federal tax regulations governing deductibility of donated easements require that the holder "have a commitment to protect the conservation purposes of the donation, and have the resources to enforce the restrictions."

An organization need not hold an easement in order to encourage an owner to grant them; other entities may possess better resources for seeing that the easement remains viable. The Waterford Foundation in Virginia, for example, has been responsible for the acquisition of more than sixty historic and scenic easements, but does not hold them. Instead, they are held by either the National Trust for Historic Preservation or one of two state agencies, the Virginia Division of Historic Landmarks and the Virginia Outdoors Foundation.

Because easements are usually perpetual, an organization should accept no easements unless there is a high degree of probability that the organization will exist for many years. Even so, the easement document should specify one or more other organizations to act as successors to the holding organization. In addition to serving as an actual successor if needed, such an organization might provide legal support in the event of any problems. If successors are not specified and the holding organization ceases to exist, a superior court judge or the state's attorney general will designate the next holder. An alternative to specifying a successor is to state that the organization holding the easement has the right to appoint an appropriate successor. In some cases, an organization may invite another organization to act as a co-holder. The Maryland Historical Trust and the Maryland Environmental Trust, for example, have jointly accepted easements over large estates with historic buildings. Each organization contributes its particular expertise in overseeing the terms of the easements: the historical trust for buildings and the environmental trust for land. The Maryland Environmental Trust also holds easements jointly with local land trusts; again, each confers unique benefits on the arrangement.

By accepting an easement, an organization accepts a continuing responsibility to ensure that easement provisions are observed. This requires periodic monitoring and communication to remind the property owner, especially a subsequent owner, of the easement's provisions. Monitoring is carried out by either on-site or aerial inspection, usually once a year. The Society for the Protection of New Hampshire Forests, for example, annually photographs from the air each of its properties under easement. Organizations should be sure they have the financial resources to monitor and enforce easements before taking them on. Upon creation of the easement, most nonprofit organizations request from the easement donor a cash donation, which is tax deductible; the money is deposited into a fund that supports the costs of monitoring the easement and potentially defending its validity in court.

Purchase of Easements

Some communities and states have embraced the idea that purchasing conservation easements is better than purchasing the property, even though buying them can sometimes be almost as expensive as buying the land outright. This is because it is often more cost effective to extinguish development rights than to pay for the roads, schools, and other services required by new residents if the land is subdivided and developed for housing. This is true of most open land far from other development, but

5.5-acre property abutting the Middle River placed 4.18 acres under permanent easement. The difference between the value of the riparian acreage before and after the easement was appraised at $1,800 per acre. Because they had recently had the property surveyed, the owners were able to use existing survey markers to delineate the area of the easement. Thus, the cost of creating the easement was only $600, for appraisal and legal and recording fees; had the owners not wished to take a charitable contribution deduction under the federal tax code, requiring the appraisal, this cost would have been even less. The owners agreed to maintain fencing and to "implement sound practices of soil, water, timber, and wildlife resource management." They also agreed not to build in the buffer zone closest to the river, although they reserved the right to construct a picnic shelter.

(See Notes to Sidebars.)

5.5
An easement held jointly by the Maryland Historical Trust and the Maryland Environmental Trust protects Lloyd's Landing in Talbot County, Maryland. The easement protects more than 1,100 acres of the Eastern Shore of Maryland as well as the early-eighteenth-century residence.

5.4 Are They Development Rights, or Are They Conservation Easements?

Nomenclature has always been something of a problem in the conservation easement business. Conservation easements have often been referred to as development rights, but recognition of the difference between development rights and conservation easements and the general preference for the term "conservation easement" indicate a growing realization that preventing development is but one task of an easement. As significant as developments like houses and roads can be in altering the natural environment, these are only some of the potentially harmful land uses that easements can prevent or mitigate. The long-term task of land stewardship, of maintaining or restoring the land's natural values, agricultural productivity, or other important characteristics, must also be addressed. The easement process is an especially flexible way to work with a property owner from the beginning to specify what the owner will do (or not do) to enhance and protect such things as wildlife habitat or water quality. Sometimes these steps are specified in a management plan, developed at the same time as the easement and referenced as a separate document, and sometimes they are addressed in the easement document itself.

Calling easements development rights can hamper easement negotiations, as the Adirondack Chapter of the Nature Conservancy learned. The conservancy joined with a timber corporation to protect land that includes former subsurface graphite mine workings now providing important habitat for an endangered species of bat. The conservancy's primary goal in undertaking the project was to prevent the timber operation from blasting shut the holes in the ground as timber was removed, which the company would ordinarily do for safety reasons. The conservancy and the corporation bought the property in partnership and then divided their interest by transferring an easement to the conservancy, to protect the bat, and ownership to the corporation. In defining the terms of the easement after the purchase, it quickly became apparent that the easement had to address much more than development rights; the corporation had thought that development rights were the only conditions involved. Tom Duffus of the conservancy recalls that "negotiating the conservation easement was a long education process":

The semantics problem got us off on the wrong foot. Key to the negotiations was crafting a conservation easement that dealt with all the potential conflicts between timber management on the surface and protecting the bat hibernaculum below. This required both sides to recognize that the easement by its very purpose had to deal with where roads would be built, how many trees would be retained around the holes in the ground, what they were going to do with water diversion—these provisions had nothing to do with development rights. You should think of an easement as a land plan for your property, put in writing and recorded in the county clerk's office. It specifies do's and don't's, mostly don't's, but the do's are also important. A well-written easement will address all land uses that are bad for the property. Simply thinking of an easement as "development rights" doesn't imply the larger potential in a conservation easement for a more holistic approach to deal with management of the land by the landowner.

(See Notes to Sidebars.)

---

the reasoning is most often applied in the case of farmland, where purchasing easements not only prevents inappropriate development but also helps to make the regional agricultural economy more secure. Under such a program to purchase easements, the land is protected, but the public bears no cost of maintenance and the land remains on the tax rolls and in productive use.

Purchase of easements is frequently referred to as "purchase of development rights" (PDR), as this phrase is thought by some to be more descriptive of a conservation easement's public purpose. A more precise term when farmland is involved is "purchase of agricultural conservation easements," or "PACE" (see Sidebar 5.4; for examples of programs to purchase easements, see Case Studies 2.1, 4.1, and 4.2).

5.5 Land Banking for Conservation

In 1984, acting on new state enabling legislation allowing Nantucket, Massachusetts, to purchase open lands with a dedicated fund raised through transfer fees (a fee paid at the time real estate changes hands), the town (pop. 6,421), created a program called land banking. Such a funding source can yield millions of dollars, even when the fee rate is set as low as 1 or 2 percent of the value of the property transferred, and creates funding out of the very reason such a program is needed: a booming real estate market. A transfer fee may be more popular with the taxpaying public than other kinds of fees or taxes, since individuals feel the bite only when they buy property.

Many public land acquisition programs are operated through capital-budget programming that allows for the purchase of specific properties. These acquisitions are typically financed through general-obligation bonds, which rely on the general income of a jurisdiction to pay back the debt, rather than on a dedicated source like transfer fees. The name

"land banking" comes from the idea, introduced in the 1970s, of a jurisdiction's establishing a revolving fund to buy land on an ongoing basis for timed release into the market for development as industrial or commercial sites. Like this concept, Nantucket's program is ongoing, but it results in the permanent retirement of open space (unless resale is approved by vote of the state legislature).

By 1995, the program in Nantucket had acquired more than 1,335 acres, or approximately 3.5 percent of the island, as permanent open space, a third of that at prices below market value. In the island's busy real estate market, property valued at $193 million changed hands in 1994. Thus, even with the transfer fee pegged at only 2 percent, the Land Bank Commission enjoys a healthy cash flow, which is used in part to acquire property and in part to retire the debt on more than $17 million in bonds issued to provide up-front financing for land purchases.

The commission has a broad range of tools at its disposal and has ac-

quired properties in fee simple and less-than-fee interests. The commission generally has preferred to buy land outright, in many cases to increase public access to open space, but it has also received four conservation easements as gifts, covering 150 acres. In addition the commission has received gifts of both cash and land, a continuing indication of the public support it received at its inception, when the town meeting voted 446 to 1 to establish the Nantucket Land Bank Act.

From Nantucket, the idea of land banking has spread to Martha's Vineyard, Massachusetts, to Block Island and Little Compton, Rhode Island, and to Hilton Head, South Carolina. The state of Washington adopted statewide enabling legislation in 1989 that allows the establishment of local land banks, and San Juan County—on an island located off the coast—has taken advantage of the new law.

(See Notes to Sidebars.)

Purchase of agricultural conservation easements is generally undertaken by local and state governments, which can issue bonds or levy taxes to obtain the necessary, usually large, amounts of funding. To date, a number of states and fifty-two counties have conservation easement programs to protect farmland. Connecticut, Delaware, Maryland, Massachusetts, Michigan, New Jersey, Pennsylvania, and Vermont have active programs; Kentucky, Maine, New Hampshire, and Rhode Island have programs on the books but lack funding.[3]

A drawback to public programs for the purchase of agricultural conservation easements is that, despite large amounts of public funds being devoted to the effort, the desire of farmers to participate far exceeds available funding. To address this problem, Howard and Harford counties in Maryland use an innovative installment purchase approach (see p. 234) that can double their limited funds, allowing them to buy more easements sooner. The twice-yearly installment payments to participating farmers consist largely of interest on the purchase price (the principal),

Bandon, Oregon:
A National Nonprofit Organization Does a
Good Turn

Bandon, Oregon (pop. 2,251), a small town and scenic harbor bordered by fir trees at the mouth of the Coquille River, was a thriving port at the turn of the century. Sailing ships, riverboats, and sternwheelers docked at the back doors of riverside businesses. The Coquille provides habitat for salmon, seals, and many bird species; Bandon's cranberry bogs have brought it the title Cranberry Capital of Oregon. When the U.S. Coast Guard decided to cease operating its historic station there, Bandon developed a creative way to acquire it, involving other publicly owned land in the community and the patient intercession of a national nonprofit organization.

Working with the Bandon Port Authority, the Trust for Public Land (TPL) undertook to save the station—a project that required six years. When the port authority told the federal government of its desire to purchase the station, it learned that the property was to revert to forty heirs of the original owner. Now, the port authority owned land across the bay from Bandon—289 acres of a salt marsh that biologists consider the second most productive in Oregon— and that property became the key to a "moneyless" transaction that secured the Coast Guard station for the port authority. Here is how it worked: (1) The port transferred the marshland to TPL; (2) TPL sold the marshland to the U.S. Fish and Wildlife Service, which will protect it in perpetuity; (3) from the proceeds of the sale, TPL paid off the forty heirs to the station; (4) TPL then transferred the station and $20,000 for its renovation to the port authority. The station today houses an apartment for the port manager, a shop, an art gallery, and a historical museum.

5.6
A view of the Bandon, Oregon, waterfront. Across the bay is a salt marsh protected by a deal among the Bandon Port Authority, the Trust for Public Land, and the U.S. Fish and Wildlife Service.

with promise of a lump sum ("balloon") payment of the remaining principal at the end of thirty years. The counties fund the balloon payments by purchasing, at a deep discount, U.S. government bonds that mature to the amount of the principal. Arrangements can be made for farmers to sell their entire interest to secondary parties if they wish to obtain full payment earlier. Farmers are willing to sell their easements for less than fair market value because taxes on their capital gains are deferred until receipt of the balloon payment, and the interest payments made by the counties are tax free.[4]

ACQUISITION OF UNDIVIDED INTERESTS IN LAND

The acquisition of an undivided interest in a property, or a percentage of ownership, gives an organization a legal interest in it, as opposed to sole ownership either of the entire property or a specific part of it. For instance, two siblings who each inherit a 50 percent undivided interest in a family farm both have the right to use the property and to divide its income between them. Each must share in the costs of operation and agree on its management and disposition. By acquiring an undivided interest, an organization may use its influence as a co-owner to insure that a property is managed properly, or even to negotiate a sale to a sympathetic buyer in a situation where multiple owners, often heirs, cannot agree on its disposition. The Vermont Land Trust received an 85 percent undivided interest in a 243-acre tract when the owners, for tax reasons, wanted to make a gift by the end of a particular year but did not have time to have the necessary surveying done. Later, the trust and the owners agreed to divide the property, with the trust taking title to 216 acres and the owners agreeing to conservation restrictions on the remainder.

OUTRIGHT ACQUISITION OF PROPERTY

In some cases, property deserving protection should be acquired outright. Some communities need additional land for public parks or to connect greenways or recreational trails; in other instances, a property may be of such outstanding ecological or historical importance that it can be adequately protected only through ownership.

An organization may also acquire properties that can be exchanged for land with conservation value. The Guilford Land Trust in Connecticut, for example, exchanged parcels in order to protect an area surrounding a popular trail. A developer had purchased a 9-acre parcel abutting lands owned by the land trust and the state, considering it an ideal site for his own home, but the homesite was visible from the trail. When approached by the land trust about selling, he challenged the trust to find him a comparable property. It took nearly a year, but the trust was able to purchase an 8-acre parcel—drier, with a better exposure, and also abutting land owned by the trust but in a more private location—which proved to be a satisfactory substitute. In making the trade, the developer paid a small cost differential.

Acquiring property, whether by purchase or through donation, is usually an expensive way to protect it. The costs are not limited to acquisition but include insurance, management, and maintenance, unless the property is resold or leased to others who assume these responsibilities. In some states, nonprofit organizations must pay property taxes as well, or, if they do not, there may be local sentiment against removing a property from the tax rolls. In particular, new organizations with limited funds need to be wary of the responsibilities of ownership, even if a property could be acquired as a gift. Many organizations do not accept gifts of property unless they are accompanied by endowments that will ensure adequate maintenance.

One kind of property welcomed by many organizations is "asset properties," which the organization may then sell for funds to support its operations. If worthy of protection, such properties can be placed under a conservation easement before sale. Donors of these properties generally receive a tax deduction based on the appraised value. (For one way nonprofit organizations handle donations of asset properties, see Sidebar 5.9.)

CASE STUDY 5.4

Brattleboro, Vermont: Financing a Purchase with Charitable Creditors

Purchases of property for conservation are typically made with cash, a mortgage, a bank loan secured by other assets held by the purchasing organization, or financing provided by the property owner. There is at least one other possibility, the use of "charitable creditors" (for another, a limited partnership, see p. 239). The Vermont Land Trust employed charitable creditors in combination with limited development to protect the Rhodes Farm in Brattleboro (pop. 12,241), a 144-acre dairy farm with 90 acres of cultivated land, the largest single block in the area. To avoid bankruptcy, the farmer was forced to put the farm up for sale. The trust then stepped in to help the owner avoid sale to a developer.

Thirty-five individuals, many of them neighbors, guaranteed a loan of $245,000 made by a local bank toward the $295,000 asking price. (The remaining $50,000 was in the form of an assumable Farmers Home Administration loan.) A small number of the charitable creditors were designated as a steering committee to advise the land trust on subsequent disposition of the farm. The land trust then sold the open land in three parcels to two other local farmers, reinforcing their farm operations. The farmhouse and barns plus a corner wood lot and a parcel along a ridge, restricted to three residential lots, were sold separately to conservation-minded buyers found by the trust. These sales covered roughly 60 percent of the purchase price plus closing costs and expenses incurred by the land trust. The charitable creditors, plus nineteen more donors who stepped in after the deals were done, donated the rest of the total cost.

Rights of First Refusal and Options

To secure the opportunity to purchase important properties, an organization can seek either a right of first refusal or an option to purchase a property. Neither technique obligates the organization to purchase the property: each simply gives it the first opportunity to buy.

By granting a right of first refusal, a property owner agrees to notify a prospective purchaser that the property is to be offered for sale and to give the purchaser the opportunity to match any bona fide offer, typically within thirty to ninety days. A sympathetic property owner may give this right to an organization or sell it for a nominal sum. A right of first refusal should be legally recorded, which assures that the property cannot be sold unless the holder of the right is notified. Intrafamily transfers often are excluded from the terms of the agreement.

Holding a right of first refusal usually means that the organization will be able to identify the other potential buyer and the buyer's intentions for the property. Rather than exercise its right to buy, the organization might be able to persuade the prospective new owner to agree to one of the other forms of protection discussed in this chapter.

An option to purchase a property usually involves paying a landowner for the guarantee that the landowner will reserve a property at an agreed upon price for a set period of time, typically ninety days to a year—although the Wildlands Conservancy of Pennsylvania has had good success in obtaining options without compensation (see p. 248). An organization can use an option to gain time, either to find a sympathetic buyer or to raise the funds necessary for purchase. Even if an organization is unsure it can afford the purchase price, it might still consider purchasing the option if the option can be transferred to another buyer who is sympathetic to conservation. The Yakima River Greenway Foundation in Washington (see Case Study 8.1) used an option in its first transaction, the acquisition of a 40-acre parcel in the river corridor from which it takes its name. The owner was willing to make an immediate bargain sale, that is, to sell the property for less than its fair market value, which offers the prospect of a tax deduction for the difference (further explained below), but the organization was just getting started and had not yet received recognition of its tax-exempt status from the Internal Revenue Service. The option allowed the organization to publicize its intention to make the purchase in order to identify the necessary funds while waiting for its IRS ruling.

CASE STUDY 5.5

Guilford, Connecticut:
A Right of First Refusal Encourages a Donation

The Guilford Land Trust in Guilford, Connecticut (pop. 20,676), used the concept of a right of first refusal in protecting land that the owner ultimately gave to the land trust. As part of its strategy for protecting a major wetland, the land trust approached the owner of a 54-acre parcel about selling, but he was not interested. However, the land trust did persuade him to sign a letter of intent to sell the property to the organization when he decided to dispose of it. Although a letter of intent is not enforceable (as a recorded right of first refusal is), the land trust was confident that continued contact with the owner would remind him of his obligation. Eight years later, the owner decided to donate the wetland portion of the property to the land trust and sell the high ground to a developer. The land trust was then able to persuade the owner to donate the entire property rather than sell any of it for development, through two gifts of 50 percent undivided interests five years apart (with a codicil in his will for the second gift in the event of his death). This method enabled him to take greatest advantage of the tax incentives for the donation.

Installment Sales and Lease-Purchase Agreements

Outright purchase is not the only way to acquire property; an organization may employ a number of creative techniques and economic incentives that may make acquisition more affordable for the buyer and more attractive to the property owner. For example, an installment sale enables the organization to spread out its expenditure of funds over time and may in some cases enable the seller to distribute any capital gains tax liability over several years. The Laudholm Trust in Maine, for instance, contracted to buy a large parcel in five installments (see Case Study 7.3), and the Big Sur Land Trust in California undertook a purchase with annual payments over ten years (see Case Study 5.7).

Another approach to acquiring property outright is a lease-purchase agreement, whereby the rent under the terms of the lease is applied toward an agreed-upon purchase price. If the leasing organization does not secure the future funding, it can terminate the agreement. Like an option to purchase, a lease-purchase agreement is useful whenever acting quickly without guaranteed funding is necessary. A lease-purchase agreement may be attractive to an owner who is anxious both to sell and to be relieved immediately of the responsibility for maintaining a property. The Yakima River Greenway Foundation used this technique to gain control of a key parcel for a park (see Case Study 8.1).

Bargain Sale

A bargain sale, sometimes called a "donative sale," allows an organization to acquire a property partly as a purchase and partly as a gift by buying property at less than its fair market value (the price a buyer pays a seller on the open market). The seller sets a price below the appraised value of the property and considers the difference to be a gift. The seller may be able to claim a charitable income tax deduction, provided the appraised value of the donation is at least 20 percent of the property's overall value; taxation on capital gains, if any, will also be lower, because the gain will be lower. The seller's compensation, therefore, is potentially in both cash and tax savings.

The Big Sur Land Trust in California used a bargain sale when a scenic 3,040-acre ranch came on the market. With a conservation-minded buyer providing the financing, the trust purchased the land at a bargain—giving the seller a tax deduction—and immediately resold the property to the buyer. Before the second sale, the trust added to the deed stringent restrictions on development, plus a right of first refusal and a provision for access to the land by the University of California for educational and research purposes. The buyer was pleased to be able to protect an important site along a famous part of the California coast and to give the trust a boost in getting established (see Case Study 5.7).

Donation

Nonprofit organizations and local governments sometimes receive gifts of property through a donation or bequest. Organizations offered such gifts should make sure they can afford the responsibility of management before they accept the property, or make sure they can sell it under the terms of the gift. Organizations should encourage potential donors to inform them in advance of their plans for bequests in their wills in order to assure that any gift is appropriate, that any restrictions imposed are acceptable, and to discuss funding for the property's maintenance and operation.

Sometimes an individual wishing to donate a property wants to continue to use it but also wishes not to delay arrangements for its long-term protection following his or her death or the deaths of specified heirs, nor to leave that protection to the terms of his or her will. The technique to accomplish this is called a "donation with a reserved life estate." Provided the property is a personal residence or meets other IRS rules, the donor is eligible to deduct the value of the gift, called a "remainder interest," at the time it is made, although the recipient will not actually take control until the donor or the donor's heirs die. There are at least two complexities to this technique. First, appraisal of such a gift must discount the present value of the gift (the value if the property were donated without the reserved life estate) by a calculation of the value of the property to the donor and any specified heirs during their estimated lifetimes.

5.7
A property given to the San Juan Preservation Trust in Washington is surveyed by Barbara Brown, then a trustee. The trust applied its acquisition criteria in receiving this outstanding 38-acre site, which includes 7,230 feet of waterfront.

5.6 Criteria for Accepting Gifts

The San Juan Preservation Trust is a private, nonprofit tax-exempt organization founded in 1979 by people who were concerned about protecting scenic, agricultural, and ecologically important lands in the San Juan Islands. Given the multiple problems caused there by tourism and population growth, and the extensive amount of land deserving protection, the trust's board of trustees agreed in 1984 to set priorities in promoting land protection. The trust accepts gifts of land and easements under the following guidelines:

1. The area is an important undisturbed natural area, or is adjacent to an important undisturbed natural area, or is adjacent to lands under conservation easements or is adjacent to Trust-owned property.
2. The property has characteristics which should be protected from development, such as scenic open space, views of water, buffer qualities, a good soil composition, or wildlife habitat.
3. The property is visible from public lands, public roads, public parks or from already Trust-protected lands.
4. The property has important historical or current land use activity, such as forestry management, farming, public enjoyment, aquaculture.
5. The protection of the property would enhance the quality of life for the community.

6. If the property is to be accepted for resale for the benefit of the Trust rather than for preservation, the property owner shall be fully informed of that purpose.
7. The owner shall be made aware that the property may be transferred to another qualified recipient.
8. Endowment funding is necessary for the long term defense of all Trust lands. An endowment fund is established for each parcel of land accepted by the Trust. It is expected that the land donor would appreciate and participate in this essential process.

(See Notes to Sidebars.)

And second, since the owner continues to occupy the property, the transaction should include careful attention to the owner's plans for management. The organization has the right to see that the property is kept in the condition expected upon final transfer; the document creating the reserved life estate usually addresses such management issues as insurance, maintenance, new construction, and timbering or farming practices.

LIMITED DEVELOPMENT

Selling land for development, with restrictions to protect special resources, can reduce the cost of acquiring properties while stimulating compatible development, a technique known as limited development. Limited development can be done directly by land trusts, by limited partnerships of private investors, or by property owners. If done by land trusts or partnerships, limited development is often a technique of last resort, when there is not the money for complete protection of a parcel. For property owners, on the other hand, planning and undertaking limited development sale may be an excellent way to gain more cash than from the tax benefits deriving from a simple easement donation, while allowing the continuation of ownership and farming, ranching, or timbering on the bulk of the property.

Vernon, Vermont:
Making Multiple Techniques Fit Together

Techniques for land protection are often used in combination to solve the problems presented by landowners' needs and the peculiarities of particular properties. Here is how it worked in the town of Vernon, Vermont (pop. 2,055).

The owner of a 273-acre dairy farm, reaching retirement age, decided that she could no longer afford to carry the farm's debts. However, she wanted to see the traditional use of the land continued, preferably by selling the farm buildings and the 76 acres of tillable land to the young farming couple already leasing them. She also wanted to remain in her home across the road. The couple, though eager to continue as farmers, could not afford to buy the property at the time she wanted to sell.

The farm owner was fortunate to be living in a community that had previously determined it wanted to preserve its six remaining farms. The town meeting had authorized a farmland protection program and had retained the Vermont Land Trust to work with a committee of townspeople in developing the program. The town also appropriated $50,000 as a revolving fund for projects that could pay their own way. And a project that paid its own way, in the end, is what the land trust was able to create out of a situation others might have thought was hopeless.

The solution, which took a year to negotiate, worked like this: The couple sold a property elsewhere, enabling them to purchase the farm buildings, including a house, and a small amount of land, converting their lease payments to comparable mortgage payments. The town used $40,000 of its revolving fund to purchase 76 acres at less than the appraised value—a bargain sale. The cash from this bargain sale enabled the owner to discharge her debts, and her charitable tax deduction offset her capital gain from selling the buildings. The town then gave the couple an option to purchase the remaining open land within four years for $40,000, which would replenish the town's fund. The couple leased the land from the town in the meantime, partially offsetting the town's temporary loss of property taxes and the loss of interest on its $40,000 and giving the couple time to pay off loans needed to expand their operation. When the four years came to a close, the couple exercised their option, with the town imposing permanent conservation restrictions and retaining a right of first refusal in the event that the couple (or their heirs) decided to sell the farm.

Nonprofit Involvement in Development

In a bargain sale, the Housatonic Valley Association in Connecticut acquired a 37-acre tract, along a tributary of the Housatonic, that had significant scenic and agricultural values and on which a developer could have built fourteen houses. To finance the $90,000 bargain purchase, the association created three residential building lots, plus a lot for a school. One residential lot of 25 acres included 8 acres of waterfront and 16 acres of farmland. The farmland was permanently restricted to agricultural use, enabling the leasing farmer, whose family had farmed the land

5.7 Financing Land Acquisition through Program-Related Investments from Foundations

For special projects or programs that will yield an income or even financial returns over costs, it may be possible to persuade a foundation to make a program-related investment (PRI). Most foundations make regular grants out of income earned from investing their principal. Federal rules governing foundations permit the investment of foundation funds, including principal, in projects related to the foundation's program—hence the name.

In practice, PRIs have evolved from simple loans into the more complicated financial instruments familiar to businesses: lines of credit, loan guarantees, and gap financing (offering coverage when a promised grant or loan from another source will be later than expected and thus enabling a project to go forward on a more timely basis). The rate of interest and other terms may or may not be more favorable than those for commercial loans; the more critical feature of PRIs is that they provide access to capital. Traditional banks are hesitant to lend to unproven applicants, or for complicated or risky projects, or for projects in which the bank's profit is significantly reduced—for instance, small loans that require considerable staff time.

for sixty years, to continue working it. Sales of the lots, which were restricted from further subdivision, brought $142,000, netting the associations's land acquisition fund $32,000 after project costs. A similar project by the Vermont Land Trust is described in Case Study 5.4.

Limited development schemes can be much larger than the Housatonic Valley Association example, provided the land trust has the resources—including a leadership willing to stick its collective neck out. Colorado Open Lands used limited development to protect the spectacular 3,243-acre Evans Ranch 40 miles west of Denver. Virtually surrounded by public lands, the 116-year-old ranch could easily have been sold for development of more than six hundred homesites. Instead, using a loan from a local foundation, Colorado Open Lands purchased the property for $4.5 million. The ranch was divided into six separate ranches, five ranging from 530 to 580 acres, each with a 40-acre designated homesite hidden from view, and a sixth ranch of 280 acres possessing two five-acre homesites, also carefully sited. Easements donated by four buyers of these properties have been transferred by Colorado Open Lands to the American Farmland Trust, complete with an endowment; the smaller site was protected by easement—also held by the American Farmland Trust—prior to its sale, and the sixth parcel is protected by lesser deed restrictions until the owner arranges to donate an easement. The historic ranch headquarters is owned in common by the property owners as an entrance to the property. Despite the generally unfavorable real estate market in Colorado at the time of this project in the 1980s, Colorado Open Lands succeeded in paying back its loan and covering its costs, and the properties have continued to hold their value in resales in the ups and downs of the real estate market in the 1990s.[5]

Limited development is not without its drawbacks, however. "The Natural Lands Trust is very cautious," says Michael Clarke, president of a Pennsylvania-based regional land trust that has been involved in a number of limited development projects. "Limited development can be a very high risk business for land trusts in terms of financial commitments, insufficient staff expertise, and public perception that the land trust is a 'developer' in disguise." The Natural Lands Trust advises owners contemplating development, usually without becoming directly involved; if the property is important and there are no other alternatives, the trust participates directly in limited development, generally as a principal rather than advisor.[6]

Development, even when limited, done directly by a land trust has other disadvantages. First, because a land trust is in business to protect land, it risks credibility in the community if it engages in the very practice many supporters think it should oppose. Neighbors, especially, may become upset at the loss of nearby open space to housing, no matter how attractively it might be designed. Second, limited development works best financially when it results in large private homesites where buyers will pay a premium to live near preserved lands with little, if any, public access. Although the public benefits of protecting a watershed, prime farmland, or a scenic view without physical access for the public may be apparent to some, others may decry the "gentrification" of the countryside and the discouragement of low- or moderate-income housing.

When limited development results in added public parkland or contributes to the ambiance of publicly used recreation areas or trails, such criticism is less likely. And planning for affordable housing can be incorporated into many projects, as it was in the Elk River Valley in Colorado (discussed further below): at a central part of the valley, where a country store now exists, a statement of intent drawn up by property owners calls for the development of well-designed affordable housing, a response to the ranchers' concerns about the ability of employees and family members to find affordable housing in a fully protected valley.[7] Community land trusts (see Sidebar 5.10), which often develop affordable housing, employ a variation of the limited development approach.

To address the technical complexities of limited development, any organization contemplating it should seek not only assistance from experts in land development but counsel from an attorney knowledgeable about tax issues for nonprofit organizations, since part of the financial appeal of limited development is that the organization's tax-exempt status allows it to avoid capital gains taxation.

Limited Partnerships

Given the risks of limited development, many land trusts have elected to refrain from direct land development. An indirect and therefore less risky way—at least financially, although still complex and time-consuming—to use limited development is to encourage conservation-minded partners to undertake the work. The Brandywine Conservancy in Pennsylvania has stimulated the formation of several limited for-profit partnerships to purchase land for conservation purchases where otherwise it would have been sold for development in the area's superheated real estate market. Return of investment capital to partners, whose risk is limited to their investment, may be in the form of cash from sales of the land (typically of large lots subdivided from the original parcel) or in the form of tax savings for the partners from bargain sales or the donations of easements or land. Fee title transfer of the land to investors may also be an option for repaying investors and may work well in the case of neighbors who are attracted to join the partnership out of concern for the fate of land slated for development.[8]

When a key property in the Rochester Gorge came up for sale, the Rondout Valley Land Conservancy of New York helped create the Rochester Gorge Limited Partnership. The 62-acre project resulted in resale within a year, a 25 percent cash return on the partners' investment, plus tax deductions from the donation of conservation easements, and it succeeded in protecting the last stretch of Rochester Creek from second home development.[9]

"Co-housing," a movement to create a new kind of housing development that offers more opportunities for community ties and activities, uses a variation of this idea of a consortium of individual investors. The investors buy and develop land directly rather than operate through a nonprofit community land trust, and their return is ownership of homes in the development, an interest in facilities built in common, and participation in the designing of the overall development.[10]

Relatively few foundations have taken advantage of PRIs, either because of a lack of familiarity with the concept, out of fear of risk, or because it is often difficult for recipients to identify income-producing activities. The New Hampshire Charitable Fund, however, one of the nation's older community foundations, has organized nearly $1 million in permanent revolving loan capital and makes it available to New Hampshire organizations for land protection, historic preservation, and energy conservation, along with loan funds for human services, education, and other purposes.

Many PRIs employed in rural communities involve purchasing land. The Sudbury Foundation, a small private foundation in Sudbury, Massachusetts, provided a line of credit to the Sudbury Valley Trustees to buy land to add to the Great Meadows National Wildlife Refuge. The Tennessee River Gorge Trust used a three-year loan from a local foundation to protect Williams Island at the gateway to the gorge in Chattanooga. After selling the 450-acre island to the state for an archeological preserve, the trust was able to repay the loan. The Gates Foundation made a loan to Colorado Open Lands for its limited development project for Evans Ranch. The loan aided in the purchase of the ranch, and the land trust was able to repay the loan through selective sales of the land (see p. 238).

(See Notes to Sidebars.)

Private Land Planning

In Colorado, limited development is part of the private, collaborative planning done by the owners of nine ranches in the Elk River Valley, a beautiful agricultural valley located eighteen miles northwest of Steamboat Springs, a ski-resort community. The owners—second- or third-generation ranchers, retirees, corporate investors, and managers of a dude ranch—had "disparate economic, conservation, and family objectives," notes Marty Zeller, a consulting planner who began work in the valley at the invitation of the dude ranch owners. Their business had been in operation for twelve years when they realized that their success depended on protecting the working agricultural character of the entire valley and thus the plans of their neighbors. As he started meeting with neighbors, recalls Zeller, he soon discovered that they shared "an amazing amount of consensus," despite their different situations. The result was the Upper Elk River Valley Compact, a statement of principles "about what people believe in and what they want to see happen with regard to conservation and development in the valley," as Zeller describes it. The compact affirms the agricultural character of the valley and calls for the use of conservation easements and a limited amount of carefully sited development to enable property owners to realize their financial objectives over time.

To date, two ranches have donated easements to the American Farmland Trust, and this private planning effort has led to Routt County's decision to create a countywide open space plan.[11] The voluntary approaches listed in the plan include conservation easements, limited development, and the establishment of a technical resource team to advise property owners.[12]

DEVELOPING A VOLUNTARY PROPERTY PROTECTION PROGRAM

The techniques described thus far deal with single properties or clusters of adjacent properties. A conservation organization generally seeks stewardship of multiple nonadjacent properties simultaneously. An overall strategy is key. Otherwise, an organization may wind up on a treadmill of emergency transactions, resulting in a hodgepodge collection of protected parcels that may be valuable only individually. It takes planning to select and pursue the protection of individual properties, like forest ecosystems, cultural landscapes, watersheds, scenic areas, or trails, that are but parts of extensive resources within a community or region.

Knowing what should be protected is an important aspect of developing a property-protection strategy. As one land trust director says, "We won't accept everything that comes along. We're not interested in loading up our inventory with meaningless property."[13] The resources inventory, discussed in Chapter 3, should form the basis of the necessary decisions. Developing a set of general criteria in advance of such decision making can aid the organization in accepting or turning down a gift and in focusing its efforts on encouraging particular owners to donate, sell, or consider some other kind of protection.

5.8 Protecting the Environmental "Goose That Lays the Golden Eggs"

One emerging idea among private initiatives to protect special resources is the community-based nonprofit organization that relies on private fees to support community conservation. The earliest examples have been established in association with large development projects in especially beautiful communities adjacent to significant natural areas—geese generating golden eggs of economic development through land development and tourism.

These communities are places where development and tourism pressures, however, have become great enough to create community concern about losing the very reason development arrived in the first place—the environment. Enhancing, rather than detracting from, such communities' appeal requires special care, and funds. They are also places that attract conscientious, imaginative developers and the significant capital required to create high-end resort developments or entire new communities. The key feature of such projects is that they can generate funds not only to pay profits to investors and provide for maintenance and reinvestment in the site, but also to be reinvested in the area's resources and the community at large.

What are the sources of private funding for conservation? Possibilities include surcharges on hotel rooms, monthly homeowner fees, ski lift or golf course greens fees, and real estate transfer fees. Deed restrictions requiring real estate transfer fees imposed by the developer are an important mechanism to assure a continual flow of funds to designated projects. For example, the Ahmanson Ranch developer in Ventura County, California, has agreed to a fee of between $600 and $1200 (depending on the type of house), to be paid by builders as construction permits are issued. These payments are placed in an endowment to provide a guaranteed source of funds for a local conservation organization associated with the development. (For a discussion of the governmental version of real estate transfer fees, see Sidebar 5.5.)

Conservation benefits from such projects can include managing open space or greenways created within the development (see Sidebar 5.11), purchasing conservation easements on nearby agricultural lands or wildlife habitat, providing affordable housing, initiating energy-efficiency programs, restoring wildlife or fish habitat or degraded streamsides, and conducting ecological research and educational programs.

The Rincon Institute of Arizona (see Sidebar 2.2) is another such organization benefiting from funding derived from development. Approximately half of its budget is connected to the Rocking K Ranch, a 3,500-acre site in the Rincon Valley adjacent to Saguaro National Park, near Tucson. The ranch and the park share a two-mile boundary. Like most national parks, Saguaro controls only part of the ecosystem it represents; given the ranch's extent, inappropriate development could easily affect natural values within the park, by reducing movement of wildlife, inducing suburban impacts (lawn grasses that compete with native plants and dogs that chase wildlife, to name but two), and altering the flow of water in the area.

Instead, development on the site has been designed to protect the sensitive desert ecosystem of the region and includes restoration of the banks of Rincon Creek and its tributaries, degraded by intensive cattle ranching. The developer has donated 2,000 acres to the national park, and the institute manages a further 2,200 acres of land, reserved as open space within the ranch, and conducts ecological research and environmental education programs. As the enormous construction project proceeds to completion following its groundbreaking in 1996, the developer will impose deed restrictions binding all future businesses and homeowners on the ranch to contribute surcharges on hotel rooms, occupancy fees on commercial and retail outlets, monthly homeowner fees, and real estate transfer fees (applying to both initial conveyances and resales) for use by the Rincon Institute.

One drawback to this idea is that a single development must be very large to provide the kind of continual funding or endowment that will support an effective organization over the long term. The idea of voluntary developer fees, however, has also been used by multiple developers to support open-space purchases by the Virgin River Land Preservation Association in Washington County, Utah. In 1995, the Southern Utah Home Builders Association endorsed the land trust's idea of collecting up to $500 per home or lot from developers working in the high-growth area near Zion National Park. To date, six developers have voluntarily committed 2,000 lots to the program.

(See Notes to Sidebars.)

Big Sur, California:
A Land Trust Learns to Seize the Moment

For 75 miles south of the Monterey Bay, California's Highway 1 winds its way between the crashing waves of the Pacific and the lofty peaks of the Santa Lucia range, suspended on the steep hills and cliffs of some of the most spectacular coastal scenery in the world, Big Sur. Named El Sur (the South) by Spanish explorers in the sixteenth century, Big Sur possesses one of the premier scenic drives in the nation, attracting more than three million visitors per year. It is also "a proud, land-loving community," in the words of one reporter. Artists and writers—Ansel Adams, Robinson Jeffers, Nathaniel Owings, and Henry Miller among them—settled there alongside families whose roots reach back through a century or more. It was no surprise that federal ownership to protect this spectacular area was proposed in the mid-1970s, when development along much of the California coast became rampant. But it also was no surprise that such a proposal attracted the fierce (and successful) opposition of property owners deeply attached to their land.

In 1978, the Big Sur Land Trust (BSLT) was formed as a homegrown solution to the long-term problem of protecting Big Sur's magnificent scenery from excessive development. BSLT got off to a running start by finding a conservation-minded buyer for a 3,040-acre ranch that had been on the market for some time (for more on this transaction see p. 234). In the next fifteen years, the land trust protected another 8,000 acres in seventy transactions, was named as a beneficiary in three wills, protecting another 800 acres, and became the beneficiary of five charitable remainder trusts.

The BSLT is in many ways a typical land trust: learning and growing with each transaction, operating in an especially beloved landscape. It does enjoy several advantages, however. Big Sur is nationally significant, and California's Coastal Commission and Monterey County's planning provide a complementary governmental framework for the land trust's activities. Moreover, the state's voters until very recently were willing to provide generous bond funding to support land trust activities in Big Sur and many other places around the state. Perhaps BSLT's greatest advantage, however, is a history of an adventurous board of trustees willing to consider a wide variety of approaches to land protection.

According to Brian Steen, BSLT's executive director, "the board of directors has the confidence to go into a transaction knowing there are risks." For example, in one early transaction, BSLT signed a sales contract to purchase 80 acres of virgin redwoods for $375,000 without the money in hand and with the imminent threat of timbering should the transaction fail. BSLT was able to raise $40,000 in the community toward the purchase and persuaded a foundation owning adjacent land to put up the remainder in exchange for the title, which BSLT transferred with deed restrictions (see Fig. 5.10).

In 1993, BSLT bought the 1,312-acre Point Lobos East Ranch from the three families who shared its ownership. The original western portion of the ranch, donated to the state in 1933, is now the Point Lobos State Reserve, jutting out into the Pacific Ocean to form one arm of Carmel Bay. The purchase of the ranch tripled the size of the reserve and preserved virginal stands of Monterey pine forest and Monterey cypress trees—the cypress grove is one of only two natural occurrences on the planet. The ranch is also home to mountain lions, wild boar, bobcat, deer, red-tailed hawks, and golden eagles. Although conserva-

5.8
Big Sur, California, looking south. Although the U.S. Forest Service owns much land in the Big Sur region, nearly all of the spectacular coastal lands, from the top of the Coast Ridge to the ocean, are privately owned.

tion minded, the owners had assumed for years that they would develop the property. They had joined forces with a developer and obtained certification of their final plan from the Coastal Commission, one of the last steps toward obtaining development permits for their planned destination resort with a conference center and a 240-unit hotel. When the real estate recession hit California, though, the owners and the land trust found a way out of what had seemingly become an intractable obligation. Negotiating the price downward from $26 million to $11.1 million was only one step in a complicated land transaction that could not have been completed without the land trust as a partner.

BSLT agreed to pay the $11.1 million in the form of a mortgage, with the sellers holding the note. BSLT leased the land to the state for management and public access; the state furthermore agreed to buy the land by paying the land trust

A key acquisition, the 437-acre Post Ranch (*foreground*), was made by the Trust for Public Land with assistance from the Big Sur Land Trust. It was then sold to the U.S. Forest Service to protect public access to the Ventana Wilderness in the Los Padres National Forest (*background*).

$1.5 million annually for ten years (a form of purchase known as an installment sale) from a 1990 state bond fund dedicated to buying mountain lion habitat. The land trust would use the money to pay its mortgage obligation—with considerable risk to both balance sheet and reputation in that, if the state were to default, the land trust would be forced either to default on the mortgage or sell some portion of the land to cover it. The promise was particularly risky because the state of California is constitutionally unable to obligate future legislatures—and so BSLT essentially stepped in to guarantee the state's financial performance from year to year. "We were able to do a deal the state couldn't do," comments Zad Leavy, general counsel for the land trust. "And we've had to go to the state legislature every year to make sure that money remains in place," bearing out the reality of the risk the land trust assumed.

In its early days, the organization had to contend with community suspicions that its members were after more than simple satisfaction in seeing land preserved. "People see us doing transactions in millions of dollars and they are intimidated, refusing to believe that BSLT has only a small amount of money in the bank and no other interests in the deal except to preserve key properties," says Steen. "It's partly to do with a lack of understanding of how a nonprofit corporation works—that no financial benefits accrue to the trustees. Also, people don't understand that the trust can make money, as long as the increment is put back into our treasury and used for land preservation."

BSLT's activities are characterized by a strong respect for community and landowner concerns. For example, although BSLT lands provide scenic enjoyment for everyone, BSLT avoids providing physical access to the lands it protects. Such access would create problems of liability and other headaches for the organization and neighboring landowners, who value their privacy in the face of the extensive tourism in the area. To maintain its options, the organization has drawn the line in respecting landowners' wishes, however. It has refused to agree never to transfer private lands to federal ownership—an idea urged on BSLT by a vocal group of property owners who oppose federal involvement in the protection of Big Sur.

BSLT's relations with local government have been excellent. It has helped the Monterey Peninsula Regional Park District purchase numerous parcels to add to its parkland inventory. Moreover, in 1986, when the county developed a land

5.10
The Big Sur Land Trust purchased this tract of virgin redwoods in 1984.

5.11
The Henry Miller Memorial Library, a home housing a collection of the famous author's books and memorabilia, was donated to the Big Sur Land Trust, with a reserved life estate, by local artist Emil White (*left*) in 1981. White, who has since died, is shown with BSLT donor and founding trustee Nancy Hopkins. White's collection is now managed by the BSLT and remains in his home, which is now open to the public.

use plan for Big Sur—required by the Coastal Commission—to protect the scenic views from Highway 1, and enacted a no-build requirement on all land visible from the road, BSLT began a campaign for a state bond act to buy land from owners no longer able to use those portions of their property. In 1988, California voters approved nearly three-quarters of a billion dollars to buy special lands around the state. A full $25 million was set aside to compensate owners in the viewshed, with the Big Sur Land Trust usually acting as the county's "land agent" for owners who wish to sell their land or development rights. Once the funds have been spent the county's plan relies on transfer of development rights to provide relief to property owners in the no-build area.

As it is for other charitable groups, the search for sources of income for

5.9 Charitable Remainder Trusts

A transaction like the acquisition by the Big Sur Land Trust (BSLT) of Point Lobos East Ranch makes just about anything else look simple—including charitable remainder trusts, or CRTs as they are known. Basically, CRTs are a way for an owner of such an asset as land, a building, or an investment (stocks, bonds, or an IRA) to donate the asset to a nonprofit organization, thereby avoiding capital gains and estate taxes and gaining a charitable income tax deduction for the value of the gift. The asset is put into the irrevocable CRT and administered by a trustee (often the beneficiary of the trust), and income from the trust is provided to the donor during the donor's lifetime or for a period of years. The asset may be sold by the nonprofit organization, subject, if appropriate, to

conservation restrictions, and the proceeds invested for greater returns. Upon the donor's death or cessation of the trust, the nonprofit organization receives the assets, or remainder, of the CRT.

This innovative financial instrument is finding its way into increasing use in the land trust community, as land trust staff gain more experience at being part of their supporters' estate and tax planning. One donor couple signed over a residential rental property in Carmel to BSLT for use in a CRT. BSLT is both trustee for and beneficiary of the trust. It sold the property for approximately $267,000—far more than the $50,000 the owners had paid many years before—holding the mortgage. The buyer's mortgage payments

form an income stream that flows through the trust to the couple until their deaths, with the BSLT entitled to a small transaction fee for undertaking the paperwork to operate the trust. The owners avoided capital gains tax on $217,000 (the difference between the sales price and the price originally paid), receive considerably more income than the property had been producing, and gained a charitable tax deduction for the value of the anticipated remainder (that which is estimated to go to the land trust upon their deaths)—all the while supporting the mission of the BSLT.

(See Notes to Sidebars.)

BSLT is never-ending. "The spectacular nature of Big Sur leads people to assume that the area is so affluent that an effort like ours would automatically be a success," says founding board member Roger Newell, who goes on to say it is not so. Even the much needed support from one prominent family has been a liability: "Here again, people falsely assume that because they're involved we've got it made," Newell comments. Steen adds, "Our experience bears out that a land trust needs a broad base of support in order to obtain funds and access to individuals in the community to carry out transactions."

Over the years, BSLT has made a couple of unusual acquisitions, which have helped to build the community support and interest any land trust needs to survive. The Henry Miller Library (see Fig. 5.11) has evolved into a community center for local artists, poets, and writers. The Mitteldorf Preserve in Carmel Valley, home to Monterey County's largest redwood tree, was purchased in 1990 to end logging there. Today, the 1,100-acre preserve is managed by BSLT, which is working to rehabilitate the portions that were logged, and is open by reservation for day hikers.

The BSLT has been opportunistic and entrepreneurial in the best sense of those words. Steen believes land trusts should take calculated risks. "There's always a landowner who's sympathetic, there's frequently a philanthropic interest, and there's always the expertise around the corner—look for it!"

Land Trusts

Land trusts are often established to protect areas of significant natural diversity or to create recreational opportunities, or both. Their work can

5.12
Colorado Open Lands divided scenic Evans Ranch into six smaller ranches. Homesites are set away from meadows and ridge lines.

lead to the protection of wildlife habitat and open space, greenways, rivers, and trail settings; some have engaged in historic preservation or forest or farmland protection as well. The Land Trust Alliance defines land trusts as "local, state, or regional" organizations engaging in "direct land protection" (Land Trust Alliance 1995, p. v). A land trust holds land and other interests in land for the benefit of the public and often undertakes educational, recreational, and scientific activities. As private organizations, land trusts have considerable flexibility in the way they can acquire property, especially in their ability to take risks and to act quickly to buy land before it is sold for development.

Revolving Funds

Revolving funds are used to purchase threatened properties which are then sold to sympathetic buyers who agree to manage, develop, or restore the properties in accordance with deed restrictions. Resale of the properties, either "as is" or with improvements, replenishes the organization's funds and allows the money to be "revolved" to new projects. Tax-exempt status from the IRS enables an organization that is operating a revolving fund to sell conservation properties without being liable for capital gains taxation.

A revolving fund may be either a freestanding organization or a portion of another organization's capital that it uses on a revolving basis. A revolving fund can effectively extend an organization's financial resources and can give it the capability to act quickly in an emergency. Many funds "revolve downward," however, since restricting the rights in a property can reduce its market value to below the price paid for it; this may be less true of open land, where subdivision, if it is an option, can increase the property's value. Revolving funds are most useful when a strong market exists for resale; otherwise, if some properties do not sell quickly, the revolving fund may soon become entirely committed.

Although a wide number of urban historic preservation organizations use revolving funds, there are few rural examples. North Carolina has several, however. The Historic Preservation Fund of Edgecombe County was the first of these, founded in 1983. Its initial project involved a frame

5.10 Community Land Trusts

A small but growing number of organizations with a social thrust have been established which are called community land trusts. Like other land trusts, a community land trust buys property or receives it in the form of gifts; unlike other land trusts, however, a community land trust usually intends to hold in perpetuity the land it acquires and to lease it to individuals who will use it in environmentally and socially responsible ways, often for affordable housing. Or, a community land trust may acquire and sell farmland with restrictions to qualified farmers, structuring the terms to reflect farm cash flow rather than market value. If a community land trust leases property, the terms also reflect its use value and not its market value, thus helping low- and moderate-income residents to afford housing or farmers to afford land. Lessees of housing can make improvements and profit from their equity in those improvements, and many community land trusts assist in financing such improvements. The land trust often receives a right of first refusal to buy the improvements if the lessee moves. Thanks to the establishment of the state-funded Vermont Housing and Conservation Fund and the collaboration among housing and land conservation interests that this program has stimulated, the most numerous examples of rural community land trust projects associated with housing are to be found in Vermont.

The Wisconsin Farmland Conservancy, established in 1988 in reaction to a wave of farm foreclosures after speculative farm prices collapsed in the 1980s, has purchased a number of farms in the central and western parts of the state. It has

house built in 1742 that had to be moved in order to be saved from demolition. The owner of the house and the owner of the land to which it was moved both donated their properties, enabling the fund to recoup its investment and gain additional funding for use in further projects. Funds from that sale, plus grants from a private foundation and the state, enabled the Edgecombe fund to begin negotiations with other owners of neglected rural homes in the county. As a result of local press coverage, many owners have gotten in touch with the fund, seeking an alternative to simply letting the old family homestead tumble down.

In Pennsylvania, the Wildlands Conservancy's revolving fund, the Wildlands Trust Fund, was begun in 1980 (for more about this fund, see p. 90). Although it is a break-even financial arrangement, Tom Kerr, the conservancy's executive director, sees major dividends in publicity for the conservancy's goals and other programs, which include stream protection and restoration projects and an environmental education program in the conservancy's home region, the Lehigh Valley.

The Wildlands Trust Fund was first built up through fund raising for individual projects. To succeed in such fund raising, an organization must have done its homework. "You have to be able to say, 'we have a project, here's a map, here's a photograph'—and you will be amazed by who will come forward to help," says Kerr. As sportsmen's clubs, civic groups, and other supporters saw the success of the Wildlands Trust Fund, they began helping the conservancy to raise funds. To date, more than four hundred such organizations are on the land trust's list of contributors. Key to this level of interest in raising funds is that money contributed in a given county stays in an escrow account for use in that county. The conservancy's work received a big boost in 1990 when an anonymous supporter bequeathed $500,000 to the trust fund.

Now that the program has been in operation for more than fifteen years, the Wildlands Conservancy has so many projects under way that it no longer raises money only for individual projects. It does, however, keep fund raising focused on individual projects to maintain an "in-your-backyard" approach, as Kerr calls it. The program has protected more than 25,000 acres, through more than one hundred separate transactions. Parcel size has ranged from 2 to 4,000 acres. Most parcels are optioned for the Pennsylvania Game Commission; the owners contribute the option and wait for the transaction to be arranged, usually a year later. "The option is then assigned to the Game Commission," explains Kerr. "At closing, we go in with our check for what the Game Commission cannot pay toward the price of the land, and the Game Commission goes home with the title." The conservancy also works with other state and municipal government entities on similar projects.[14]

Public-Private Cooperation

A technique called "pre-acquisition" or "pass-through" involves close cooperation between a nonprofit organization and a government agency that ultimately will acquire and manage a property. The nonprofit organization buys the property in advance of an agency's ability to come up with the funds. Or, as the Wildlands Conservancy example above illustrates, sometimes the nonprofit organization does the legwork in identifying the property, negotiating a price, and arranging the transaction—without actually possessing the land. The more flexible nonprofit organization can move quickly when a property comes on the market, using any of the techniques described above, such as bargain sales, options, and a revolving fund. If it purchases the property, the organization can usually structure the transaction so that all or some of the costs are recovered when it sells the property to the agency. National groups such as the Nature Conservancy and the Trust for Public Land and many local groups have used this approach in working with park agencies, the U.S. Fish and Wildlife Service, and the U.S. Forest Service (see Case Studies 2.5 and 5.3).

Alabama's Coastal Land Trust was launched in 1983 with a loan from a major foundation, working through a national nonprofit organization, to purchase land in the heart of the Mobile-Tensaw Delta. The land trust repaid the loan several years later when the U.S. Army Corps of Engineers, under federal legislation for the Tennessee-Tombigbee Waterway mitigation program, bought the land and signed it over to the state's natural resources agency. Through various publicly funded programs, donations, and other means, the land trust has continued to acquire property in the delta and, where appropriate, has resold the land to public agencies to manage for hunting, outdoor recreation, and wildlife habitat. To date, the land trust has seen to the protection of nearly 40,000 acres, retaining only 6,000 acres under its own management.[15]

As compared to many environmental and historic preservation organizations, which take stands on local ordinances, state legislation, and local and state permits, most land trusts are careful to remain neutral on political issues, including local planning decisions, to guard against alienating potential donors and supporters. A growing number of land trusts, however, do encourage local governments to improve their land use regulations.[16]

The Upper Valley Land Trust, which serves New Hampshire and Vermont along the upper reaches of the Connecticut River, published and distributed to towns in Vermont a guidebook on inventorying natural, scenic, and historic lands. "Believing that what constitutes lands of critical conservation interest ought to be mainly a local decision, we decided to become not open space planners but teachers and promoters of planning," says Timothy O. Traver, who was executive director of the land trust at the time the guidebook was completed. The response was strong; one community even went beyond the manual to locate people with traditional skills who maintain the landscape as a working landscape. The land trust's outreach has led to other benefits besides improved town planning: "The manual has sparked quite a bit of interest among local groups and given us a foothold in the planning processes in our region. . . . Meetings have ranged from informal discussions at regular town board meetings to more formal presentations of both the inventory process and land protection work," comments Traver.[17]

Municipalities and other government agencies are only just beginning to make creative responses to the possibilities inherent in private, voluntary land conservation. In Maryland, pursuant to special state legislation, Calvert County has established a fund from general public revenues to provide loans to any nonprofit organization acquiring land for public

worked closely with sellers, buyers, bankers, and community supporters to develop "land trust models" that support permanent dairying operations, assist beginning farmers, and create local community land trusts. In one of its first transactions, the conservancy bought a farm under threat of foreclosure by acquiring the bank's interest in the property at a discount—which the bank was willing to do in order to avoid the costs of foreclosure—and then leased the farm back to the original farmer on an affordable basis. In another case, the conservancy used funds from a socially conscious loan fund to purchase a dairy farm from a retiring farmer at a very affordable price. The conservancy then leased it to a couple, who assigned portions of their milk checks to the conservancy for rent and to the retiring farmer to pay for the cows and equipment. After five years, the couple had built enough equity in the farm operation to qualify for conventional financing. The conservancy sold them the farm and retained a conservation easement.

The conservancy is also developing new community partnerships that can protect farmland and provide opportunities for a new generation of farmers. It is working with several community-supported agriculture farms (CSAs) (see p. 282) to assist them in purchasing farmland. CSA members are organizing pledge drives to raise donations to the conservancy to purchase easements that will lower the cost of a farm purchase for the CSA farmer and assure that the land is permanently protected. The conservancy is also working with retiring farmers to plan farm protection and sales agreements that provide tax savings and allow their farms to be more affordable to new farmers.

(See Notes to Sidebars.)

3315 N. Alexander Street

Charlotte
See (G) on map
$45,500

The Historic Preservation Fund is offering for sale a 1903 mill worker's cottage in Charlotte. Following a design produced by New South industrialist D.A. Tompkins the house served the nearby Mecklenburg Mill until it was sold to private owners. The North Charlotte neighborhood, in which the house is located, is a National Register Historic District, and an emerging arts district. The house which is currently under reno-vation will be completely restored to include a new gas furnace, central air, electric water heater, updated kitchen, and bath with new fixtures. This two bedroom house is sited on a corner lot.

Square feet: approx. 1000
Contact: Charlotte-Mecklenburg Historic Preservation Fund
PO Box 35434
Charlotte, NC 28235
704/375-6145,
Fax 704/372-4584

Thaddeus S. Wilkinson Log House

4815 Mooresville Road,
Kannapolis
See (F) on map
$31,000

Thaddeus S. Wilkinson is said to have erected ca. 1848 the original one story log section of this farm house, which later received a frame second story and a rear ell. The interior of the seven room, one bath home is sheathed in random flush boards and random-width heart pine floors. All the timber is said to have been logged on the farm. The original log portion is arranged in a three-room Quaker plan with a large living room and two smaller adjoining rooms. A variety of simple Federal and Greek Revival trim, including a fireplace mantel and board and batten doors is evident in the home. An enclosed staircase leads to two second floor bedrooms. The home will require interior and exterior repairs, updating of plumbing and wiring, and a central heating system. Kannapolis in Cabarrus County is located on I-85 twenty-five miles north of Charlotte.

Square feet: 1,910
Lot: .92 acres with additional 5 acres available
Contact: Preservation NC
Box 27644
Raleigh NC 27611
919/832-3652

Henry Walker House

Cress Road, Cabarrus County
See (F) on map
$18,000

The Walker House is an early 19th-century, two-story, three-bay, Greek Revival structure, one room deep with a central hall on each floor and a two-room shed addition. The interior has tongue-and-groove sheathing throughout. The vernacular post-and-lintel Greek Revival mantels and two-panel interior doors have been stored for safekeeping. The staircase has a molded banister with octagonal newel post. The doors and windows have simple Greek Revival corner blocks. The house will need a total rehabilitation including new clapboard, windows, and mechanical systems. It is less than 20 miles from Charlotte and about 5 miles from Concord.

Square feet: Approx. 2,100
Lot size: 2 acres, with additional land available
Contact: Preservation NC
PO Box 27644
Raleigh, NC 27611-7644
919/832-3652

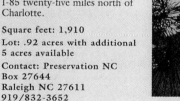

access. The loans are made at no interest for up to ten years, with a one-time charge of one percent to cover administrative costs. The program was established in 1994, when the newly formed Plum Point Environmental Land Trust needed up-front financing to buy a very expensive 185-acre parcel on the Chesapeake Bay. More than 85 percent of the property lies within a state-regulated critical area along the shoreline; the land trust plans to establish trails and beach use and will be responsible for managing the property and the public access. The loan will be repaid by sales of three small lots outside the critical area and of development rights for transfer to sites elsewhere in the county (see p. 188).[18] Descriptions of other forms of cooperation between local government and land trusts are found in Sidebars 5.3 and 5.11 and in Case Study 4.1.

Administering a Program

A successful program for voluntary land conservation may be run by volunteers, a paid staff, or both. Volunteers usually can handle simple programs and even manage an easement or acquisition program for a small number of properties. A paid staff, however, can help considerably by managing the day-to-day details and following up on negotiations. Once a program involves multiple properties, constant monitoring, or numerous transactions, paid staff is usually essential. Even with staff, volunteers remain important, as they can contribute familiarity with the community and personal acquaintance with property owners and can extend the reach of the paid staff in accomplishing all of the organization's activities.

Consultants are needed from time to time. For example, attorneys are essential for most real estate transactions; landscape architects may be helpful in designing the boundaries of an easement to protect scenic views; a botanist, wildlife biologist, or ecologist may be helpful if rare plant species or the habitat of endangered wildlife are to be protected; and an archeologist or architectural historian may help in developing management plans to protect archeological sites or historic buildings. On occasion, simply consulting with more experienced staff members of another land trust may be useful.

Most organizations find it helpful to develop a brochure outlining their goals and objectives and explaining various protection techniques. "For young organizations, especially, a brochure should mention the names of board members and advisors," whose names might lend credibility to a new effort, comments one land trust advisor.[19] The brochure should address the major concerns of most property owners, who are likely to ask: "How may I best protect the natural, historic, and scenic qualities of my property? Provide for my own and my children's future needs? Take advantage of tax deductions?"

As useful as a brochure is, it cannot substitute for personal contact. Persuading people to participate in a land protection program can require several on-site visits and many discussions. It is customary to hold discussions with a property owner over the course of several years, to develop an appropriate protection strategy. Developing and implementing a protection plan for an owner requires not only a thorough knowledge of the resources to be protected and of land use and tax law but also a great

5.13
Opposite: The mission of Preservation North Carolina is to protect and promote buildings, sites, and landscapes important to the heritage of North Carolina. Revolving funds in small towns around the state belong to its Association of Revolving Funds and are offered, among other services, one free advertisement per issue in its newsletter, *North Carolina Preservation.*

5.11 Regulatory Easements

Elsewhere in this chapter the conservation easements we discuss are generally voluntary ones—usually donated or, less often, purchased from willing sellers through programs to protect agricultural or other open lands. But it is also possible for local governments to require developers to record easements as part of the land development process. Called regulatory easements, or developer easements, these are often used in cluster developments, where significant portions of the property are set aside for ownership in common by homeowners associations (for more on cluster development, see p. 180 and Sidebar 4.10). Most states allow communities to require conservation easements as a condition for their approval of such development applications as subdivisions, site plans, special permits, variances, and rezoning of properties.

Regulatory easements can also be required by state regulations to preserve sensitive environmental areas such as floodplains, wetlands, and forests. For example, the Maryland Forest Conservation Act, adopted in 1991, requires developers to set

aside a certain portion of their developable forest land for long-term protection. Some counties in Maryland allow this requirement to be satisfied using conservation easements.

To assure that conservation lands are managed properly, and to reassure community residents doubtful that land left open under governmental regulation will remain so over the long term, some ordinances require that mandatory easements be granted to a third party (besides the developer and the homeowner's association). Who accepts them? Local governments often do. Many local governments and developers, however, are increasingly asking land trusts to step into the process. Land trusts are more experienced with requirements of protecting open lands, crafting easements, and monitoring them. As is the case with easements received in other ways, land trusts frequently receive endowments for regulatory easements, to cover costs of managing the land.

What are some of the other issues involved? For one, conventional developers may be reluctant to cooperate fully in designing appropriate ease-

ments, since they typically want to reserve the "worst" unbuildable land for conservation—when portions of the buildable land may be highly desirable according to a land trust's criteria. For another, land trusts must be careful not to seem to endorse land development, and must stick to their guns on the matter of what is acceptable in terms of both the land as a whole and the restriction provisions.

Tom Saunders, director of the Maryland Environmental Trust, which has sponsored meetings among local land trusts in the state on the question of regulatory easements, believes that for regulatory easements to be effective, long-term planning must be the basis for their implementation. "It doesn't really help to have regulatory easements on patchwork, scattered parcels of land between numerous developments," he notes. "A better idea is to plan and arrange easements on the land so that the protected parcels abut one another, creating larger areas of protected open space and habitat that better achieve the desired goal."

(See Notes to Sidebars.)

deal of patience and personal attention to both the owner and his or her attorneys, tax consultants, and other advisors. The president of the Berkshire County Land Trust in Massachusetts, for example, has been working with one family for more than twenty-five years to protect property overlooking Lake Mahkeenak. The family made gifts of land in fee in 1971, 1976, and 1979, donated an easement in 1993, and is currently considering a further easement. "These continuing gifts might not have been possible without the long-term relationship of trust established between the land trust and the family," commented one family member.

CONCLUSION

There is much excitement and vigor, and many creative ideas, in the nonprofit conservation movement. For rural communities, nonprofit action offers great hope for achieving protection of land and historic build-

5.12 Deal-Making Ground Rules

Skill in the art of negotiating is vital for property conservation organizations. Regardless of who does the negotiating, there are a few ground rules that may make "making a deal" easier:

• *Before talking to the owner, develop a profile of his or her stewardship record and approximate income, and of the family history associated with the property. Estimate the land's value, determine its zoning, and investigate local real estate trends.*

• *Your first contact should be a simple, friendly gesture. A brief letter or telephone call and a follow-up visit to answer questions may be sufficient to establish contact.*

• *Time your visits carefully. Avoid intensive work periods for farmers, and times of stress such as illness and death, unless the owner specifically requests the visit because the information may be helpful in making decisions during such a period.*

• *For a first visit, go with a friend, relative, or neighbor who knows the owner. The primary purpose of the first visit should be to explain the organization's interests and help you size up both the owner's commitment to protection and any potential threats to the property.*

• *Be prepared to spend a lot of time with a property owner, over a number of visits—even years. Be a good listener and be patient. Don't try to rush anyone into making a decision. The owner is being asked to make a decision about a property that may be the family's principal asset, that may have been in the family for generations, or that may have some other significance to the owner that you know nothing about.*

• *Always know what it is that you want to protect on a particular property; let the owner know that you are most concerned about protecting the wetland or the Greek Revival farmhouse or whatever. An owner who hesitates to protect the entire property may be receptive to protecting the part where the most critical resources are located. Don't think of the organization as saving the property: you are seeking a way for the owner to save the property. Remember that the only reason the resource is still there is because of the actions (or inaction) of the owner.*

• *Information about the property from the community's environmental inventory, such as maps, photographs, or written narratives, may be useful in highlighting the importance of the property. As a first step, you might suggest that the owner draw the property's boundaries and point out special features on an aerial photograph.*

• *Follow up quickly. Write a thank you note after a visit and answer any questions that were left unanswered during the visit.*

• *The setting is important. The kitchen table may be a far more successful site than a lawyer's office; holding meetings on the owner's turf reduces any sense of intimidation. If you are dealing with multiple owners, use hosts in the neighborhood.*

• *Appearances are important: dress for the occasion. Ask yourself how the landowner will interpret what you wear; casual wear, office dress, or a uniform can each be appropriate or inappropriate. "Bib overalls aren't necessary," comments Mark Ackelson, an Iowa land trust negotiator. "But I have been known to slip on a pair to help repair a combine while I talk with a farmer."*

• *Strive to project confidence and build respect and trust. Be honest, positive, and open. Don't hide anything; doing so can destroy a carefully built relationship and hurt you with others. If you are not an expert, do not try to appear to be one.*

• *If an owner has difficulty understanding the options, suggest that an advisor—a relative, friend, family attorney—join the discussion.*

• *Take careful notes about what the owner and the family members say, and what the owner agrees to. Later, these notes may prove helpful in developing an agreement or clarifying the donor's intent once the agreement is in place.*

(See Notes to Sidebars.)

---

ings. Perhaps the best way for you to begin is to learn from experienced organizations elsewhere in your state or region. You should not let the thought of emulating a well-established organization intimidate you. As these organizations have grown, so have their funding and their ambitions—from little acorns great oaks grow. Your knowledge of the potential for private action in your community can start you on the way toward duplicating the successes of others and creating successes unique to your community.

And remember—to embark on an initiative to stimulate voluntary conservation is to give more to your community than simply land. The remarks of Jon Roush, former president of the Wilderness Society, apply not only to land trusts but to all efforts to protect the treasured assets in rural communities:

> A community with an active land trust is rich in more than land. It is blessed with a group of people who give what could never be bought. . . . To help make one's community a better place, to be personally challenged, to increase concord and decrease discord, to build for the future—to do any of those is to enrich one's life with meaning. A chance to do them all is a rare gift. . . . Land trusts cannot address all conservation needs, but they can meet needs beyond the reach of any other institution, public or private. In doing so, they have created vehicles for participation by people of all classes and political leanings. They have created a unique grassroots movement. . . . Its message is that responsive private institutions can help build livable communities.[20]

Economic Development and Rural Conservation

6

INTRODUCTION

As we discussed in Chapter 1, some rural communities are experiencing growth—even rapid growth—while others are losing population and sources of employment. If your community is growing, you will likely want to control development, or at least channel it in ways that will protect and enhance your community's special resources. If your community is declining, attracting economic development is probably a major concern.

Not all economic development strategies are compatible with conservation. Indeed, many of the industries that communities seek to recruit are sources of pollution that harms the natural environment, and development that causes too much growth too fast can destroy the character of a rural community. Rural communities can, however, adopt an economic development strategy that is fully compatible with rural conservation. Strengthening the core of a commercial downtown, for example, can serve to combat sprawling development on the edges of the community; if your downtown is strong and viable, businesses will have less incentive to locate outside of town. Similarly, economic development that focuses on heritage tourism and the unique resources of the community can lead to large-scale beautification efforts and these, in turn, can lead to conservation initiatives. For a conservationist, working with the development community can win you valuable allies and assure that both your goals and theirs are met.

Economic development does not necessarily equal growth. Rather, economic development may be a restructuring of the economy, a stabilization of the economy, or a stemming of revenue and population loss. Often, however, economic development does result in growth. Communities interested in economic development should consider first whether they really want growth. What impact will it have on your community? Who will benefit and who will lose? What indirect consequences of growth may occur in the long run? Communities must realistically assess the costs and benefits of growth. All too frequently communities undertake an economic development strategy thinking only of the revenues it will provide, not of the costs. Yet each of the various types of economic development has particular consequences and impacts on a community and must, therefore, be carefully considered.

This chapter introduces five types of economic development that rural communities often turn to. Four of these—downtown revitalization, heritage tourism, farmers' markets, and heritage area development—are generally compatible with community conservation. The fifth—gambling—may be compatible but often is not. We include a discussion of gambling because of its increasing popularity as an economic development strategy and because of its ties to heritage tourism and downtown revitalization.

RURAL ECONOMIC DEVELOPMENT

Rural economic development in the 1990s is more of a challenge than ever before. Rural America is part of the global economy and must compete with suppliers and markets overseas. In a global economy driven by rapidly developing technologies—especially telecommunications technologies—rural communities must struggle to keep pace with metropolitan America. Indeed, many economic development theorists believe that only by developing telecommunications linkages with metropolitan areas can rural communities thrive.

The term "economic development" covers a wide range of approaches and activities. Basically it implies a social goal and encompasses notions of what American society should be and how value in a community can be maintained. Economic development includes the provision of infrastructure, housing, education, and basic social services, as well as industrial, retail, and service development that provides jobs and adds income to the economy. These types of investment in a community spur additional investment—or multiply existing investment—as available resources increase. Although frequently used interchangeably with "growth," "development" suggests not only an *increase* in infrastructure, jobs, income, and well-being but also a *change* in the structure of the social and economic delivery system. Development may also be reflected in less tangible indices of community character; as a place prospers, its residents invest in its appearance and express a spirit that is reflected in numerous community activities.

Particularly for economically depressed communities, providing new or improved infrastructure can be an important economic development strategy. Installing, upgrading, or extending water and sewer lines provide the bases for commercial and residential development; road construction and improvement heighten the accessibility of rural areas and facilitate interaction within and between communities.

Today the most important infrastructure may be telecommunications; rural communities with access to information are the ones most able to grow and develop economically. Fiberoptic cable, satellites, modems, and computers compose the telecommunications infrastructure that can link rural areas to urban areas instantaneously. Telecommunications allows rural communities to provide back-office functions, including telemarketing, bill and check processing, catalog sales, and reservations processing. Even so, there is growing evidence that infrastructure improvement alone cannot provide a sustainable economic development strategy. To be economically competitive, rural communities must be flexible, and placing too much capital in infrastructure may restrict flexibility.

Attracting a new industry or a facility such as a prison, hospital, or landfill, is another common economic development strategy that rural communities adopt. Bringing in a new industry is one of the most obvious ways to increase employment and, therefore, income. Although manufacturing employment overall is declining in rural areas and manufacturing generally as part of America's economic production is declining in importance, some rural communities have had considerable success recruiting new business. Yet for many communities, importing a new industry or facility is only a "quick fix" approach to economic development and may not provide sustainable revenues and quality of life over time.

"Sustainable development": this surely is one of the most commonly used terms of the 1990s. Although the term has been sometimes misapplied, its key principles are important for rural conservationists to keep in mind. Sustainable development means development that continues in the long run, without the loss of unreplenishable resources and without damage to the environment. A community can sustain itself over time without attracting new industries, new residents, or visitors; it can simply invest more in itself and become more economical and efficient in the way it does business. Too much growth may threaten to destroy the very resources that a community sets out to conserve.

Another critical concept for rural communities is self-development—locally initiated, not from the outside. The most successful rural communities have achieved economic development through their own initiative, by strong leadership, careful self-assessment, and development of the right market niche. Self-development—which involves local organizations and local government, invests local resources, relies on local goods and services, and results in an activity which is locally controlled—is the most sustainable in the long run. Thus, recruiting an outside industry or special facility to relocate in the community is not self-development and, although such development may bring jobs and new revenues, there may not be a local base to sustain them over time. Indeed, an imported industry controlled from outside may increase a rural area's dependence.

Whatever economic development strategy a community chooses, it must realistically assess the advantages and disadvantages and the costs and benefits of each. It must seek to find the right fit between the community and a particular development strategy. Whether a community succeeds economically is a function of several factors: location, leadership

6.1 Calculating the Economic Multiplier

In calculating the benefits of economic development, communities should recognize that revenues coming into a community multiply. The additional indirect benefits of an investment can be calculated as the multiplier effect. For every dollar received by a local business or industry, purchases are made for support goods and services that would not be made otherwise. For example, a historic house museum may hire local people to serve as guides and may print brochures—thus spending money in the local economy. The people hired and the firm printing the brochures likewise spend additional money locally. This indirect impact can be calculated as some multiple of the initial direct expense. It is usually expressed in decimal form: a multiplier of 1.5, for example, means that for every dollar directly invested, 1.5 dollars additional are spent.

Mathematical models have been developed to calculate the total impact—direct and indirect—of expenditures. One of the most frequently applied is the IMPLAN (Impact Analysis for Planning) model, developed by the USDA Forest Service and the Federal Emergency Management Agency.

6.2 20 Clues to Community Survival

The Heartland Center for Leadership Development, Lincoln, Nebraska, lists the following traits that characterize communities that survive:

1. *Evidence of community pride*
2. *Emphasis on quality in business and community life*
3. *Willingness to invest in the future*
4. *Participatory approach to community decision-making*
5. *Cooperative community spirit*
6. *Realistic appraisal of future opportunities*
7. *Awareness of competitive positioning*
8. *Knowledge of the physical environment*
9. *Active economic development program*
10. *Deliberate transition of power to a younger generation of leaders*
11. *Acceptance of women in leadership roles*
12. *Strong belief in and support for education*
13. *Problem-solving approach to providing health care*
14. *Strong multigenerational family orientation*
15. *Strong presence of traditional institutions that are integral to community life*
16. *Attention to sound and well-maintained infrastructure*
17. *Careful use of fiscal resources*
18. *Sophisticated use of information resources*
19. *Willingness to seek help from the outside*
20. *Conviction that, in the long run, you have to do it yourself*

and organization, natural resources, and the character of the economic base. All these factors must be evaluated in planning for economic development, so that the community's chief assets, deficits, opportunities, and realistic choices are clear.

DOWNTOWN REVITALIZATION

Most small town or rural Main Streets have traditionally served as market centers—places where the surrounding population purchases goods and services. Maintaining and enhancing the commercial cores of America's rural towns and villages is one of the most powerful rural economic development strategies. With the acceleration of strip development and the proliferation of giant discount department store chains and warehouse shopping clubs, keeping traditional Main Street commercial districts viable is all the more critical. Contrary to the common perception that Main Street must fall victim to changes in technology and marketing, rural Main Street *can* survive—provided its merchants become knowledgeable about the competition, develop a targeted strategy, form partnerships with other community groups, and capitalize on the special resources the community offers. Main Street revitalization can be an effective tool for combating sprawl and, thus, conserving the open lands and natural resources of a community.

Strengthening Downtown Commerce

Revitalizing a downtown involves developing a broad strategy that combines historic preservation and smart business decisions. It is not enough simply to repair or refurbish the facades of downtown buildings, plant street trees, or decorate the sidewalks with flowers and benches. For Main Street to survive and thrive there must be a viable mix of businesses, a strong organization and commitment from business owners, and a market strategy that is responsive to customers' needs.

The beginning of a Main Street revitalization effort is often a crisis, as it was in Bonaparte, Iowa, where four of the main buildings in the small, already deteriorating downtown were put up for sale. When the survival of downtown is seriously threatened, business owners and citizens who may not have previously cooperated with each other find it in their best interest to work together. A town's commercial revitalization is usually based on partnerships and a strong organization of interests. The community must seek Main Street's revitalization as a whole, not just the preservation of individual businesses. For example, in Hannibal, Missouri (pop. 18,105), the tourist-oriented businesses and the local-serving businesses, which had each pursued their own marketing and development strategies, joined forces in a downtown revitalization effort.

Frequently, chambers of commerce take the lead in revitalizing a commercial downtown, but nonprofit organizations, business associations, or even local government agencies can provide Main Street revitalization leadership. In Kosciusko, Mississippi (pop. 7,161), revitalization began when several young businessmen acquired, restored, and painted three downtown buildings; these actions had a domino effect. Other businesses began to improve their appearances, and eventually the county government appropriated funds to landscape the courthouse lawn. Obviously, the more downtown merchants involved in a revitalization plan, the better. However, bringing a downtown back to life involves more than just the merchants; garden clubs, civic associations, historic preservation and conservation organizations, and youth groups can also contribute substantially. The best Main Street revitalization efforts involve a partnership of local interests who work together for a common goal.

One of the first steps to downtown revitalization is taking stock of what the commercial district of the community offers. What businesses are there? Why do customers come to shop on Main Street? If the post office is located downtown, it can be a draw for other businesses—restaurants, a drug store, and the like. If the post office has been relocated to the edge of town, what other important draws does the downtown have? Is there a good mix of stores, or are critical elements missing?

Main Streets cannot compete with large discount retailers, and should not try to; instead, they must find special market niches that the discounters cannot offer. This may require some economic restructuring of the downtown. Stores may have to feature new product lines, and new businesses may have to be recruited to replace the obsolescent services.

For smaller communities with, say, populations of under 5,000, downtown revitalization may be more of a challenge. Smaller towns have fewer resources—in terms of both volunteers and funding. Smaller towns, too, may not be able to achieve an ideal mix of businesses, and their market areas may be limited. In small communities, however, the percentage of people involved in Main Street is higher and, therefore, the overall commitment may be relatively greater, as is the case with Bonaparte, Iowa (see Case Study 6.1).

Often, for a small town, the strategy is to find the right market niche; specialization is frequently the key to commercial success for towns of fewer than 5,000. For example, McCormick, South Carolina (pop. 1,701), which in 1982 was labeled one of "The Real Ghost Towns You

6.3 Principles of Sustainable Economic Development

According to Michael Kinsley of the Rocky Mountain Institute in Snowmass, Colorado,

> *communities pursuing sustainable futures focus their development efforts on four principles: First, plug the unnecessary leakage of dollars and resources through import substitution, resource efficiency, buy-local programs, and a strong informal economy. Second, support existing business through such efforts as training, downtown revitalization, business networks, and community development corporations. Third, encourage new local enterprise through such projects as adding value to local products, business incubators, and creative financing. The last principle, recruit compatible new business, speaks to the caution that any community should employ in its development efforts. It should ensure that new business will provide the community with a net gain after possible side-effects are considered.*

6.1
The historic Tabor Grand Hotel on the main street of Leadville, Colorado, was rehabilitated for affordable housing in 1991. Residents of the Tabor Grand work at nearby ski resorts of Vail, Copper Mountain, and Beaver Creek but cannot afford to live at them. Revitalizing this prominent downtown structure has brought new life to the main street of Leadville.

Never See in Movies" by *U.S. News and World Report* magazine, has learned to take advantage of the 4,000-acre retirement community under development on nearby Lake Thurmond. It has broadened its commercial base for tourists and retirees, and gained four hundred jobs between 1988 and 1994.[1]

Ponchatoula, Louisiana (pop. 5,934) is another example of small town Main Street specialization. In early 1989, 85 percent of the buildings in downtown Ponchatoula were vacant, as business moved to the nearby Interstate 55 interchange or the regional mall. Still, the town had an existing base of antique shops and had become known for its annual spring antique festival. The enterprising president of the chamber of commerce and a realtor put together a plan to make Ponchatoula what it is known as today, America's Antique City. Over the course of a year, a citizens group, guided by the chamber of commerce, leased all the downtown stores and advertised their availability to antique buyers and dealers across the country. Within four years, the revitalization effort added fifty-two new businesses and four hundred new jobs to Ponchatoula.[2]

Main Street commercial space can and should be marketed as an ideal location for small businesses, start-up companies, or enterprises that depend on computerized technology or mail order. Most businesses in the United States, and certainly the fastest growing businesses, employ fewer than 20 people at a site. Figuring 250 square feet per person, these businesses require only 5,000 square feet—about two floors of a typical Main Street commercial structure.[3] Businesses that reach customers by mail order, express delivery, modem, or telephone are ideal Main Street enterprises. All the services they require—a post office, bank, office supply store, government offices—are generally located conveniently downtown.

All communities undertaking a revitalization strategy should think of ways to keep the downtown active after 5:00. If the downtown has a movie house, theater, or community center, residents will be drawn downtown, at least on occasion. Often business leaders decide collectively to keep stores open until 8:00 or 9:00 on certain nights. Restaurants can offer special attractions to bring residents and visitors to Main Street.

CASE STUDY 6.1

Bonaparte, Iowa:
A Small Community Invests in Its Downtown

Located on the Des Moines River in southeastern Iowa, Bonaparte, with a population of 478, is a robust, active, and determined town that has saved itself from the demise to which many other rural communities have acquiesced. Bonaparte invested in its own resources and, as a result, has received state and federal development funding as well as national attention.

In the fall of 1986, Rollo and Helen White, owners of four historic but dilapidated buildings on First Street, along the river, closed down their retail businesses to retire. These businesses covered more than 8,000 square feet of ground-floor space—including the original market, opera house, and four retail shops. Although Bonaparte's main industry, Riverside Plastic, was unaffected by the stores' closing, it was a devastating blow for the downtown.

The abandonment of these buildings, in a downtown only two blocks long, might well have been the death of the town's core were it not for four enterprising and concerned business leaders. The four—Mike Gunn, vice president of Riverside Plastic Company, Steve Hainline, owner of Hainline's Phillips 66 station, Steve Reno, Van Buren County attorney, and Bill Easter, a woodcarver and craft shop owner—developed the idea of purchasing and restoring the buildings. None had ever been involved in professional development before.

The Whites were asking $36,000 for their buildings, which they wanted to sell as one package. Because none of the four businessmen individually could afford to buy and fix them up, they formed a for-profit corporation, called Township Stores, and raised the money through the sale of shares of stock to members of the community, and they did all this within about ten days. Shares were sold for $2,000 each, and, in order to minimize the risk to anyone, no one could buy more than one share. A community meeting was held, pledges were made, and $100,000 was raised within one week.

Renovation of the structures began in the spring of 1987 and proceeded through the year. The corporation continued to sell shares as well as borrow funds from a local bank. The first renovated space was leased for a grocery store, hardware store, and office space, and two apartment condominiums were sold. The corporation then renovated the old opera house in the center of the downtown block for a beauty shop and offices. The town of Bonaparte purchased a portion of the building for a community meeting room. Altogether, by 1989, nearly $500,000 had been invested in the buildings—all from local sources.

Although at the time Bonaparte was too small to qualify for the National Trust's Main Street Program, in 1987 it formed its own Bonaparte Main Street Program, modeled on the national program's four points (see Sidebar 6.5). Through various fund-raising efforts, including dinners and auctions, the program was successful in hiring an architectural historian who in 1988 prepared a nomination of most of downtown Bonaparte to the National Register of Historic Places as a historic district.

Initial revitalization led to larger communitywide development plans. In the fall of 1987, under the leadership of the mayor, Rebecca Reynolds-Knight, who believed that Bonaparte needed to take responsibility for itself and initiate its own development, the city passed a historic preservation ordinance, establishing a historic preservation commission to conduct inventories and adopt regulations. In 1988, the town pursued designation, and met the standards to qualify, as a Certified Local Government. It passed several ordinances, including a nuisance ordinance, junk car ordinance, and mobile home ordinance, to maintain the appearance of the town. Bonaparte established a design review board to oversee the historic district and instituted several volunteer programs, including a tree planting project that began by planting 500 trees.

One good thing led to another. In 1990, Bonaparte was incorporated into the National Trust's Main Street Program, becoming the smallest official Main Street town in the nation. Sidewalk improvement and street light improvement were undertaken with funding from Iowa's Historic Resource Development Program. In 1990 the city received a $46,000 grant from the Iowa Resource Enhancement and Protection program for its park—to restore lock walls along the river, restore the 1926-era band shell, build fishing and boating areas, and develop a garden to attract butterflies. Between 1990 and 1995, Bonaparte's Main

Street gained five new businesses and thirteen new jobs and rehabilitated ten commercial buildings. Bonaparte has also received three $200,000 Community Development Block Grants to rehabilitate residences for low- and moderate-income housing.

The can-do spirit in Bonaparte carried the town through the severe Midwest floods of 1993. The entire historic district was inundated. Mark Meek, usually a rural mail carrier, became full-time mayor during the flood. Under his leadership and using its fund-raising skills, the town applied for and received nine separate flood relief grants—from the Federal Emergency Management Agency, the National Trust for Historic Preservation, Community Development Block Grant funds, and Iowa's Historic Resources Development Program. These grants—totaling over $609,000 by spring 1995—enabled the town to restore City Hall and other buildings throughout the historic district. The grants also acted as a catalyst for private investment in the downtown. Four flood-damaged buildings that were vacant or housed declining businesses were restored for new business enterprises.

Bonaparte also began to get more involved in tourism development. In 1994 the first bed-and-breakfast opened in town, and a downtown building was bought for a hotel that will cater to hunters and fishermen. In the words of Thom Guzman, state coordinator for Main Street Iowa, Bonaparte "is a little community that just doesn't give up. The community has an uncanny ability to rebound." The story of Bonaparte demonstrates that, even for a very small town, local investment in a community's resources and strong determination to survive can bring state and national investment and recognition.

Main Street as the Social Focus of the Community

Traditionally, Main Street was not just a community's commercial center; it was the social core as well. Main Street was where people came to meet each other and catch up on the news of the day. Main Street was where the post office, bank, and local cafés were located—where people not only transacted business but also congregated socially. Main Street was where parades occurred, festivals were held, and politicians ran for office. Revitalizing Main Street requires that some of its most important social functions be restored.

One reason that many Main Streets have lost their vitality is that the residential dwelling units that used to be in the second and third stories over the stores are no longer allowed by most zoning ordinances, which separate residential and commercial uses. Restoring residential space to the commercial downtown can be a critical component of a revitalization strategy. Downtown residents require services—including groceries, restaurants, dry cleaners, and banks—and can provide a base of customer support for downtown businesses. Restoring residences to Main Street may require not only changing the existing zoning ordinance but also working with developers and financial institutions to make rehabilitation of the second- and third-story space profitable. In Albany, Oregon (pop. 31,785), the downtown association began drawing attention to the vacant space above its stores and in May 1993 had its first "Living on Main Street Tour," for which it opened upstairs apartments—both occupied and unoccupied—for view. Since its campaign to attract residents to upper-floor space began, more than twenty units have been occupied. The association also identified an area along the river that was zoned for industrial use which they were able to get rezoned for residential and mixed-use occupancy.[4]

Another technique for restoring the social vibrancy of downtown is improving or creating new parks or greenways. Green space and opportunities for recreation are important elements in a vibrant community. Sometimes even a small park, established on a previously vacant lot, can provide social space for conversation and children's play.

Scheduling events on Main Street also helps bring the community together and focuses attention on the downtown. Festivals, parades, dramas, all can be located downtown. A farmers' market every Saturday at a downtown location can be a strong contribution to a revitalization strategy (see p. 280).

The South Carolina Downtown Development Association (SCDDA) has developed a program called Downtown as a Classroom. Towns participating in this program establish a partnership between the local schools and the downtown, whereby students use the downtown as a classroom and laboratory through lessons on history, the arts, civics, communications, and mathematics. Bill Steiner, SCDDA's director, says the participating towns have done wonderful things.[5] Students in Orangeburg, South Carolina (pop. 13,762), for example, researched the history of the downtown during World War II and prepared a book, based mostly on oral histories, which they sold. The project enhanced their appreciation not only for the downtown but for the elderly citizens of the community as well.

Appearance and Design

Although an attractive appearance and good design alone are not enough to assure a vital downtown, clearly the look of the buildings and the streetscape of communities is critical to keeping Main Streets strong. Buildings in disrepair, unsightly modern metal facades (which may be covering historic buildings), unpainted storefronts—all discourage shoppers. Restoring the look of Main Street buildings to their original appearance, for instance by removing aluminum siding that was put up in the 1960s, can be instrumental in turning the economic tide. New awnings over the windows and doorway bring an old building a lift. Sometimes, simply applying new paint can make a dramatic difference in a storefront.

Small details can add a great deal. Clean streets, benches along the sidewalk, attractive street lights, well-tended flower plantings, small parks—these can contribute substantially to the appearance of a street and to its appeal to businesses and customers. Sweet Home, Oregon (pop. 7,400), faced with the closing of local timber mills, undertook an aggressive business recruitment campaign to diversify its economy. Overwhelmingly, the businesses being recruited had negative things to say about the run-down appearance of the town. This prompted Sweet Home to begin a downtown face lift. Within three years, the community had raised over $750,000 to undertake facade restoration, the addition of concrete planters filled with flowers along the median strip of Main Street, and the painting of nine murals on the blank walls of 1950s- and 1960s-style buildings. This beautification effort is part of a comprehen-

6.2
Massive columns support what was originally the Greek Revival courthouse of Newberry, South Carolina, in the heart of its downtown. It is now the community center. Newberry participates in South Carolina's Downtown Development program.

6.4 18 Ways to Improve Community Appearance

The Tourism Center of the Extension Service of the University of Minnesota suggests the following actions that a community can take to repair and enhance it appearance:

1. *Eliminate trash and accumulated junk, eyesores, old signs, graffiti.*
2. *Mow or control weeds on streets and ditch banks early in the season and during the summer before weeds become large.*
3. *Grade unpaved streets and ditch banks.*
4. *Repair or replace nonworking, bent or dilapidated traffic signs, street lights, trash receptacles, benches, fences.*
5. *Paint, on an ongoing basis, homes, porches, fences, benches, storefronts, park and public facilities.*
6. *Remove debris from streets and develop a street-sweeping campaign.*
7. *Screen objectionable sights, such as junkyards and gravel pits, from view with landscaping, fences, shrubs and trees. Better yet, relocate unsightly activities to a less prominent area.*
8. *Formulate a community street tree planting policy and initiate a planting program.*
9. *Develop creative designs for community entrances, public trails, public waterfront, scenic highways, boulevards and streets.*
10. *Control storage of boats, recreational vehicles, cars, trucks, and other large equipment in streets and front yards.*
11. *Create a lighting plan for special features (statues, fountains, trees, waterfronts, trails, etc.)*
12. *Protect special features: create historic zones, buffer areas around*

sive development strategy that also includes converting a mill site, building some flexible manufacturing space, and creating new tourism attractions. As a result of the effort, a new modular home construction business employing more than one hundred people located at the converted mill site, and several new galleries and tourist-oriented businesses located on the main street of town. According to Craig Smith, a regional community development coordinator, the face lift has "totally changed" Sweet Home's attitude. "Now people are very proud of the community; it's like night and day."[6]

Limitations to Downtown Revitalization

Commercial revitalization of the downtown is not a panacea for all rural towns in decline, and it requires continuous dedication, organization, and hard work on the part of downtown merchants, civic groups, and the local government. Further, it may not be successful if it is too limited in scope. Many communities may also need to deal with issues of residential development and housing availability. In addition, although a strong and vital Main Street can work to minimize sprawl on the edges of town, focusing only on the commercial core is usually not enough. Ideally, downtown revitalization should be undertaken in concert with other measures, in order to preserve the character of the community. In Baker City, Oregon (pop. 9,731), for example, a committee of conservationists is working to develop a 3-mile greenway trail along the Powder River that will connect the downtown to residential neighborhoods. Development of the riverfront path complements downtown revitalization efforts and extends the reach of revitalization into the outlying community.

Particularly when coupled with other development strategies and broad conservation efforts, Main Street revitalization can make a significant contribution to rural economic development and, because it builds on the strengths of local residents rather than outside resources, is usually much more sustainable in the long run than other types of economic development strategy.

TOURISM DEVELOPMENT

Especially in the last ten years, many rural communities have sought to develop tourism as a way to create new jobs and bring in revenue. These efforts take different forms. A community may develop a festival that celebrates a local historic event or hero, or they may open a museum, establish a center to market local crafts, or develop a walking tour of the town. Indiana, Pennsylvania—birthplace and hometown of actor Jimmy Stewart—hoping to attract thousands of new visitors, in 1995 opened a museum dedicated to Stewart, on the top floor of the public library. A group in Walterboro, South Carolina, established the Edisto River Canoe and Kayak Trail and the annual Edisto Riverfest to promote and protect the river, which in 1994 attracted some 3,000 paddlers. Often, as in Jonesborough, Tennessee, one successful aspect of tourism—in this case the National Storytelling Festival—proves to be the catalyst for numerous other tourist-oriented community activities (see Case Study 6.2).

Most rural communities have sought tourism development that builds on and complements the rural character of the community. This type of tourism includes eco-tourism, or "green tourism," and heritage or cultural tourism. Eco-tourism is travel to natural areas with a focus on education and conservation. A canoe trip down Pennsylvania's Lehigh River, a hiking vacation in Vermont, or a week at a nature camp in Idaho all may be classified as eco-tourism, as long as there is some educational component. Heritage or cultural tourism, on the other hand, is traveling to historic sites and cultural attractions specifically to learn about the past. Frequently, visitors seek out places that combine natural and cultural resources; thus, these two types of tourism are often considered together and are highly complementary. In Tyrrell County, North Caro-

key attractions, such as waterfronts.
13. *Obtain public access to waterfront areas.*
14. *Develop hiking and biking rights of way and trails.*
15. *Control sign and billboard proliferation. Adopt a community signage plan; consider a uniform logo sign program and billboard elimination.*
16. *Develop a plan to eliminate overhead wires in downtown and other areas.*
17. *Develop a scenic easement plan and purchase or obtain scenic easements.*
18. *Develop a local scenic highway program.*

(See Notes to Sidebars.)

MAPLE SUGAR MAKING, EAST PITTSFORD, VT.
Made Expressly for Nelson's Five Cent Store.

1771 Point Pinos Lighthouse, Pacific Grove, California.

6.3 & 6.4
Rural America has been a popular tourist destination for many decades, as evidenced by these historic postcards.

6.5 The National Trust's Main Street Program

The Main Street program started at the National Trust in 1977 with a pilot project involving three midwestern towns—Galesburg, Illinois; Madison, Indiana; and Hot Springs, South Dakota—which had been selected from among seventy applicants. The project proved successful, and in 1980 the National Main Street Center (NMSC) was established. Since then, Main Street staff have worked in some 37 states and nearly 900 communities. The Main Street program cites impressive economic results: by 1994, some 86,000 new jobs had been created, a net number of 21,000 new businesses established, and over $3.6 billion reinvested.

The Main Street program concentrates on four aspects of downtown development, trademarked as the Four-Point Approach. The four points are

1. Promotion—Create a positive image for the downtown district; make people regard and use it as a shopping destination so that retail sales are improved.
2. Economic restructuring—Strengthen the town's commercial assets and diversify business. Retain and expand existing businesses; provide a balanced commercial mix. Sharpen business owners' merchandising skills.

3. Design—Enhance the visual quality of downtown. Focus on the physical elements: the storefronts, signs, public spaces, landscaping, displays, and promotional materials. Stress the importance of the quality of design.
4. Organization—Build consensus and cooperation among partners for effective management; increase public-private cooperation.

The Main Street program operates according to eight principles:

1. Comprehensive. A single project cannot revitalize a downtown or commercial neighborhood. An ongoing series of initiatives is vital to build community support and create lasting progress.
2. Incremental. Small projects make a big difference. They demonstrate that "things are happening" on Main Street and hone the skills and confidence the program will need to tackle more complex problems.
3. Self-help. The NMSC can provide valuable direction and hands-on technical assistance, but only local leadership can breed long-term success by fostering and demonstrating community involvement and commitment to the revitalization effort.
4. Public-private partnership. Every local Main Street program needs the support and expertise of both the public and the private sector. For an

effective partnership, each must recognize the strengths and weaknesses of the other.
5. Identifying and capitalizing on existing assets. One of the NMSC's key goals is to help communities recognize and make the best use of their unique offerings. Local assets provide the solid foundation for a successful Main Street initiative.
6. Quality. From storefront design to promotional campaigns to special events, quality must be the main goal.
7. Change. Changing community attitudes and habits is essential to bring about a commercial district renaissance. A carefully planned Main Street program will help shift public perceptions and practices to support and sustain the revitalization process.
8. Action-oriented. Frequent, visible changes in the look and activities of the commercial district will reinforce the perception of positive change. Small but dramatic improvements early in the process will remind the community that the revitalization effort is under way.

(See Notes to Sidebars.)

---

lina, residents are developing a tourism program that aims to lure visitors to its wetlands, wildlife refuges, and waterways and, at the same time, to a restored plantation, a historic waterfront, and a gallery for local artists (see Case Study 2.3).

These new concepts of tourism appeared, in part, as a backlash from perceived excesses of "mainstream" tourism. Immediately popular, they soon prompted new marketing and new tourism products. They also led to valuable efforts to define the ethical dimensions of what environmentally sensitive tourism should be. In exploring these new types of tourism, rural communities should employ terms that suit their own circumstances. Here we will refer simply to "heritage tourism" or "tourism," recognizing that communities have a mix of natural, cultural, historic, and other resources to capitalize on.

Heritage tourism is a growing segment of the tourism market. Annually, 45 percent of all travelers in America seek out historic sites, and such visitation ranks among the top five tourist activities.[7] The growth reflects recent changes in demographics and social and economic forces in America. The country's population is generally aging, which means that more retirees are seeking leisure pursuits. Senior citizens, enjoying their retirement, are relying increasingly on bus tours, and many are interested in history, antiques, museums, and genealogy. In most preretirement households, two family members work, which means that long, extended vacations are more difficult to take; in general, people are traveling more frequently, for shorter periods of time, and over shorter distances. Thus, there is more demand for sites that are close at hand and can be visited in any weather. Today's travelers are generally more educated and sophisticated than in the past, and both national and international travelers seek out the *real* America.

The Importance of Authenticity

Heritage tourism should be based on the resources and stories that are true to a community's history. It should not be imitative or rely on false buildings or borrowed legends to attract visitors. If a tourist attraction purports to be something it is not, today's heritage tourist will be discerning enough to recognize the falseness.

Most communities celebrate important historic events through annual festivals, many of which are designed specifically to attract visitors. As with other tourist attractions, authenticity counts. Festivals can bring millions of dollars to a site but will probably be unsuccessful if their only goal is revenue. There must be something in the community worthy of celebration—a genuine reason behind the festival. For example, Superior, Nebraska (pop. 2,288), achieved renown as the "Victorian Capital of Nebraska" largely as a result of the Lady Vestey Festival, named after a town resident, Lady Vestey, who married a British nobleman after amassing a fortune in the meat packing industry. The festival began Memorial Day weekend in 1992 to celebrate the more than one hundred residences of Superior built during the Victorian era.

This is not to say that inauthenticity necessarily fails in the marketplace. For example, Helen, Georgia (pop. 315), located in the Appalachian Mountains in the northern part of the state, set out to develop tourism by dressing up as a Bavarian town—and it succeeded. Helen was established as a sawmill town but since the 1930s had experienced economic decline. In 1969, a small group of businessmen decided to do something about the dreary block buildings of Main Street in order to attract the recreational travelers on their way to the north Georgia mountains. A local artist drew sketches of what Helen could look like if it took on an Alpine style reminiscent of Bavarian architecture. The group liked what they saw and set about transforming the first buildings.

Gradually, over the decades, the whole town has achieved an Alpine appearance—old buildings and new—and is marketed as a tourist desti-

6.6 The National Trust's Heritage Tourism Program

The Heritage Tourism Program, created in 1989, developed five principles of heritage tourism that both distinguish heritage tourism from other kinds of visitation and provide advice for communities to follow in developing a heritage tourism program.

1. *Focus on authenticity and quality. Tell the true story about your area, the authentic contributions previous generations have made. The true story will reveal what distinguishes your community from others.*
2. *Preserve and protect resources. It is essential to protect the resources that attract the heritage tourist; investing in preservation is investing in your future.*
3. *Make history come alive. Visitors want to discover the human drama of historic places. Developing interpretive materials and communicating in a lively and exciting way are key elements of tourism development.*
4. *Find the fit between tourism and your community. Each community must assess its heritage tourism resources and its ability to sustain tourism over time.*
5. *Collaborate. A strong heritage tourism is based on partnerships among political leaders, the business community, artists and craftspeople, and other groups. Regional partner-*

6.5
The center of downtown Helen, Georgia, reflects the uniformity of its Bavarian-style architecture. Helen's economy is based entirely on tourism.

nation. The town has some 250 retail establishments, including outlet stores. Helen is, indeed, a curiosity. Over two million visitors a year come to drink German beer, eat Bavarian food, shop, and gawk. But some hard retail lessons have been learned. New businesses have failed, in large part because of the seasonalness of the tourist trade. What is worse, most of the town's original families have left Helen, dismayed and embarrassed with the "ersatzification" of their town.[8]

In the long run, Helen's success will always be limited, because it is an inauthentic place. The town offers nothing but the opportunity to drink, eat, and shop; there is no effort to educate visitors about the real history of Helen or orient them to the history, culture, and recreational opportunities of the region. The same can be said of most "dressed up" tourist villages, like Sisters, Oregon (with a faux historic Western theme) and Leavenworth, Washington (another Bavarian village).

Getting Started

Getting started in tourism is a process that takes up to five years and involves determination of tourism potential, assessment of resources, leadership and organization, planning of tours and other educational devices, and marketing.

DETERMINING TOURISM POTENTIAL

The first step to getting started in heritage tourism is figuring out what the community's potential is. A community must know its competitive advantage, the relative quality of its resources and support services, and what its special market might be. All too often communities develop marketing brochures first, without thoroughly assessing their resources or gauging their current and potential audiences.

Each community must determine what kind of tourism is appropriate, how much visitation it wants, and when and how often it wishes visitors to come. A community must ask, for example, whether it would be com-

fortable with visitors every day, every weekend all summer long, or only once or twice a year at major events. Waterford, Virginia, for example concentrates almost all of its tourist visitation in one festival weekend (see Case Study 8.3). How much tourism will be required to make a measurable difference in your community? How much is too much? Does your community want to host motor coach tours, or would you prefer visitors to arrive by car, boat, or even bicycle?

ASSESSMENT OF RESOURCES

The process of getting started in heritage tourism also includes conducting a communitywide assessment of tourism resources: attractions and destinations as well as support facilities. A community must ask, What will visitors come to see and do? Will there be enough to educate and entertain them? A comprehensive list must be compiled of the important historic sites, museums, cultural events, and festivals, and of special natural areas, outdoor activities, tours, and shopping opportunities. These should be examined in terms of both quantity and quality. Does the community have a diversity of high-quality offerings to visitors so that they will want to come back? How do the resources relate to each other? Do they tell a story? Claiborne County, Mississippi, for example, is trying to weave together through interpretation and marketing the various aspects of its heritage for tourism: its African American heritage and the story of early European settlement, along with the Civil War heritage for which it is already known (see Case Study 4.3).

A community must also ask, Where will the visitors stay? Where will they eat? An inventory of hotels, motels, bed-and-breakfast inns, and restaurants should be undertaken. How many visitors can these facilities support, and are they of sufficient quality? If visitors want to picnic, are there roadside tables and benches for them? Communities must also examine tourist-oriented signage. Can visitors easily find their way into and around town? Are the attractions well advertised and the routes to them well marked? The inventory should serve as a guide for tourism development; weaknesses as well as strengths will become apparent, and where there are needs, the community can work to fill them.

An inventory and assessment of tourism support facilities and services should also include an analysis of the road system, parking facilities, water and sewage systems, and wastewater treatment facilities. Are these adequate to support an influx of visitors? Important, too, are the police and fire departments, public health facilities, and emergency care providers. Is there an adequate number of public restrooms and pay telephones?

In 1994, Mount Pleasant, Utah (pop. 2,333), decided, as a goal of its Main Street program, that it wanted to develop its heritage tourism potential. Settled as a Mormon pioneer community in the 1850s, Mount Pleasant has a historic district listed in the National Register. The town, located in a basin between two mountain ranges, possesses an abundance of natural scenery and recreational opportunities, for both summer and winter. However, Mount Pleasant was not a destination but, rather, a town that travelers passed through on their way to the county's major attraction, the Mormon temple in Manti.

An initial assessment by a resource team from the National Trust's

ships are also useful to heritage tourism efforts.

These principles address the special niche of heritage tourism. It is based on real history—real places and real people. For the visitor, historic structures and sites are the tangible evidence of this history; people want to visit these places and learn the stories such places convey. For the host community, heritage tourism is a strategy the majority of the community needs to support—in a scale that is appropriate to the individual place.

The program's four basic steps in developing heritage tourism are:

1. Assess the potential. Evaluate your attractions, visitor services, organizational capabilities, protection of resources, and marketing.
2. Plan and organize. Make good use of human and financial resources. Develop a strong partnership organization and establish a realistic timeline.
3. Prepare, protect, manage. Look to the future and make sure your plans for tourism will protect the community in the long run. Protect resources, prepare interpretive materials, educate the community about tourism, and evaluate your successes.
4. Market for success. Develop a multiyear, many-tiered marketing plan through public relations, advertising, graphic materials, and promotions to reach your target market.

(See Notes to Sidebars.)

National Main Street Center revealed that Mount Pleasant was not equipped to attract or support tourism. Although there were two small bed-and-breakfast establishments in town, there was no motel and no restaurant serving full-course meals in attractive surroundings. Indeed, there were no public phones on Main Street, no automatic teller machines at the local banks, and virtually no interpretive information for visitors. A traveler stopping in Mount Pleasant could not find a brochure about the history or sites of the town.

Since then, Mount Pleasant has developed a motel with a restaurant attached. The town has received a $75,000 grant through ISTEA (Intermodal Surface Transportation Efficiency Act) to rehabilitate the historic train depot and convert it to a visitors' center. The Main Street program raised another $50,000, which will help fund the development of marketing and business recruitment brochures.

LEADERSHIP AND ORGANIZATION

Successful tourism development relies on strong leadership and organization. Building a heritage tourism program should involve as many of the stakeholders in the community as possible, ideally everyone upon whom tourism will have an impact. Stakeholders include not only the hotel, motel, restaurant, and retail community, but the residents, planners, preservationists, and elected officials of the town. It is good to conduct a survey to learn residents' opinions about tourism. For example, a resident attitude survey conducted in Centerville, Indiana, in 1994 revealed that 76 percent of the town's population wanted to see more visitors; whereas, only 7 percent of the residents wanted no more tourism. Community design charettes—workshops where groups of people design solutions to physical problems—or local forums on heritage tourism are also good ways to involve the whole community. Ultimately, the community's comprehensive plan, zoning ordinance, and other development guidelines and ordinances should be made compatible with tourism development. For example, if special areas need protection *from* tourist visitation or protection to preserve community character *for* tourism, it should be built into the comprehensive plan and community ordinances. Lindsborg, Kansas (pop. 3,272), settled by Swedish pioneers, depends on its Scandinavian wooden architecture to attract visitors. The town has therefore developed strict design guidelines that govern new construction and rehabilitation and a sign ordinance that prohibits neon and emphasizes natural wood. Rugby, Tennessee, limits tourist visitation to fit within its master plan, developed in 1986 to preserve the historic fabric of the utopian planned community (see Case Study 8.2). Although new visitor-oriented buildings have been constructed using materials and designs in keeping with the original Victorian look of the town, both construction and reconstruction occur only when there is an immediate need for the building.

It is wise to work from the beginning in partnership with a local or regional convention and visitors' bureau and with the state tourism office to develop a tourism program. Virginia, for example, has a Tourism Accreditation Program to help communities conduct self-assessments of their readiness to engage in competitive tourism and to develop courses

Nelson County, Virginia, promotes its rural landscape to visitors. The Nelson County tourism brochure advertises the county's "unspoiled natural beauty" and complete lack of traffic lights.

of action in tourism development. Rural Nelson County was one of the first communities to take advantage of this program's eighteen-month process. Nelson County focused on its unique assets—the beauty of the Blue Ridge Mountains, its remoteness from urban life, its agricultural products, and its quiet inns—and developed marketing materials that reflect the special attractions of the place (see Figure 6.6). Indiana has the Hoosier Heritage Development program, which offers technical assistance to emerging heritage tourism attractions across the state. And Tyrrell County, North Carolina, is developing its tourism program as part of the state's Coastal Initiative, which promotes the tidewater region of the state (see Case Study 2.3).

Rural communities may also benefit by working in partnership with neighboring communities, promoting a region or corridor rather than one particular town as a destination. The more visitor activities available, the more tourists will find the area appealing. In northern Minnesota, the Northern Lights Tourism Alliance, with a $500,000 budget from regional industrial revenue bonds, works to promote the multiple resources of a seven-county region and recently developed a new emphasis on heritage tourism. The marketing efforts of the alliance make it easier for a small town like Embarrass (pop. 776) to attract visitors to its remarkable collection of nineteenth-century Finnish log buildings. In Texas, communities along the Alamo–La Bahia Corridor, which parallels the San Antonio River for 90 miles, from San Antonio to Goliad, have developed a partnership to promote economic development focused on tourism. Two annual events—a classic car cruise in the spring and a Christmas fiesta with Pony Express couriers—promote sites and events throughout the corridor and link communities as a visitor destination. And eighteen counties of western North Carolina worked with the city of Asheville and the Biltmore Estate (the state's most visited site) to establish the region as an arts and crafts mecca. Their HandMade in America program focuses on building regional tourism, fostering economic development, promoting cultural development, and educating visitors and residents.

TOURS

Tourism development can begin with self-guided walking or driving tours. In rural areas, scenic driving routes are very popular with visitors. An easy-to-follow map illustrating auto routes can guide visitors through the most attractive areas of a community. Fall-color driving tours are especially popular. Walking tours are popular with heritage tourists, as Jonesborough, Tennessee, discovered with its Times and Tales tour (see Case Study 6.2). A brochure with a map linking the ten or fifteen most interesting historic and scenic places in town can guide visitors around and educate them easily. Such a tour might also include suggestions (or advertisements) for places to eat or rest along the way. Cazenovia, New York, developed two brochures—the "5 Walks" in the village of Cazenovia and the "5 Drives" in the town of Cazenovia (Figure 8.6).

An increasingly popular kind of tour for rural communities is one based on the local products of the area. Visitors frequently like to buy locally produced goods—jams and jellies, candy, wine, pottery, wood carvings, and the like. A tour based on local products takes the visitor a step further—to see the actual sites of production and to watch the products being made. For example, Marion and Polk Counties, Oregon, have collaborated on "We Make It Here," a brochure that invites visitors to tour local gardens, farms, fish hatcheries, mills, and factories to see products being harvested or made.

Some communities may wish to develop group motor coach tour packages, especially popular with older, well-educated travelers who are generally retired from white-collar jobs. Historic areas are among the top five vacation choices for motor coach visitors. A community considering group tours must assess whether it has parking space and turning space for busses, as well as adequate restaurant and restroom facilities to serve forty or more people getting off a bus at one time. To attract group tours, communities and individual sites should contact the state travel office, regional convention and visitors' bureaus, and the National Tour Association.

INTERPRETATION

A critical component of tourism development is interpretation: telling the story of the community to visitors. Good interpretation is an integral part of historic and environmental sites and tours; without it, visitors may not understand or appreciate what they have come to see. Interpretation can take a variety of forms; a story can be told through a narrative on paper, panels and other stationary displays, a slide show or video, or a live drama. Communities developing interpretive materials would do well to consult with experts in interpretation, perhaps by contacting a state historical society, the history, natural resources, or anthropology department of a nearby university, or a local arts agency. Bringing together interpretive specialists, local experts, and others familiar with a site for a brainstorming session may result in a clear articulation of the

6.7
In Vermont, uniform signage is required for all businesses, to orient both visitors and residents. Such signage reduces visual disorder and maintains the well-kept appearance of roadsides.

6.8
Florence, Oregon, offers attractive public restrooms in the heart of its downtown.

major themes to be interpreted and the best means of telling the story. The American Association for State and Local History may also be able to provide technical assistance in interpretation.

MARKETING

The final step to tourism development is developing a marketing plan—a strategy for promoting visitor attractions to those most likely to use them. One of the first steps in developing a marketing plan is to identify the special niche in the marketplace that a community believes it can fill. Working with the local convention and visitors' bureau and the state tourism agency, a community can identify a target market. Is the community hoping to attract visitors from neighboring towns, from the region, or from a much broader area? Who are the typical tourists

6.7 Visitor Surveys

Surveys of visitors can provide valuable information on who visits an area, why they came, what their perceptions are, and what improvements can be made to the community. The Heritage Tourism Program of the National Trust for Historic Preservation advises obtaining the following information from visitors:

- *Where the visitors are from*
- *What their chief destination is*
- *Purpose of their trip*
- *Number of people in the party*
- *Type of accommodations booked*
- *Number of nights stayed*
- *Specific sites visited*
- *Amount of money spent*
- *An evaluation of their visit*
- *How they would describe the area to others*
- *Whether they would recommend that friends visit the area*
- *What improvements could be made for visitors*

the community expects to attract? What are their characteristics? Are they families with small children? Retirees? Day visitors?

Administering a simple visitor survey at key destinations can provide useful information, both about the visitors themselves and about their perception of the area visited. For example, a detailed visitor survey was developed for the Katy Trail State Park in Missouri, a hiking and biking trail along the Missouri River, both to assess who used the trail and to gauge what improvements visitors thought would be desirable. The results of the survey revealed a user population of fairly affluent, well-educated trail enthusiasts coming principally from St. Louis and the adjoining counties for the purpose of cycling. They most often cited water, restrooms, printed trail guides, and restaurants as needed services. Based on the survey results, a marketing plan was developed for the Katy Trail specifically to target predictable users and to address their service concerns.

Many marketing techniques are simple and inexpensive. Certainly, a brochure is one of the most common marketing tools—a pamphlet that summarizes the attractions of the community and the basic where/when/how-much-does-it-cost facts. Other techniques for advertising local attractions are announcements in the newspaper or on radio and television. Newsletters can also serve as marketing tools. More sophisticated techniques include advertisements in regional or national magazines, familiarization ("fam") tours for travel agents, writers, or promoters, and computerized marketing—for example, advertising through the World Wide Web or the Internet. (See Chapter 8 for more information on public relations and marketing techniques.)

Benefits and Costs

Many communities develop tourism attractions and programs because tourism appears to be a relatively easy and lucrative economic development strategy—almost a free wave to ride. The economic benefits of tourism, which are frequently touted, seem impressive. Travel and tourism are cited as the third largest retail industry in the United States (the fastest growing sector of the economy), accounting for billions in annual expenditures. Even for states or localities, the figures on jobs created or taxes collected from tourism would tempt many communities to grab a piece of the tourism pie. However, like other economic development strategies, tourism requires substantial investment by the local community. Even after sites and tours have been developed, it may take five years to realize a solid return.

Cultural tourism, as a special segment of tourism, appears to offer favorable economic returns. Heritage tourists may prefer to stay in small, locally owned bed-and-breakfast inns, instead of chain motels, and to seek out authentic, locally prepared cuisine. Obviously, then, revenues accrue to the local establishments. Because heritage tourists are generally better educated and more affluent, on average, than other visitors, they may frequent more expensive sites and appreciate more costly merchandise.

If done well, heritage tourism, like downtown revitalization programs, enhances a community's sense of place and pride. The need to put on a

6.8 Benefits and Costs of Tourism

The development of tourism has been shown to deliver a variety of benefits to communities. Sarah L. Richardson, in the Colorado Community Tourism Action Guide, *described some of them:*

Economic Benefits

• *Tourism brings new money into the economy through visitor expenditures.*
• *Tourism helps to diversify and stabilize rural economies. It may help attract additional industry to your community by creating a larger business base and increasing visitors' recognition of opportunities.*
• *Tourism creates jobs and incomes through business expansion and new business start ups.*
• *Tourism contributes to the state and community tax base.*
• *Tourism helps support business services and products that could not be supported by the community's existing retail trade area.*

Social Benefits

• *Tourism dollars help support community facilities and improvements that could not be supported within the existing trade area.*
• *Tourism can help enhance a community's "sense of place" through the development of festivals, museums, and other interpretive activities that help document and celebrate a community's resources.*
• *Tourism encourages community civic involvement and pride.*
• *Tourism provides cultural exchange between community and visitors and brings new ideas into the community.*

Environmental Benefits

• *Tourism can foster conservation and preservation of natural, cultural, and historical resources.*
• *Tourism may encourage community beautification and revitalization.*

Although tourism delivers many benefits, it is not developed without costs. The following describes some of the costs and liabilities associated with hosting more tourists in your community.

Economic Costs

• *Tourism requires organization that will incur operational costs for personnel, administration, promotion and marketing, research and other developmental costs.*
• *Tourism places demands on public services and facilities that are tax supported. Services may need improvement and upgrading to maintain public service standards.*
• *Tourism may inflate property values and the price of goods and services.*

• *Tourism may require training of service employees, business owners, and community residents in order to produce a competitive tourism product.*
• *Tourism can be seasonal and depends on forces outside direct community control (for example, recession).*

Social Costs

• *Tourism may attract visitors whose lifestyles and ideas conflict with those of your community.*
• *Community residents will need to share important community resources with outsiders.*
• *Tourism may create crowding and congestion.*
• *Tourism may bring an increase in crime.*
• *All community residents will not share the benefits equally, so conflicts may emerge between those who benefit and those who do not benefit from tourism.*

Environmental Costs

• *More tourism may degrade the quality of important natural and historic areas in a community.*
• *Litter, noise and pollution may increase with tourism.*

(See Notes to Sidebars.)

---

good appearance for outsiders often fosters landscaping programs, the improvement of streetscapes, conservation of natural resources, and the rehabilitation of historic buildings, all of which heighten community awareness and sense of accomplishment. In turn, seeing others appreciate the assets of a place raises community spirit.

Tourism can also have negative impacts on rural communities, principally through loss of community character, but there may be negative economic impacts as well. Too many visitors create crowded conditions, excessive traffic, noise, and pollution, especially on rural roads. Parking can become scarce, and pressure may be placed on existing infrastructure and services, such as police and fire protection. Too many visitors can harm the resources they've come to enjoy. Many rural communities that become popular tourist destinations, such as Park City, Utah, also experience second-home and even permanent-home development. Visitors may turn into long-term residents!

Although tourism may bring increased revenues to a rural community, the issue of income distribution must be considered. Who will benefit from increased tourism? National chains or investors who do not live in the community may be the beneficiaries. Although tourism may create new jobs, most restaurant and hotel jobs are low paying, provide minimal if any benefits, and provide limited opportunities for advancement. All community residents will not share the benefits of tourism equally—there will likely be a disparity between those who benefit directly and those who do not.

As with all other economic development strategies, weighing the costs and benefits of tourism is an important task for communities to undertake. Some rural areas will prosper from heritage tourism; some will invest a lot and achieve only modest or even token gains; and others, unfortunately, will be overwhelmed by tourism, so that the fundamental nature of the community may be threatened. Again, a strong zoning ordinance and other protective measures, such as were developed in Park City, are critical to managing large-scale tourism development.

CASE STUDY 6.2

Jonesborough, Tennessee: The National Storytelling Festival

Jonesborough (pop. 4,380), located in the foothills of the Southern Appalachian Mountains in northeast Tennessee, is a little town that has achieved nationwide status and acclaim for its annual festival and interpretive heritage tourism programs. The first township in Tennessee, settled in 1779, it is the site of the National Storytelling Festival, a three-day event that draws some 8,000 visitors every October.

The storytelling festival was a serendipitous outgrowth of local efforts to revitalize a decaying historic Main Street. By the late 1960s, Jonesborough had lost much of its business activity to the strip shopping centers in nearby Johnson City, but town leaders developed plans to restore their Main Street and build an economy based on heritage tourism. They formed the Jonesborough Civic Trust in 1973 and within two years sponsored a weekend-long festival, Historic Jonesborough Days. The festival was such a success that the town began to search for additional ways to promote and celebrate Jonesborough.

Jimmy Neil Smith, a local high school journalism teacher, came up with the idea of a storytelling festival and proposed it to the Jonesborough Civic Trust. Received with encouragement, Smith set about planning the event, which he boldly named the *National* Storytelling Festival. It was held in October 1973. On Saturday night, Jerry Clower, renowned Mississippi storyteller, told tales to an enthusiastic audience of over 1,000. The next afternoon, some 60 people

6.9
The National Storytelling Festival in Jonesborough, Tennessee, is an annual event which draws crowds of visitors from across the country. Ray Hicks of North Carolina has performed at every storytelling festival since 1973.

gathered around a wagon in the courthouse square to tell and listen to stories. This afternoon gathering became the model for the annual festivals to follow.

The festival has continued, year after year growing in participation and attendance. Even more remarkable, it gave birth to a national storytelling movement that has spawned other festivals and conferences across the country. In 1975 the nonprofit National Association for the Preservation and Perpetuation of Storytelling was founded in Jonesborough. It has a full-time staff of twelve and a budget of nearly $2 million, and Jimmy Neil Smith serves as its executive director. The association's mission is to promote the traditions and practice of storytelling and encourage its use to enrich our lives.

The festival has been a powerful economic development tool for the association and for Jonesborough. In 1992 at the twentieth anniversary of the festival, attended by some 9,000 people, more than $2 million worth of products and services were sold, bringing in $700,000 in revenue to the association and nearly $250,000 in state and local taxes. Sue Henley, proprietress of the Cherry Tree gift shop, reports that she makes more in the three days of the festival than in most entire months. She enthusiastically describes the event's success: "The people who come totally fall in love with Jonesborough. It's like family coming home every year."

The festival also gave impetus to further heritage tourism efforts in Jonesborough. In 1992, an interpretive tour of Jonesborough was developed called Times and Tales. This was the inspiration of Robert Browning, town administrator, who had been disappointed in the historic tour he was offered in another southern town he visited. Browning decided that Jonesborough needed a tour which played on the storytelling theme and brought history to life. Times and Tales tells the stories of the people who lived in the historic buildings on the award-winning tour.

In conjunction with the town of Jonesborough, the national storytelling association is developing a national storytelling center on three acres of land in the downtown historic district. On this site stands the 1797 Chester Inn, which is being rehabilitated by the Tennessee Historical Commission. A portion of the property will be developed as a park, and a museum and interpretation center will be constructed, featuring a welcome center, storyteller's café and gift shop, exhibits, a library, and meeting space. The association and the town received a $260,000 transportation enhancements grant from the state through the Intermodal Surface Transportation Efficiency Act (ISTEA); the funds will be used for construction of a trail linking the facilities on the three-acre site.

Jimmy Neil Smith believes that the association and the town have been successful in large part because their work builds on the authentic history of Jonesborough. "We're trying to capitalize on what is special about Jonesborough," Smith said, "the heros, the architecture, and the history." In Jonesborough, historic preservation and heritage tourism based on authenticity have not only benefited the economy but enhanced community pride as well.

C A S E S T U D Y 6 . 3

Park City, Utah: Protecting a Community's Assets from Too Much Tourism

Over the past twenty-five years, Park City, Utah (pop. 6,188), has been transformed from an impoverished, isolated silver mining town in the Wasatch Range to one of *the* places to ski and vacation in the mountain West. This transformation has been achieved largely through the marriage of tourism and historic preservation. With the community's success has come considerable controversy and growing pains, as Park City continues to struggle with rapid growth and change.

Prior to the development of the ski industry in Park City in the 1960s, the town was a collection of neglected, boarded-up buildings—many of them miners' cottages from the nineteenth century. Ski development was a welcome economic boon. All of it—lifts, runs, new motels and restaurants—was on private land; a new resort area outside the town was created. In comparison, the old downtown was a source of civic dismay. The community removed the historic iron streetlights and replaced them with modern freeway lights.

In the late 1970s, in an attempt to attract more skiers to the area, the Park City Chamber of Commerce developed a visitor survey which was administered as people got on and then off the chair lift. The essential question the survey asked was Why did you come to Park City to ski? Everyone was surprised by the answer: people came because of the historic buildings! Skiers found Park City a real place, where history had actually happened.

The results of this survey provided the impetus for a fifteen-year-long program of historic preservation in Park City. Suddenly there was economic justification for preserving and rehabilitating the old buildings that people had allowed to deteriorate. Business owners slowly began to realize that it was in their best interests to save the environment they had formerly eschewed. In 1980, although it was very controversial at the time, Park City established its historic district, with a commission and design guidelines, developed in 1983, that deal with issues of building height, bulk, mass, roof shapes, and color. The community identified a redevelopment district and in 1987 began a historic district grants program that provided matching grants of $5,000 for residential and $10,000 for commercial building rehabilitation.

With private preservation under way, Park City began its public building restoration campaign, led by city council member Tina Lewis. First, the city pro-

6.10
The streets of downtown Park City, Utah, bustle with wintertime visitors. The town has gone to great lengths to preserve its historic character in the face of growing tourism and second-home development.

posed a $750,000 bond referendum to rehabilitate the old miners' hospital for a public library. The bond issue divided the community: many objected to the tax increase that would result from the financing; others felt the building was too dilapidated to restore. The referendum passed by only about fifty votes. The building became a landmark in Park City. The library subsequently outgrew the space, and the building now functions as the town's community center.

With one success achieved, rehabilitation of other buildings continued. The old city hall on Main Street was restored as the Park City Museum; an old elementary school was rehabilitated for city offices, as was the high school, now the town library and educational center.

Park City didn't just save buildings; it developed one of the toughest demolition ordinances in the United States. The ordinance gives the city the leverage to ensure that before a permit is granted for a historic building to be demolished, every alternative option will have been explored. The city has also developed a sensitive-lands ordinance to deal with development on hillsides, wetlands, and entry corridors. The town has no lack of developers and some 400 real estate agents, and there is plenty of development pressure, but people have generally respected the toughness of these regulations, because property values have been shown to be so clearly tied to historic preservation.

"Without tourism, Park City would have been lost," says Myles Rademan, the town's director of public affairs. However, with increased visitation from tourists have come substantial second-home development and new settlers. Park City has a permanent population of around 6,000 (double what it was thirty years ago), but its winter population swells to nearly 25,000 and its summer population to 15,000. Over the years, property values have soared. The tiny miners' cabins, most of which are less than 10,000 square feet in living space and which used to sell for about $10,000, are now chic and cost up to $500,000. According to Tina Lewis, Park City is experiencing "roaring growth" outside the town boundaries. The Deer Valley Resort was built adjacent to and is incorporated within Park City. Summit County grew nearly 80 percent between 1980 and 1992. As Lewis says, success was "like creating a monster." Park City will be participating in many of the ski events of the 2002 Olympics, so growth can only be expected to continue.

With the growth and economic change have come social changes as well. Newcomers have brought different attitudes and values. Park City had long had a tradition of rebellion from the mainstream Mormon culture of Utah (Mormons were forbidden to participate in mining); here was established the first Catholic church in the state, and here prohibition was ignored and prostitution flourished. Even in the 1970s, Park City had, as Lewis says, "a rip-roaring reputation." Now the demographics have changed. Many of the newcomers to Park City and the areas around it are suburban commuters. Tina Lewis says that, although historic preservation is much of what accounts for visitors and new residents coming to Park City, there is a "nostalgic feeling for the days before preservation was here." Although Park City has accommodated growth and change very progressively, it is socially and economically a much different place than it was two or three decades ago.

USING AGRICULTURE FOR COMMUNITY DEVELOPMENT

As farm fields give way to residential and commercial development and the number of farms and farmers continues to decline, communities across the country are discovering ways to offset these trends. Responding to a growing demand for locally grown, organic, and specialty produce and the desire of many people to reconnect with the land, farmers' markets, community-supported agriculture, and specialty farming are becoming increasingly popular. They provide a new means to help farmers stay in business, thereby encouraging farmland retention on the periphery of towns, where it is disappearing most rapidly. Obviously there are other ways agriculture can be promoted, but the techniques described here have special relevance to those working to retain agriculture on the urban fringe.

Farmers' Markets

During the 1980s, farmers' markets enjoyed a return to popularity. Farmers' markets provide city residents with a reason to support farmland retention and rural·conservation leaders with a good opportunity to cooperate with a nearby town.

Traditionally, most towns had markets where farmers sold their produce directly to the public. Such markets were lively places that provided

6.11
Farmers' markets not only provide
city residents with fresh produce but
also help farmers on the urban fringe
to stay in business. This is one of
thirty-one farmers' markets operated
by Greenmarket, a nonprofit organization in New York City.

both town and country people an opportunity to visit as well as to conduct business. Farmers' markets all but disappeared with the rise of the
supermarket, but consumers in the 1970s and 1980s, tired of hard toma-
toes, waxed cucumbers, and tasteless strawberries, learned to appreciate
farm-fresh produce. Such markets provide an outlet for farmers whose
quantities of produce may not be sufficient to interest a corporate food
processor or distributor.

Some farmers' markets are no more than downtown parking lots
where farmers are allowed to sell from the backs of their trucks; others
have stands or are located in market buildings and feature baked goods,
home-cooked meals, crafts, and flowers as well as fresh produce. Some,
such as the Saturday market on the square surrounding the state capitol
building in Madison, Wisconsin, are seasonal, while others are year-
round. A sense of permanence fosters confidence, an important ingredient for farmers and customers alike. Markets have worked best in towns
that have allocated permanent space or a building for the market, as
Lancaster, Pennsylvania has done. Most markets are on public land, but

sometimes private landowners are willing to lease or donate land for farmers' markets. Wherever they are, markets should be visible and accessible to both pedestrians and vehicular traffic, and ample parking space should be available for both vendors and customers. It is also important to limit participation, generally to vendors who are actually selling produce from their own farms.

Some markets are sponsored by town governments, state departments of agriculture, farmers' associations, or chambers of commerce. Others, like the thirty-one markets run by Greenmarket at twenty-four locations in New York City, are operated by nonprofit organizations. Greenmarket has as one of its primary purposes "to support agriculture and conserve farmland in the region." Greenmarket director Barry Benepe reports that the markets bring in a gross revenue of $40 million a year and are helping to preserve some 16,000 acres of regional farmland.[9]

Several state departments of agriculture, including those in California, Massachusetts, New York, and Texas, offer assistance to communities in establishing farmers' markets. Pennsylvania passed legislation in 1995 to allow farmers to sell produce at Pennsylvania Turnpike travel rest stops. The Cooperative Extension Service may also be able to assist in establishing farmers' markets.

Many cities, among them Shelby, North Carolina, have found that farmers' markets can draw people downtown for other shopping and be a major factor in downtown revitalization. Pasco, Washington, rebounded from years of downtown decline after establishing a farmers' market in the mid-1980s. Today the market draws some 7,000 customers on a busy Saturday (Spitzer and Baum 1995, p. 23). In addition to farmers' markets, other public markets, such as crafts markets and flea markets, are helping communities attract people back to the public spaces of their downtowns and neighborhoods.

Community-Supported Agriculture

Community-supported agriculture (CSA) is an innovative way to connect local food producers with local food consumers who want fresh, regional produce. In community-supported agriculture, participating households buy "shares" of a farm's harvest before it is even planted. The money paid for these shares is used to pay for all food production costs (seeds, equipment, fertilizer, and the like) and a salary for the farmer or gardener who tends the crop. For one share of the harvest, each participating household receives a bagful of local, same-day-fresh produce, typically organic vegetables and herbs, once a week during the summer months. If a root cellar or cold storage is available, members can also receive produce during the winter months. The land used for the community-supported operation can be either privately owned or leased by the member participants.

The benefits of community-supported agriculture are many. First, because there are participating households buying shares of the harvest, the cost of production is spread out, which keeps a single farmer from having to advance all of the money for the season's crops. By the same token, the risk of failure is spread out among the shareholders. For example, during the first CSA year at Indian Line Farm in South Egremont, Massachusetts, a freak thunderstorm dropped eight inches of rain in three hours and ruined many of the crops. This translated to a $35 loss on each share purchase, but would have been a $3,500 loss to the family that owned the farm. In addition, in a CSA operation, the farmer is paid a regular salary, instead of having to wait until harvest time to see the financial reward for a whole season's work. Therefore, community-supported agriculture is often an excellent solution for individuals or communities who are working to keep agricultural land in production but who could not afford to do it using standard farming methods.

For the shareholders, the most obvious benefit of CSA is the produce. In return for their investment, participants get a wide variety of fresh produce for a fair price. In addition, many participants volunteer their labor and enjoy being part of a community farming experience. CSA keeps food dollars in the local economy and lends to the continuation and establishment of more regional agriculture production.

Specialty Farming

Specialty farming is a recent trend in agriculture that is helping to keep many farms, particularly small ones, in production. The rising demand for specialty products such as herbs, fresh cut flowers, mushrooms, berries, grapes, and lesser-known varieties of vegetables is even helping many small farmers to prosper. In addition, many farmers are turning to raising game animals, such as quail, pheasants, and fallow deer (which produce venison for restaurants), instead of traditional dairy cattle.

Specialty farming usually works best on the fringes of growing metropolitan areas, where demand for fresh and unusual produce is high. According to Maria Price, who with her husband specializes in herbs and flowers while also raising horses, sheep, and goats on a 40-acre farm on the Eastern Shore of Maryland, "there seems to be a real general interest in learning about herbs."[10] The growth in the number of farmers' markets across the nation during the past decade has also helped specialty farming to grow.

One of the greatest benefits of specialty farming is that it allows farmers to make a living on much less land than traditional crops, such as corn, require. For instance, by growing land-intensive specialty products, it is possible to gross as much as ten to fifteen times more per acre than a traditional crop would bring. By raising specialty animals instead of cattle, a dairy farmer can make up to three times as much per acre. Therefore, specialty farming can be the difference between keeping a farm in production and having to sell it to developers.

It is not only individuals, small stores, and farmers' markets that are driving the specialty market. Many large supermarket chains, especially those in metropolitan areas, are also helping to enlarge the specialty farming market, by buying much of their produce from local farmers instead of large-scale distributors.

GAMBLING

Gambling is a special case of rural economic development—a combination of tourism and new industrial development. Yet gambling is different from both tourism and industrial development in the extent of impact it has on a community. With gambling, the stakes are higher, for both the visitor and the community. The possibility of big windfalls and big losses distinguishes gambling from other development; it can bring major changes to a community, for better and for worse.

Gambling Revenues

Revenues from gambling come from a number of sources, including mooring fees for floating casinos, business licensing fees, and device fees (a charge per slot machine, poker table, and blackjack table). Most of these revenues are collected by the state, but some are redistributed to local jurisdictions. For example, in fiscal year 1992, of South Dakota's $7.5 million in total revenue from gambling, 68 percent was returned to Deadwood and 4 percent to Lawrence County, in which Deadwood is located.[11] In some cases a portion of these revenues is set aside specifically for historic preservation. In Colorado, for example, 28 percent of the revenues to the state gaming fund go to the Colorado Historical Society, which distributes 20 percent of what it receives to the three gaming towns—Cripple Creek, Central City, and Black Hawk—and the remainder for preservation elsewhere in the state.

Other sources of local revenues from gambling include increased property taxes from commercial developments, as well as increased sales taxes. Also, gambling creates local jobs. After the introduction of riverboat gambling in Tunica County, Mississippi in 1992, unemployment dropped from 25.1 percent to 6.8 percent.[12] Before casinos, 20 percent of Tunica's residents received cash welfare payments; in 1995, 12 percent did.[13] In Gilpin County, Colorado, nearly 1,100 new jobs were added in 1992, one year after gambling was legalized in Central City and Black Hawk.[14]

The only revenues that should properly be counted in a community's assessment of the benefits of gambling, however, are the *new* money coming into the area from visitors. Money spent by local residents on gambling is money diverted from other discretionary spending—for other entertainment, for example. In fact, it can be argued that, overall, gambling is a zero-sum industry—it does not increase gross expenditures but, rather, takes away from other types of expenditure.[15]

One year after riverboat gambling was introduced in Natchez, Mississippi (pop. 19,280), nearly half of the downtown retailers reported a drop in revenues of 10 percent or more, and revenues from the town's annual house tours decreased more than 20 percent.[16] Moreover, most gamblers spend money only within the gaming establishments themselves, not in the surrounding community. Riverboat casinos, especially, detached as they are from the community, are not in the business of serving the local economy; it is in the interest of casino owners to keep visitors on their boats or in their casinos as long as possible. Gamblers generally do not contribute to the local economy; rather, they are mostly day-trippers who gamble, eat, drink, enjoy entertainment on the river or in the casinos, and then depart. Communities eager to attract gamblers to eat and shop in their towns must provide worthy attractions to get them off the boat or out of the casino—specialty boutiques, unusual res-

6.12
When gambling was legalized in Black Hawk, Colorado, construction began immediately. For months, residents' lives were disrupted with noise, dust, and congestion.

6.13
This sign advertising the Pojoaque Casino in New Mexico can be seen from miles away.

taurants, or other amusements. In Natchez, however, although downtown retailers distributed discount coupon books featuring Main Street businesses to riverboat patrons, they felt gambling had no effect or even a negative effect on sales.[17]

Costs of Gambling

Legalized gambling also comes with serious community costs. These include economic costs, such as expenditures on infrastructure (roads, parking facilities, water and sewer lines) and other municipal services. The city budget of Black Hawk, Colorado, where legalized gambling

6.14
On the banks of the Mississippi River at Natchez, Mississippi, the Lady Luck Casino attracts visitors away from downtown stores. After the casino opened in 1993, downtown retailers reported a decline in sales, while hotels, motels, and restaurants experienced little increase in business. Most visitors to the casino come from within 50 miles and spend their money on the riverboat, not in Natchez.

started in 1990, went from $150,000 to $16 million over a four-year period. Before gambling, there were no municipal law enforcement officers; in 1994, there were 27.[18] Gambling brings physical and social costs as well. Crime in the community may increase. In Black Hawk, for example, arrests for driving under the influence of alcohol and for prostitution increased dramatically. Gambling development often brings traffic congestion, the displacement of residences and shops, a loss of population, and air, water, and noise pollution. Casinos can intrude on rural quality of life. Residents near the Sandia Casino in New Mexico, for example, are irritated by the strobe lights that flash twenty-four hours a day. The social costs of gambling may be serious as well. Although residents of Black Hawk still regard their town as a good place to live, many report a loss of sense of community since the introduction of gambling—a feeling of living in an adult theme park.

Communities have choices about whether they want the kind of transforming changes that gambling brings. Residents must decide in advance whether and how gambling will fit into their vision of what they want the community to be. Rural communities facing gambling development must plan early and comprehensively; they must put appropriate ordinances and design guidelines in place. Communities participating in gambling must recognize that its impacts are more uncertain than those of traditional land uses. Even if comprehensive planning is undertaken well in advance, unexpected developments may occur. Citizens of Natchez, Mississippi, for example, developed a strong waterfront development plan before riverboat gambling was initiated in February 1993. Subsequently, the city amended the plan to allow construction of a previously prohibited 550-car parking lot within the proposed boundaries of the Natchez National Historical Park.

In the long run, it is difficult to predict whether gambling will prove to be a dependable rural economic development tool. It does not necessarily ensure opportunities for local economic success. The competition for

6.15
The Sandia casino in New Mexico
shines its lights twenty-four hours a
day. Neighboring communities have
found such lighting intrusive.

gambling revenues is fierce, and there is no guarantee that any one location will continue to be favored over another. In fact, it is possible that,
in the long run, rural communities will not be able to compete with large
cities and metropolitan areas that offer gambling as well as other diver-
sions. Again, the stakes are high and must be carefully considered.

CASE STUDY 6.4

Deadwood, South Dakota:
Making Gambling and Historic
Preservation Compatible

Deadwood (pop. 1,930), in the Black Hills of South Dakota, has a renowned
gambling history and today is the only town in South Dakota where organized
gambling is legal. Founded during the gold rush of 1875, Deadwood was home
to Wild Bill Hickok, Calamity Jane, Wyatt Earp, and other famous characters of
the Old West. Hickok was killed in Deadwood, while playing poker. The hand
he was holding at the fatal moment—black aces and eights—is still known as
the Deadman's Hand.

   Deadwood is the county seat of Lawrence County, located near the state's
western border. Deadwood's biggest boom years were at the turn of the century.
The town flourished until World War II, when gold production ceased. By the
1960s, tourism was Deadwood's main attraction. Deadwood's downtown, declared a National Historic Landmark in 1961, then attracted visitors seeking
the ambiance of the nineteenth-century gambling town. Unfortunately, over the
next three decades, a series of fires destroyed more than a dozen significant historic buildings, and by 1988, what was left of the downtown appeared shabby
and neglected.

6.16
Most of the downtown of Deadwood has been restored since legalized gambling came to town. Big Jake's Cardroom and Sophie's Slots and Sodas are in a historic building which operated as a grocery store from 1882 until 1990. The street paving bricks were placed there in 1991 through funds derived from gambling.

The efforts of the Deadwood You Bet Committee resulted, in November 1988, in a statewide referendum on a constitutional amendment to allow limited-stakes gambling within Deadwood's city limits. Sixty-four percent of the voters approved the measure.

Gambling began in November 1989 in five establishments and was an immediate visitor attraction. Within a year about 70 percent of the historic commercial buildings in the city's downtown historic district had been converted to casinos. Gambling has its limits in Deadwood. Each gambling establishment may have no more than thirty devices (slot machines or tables), and no single licensee may have more than ninety devices in his or her name. Gamblers may wager no more than $5 in any single bet. A requirement that gambling be associated with a secondary business, such as food, liquor, or gifts, was quickly found to be unenforceable and was eliminated.

Parking, congestion, and public services became immediate concerns as the town struggled to cope with unexpected demand. The city issued revenue bonds obligating its share of gaming taxes to pay for three parking projects, a new city hall, a fire station, a restructuring of utilities, sidewalks, and brick resurfacing of Main Street, among other projects. The economic impacts of gambling on Deadwood and surrounding Lawrence County have been considerable. After the first year of gambling, more than 1,000 new gambling-related jobs had been created and city sales tax receipts had increased by 73 percent. By 1992, Lawrence County had nearly 3,000 workers in the tourism industry. Annual visitation increased from less than 500,000 to more than 1.5 million.

In 1992, Deadwood received over $5 million as its share of gaming tax and license fees. All of the gambling revenue returned to Deadwood is used for historic preservation activities. The town's accomplishments include the restoration of museums, street improvement, restoration of a 1930s log rodeo grandstand, water and sewer systems, refurbishment of the city's 1912 recreation center, and restoration of a 1904 Carnegie library. Deadwood established a $2 million low-interest revolving loan fund which has supported the restoration of historic private residences and commercial buildings. The Gilmore Hotel, built in 1892, has been rehabilitated for low- and moderate-income housing through the use of the loan fund. The city's gaming revenue has also supported painting of historic homes, construction of a trail along the creek from one edge of town to the other, walking-tour signs, and development of an archive facility to house historic documents and artifacts relating to Deadwood's history.

With their businesses located on Main Street, most of the casino owners—even though they may not live in Deadwood—have been involved in community issues and regularly attend community meetings. A survey of the town's citizens conducted by the Aspen Institute two years after gambling was introduced revealed general community support for gambling, a feeling that gambling is appropriate, and a sense that, although traffic congestion had increased substantially, citizens felt safe. Deadwood's neighborhoods appear to be stable, with only 6.5 percent of residences changing owners each year since gambling began. After holding a series of neighborhood meetings in 1995, Mark Wolfe, Deadwood's historic preservation officer, found strong positive feelings for the community. Most people, he said, "love where they live; they wouldn't live anywhere else." Although some residents lament the loss of the small-town friendliness that prevailed before gambling (some have said Deadwood now feels like a town full of strangers,), for the most part, gambling, it seems, has been a successful economic development strategy for Deadwood.

In terms of lessons learned, Wolfe believes that rural communities pursuing gambling must do as much advance planning as possible. "The industry is very competitive, and [casino operators] want signs, lights, and noise. A community must have its zoning, sign, and preservation ordinances in place first; otherwise, it will be too late." Second, Wolfe says, communities must make sure that the industry people coming in buy into the community's vision of what it wants to be. "They need to understand the connection between gambling and preservation—that is their market."

HERITAGE AREA DEVELOPMENT

A number of rural communities have found that economic development is best approached on a regional basis and with a combination of complementary goals. Such efforts to unite job and income creation with historic preservation, tourism, natural resource conservation, and recreational development across several communities are frequently structured around the concept of "heritage areas." A heritage area is both a geographic region and a framework for heritage conservation and development; the concept belongs both to the region and to the process of organizing for and implementing heritage conservation. Establishing a heritage area is a way of protecting resources that are nationally distinctive and representative of the national experience but should remain in private ownership.

Some heritage areas have been designated by the federal government through acts of Congress and have received federal funding and technical assistance from the National Park Service. Assistance has included developing feasibility studies and management plans, building interpretive facilities, and providing staff. An important benefit of federal designation is national recognition; to be a National Heritage Corridor, for example, conveys a special significance to residents and visitors alike. As of this writing, Congress is considering generic legislation that would authorize the Park Service to administer a national heritage areas program.

Several states have also developed heritage area programs—Maryland, Massachusetts, New York, and Pennsylvania—and have designated specific areas within the states. Pennsylvania's heritage parks are eligible for technical assistance and grants from the state both before and after official designation, but they must compete for the grant funding through a competitive application process.

Other heritage areas are created by local governments or nonprofit organizations, often several entities working in partnership. Although outside recognition may help, becoming a heritage area basically requires that a group of communities in a well-defined region share a common vision of the future and agree to cooperate to build that future. Heritage areas are about building partnerships, bringing together interest groups that, each with its own agenda, can work together toward a shared set of goals.

Defining a Heritage Area

A heritage area is a region with a strong sense of place, where natural and cultural forces have combined to produce a distinctive, special landscape. Heritage areas are often organized around large-scale physical resources—such as a river, a valley, a lake, a range of hills—which are readily recognizable and which have helped to shape the culture of the region. For example, the Quinebaug and Shetucket Rivers in Connecticut form the organizing element behind the heritage area of the same name, which was designated by Congress in 1994. Here, a distinct settlement

6.17
This view of Lake Ocoee from the Chilhowee Overlook shows the rugged terrain and scenic beauty of the Tennessee Overhill heritage area.

pattern of small farms and scattered villages evolved along the quiet rivers; the region has remained remarkably intact and is often referred to as the "last green valley" between Boston and Washington, D.C. The heritage area called Tennessee Overhill was so named by the British, because it is just west of the Southern Appalachian mountains, settled by one group of Cherokees "over the hill" from the coastal Cherokee community (see Figure 6.17). The LBJ Heartland refers to the hill country of Texas, a crescent-shaped area along the Balcones Escarpment where President Johnson's LBJ Ranch is situated.

Because most heritage areas are rooted in some aspect of physical geography, transportation networks—canals, railroads, roads, and trails—frequently play an important role in the growth and development of a heritage area and may, in fact, be the unifying feature of the region, such as the Illinois and Michigan Canal in Illinois or the Lincoln Highway in Pennsylvania. Heritage areas may be urban as well as rural, and often they link rural and urban places. For example, the Ohio and Erie Canal Corridor extends from Cleveland in the north through Akron to the rural farming town of Zoar 87 miles to the south. And Tracks Across Wyoming follows the line of the Union Pacific Railroad across the southern part of the state and links Cheyenne, the capital, with rural Wyoming railroad communities.

Heritage areas often come into being because a particular region with a strong and distinctive history has experienced some kind of loss—of an industry, a resource base, population, or sense of well-being. In such cases, communities, aware of the heritage of the past, unwilling to let it be forgotten, and eager to reestablish a sense of place, form a heritage area to restore economic vitality and draw attention and investment to the region. The Blackstone River Valley in Massachusetts and Rhode Island, where the water-powered textile industry was flourishing in the late eighteenth century, was largely abandoned by the mid-twentieth century, the river polluted and the mill villages empty. Its congressional designation as a National Heritage Corridor in 1986 evolved from years of efforts by local communities, both states, and the National Park Service to plan for and develop the unique resources of the region. Numerous heritage areas celebrate the role of industry in their past: the mining of coal and iron ore, for example, or the manufacturing of steel. In Pennsylvania's statewide heritage park program, each park reflects some aspect of the state's industrial heritage. West Virginia marks its coal history through several heritage areas. And the Southwest Montana Heritage Area, focused on Anaconda and Butte, honors the role of copper mining in the state's economic development.

Not all heritage areas are generated from a sense of loss and abandonment, of course. The LBJ Heartland Council, an organization seeking to preserve and promote the hill country region of Texas, began as a group of supporters of the LBJ State and National Historic Parks, assembled to consider ways of accommodating change in the face of growth pressures from nearby San Antonio and Austin. Today the LBJ Heartland Council is a regional educational and planning organization promoting both the protection of resources of the region and economic development. The John Singleton Mosby Heritage Area in the northern Piedmont of Virginia (named after a renowned Confederate soldier who conducted raids throughout the region) was created in response to development and road-widening threats. Local community leaders, looking for a way to proclaim how special they believed their region to be, but sensitive to local concerns about property rights and the burdens of new zoning requirements, decided that establishing a heritage area would serve their purpose best. Here, after a year of planning, citizens sought the endorsement of local government and business organizations and produced an opening event, to which they charged admission, to proclaim the heritage area's existence. The heritage area designation requires no changes to local comprehensive plans or zoning ordinances, and the boundaries are loosely defined. Thus, in the Mosby Heritage Area, the emphasis is on voluntary inclusion, and the purpose is educational and celebratory.

CASE STUDY 6.5

Tracks Across Wyoming: Linking Communities along a Historic Transportation Corridor

In 1992, after a ten-year hiatus, Amtrak restored passenger service along the lines of the Union Pacific Railroad in southern Wyoming. This event sparked an unprecedented series of meetings and cooperative ventures among the communities linked by the railroad and gave birth to a new heritage area—Tracks Across Wyoming.

The reintroduction of passenger service along the 400-mile-long route across the state gave new life to the six Wyoming communities whose settlement and economic livelihood had once been based on rail transportation. All still had historic railroad depots, some recently rehabilitated. In 1992, with the help of the National Trust and the Wyoming State Historic Preservation Office, the communities held a heritage tourism forum, focused on the role of the transcontinental railroad in the history of southern Wyoming. Tracks Across Wyoming was created to carry the group's enthusiasm forward.

Through a series of initial meetings, the group got organized, developing articles of incorporation, by-laws, a board of directors, a membership structure, a vision statement, a mission statement, and short- and long-term goals. The vision statement of Tracks Across Wyoming expresses the multiple interrelated reasons why heritage areas get started:

> Tracks Across Wyoming will preserve, interpret and celebrate Wyoming's historic resources, natural beauty, quality of life and spirit, with first-class, authentic preservation and interpretation of historic sites. The corridor will be a "cerebral tourism" experience, with opportunities for visitors to learn about the rich history and culture of southern Wyoming. The cooperative effort among communities will improve the image of the southern area of Wyoming and will improve economic stability for the region.

The fledgling organization received from the Wyoming Department of Economic Development a grant, matched with cash and in-kind contributions from all six counties along the corridor, to develop a strategic plan. The plan set an agenda of actions to be accomplished each year. In 1994, for example, the plan

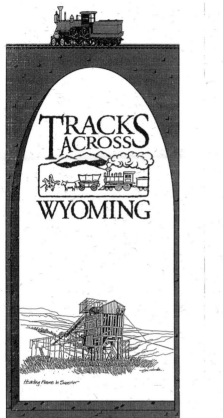

MEMBERSHIP
APPLICATION

NAME

ADDRESS

CITY   STATE   ZIP

TELEPHONE

CHECK FOR $ _____ ENCLOSED
(PAYABLE TO TRACKS ACROSS WYOMING,
INC.)

**PLEASE SEND INFORMATION
ON THE FOLLOWING:**

☐ Volunteer opportunities

☐ Committees

☐ Corridor Events

VISION

Tracks Across Wyoming will preserve, interpret and celebrate Wyoming's historic resources, natural beauty, quality of life and spirit. With first class authentic preservation and interpretation of historic sites, the corridor will be an exciting tourism experience, with opportunities for visitors to learn about the rich history and culture of southern Wyoming. The cooperative effort among communities will improve the image of the southern area of Wyoming and will improve economic stability for the region.

JOIN TRACKS ACROSS WYOMING TODAY!
Tracks Across Wyoming, Inc.
1200 Main Street
Evanston, Wyoming 82930
(307) 789-9690

6.18
Tracks Across Wyoming developed a membership brochure which displays its logo boldly on the front. Memberships in Tracks Across Wyoming start at $20, but benefactor memberships are also offered: Mountain Man, $100; Railroad Builder, $250; Miner, $500; Rancher, $1,000; and Territorial Governor, $5,000.

called for, and the group accomplished, production of a brochure and a map of the corridor showing the major communities and attractions. Forty thousand copies of the map were printed and distributed.

The board of Tracks Across Wyoming meets four times a year, alternating locations along the railroad line. Twice yearly, educational meetings for members feature a guest speaker. The group continues to undertake new projects. It produced a slide show and script describing the corridor which was distributed to each county; it developed a speakers bureau; it produced and distributed a membership brochure. In 1993 Tracks developed a five-day media familiarization bus tour for the press. This resulted in articles about the corridor in *American Heritage* magazine, the *Laramie Daily Boomerang,* and the (Cheyenne) *Wyoming Eagle.*

Over the years, the focus of Tracks on the railroad linkage has diminished. Rather, the communities involved in Tracks emphasize the many linkages among them—the early trails (the Oregon Trail, the Mormon Trail, the Overland Trail, the stagecoach route, and the route of the Pony Express), the Lincoln Highway, as well as Interstate 80. In 1995 Tracks produced a 90-minute audio cassette that takes visitors from east to west and west to east along the corridor. Funding to develop the cassette came from lodging tax receipts contributed by some of the towns, the Wyoming Division of Tourism, and city and county governments.

Tracks publicity has heightened the awareness of the state and western travelers to the attractions of southern Wyoming. Relates Mary Humstone of the National Trust, who worked closely with Tracks, "the region is getting known as

6.19
Tracks Across Wyoming encompasses several generations of transcontinental transportation, including the Overland Stage Route, the Union Pacific Railroad, and Interstate 80, all pictured here. The stabilized ruins of the Point of Rocks State Station, east of Rock Springs, Wyoming, is one of the attractions in the Tracks corridor.

more than the fastest way to get across Wyoming." But more important, she feels, is the cooperative spirit that the heritage area embodies. "Counties and communities that have been rivals are working together." Jim Davis, executive director of Tracks, agrees. "It's the networking and creating partnerships that have been most beneficial. For us, with a 400-mile-long corridor, the logistics have been tough, but the partnerships and friendships will be there for a long, long time." There is a heightened awareness of preservation along the corridor, and a sense that each community belongs to something much bigger than itself. Says Davis, "We are just getting started."

Building Partnerships

Establishing heritage areas almost always serves several purposes. Communities seek new recognition and investment but recognize that these goals can best be achieved on a regional basis and through a combination of means and an alliance of interests. When diverse groups work together for a common vision, much more can be accomplished than when one interest group acts alone. In heritage areas, the various interests and goals complement and bolster one another. For example, in Essex County, Massachusetts, the Essex Heritage Ad Hoc Commission, which includes representatives of business and government from thirty-four cities and towns, works in partnership with the North Shore Chamber of Commerce, the North of Boston Visitor and Convention Bureau, the Lynn Business Partnership, and numerous smaller organizations and private individuals, to promote the assets of the region.

The multiplicity of goals involved in heritage areas logically calls for partnerships of interests to carry them out. Local nonprofit groups established to focus on particular interests or projects cannot achieve the goals alone; they must cooperate with the business community as well as local government and other interested parties. Local governments need private interests and nonprofits because of their flexibility and entrepreneurial spirit. Whereas, private interests need the buy-in of local governments because of the scope and magnitude of heritage areas and the goals they undertake.

The organization that takes the lead in establishing a heritage area and implementing its goals—the management entity—can take many forms, but it is always a partnership or works in tandem with other organizations in a partnership arrangement. For example, in Pennsylvania's heritage parks, the management entity most often is a nonprofit corporation created from diverse community interests, including leaders of the business community, specifically to oversee implementation of the heritage area plan. Tracks Across Wyoming's eleven-member board works with the State Historic Preservation Office, the Wyoming Division of Tourism, the Wyoming Department of Economic Development, the Bureau of Land Management, and the National Trust.

Building partnerships in a heritage area is an ongoing process—in fact, it is probably the most important function a heritage area serves. To be successful, management entities must recognize the importance of involving all the interest groups of the community—business leaders, the chamber of commerce, local government officials, nonprofit organizations, civic groups, anyone who has a stake in the region's future. The greater the number of groups that invest their time, energy, and money toward the region's goals, the more will be achieved.

In Easton, Pennsylvania, where the Lehigh River flows into the Delaware River in the Delaware and Lehigh Canal National Heritage Corridor (a federally designated heritage area as well as a state heritage park), a canal museum had been operating since 1970 through a partnership of the city, a local park commission, and the Pennsylvania Canal Society. However, its exhibit and visitor space was inadequate, and the state legislature had pledged funds to build an expanded museum. The Delaware and Lehigh Management Action Plan, developed in 1993, designated the museum as a potential "landing," or visitors' center, a focal point for revitalization in the corridor. By the late 1980s, Easton's downtown stores were nearly two-thirds vacant, and Orr's, the local department store, had closed down its 80,000-square-foot building on the town square. Economic studies for Easton suggested that the downtown needed a major new visitor attraction, and Easton's new mayor, Tom Goldsmith, was committed to downtown revitalization.

Binney and Smith, the maker of Crayola crayons, which has its factory in Easton, offered to join with the city to locate its planned Crayola Factory visitors' center in Easton's downtown—in fact, in the abandoned Orr's building. The canal museum joined forces with Binney and Smith and the city and offered to locate the canal museum downtown. Together, with funding from the state, the city, and Binney and Smith, Orr's was acquired and rehabilitated to create Two Rivers Landing, which contains the Crayola Factory center—featuring company history, manufacturing, and creative art activities—a Delaware and Lehigh Heritage Corridor visitors' center, and the National Canal Museum—a showpiece of heritage tourism and economic development central to the corridor. Into another nearby building, Binney and Smith is locating a Crayola-brand store and the city of Easton is relocating its city hall.

INTRODUCTION

Welcome to the Tennessee Overhill – so named because it was home to the Cherokee Towns that rested on the western slopes of the Appalachian Mountains – overhill from the Lower Cherokee settlements.

The Tennessee Overhill is best known for its rivers–the Ocoee, Hiwassee, Tellico and Little Tennessee. These rivers, along with Lake Ocoee, Tellico Lake and other smaller lakes and streams, offer more than enough for a vacation of whitewater rafting, floating, canoeing, sailing, fishing and water skiing.

Visitors can follow rivers and trails to explore the Cherokee National Forest by car, foot, horseback or boat. For those who love adventure, there is gliding, rappelling, caving, gold panning and hunting.

And there's more. Outdoor recreation is just one offering of the Tennessee Overhill. Museums, historic sites and reenactments spin tales of Cherokee Indians, fur traders, settlers, loggers, miners, railroaders, textile workers, farmers and sharecroppers - the people who came together to sculpt the cultural legacy of the Tennessee Overhill.

Sequoyah, inventor of the Cherokee alphabet. His life and the Cherokee culture is celebrated in the Sequoyah Birthplace Museum at Vonore.

You won't find high rises or glass and steel buildings. Many of the points of interest lie along highways and backroads surrounded by streams, mountains, forests and small towns.

Selected by the National Trust for Historic Preservation and the Tennessee Department of Tourist Development as one of sixteen heritage tourism demonstration areas, the Tennessee Overhill is comprised of the Southeast Tennessee counties of McMinn, Monroe and Polk, as well as the southern portion of the Cherokee National Forest. The mission of this non-profit organization is to promote and preserve the historical and cultural character of the Overhill.

This publication is offered as a traveling companion to guide you through the Overhill. For additional information contact Chamber of Commerce offices or the Tennessee Overhill office listed on page 20.

▥

CONTENTS

▥

Cover Painting "Lake Ocoee"/Oil on Canvas, Carolyn Jones

A special thanks to Murray Lee/Tennessee Photo Services and Nell Griffin/Bellevue Frame & Art Gallery of Nashville, Tennessee.

1

6.20
The visitors' guide to the Tennessee Overhill introduces visitors to the various attractions of the region.

Heritage Development

The goals of most heritage areas integrate tourism and recreation development with historic preservation, education, and land conservation; thus, "heritage development" conveys well what heritage areas are formed to accomplish. Measurable results in heritage development take time, so, communities should temper enthusiasm with patience and boosterism with realistic expectations. In part, the amount of time involved relates to the complexity and number of the project's goals; in part it is a function of the multiplicity of interest groups and, perhaps, of jurisdictions that are trying to work together. Heritage area success begins with small steps. A brochure published, a grant received, a new festival successfully accomplished, a new business opened for tourists—these are the beginning. But these small steps lead to larger ones and feed into one another.

First, heritage development builds local awareness and pride. In the LBJ Heartland, one of the greatest accomplishments has been saving and rehabilitating the Blanco County Courthouse. Designed in 1886, the courthouse had been acquired by a developer, who was going to move it, brick by brick, to his ranch. A local preservation group that organized to stop the effort linked forces with the LBJ Heartland Council and together they raised the funds to buy out the developer. Saving the courthouse was a symbolic achievement that gave hope and pride to the community. The building is now being used for council offices and as a discovery center, where visitors can learn about the area's special natural and cultural resources.

In the plan developed for the Lackawanna Valley heritage area, Pennsylvania's first state heritage park, six interpretive sites were identified to tell the story of the anthracite coal industry in the region. Two of the sites where revitalization efforts are focused are Olyphant (pop. 5,298) and Carbondale (pop. 10,338), former coal towns with faltering downtown economies. Olyphant is planning to develop a folklife center to interpret the multiple cultures that settled the region, and Carbondale is planning to develop a visitors' orientation center, which will introduce visitors to the whole valley. In the meantime, however, heritage development efforts have been concentrated on building local pride and investment. For Halloween 1995, a special excursion "ghost train" traveled on the freight line between Olyphant and Carbondale for six nights in a row, bringing some 10,000 visitors from the region to towns whose normal Saturday night populations are only 500. More significant than dollars spent were the spirit and energy evident in the cooperative effort among the towns, the region, and the state.

In the Blackstone River Valley, a forty-nine-passenger riverboat, the *Blackstone Valley Explorer,* was constructed with funds raised by the Blackstone Valley Tourism Council from local corporations, communi-

6.21
The *Blackstone Valley Explorer* takes visitors past the Glenark Knitting Mill, in Woonsocket, Rhode Island. The mill, constructed shortly after the Civil War, has been rehabilitated for low-to-moderate income housing.

ties and private citizens, and a matching grant from the National Park Service. The boat is used by the council to introduce local residents and visitors to the valley. Its River Classroom program takes school children out on the river to learn about the ecology, hydrology, and culture of the valley. Within two years after the boat was launched in 1993, more than 50,000 passengers had seen the Blackstone Valley from the deck of the *Explorer.*

Many heritage areas, wishing to attract attention and new revenues, focus their heritage development goals on increased tourism. To bring visitors to the area and to encourage new local investment, there must be something to see and be proud of, as well as a story to tell. For this reason, heritage areas often start by developing tour routes: maps and brochures to guide visitors through the region by car or by walking. Maryland's Lower Eastern Shore developed a self-guided driving tour along the Beach-to-Bay American Indian Trail, which ties together parks, historic sites, and natural areas. In the Quinebaug and Shetucket Rivers National Heritage Corridor, the Association of Northeastern Connecticut Historical Societies published a brochure guiding visitors to hill towns and mill villages of the region along historic Route 169.

Much of the information and advice given about tourism in the previous sections of this chapter applies to heritage areas. Emphasizing what is authentic about a particular place is the key to heritage area development. In the Tennessee Overhill region, a grant from the National Endowment for the Arts through the Tennessee Arts Commission enabled the Tennessee Overhill Heritage Tourism Association to hire a full-time folklorist for three years. He works with local arts organizations on interpretation and develops programs on indigenous art forms and artists. Early in his tenure, he discovered that the Overhill area had a long tradition of blademaking—all kinds of blades—and he is now helping local groups to celebrate that heritage and interpret it to visitors.

6.22
On a back road in the Tennessee Overhill, Trew's General Merchandise, operating since 1890, is still open for visitors and locals. The store is listed in the National Register of Historic Places. Mortimer Trew, proprietor, holds a montage of photographs and clippings about the store, which includes a representation of Trew's ancestor, Return Meigs, one of the first Indian agents in the area.

6.23
Illinois and Michigan Canal stone locks provided passage for the long, narrow canal boats. Just north of this lock is the Aux Sable aqueduct which has been rebuilt in concrete. The Illinois and Michigan Canal National Heritage Corridor was the first heritage corridor designated by Congress.

The Illinois and Michigan Canal National Heritage Corridor offers many examples of how heritage areas can provide a framework for development. Since its designation in 1984, the I&M Canal Corridor has received more than $130 million in state, local, and private investment. Most of this money (some $95 million) has gone into recreation and tourism projects, and about $34 million has been invested in historic preservation.[19] One of the proudest achievements of the corridor organizers is the progress made on the longstanding dream of constructing a bike and pedestrian trail the entire length of the corridor. In 1994, 60 miles of trail existed between Joliet and the LaSalle-Peru area, along a historic towpath that parallels the canal. With help primarily from ISTEA transportation enhancements funds, another 23 miles of trail will be complete in 1998. One part of this new trail is through Heritage Park, a previously inaccessible 260-acre site that contains old quarries, blast furnace ruins from a steel plant, and remnants of prairie. Here, the industrial history of the corridor will receive special interpretation.

Heritage areas can bring together various approaches to development—heritage tourism, historic preservation, and Main Street revitalization. But the heritage area approach is even more holistic, for it integrates natural resource conservation and recreation—often through the development of trails, riverways, and scenic byways—with the preservation of the cultural environment. Heritage areas aim to link all the assets of a region and both promote and protect them in a balance of preservation and development. It may be difficult to achieve, but it is a goal well worth striving for.

CONCLUSION

If your community is seeking or confronting economic development, finding the balance between development and rural conservation will be a challenge. Too much development or development of the wrong kind can destroy a community's rural character. This is particularly the case with large-scale industrial development but may also result from tourism and gambling. Too many visitors can transform a community from a quiet, peaceful place to a bustling boom town; too many residents can change a community to an appendage of suburbia.

It is important to remember the principles of self-development and authenticity. Your community will sustain development in the long run if you rely on your own inner resources—the people, and the natural and cultural features—that make your community special. Communities should also keep in mind that no one development strategy is likely to succeed as well as several pursued simultaneously. That is, downtown revitalization coupled with a farmers' market that brings in new visitors, coordinated with an agricultural and craft festival, not only promises a greater return on investment but also assures that, if for some reason one aspect of the development strategy fails, success will still be achievable.

Getting Help from the Outside

INTRODUCTION

Unless a nationally significant resource is at stake, most rural conservation programs depend primarily on local initiative and financing. Using the techniques described in the previous five chapters, you can go a long way toward protecting your community's natural areas, historic sites, scenic vistas, farmland, and economic vitality. Assistance from national, state, and regional agencies and nonprofit organizations can certainly help, however. Communities diligent in seeking outside funding, advice, and the application of state and federal regulations are generally more successful than those that try to handle all their programs alone.

Don't assume, however, that you will necessarily get the help you need from outside sources. State and federal agencies and national nonprofit organizations often have their own agendas; your needs may or may not fit in with their priorities at the time you request assistance. Furthermore, many state agencies and national nonprofit organizations are operating with diminished budgets and staff, so they may simply be spread too thin to offer help or provide it when asked.

Federal and state laws and programs change frequently. For example, new legislation may be enacted or existing laws amended or repealed; laws may apply only for a certain number of years; over time, the courts and executive administrations vary in their interpretation and enforcement of laws; and the amount of funding available for grants and their eligibility requirements rarely remain constant. Also, nonprofit organizations often change their focus over the years as leaders change, funds become available from different sources, and organizational philosophies evolve. For these reasons, we cannot provide a comprehensive listing of current laws and programs; instead, we have attempted to give you ideas about the types of laws and programs that may be available to you and the strategies your organization may use when it seeks help.

After discussing the nature of outside help and of lobbying, we describe those laws and programs that are of greatest relevance to most rural communities. In Appendix 2 you will find basic information on all of the federal agencies and national nonprofit organizations described in this chapter, as well as others. Many more, plus state agencies, are described in the National Wildlife Federation's annual *Conservation Directory*. Although our focus here is on federal agencies and national nonprofit organizations, state agencies and organizations will in many instances be more responsive. Indeed, many of the federal laws and national programs have their antecedents in innovative approaches first tried at the state level, and states often carry out federally established programs.

THE NATURE OF OUTSIDE HELP

There are several varieties of environmental laws. Some prohibit actions that may be harmful to the environment or require review procedures before certain types of activities can occur; others enable state or local governments to undertake programs to protect the environment. Several federal environmental laws provide partial funding to states or communities for their implementation. In some instances, such as requirements for environmental impact statements, states may have statutes paralleling the federal laws; in other instances, such as laws regulating air pollution, states may have laws that are stricter than federal regulations. Of course, not all governmental programs promote rural conservation. State and federal agencies may carry out agendas that do not conform to a rural community's vision of the future. They may not involve communities in their planning process and may not ask if communities approve of their proposed actions (see Case Study 7.2). Many governmental programs actually work against rural conservation. For instance, federal funds have often been used to finance highways, housing developments, and shopping centers that contributed to sprawl or consumed prime farmland.

Federal agencies are as varied as the laws they administer. Many, such as the Federal Energy Regulatory Commission, are centralized, have relatively narrow mandates, and have little citizen contact. Others—notably the Cooperative Extension Service, the Rural Housing and Community Development Service (part of the former Farmers Home Administration), and the Natural Resources Conservation Service (NRCS)—have broad mandates and are decentralized with many field offices to serve citizens and community groups. These federal agencies are often good initial contacts for community leaders seeking help in starting a rural conservation program.

There are also numerous nonprofit environmental organizations with differing approaches. Some, such as the Natural Resources Defense Council and the Environmental Defense Fund, are primarily concerned about large-scale environmental issues, federal policy, legislation, and precedent-setting litigation. These organizations have the resources to offer only limited assistance to community leaders. Others, such as the Land Trust Alliance, the National Trust for Historic Preservation, River Network, and the American Farmland Trust, enthusiastically assist community projects. Organizations such as the Sierra Club are interested in a variety of issues, while others, such as Clean Water Action, are more narrowly focused. Many, like the National Audubon Society, are membership organizations, while others, like the Trust for Public Land, are not. A few, most prominently the Nature Conservancy, protect land by acquiring and managing it; most, however, do not get involved in real estate transactions. Finally, help may be had from a number of statewide nonprofit organizations, such as Preservation North Carolina, the Iowa Natural Heritage Foundation, the Maine Coast Heritage Trust, and chapters of national organizations like the National Audubon Society, the National Wildlife Federation, and the Sierra Club.

There are many publications on federal and state laws and programs and about the work of nonprofit organizations. Reading about programs, however, is no substitute for talking with knowledgeable officials or representatives of organizations. Many agencies and organizations have current information on the relevant laws and programs for a particular issue. For instance, if a community is concerned about protecting a river, the first organization to contact may be River Network. For housing programs, the Housing Assistance Council and the county office of the Rural Housing and Community Development Service are the best bet.

As for potentially harmful government action, citizen vigilance is essential. Sometimes, a public notice published in the classified section of the local newspaper is the first indication a community receives of a proposed activity that may be of concern. If volunteer conservationists in Transylvania County, North Carolina, had not seen a notice about a proposed diversion of the waters of the Horsepasture River, that stream might not be free-flowing today (see Case Study 7.2). Fortunately, government agencies are required to publish notices for many proposed actions that affect the environment, but even earlier intelligence gathering may be important (see p. 100). Moreover, many agencies maintain mailing lists of individuals and organizations interested in receiving notifications of proposed activities.

LOBBYING

Rural conservation leaders should keep their elected representatives informed about their activities, even when there is no crisis. Officials should be invited to visit the community to learn first hand about its assets and to take part in awards ceremonies, festivals, and other events. They should regularly receive any newsletters or bulletins that the community may publish. It is wise to get elected officials interested and involved in projects from the beginning. Having a champion in Congress or the state legislature can be a critical asset.

Congressional representatives can help if a federal agency is not being responsive to a community's needs. A letter should be sent to a U.S. senator or the House member for the district, specifying what information or action is being requested of the agency. Elected officials usually forward letters from constituents to the appropriate agency and ask for clarification. Such letters generally receive high-priority handling in federal agencies. Letters to the Maine congressional delegation, for example, were pivotal in getting the National Oceanic and Atmospheric Administration to approve funds for the purchase of Laudholm Farm (see Case Study 7.3). The same approach, of course, can be used with state legislators if state agencies are not responsive. If all else fails, a lawsuit brought against an uncooperative agency may help, as Michigan's Citizens Concerned about Interstate 69 discovered (see Case Study 2.4).

If there is no relevant federal or state law, rural groups can consider working to enact a law, as did the Naturaland Trust in South Carolina when it persuaded the state legislature to approve enabling legislation for easements. The Friends of the Horsepasture persuaded Congress to request a study of the river for potential designation as a National Wild and Scenic River and to appropriate funds for land acquisition. And local organizations in Connecticut, Illinois, Louisiana, Massachusetts, Pennsylvania, and Rhode Island have obtained congressional legislation designating individual heritage areas within their states.

STATE LAND USE PLANNING AND REGULATION

Although the power to regulate the use of private land belongs ultimately to state governments, most regulation has traditionally been delegated to local governments. Since the 1970s, a number of states, faced with unprecedented growth, took direct control of certain land use decisions. Some, Oregon and Rhode Island among them, require local governments to prepare land use plans; others, such as Connecticut and New Jersey, have state plans and urge local governments to conform their own plans to the state's; and Georgia provides strong incentives for local governments to prepare land use plans. Other states regulate land that is considered critical, such as wetlands, floodplains, prime farmland, and coasts.

States with more comprehensive laws include Florida, Hawaii, Oregon, Vermont, and Washington. In Hawaii, all land is zoned by the state and placed in one of three categories: urban, agricultural, or conservation. Land in agricultural and conservation areas is regulated by the State Land Use Commission, and urban expansion is more contained as a result. In Washington, the fastest-growing counties must designate urban growth areas to contain sprawl.

The Vermont Environmental Control Act of 1970 (usually referred to as Act 250) provides for state review of proposed subdivisions of more than ten units, commercial development of more than ten acres (or more than one acre in towns lacking zoning regulations), and all construction above an altitude of 2,500 feet. District environmental commissions, appointed by the governor, review proposed developments covered by the act. Before issuing a permit, a commission must discern that a proposed development "will not have an undue adverse effect on the scenic or natural beauty of the area, esthetics, historic sites, or rare and irreplaceable natural areas." In Florida, the Environmental Land and Water Management Act of 1972 authorizes designation of "areas of critical state concern" that contain significant environmental, historical, or natural resources. If local governments do not protect these areas, the state can assume authority and regulate them. Florida also has "concurrency" legislation mandating that appropriate infrastructure be in place to handle local growth (that is, infrastructure construction must be concurrent with growth). Vermont's and Florida's laws have helped to control major developments, but small-scale developments that do not come under the purview of the laws have often gone unchecked. Vermont passed the Growth Management Act of 1988, known as Act 200, to establish a broad statewide planning framework for all land use decisions. In addition to setting state planning goals, Act 200 requires regional planning commissions to adopt plans, and provides incentives for towns to adopt local plans.

In Oregon, the Land Conservation and Development Act of 1973 requires local governments to prepare comprehensive plans that must meet the conservation goals set by the state Land Conservation and Development Commission to protect such resources as coastal areas, farmland, and historic resources. The plans must delineate urban growth boundaries and designate prime farmland beyond the boundaries for "exclusive farm use." Oregon's law has withstood numerous legal challenges over the years from groups and property owners dissatisfied with the level of regulation.

Other states have designated certain areas as critical and have established comprehensive controls over them. For instance, New York enforces controls over 3.7 million acres of private land within the boundaries of the Adirondack Park. For more than a million acres in the park's resource management zone, the state-zoned minimum lot size is 42 acres. New Jersey, in cooperation with the federal government, has established controls over private lands in the Pinelands National Reserve. Maine's Land Use Regulation Commission plans and zones private land in the state's sparsely inhabited northern woods. In the 1980s, both Maryland and Virginia passed laws to protect the Chesapeake Bay and the land around it. Under Maryland's Chesapeake Bay Act, local governments must implement programs that limit certain land uses and require performance standards for lands within 1,000 feet of the bay's tidal wetlands. Virginia's Chesapeake Bay Preservation Act requires local governments in the tidewater region of the state to enact mechanisms to protect water quality and to manage stormwater through their comprehensive plans and zoning and subdivision ordinances. Maryland's Planning Act of 1992 requires local jurisdictions to identify all "sensitive areas," including streams, stream buffers, one-hundred-year floodplains, endangered species habitat, and steep slopes, and to describe how they will be protected.

7.1 Environmental Impact Statements

The National Environmental Policy Act (NEPA) requires all federal agencies to include in every recommendation for "major Federal actions significantly affecting the quality of the human environment," a detailed environmental impact statement (EIS) that describes

- *the environmental impact of the proposed action,*
- *any adverse environmental effects that cannot be avoided should the proposal be implemented,*
- *alternatives to the proposed action,*
- *the relationship between local short-term uses of the environment and the maintenance and enhancement of long-term productivity, and*
- *any irreversible and irretrievable commitments of resources which would be involved in the proposed action should it be implemented.*

In 1978, the Council on Environmental Quality established regulations for the application of the NEPA and EISs to the work of federal agencies. If more than one federal agency is involved, one of them is designated as the "lead agency." Other federal agencies and state and local governments can become "cooperating agencies." As a first step, the lead agency must prepare an environmental assessment for all projects that may have significant effects on the environment. This assessment provides the lead agency with the information it needs to determine whether a full EIS is needed. Federal agencies must elicit public comment in the process of making an environmental assessment.

If the lead agency determines that an EIS is necessary, it must involve interested parties in "scoping"—or "determining the scope of issues to be

Obviously, any rural community considering a plan or drafting land use ordinances should consult with the appropriate state officials to determine the requirements state governments have imposed. State officials may also be able and willing to assist in the preparation of the local plans and ordinances. There are many statewide nonprofit organizations that are concerned with land use issues. The Vermont Natural Resources Council and 1,000 Friends of Oregon, for example, have been particularly active in monitoring statewide land use laws, and the Pennsylvania Environmental Council has issued a detailed guidebook on land use regulations in Pennsylvania.

THE NATIONAL ENVIRONMENTAL POLICY ACT AND STATE EQUIVALENTS

With the passage in 1969 of the National Environmental Policy Act (NEPA), as amended, the United States embarked upon a national program of environmental protection. NEPA, which states that the federal government must make it possible for the nation to "preserve important historic, cultural, and natural aspects of our national heritage," is arguably the most comprehensive and significant federal law governing the environment in the nation's history.

NEPA's key provision is the requirement that all federal agencies prepare an environmental impact statement (EIS) for proposed federal actions and permits that might affect the environment (see Sidebar 7.1). An understanding of the EIS process is important for rural conservation leaders, since few communities are immune from federal actions. Projects undertaken by the private sector but requiring federal funds for a portion of their financing—as is the case for many large-scale construction projects—are also covered by NEPA. It is important to note that the preparation of an EIS does not stop the federal government from harming the environment. The law simply requires that the government take environmental values into account when planning projects.

Rural conservation leaders who understand the EIS process can ensure that their concerns are brought to the attention of the appropriate federal officials. For instance, farmers in Eaton County, Michigan, who were concerned about a new interstate highway that would have consumed prime farmland made good use of the EIS process to force the state highway department to change the road's alignment (see Case Study 2.4). Conservationists should determine whether the EIS has been prepared by qualified persons, covers all of the resources the community is concerned about, is accurate, and objectively presents the alternative courses of action. If a federal agency fails to prepare an EIS or prepare it adequately, citizens' groups can seek a court injunction to halt work on a project until NEPA has been complied with.

Many states have passed their own general environmental statutes, often referred to as "little NEPAs." They require documents similar to an EIS for actions of state and local governments (not covered by the federal NEPA) that may have an impact on the environment. For projects that involve both federal and state or local funds, the impact statements are generally prepared in coordination with the federal agency.

To facilitate cross-referencing, programs to deal with the following resources and problems are described in the same order in which they appear in Chapter 1.

WATER AND RELATED RESOURCES

Water Supply and Quality

The principal federal laws that protect water quality are the Clean Water Act of 1972, as amended, and the Safe Drinking Water Act of 1974, as amended. Both are administered by the Environmental Protection Agency (EPA), but the EPA delegates much of its authority to state agencies when their programs meet the EPA's approval. States are eligible for EPA grants to administer these two acts. There are also many state water-protection laws, some of them stricter than the federal laws.

The objective of the Clean Water Act is "to restore and maintain the chemical, physical, and biological integrity of the Nation's waters." Under the act, EPA has developed water-quality guidance to protect aquatic life and human health. The guidance specifies the maximum amount of certain pollutants that can be present in water without harming ecosystems or human health. Each state must set water-quality standards for its surface waters. To aid in meeting the standards, the Clean Water Act established the National Pollutant Discharge Elimination System, which requires all dischargers, including municipalities and industries, to obtain permits—commonly called NPDES permits—from EPA or approved state agencies before pollutants can be discharged into "the waters of the United States," defined to include wetlands. The quantities of pollutants that are discharged may be limited and required to be monitored.

The Clean Water Act addresses groundwater pollution, a growing concern of many rural communities, and "nonpoint source" pollution, from farmland, grazing areas, or parking lots, for example. Nonpoint pollution degrades more waters than point pollution. Section 319 of the Clean Water Act funds demonstration projects to control nonpoint source pollution as well as a grant program to help states control and abate nonpoint source pollution. All fifty states have developed nonpoint source management programs approved by EPA. Arizona's program builds partnerships interested in controlling nonpoint source pollution. In its Chino Winds Demonstration Project, for example, various individuals, state and federal agencies, and the University of Arizona are working on a system of rotational grazing that concentrates animal waste, controls water, and promotes more uniform rangeland.

Under the Clean Water Act, EPA has also developed regulations known as "antidegradation standards" which require states to preserve the water quality of streams. In the highest quality streams—"national resource waters"—there can be no new or increased discharges. In streams of above standard quality, discharges cannot degrade the water below the standard. By late 1995, twenty-four states had drafted laws implementing the antidegradation standards.

addressed" in the EIS. To facilitate review and comment by the public, the EIS must be written in "plain English" and for most projects be limited to 150 pages of text. There are specific requirements for format and the topics to be covered. The lead agency must circulate the completed EIS to all organizations, agencies, and people affected by or interested in the project to elicit their comments. Finally, once the lead agency has made its decision, it must maintain public records stating the agency's plans for ensuring mitigation of environmental impacts.

If the proposed federal action might affect historic, cultural, or archeological resources, a Section 106 review is often conducted simultaneously *(see p. 325).*

For further information on the NEPA process, contact the Council on Environmental Quality. The council's annual report summarizes regulation updates.

By providing grants and loans for construction of sewage treatment plants, the Clean Water Act has helped to solve many problems associated with harmful discharges. The original act has also created incentives for development in some rural areas, however, by requiring construction of sewage treatment facilities that exceeded the community's current needs. For instance, planners in Mecklenburg County, North Carolina, have found efforts at farmland retention thwarted by the presence of added sewer lines that are attracting development. The 1981 amendment to the act ameliorated this problem by stating that, after October 1984, grants would not be made "to construct that portion of any treatment works providing reserve capacity in excess of existing needs." EPA operates a state revolving loan fund program whereby states provide loans for sewer lines and sewage treatment plants.

While the Clean Water Act seeks to prevent or control water pollution at the source, the public water supply provisions of the Safe Drinking Water Act control it largely at the point of consumption. The act requires EPA to establish standards for specified pollutants in public drinking water supplies. Under the act, EPA also regulates the injection of pollutants into groundwater and designates aquifers that should be protected. If EPA designates an aquifer as "the sole or principal drinking water source for an area," no federal funds can be spent on projects that would contaminate it. Very few sole-source aquifers have been designated, though many exist. The Safe Drinking Water Act also established a national program to encourage the states to develop wellhead protection programs, and grants are available from EPA to protect wellheads and groundwater. Although the Safe Drinking Water Act has great potential for protecting groundwater supplies from pollution before treatment, enforcement has most often been ineffective.

Other bills that protect water quality include the Coastal Zone Management Act and the Federal Agricultural Improvement and Reform Act (FAIR) of 1996. The 1990 amendments to the Coastal Zone Management Act contain provisions that require states with coastal zone management programs to develop coastal nonpoint source pollution programs. FAIR established the Environmental Quality Incentive Program, which provides $200 million in mandatory spending for farming practices and structures—such as animal waste containment facilities—to reduce the impact of agricultural production on water quality and other environmental elements.

The best sources of information about water pollution control are the regional offices of EPA and state agencies charged with protecting water quality. Numerous national organizations, such as the Natural Resources Defense Council, the Sierra Club Legal Defense Fund, the Environmental Defense Fund, the National Audubon Society, the Izaak Walton League, the Groundwater Foundation, and Clean Water Action, work on legislation, litigate on clean water issues, and may be good sources of information, but they do not generally get involved in local issues unless there is the potential to set a national precedent.

Middlesboro, Kentucky:
Yellow Creek Concerned Citizens Insist on
Clean Water

An example of a local group that has used the Clean Water Act to curb water pollution is Yellow Creek Concerned Citizens, in Middlesboro, Kentucky (pop. 11,826) For years a local tanning company had dumped chemical wastes into the creek. The stench was often overpowering. Fish died and wildlife disappeared. Residents along the creek objected, but to no avail. The tannery was the major employer in town, and the city government and the courts seemed reluctant to force the company to stop polluting. A newly renovated city wastewater treatment plant, partly funded under the Clean Water Act, went on line in 1975 and received the tannery's waste but could not adequately treat it.

For Larry Wilson, who lived nearby, the final straw was when his pigs, goats, and cattle died after drinking creek water. In July 1980, Wilson and his neighbors came together to form Yellow Creek Concerned Citizens to combat the problem. The group incorporated and elected Wilson president.

A few months later, the Environmental Protection Agency (EPA) held hearings on reissuing a discharge permit to the Middlesboro Sewage Treatment Plant. The Concerned Citizens objected, saying the city should be denied a permit until it could prove that it could effectively treat the company's waste. A number of other hearings followed. The Concerned Citizens gained membership and, more importantly, became regarded as a responsible, well-informed organization. Wilson states: "We use the old accounting principle of understatement rather than overstatement. When people start investigating what we said, most of the time they'll find it's worse than the way we stated it." The group even took its case to Washington, D.C., testifying in 1982 at congressional hearings on the Clean Water Act.

After being presented with much evidence of an alarming incidence of cancer and other diseases among residents living along the creek, local and state officials finally concluded that wells near the creek were unsafe. In September 1982, the state government and the Farmers Home Administration agreed to finance a new water system.

But the Concerned Citizens also wanted to stop the pollution itself. That November, the EPA ordered the city to do a better job of cleaning up the effluent. The Concerned Citizens also pressured the EPA to sue the city and the tannery for violating the Clean Water Act. The city was forced to pay $50,000 in damages.

In 1983, the group filed a class action lawsuit against the company and the city, asking for $31 million in damages. The city of Middlesboro was dropped from the suit in 1988 after it imposed stringent regulations on the tannery, paid $390,000, and built a new sewage treatment facility. In 1989 the tannery filed for bankruptcy, but the suit was brought against the four individual owners of the company. Finally, in February 1995, the suit was brought to court. The jury heard the case for eleven days then ruled in favor of the plaintiffs. The court awarded them $15.1 million—$11 million for a medical monitoring fund to test the residents living along Yellow Creek and $4.1 in punitive damages, both of which the plaintiffs had requested during the course of the suit.

The tannery is still in operation by one of the original owners and new partners—but with much more stringent permits. In addition, the new sewage treatment plant has helped the situation considerably. The Yellow Creek Concerned Citizens stay active, with some 450 members, monitoring environmental quality in the valley. According to Shelia Wilson, who testified in court about the health difficulties her family had suffered, although the water in the creek is beautiful, the sediment is still toxic. Nevertheless, wildlife—especially deer and beaver—are beginning to return to the banks of Yellow Creek. "It is recovering; it's amazing."

As one observer has noted, "the same story is endlessly repeated of citizens groups believing at first that all they need do is demonstrate a serious problem in violation of the laws for somebody somewhere to do something. But typically it is shrewd political pressure, as was brought to bear in Middlesboro, that gets results."

Rivers

Most rivers are located in more than one town or county. Consequently, efforts to protect them are usually undertaken by organizations working at the regional or state level or by an organization set up for the specific purpose of protecting a particular river or a watershed. The James River Association in Virginia spans dozens of counties, and the Mississippi River Basin Alliance covers all ten states drained by the Mississippi.

The 1968 Wild and Scenic Rivers Act, as amended, states that it is federal policy to preserve rivers that "possess outstandingly remarkable scenic, recreational, geologic, fish and wildlife, historic, cultural, or other similar values." The law sets up a mechanism to designate and protect any sections of those rivers that meet at least one of the above criteria, are relatively undeveloped, are free-flowing (i.e., are not dammed), and have good water quality.

In being designated, rivers are classified as "wild," "scenic," or "recreational," depending on the ease of access and the amount of development along them. Management plans prepared by the federal government for designated rivers are strictest for wild rivers and the most flexible for recreational rivers. Designated rivers are also protected from federally funded, assisted, or licensed dams, channelization, and other water projects. The act authorizes the federal government to acquire land or easements along their banks. As of 1995, 150 river segments (10,734 miles) had been designated by Congress.

There are two routes to securing designation under the Wild and Scenic Rivers Act, and two steps in each process. In one, Congress must first authorize study of a river for its potential addition to the system. The eligibility of the river for designation is then reviewed by the Department of the Interior, or the Department of Agriculture for rivers on Forest Service land. During this time, public comment is solicited. After the studies are complete, they are submitted to Congress for legislative action on their designation. As of 1996, of the eighty-three "study rivers," as they are called—those deemed eligible for designation—forty have been added to the system. Failure of a river to be designated usually results

7.1
Opposite: This map shows the rivers protected under Michigan's Natural Rivers Act.

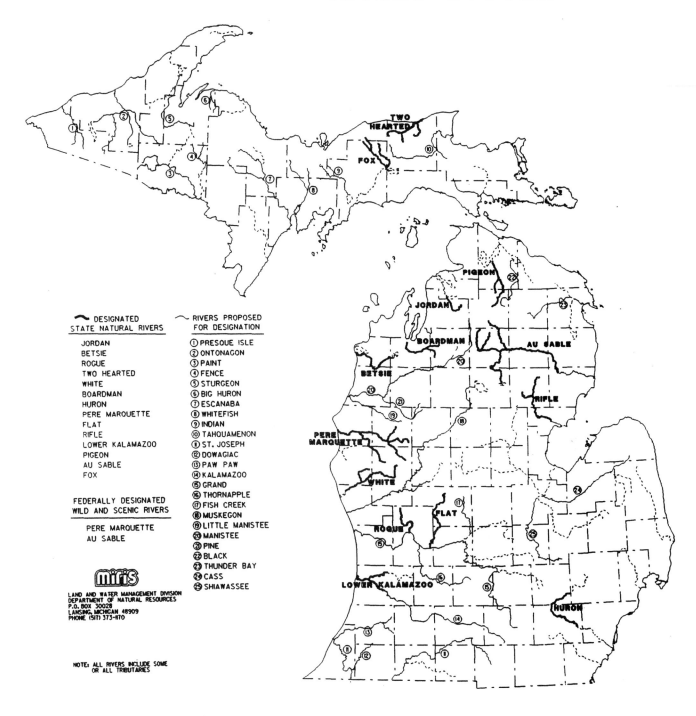

MICHIGAN'S NATURAL RIVERS SYSTEM

DESIGNATED STATE NATURAL RIVERS

JORDAN
BETSIE
ROGUE
TWO HEARTED
WHITE
BOARDMAN
HURON
PERE MARQUETTE
FLAT
RIFLE
LOWER KALAMAZOO
PIGEON
AU SABLE
FOX

FEDERALLY DESIGNATED WILD AND SCENIC RIVERS

PERE MARQUETTE
AU SABLE

RIVERS PROPOSED FOR DESIGNATION

1. PRESQUE ISLE
2. ONTONAGON
3. PAINT
4. FENCE
5. STURGEON
6. BIG HURON
7. ESCANABA
8. WHITEFISH
9. INDIAN
10. TAHQUAMENON
11. ST. JOSEPH
12. DOWAGIAC
13. PAW PAW
14. KALAMAZOO
15. GRAND
16. THORNAPPLE
17. FISH CREEK
18. MUSKEGON
19. LITTLE MANISTEE
20. MANISTEE
21. PINE
22. BLACK
23. THUNDER BAY
24. CASS
25. SHIAWASSEE

miris

LAND AND WATER MANAGEMENT DIVISION
DEPARTMENT OF NATURAL RESOURCES
P.O. BOX 30028
LANSING, MICHIGAN 48909
PHONE (517) 373-1170

NOTE: ALL RIVERS INCLUDE SOME
OR ALL TRIBUTARIES

from insufficient local support, which translates into insufficient congressional support.

The second route is for rivers to be nominated for designation by state governments. The state legislature must designate the river for protection under state law and provide for its protection. Then the governor may request that the Secretary of the Interior add the river segment to the national system. Congressional approval is not required.

Thirty-one state governments have their own river conservation programs and have designated more than 12,000 miles of streams. Some states, including Oklahoma and California, have strict controls on dams on designated rivers but do not regulate land adjacent to rivers. Oregon, on the other hand, regulates a corridor one-quarter mile wide along its designated rivers. Other states, Minnesota among them, have acquired land along designated rivers.

The Federal Energy Regulatory Commission (FERC) approves the construction, licensing, and relicensing of hydropower projects and dams and, therefore, may affect not only streamflow but also settlements and landscapes in a river corridor. When an electric power company applied for a FERC permit to divert water from North Carolina's Horsepasture River for power generation, local activists organized to prevent such action and to protect the river's free-flowing beauty. During the 1990s, many dams constructed in earlier decades are being considered for relicensing. Citizens groups should determine if a nearby project is due for relicensing and work with American Rivers or River Network to ensure that the relicensing agreement includes appropriate provisions for conservation, streamflow, and recreational access.

CASE STUDY 7.2

Horsepasture River, North Carolina: Halting a Plan to Divert a Scenic River

The Horsepasture River tumbles 1,700 vertical feet in just two miles as it descends from the forested eastern escarpment of the Blue Ridge Mountains. Six waterfalls along its course have long been favorites of hikers in Transylvania County. The pools below the falls are popular swimming holes. Thanks to the Wild and Scenic Rivers Act and concerted local conservation leadership, the Horsepasture should continue to be free-flowing for many generations of hikers and swimmers to enjoy.

A different fate awaited the river in 1984, when an electric power company applied to the Federal Energy Regulatory Commission (FERC) for a permit to divert most of the water to a generator.

Permission might have been granted quietly if Stuart Rabb had not read a public notice in the local paper about FERC's intention to grant a permit. At the same time, Bill Thomas, another county resident and an active member of the Sierra Club, heard about the project through a magazine article, made inquiries, and obtained a copy of the power company's application to FERC. Thomas developed a slide show on the Horsepasture and he, Rabb, and others started talk-

7.2
An electric power company proposed diverting most of the water flowing over the spectacular falls on the Horsepasture River. As a result of citizen action, the Horsepasture is now protected by the Wild and Scenic Rivers Act.

7.3
Sometimes conservationists can obtain help from Congress and federal agencies. In 1984 Bill Thomas (*left*), chairman of Friends of the Horsepasture, met with congressional candidate Bill Hendon (*center*) and U.S. Secretary of Energy Donald Hodel to discuss a proposed hydroelectric plant. The two agreed to assist in protecting the river.

ing about the need to protect the river. They believed the relatively small amount of power to be generated and its cost did not warrant diminishing the spectacular power of the falls and the potential damage to fish habitat and water quality.

In April 1984, Thomas and others organized the Friends of the Horsepasture—or FROTH, as they called it for short—which quickly became an informal but effective lobbying group. They started a newsletter and within months had 800 members. On the advice of the Sierra Club, they requested a hearing with the state natural resources department and the county commissioners, held on September 24, 1984, in the local high school auditorium. Seven hundred and fifty residents showed up at the largest public hearing in the county's history.

FROTH's timing was excellent. Both Congressman James Clarke and Senator Jesse Helms were facing tough elections that November and could not afford to ignore these vocal voters. Congressman Clarke introduced legislation to have the Horsepasture studied for designation as a wild and scenic river. The study bill passed the House of Representatives on September 24, the very day of the public hearing. When Clarke's assistant at the meeting announced the vote, "the roof blew off the place," according to Thomas. "I still get choked up thinking about it. It was the most incredible evening I have ever spent. As soon as this great roar went up, all of the politicians jumped up in turn." Bill Hendon, the Republican candidate for Clarke's seat, was at the meeting and promised his support. An assistant to Senator Helms promised similar action in the Senate. As luck would have it, then Secretary of Energy Donald Hodel, who controlled FERC's budget, was campaigning for Hendon in Asheville two weeks later. Thomas met with Hodel, who promised his help in heading off the project.

Hendon and Helms won their elections and lived up to their commitments, supporting not only legislation to designate the river but also to appropriate $1 million to acquire 435 acres along the river to add to the Nantahala National Forest. Early in 1985, the Trust for Public Land (TPL), at the urging of FROTH, purchased an option on the tract from the owner. Later that year Congress passed the necessary legislation, and in February 1986, TPL purchased the land and resold it for the same price to the Forest Service.

Bill Thomas and his colleagues have continued working to protect other streams in the same Jocassee watershed. Nearly 60,000 acres of land there are owned by Duke Power Company, in all likelihood for the potential for generating hydroelectric power, and there is an ever-present threat that the power company will act on that potential. In fact, in 1987 Duke Power announced plans to build a pump storage reservoir in the Jocassee watershed. Thomas, together with Jerry Beck of the South Carolina Sierra Club, organized the Jocassee Watershed Coalition and commissioned a study which demonstrated that combustion turbines would be more cost-effective than pump storage. In 1988, Duke Power dropped its plans. As Thomas states, the coalition "made them think really hard about the economic alternatives."

From an organization focused on one project on one river, Thomas, Rabb, and their associates have broadened their mission to monitoring the management of the Pisgah and Nantahala National Forests and looking for opportunities of designating new wilderness areas.

Increasingly, conservation groups are focusing their efforts not just on river segments but on whole watersheds. Thus, land use issues become critical in protecting water quality and quantity. The Rivers, Trails, and Conservation Assistance (RTCA) program of the National Park Service provides technical assistance to communities, by bringing together state and local agencies and nonprofit organizations to develop and implement a protection program for a watershed or river. Working with community groups and public officials, RTCA staff have helped revitalize the waterfront of the Little Sioux River in Cherokee, Iowa, mitigate the effects of a hydroelectric dam along the Au Sable River in Michigan, and develop trails along the Yampa River in Colorado. Other watershed conservation groups work with state programs and such organizations as the Izaac Walton League and River Network. Through Maryland's Save Our Streams program, for example, an extensive network of volunteers organizes stream cleanups, monitors changes in the water quality of selected streams, and helps educate the public about watershed protection.

Wetlands

In the past, the Natural Resources Conservation Service assisted farmers in draining wetlands, and projects by the Army Corps of Engineers and the Bureau of Reclamation destroyed many more wetlands. President Carter's 1977 Executive Order 11990, entitled "Protection of Wetlands," signaled a change in federal policy by requiring all agencies to protect wetlands. Since the National Wetlands Policy Forum in 1987, both Presidents Bush and Clinton have pledged a national policy of "no net loss" of wetlands and a long-term goal of increasing the quantity and quality of the nation's resource base.

Several federal laws now offer a degree of protection to wetlands. Section 404 of the Clean Water Act states that a permit from the Army Corps of Engineers is necessary to discharge "dredge or fill material" into the nation's waters, including wetlands. The Environmental Protection Agency can overrule the corps and stop a 404 permit from being issued if it will have an unacceptable effect on wetlands. Other federal laws offering protection to wetlands include the 1982 Coastal Barrier Resources Act, the 1985 Food Security Act, and the 1986 Tax Reform Act, which reduced incentives for draining wetlands.

One of the provisions of the Farm Security Act of 1985 allows the Consolidated Farm Service Agency to obtain perpetual conservation easements to protect or restore wetlands in exchange for a portion of a loanholder's federal indebtedness, and the 1990 Farm Bill created a Wetland Reserve Program whereby the U.S. Department of Agriculture purchases conservation easements from willing landowners, with the goal of protecting and restoring up to one million acres of wetlands by the year 2000. Landowners retain control of public access, maintain the easement areas, and are allowed to engage in compatible economic activities on the land under easement.

The NRCS and the U.S. Fish and Wildlife Service, through the latter's Partners for Wildlife program, offer technical assistance on habitat restoration to landowners through voluntary partnerships. The North American Waterfowl Management Plan, relying on partnerships with numerous other conservation organizations, such as Ducks Unlimited, the Land Trust Alliance, the National Audubon Society, the Sierra Club, and the Nature Conservancy, as well as with all levels of government, aims to conserve and restore wetlands and waterfowl populations across the United States, Canada, and Mexico. Since 1987, nearly 2.5 million acres of wetlands and associated uplands have been restored or enhanced in North America in cooperation with nearly 13,000 landowners.

In addition to these national initiatives, many states and more than three thousand local governments have programs to protect coastal wetlands in conjunction with coastal-zone management plans. Some also regulate or offer incentives to protect inland wetlands. Massachusetts, for instance, requires the review of proposed alterations to wetlands by municipal conservation commissions. In Oregon, property owners may receive an income tax abatement on land they own that borders streams if their plan for managing that land is approved by the Oregon Department of Fish and Wildlife.

Advice on protecting wetlands is available from the U.S. Fish and Wildlife Service (which is mapping the wetlands and deepwater habitats in the United States), from EPA's Wetlands Information Hotline, from the Natural Resources Conservation Service, and from the U.S. Army Corps of Engineers district offices. The Environmental Law Institute, a non-profit organization, has a particular interest in wetlands policy issues. Ducks Unlimited and Pheasants Forever are two of the national groups advocating wetlands protection.

Floodplains

The Corps of Engineers, the Natural Resources Conservation Service, and the Bureau of Reclamation all have programs to protect floodplains. The National Flood Insurance Program, administered by the Federal Insurance Administration of the Federal Emergency Management Agency (FEMA), is a key federal program to protect floodplains. FEMA works with state and local governments to map one-hundred-year floodplains (areas that have at least a 1 in 100 chance of flooding in any given year). Through the insurance program, all residents in a participating community can receive federally backed flood insurance if their local government agrees to implement programs to reduce future flood risks. The local government must adopt and enforce a floodplain management ordinance that includes, among other things, zoning and subdivision controls that meet FEMA's standards. The controls on floodways, where flood waters are deepest and fastest, are stricter than in flood fringe areas. Typically, floodway land is limited to uses that will not reduce peak flow during a flood, such as agriculture, parks, and golf courses. Construction in flood fringe areas is often permitted if the buildings are elevated or otherwise protected. Communities that fail to adopt flood-control measures may lose eligibility for disaster assistance, flood insurance, and certain federally subsidized loans. More than 18,500 communities have established controls meeting FEMA standards and participate in the National Flood Insurance Program.

Federal advice on flood control is also available from the Natural Resources Conservation Service, the Corps of Engineers, and the Bureau of Reclamation. These agencies can construct dams and levees to protect certain areas from floods, but these measures may worsen flood damage in other areas of the floodplain.

Many states also now have laws that regulate floodplains, and each state has a flood insurance coordinator. The Floodplain Management Resource Center in Boulder, Colorado, serves as a library and referral service for floodplain management publications. The Association of State Floodplain Managers serves as an information clearinghouse on floodplain issues.

Coasts

The principal federal legislation protecting America's coasts is the Coastal Zone Management Act of 1972, as amended. The act declares that it is national policy "to preserve, protect, develop, and where possible, to restore or enhance, the resources of the Nation's coastal zone." Rather than impose federal regulation, the act gives incentives to states that plan and implement regulations based on the plans. The act requires that states give "full consideration to ecological, cultural, historic, and aesthetic values." The coastal zone, as defined by the act, extends over 95,000 miles and includes all beaches, estuaries, bays, wetlands, and islands along the Atlantic and Pacific Oceans, the Gulf of Mexico, and the Great Lakes.

The thirty-five coastal states and territories are eligible for grants from the National Oceanic and Atmospheric Administration (NOAA) of the U.S. Department of Commerce to develop management programs for land and water resources in their coastal zones. States with approved programs are eligible for additional grants from NOAA to implement the plans, and states can transfer the funds to groups for local projects. Funds can be used to protect areas important for "their conservation, recreational, or aesthetic values." Property acquisition, construction, and the rehabilitation of historic buildings are eligible activities. Federal agencies undertaking or licensing projects in the coastal zone must ensure that the projects are consistent with approved state management programs.

Many states have regulated new construction near their coastlines. North Carolina has one of the strictest laws; the distance new construction must be set back from the vegetation line takes into account the erosion rate at that point along the coast. This helps to protect dunes but does not relieve development pressure behind that setback line. North Carolina also prohibits all "hardening structures," such as jetties and sea walls, along the beach, except to protect historic structures or to facilitate navigation. The California Coastal Zone Conservation Act of 1972 gave the control over most construction along the state's coast and up to 1,000 yards from the coast to those state and regional commissions empowered to grant or deny permits for development.

Conservationists near coasts should determine from the appropriate state government office whether any part of their community is within the designated coastal zone. In Florida and Delaware this is easy: the entirety of both states is included. For communities within the coastal zone, there are likely to be special state laws that can be used to protect coastal resources, and there may be funds designated for coastal areas that a community can use for conservation projects. Another federal statute that protects coasts is the Coastal Barrier Resources Act of 1982. The act prohibits federal funding, including flood insurance, for projects that would result in development on specified barrier islands. The Coast Alliance can provide information on coastal management and protection.

Wells, Maine:
Saving a Saltwater Farm

The Laudholm Trust in Wells, Maine, is an example of a nonprofit organization that took advantage of the Coastal Zone Management Act and has formed a partnership with federal, state, and local agencies to protect a significant natural, scenic, and historic property. In the late 1970s, conservation leaders in Wells, concerned about the protection of the Laudholm Farm, discovered that the National Estuarine Sanctuaries program (renamed the National Estuarine Research Reserve Program in 1986) could be of help. Through this program the National Oceanic and Atmospheric Administration (NOAA) has designated twenty-two reserves by providing 50 percent matching grants to states for acquisition and management.

The scenic 313-acre saltwater Laudholm Farm, with its historic farmstead, borders two estuaries and was the only large undeveloped private property left along the southern Maine coast. When the farm came on the market in 1978, a group of Wells citizens got together to see what could be done to protect it. They established the Laudholm Farm Committee, but their task seemed hopeless: the owners were asking $2 million for the property and had already started to subdivide.

Then, in 1980, committee members received a notice from the state planning office asking for nominations of a property that could be acquired with NOAA funds as a National Estuarine Sanctuary. The town's selectmen were supportive of nominating the Laudholm Farm so long as it would not cost the town money. After reviewing forty applications, the state and NOAA chose the Wells site.

Three major hurdles remained: moving final approval for the project through

7.4
The Laudholm farmstead in Wells, Maine, was rehabilitated and is used as the visitors' center for the Wells National Estuarine Research Reserve.

the NOAA bureaucracy, raising the necessary 50 percent matching funds, and negotiating a sales agreement with the owners. The citizens committee received invaluable assistance in dealing with NOAA from the regional planning commission. Despite this help, final approval was slow in coming. Mort Mather, a former New York stage manager, became increasingly frustrated by the inaction: "Finally, in early 1980, I said O.K., I'll have a meeting at my house. From that meeting everyone went home and wrote letters to their congressmen, to NOAA, and the editor of the paper." This did the trick. NOAA officials came up for a hearing, primarily because of the letter-writing campaign, and in 1982 awarded the first of three acquisitions grants, totaling $1.2 million.

Anticipating the federal grant, the committee members incorporated the Laudholm Trust in 1982, with Mather as president, to raise funds and acquire the property. The trust raised more than $800,000 in cash, mostly from its members, and was given 37 acres of land plus several building lots. The state supplied $250,000. The trust then negotiated with federal, state, and local agencies to include the state-owned Laudholm Beach and 1,350 acres protected by the U.S. Fish and Wildlife Service through the Rachel Carson Wildlife Refuge within the 1,690-acre reserve.

The Wells Reserve was dedicated in 1986. In the early 1990s the Laudholm Trust developed a management plan for the property and, through hard work over several years, raised another $3.5 million. Some of this money came from NOAA, but most was raised from individual donors and private foundations. The funds raised paid for a seven-mile trail system and the rehabilitation of the historic farmhouse for a visitor center and offices, and of the barn and several outbuildings.

In 1995 Mort Mather left the trust to help other organizations as a consultant. He left an operation with an annual budget of more than $900,000— $110,000 of which comes from NOAA and the rest from donations, memberships, and foundations. The trust has a fourteen-person staff, most full-time, a 3,000-person membership, as well as educational programs and a budding research program. Twenty-five thousand people visit the Wells Reserve annually. "When I look at what has happened here since the farm was saved, I am amazed," Mather has said. "I think the beauty of this site and the magnificent complex of historic buildings attract capable people and then inspire them to excellence." Trudy Cox, director of NOAA's Office of Ocean and Coastal Resource Management, called this reserve the jewel in the crown of the reserve system. It is a partnership effort that has succeeded beyond the trust's wildest imaginings.

THE LAND

Soils

The federal agency responsible for soil conservation is the Natural Resources Conservation Service. An agency of the Department of Agriculture, NRCS maps soils and provides technical assistance to individuals, organizations, and local governments in conserving soil and water resources. NRCS provides its services through local Soil and Water Conservation Districts. To date, nearly three thousand districts have been established across the country. The districts generally follow county lines. Conservation districts are units of government organized under state laws and supervised by locally elected boards. Most districts have one local district employee as well as the NRCS district conservationist, and sometimes other staff who give advice and assistance not just to farmers but to all land users. For instance, NRCS provides guidelines on controlling erosion on construction sites and information about soil types considered unsuitable for housing developments.

Given its decentralization, NRCS is an invaluable source of assistance to many rural conservation programs. Cazenovia, New York (see Case Study 3.1), and many other rural communities have made extensive use of NRCS, not only for help in conserving soil, but also for natural resources protection in general. NRCS is most easily contacted through its county offices.

Farming and Farmland

In 1981 the National Agricultural Lands Study concluded that many federal programs contributed to loss of farmland. For instance, as mentioned above, grants to build sewer lines through farmland might create an incentive for more development, and grants for highway construction might also result in farmland loss. In response, Congress in 1981 passed the Farmland Protection Policy Act. The act directs all federal agencies "to identify and take into account the adverse effects of Federal programs on the preservation of farmland" and to consider alternatives that would lessen those effects.

Congress went further when it incorporated conservation concerns into the 1985 Food Security Act. The so-called "sodbuster" and "swampbuster" provisions of the act specify that farmers who cultivate highly erodible land and wetlands could lose federal financial assistance. In the past, farmers could receive assistance regardless of the suitability of their land for agriculture. (These programs were both renewed under the 1990 and 1996 farm bills.) Under the Conservation Reserve Program established by the Food Security Act, the Department of Agriculture pays rental income to farmers who agree to take highly erodible and other environmentally sensitive land out of crop production for ten years. Nearly 37 million acres have already been placed in the reserve; many come up for renewal by the turn of the century. The 1996 Federal Agricultural Improvement and Reform Act renewed the Conservation Reserve Program.

Federal protection for farmland remaining in production has been focused on the Agricultural Resource Conservation Demonstration Program established by the 1990 Farm Bill. As a pilot program, interest-free loans were provided to Vermont to acquire agricultural conservation easements. Many states have farmland protection laws that reduce taxes on farmland, establish agricultural districts, protect farmers from nuisance suits, protect them from assessments for sewers and other public improvements not related to agriculture, and make funds available for the purchase of development rights. These programs, which generally require local initiative, are described more fully in Chapter 4. The states in general, but particularly California, Delaware, Maryland, Michigan, New Jersey, Pennsylvania, and Vermont, have gone further than the federal government in protecting farmland.

The 1996 farm bill authorizes the Department of Agriculture to provide funds to help qualifying state and local governments acquire devel-

7.5
Opposite: The Barn Again! program sponsored by the National Trust for Historic Preservation and Successful Farming magazine provides awards and technical assistance for preserving and using older farm buildings for today's farming needs. The program has documented hundreds of examples of barns that have been rehabilitated for new uses. Even barns that are no longer useful for agriculture can be adapted for shops, commercial storage, or retail sales. Since 1988 Barn Again! has awarded cash prizes to farmers for the best examples of older barns and even entire farmsteads that have been preserved and adapted for new farming uses. The program provides advice to barn owners through publications and a hotline. Barn Again! also works with states and communities to develop local barn preservation programs. Kane County, Illinois, developed That Darn Barn, a countywide barn preservation program modeled on Barn Again! Through recognition, technical assistance, and demonstration projects, that program encourages farmers to preserve their older buildings.

opment rights to keep farmland in productive use. Information on farmland retention programs can be obtained from the Cooperative Extension Service agents, Natural Resources Conservation Service district conservationists, state departments of agriculture, and the American Farmland Trust.

Forests and Rangeland

The Forest Service of the Department of Agriculture is the principal federal agency responsible for forest resources. It is a decentralized agency, vesting considerable authority in forest supervisors, one of whose jobs is to prepare multiple-use management plans for national forests, incorporating public comments. In rural communities where a large percentage of the land is in national forests, it is important for conservation leaders to know their forest supervisors or district forest rangers and become involved in the planning process for national forests. Also, Forest Service personnel can advise communities about protecting forests adjacent to national forests.

In addition to overseeing national forests, the Forest Service, under the terms of the 1978 Cooperative Forestry Assistance Act, aids local governments, nonprofit organizations, and private landowners. In some states this assistance is offered directly by the Forest Service; in others it is offered through state agencies or the Cooperative Extension Service.

The Bureau of Land Management (BLM) of the Department of the Interior manages 170 million acres of federally owned rangeland in eleven western states. Approximately nineteen thousand livestock owners pay BLM for the right to graze livestock on these public lands. Conservation leaders should contact BLM district and resource area managers if they wish to comment on BLM's plans for rangeland. Although BLM does not provide advice on range issues off federal lands, the Natural Resources Conservation Service, the Forest Service, and the Cooperative Extension Service have specialists on range issues who can assist community groups.

Both the Sierra Club and the Wilderness Society work to protect forest and range resources on public lands. In addition, the American Forestry Association and American Forests are concerned with forest protection.

WILDLIFE AND ENDANGERED SPECIES

Wildlife

The federal agency most directly involved in wildlife protection and management is the U.S. Fish and Wildlife Service of the Department of the Interior. It administers more than five hundred wildlife refuges across the country that comprise nearly 90 million acres. They provide habitat for hundreds of species of wildlife, many of which are endangered. Many refuges are located along the major flyways of migrating birds.

The Fish and Wildlife Service also evaluates the effects of development on wildlife habitat outside its refuges and offers assistance to state and local conservation programs. Expert advice on wildlife and fisheries is available from refuge managers and through the service's seven regional and numerous field offices. In addition, state fish and game departments can be of assistance. In the past, these offices were primarily interested in species that were hunted or fished, but this is changing.

Numerous national and state nonprofit organizations are concerned with protecting wildlife. Three of the largest are the National Audubon Society, the National Wildlife Federation, and the Nature Conservancy; all have chapters throughout the country.

Endangered Species

The Endangered Species Act of 1973, as amended, is one of the strongest American environmental laws. The act gives the Secretary of the Interior, acting through the Fish and Wildlife Service, broad powers to protect endangered plant and animal species and the habitat on which they depend. It gives the Secretary of Commerce similar authority to protect endangered marine species. According to the act, endangered species—defined as "any species which is in danger of extinction through all or a significant portion of its range"—and threatened species—any species which is likely to become endangered—may be added to the U.S. List of Endangered and Threatened Wildlife and Plants. After review, the appropriate department decides whether to list the species. Once listed, an ani-

7.6 & 7.7
Most endangered species are plants and invertebrate animals. Many have yet to be officially listed or protected. Here botanist Donna M. E. Ware of the College of William and Mary measures and records small whorled pogonias (*Isotria medeoloides*) in Virginia's deciduous woodlands as part of a study of the ecology of this rare native orchid. The study is an element in the U.S. Fish and Wildlife Service's recovery plan for this endangered species. The privately owned 200-acre site is leased by the Nature Conservancy for a nominal sum.

mal species cannot be removed from its habitat, harmed, pursued, hunted, transported, or traded in interstate or foreign commerce without special permission. For endangered plants, a less stringent set of prohibitions applies, but only on federal land or to actions that also violate state law.

When federal agencies authorize, fund, or carry out any action that might adversely affect the continued existence of a listed species or its critical habitat, they must consult with the Fish and Wildlife Service. When there is no federal authorization or funding involved in an action that might have such an effect, the landowners may seek relief from possible prosecution under the act through the Habitat Conservation Planning process, whereby a landowner undertakes mitigation or other conservation actions to balance the adverse effects.

The principal goal of the Endangered Species Act is to restore the populations of listed species so that they are no longer endangered or threatened. Recovery plans may include acquisition and improved management of habitat. As of 1996, 959 endangered and threatened U.S. species were listed. The program has had some remarkable successes—for example, the return of the bald eagle. During the 1960s there were slightly more than 400 nesting pairs of bald eagles; by 1995, 4,500 nesting pairs were counted in the continental United States. As a result, the status of the eagle was upgraded from endangered to threatened. Unfortunately, most scientists agree, there are many more known and unknown species that should be listed.

Some states, including California, Florida, Hawaii, Michigan, Minnesota, Pennsylvania, and Wisconsin, have lists of species of special concern at the state level. The Nature Conservancy works with natural heritage programs in all fifty states to inventory exemplary, rare, or endangered species (p. 136).

SPECIAL RESOURCES

Natural Landmarks

The National Natural Landmarks Program was established by the Secretary of the Interior in 1962 "to identify and encourage the preservation of nationally significant examples of the full range of ecological and geological features that constitute the nation's natural heritage." Sites that are designated as landmarks represent, within a given natural region, the best examples of that region's ecosystems, geologic features, or paleontologic sites. They are listed in the National Registry of Natural Landmarks. Among the approximately six hundred sites designated are Okefenokee Swamp in Georgia, Franconia Notch in New Hampshire, and Point Lobos in California.

The National Park Service, which administers the registry, conducts inventories of natural areas to identify potential landmarks. The Park Service nominates eligible sites to the Secretary of the Interior, who confers the designation at his discretion.

Both publicly and privately owned sites are eligible. Designation does not affect ownership of a site, nor its management and use. Nevertheless, owners of landmarks are invited to enter into voluntary, nonbinding con-

7.8
Rock City in central Kansas is a designated National Natural Landmark. It consists of some 200 spherical sandstone concretions on 14 acres of a 40-acre town park, in the midst of rolling farmland. Some of the rocks are 12 feet high and up to 27 feet in diameter.

servation agreements with the Park Service to protect the features for which their properties have been recognized. The Park Service monitors landmarks, and federal agencies are required to take their status into account when preparing environmental impact statements. The Park Service works closely with the Nature Conservancy and state natural areas programs.

Historic and Cultural Resources

The basic federal law protecting historic and archeological resources is the National Historic Preservation Act of 1966, as amended. The act authorized the National Register of Historic Places, made funds available to states and the National Trust for Historic Preservation, and established the federal Advisory Council on Historic Preservation.

The National Register, administered by the National Park Service, is composed of "districts, sites, buildings, structures, and objects that are significant in American history, architecture, archeology, engineering, and culture." The more than sixty-five thousand properties in the National Register are given national recognition, which can be an incentive for their protection. An important aspect of the National Historic Preservation Act is the requirement that all federal agencies consider the impact of their proposed undertakings on historic properties. There are no restrictions, however, on private owners of listed properties unless they receive federal funds or tax benefits.

Properties that are of outstanding national significance can be designated by the Secretary of the Interior as National Historic Landmarks. National Register regulations apply to these properties. In addition, the Park Service monitors the condition of landmarks and provides their owners with advice about their preservation.

Nominations to the National Register are usually made by state governments or, in the case of federally owned properties, by federal agencies. (The criteria used in evaluating nominations are described in the Sidebar 3.6.) Wherever possible, the Park Service urges that nominations be of districts that include contiguous properties. After review by the Park Service's staff, the Keeper of the National Register enters the properties in the register. Owners must be informed if their property is being nominated to the register. If they object, the property is not listed. In the case of a district, if more than 50 percent of the property owners object, the district is not listed.

At the state level, the National Register program is administered by State Historic Preservation Officers (SHPOs), who are appointed by the governors. The SHPOs, or their staffs, assist local governments and nonprofit organizations in preparing nominations, sometimes making funds available to assist in this work.

Under the provisions of Section 106 of the National Historic Preservation Act, federal agencies must afford the SHPOs and the Advisory Council on Historic Preservation the opportunity to comment on any federal, federally assisted, or federally licensed "undertaking" that may affect properties listed or eligible for listing in the National Register. Undertakings include a wide variety of federal actions, including issuing a permit to mine, widening a highway, granting a hydropower license, and closing a post office in a historic building. The federal agency, the council, and the SHPO then attempt to identify ways to avoid or minimize adverse impacts. Federal agencies are required to give even greater consideration to National Historic Landmarks. In the final analysis, federal agencies are free to proceed in spite of objections by the council. Although it is the legal responsibility of the federal agency involved to inform the council of proposed actions, agencies often fail to do so in a timely manner. The council therefore welcomes information from the public about potential federal projects.

Section 106 is reinforced by a requirement in the National Environ-

7.9
The owners of the Spring Hill Ranch in Chase County, Kansas, qualified for rehabilitation tax credits when they restored the 1880s ranch for continued use. The buildings, constructed of locally quarried limestone, are listed in the National Register of Historic Places. This drawing, done shortly after the complex was built, provides invaluable documentation on the history of the ranch.

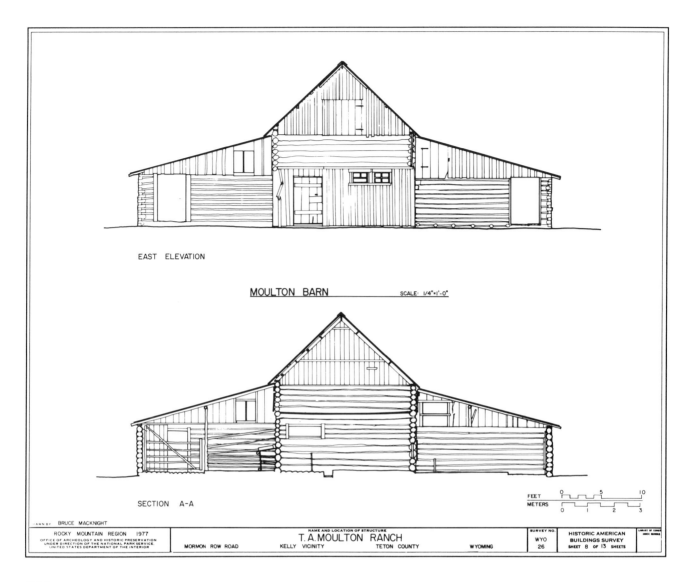

EAST ELEVATION

MOULTON BARN   SCALE: 1/4"=1'-0"

SECTION A-A

DRAWN BY BRUCE MACKNIGHT

ROCKY MOUNTAIN REGION 1977 OFFICE OF ARCHEOLOGY AND HISTORIC PRESERVATION UNDER DIRECTION OF THE NATIONAL PARK SERVICE. UNITED STATES DEPARTMENT OF THE INTERIOR	NAME AND LOCATION OF STRUCTURE T. A. MOULTON RANCH	SURVEY NO. WYO 26	HISTORIC AMERICAN BUILDINGS SURVEY SHEET 8 OF 13 SHEETS
	MORMON ROW ROAD KELLY VICINITY TETON COUNTY WYOMING		

7.10

T. A. Moulton homesteaded in Jackson Hole in 1908. In 1960 the National Park Service purchased his 160-acre ranch to add it to Grand Teton National Park. The Historic American Buildings Survey division of the National Park Service documented the ranch through measured drawings.

mental Policy Act that historic and cultural resources, including aspects of folklife, be considered in environmental review (see Sidebar 7.1). Studies done for Section 106 and NEPA reviews are often executed together. Another explicit protection for historic resources is Section 4(f) of the Department of Transportation Act of 1966 as amended (see below under "Highways").

The Archeology Resources Protection Act (ARPA) of 1979, as amended, affords further protection to archeological sites on federally owned and Native American land by prohibiting unauthorized excavation and establishing a permit system to conduct archeological excavations. It imposes criminal penalties for removal of archeological artifacts without a permit. Amendments made to the act in 1988 require federal land management agencies to develop public awareness campaigns about the significance of archeological concerns regarding public lands and to prepare plans for surveying agency-owned land for archeological resources. Although ARPA does not explicitly protect archeological resources on private lands, it does prohibit the interstate transportation of stolen archeological artifacts, which may have been stolen from privately owned land. Most states have statutes that reinforce or complement ARPA. Many State Historic Preservation Offices with state archeologists on staff have programs to educate the public about archeology and to protect sites.

Another important federal law that promotes historic preservation is the Tax Reform Act of 1986, which provides a tax credit for owners of income-producing buildings listed in the National Register or within National Register districts who rehabilitate those properties. If the rehabilitation qualifies, the owner may claim a 20 percent tax credit for the work. Thousands of commercial properties have been rehabilitated using tax credits, mostly for rental housing. Although most of the projects have been in cities, many small town and rural properties, including barns, have been rehabilitated using the tax credits. To qualify, the building must be a certified historic structure that is listed in the National Register or certified as contributing to a registered historic district. The rehabilitation work must meet standards set by the Secretary of the Interior (see Sidebar 4.15).

Included in the Intermodal Surface Transportation Efficiency Act of 1991 (ISTEA) was provision for a 10 percent set-aside from state highway funds for transportation enhancement activities that include historic preservation (see p. 336).

The principal sources of assistance in historic preservation are the SHPOs, various offices of the National Park Service, regional offices of the National Trust for Historic Preservation, state historic preservation organizations, and historic preservation programs in colleges and universities.

7.2 State Historic Preservation Officers

State Historic Preservation Officers (SHPOs) have the following responsibilities:

- *To nominate properties to the National Register of Historic Places.*
- *To conduct comprehensive inventories of historic properties in the state. Inventoried properties may or may not be eligible for the National Register.*
- *To administer state registers. Many states have established their own registers that may protect properties from the actions of state and local governments. Often, as is the case in New Jersey, the nomination process is the same as for the National Register.*
- *To prepare state preservation plans.*
- *To review and give preliminary approval for rehabilitation being done for federal tax credits.*
- *To advise local governments, non-profit organizations, and individuals on historic preservation. Many SHPOs have staff members who can visit communities to give advice. SHPOs frequently publish newsletters and conduct conferences and training programs for community preservation leaders.*
- *To advise federal agencies on avoiding or minimizing harm to National Register properties through their projects.*
- *To administer state and federal grant and loan programs, when available.*

7.11
New Market, Virginia, is one of the Shenandoah Valley's important battlefields. Much of the hallowed ground, seen here from Shirley's Hill, is outside the boundaries of the battlefield park established by the Virginia Military Institute and is threatened by development along I-81.

7.3 Battlefields

Battlefields are special resources, representing tangible evidence of the hostilities, casualties, and heroism that formed the United States through the Revolutionary and Civil wars. In a sense they are sacred places of the nation, valued for their historical significance and for the parklike open space most of them provide.

In 1988, Congress appropriated $135 million for the National Park Service to acquire 542 acres adjacent to the Manassas National Battlefield Park, on which 560 houses and a large regional shopping center were to be built. Although the development had been approved by the county planning commission and zoning authority, the proposed development had raised local, state, and finally national outrage that a devel-

opment of that magnitude could be located so close to a national battlefield park. Ultimately, the only recourse to stopping the development was the federal buy-out.

The battle over Manassas raised the issue of battlefield protection nationwide. Clearly, not all lands adjacent to battlefields could be acquired by the federal government, or any government. In 1990 Congress established the Civil War Sites Advisory Commission to identify and evaluate America's historically significant Civil War sites, assess threats to their integrity, and recommend alternatives for protecting them.

The commission's report identified 384 primary Civil War sites (Civil War Sites Advisory Commission 1993). The commission determined

that more than half the sites were seriously threatened by development. It recommended a series of mechanisms for protection, largely through public-private partnerships at all levels.

The National Park Service's American Battlefield Protection Program is focused on battlefield protection. It has no acquisition function but, rather, provides technical assistance in researching, documenting, mapping, and protecting battlefields.

The Association for the Preservation of Civil War Sites, the Civil War Trust, and the Civil War Battlefield Campaign of the Conservation Fund all work for the preservation of Civil War battlefields through acquisition, easements, and other protection mechanisms.

Scenic Areas

Scenery is protected to some extent through many federal and state laws. The National Environmental Policy Act and Vermont's Act 250, for instance, include scenery among resources to be protected. Federal agencies such as the U.S. Forest Service take steps to identify and protect scenic resources that might be damaged by their activities or the permits they issue.

Nearly all states and some local jurisdictions have scenic roads programs. Some programs, such as Tennessee's, merely designate roads as scenic, while others, such as California's, require management plans that may restrict development along the road corridors. The National Scenic Byways Program, authorized by the Intermodal Surface Transportation Efficiency Act of 1991 and inaugurated in 1995, designates National Scenic Byways and All-American Roads. Nominations of roads come from local communities through the state agency responsible for the program, usually the department of transportation. Roads can be designated for their scenic, historic, cultural, natural, recreational, or archeological importance. Each designated byway must have a corridor management plan prepared by the local community nominating it. All-American Roads are designated for having at least two of the intrinsic qualities cited above representing the best of the nation, being destinations unto themselves, and providing exceptional driving experiences.

Since the passage of ISTEA, numerous citizens groups have been

7.12
These pine trees were cut down only because they hindered the visibility of a billboard. Current federal legislation inadequately protects federally funded highways from such visual blight.

working to develop corridor management plans for scenic byways. Some of these efforts have been initiated with the support of the state. For example, as part of developing their state scenic byways programs, Colorado, Connecticut, and Indiana have provided support and technical assistance to local groups developing corridor management plans.

The federal government and all states have laws regulating billboards. Lady Bird Johnson provided much of the leadership for the Highway Beautification Act of 1965, which states that "the erection and maintenance of outdoor advertising signs, displays, and devices in areas adjacent to the Interstate System and primary system should be controlled in order to protect the public investment in such highways, to promote the safety and recreational value of public travel, and to preserve natural beauty." (The "primary system" generally consists of U.S. numbered highways.)

The law requires states to remove illegal signs and maintain "effective control" over outdoor advertising or be subject to a 10 percent reduction in their federal highway funds. In rural areas outdoor advertising must be controlled within the limits of visibility. Certain signs, such as those advertising goods or services on the premises where the sign is located, official signs, and signs in areas either zoned or used for industrial or commercial use, are allowed. So are those of historic or artistic significance, such as the "Chew Mailpouch Tobacco" signs painted on barns. States are required to compensate sign owners when legally erected signs are removed.

Unfortunately, the law has not been effective. Many rural areas have been rezoned commercial or industrial at the request of billboard owners to allow for billboard construction. In some areas, sham businesses have

7.13
This travelers' information sign in New Mexico is a simple, effective alternative to billboards and allows local businesses to advertise their presence without detracting from the scenery.

been established to allow for billboard construction. The cash compensation provisions make the act prohibitively expensive to implement. Some states even allow billboard owners to cut trees that block the view of their signs. The billboard industry continually exerts considerable pressure on the states and Congress to change existing laws and has attempted to preempt local zoning in favor of weaker federal laws.

The ISTEA provision that no new billboards may be erected on state scenic byways that are part of the interstate system or primary system applies also to roads that are designated National Scenic Byways or All-American Roads.

Several states—notably Alaska, Hawaii, Maine, Oregon, Vermont, and Washington—have established strong controls on outdoor advertising that go well beyond the federal law. (Alaska, Hawaii, Maine, and Vermont have no billboards at all.) In other states, many counties and towns have enacted ordinances to prohibit or limit billboard placement. Some have begun taxing billboards under property tax laws that recognize the income of the sign, rather than the value of the land on which the sign stands. The national organization Scenic America promotes sign control and assists communities in their efforts to protect scenery along roadways.

Outdoor Recreation and Greenways

The National Park Service assists communities in establishing trails and greenways. The National Trails System Act of 1968, as amended, established a nationwide system of recreational, historic, and scenic trails and encourages volunteers' participation in their development and management. The legislation also encourages the conversion of abandoned railroad rights-of-way into trails. These trails often have the advantage of being accessible to urban residents, bicyclists, and the handicapped.

Congress must authorize studies to determine the desirability and fea-

7.4 Special Planning and Design Assistance Programs

A number of programs have been developed through partnerships of non-profit organizations, public agencies, and universities that offer help to rural communities with planning and design. These take the form of workshops and exchanges, which bring together professionals from the outside and local community leaders to confront the problems facing rural areas.

One such program is the International Countryside Stewardship Exchange, developed by the Countryside Institute. The exchange brings teams of domestic and international experts to consult with small communities on problems defined by the communities. A community may be only one town or may include a whole valley or watershed, for example. The teams visit communities for a week and are provided lodging, food, and transportation by local hosts. At week's end, after immersing themselves in community issues, the team members present recommendations for further action in the community and prepare a report of

their findings. This report can provide a boost for planning already done in the community and point the way for more information-gathering and action. Often, simply having outsiders ask penetrating questions can change the community's perspective on its problems and infuse new vigor into stale patterns of community give-and-take. Exchanges have taken place in selected communities across New England, the Mid-Atlantic, and the South.

Your Town: Designing Its Future is a program developed by the National Trust and the Faculty of Landscape Architecture at the State University of New York at Syracuse through the sponsorship of the National Endowment for the Arts. This program brings together rural community decision makers from across a region for a three-day intensive workshop on the role of design in community planning. The curriculum includes presentations on resource assessment, the design process, graphic communication, and getting design assistance. The special feature of the

workshops is a small-group problem-solving exercise on a hypothetical "Your Town," modeled after a real town of the region. Groups present their design solutions both graphically and orally to the workshop participants. Your Town workshops have taken place in all regions of the United States.

The Minnesota Design Team is an example of a state-based design assistance program. It is a volunteer organization of professionals who donate at least one long weekend each year to help communities in Minnesota plan their future. After months of preparation, a team visits a community for a three-day design exercise focused on the issues of most concern to the community—whether they be downtown revitalization, farmland loss, tourism development, or whatever. As with the Countryside Stewardship Exchange, the team members are hosted by the community and immerse themselves in community issues. The exercise ends with a team presentation at a town meeting.

sibility of designating scenic and historic trails. Studies are generally conducted by the Park Service. The Secretary of the Interior then proposes to Congress which trails should be considered for designation. As of 1995, Congress had designated eight National Scenic Trails, totaling over 14,000 miles, and eleven National Historic Trails, totaling more than 23,000 miles (see Case Study 7.4). Recreation trails may be designated by the Secretary of the Interior, or by the Secretary of Agriculture if the trail is on Forest Service land. In 1995 there were eight hundred recreation trails, totaling over 8,500 miles. Following designation, the federal agency responsible for the trail prepares a management plan. The act encourages state and local governments to protect trail portions on non-federal land either through agreements with property owners or by acquisition.

The Rivers, Trails, and Conservation Assistance (RTCA) program of the National Park Service provides technical assistance to communities in developing local trails or greenways for recreation, wildlife habitat, and maintenance of water quality. Operating out of offices across the

7.14
The Washington and Old Dominion Railroad Regional Park in Virginia is a greenway running 45 miles from the Potomac River to rural Purcellville. The paved path for pedestrians, bicyclists, and roller-bladers is paralleled by a trail for horseback riders that runs a considerable length along the railroad's route.

country, RTCA staff can help communities plan a greenway or system of greenways, protect riverbanks for a greenway, turn an abandoned rail line into a trail, and plan bikeways. RTCA staff have helped numerous communities across the country with greenways projects, including the Huerfano–Las Animas Greenway Corridor in Colorado and the Pumpkinvine Trail from Goshen to Middlebury, Indiana.

The Rails-to-Trails Conservancy is a national nonprofit organization that works with nonprofit citizens groups, public agencies, and the railroads to transform abandoned rail lines into linear corridors for recreation, wildlife protection, and open space preservation. A few states, including Illinois, Michigan, Ohio, Pennsylvania, and Washington, have Rails-to-Trails chapter offices.

For further information on creating trails or greenways, rural conservation leaders should contact regional offices of the National Park Service, the American Hiking Society, the Rails-to-Trails Conservancy, and the American Greenways program of the Conservation Fund. The 10 percent ISTEA set-aside for transportation enhancement activities can be applied to trail-building (see p. 337).

CASE STUDY 7.4

Wisconsin:
Establishing the Ice Age Trail

Trails designated under the National Trails System Act generally extend through many communities. Consequently, the organizations that have urged their desig-

7.15
The Ice Age Trail, following the periphery of the former Wisconsin Ice Sheet, traverses the land conservationist Aldo Leopold loved and wrote about in A Sand County Almanac, and goes by the site of the boyhood home of Sierra Club founder John Muir. Here, hikers enjoy the trail near Madison, Wisconsin.

nation and work for their protection tend to be statewide or regional in scope. Many have local chapters that concern themselves with the trails in particular counties or areas. The Ice Age Park and Trail Foundation in Wisconsin is such an organization. Through its twenty local chapters and with assistance from other trail clubs and local government agencies, the foundation is making the 1,000-mile Ice Age National Scenic Trail a reality.

Since the 1950s, trail enthusiasts have worked to protect and make available to the public some of the finest scenic and ecologically varied drumlins, kames, eskers, moraines, lakes, bogs, marshes, and gorges created by the Wisconsin Ice Sheet 12,000 to 20,000 years ago. The Wisconsin Ice Sheet, which covered the northern and eastern parts of the state, was the last great glacier of the Ice Age to advance into what is now the United States.

In 1958, concerned citizens of Wisconsin established the Ice Age Park and Trail Foundation to promote the creation of a national Ice Age glacial park. As a result of this citizen lobbying, Congress in 1971 established the Ice Age National Scientific Reserve, which protects and interprets some of Wisconsin's finest glacial features and landscapes. In 1980 Congress designated the Ice Age National Scenic Trail, which follows the moraines and other features marking the Wisconsin glaciers' farthest advance. Although Congress has not appropriated any funds for acquisition of trail land, the National Park Service guides the planning and management of the Ice Age Trail.

Both before and since its designation, volunteers have worked to complete the Ice Age Trail. County chapter volunteers contact landowners to gain their permission for public access and do most of the work in laying out, constructing, and maintaining the trail. So far, approximately 500 miles of the Ice Age Trail have been opened to the public for hiking and skiing.

Most of the land needed to complete the trail is privately owned. The foundation established a partnership with the state and several counties to share in funding the acquisition of the trail. In 1987, the Wisconsin legislature designated the Ice Age Trail the state's first scenic trail and gave the departments of Natural Resources and Transportation responsibility for assisting in its development. In 1988, the legislature established a matching grant program to acquire trail land and subsequently allocated $500,000 a year from a statewide stewardship program to purchase lands along the trail.

Some communities have taken advantage of the stewardship program to protect the trail and integrate it into their own planning efforts. In Dane County, for example, 57 acres of land were protected through a partnership among the state stewardship program, county, city of Verona, Madison Area Youth Soccer Association, and the foundation. A wide greenway along the trail not only provides a coherent recreational and environmental resource for the county but also acts as a growth-management tool in buffering the edges of Madison from outlying communities. Forty acres of the 57-acre parcel are used for soccer fields, while the remaining 17 acres (along with 80 acres of an adjacent property) are being restored to their native prairie grassland habitat.

Other partnerships are designed around trail building. The foundation has developed a program called Project RELIANT—Restoring, Exploring, and Learning on the Ice Age National Trail—which employees the labor of youths performing court-ordered community service. In 1995, ninety-six youths built 9 miles of new trail, rehabilitated 86 miles of existing trail, and laid out 42 miles of future trail. "It takes a lot of money to build and maintain the Ice Age Trail," says Kathy Bero, executive director of the foundation, "in fact, . . . up to $4,000 per mile. With Project RELIANT, we can build the trail and the self-esteem of young people at the same time."

In the mid-1990s, over two million people walked some segment of the Ice Age Trail, making it Wisconsin's most popular outdoor recreation resource. Gary Werner, who facilitated the acquisition of the 57 acres in Dane County, points out that the Ice Age Trail provides an opportunity to "bring people together and give them a feel for the natural and cultural history of the land and the region. By getting people out and connecting them with the land, we can help instill a land ethic and a sense of stewardship for this property." He hopes that community residents will begin to view the land in the way that two fa-

7.16
Volunteers are the backbone of most rural conservation efforts. Here Sierra Club and Ice Age Trail Council volunteers install a marker post.

mous Wisconsin-born conservationists, Aldo Leopold and John Muir, looked upon it years ago. Werner sums up the motivation behind both the Ice Age Trail and the Dane County project: "As John Muir once stated, we must sustain our land to sustain ourselves. We must realize that everything is connected to everything else." The partnerships working for the Ice Age Trail are helping to make that vision a reality.

Public Lands

The Federal Land Policy and Management Act of 1976 declared that "the national interest will be best realized if the public lands and their resources are periodically and systematically inventoried and their present and future use is projected through a land use planning process." The act further requires that "the public lands be managed in a manner that will protect the quality of scientific, scenic, historical, ecological, environmental, air and atmospheric, water resource, and archeological values."

For conservationists concerned about federal public lands, the best point of contact is generally the local manager: the forest supervisor, the park superintendent, or the Bureau of Land Management manager. These individuals should be able to supply information about the environmental resources on the land they supervise and to incorporate the recommendations of community leaders into their management plans. In many cases they are required by legislation to do the latter. Furthermore, these individuals can frequently provide assistance to community leaders in inventorying and protecting resources throughout the community. In addition, many national nonprofit organizations, including the Natural Resources Defense Council, the Sierra Club, and the Wilderness Society, have a particular interest in the protection of federal lands.

Along with addressing concerns about protecting publicly owned land, rural conservation organizations may wish to work with federal,

7.5 States and Localities Are Going for the Green

In state after state across the nation, organizations concerned about community resources, parklands, and open space have teamed up with state and local agencies to devise major funding for land acquisition. They may pass entirely new programs—such as Vermont's hybrid Housing and Conservation Fund, funded by state appropriations and a real estate transfer tax (see p. 346), or Pennsylvania's cigarette tax to pay for its PACE (purchase of agricultural conservation easements) program—or continue support for such older programs as Maryland's Program Open Space, funded by real estate transfer fees, or New Jersey's Green Acres bond funding. In recent years, Arizona, Delaware, Florida, Wisconsin, and Washington have all seen state budgets healthy enough to establish major bond funding or other appropriations for land acquisition. Even cities and counties have gotten into the act: Chester County, Pennsylvania, passed a $100 million bond fund to purchase conservation lands, and residents of Scottsdale, Arizona, voted for a thirty-year sales tax toward raising the $240 million needed to protect views of nearby mountains.

What is the formula for success in this public-private advocacy? Here's how Phyllis Myers, president of State Resource Strategies and editor of Green Sense, *describes it:*

• Position the program as bipartisan and nonpartisan.
• Respond to legitimate concerns: In Maryland, after it had argued successfully to exempt first-time home buyers from taxes under Program Open Space, the real estate lobby supported the program in the face of

state, or local governmental agencies, as well as with the appropriate national conservation organizations, in acquiring additional land, or easements on land, that should be protected. For instance, the La Plata Open Space Conservancy in Colorado worked with the Trust for Public Land to secure protection of a 530-acre parcel within the boundaries of the San Juan National Forest near Durango. The parcel was a wetland, a winter elk habitat, and a site of archeological significance. The trust crafted the real estate deal with the landowner, the La Plata Conservancy raised money from the local community and brought political pressure to bear, and the Forest Service was able to secure the funding to acquire the parcel.

POTENTIAL PROBLEMS AND OPPORTUNITIES

Highways

Many highway projects involve the allocation of federal and state funds. The principal federal legislation protecting the environment from the adverse effects of highways is the National Environmental Policy Act (NEPA) and section 4(f) of the Department of Transportation Act of 1966, as amended. The latter states that "the Secretary shall not approve any program or project which requires the use of any land from a public park, recreation area, wildlife and waterfowl refuge, or historic site unless (1) there is no feasible and prudent alternative to the use of such land, and (2) such program includes all possible planning to minimize harm." A historic site can be one of local, state, or national designation. The 4(f) provision makes the Department of Transportation Act one of the strongest federal environmental protection laws.

The federal and state agencies involved generally conduct the NEPA and 4(f) reviews simultaneously. Although each makes a separate finding, the documentation is sent out for public review bound in the same volume. The Federal Highway Administration (FHWA) is ultimately responsible for preparing the documentation and making the final determination on environmental impact, but since the agency is decentralized, it works primarily through the state highway agencies. The state highway agency and the FHWA division office (always in the same city as the state agency) are often the first points of contact for citizens.

Most federal highway funds are allocated to the states according to a formula. In addition, there are some demonstration projects that are specifically earmarked in the federal legislation, often the result of pressure from a particular congressional delegation or lobbying group. FHWA oversees the projects, which are either selected by the states or federally mandated.

The Intermodal Surface Transportation Efficiency Act of 1991 changed transportation planning in the United States. With its goal of developing an efficient and environmentally sound transportation system, ISTEA emphasizes linkage among various methods of transportation—such as rail and bicycle—and shifts the decision making about federal transportation funding from the state departments of transportation to a cooperative effort of state and local entities. Communities have the opportunity to develop transportation programs that complement community goals and plans; the planning process must consider the overall social, economic, energy, and environmental effects of transportation decisions. Under ISTEA, there is greater public involvement in transportation planning and more consideration of alternatives to the construction of highways.

Under ISTEA, each state develops a State Transportation Improvement Program (STIP). The STIP must include at least a three-year program of projects at the metropolitan level and a two-year program at the state level, the projects being listed in order of priority and tied to specific sources of funding. The STIP must also take into account all transportation projects that could significantly affect air quality, including privately funded projects and public-private initiatives.

Through required public involvement, citizens have an opportunity to influence transportation investments by shaping the STIP. During the first years after the passage of ISTEA, most state departments of transportation funded projects that had long been planned and were, therefore, advanced in the design and environmental review processes. This put a damper on initial citizen efforts to become involved in decision making. In some states, it has been difficult for rural areas and small towns to be actively involved in the planning process. Other states, however, were quick to welcome the new flexibility allowed by ISTEA. In Vermont, for example, the state department of transportation established cooperative agreements with the state's twelve regional planning commissions to support local citizen planning, and the project selection process was modified to reflect the results of local planning.

One of the most innovative aspects of ISTEA is the provision for a 10 percent set-aside from state allocations for what the act calls Transportation Enhancement Activities. These activities include provision of facilities for bicycles and pedestrians, acquisition of scenic easements, landscaping, historic preservation, the rehabilitation of historic transportation buildings, the conversion of abandoned railway corridors, archeological planning and research, and control of outdoor advertising. Funds for enhancement activities may not be used for business-as-usual highway projects, such as minimal landscaping, but must be in addition to standard enhancement procedures. As of June 1995, nearly 37 percent of transportation enhancement funds had been spent on bicycle and pedestrian facilities, 18 percent on landscaping, 16 percent on historic transportation facilities, and 15 percent on rail-trails.

ISTEA also established the National Scenic Byways Program (p. 328). In addition, it provides that under certain circumstances other federal funds can be used to preserve a scenic or historic road. The Federal-Aid Highway Act of 1987 specifically authorizes funding for the rehabilitation of bridges listed in or eligible for listing in the National Register of Historic Places. This act further provides that a bridge slated for demolition, if it is movable or on an abandoned right-of-way, must first be offered to a unit of government or "responsible private entity" willing to preserve it. The funds that would have been spent on demolition can be applied towards a bridge's restoration. This happened in Kent County, Michigan, where a single-lane metal truss bridge was moved to a bike trail in a neighboring county. There it was rehabilitated and is now managed by the City of Portland's park authority.

anti-tax arguments, as a major force for improving the quality of life in the state's communities.

• Be accountable: state how the money will be spent, and then provide solid facts about program accomplishment.

• Choose projects that leverage public funds: the promise of matching private funds encourages the careful spenders among voters and legislators.

• Involve willing sellers: newer programs never include condemnation authority, and often encourage the use of nonprofit organizations as intermediaries.

• Nurture strong coalitions: it takes work among advocates for such programs to remain focused on funding when they may disagree on other environmental issues.

(See Notes to Sidebars.)

The National Trust for Historic Preservation and Scenic America have a particular interest in preservation and conservation issues relating to highways. The Surface Transportation Policy Project provides information and training on all aspects of transportation affected by ISTEA.

Snickersville Turnpike, Virginia: Maintaining the Integrity of a Scenic and Historic Road

Snickersville Turnpike—Route 734 in rural Loudoun County, Virginia—is a two-lane historic road winding 14 miles through the rolling Piedmont from Aldie to Bluemont, both National Register districts. Originally an Indian trail, Snickersville Turnpike became a route of colonial transportation in the early eighteenth century and today retains almost all its original alignment. It winds through farm fields lined with stone walls and wood fences and, as it travels from east to west, offers spectacular vistas of the Blue Ridge Mountains. In 1988 the state designated it a scenic Virginia Byway.

In April 1994 some of the citizens living along Snickersville Turnpike noticed stakes along a portion of the road, placed there by the Virginia Department of Transportation (VDOT). Upon inquiry, they learned that VDOT was planning to "improve" 1.7 miles of the road near Aldie by widening it from the road's average of 18 feet to 22 feet, installing 3-foot-wide gravel shoulders, and doing considerable ditch and excavation work beyond that. Several years before, a handful of citizens had expressed some concern about the road's maintenance, as there were a number of potholes and the edges were crumbling. This concern

7.18
The Snickersville Turnpike in rural Loudoun County, Virginia, is threatened with road widening and other "improvements" that would alter its historic and scenic qualities.

became expressed as an improvement project in Loudoun County's six-year plan, and now VDOT was implementing the project. Only shortly before, VDOT had replaced a one-lane bridge along the turnpike with box culverts and, in the process, had clear cut the banks, removed mature trees, and changed the look and feel of the road, to local dismay and protest. Residents were now alarmed about what VDOT might do in widening the road.

Several citizens called a public meeting in Aldie and, discovering that many shared their concern, scheduled another meeting at the other end of the road in Bluemont, which was attended by some 300 people. Kathy Mitchell and Susan Van Wagoner—who both lived along the road but had never met before—took the lead in organizing the Snickersville Turnpike Association. In the age of the Intermodal Surface Transportation Efficiency Act, they were determined to participate in the transportation planning process. According to Van Wagoner, the association "made it possible for a lot of voices to be heard—voices that otherwise would have remained silent." And they sought help from national, state, and local conservation and preservation organizations. The Advisory Council on Historic Preservation provided advice on dealing with state departments of transportation, and the National Trust and Scenic America linked them with communities dealing with the same types of transportation issues. Thus began an intensive political campaign to raise public awareness at the local, county, and state level about Snickersville Turnpike as a special resource and about the threat VDOT's plans presented to the community. Mitchell and Van Wagoner targeted the county board of supervisors, delegates to the state legislature, and a local representative on the Commonwealth Transportation Board, the statewide body that approves all road projects.

Discovering that simply protesting VDOT's plans for Snickersville Pike was not enough, Mitchell and Van Wagoner developed their own plan for Snickersville Pike. They looked carefully at the safety issue, trying to counter the argument that the road must be widened to 22 feet. Snickersville Turnpike carries only 1,000 cars per day, essentially local traffic. Mitchell and Van Wagoner discovered that no fatalities had occurred on the road over the previous ten years, and in preceding eighteen months there had been only two accidents. They talked to fire and rescue personnel and school bus drivers, all of whom felt the road needed only a new surface. Although some residents had been concerned about potholes, crumbling shoulders, and the speed at which some people traveled, no one had complained that the road was too hilly or narrow or curvy, or that there was nowhere to pull over. The association continued to rally community support. Says Mitchell, "There was a real community spirit involved in the process, because our roads are a visible, physical part of our environment and something we all share." A straw vote taken of the road's users, in which 247 of 267 residents and landowners along the road were contacted, revealed that all but two did not want the road widened significantly, did not want it realigned, and did not want trees or stone walls removed. How could VDOT justify the claim that the road needed to be widened?

The Snickersville Turnpike Association presented their positive arguments in a beautifully written and photographed document which they distributed far and wide. By the end of 1994, everyone who could possibly be influential in persuading VDOT to change its plans was well aware of the issues. Members of the association also met repeatedly with VDOT engineers, walking the roadway, reviewing drawings, and discussing alternatives.

Mitchell and Van Wagoner also took exception to VDOT's plans to replace Hibbs Bridge, a 170-year-old double-arched stone structure, with a 400-foot-long span. With advice from transportation engineers, they challenged VDOT's assumptions about the structural integrity of the bridge and offered alternatives for its improvement.

Meanwhile, the association applied for, and received, an ISTEA transportation enhancements grant of $70,000 to replant the road banks where VDOT had replaced the one-lane bridge with a box culvert, and to provide access to, and interpretation of, a historic Union monument along the road. The association is also preparing a nomination of the Snickersville Turnpike to the National Register and may even submit a nomination of a National Register district for the corridor.

In the face of fierce local sentiment and unrelenting attention by the Turnpike Association, VDOT softened its position and in late 1995 proposed a 19-foot-wide pavement with 2 1/2-foot gravel shoulders as a compromise. The association argues for grass shoulders but would be willing to compromise on gravel with some soil mixed in so that grasses could grow.

VDOT's concession may appear small—a reduction in road width from 22 to 19 feet, a slight reduction in shoulder width, and a willingness to negotiate on the material of the shoulders—but these details make all the difference in the appearance of a scenic and historic road; in whether it will maintain its three-century integrity or will look like any suburban commuter route. And, perhaps more important, the Snickersville Turnpike Association achieved a sense of community about the issue of the road. Says Van Wagoner, "Most people feel as though they can't do anything about what's going on around them. When you pull a citizens' group together, you empower everyone."

Mining

Surface coal mining and the environmental effects of underground coal mining are regulated through the Surface Mining Control and Reclamation Act of 1977 (SMCRA). The Office of Surface Mining within the Department of the Interior administers the act. States may retain primary responsibility for regulating surface mining, but only if their regulations are as stringent as those required by SMCRA.

Under the provisions of SMCRA, states must identify areas that may be unsuitable for surface mining because they possess historic, natural, or other resources, or present hazardous mining conditions. Pennsylvania, Ohio, and Tennessee have been diligent in doing so; however, many states, especially those in the West, have not. SMCRA requires each state to establish a regulatory procedure for granting permits for mining activities. Permit regulations must include environmental protection performance standards based on the minimum federal standards set forth in the act. The states must conduct regular inspections of each mine and cite the operator for violations of regulations. Unfortunately there are loopholes in the law, and enforcement of SMCRA has frequently been lax. The Environmental Policy Institute is the nonprofit organization most directly concerned with surface mining.

SMCRA also established the Abandoned Mine Reclamation Fund, to which all coal mine operators must pay a reclamation fee per ton of coal produced. The Secretary of the Interior distributes these funds among the states that have approved regulatory programs. These funds may be used for reclamation and restoration of land and water resources adversely affected by coal mining prior to 1977, for acquisition and filling of shafts or pits, for acquisition of damaged or adjacent land, and for other reclamation activities. Kentucky has used some of its funds to build new water systems for people whose drinking water has been polluted by mining activities. The funds also support research and development efforts to find effective low-cost methods of treating acid mine drainage, such as adding alkaline materials to neutralize acid-producing waste. The Secretary of the Interior may also transfer annually up to one-fifth of the fund to the Secretary of Agriculture to control erosion damage on lands mined before 1977 and to conserve soil and water resources on lands affected by mining.

There is no federal legislation governing the mining of minerals other than coal, yet hardrock mining—of gold, silver, copper, molybdenum, phosphate, and lead, for example—is more destructive to water quality than is coal mining. Some sections of the Clean Water Act and the Clean Air Act regulate some *effects* of hardrock mining, and some states have laws that regulate aspects of hardrock mining. However, nearly all of these laws have loopholes and have been largely ineffective in preventing water and air pollution. The mining of minerals for construction—sand, gravel, limestone, and granite, for example—is regulated at the state and local levels.

The Mineral Policy Center is the nonprofit organization most directly concerned with all mining issues. The Citizens Coal Council is concerned specifically with coal mining.

Hazardous Waste

The disposal of hazardous waste is governed by the Resource Conservation and Recovery Act (RCRA) of 1976, while the cleanup of abandoned waste sites is covered by the Comprehensive Environmental Response, Compensation, and Liability Act (CERCLA) of 1980 and by the 1986 amendments to CERCLA known as the Superfund Amendment and Reauthorization Act.

Through RCRA, the Environmental Protection Agency has instituted a national program to control hazardous and solid waste from its point of generation through treatment, storage, and finally, disposal. The federal requirements of RCRA are actually carried out at the state level by programs approved by EPA. Under state programs, companies that generate waste must first determine whether it is hazardous according to criteria established by EPA. Those businesses that are producing hazardous waste must then use EPA-approved procedures for the treatment, storage, transport, and disposal of that waste and must establish a manifest system to track the waste from point of origin to point of disposal (known as a "cradle to grave" tracking system). RCRA provides for public participation by enabling citizens to take legal action against anyone involved in the mismanagement of hazardous waste; it also ensures that citizens will be notified about hazardous waste issues.

CERCLA, now better known as Superfund, authorizes EPA to respond directly to the discovery of hazardous substances at uncontrolled waste sites. Through Superfund's emergency response program, EPA can act upon immediate threats to human health, such as a truck or train accident in which chemicals have been spilled. In addition, EPA also performs

Surface-mined land can be reclaimed successfully, as before and after photographs taken in Tioga County, Pennsylvania, illustrate. The reclamation was done under the provisions of the U.S. Department of Agriculture's Rural Abandoned Mine Program.

long-term cleanups at hundreds of contaminated, and often abandoned, hazardous waste sites. Some states, such as Pennsylvania, also have state-level superfund programs to address sites that do not meet federal criteria. While the goal of CERCLA is to make responsible parties clean up their own hazardous waste, it is not always possible to find out who the responsible parties are or to get them to cooperate. This is why Superfund was set up and financed through taxes on petroleum and chemicals.

At the national level, the Sierra Club and the National Audubon Society have a particular interest in legislation concerning hazardous waste. The Citizen's Clearinghouse for Hazardous Waste provides technical, legal, and organizing assistance to community groups.

Solid Waste

In addition to hazardous waste, RCRA governs the treatment and disposal of solid waste. It does this principally through regulations on landfills. Federal regulations governing landfills deal with their location, design, operation, and closure. Generally, landfills may not be located in areas near wetlands or in areas prone to flooding, instability, landslides, mudslides, or seismic activity. Hazardous wastes are excluded from landfills, and the deposition of some other materials must be managed or restricted. In addition, landfill operators must install systems to preclude and monitor ground water contamination.

Under RCRA, states are required to develop their own solid waste disposal programs; if a state's program is approved by the EPA, the state is granted some flexibility in applying RCRA regulations. Some flexibility also exists at the local level. For instance, municipalities can be granted exemptions from some of the more costly requirements of landfills, as long as the landfill serves fewer than 10,000 people and does not pose a threat to groundwater.

Over the past decade there has been a growing movement to keep more solid waste out of the nation's landfills through recycling. The federal government has promoted the recycling of materials such as paper, glass, steel, aluminum, and plastics, but it has left localities to set up their own household recycling programs. In addition to recycling, many localities have now established programs for the collection and safe disposal of hazardous household substances.

Air Pollution

The Clean Air Act of 1970, as amended, aims to protect and enhance the quality of the nation's air. While the legislation gives the Environmental Protection Agency the authority to set limits on air pollution anywhere in the United States, it is the individual states that do much of the actual work in carrying out the provisions of the act. Each state must develop an EPA-approved state implementation plan that outlines the regulations to be used in cleaning up polluted air.

Amendments to the Clean Air Act passed in 1990 have been successful in strengthening the legislation in several ways. One of the major provisions of the act as amended is to establish a permitting program for both existing and new large sources of pollutants. These permits include information on which pollutants are being released, how much of each pollutant may be released in the future, and what steps the source's owner is taking to reduce pollution. The 1990 act also gives EPA added enforcement authority by allowing it to fine violators. In addition, the act sets deadlines for states, local governments, and businesses to achieve air quality standards and establishes a public participation process for state and local implementation of the act.

Communities suspecting that they have dangerous levels of air pollution from automobiles, nearby power plants, or factories may want to commission an air quality study or persuade the state agency responsible for monitoring air quality under the provisions of the Clean Air Act to investigate.

The best sources of information about air pollution programs are the regional offices of EPA and appropriate state, county, or municipal air pollution control agencies. In addition, national environmental and public health organizations such as the Natural Resources Defense Council, the Clean Air Action Network, and the American Lung Association take a particular interest in air pollution.

RURAL DEVELOPMENT AND HOUSING

There are numerous federal and state programs designed to promote rural development and improve housing. Although much has been done in the past fifty years to alleviate rural poverty and promote community development, in recent years there has been a marked decline in funding for these programs.

Rural Development

A good general source of assistance on rural development is the Cooperative Extension Service, established by Congress in 1914 as a partnership between the U.S. Department of Agriculture, state land-grant colleges, and county governments. Approximately ten thousand county extension agents and other specialists offer advice and practical education programs at the county level across the nation. Best known for the assistance it gives to farmers, the Cooperative Extension Service also promotes rural development and the protection of natural resources. Depending on their individual abilities and interests, Extension Service community development specialists can help a community undertake economic development and land use planning, organize workshops, provide leadership training, and get people together to discuss community problems. Extension agents, particularly those charged with community development, have assisted many rural conservation efforts, including the Oley Resource Conservation Project in Pennsylvania (see Case Study 2.1).

The Resource Conservation and Development (RC&D) program in the Department of Agriculture is a multipurpose initiative of the Natural Resources Conservation Service. Through nonprofit councils composed of local citizen volunteers and staffed by the NRCS, RC&D combines economic and community development, land conservation, water management, and cultural resource protection. For example, the Mammoth Cave RC&D in Kentucky provided funds and technical assistance to establish the African American Heritage Center in Franklin, Kentucky; RC&D also provided funds to Edmonson County, Kentucky, to install new, pressurized fire hydrants across the county, reducing property owners' insurance rates by 40 percent.

The Rural Utilities Service within the Department of Agriculture provides loans and grants for basic community infrastructure, specifically for water and waste disposal, solid waste management, emergency water assistance, and electric and telephone service. The Rural Business and Cooperative Development Service (RBCDS) provides financial assistance, business planning, technical assistance, research, education, and general information to rural areas through loans and grants for business and industrial development, business feasibility studies, job creation projects, and similar development initiatives.

The largest source of general-purpose federal grants to rural communities is the Community Development Block Grant (CDBG) program of the Department of Housing and Urban Development. Grants are generally made through the states to local governments for community development, economic development, public facilities, and other projects that will benefit low- and moderate-income residents. Several rural conservation organizations have received CDBG funds by making persuasive cases that their projects would benefit low- and moderate-income citizens. Historic Rugby persuaded a neighboring town in Tennessee to apply for CDBG funds so that the two together might restore several structures in the Rugby historic district (see Case Study 8.2). As a result of the $456,768 CDBG grant and the restorations, tourism has grown substantially and has brought increased employment and income to this economically depressed area. In Bucks County, Pennsylvania, the Office of Community Development provides CDBG funds to local organizations and municipalities for the rehabilitation of historic buildings (see Case Study 5.1). Eligibility for funding is determined by eligibility for listing in the Bucks County Heritage Conservancy's register.

The Economic Development Administration (EDA) in the Department of Commerce provides grants for the construction of public facilities, such as water and sewer systems and site improvements for industry. EDA also provides grants for economic development planning, loans to businesses, and for development and implementation strategies to mitigate the impacts on a community from severe economic decline or major job losses.

Economic development grants and loans from a number of sources may be applied to the development of rural commerce. Community Development Block Grants, for example, have been applied to the rehabilitation of small town buildings and to streetscape improvement. The Intermodal Surface Transportation Efficiency Act has provided another good source of funding for Main Street and tourism projects. In Jonesborough, Tennessee, for example, an ISTEA enhancement grant funded construction of a trail linking the facilities of the National Storytelling Center, one of the major attractions of the community (see Case Study 6.2). The U.S. Forest Service and the Cooperative Extension Service both provide technical assistance on tourism development. The Rural Business and Cooperative Development Service funds the OuR-TOWN Tourism Development Project to assist communities in building local tourism capacity.

The Rural Information Center at the National Agricultural Library, in Beltsville, Maryland, provides information on a wide range of rural development issues. The Center for Rural Affairs and the Rural Coalition give assistance to rural communities and seek legislation to help rural residents. The National Trust for Historic Preservation's National Main Street Center provides technical assistance on small town revitalization through state programs and local contracts (see p. 266). The National Trust's Heritage Tourism Program offers technical assistance on the development of heritage tourism, and most state tourism offices offer technical assistance or grants for tourism development. Several state departments of agriculture—including those of California, Mississippi, New York, and Texas—offer assistance to communities in establishing farmers' markets.

Housing

The principal federal agency that provides housing assistance in rural communities is the Rural Housing and Community Development Service (RHCDS), which is within the Department of Agriculture. RHCDS employees serve rural communities from close to two thousand county offices across the country. The agency provides loans and grants to help low- and moderate-income residents purchase, build, repair, improve, and renovate homes. These loans are often available when funding from other sources is not. RHCDS also subsidizes rents and refinances mortgages for eligible families. Moreover, RHCDS makes loans and grants to nonprofit organizations involved in housing. Although these programs have assisted many rural Americans in obtaining decent housing, the housing has not always been well planned and has frequently contributed to sprawl and its associated problems. Also, RHCDS officials have been reluctant to use funds for the rehabilitation of historic buildings. The agency also operates programs to aid construction and improvement of community facilities and watershed improvement. The Department of Housing and Urban Development also has a number of grant and loan programs for housing in rural as well as urban areas.

Vermont has a unique program that combines the provision of affordable housing with land conservation efforts. It was established by the state legislature in 1987 after advocates of affordable housing and state conservationists, who had been competing for state funding, formed an alliance to lobby for a fund that would support both groups. The Vermont Housing and Conservation Board (VHCB), supported by state appropriations and a real estate transfer tax, provides grants and loans to nonprofit organizations and municipalities for projects that conserve natural resources and, at the same time, rehabilitate or develop affordable housing. For example, a VHCB grant allowed the Central Vermont Community Land Trust to acquire a remainder interest in the 320-acre Smith farm and two lots on which they will eventually build affordable housing. Smith, who also donated conservation easements on his farm, will remain on the farm until his death, when it will automatically transfer to the land trust, which will sell it to another farmer (subject to the easements). Smith kept two other lots for himself, to sell or develop; but if he does neither, the lots will revert to the land trust for development of more affordable housing.

A leading national nonprofit organization that assists rural communities with housing programs is the Housing Assistance Council. The National Rural Housing Coalition works on rural affordable housing and community service issues. Habitat for Humanity is a nonprofit ecumenical organization that provides affordable housing for people in need. Through volunteer labor and donations of capital and materials from individuals, organizations, and governments, Habitat assists homeowners in the financing, planning, and construction of their homes. Habitat for Humanity operates through nearly 1,200 affiliates around the country. There are numerous statewide and local nonprofit organizations concerned with housing, such as Self-Help Enterprises in California and Rural Housing Improvement in Massachusetts. Although the goal of most affordable-housing organizations is to provide decent housing, whether new or rehabilitated, many are receptive to the possibility of rehabilitating historic buildings.

Union, South Carolina: Rehabilitating Historic Buildings for Low- and Moderate-Income Housing

In 1985, the town of Union (pop. 9,830), on the edge of the Sumter National Forest in South Carolina, was delighted when a local bank foreclosed on the Fairforest Hotel and gave it to the town. The sixty-nine-room hotel, built by local investors in 1927, was a beautiful structure—listed in the National Register and located in the downtown historic district—but it was now a run-down haven for itinerant workers and an eyesore. The town wanted to rehabilitate the building as a fine hotel.

Twice, rehabilitation plans were made for adaptive reuse of the building as a hotel, but developers deemed the project to be financially infeasible. The town had also acquired two adjacent historic buildings which it planned to tear down in order to construct parking lots for the hotel with Community Development Block Grant funds. Because federal dollars were involved, the State Historic Preservation Office was notified of the project. It objected to the destruction of the historic buildings. With repeated failed attempts to move the project forward, the town vowed to get out of the real estate business. In 1988, Union put the Fairforest Hotel up for sale.

DeWayne Anderson, a developer who specializes in rehabilitating historic buildings for low- to moderate-income housing, offered an option to buy the building. To Anderson, Union—a mill town with a large proportion of the population qualifying for low- to moderate-income rental housing—was a good market for the project.

Union, wanting to sell the hotel outright, turned Anderson's offer down and sold the hotel and the two adjacent buildings to a speculator. The structures continued to stand vacant. Finally, the Downtown Union Revitalization Association got involved. Its director, Fred Delk, put Anderson directly in touch with the speculator. Anderson bought the buildings, and the rehabilitation project was under way. The hotel would become an apartment for the low-income elderly, with nonresidential uses in the storefronts.

It took a full five years for Anderson, working in partnership with the Downtown Association and the City of Union to structure the financing package and accomplish rehabilitation. Financing for the $2.6 million project came from a Section 515 Rural Rental Housing loan from the Rural Housing and Community Development Service, a Community Development Block Grant, the South Carolina Housing Trust Fund, and the City of Union, as well as equity from the sale of low-income tax credits and historic rehabilitation tax credits. It was the first time in South Carolina that a Section 515 loan had ever been used with the historic rehabilitation tax credits, and the bureaucratic wheels turned slowly. When the rehabilitation was complete, however, it was an immediate success; its forty-one attractive and spacious apartments filled right away. "It is a classy place," reports Delk. "Residents congregate in the lobby; it is a social place." The lobby, verandah, and other public spaces are frequently used by the community for weddings, parties, and meetings. All of the four store fronts are occupied.

Once construction on the hotel began, the city council got interested in real estate again and began to examine what could be done with Poverty Flat, a row of six buildings around the corner from the Fairforest Hotel that had once served as cotton and general warehouses and a bottling company. With Anderson, the city used federal, state, and local funds combined with private equity to rehabilitate the buildings into nineteen moderate-income apartments. The city then went on to capture the new taxes paid by the development and assemble some $800,000–$250,000 of which came from an ISTEA enhancements grant— to reconstruct a historic streetscape, with concrete sidewalks, decorative lighting, and trees.

According to Delk, now planning coordinator for Union as well as director of the Downtown Association, the rehabilitation projects have "made a tremendous difference for downtown. In 1995 there were eight more businesses downtown than a year before, and the vacancy rate is constantly dropping." People who needed affordable housing have it, and their presence strengthens the downtown. Moreover, the project has significantly changed the attitude in the community; the town, which had been reluctant to take an active role in its own development, is much more willing now to invest in the future. As Anderson says, "the Union projects are excellent examples of how public and private interests can work together to meet community development needs and to preserve a locality's unique character."

CONCLUSION

Don't let the number of laws and programs described in this chapter overwhelm you. Obviously you need to choose those that address the issues most important to your organization. As the case studies make clear, it is the organizations that complain, lobby, cajole, threaten, and generally refuse to take no for an answer that get results. When it comes to getting help from the outside it is the squeaky wheel that gets the grease.

Community Education and Support

8

INTRODUCTION

Education is vital to every successful conservation organization's program. If residents in your community do not appreciate the significance of prime farmland, historic farmsteads, wetland habitat, or scenic vistas, it will be difficult to establish a program to protect them. Not only must you educate residents about the importance of these resources to your community's future; you may also need to persuade them to contribute money or property, embark on a visioning exercise, agree to rezoning, or possibly forgo employment opportunities by keeping out an industry that would pollute. Persuading people to contribute to the common good—particularly when it involves sacrifice of time or money or a change in the status quo—is never easy and calls for all of the ingenuity a conservation organization can muster.

Education takes many forms. It can be formal or informal. It may consist of a media campaign, newsletters, lectures, workshops, programs for schools, special events, museum exhibits, or even a county fair or farmers' market, all of which are discussed in this chapter. Obviously, many of the programs discussed in previous chapters also entail education. In fact, there is little a conservation organization does that does not involve education. The same is true of many public agencies involved in conservation, environmental protection, and community development. In addition to serving your immediate goals, however, education projects can build a foundation for greater civic collaboration—creating low-key, perhaps long-term, even entertaining means of building personal relationships. As they grow more skilled in working with one another on an educational project, participants are also preparing the way for tackling other, larger, more complex efforts through their own or other organizations.

The first step in developing an education program is determining who needs to be educated about what and why. Do farmers need to learn about a new transfer of development rights program, school children about the importance of protecting wetlands, or property owners about easements? Once an organization has identified both its audience and subject matter, it can choose an appropriate educational activity. An organization will probably conduct different activities for its board members, for government officials, for children, and for the general public.

For nonprofit organizations, community education goes hand-in-hand with fund raising. If your organization communicates its mission successfully, people will be willing to contribute to its future activities; the more good press coverage an organization can get, the easier it will be to persuade individuals, businesses, and foundations to support its activities. Although funds for rural conservation are often raised through grants from public agencies and private foundations, much of an organization's funding comes from individuals and local businesses. Thus, writing good newsletters, brochures, and membership letters and producing special events are integral to successful fund raising. For public agencies, the test of success in community education lies not in direct fund raising but in building a supportive constituency.

CASE STUDY 8.1

Yakima, Washington: Selling the Yakima River Greenway

"To make land conservation work, a land trust must sell its program," asserts Marc Smiley, the first executive director of the Yakima River Greenway Foundation. "It must sell its goals to the local community that ultimately determines success or failure for the program."

The greenway is a river corridor along 10 miles of the Yakima River and 3 miles of the Naches River in Yakima County, Washington. Interest in protecting this significant scenic and recreational resource in the midst of a rapidly urbanizing area dates back to the 1960s. Finally, in 1979, the county commissioners established a task force to investigate how a linear park could be established. The task force, after receiving advice from the Trust for Public Land, recommended the establishment of a private, nonprofit land trust. The commissioners accepted the recommendation, and in 1980 the Yakima River Greenway Foundation was incorporated. The initial board consisted of representatives of community groups and interested government agencies and citizens at large. The board decided that the initial focus had to be the further development of several existing parks and pathways that gave the community the opportunity to experience the values that made the entire greenway important to protect.

"When the Yakima Greenway Foundation was established in 1980, it quickly learned that a vision was not enough to turn a greenway dream into re-

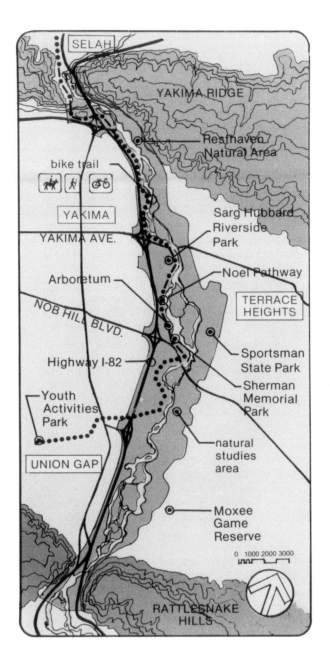

8.1
The Yakima River Greenway Foundation in Washington State is working to protect a 10-mile corridor between Yakima Ridge and Rattlesnake Hills, including two parks and a series of trails (dotted line) to be built along the river. The foundation's successful educational program has resulted in a committed local constituency and donations of funds, land, and volunteer labor.

ality," relates Cec Vogt, present executive director of the land trust. "In order to raise the funds to carry out our ambitious project, the community had to be able to *see* it. Seeing truly is believing, because the more that we put on the ground, the easier it is to get the message out to the community and build a strong constituency."

Over the years, the foundation has found a number of ways to publicize its program. It has organized public meetings, held fund-raising banquets, invited VIP speakers, enlisted the help of service clubs, recognized volunteers, awarded plaques to donors, had booths at state fairs, arranged rafting trips for influential officials, created special events focused on the greenway, published a newsletter, written brochures, and prepared slide shows and a video. Contacts with the

8.2
The Yakima River Greenway Foundation's annual Gap to Gap Relay race includes bicycle riding, canoeing, and running. The contestants and spectators gain an appreciation of the resource, and the publicity that results has greatly increased support for conservation.

press have been key. Media sponsorship of events, news conferences, press releases, and open communication have been an integral part of getting the message to the community.

Many of the foundation's most successful educational projects date from a board retreat in 1984, when the members decided they needed to do a better job of getting their message out. The board established a public relations committee and prepared a public relations plan that would be updated annually. The plan included attention to press, lectures, exhibits, collaboration with civic organizations, and special events.

One of the foundation's most successful projects has been the Gap to Gap Relay. This annual race, which includes bicycle riding, canoeing, and running along the river corridor, began in June 1985 as a way to build community awareness, showcase the greenway, and possibly raise some money. Since then the race has grown into a full weekend of events with a Junior Gap to Gap, festival, and fun walk involving 500 volunteers and 1,000 participants. About 100 local businesses donate services, goods, and money. The event has netted the Greenway Foundation up to $50,000. According to Vogt, "the publicity the event brings the greenway is invaluable. It is extensively covered by the local newspaper, which is a sponsor, and all the TV and radio stations. We couldn't afford to pay for such visibility, but they all want to cover it."

As a result of fifteen years of continuous promotion, networking, building partnerships, fund raising, holding special events, and educating the public—and with the support of hundreds of dedicated volunteers—the Greenway Foundation has acquired 209 acres of mostly undeveloped land, restored and protected a degraded river corridor and, in 1994, on 200 acres of land protected by easements and agreements with landowners, built three large parks, seven miles of paved pathway, four river landings; and a fishing lake with facilities for the disabled. The greenway is fondly known as the jewel of Yakima by a proud community.

NEWS MEDIA

Informing the community about activities through the local news media is one of the most effective ways of developing support. News coverage can enhance the group's credibility as well as increase its visibility. The right publicity at the right time can help pass an ordinance or law and can help raise money at a critical moment. Coverage in the closest city also informs the region about the community's programs. Occasionally, residents of a nearby city who become aware of concerns will offer

Cazenovia Republican

Cazenovia's Oldest Industry - Established 1808

USPS 095-260

All About Cazenovia — — What Makes It Special?

This is the first in a series of articles written by members of the Cazenovia Community Resources Project, a study assisted by the National Trust for Historic Preservation. Protection of the resources and the rural character of Cazenovia, while still accommodating growth, is the aim of the project. In this article Don Callahan, supervisor of the Town of Cazenovia, discusses Cazenovia's "quality of life."

By Don R. Callahan

You have heard the axiom, "the whole is greater than the sum of its parts." In many ways this is true of Cazenovia. The ridges and rolling hills, the gorges and waterfalls, the streams and lake, the woodlots, wildlife, meadows, productive farms, historic settlements and buildings, splendid views — together these aspects are a part of what makes Cazenovia a nice place to live.

In addition to these physical characteristics, there is a sense of community that has evolved over the years. Witness the mingling of people in the streets and shops, and enjoying the parks, countryside and the lake. The number of active community organizations in Cazenovia is a good indication of the strong community feeling that exists.

Cazenovia has a good mix of people — youth, young married couples, families, farmers, tradesmen, businessmen, professionals, the retired and the elderly. We all enjoy some aspect of our surroundings, the views, the countryside, recreation, the people. Together, our environment and our community create a quality of life that is unique to Cazenovia.

These qualities, however, are disappearing in many rural communities especially those on the urban fringe.

How can we protect this quality of life as Cazenovia grows and moves into the future? This is the question that the Cazenovia Community Resources Project has been studying since June 1980 when 200 volunteers began collecting information for an extensive inventory of local resources. This article is the first in a series describing what we have learned.

The series will discuss Cazenovia from the early movements of the earth's crust which has resulted in the shape of the land, the soils, water, vegetation, and wildlife, and the large part that these resources played in the settlement of the area and the human activities which have shaped the community into what it is today.

We are all part of a system of interrelated resources. Each part of our environment determines and is dependent on other parts.

Some parts of the environment are beyond our control, such as the weather, but we can control the kind and degree of change which occurs in the environment as a result of human activity.

As we move into an age of scarcity, we should pay more attention to local resources. Many communities have learned that growth is not necessarily synonymous with lower taxes and a better quality of life. Uncontrolled growth can often cost more in services. As a result, the wise use of resources and the consideration of the capacity of the land for certain uses is a policy more and more communities are adopting. Careful siting of housing, business, and industry can help maintain the quality of the environment and the health of the community.

We enjoy Cazenovia as it is now. But we must consider the whole in relation to the parts, we must consider the community and the environment as we grow and change so that future generations will enjoy Cazenovia as we do today.

June 23, 1982 Cazenovia Republican

Don R. Callahan

8.3
Press coverage of conservation issues and activities is important to any conservation organization. A series of thirteen articles written by Cazenovia Community Resources Project volunteers for the *Cazenovia Republican* helped broaden the base of support for new conservation initiatives in the upstate New York township. This was the first article, written by Don Callahan, Cazenovia's town supervisor. Other subjects covered in the series included geology, soils, the lake, wetlands, trees, wildflowers, agriculture, architecture, and history.

their services, donate funds, or help in some other way. The Amana Heritage Society, for example, routinely informs the media in nearby Cedar Rapids and Iowa City of its programs and as a result has received donations and drawn attendance from Amana's urban neighbors.

The interest of the news media, however, is sometimes a hindrance rather than a help. Intense, premature coverage of a proposed conservation project in a New Jersey township fanned the fires of controversy and influenced citizens to oppose the project before they had learned what it could do for them. Even positive publicity can have a negative impact, especially if it results in increased visitation to a fragile area. Most archeologists, for example, avoid naming the specific locations of sites because of the danger of damage or looting. Similarly, biologists may not wish to disclose the location of endangered species. Biologists in western Virginia are concerned that increased caving as a result of press publicity is disturbing the hibernation of endangered long-eared bats, causing a serious reduction in their population.

Small communities may be unable to handle the increased visitation from outsiders that might result from publicity, or they may fear excessive new development to accommodate visitors. Such communities may prefer not to publicize their assets. The historic village of Waterford, Virginia, has developed a happy compromise. The Waterford Foundation concentrates news coverage in the period preceding its annual Homes Tour and Crafts Exhibit. While visitors are encouraged to come to that event, there is little publicity outside the community during the rest of the year (see Case Study 8.3).

The first steps in establishing a media program are to identify which audiences are most important and which newspapers, periodicals, radio stations, or television programs are most likely to reach them. Although the printed word is more appropriate for detailed information, some people are more likely to pay attention to what they see or hear on television and radio.

In addition to getting the organization's message across as part of the news, it may be possible to arrange for a public service advertisement or announcement. Most newspapers and radio and television stations offer space and time for "PSAs" to nonprofit organizations and may even help to prepare them.

Most organizations need someone to act as press coordinator or spokesperson. The Amana Heritage Society chose a volunteer who had experience with the League of Women Voters and other organizations to coordinate its effective public information program. The coordinator should be well-organized and a good communicator both in person and in writing. The coordinator needs to develop a relationship of mutual trust with reporters, since reporters are likely to get in touch with a spokesperson only if they believe they will get reliable information. Reporters have an obligation to present both sides of a story, and a spokesperson should be prepared to answer questions about opposing points of view.

A group should periodically evaluate its use of the media. The press coordinator should keep a notebook of newspaper and other clippings and a record of radio and television broadcasts mentioning the group. The group can use the notebook to determine the frequency and extent of local coverage and make judgments about what types of coverage to pursue in the future. The notebook can also be used to brief community leaders, funding sources, visitors, and others about the organization.

Newspapers

Newspapers are usually the most important and available news medium for conservation organizations. Some rural communities have their own daily or weekly newspapers. For the many that have none, the press coordinator must identify the papers most people read. These may include the state's major newspaper, the paper of the closest city, or a free weekly advertiser.

Developing a contact person at each newspaper is useful: at a small paper, it might be the editor-in-chief; at a large paper, one reporter might be assigned to news in a particular community. A personal visit to an editor or reporter helps establish a relationship with the newspaper. In face-to-face meetings, the reporter can better understand the community's issues and needs and the community representative can better appreciate the journalist's particular interests. It is helpful to leave with the reporter a fact sheet or press release giving background information.

Many newspapers welcome general interest stories that are not tied to a specific event. Others may run special supplements several times a year in conjunction with local events or particular seasons. The Oley Resource Conservation Project in Pennsylvania, for example, was covered in a special section of the *Boyertown Area Times*. In New York, the Cazenovia Community Resources Project volunteers wrote a series on rural conservation issues for the weekly *Cazenovia Republican*. A sympathetic editor might be asked to write an editorial or a group's leader to write a guest column.

From time to time, an organization may wish to grant an exclusive story to one newspaper. An exclusive may result in a more comprehensive article, which can be more effective than minimal coverage in several papers. Exclusives should not always be given to the same newspaper, as granting an exclusive to one paper may damage your standing with others.

Radio and Television

Radio is an especially good way to publicize upcoming events. Morning and late afternoon news programs appeal to many people, especially to commuters, who can find out about last night's rezoning or the upcoming fair while driving to and from work. Any press releases submitted to a radio station should include a brief statement that can be read over the air exactly as it is written. Many radio stations produce talk shows for which a feature on rural conservation issues would be appropriate. Such a forum would offer more extended coverage and allow an interview with a group's leaders. Because radio talk shows are increasingly popular and usually have a faithful following of listeners, they can be effective means of getting the word out.

Rural stories with regional appeal can provide interesting material for television. Television stations look for action in the subjects they cover. Tree planting or litter collection along a highway may have more appeal than an interview with an organization's president. When the Yakima Greenway Foundation organized a trip on the Yakima River for state Park Commission members, all three local television stations covered the event. The outing and the publicity helped to persuade the commissioners to continue state funding for land acquisition along the river.

Press Conferences

Press conferences sound intimidating and bring to mind images of the President sparring with reporters at the White House. But even a small organization may find it useful to hold a press conference occasionally for big announcements, such as the acquisition of a major property or

8.1 Press Releases

Press releases should be concise and typed double-spaced. Include the following information:

- *The name and telephone number of a contact person*
- *The date the story should be published if the press release is sent out before the event; "For Immediate Release" indicates it can be published at any time*
- *A brief title and a short, interesting, but objective account*
- *Several direct quotes*
- *The names and titles of all persons and groups involved, double-checked for accuracy*

Accompanying photographs should be 8-by-10-inch black-and-white glossy prints, labeled on the back with the names of people and places in the photograph, date taken, and name of the photographer. Photographs that show people in action—a naturalist leading a hike, a history student interviewing an old-timer, or a soil scientist taking a sample—have more appeal than those that show only buildings and landscapes, or people lined up in a row.

The press release can also be accompanied by background information on the community, conservation issues, and the organization's accomplishments. It may be helpful to summarize this information in a fact sheet that can accompany all press releases.

8.2 Photographing the Countryside

Photographs are an important part of any community's environmental inventory and education program. They can be used to document the status of resources, to illustrate publications, and in public presentations. Photographs are essential in historic preservation surveys; they allow a community to document the current status of a historic building and monitor future alterations. The Cazenovia Community Resources Project in New York documented all of its historic buildings with photographs and prepared a popular slide show covering all of the community's resources.

In some cases it is worth the investment to hire a professional photographer. However, amateurs can be of great assistance in many situations.

Good-quality photographs can greatly enhance public presentations and publications. Here are some recommendations regarding their preparation:

• Slower film yields sharper pictures, but you must guard against camera movement. Whenever possible use a tripod.
• Color is great for slide shows, but black-and-white is often necessary for publications. Converting color shots to black-and-white is an iffy

the completion of a comprehensive plan. The advantage of a press conference is that it highlights the importance of the news and avoids having to tell the same story several times. Conservationists should be certain that the news justifies the event; the press will eventually ignore groups that repeatedly hold press conferences for marginally important stories.

Press conferences should be held at a location and time convenient for the invited news media. A one-page memo sent well in advance and follow-up phone calls a day or two before the scheduled conference can help a great deal. When the reporters arrive, each one should be greeted and thanked for coming. These courtesies will be appreciated, and the media will be more responsive to future press conferences the group calls.

BROCHURES

A brochure is often the first tangible product that a rural conservation organization develops as a way to get its message across. Brochures serve many purposes; they are used in direct mailing for fund raising, may be handed out at press conferences or other events, and may be displayed in public facilities for visitors to pick up. Because brochures are so integral to the way the group will be perceived, it is important that they be well written and well designed.

The first step in preparing a brochure is deciding exactly what message the organization wants to convey. Once this has been decided, the message should be expressed as concisely and clearly as possible and should convey a sense of immediacy, even urgency. In fact, the message should be condensed into one phrase, if possible, to be used on the brochure's cover. The reader needs to be drawn in by the cover and made to sense the importance of reading the material inside.

Text should take up no more than one-third of the brochure's paper surface; graphics are critical to a brochure's success. Pictures or illustrations that convey the organization's message immediately and clearly are invaluable. Dark colors and tiny images should be avoided; instead, bold and vivid pictures, symbols, and lettering should be used.

Ideally, brochures should be designed by graphic artists. Design services may be available from a community volunteer, but if no one with graphics skills is available, it may be well worth the cost to hire a professional designer.

NEWSLETTERS

A newsletter is an effective way to communicate information promptly, especially when there is no local newspaper. Newsletters can include such features as photographs or drawings of local scenes, practical advice on gardening, contests to identify the individuals or sites shown in historic photographs, and a calendar of upcoming community events.

Newsletters should be written with brevity in mind. Concise writing is the key to effective newsletter communication. It is important to accompany the words with graphics. What maps, illustrations, photographs, or charts will best convey the message the organization is trying to get across?

A newsletter can be an excellent project for volunteers. A printer or someone from a local newspaper can often provide advice on how to lay out the newsletter. Computer programs can be used to prepare camera-ready copy and graphics. An art teacher may be able to help with graphics or show volunteers how to use art supplies. An editor, perhaps an English teacher or newspaper reporter, who can spot faulty grammar and poor syntax is essential.

An up-to-date mailing list is important for both newsletters and other bulletins. If the list is long, a computer program that can store mailing lists, sort addresses by zip code, and prepare labels can be an assist. Non-profit organizations can save postage costs by obtaining bulk mail permits. Dividing the mailing list into different categories—such as members and nonmembers, residents and outsiders, local officials, donors, and press—simplifies sending out mailings aimed at particular audiences. In-

The Uwharrie Lakes
Newsletter

Winter 1995/96

U-Where? Uwharrie...A Heritage Area In The Making

by Alex Cousins, Associate Director

Each of us can think of a region in this country where the landscape, the cities, and towns have a particular character to them. They have evolved over time in harmony with the way of life of the residents, and the residents in turn value the history and culture of this shared landscape. The Mississippi Delta comes to mind — as do the Brandywine Valley, the Shenandoah Valley, and the Texas Hill Country.

There is a name for these regions: *heritage areas*. Heritage areas often are built around natural features, such as a river or mountain range, or man-made features, such as a canal or trading route. They tie together cities, counties, and sometimes states — linking historic sites, natural landscapes, and small towns. Their vitality comes from a new coalition of leaders and constituents, some committed primarily to historic preservation, some to the natural environment, others to recreation, and most of them to compatible economic development. The resulting collaboration is the promotion and development of an

area with a "shared sense of place".

The Yadkin/Pee Dee regional strategic planning process culminated with the idea of just such a place — *The Uwharrie Lakes Region*. Here were seven North Carolina counties sharing much in common: a river, six man-made reservoirs, America's oldest mountain

range, Native American archeological sites, a pioneer history, and an industrial heritage that includes gold mining, textiles, and railroading. So on target were the leaders spearheading the strategic plan that they created a "heritage area" before the movement was even recognized nationally. The Uwharrie Lakes Region is now part of a

growing movement of over 100 distinct heritage areas in the U.S.

The Uwharrie Lakes Region was created from individual parts. The Yadkin/Pee Dee Lakes Project has been fashioning those parts into a whole. How are we doing this? By using the strategic plan as a blueprint, we are putting into place the recommended tourism strategies that will physically unite the region and reinforce its "sense of place."

The 350-mile Uwharrie Lakes Byway will go a long way toward accomplishing this goal. The byway will connect the historic sites and attractions of all seven counties through a network of scenic back roads. For the first time, a family visiting the NC Zoo will have a physical link that connects them to the many other assets in the region. For example, that family may decide to head back to Charlotte via the byway, instead of the interstate. In doing so, they will travel through and spend their dollars in places like Seagrove, Badin, and Mt. Gilead.

Continued on page 2

Continued on page 2

Randolph County Becomes Newest Member Of The Uwharrie Lakes Region

The Yadkin/Pee Dee family grew to seven in September when the Randolph County Board of Commissioners voted to join Anson, Davidson, Montgomery, Richmond, Rowan, and Stanly counties as a member of the Uwharrie Lakes Region. The strategic planning process originally focused only on those counties that bordered the Yadkin/Pee Dee river, thus excluding Randolph. However, because the county comes within 2 miles of Badin Lake, contains the NC Zoological Park, the Seagrove area potteries, and 9,179 acres of Uwharrie National Forest, Randolph has been included in the implementation of the strategic plan. "The county has really been an unofficial partner in our efforts all along," said Judy Stevens, chairman of the Yadkin/Pee Dee Lakes Project. "We are delighted that the county commission has decided to cement this relationship and we look forward to working with their leadership." Randolph County has made a $2,500 fair-share contribution to the Project's operating budget and it now has three representatives on the Project's Board of Directors (*see related article on page 4*). Join us in welcoming beautiful Randolph County to the Uwharrie Lakes Region!

---

proposition. For color photographs in publications, slides yield better results than prints.

• The best lighting for photography is in the early morning and late afternoon. Midday photographs tend to be flat in tone and lack the shadows that provide good contrast.

• In checking the exposure, point the light meter at the most important part of the picture. Avoid pointing it at the sky.

• A filter that cuts haze enhances detail and emphasizes clouds. It also protects expensive lenses.

• Backlighted photographs, with the sun beaming into the camera, are generally to be avoided.

• In terms of composition, overall scenes are useful, but so are details, such as a single fern or a building cornice. Minimize distracting foreground, such as pavement and too much sky.

• Use a good lab for developing. Avoid drugstores and discount shops. When ordering prints, ask for reproduction-quality enlargements. Have color film processed by the film's manufacturer.

• Identify all photographs with the subject, location, date, and photographer.

• Never touch the picture area of a negative or transparency. Negatives should be stored in acid-free envelopes.

(See Notes to Sidebars.)

8.4
A newsletter is an effective way to communicate information promptly, particularly when there is no local newspaper. Many, like this one from the Yadkin/Pee Dee Lakes Project, headquartered in Badin, North Carolina, are published by volunteers.

8.3 10 Steps to a Successful Brochure

Richard Beamish, a very experienced communications consultant to conservation organizations, offers these guidelines for creating a good brochure.

1. Decide what you want to say, and then say it as clearly and concisely as you can. After you do a first draft, go back over the text and boil it down to about half that size. Then go over it again and cut out more words. (Be ruthless with that red pencil!)

2. Condense your message into one phrase (the theme) to be used on the cover or as the first words your reader is drawn to inside. State your theme at the outset, and let the text and graphics flow from there.

3. Tell your story in logical, narrative sequence—and don't be afraid to tug at your reader's heart strings.

4. Use graphics that illustrate, inform, enliven, and tell most of your story at a glance.

5. Use pictures with emotional impact—pictures that will move your reader—and play the pictures big.

6. Use high-quality professional photographs with sufficient contrast to reproduce well.

7. Stress graphics over text. Be generous with the size of your pictures and the amount of white space. (White space is not wasted space.) Be bold with your headlines. Devote at least two thirds of your brochure to pictures, headings, white space, and other visual enhancements.

8. Choose a typeface (font) that is big enough and dark enough to be read easily. Strive for sharp contrast

dividuals and organizations that have helped the group, or are expected to help in the future, should be included, as should elected representatives and regional, state, and national organizations that may share the group's concerns.

EDUCATIONAL PROGRAMS

Many people, both adults and children, are hungry for the kinds of educational experiences rural conservation organizations can offer. Hands-on activities, organized not for fund raising but to get something done—an elderly owner's home freshly painted, a roadside freed of litter, a stream's eroded banks stabilized and newly planted with trees—provide excellent opportunities to learn about the organization, about the community's civic structure or history, or about the environment in general. People also engage in educational activities in order to meet other people or simply to show support for the organization. In choosing what kinds of educational events to sponsor, it is well to bear these multiple motivations in mind and to provide a range of opportunities matched to the interests of different audiences.

Lectures, Slide Shows, and Videotapes

Talks by both local leaders and outsiders are effective educational tools. The topic should be as relevant and appealing as possible to the audience. Farmers may be more interested in a talk entitled "The Economic Benefits of Agricultural Districts" than in one called "Conserving Our Farmland." A talk on agricultural districts can, of course, impart a strong conservation message. It is important to select a time and place that are appropriate and convenient. To reach local realtors, a luncheon meeting might be best; farmers might prefer an early morning breakfast at the local café.

Civic, fraternal, and other local organizations, such as libraries and churches, often are seeking interesting and timely topics for their meetings. Booking speakers for these organizations is an effective way of gaining community visibility and educating a broader population about rural conservation. The Cherokee Nation in North Carolina developed a brochure listing tribal members who were prepared to talk about their cultural traditions to school groups and other audiences.

Inviting a speaker from a well-known organization can attract a large audience and lend credibility to the local group sponsoring the speech. If, for instance, a State Historic Preservation Officer praises a historic farm, the group may win supporters in a fight to prevent a road widening.

Good slide shows and videotapes may be rented or borrowed from many state and national organizations. Alternatively, an organization can develop its own slide show or video, to focus attention on its goals and programs and also on the community's resources. If an organization will be showing the same slides many times, it might consider transferring the slides to videotape, creating a slide-tape show. The presentation should be short enough to allow for questions and discussion within the program time.

Although videotapes can be effective, they are more expensive to produce than slide shows and cannot be altered easily to take into account changing circumstances. Videos can be an effective way to lobby or solicit contributions, but organizations considering making one should have a very clear vision of the purpose and the message to be conveyed. Critical, too, is a plan for distribution of the tape. How will it reach its intended audience? Some communities have used videotape successfully. The Yakima Greenway, in cooperation with the three local television stations, prepared an 8-minute video presentation narrated by a well-known local TV personality. The video exemplifies the numerous collaborative efforts within the greenway and the many community entities that helped build the greenway and continue to foster it.[1]

Field Trips

Every community's environment provides a learning laboratory in which to explore such matters as natural resources, architectural styles, and farming methods. There is no substitute for getting people out in the field, to see the resources that need to be protected or how conservation and development can complement each other if done with care. Reading about farmland loss in a community is instructive, but it does not have nearly the impact of visiting a farm and learning about its operations from the farmer. Nonfarm residents will then better understand the importance of agriculture in their community; and they may also become personally committed to assuring that the farm family they met, and their neighbors, can stay in business.

Many groups organize regular outings for their members and for others in the community. An outing might consist of an hour's walk through the village historic district led by a local historian, an afternoon's nature hike in a local preserve led by the high school biology teacher, or a day's tour of farms led by the Natural Resources Conservation Service's district conservationist.

by using dark ink on a light background. Keep in mind that white letters on a dark background can dramatically highlight a cover message or principal headline inside.

9. *Consider using a second color to accentuate headings, backgrounds, and graphic features.*

10. *Collect brochures and other printed material that appeal to you, and adapt useful ideas and techniques to your own communications. Find out who did the designing and the printing, check into the cost of these professional services, and employ these services if you possibly can. Use the best printer (who does the best photographic reproductions) you can afford. And remember that the best really does not cost much more than the worst.*

(See Notes to Sidebars.)

8.5
There is no substitute for getting a community's residents out to see the resources that need to be protected. Here a science instructor points out the many features of good wetland habitat in Kandiyohi County, Minnesota.

Each year since 1973, the all-volunteer Plymouth County Wildlands Trust in Massachusetts has organized "First Sunday" nature walks on one or more of its fifty-five parcels, which include lands bordering coastal inlets and ponds, Native American sacred sites, colonial industrial sites, and a variety of woodland and meadow lands. These monthly rambles are each led by an expert on local fauna, flora, geomorphology, or history. The walks, as well as path and parking maintenance, are all performed by volunteers. The trust publishes a guide to its most popular walks, *Lands in Trust*.

In addition to sponsoring field trips, organizations can prepare booklets for self-guided tours. For example, student interns from the Yale University School of Forestry and Environmental Studies working for the Roxbury Land Trust in Connecticut prepared publications for self-guided nature walks in that trust's holdings.

Workshops

Workshops can provide more detailed information than lectures and are typically on subjects that have practical application. For property owners, the advantages of agricultural districts, rehabilitating an old house, or the benefits of easement donation are examples of worthwhile

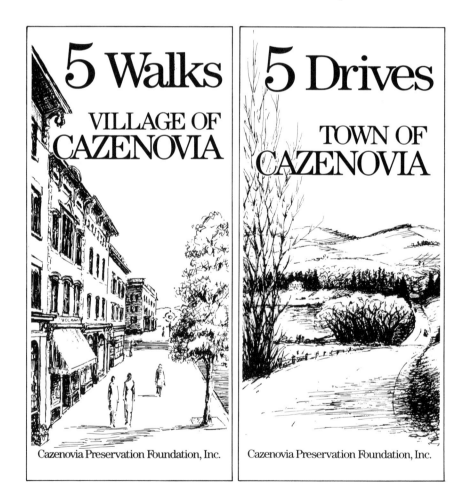

8.6
Booklets providing self-guided tours encourage residents and visitors to experience the environment first-hand. Dorothy Riester wrote and illustrated these pamphlets for the Cazenovia Preservation Foundation. The guides include maps and short descriptions of significant sites along the way.

topics. A workshop usually includes more than one speaker, allows ample opportunity for discussion, and provides participants with instructional materials to take home for future reference. Sessions can be held over a series of evenings or on a weekend. For instance, THRIFT (Tug Hill Resources—Investment for Tomorrow), in upstate New York, sponsored two Saturday workshops to inform landowners about forest management. Owners learned to identify trees, received guidance on woodlot management, discussed the protection of wildlife habitat, and observed sawmill operations.

Leadership Training and Member Education

The education of leaders and potential leaders of both nonprofit organizations and local governments pays off in informed decision making. Attending conferences, workshops, and short courses and visiting other communities that have undertaken rural conservation programs are all good ways for leaders to gain new skills and insights. Workshops designed to increase management and fund-raising skills or to provide detailed information about ecology, historic preservation, good design, or land use law can help to improve leaders' effectiveness. A group might pay the registration costs for a county supervisor to attend a national conference on farmland retention; a more knowledgeable supervisor may later encourage the county to take action on that issue.

In-house educational activities may be structured or unstructured, limited to selected participants, such as board members or committee chairs, or open to all members of an organization. Some organizations conduct retreats or seminars. Collecting and making available a basic rural conservation library is a simple educational activity that all groups can conduct. The Cazenovia Community Resources Project in New York collected useful publications and placed them on a special shelf at the local library.

Activities for Children

Sponsoring events for children is a good way to build and keep community awareness. An added benefit is that parents often become involved in community affairs through their children. The Amana Heritage Society in Iowa found that its membership increased substantially after it began sponsoring programs in community schools, and students participating in the state arts council's architect-in-schools program in Rolfe, another rural Iowa community, were responsible for awakening interest in their deteriorated downtown. The Rolfe students developed oral histories for each building, took photographs, and traced deeds as part of an exhibit on the downtown for the school fair. Another group of Rolfe students suggested improvements to building facades that resulted in a new use for a historic bank building.

Programs for children should provide hands-on experience. An occasional slide show or video is an interesting diversion from classroom work, but tours, games, and research projects that allow children to discover things on their own are generally more instructive. Every community has sites to visit that will interest children. Moreover, many museums and nature centers have programs specifically designed for children.

A sixth-grade class in Lakefield, Minnesota, participates in Environmental Clean Up Day, in cooperation with the county's Soil and Water Conservation District. Projects for children increase their interest, and that of their parents, in conservation.

The Housatonic Valley Association in Connecticut, for instance, has made a major commitment to environmental education through its Watershed Environmental Resource Center. The association helps high school teachers throughout the valley integrate environmental education into the curriculum. It provides a computerized bulletin board for teachers and students, teacher workshops, classroom programs, and information on published curricular materials and about the people who are available to make classroom presentations or lead field trips. The resource center also hosues a library of reference sources on the Housatonic watershed which is available to students, teachers, and the general public. The association also conducts an annual watershed-wide cleanup of the Housatonic River and its tributaries, which gives students an opportunity to serve their community and learn about the river at the same time.

At the national level, the National Audubon Society and the National Wildlife Federation publish environmental magazines for children and supply teachers with curriculum materials.

EDUCATIONAL FACILITIES

Many rural conservation organizations undertake long-term educational programs that require permanent facilities like museums, living history programs, and nature centers. These programs can be very effective, but they take a considerable investment of time and money and require trained staff. Often the necessary real estate can be acquired through one of the techniques described in Chapter 5.

Museums

A museum may consist of a room in the county courthouse, town library, or Grange hall, or it may be something more elaborate. It can be

8.8
The Historical Society of Carroll County, Maryland, promotes its image by publishing a Heritage Calendar, financed in part by the businesses listed on the pages. In addition to displaying historical prints and photographs, the calendar marks the dates of important events in area history and of upcoming community activities.

JANUARY

SUNDAY	MONDAY	TUESDAY	WEDNESDAY	THURSDAY	FRIDAY	SATURDAY
		1 New Year's Day	2	3	4	5
6	7	8	9	10	11	12
13	14	15 Martin Luther King Jr.'s Birthday	16	17 Carroll County Birthday Observance	18	19 Carroll County's 148th Anniversary
20	21	22	23	24	25	26
27	28 C.C. Genealogical Society Film	29	30	31		

DECEMBER 1984
1
2 3 4 5 6 7 8
9 10 11 12 13 14 15
16 17 18 19 20 21 22
23 24 25 26 27 28 29
30 31

FEBRUARY 1985
1 2
3 4 5 6 7 8 9
10 11 12 13 14 15 16
17 18 19 20 21 22 23
24 25 26 27 28

Taneytown Bank & Trust Company
SINCE 1884
756-2655   TANEYTOWN • UNIONTOWN • WESTMINSTER, MARYLAND   876-3787

Your Neighbor For 100 Years
A Century of Service To Our
Community

a historic plantation, such as Sully in Fairfax County, Virginia, or even an entire community, such as Old Sturbridge in Massachusetts, where visitors can observe all aspects of life in an early-nineteenth-century rural New England village. In some cases the buildings are historic; in others, they are reconstructions. The buildings may be in their original locations, or they may have been moved in from the surrounding countryside, as is the case at Trail Town in Cody, Wyoming.

8.9 & 8.10
Project Seasons, a book of 152 environmental activities for children, was designed to assist classroom instructors in teaching children to appreciate the natural and agricultural resources of the Northeast. The activities, one of which is reproduced here, are organized by topic according to season of the year. Fall activity titles include "Harvest," "Farm Life and History," "Leaf It to Me Designs," and "The Soil Chef." The book is published by the Stewardship Institute, which also offers teacher training at Shelburne Farms, a historic estate in Vermont.

It is best to preserve buildings in their original settings, where they can be interpreted as part of the original landscape. In some instances, however, particularly in areas where farmsteads are being abandoned or where major new development is imminent, moving a building and recreating its landscape may be the only alternative to demolition. Further information on creating, operating, and working with museums is available from the American Association for State and Local History and the American Association of Museums.

Living History Programs

Living history farms, where the public can see the farming operations of a particular period, have a special relevance for rural communities. The farm may depict the life of one family at one time in history, as does

The Soil Chef
· EXHIBIT ·

Materials:

Old clothes (preferably white) including two or three aprons and a chef hat; newspapers for stuffing a three-dimensional chef; small table and chair; binder labelled as soil cookbook; mixing bowl; measuring spoon and cups; mixing spoons and other kitchen utensils; shopping bag filled with soil ingredients (see list below); index cards or paper designed for use as recipe cards.

Activity:

1. Have students work in pairs. Have them sort through the ingredients in the shopping bag and place those chosen into the mixing bowls. Have extra aprons on hand for the budding soil chefs to wear while concocting their new recipes. Then have them refer to the sample recipe card in the binder to write up their own recipe complete with directions.

POSSIBLE SOIL INGREDIENTS
(sealed in plastic sandwich bags)

stones	dried orange peels
twigs	bag filled with
dried leaves	colorful paper dots,
grass clippings	labelled bacteria
pieces of bark	blown-up bag labelled
various types of	air
soil	and a clear plastic
compost	jar filled with water.
peat moss	
gummy worms to	Other items to trick
represent earth	them might include
worms	an old tin can,
selection of plastic	old sock, Styrofoam
insects	cup or other non-
plastic mushrooms	biodegradable waste.

Design:

1. Have the students help create a three-dimensional soil chef. Ask them to bring in old clothes and use newspaper to stuff the chef. Seat the chef on chair behind table and be sure to add a chef's hat and apron to complete the look.

2. Set mixing bowls, measuring cups, spoons, and utensils on the table. Label a binder as the class soil cookbook, insert a sample soil recipe in the front and place it on the table.

3. On one corner of the table set a large sturdy shopping bag filled with a selection of possible soil ingredients (see list) plus a few tricks and surprises.

4. Write the following directions on or near the exhibit:

> *Welcome to Shelburne Farms Restaurant (substitute your own name). Today we are featuring a smorgasbord of soil dishes for your plant's dining pleasure. Tie on an apron, sort through the ingredients in the bag and mix together your own special recipe in the mixing bowl provided. Then name your recipe, write down the ingredients, list important directions on the recipe cards provided, and add it to the class collection. Bon Appetit!*

---

the early-twentieth-century Howell Living Historical Farm in Titusville, New Jersey; or of many different farms, as does Old World Wisconsin, with its series of farmsteads reflecting the state's ethnic diversity; or may present a progression through historical periods, such as Iowa's Living Historical Farms in Des Moines, which depicts rural life in that state from 1840 to the present. At some farms, for example Norlands in Livermore, Maine, visitors can assume roles on the farm, to experience firsthand the life of an earlier era. Living history farms, such as the Oliver H. Kelley Farm in Elk River, Minnesota, have also played an important role in propagating old breeds of animals and strains of plants, which may be more resistant to disease than many of the hybrids that are used in modern agriculture.

A living history farm can become a focus for a community's conserva-

8.11
The Garfield Farm Museum in Kane County, Illinois, is just forty miles west of Chicago. A portion of the 250-acre property is interpreted as an 1840s farm and inn. Fortunately, three of the farm's buildings from that era survive, as does much of the correspondence and other records of the Garfield family. Here a couple demonstrates for visitors the setting of bean poles. The museum operates in conjunction with Campton Historic Agricultural Lands, Inc., a land trust that encourages the protection of farmland in the area through the donation of easements.

tion efforts. Protecting the countryside around the farm not only enhances the visitors' experience and the scenic beauty of the area but also provides a model for protecting other areas in the community. Additional information on developing living history farms can be obtained from the Association for Living Historical Farms and Agricultural Museums.

In addition to farms, rural communities can develop other living history programs. The Waterford Foundation developed a free program for area schools which gives third- and fourth-graders studying Virginia's history the opportunity to spend a day at the Waterford One-Room School, taking on the roles of specific nineteenth-century children. The foundation has prepared biographies of actual students who attended school there in the 1880s, and these are given to the visiting children before they arrive, to allow them to prepare for their roles. The foundation supplies teachers with educational kits, including activities to be conducted in the classroom before and after the visit.

Nature Centers

Many rural conservation organizations, typically land trusts and local park authorities, operate nature centers, which usually include both a building with exhibits and adjacent land that is protected. The best centers relate exhibits to the surrounding environment and encourage visitors to explore that environment. Many centers have programs geared to science curricula at neighboring schools. Like a living history farm, a nature center can provide a community with a focus for its rural conservation program. The National Association for Interpretation and the

Natural Science for Youth Foundation offer information on creating nature centers and exhibits.

8.12
The Finnish farmstead at Old World Wisconsin in Eagle annually gives tens of thousands of visitors a feel for Finnish heritage in America.

FUND RAISING

Of all of the tasks confronting local conservation groups, fund raising is often the most daunting. Yet Phoebe Hopkins of the Oley Project in Pennsylvania recalls, "It was easier to raise money than I thought. Knowing exactly what the money was to be used for and having a list of groups and individuals to ask for a donation really helped. It got easier each year, too."[2] The development of a realistic fund-raising plan is the first hurdle. The plan should identify both potential sources of funds and the amount of money to be raised in a set period of time, linking this goal to the organization's budget. It may also call for training the board and other volunteers in various aspects of fund raising; training is available from such nonprofit organizations as the Institute for Conservation Leadership.

In most communities a nonprofit organization can obtain donations more easily than can the local government. Although donations to both may be tax deductible, many residents are reluctant to contribute funds

8.13
The Little Traverse Conservancy sponsors a nature center at the Thorne Swift Nature Preserve in northern Michigan near Harbor Springs. Since 1972, the conservancy has acquired more than 1,700 acres of forest, dunes, swamp, and rugged Lake Michigan shoreline. In an innovative cooperative arrangement between a private nonprofit organization and local government, the conservancy in 1982 leased the Thorne Swift Nature Preserve to West Traverse Township for an initial period of five years, for one dollar a year. The conservancy and the township jointly prepared a plan for the preserve, which was approved by the township board after several public hearings, and as part of that plan built a nature center now managed by the township. In addition to the nature center, the preserve incorporates a much-needed public beach.

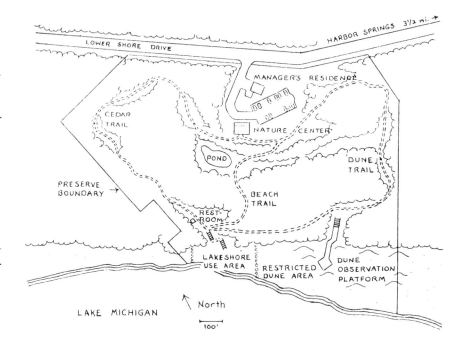

to a local government that is also taxing them. If a local government needs voluntary contributions for a rural conservation effort, it may be more successful if it raises the necessary funds through a cooperating nonprofit organization.

Individual contributions, both large and small, are the best sources of funds in most communities. Thus, it is wise for organizations to develop a solid membership base. One key to membership development is a solicitation letter that is simple, specific, and friendly. The Southern Appalachian Highlands Conservancy began its 1994 membership letter by telling each "friend" about the organization's specific accomplishments over the past year and the goals of the year ahead that donations would directly fund. Membership letters must convince readers of the urgency of the organization's mission in an upbeat, positive way. Further information on membership development is available from the Institute for Conservation Leadership.

Local businesses and corporations, or national corporations with local facilities, are also good potential sources of funding. In reaching out to the business community, the Little Traverse Conservancy in Michigan, for example, had a committee of business owners write letters to affiliated businesses, simply informing them of the conservancy's work; then, several months later, the conservancy sent a solicitation letter to the contacted businesses—which raised over $5,000. The conservancy announces new business members in each of its newsletters and publishes an annual roster of all business and professional members.

When looking outside the community, an organization will usually have more success starting with regional or state sources. Large gifts from national foundations, for all of the publicity they generate, are the least likely sources of funding, particularly the kind of steady, year-to-year unrestricted contributions that keep an organization running. Success in fund raising on the national level generally requires resources or issues of national significance and evidence of successful local fund raising.

Research on sources of both private and government grants is not hard to do—it just takes time, organization, and persistence. The Foundation Center operates libraries in several locations around the nation, along with collections that are often housed in state university libraries. These collections include indexes to foundations and files of information on specific foundations, including their most recent guidelines for applicants. Grants from state and federal agencies (see Chapter 7) may also be indexed in various sources; local staff of these agencies may know of useful guides. Grant writing is a specific skill, one that takes practice but for a good writer is not hard to learn. Most organizations, like Historic Rugby, learn grant writing by experience (see Case Study 8.2). Training courses are often available for grant writing, and the Grantsmanship Center publishes useful how-to information on this topic.

In recent years, consortia of environmental organizations have begun organizing workplace donation programs modeled after the United Way. Such programs may welcome the participation of local nonprofit organizations.

Another source of funding not to be overlooked is the community foundation, the fastest-growing sector of the foundation world. Commu-

---

8.4 Hints on Fund Raising

Here are a few suggestions from community organizer Pat Munoz for getting your organization's fund raising off to a good start:

• Develop a positive public image before trying to raise money.
• Use every contact imaginable—neighbors and friends of board members, officers of local corporations and civic groups, wealthy people who grew up in the area but moved away, people owning second homes in the community.
• Make personal contact with a prospective donor. If the person making the visit or telephone call or writing the letter knows the donor, personal contact should be even more effective. "Asking for money in person is at least twice as effective as asking by telephone, and almost always results in larger gifts," says one advisor to nonprofit organizations.

• Talk or write about the program before requesting a donation. Why is it needed? How will it benefit the community? What will it cost? Be brief, be direct, and don't be embarrassed by having to ask for money.
• Ask for specific amounts or items. Try to judge in advance what a donor can afford.
• Keep careful track of donations. Identify those willing to give larger amounts than usual and target them for extra giving and increased annual donations. Remember the old "80-20" rule may apply: as much as 80 percent of your giving could come from as little as 20 percent of your members. Know which 20 percent to target.
• Don't simply ask for a contribution. Ask the donor to identify the part of your program in which the donor would like to invest, and ask for advice and help in obtaining support from others.

• Write your donors immediately to thank them personally, and recognize them in your annual report or newsletter. Offer major donors (giving more than $50 or $100) premiums or "donor clubs" with special benefits.
• Keep donors informed of the organization's progress and invite them to events. Once people have given money, they have a vested interest in its success.
• Keep records of volunteer time as an indication of one form of community support. Occasionally, volunteer time can be used as an in-kind match for grants.
• Don't give up in the face of delays and rejections. Fund raising requires patience as well as energy.

(See Notes to Sidebars.)

nity foundations provide operational assistance to sometimes numerous independent foundations or family funds that are too small to operate efficiently as freestanding grant makers. Their donors are often interested in conservation issues. Some community foundations are statewide or regional in their focus, although many are based in cities.

Most organizations find it more difficult to raise money for general operating expenses than for special projects. People (and foundations) like to see specific results from their money. Helping to buy an endangered property is more exciting than donating money for office rent and telephones. The Lake Forest Open Lands Association, a land trust that owns or manages more than 300 acres for public access near Chicago, has capitalized on this human tendency to want to know how one's cash donation is spent. It publishes a "gift catalog" that has allowed donors to "buy" needed items to support its land management, including benches, trails, a foot bridge, and prairie and woodland restoration by the square foot.[3]

There are several effective ways to generate operating expenses. Membership dues are a prime source, together with appeals to members for special needs and end-of-the-year gifts. Sometimes a local government will contribute, especially if it sanctions the rural conservation effort in question. Many community-based organizations rely on an annual event or benefit, such as a festival, auction, flea market, or crafts fair, to raise a substantial portion of their expenses. The Kennebunkport Conservation Trust in Maine has raised money through bean suppers, auctions, softball tournaments, raffles, post cards, clam bakes, and lectures. Although it may take time and practice to make such an event a paying proposition, it may have other benefits, in the form of community goodwill and education, as an outlet for local craftspeople, or as a way of highlighting community assets. Sale of publications or such other typical items as calendars, coffee mugs, or T-shirts can also provide unrestricted income, while helping to keep the organization's name in front of its public.

Gifts "in kind"—donations of equipment, office supplies, and materials needed to put on events—can be a helpful source of support in any community. A national program that coordinates such gifts is Gifts In Kind America, which was created by the United Way.

CASE STUDY 8.2

Rugby, Tennessee: One Fund-Raising Success Leads to Another

Historic Rugby is an organization that has successfully used a variety of grant and funding sources to achieve historic preservation and build a heritage tourism industry.

Rugby (pop. 80) was established on the scenic Cumberland Plateau of northeastern Tennessee in the 1880s by Thomas Hughes, the English social reformer and author of *Tom Brown's Schooldays*. Hughes founded Rugby as an experiment in classless cooperative living, for the younger sons of English gentry in particular. All land use in the model community was planned, with scenic areas being left in their natural state. Since Rugby was built at the convergence of two river gorges that intersect an uplifted plateau, the community affords views of a surrounding terrain that varies from 1,200 to 1,500 feet above sea level.

Although crop failures, disease, and bad management soon led to the demise of Rugby as a social and economic model, the small unincorporated hamlet survived. The spectacular scenery that first attracted Thomas Hughes, and the twenty-two surviving original Rugby buildings have now become a major tourist attraction.

In 1966, concerned citizens in the area established Historic Rugby to protect Rugby's historic resources and natural setting and to revitalize the community. In 1972, a 900-acre Rugby Colony historic district was listed in the National Register; Historic Rugby researched and wrote the nomination. The organization has restored, reconstructed, or built fourteen buildings in the town; eight of the buildings are original, three have been reconstructed, and three are new infill projects that are historically compatible. Historic Rugby conducts tours throughout the year and attracts thousands of visitors for its spring music and crafts festivals and its fall Rugby Pilgrimage house tours. It is the major employer in the area and a source of income for related business.

In the early 1960s, Congress authorized the U.S. Army Corps of Engineers to build a dam on the Big South Fork River, downstream from Rugby. Although the impounded water would not have inundated Rugby itself, it would have destroyed the spectacular Devil's Jump Gorge below the town. As a result of effective lobbying by conservationists, Congress in 1974 deauthorized the dam. In its place Congress authorized the 125,000-acre Big South Fork National River and Recreation Area, which was planned, acquired, and developed by the corps and then turned over to the National Park Service. This major recreation complex on the Big South Fork has greatly increased visitor traffic to Rugby.

At the request of the State Historic Preservation Officer, the Advisory Council on Historic Preservation held discussions in 1979 with the corps on mitigating the potential adverse impacts of increased tourism on the Rugby historic district. The corps agreed to fund the Master Plan for the Development, Management, and Protection of the Rugby Colony Historic Area. After a series of workshops with local residents and the general public during the early 1980s, it became clear that the goal of the master plan was to specify historic preservation measures while at the same time encouraging compatible development. The master plan was completed in 1988 and has since become the cornerstone of Historic Rugby's preservation efforts. The plan's goals and objectives statement, updated in 1993, has insured that economic development and tourism are compatible with managing the historic district.

Perhaps the most impressive accomplishment of Historic Rugby has been its ability to win grant and loan funds, which have been invested in community improvements. After the Big South Fork project was authorized in 1974, the U.S. Department of the Interior and the Corps of Engineers became the first significant sources of grant funds and technical assistance. Since then, the Historic Rugby staff has actively pursued a variety of funding sources. The largest grant came in 1985: a Community Development Block Grant of over $450,000 for the restoration and construction of buildings, sponsored by the neighboring incorporated town of Allardt.

Additional grant funds have come from the Institute for Museum Services, used for general operating support and to survey conditions and recommend management practices in the restored Thomas Hughes Library. Funds have been contributed by various state agencies, including the Tennessee Arts Commission, which has supported crafts programs, and the Tennessee Historical Commis-

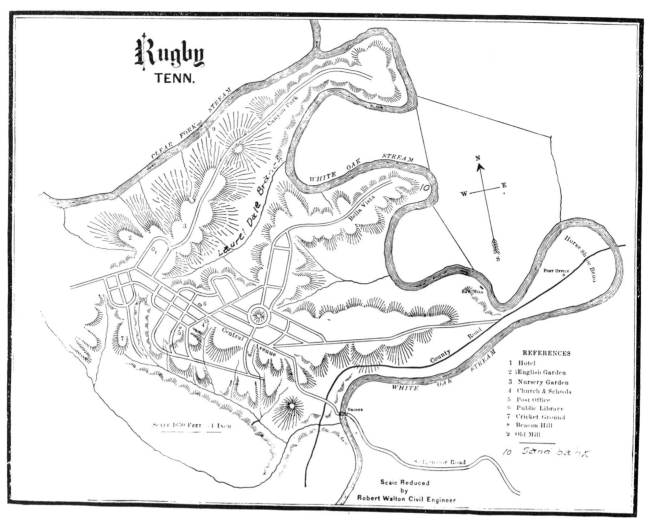

8.14
Rugby was established as a utopian community on the Cumberland Plateau of Tennessee in the 1880s. The village, which has retained its original street pattern, is now protected by Historic Rugby, a nonprofit organization. In 1979, the U.S. Army Corps of Engineers undertook a historic preservation plan for Rugby.

sion, which has provided grants for the restoration of the library and other buildings. The Tennessee Committee for the Humanities awarded grants to develop a traveling exhibit using Rugby as an example of community development and protection through historic preservation.

In addition to federal and state agencies, regional development agencies have provided aid, including a $62,000 Special Opportunities grant from the Tennessee Valley Authority (such grants are used to support economic development in disadvantaged counties) which was used as start-up funds to open a café and a bed-and-breakfast in the historic district.

Over the past twenty-three years, Rugby has received a total of $1.4 million in grant money from eighteen different federal, regional, state, and private agencies and organizations. In addition to grants, individual gifts and bequests have helped Historic Rugby build an endowment fund to support the continued maintenance and development of its properties. A cornerstone of the endowment fund has been the multiyear Second Century Campaign, which was started in 1987 to raise $1 million for the restoration and development of educational facilities in Rugby.

Historic Rugby has also used loans to further its cause, including a low-interest loan from the National Trust for Historic Preservation to help purchase a 151-acre tract of land that will extend Rugby's trail system while functioning as a buffer between the historic district and nearby commercial development.

According to Barbara Stagg, the executive director of Historic Rugby, the organization's success in obtaining grants and loans from so many different sources over the years can be attributed to both persistence and diversification. "We have been fortunate because we have been able to diversify and fit ourselves into many different niches where money is available. We have been able to market ourselves to grant sources for museums, historic preservation, environmental and open space preservation, economic development, and crafts. It requires being entrepreneurial, but it pays off by giving you more potential sources of funding." Stagg advocates "tracking down every lead, following up every possible source, and networking as much as possible. In 1994, we received a $2,000 grant from the Tennessee Horticulture Society after we read a small blurb about them in a Nashville newspaper. We never even knew about them before that."

Even with Historic Rugby's success in obtaining grants and donations, the majority of its operating budget (approximately 65 percent) comes from on-site

8.15
Listed in the National Register of Historic Places, Rugby is a major tourist attraction. Here visitors explore the Thomas Hughes Free Public Library, unchanged since its 1882 opening. The original 7,000-volume collection is still on the shelves.

tourism-related activities such as admissions, lodging, craft sales, and food service.

Looking toward the future, Historic Rugby is using a loan from the Morgan County Industrial Development Board, with the approval of the TVA's Special Opportunities for Counties loan fund, to develop new housing that is compatible with Rugby's historic design. Beacon Hill, a part of Rugby's original town plan that had not been built, was opened for the construction of new homes in 1993. The twenty-eight-lot development is being carried out by Historic Rugby to restore more components of the original town plan, repopulate the community, and help enhance the economy of the community and the region.

SPECIAL EVENTS

An organization may stage a special event in order to raise money, provide residents with a social or cultural occasion, involve members or recruit new ones, obtain publicity, thank volunteers, or generate community support. Whatever the goal may be, the occasion should be enjoyable. Successful events require a lot of work. Leaders need to be sure of the enthusiasm and commitment of members to ensure that the endeavor complements and does not preempt the organization's other activities. An event that is well attended, well organized, and fun reflects positively on the organization's ability to get things done.

While a fish fry or rodeo may work in one community, a square dance or canoe race might be more appropriate in another. Some community groups have found that reviving past traditions, such as homecomings, harvest festivals, and parades, can be successful. The events already being sponsored by an area's church and civic groups indicate what kinds of events are popular with residents. Adding special features such as a barbecue, watermelon-eating contest, or bluegrass band can enliven a routine event.

Organizations will need to advertise whatever occasion is planned. Messages reach people in a variety of ways—newspaper, television, and radio announcements, posters and fliers, inclusion in the organization's

8.16
An information center at the annual Oley Fair in Pennsylvania was effective in giving the Oley Resource Conservation Project broad community exposure. Equipped with a continuously running slide show, handouts, and volunteers who were able to answer questions, the information center provided residents with basic information about Oley's resources and the efforts to protect them. Several visitors to the booth later became project volunteers.

own and other groups' newsletters. Some groups herald an upcoming event with promotional items such as buttons and bumper stickers.

Exhibits

Rural conservation organizations may prepare exhibits or arrange for demonstrations at a community event or in conjunction with a lecture or a workshop. Store windows, shopping centers, and the lobbies of such buildings as banks, the county courthouse, and the town hall are good display locations.

Each year since 1983, the Yakima Greenway Foundation has had a booth at the Central Washington State Fair. One year the booth "was decorated with plants and shrubs (lent by a local nursery) to resemble a small park and had information posters, photographs, brochures, and a large diorama of the proposed Greenway."[4] In recent years the fair booth has focused on one of the Greenway's primary fund raisers, the Great Yakima Duck Race, when people place $5 bets on rubber ducks that float down the river. Publicizing the race annually at the state fair keeps the foundation in the public's eye and helps to raise much-needed maintenance funds.

The simplest exhibits are often the most successful, although good lighting and attractive, high-quality graphics are essential. Not many people, for example, will read long architectural descriptions as part of a display on historic farms, but they probably will look at photographs of farmers at work, a map showing the layout of a farmstead, or a model of an interesting barn. Successful exhibits have distinct themes, such as the changing rural landscape, endangered species, the restoration of a prominent landscape, or the loss of farmland.

Tours

Village walks, nature hikes, farm visits, open houses, and spring garden tours are popular. Some groups find tours profitable; others conduct them primarily for educational purposes. Refreshments using local recipes and locally produced items, audio-visual presentations, and opportunities to purchase crafts or promotional items can be incorporated into the tour agenda. In Oley, Pennsylvania, for example, tours of selected homes in the valley, begun in 1985, have helped raise funds toward a project to record Oley's unusual outbuildings through measured architectural drawings. Over the years, the association has held a summertime walking tour of Oley Village, complete with craft demonstrations on front porches, and has devised theme tours of mills, one-room schoolhouses, and iron furnaces. The tours are the Oley Valley Heritage Association's main source of income.

A nature walk or a village tour requires a knowledgeable leader and good publicity, but it may not require a great deal of other advance work by the sponsor. Tours that entail visiting private property, renting buses, or serving food, however, can require considerable planning and coordination. Occasionally, residents will not allow visitation on their property, because they are concerned about liability, theft, or vandalism. The sponsoring organization may need to obtain insurance, post signs, arrange for parking, instruct visitors not to walk or to take photographs in certain areas, prepare maps, and provide rest room facilities and other services that will make the tour enjoyable for visitors and protect the community's resources and owners' privacy.

Waterford, Virginia: Homes Tour and Crafts Exhibit

The Waterford Homes Tour and Crafts Exhibit, in Waterford, Virginia, is one of the nation's most successful fund-raising events conducted by a nonprofit rural conservation organization. Held annually for more than fifty-two years, the fair started small but has expanded to the point that it generates approximately $200,000 each year for the Waterford Foundation.

Waterford is a village of 250 residents surrounded by farmland and located 50 miles west of Washington, D.C. It began as a Quaker settlement that grew up around a mill established early in the eighteenth century on Catoctin Creek. Today the community is composed of more than 120 structures, most from the eighteenth and early nineteenth centuries. The entire village, and much of the farmland that can be seen from the village, is included in a National Historic Landmark district.

In 1943, residents established the Waterford Foundation to protect the village's cultural and architectural heritage. Over the years it has purchased or protected both land and buildings. Today it owns more than 35 acres of land and ten buildings. It has also arranged for sixty easements on houses in the village itself and on some 250 acres of open land. In 1981, the foundation hired an executive director to manage its increasingly complex programs. Currently, two people work full-time and three work part-time for the foundation. The foundation board delegates much of the authority for organizing the Homes Tour and

8.17
The Waterford Foundation in Virginia was established in 1943 to protect Waterford's cultural and architectural heritage. The Patriots of Northern Virginia Fife and Drum Corps perform at the Waterford Foundation's annual Homes Tour and Crafts Exhibit. The event, which attracts thousands of people and is a major source of income for the foundation, also educates visitors about the importance of protecting the village and its rural setting.

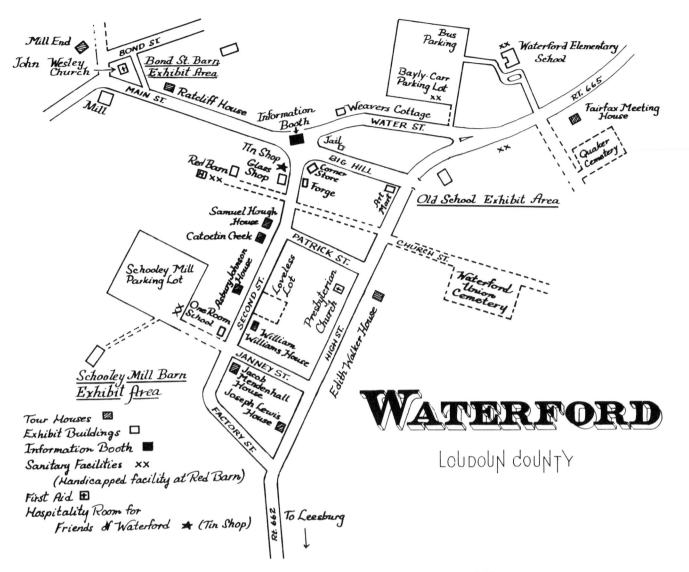

Map labels:

Mill End
John Wesley Church
BOND ST.
Bond St. Barn Exhibit Area
Mill
MAIN ST.
Ratcliff House
Information Booth
Weavers Cottage
WATER ST.
Bus Parking
Bayly-Carr Parking Lot
Waterford Elementary School
RT. 665
Fairfax Meeting House
Quaker Cemetery
Tin Shop
Glass Shop
Red Barn
Jail
Corner Store
Forge
BIG HILL
Art Mart
Old School Exhibit Area
Samuel Hough House
Catoctin Creek
PATRICK ST.
CHURCH ST.
Waterford Union Cemetery
Schooley Mill Parking Lot
Asbury-Johnson House
SECOND ST.
Loveless Lot
Presbyterian Church
HIGH ST.
Edith Walker House
One Room School
William Williams House
JANNEY ST.
Jacob Mendenhall House
Joseph Lewis House
FACTORY ST.
RT. 662
To Leesburg

WATERFORD

LOUDOUN COUNTY

Tour Houses
Exhibit Buildings
Information Booth
Sanitary Facilities xx
(Handicapped facility at Red Barn)
First Aid
Hospitality Room for
Friends of Waterford ★ (Tin Shop)

8.18
Visitor's map for the Waterford Foundation's Homes Tour and Crafts Exhibit. The large event requires careful planning and involves volunteers from many community groups.

Crafts Exhibit to a paid fair chairperson. Subcommittees handle such arrangements as selecting and communicating with the artisans who exhibit.

The annual Homes Tour and Crafts Exhibit is responsible in large part for the positive image that the Waterford Foundation commands locally and regionally. The three-day event, which takes place throughout the village, consists of tours of historic homes and buildings, craft demonstrations, art and photography shows, entertainment, including performances by traditional dancers and musicians on the village's streets, Civil War reenactments, and the sale of baked goods, preserves, dried flowers, crafts, and other local products. In addition to being entertained, the 30,000-plus visitors who attend each year come to appreciate the village's historic and scenic environment and the efforts to protect it.

"We really stress the educational aspects of the fair," says Constance Chamberlain, the foundation's former executive director. "The visitors are a captive audience, and in addition to giving them a good time, we make sure they go away knowing something about the significance of Waterford and the need for preservation." Each year features a special exhibit focused on an important aspect of eighteenth- or nineteenth-century village life. Exhibits have featured the area's agricultural heritage, the Hough furniture factory and a collection of furniture made in Waterford in the nineteenth century, and a textile exhibit with old and new textile craftsmanship. Every visitor receives an illustrated booklet about the history of Waterford, its historic buildings, the fair, and the foundation's preservation program.

Not only is the fair a financial success, but it is also a model of community cooperation and a well-organized event that continues to be educational and entertaining year after year.

Festivals and Fairs

Many rural organizations sponsor successful festivals, fairs, and crafts demonstrations, focusing on what is authentic and appropriate to the area. These events require considerable advance planning and careful coordination. Some of them, such as the Waterford Foundation's annual Homes Tour and Crafts Exhibit, attract large numbers of outsiders and make considerable money. Others are more low-key. The Calvert Farmland Trust in Maryland teamed up with a local agricultural heritage group, Funding to Assist Rural Management, to sponsor a day-long music festival for farmland preservation. The fund raiser, featuring local musicians, raised $250,000 for a land acquisition fund established by the trust.

Organizing a community event takes substantial time to plan and requires the completion of many tasks. It can seem overwhelming, but developing a budget and timetable helps to make an event run smoothly. The community of Quitaque, Texas, starts planning for its annual National Trails Day celebration, which attracts some 3,000 visitors, a full year in advance. It is a good idea to be liberal in estimating expenses and conservative in projecting revenues, to allow for such circumstances as a low turnout in poor weather. In general, a group should not depend on a first-time event to provide the major portion of its funding. Only well-established events like the Waterford Foundation's Homes Tour and Crafts Exhibit are dependable, "and even we are scared to death of rain," adds its former executive director.[5]

Recognition and Awards Ceremonies

Occasionally, a group may elect to host an event honoring individuals or recognizing a significant property. Such events may range from a formal ceremony during which a plaque is affixed to a building, to social affairs with music, dancing, and refreshments. In Pennsylvania, the Oley Resource Conservation Project planned a public ceremony for the presentation of the certificate showing that the township had been listed as a historic district in the National Register of Historic Places. The ceremony included representatives of the organizations that had assisted Oley in preparing the nomination, local officials, the district's member of Congress, and the state's secretary of agriculture, who praised the town's leaders for their work in protecting the community and thanked its many volunteers.

As well as honoring deserving individuals, recognition and awards ceremonies call attention to the organization's goals and programs, although a potential risk is offending those not honored. Criticism can be deflected by setting clear criteria for the award, naming an impartial selection committee, and presenting the award annually. An organization can also spread the credit by holding a reception honoring all of the individuals who have contributed to conservation efforts in the past year. When a group does give an award, the prize need not be elaborate or expensive: a plaque, medal, photograph, or book will do. As a recipient of the Amana Heritage Society's Lantern Award for outstanding contributions to preservation efforts said, "It's the thought that counts; knowing that the group thinks I made a difference is reward enough."

Public Service

Through public service a group can make a substantial contribution to the community and receive favorable publicity. For instance, in areas where there is an abundance of litter and clutter, a rural conservation group can perform a service by sponsoring a regular community cleanup day.

In addition to the public service a conservation organization's members can undertake, service clubs in the community may be willing to work with the organization on conservation projects. Most service clubs select community projects each year to support through fund raisers and volunteer work. For instance, the Kiwanis Club raised over $30,000 for an irrigation system and trees for a park managed by the Yakima Greenway Foundation in Washington. Kiwanis members also donated their time to install the irrigation system, and local businesses provided services and equipment at cost. The Rotary Club raised over $25,000 and in 1994 coordinated 2,000 volunteers to build a park and playground, a $250,000 facility that no single organization could so readily have built. Such endorsements by service clubs can significantly increase long-term public support for a conservation organization.

Boy Scouts, Girl Scouts, 4-H Clubs, and Future Farmers of America are examples of youth organizations that volunteer their services. In Amana, Iowa, one Boy Scout directed the establishment of a "community attic" for discarded building materials that could be used in restoration projects. Another Scout conducted a tree-planting beautification project.

One public service that many local governments and nonprofit organizations have found popular is to publish an annual directory of local organizations and units of government that are involved in conservation or that provide community services. Such a directory can also include emergency telephone numbers, a calendar of community events, and information on municipal services. Advertising often covers much of the publication cost.

8.5 Recognition Ceremonies

Special events of recognition can be used for a variety of purposes. Among them are these:

• To thank volunteers and others who have made substantial contributions

• To honor outgoing board members, officers, or staff

• To recognize a particular group of properties, such as century farms (farms that have been in the same family for 100 years or more)

• To announce a special designation, such as a National Natural Landmark listing, entry in the National Register of Historic Places, or the establishment of an agricultural district

• To recognize individuals who have protected their properties by some action such as donating an easement or rehabilitating a dilapidated house

• To recognize the winner of a youth essay contest or the organization's logo contest

CONCLUSION

Fund raising and community education are necessary parts of keeping a rural conservation program viable. Although the purpose of educational programs is serious, they can and should be enjoyable and satisfying. Both education and fund raising call for much creativity and fortunately can make use of the varied skills of many community residents. Moreover, the teamwork required in setting up such programs can be a major factor in developing an organization's esprit de corps.

Conclusion: Putting It All Together

How do you go about applying the ideas in this handbook? Let us start with a framework for those ideas. Planners talk about following this simple process: inventory the community's resources, analyze the problems and potential solutions, and act. In life, nothing is quite so simple. Complexities deriving from personalities, culture or custom, government, and changes in land uses render the process never-ending and constantly open to adjustment to new factors.

Below, we suggest ways to approach the process effectively. You need to think broadly, think in terms of coalition building, think about the long term, and think positively. You also need to be willing to approach rural conservation creatively, in terms of solving your community's particular problems rather than offering off-the-shelf solutions. Finally, you need to be willing to take risks. Let's take up each of these points one by one.

Think broadly. Rural conservation as we define it in the Introduction to this handbook requires that you consider all of a community's assets. In addition to its natural and historic resources, a community has other assets: its people, its governmental structures and officials, its organizations. Segments of the economy may have certain strengths: tourism, agricultural services, forest products, regional retailing. People may take special pride in certain aspects of the community, such as having the best drinking water in the county or the best schools. Understanding these assets and figuring out how to capitalize on them requires you to think broadly.

A historic ranch adds to the scenic quality of Red Rock Lakes National Wildlife Refuge in Montana.

Think about building coalitions. Thinking broadly includes thinking in terms of building coalitions. One well-organized group in an area can make all the difference in helping good ideas take root; even better is broad community understanding of and cooperation toward your goals. Learn to identify mutual interests among the people, organizations, and business interests involved in your community, and learn to approach problems cooperatively, through governmental, nonprofit, and private entities—whatever will get the job done. Build multiple strengths in your community. If there is a planning void in the public sector, then develop ways to address it through nonprofit action, and be prepared to acknowledge and support changes in the attitude of public officials once they see the light. There is an old saying that pertains here: You can get many things done if you don't care who gets the credit.

In thinking about building coalitions, you should not lose sight of action at the regional or state level. Tracks Across Wyoming brought together communities across the state to promote historic preservation and tourism development through the creation of a heritage corridor (see Case Study 6.5). In Michigan's Upper Peninsula, fifteen counties banded together to inventory their forest lands and created resource maps that could be used by property owners. They received a grant from the U.S. Forest Service to carry out the work. For another example, the Trust for New Hampshire Lands was a broad—indeed, unprecedented—coalition of 127 businesses, foundations, conservancies, other nonprofit organizations, and governmental entities, all joined around the creation and administration of a state-sponsored Land Conservation Investment Program to protect up to 100,000 acres of "New Hampshire's most cherished natural lands" through voluntary negotiations with landowners. The trust served as a land agent, using the state program's $20 million trust fund, and now works with the state's communities to accomplish similar protection for locally valued lands. The bond act also required statewide approval by voters. A simpler example of an effective statewide coalition is in Virginia, where ten local and state conservation and preservation organizations and state agencies sponsored publication of a handbook on stewardship of natural resources. While the focus of our book has been on what local community leaders can do to achieve conservation, clearly for conservation to work there will need to be changes at the regional, state, and national levels as well. What better way to achieve these changes than through coalitions built at the grass-roots level?

Think about the long term. It is all too easy to allow immediate demands to overwhelm your ability to address what is truly important—or, as another saying goes, When you're up to your ears in alligators, it's hard to remember that your objective is to cross the river. In Chapters 2 and 4 we discussed envisioning your community's future and setting goals: defining for yourself, your organization, or your community what you are setting out to achieve over the long term. It does not matter what you call the process or its result—plan of action, master plan, strategy—and there are any number of variations in how you do it. What is important is developing a sense of who and where you are, and where you are going. Such an understanding will help you maintain the patience and persistence you will need to make the changes you believe are necessary in your community. Although your conservation work will never be complete—there is no such thing as a rural community that has achieved complete conservation—you can at least establish a framework for dealing effectively with future challenges and problems.

Think and act positively. This is not a mini-lecture about the power of positive thinking but rather a caution about approaching the problems in your community in a negative manner. It may be obvious to you that your nonprofit organization or your community's planning board is ineffectual. Simply offering criticisms without constructive ideas for their solution can easily create enemies where you most need friends. In addition, it is all too easy to forget to consider the opinions of others; those who resist your ideas may view your community, the problem, or possible solutions in entirely different ways. Your constructive ideas should, whenever possible, include specific steps your organization or government officials can take, but you must also be artful in communicating with others and in developing community consensus in a positive way. It may well be that others do not agree that a problem exists in the first place—which leads us to the next point.

Be a problem solver. Do not let your efforts to achieve rural conservation get sidetracked by debates about solutions. The first level of public debate should be about whether the community has a problem, and it should move toward developing a sense of widespread agreement among whatever different interests are present in the community. The debate about the problem should direct the design of any solution to be proposed. Jumping prematurely into a discussion of the merits of zoning in protecting farmland, for example, may unnecessarily polarize the community. While it may seem easy to propose some kind of solution "just to get a reaction"—and, indeed, others may ask you for your ideas in order to understand your position—it is well worth resisting the temptation to advance a solution before there is consensus about the problem.

Being an effective problem solver requires you to approach rural conservation creatively. To continue the example above, rather than simply resorting to zoning to address the problems of growth in agricultural areas, you might consider some combination of the techniques discussed in Chapters 4 and 5. Your evaluation of potential techniques plus your understanding of what your community is likely to accept should allow you to choose the techniques best suited to your needs. Cost and the community's ability to implement a new technique are obviously factors to consider in evaluating potential solutions. In borrowing successful ideas from other communities, use your problem-solving approach to adapt these ideas to your community.

Be a risk taker. In initiating rural conservation programs in your community, be willing to try something new. There just are not enough communities working hard at rural conservation that you can rely on having a neighbor you can safely emulate. You may not learn what works best in your community without trial and error, even after a careful assessment of what you want to do, how you should go about it, and what risks are involved. Among the risks are court challenges. Some communities seem immobilized by the fear of litigation, but doing nothing can have its cost too. Be ready to capitalize on your opportunities despite the apparent risks: good timing may help you carry the day. Plan as wisely as you can, and then invest the resources needed to make your risk pay off. People, time, energy, money, or help from the outside are all things you may have to invest in your programs.

In rural conservation, what is success? As authors, we seek to be like the soldier in the old European folk tale of stone soup, helping you find the answers that lie within your communal reach. In the story, a soldier visits a war-ravaged village and asks for food. The villagers are unwilling to share their meager stores with the stranger—or, it appears, with each other. He then asks for a pot, some water, and some stones, which they freely provide. Curious, they ask him what he is doing. "Making stone soup," he replies. "But it would taste better if I had an onion." Someone recalls that she might, in fact, have an onion after all. And so it goes, with villagers eagerly adding other ingredients, removing the stones, and sharing all around in the end.

A Checklist for Sustaining Rural Communities

VISIONING: a vision of the community's future. *Does the community understand its resources, its needs, its threats, and its opportunities, and has it developed a vision for its future that involves the entire community?*

GROWTH MANAGEMENT: policies and procedures to deal realistically and fairly with community change. *Does the community have a land management system to deal with the impacts—good and bad—of growth? Is the system equitable, and flexible enough to reflect changing conditions? Do citizens and civic groups monitor the system's effectiveness, incorporate new ideas, and provide leadership in making changes?*

LAND TRUSTS: a means of working with property owners to support the vision and growth management system. *Does the community have a land trust or a relationship with a private land conservation organization in the region, or both, and are they together working on the long-term conservation and management of natural lands and special properties? Do these organizations provide owners with advice and multiple options for responsibly protecting and developing their properties, as appropriate?*

RESOURCE STEWARDSHIP: a means of encouraging owners to maintain and restore natural systems, recreation opportunities, and historic resources. *Does the community understand its resources and assets and any threats to their long-term health? Does the community work with property owners on watershed restoration, timber management, wetlands mitigation, and other land management issues? Does it make technical expertise available to owners of buildings and land to help them assess their condition and make plans for maintenance and improvement?*

ECONOMIC DEVELOPMENT: a means of encouraging sustainable economic development through support for individual opportunities and creation of communitywide programs while protecting the environment. *Does the community recognize the economic potential in emphasizing community assets, including its environment—both natural and built—and existing human resources and businesses? Does the community have a plan to support small businesses as well as large, agriculture and tourism as well as commerce and manufacturing?*

EDUCATION AND TRAINING: continuing education for both leaders and activists, and the public at large. *Does the community keep current its knowledge of trends and techniques? Does the community regu*larly recognize and celebrate its environment, heritage, and traditions? Do organizations in the community invest in training for leaders, staff, and volunteers?*

A CIVIC FORUM: a means for all interests in the community to work together on social, economic, conservation, and other needs of the community. *Through one or more organizations, does the community encourage communication and collaboration among civic leaders—in public and private organizations, in businesses—to support sustainable economic development, encourage and celebrate traditional ways of life, improve the quality of life for all citizens, enhance civic participation, and reduce conflict?*

INTERGOVERNMENTAL AND REGIONAL ACTION: ways to reach out to neighboring communities and other levels of government. *Does the community have the ability, both governmental and nongovernmental, to work effectively on issues of common concern across the region? How do communities in the region address the protection of watersheds, scenic roads, cultural landscapes, or other large, regionally shared resources? Does the community participate in or seek to create forums that allow for intergovernmental partnerships?*

(See Notes to Sidebars.)

On one level, the tale of stone soup is about a trickster who overcame the traditional distrust of the outsider, but on another, more important level, it is about a community that discovered it could cooperate to feed its hungry citizens. Your own success may lie more in developing just such ways for your community to cooperate effectively than in actual acres or buildings. Just being nimble or creative at stimulating a useful process or understanding the many techniques outlined in the foregoing chapters is not enough. You must have an idea of what you want to accomplish—where your hard work and determination should ultimately lead your community. In the sidebar on p. 385 we suggest, in the broadest possible terms, the elements of a program we believe will help you achieve rural conservation and sustainability in your community.

Aldo Leopold, the scientist and author who helped formulate a land conservation ethic, defined conservation as a state of "harmony between man and the land." Leopold also recognized, however, that harmony is "an ideal—and one we shall never attain." [1] Yet he had faith, as we do, that in seeking that ideal, it is possible to treat the land, and the human community that is a part of the land, in the best way we can.

In conclusion, we encourage you to dream . . . a little, or a lot. What kind of out-of-the-ordinary state legislation or local ordinances would you like at your service? What makes you the maddest or saddest about opportunities you have lost, and what would you have needed to be able to seize them? (If your answer is "money," explore a little deeper; there were probably other roadblocks.) There is strength in numbers, and salvation of a kind for those stretched thin at the local level who can discover peers nearby: Where are others like you at work, and what do you have in common? What are you doing differently from each other, and why? If you could combine and use one-quarter of the ideas in this book, which ones would they be? If you had to convince outsiders to join your efforts, how would you induce them? What are your community's people strengths? Your other resources? Your weaknesses? Think about what is ahead for your community, your state, region, and nation. What can you achieve locally? What would require coalitions at the state or national level?

This handbook gives you some of the tools and ideas you need to refine and implement the vision of your community that you must develop. If we have helped you to dream about what you might do to make your community a better place in which to live, work, and play, we have accomplished our own vision for this handbook. The rest is up to you. It is never too late, or too soon, to start.

Educational Programs on
Rural Conservation

Saving America's Countryside has been used as the basis for short courses for community leaders wishing to be trained in the principles of rural conservation. It has also been used at the undergraduate and graduate levels as a text for planning, environmental studies, and landscape architecture courses. Although there are many publications that can be used to teach the principles of planning and the techniques that local government and nonprofit organizations can use to protect resources, *Saving America's Countryside* is particularly helpful in teaching about how techniques interrelate and what community leaders can do relying primarily on their own resources.

Involvement by course participants or students in class discussions is valuable, as is discussing specific communities. Participants who can draw upon rural communities they are from or are knowledgeable about can greatly enrich class discussion. If possible, the curriculum should include field trips and field exercises so that the entire class can discuss one or more communities with which they can all become familiar.

During field visits, hearing accounts from local officials, representatives of nonprofit organizations, and concerned residents is important, but the trips will be much more valuable if class participants have an opportunity to figure out some things for themselves.

CHAPTER STUDY NOTES

Study notes for each chapter follow. The classroom discussion sections list some of the questions that might be asked to help course participants synthesize the material. Listing responses on a flip chart, blackboard, or overhead projector for all to see is useful. The field project sections list questions and hands-on projects for class participants exploring or working in a particular community.

Chapter 1

Classroom Discussion. What resources and issues are important in your rural community (or one you are familiar with)? Answering this question not only can help class participants think about their communities in new ways but also can help them get to know each other at the start of a new course.

Field Project. What resources make the community being studied special? If the community is changing, what is causing the change? What other issues does the community face? On what issues is there consensus among different sectors of the population? Disagreement? Sectors to look at might include farmers or ranchers, village residents, long-term residents, recent arrivals, young people, older people, business owners, developers, year-round residents, and people who spend the summer. Ask class participants to collect basic information on the community's demographics, history, resources, land use, form of government, and nonprofit organizations. Some could interview residents, leaders, and officials. Others could collect documentation from the local library, town or county office, nonprofit organizations, the extension agent, and the district conservationist. Still others might photograph or sketch significant resources. (See also Sidebars 3.1 and 8.2)

Chapter 2

Classroom Discussion. What are the advantages of working through a nonprofit organization? Through local government? In what ways can the two cooperate?

Field Project. What are the roles of local government in the community? What nonprofit organizations are working in the community whose work might relate to rural conservation? How successful have they been and why? Could these organizations take on a larger role in rural conservation? What might be the steps in starting a visioning process for the community? For a particular organization? Is there a need for a new organization? If so, what should its mandate be? What geographic area should it cover? Who will support and who will oppose it? What opportunities are there for regional cooperation?

Chapter 3

Classroom Discussion. How can inventory information be used in a rural community? What are the advantages and disadvantages of different types of inventories? To what uses can a soil survey be put?

Field Project. What resources have been inventoried in the community? What ones should be inventoried? What should be mapped and how? Who should undertake the inventory? If a course will last for a semester or longer, it may make sense for class participants actually to become involved in undertaking portions of an inventory. A class could also take data from an existing inventory and put it on a GIS.

Chapter 4

Classroom Discussion. What are the functions of local government in a typical rural community? What are the advantages and disadvantages of zoning? Have class participants describe such techniques as cluster development and TDR, perhaps pretending their fellow participants are skeptical rural residents.

Field Project. What planning has been done in the community? What protections do the zoning and subdivision ordinances provide? How effective are they? Develop zoning recommendations or design guidelines for a particular section of the community. Prepare a plan to develop a particular property within existing zoning while protecting its most significant resources, assuming the owner is sympathetic to conservation but cannot afford to lose equity in the property.

Chapter 5

Classroom Discussion. In a campaign to achieve rural conservation, what are the advantages of different forms of nonprofit organizations: Advocacy organization with members? Land trust with no members? For a conservation organization, what are the advantages and disadvantages of fee ownership, easement acquisition, and recognition programs as ways of protecting significant properties?

Field Project. What techniques have been tried to protect particular properties? How effective have they been? Develop a protection plan for a particular property, assuming the owner is willing to lose some, but not all of the value of the property in the interests of conservation.

Chapter 6

Classroom Discussion. Under what circumstances does it make sense for a conservation organization to get involved in economic development? What are the advantages and disadvantages of tourism?

Field Project. What economic development strategies would class participants recommend: A downtown revitalization program? A tourism initiative? A farmers' market? Would a heritage area make sense? Should it include neighboring communities? How should it be promoted and administered?

Chapter 7

Classroom Discussion. What are the advantages and disadvantages of seeking help from the outside?

Field Project. What help has the community received from the outside? How valuable has this assistance been? What are local attitudes toward help from the federal government? State government? National or statewide nonprofit organizations? How successful have federal or state regulatory programs been in protecting resources? What agencies or organizations might the community consider applying to for help?

Chapter 8

Classroom Discussion. What are the advantages and disadvantages of the various ways rural communities can promote their activities? How can they best raise the funds they need?

Field Project. What newspapers, television stations, and radio stations cover the community? How likely are they to cover conservation activities in the community? What kinds of special events would prove popular? What special fund-raising opportunities exist in the community?

Conclusion

Classroom Discussion. What attitudes, laws, and programs will be needed to promote widespread rural conservation in the United States during the next decade?

Field Project. How does the community rate on the checklist for sustaining American communities (see p. 385)?

HANDS-ON EXPERIENCE

Gaining experience applying the lessons learned in the text is an invaluable addition to reading about techniques. It can be accomplished by working in a particular community that is within a reasonable drive of the course location, using the field project suggestions listed above. The class may also work with an invented community. Both have their advantages. With an invented case study: materials can be prepared in advance; materials can be reused for other courses; there is more flexibility to make sure all types of situations are covered; and there is no risk of offending community residents or taking up too much of their time. Class participants can feel free to be as imaginative and creative as they wish. The advantages of working in a real community include that: participants can go out and see the community and properties in question and talk with the players; the exercise will seem less academic and may better keep the attention of the participants; and the participants may come up with recommendations that can actually be implemented. Of course, these two approaches are not mutually exclusive.

If you choose a real community, think about whether a particular exercise will primarily benefit the class participants or the community and be honest with community leaders about who stands to benefit and how much. For instance, if class participants become involved in the inventory or planning phases of the rural conservation effort, will their work contribute more to the community than the time it will take community leaders to brief them? Will the work of the class mean that members of the community will become less involved and committed? What specific products, if any, will the class present to the community? Be careful not to promise the community more than you can deliver. It is difficult, but not impossible, to plan a field experience that will benefit both community and class participants. In any case, avoid taking a class to the same community too many times. Their visits may be welcome at first, but be looked upon as a burden if repeated too often (see Sidebar 2.7).

As an alternative to working in a particular community, course participants can consider recommendations for a hypothetical community. The case study might include several rural properties near a growing town. These properties should include a variety of environmental, agricultural, scenic, and historic resources that should be protected. Some of the properties should include areas that are appropriate for development. The area should be large enough for the participants to consider communitywide resources, concerns, and solutions, and small enough for them to consider the challenges facing a particular property owner. Prepare bird's-eye views and maps in advance for a couple of square miles of the community, as well as for one or more particular properties within that area. Give the participants written information about the case

study community and properties, including descriptions of resources, proposed developments, existing planning and zoning ordinances, nonprofit organizations, and attitudes of citizens. Ask participants to consider how this area (and these properties) can be developed in such a way as to assure that important community resources are conserved. Participants can make design recommendations that can be noted on the maps. As a variation, they can construct a model of a new community, or in-fill buildings in a historic community, using cardboard models. They can also make notes on flip charts about the needs for ordinances, concerns about fiscal impacts, and possible roles for a land trust. Set rules and answer questions about the community, but allow the participants to come up with their own solutions, which they can later report on. Ten is probably the largest number of participants that can work together effectively on a project like this. If there are more than ten participants, they can be broken into groups and then report out their solutions to the entire class.

Participants could also do role playing about a proposed development in the case study community. Each participant would be given a role to play during an imagined meeting of the planning board. The purpose is to help participants gain increased understanding of the concerns of people with different points of view in the community. The roles could include: property owner, neighbor, developer, county planner, director of the historical society, president of the land trust, four members of the planning commission—two pro-growth and two anti-growth—and the planning commission chair. Each would be given a briefing sheet on his or her role and concerns. The planning commission chair would assure that everyone is heard from and given equal time.

PAPER TOPIC

A paper topic that helps students of for-credit courses integrate what they have learned is as follows: Evaluate how well historic, natural, agricultural, recreational, and scenic resources are being protected in a rural community with which you are familiar. How effective is the local government and any local nonprofit organization in applying the techniques described in *Saving America's Countryside?* Include a brief history of the community and a description of its assets and the issues it faces. Also include a map showing the location of the community's most significant resources and problem areas. The map can be copied from a planning report or be a rough hand-drawn version. What recommendations would you make for rural conservation in the community? Review appropriate documentation (such as inventories, plans, ordinances, and reports of nonprofit organizations). If possible, interview people involved in conservation in the community. Include a list of sources consulted, both publications and people.

Sources of Assistance

PRIVATE NONPROFIT ORGANIZATIONS

Those national nonprofit organizations that are most likely to be of assistance to local governments and nonprofit organizations are listed below. There are many other important national organizations doing research, lobbying for national legislation, and litigating. There are also many helpful statewide organizations. For a more complete listing of conservation organizations, see the National Wildlife Federation's *Conservation Directory* (Suggested Reading for Chapter 7). Many of the following organizations have regional and state offices. Their addresses can frequently be found in the *Conservation Directory*.

American Association for State and Local History: membership organization; represents history museums, archives, and historical societies; offers technical assistance. *History News,* bimonthly magazine; *History News Dispatch,* monthly (530 Church Street, Suite 600, Nashville, TN 37219).

American Association of Museums: membership organization; represents museum professionals and museums; offers information on programs and technical assistance. *Museums News,* bimonthly magazine; *Aviso,* monthly newsletter (1225 Eye Street, N.W., Suite 200, Washington, DC 20005).

American Farmland Trust: membership organization; promotes farmland preservation and soil conservation; demonstrates preservation techniques; administers a revolv-

ing loan fund for farmland acquisition and protection; works to influence public policy; issues publications. *American Farmland,* quarterly newsletter (1920 N Street, N.W., Suite 400, Washington, DC 20036).

American Forests: membership organization; plants trees in forests damaged by forest fires, hurricanes, or human abuse. Also educates people on how to plant and care for trees. *American Forests,* quarterly magazine (1516 P Street, N.W., Washington, DC 20005).

American Hiking Society: membership organization; information clearinghouse on trail programs; promotes trail-building legislation; conducts training. *American Hiker,* bimonthly magazine (P.O. Box 20160, Washington, DC 20041).

American Planning Association: membership organization; monitors developments in planning, sponsors educational programs, prepares publications, and lobbies on planning issues; has committees for rural and small town planning, historic preservation, and environmental planning. *Planning,* monthly magazine; *Small Town and Rural Planning,* quarterly newsletter; *Zoning News,* monthly newsletter (1776 Massachusetts Avenue, N.W., Washington, DC 20036. For publications write: 122 S. Michigan Avenue, Suite 1600, Chicago, IL 60603).

American Rivers: membership organization; fosters a river stewardship ethic; monitors federal and state protection legislation; provides information on developing wild and scenic river protection programs. *American Rivers,* quarterly newsletter (801 Pennsylvania Avenue, S.E., Suite 400, Washington, DC 20003).

American Society of Landscape Architects: membership organization for professional landscape architects; informs the public about landscape design, planning, and management issues and has an Open Committee on Rural Landscape; *Landscape Architecture,* monthly magazine (4401 Connecticut Avenue, N.W., Washington, DC 20008).

American Trails: membership organization working to build trail networks for all Americans; organizes the National Trails Symposium, educates the public about trails, and supports grassroots trail efforts. *Trail Tracks,* quarterly (P.O. Box 200787, Denver, CO 80220).

The Archeological Conservancy: membership organization; works with private landowners and developers to protect endangered archeological sites, largely through acquisition and donation to a public agency. *Archeological Conservancy Newsletter,* quarterly (5301 Central Avenue, N.E., Suite 1218, Albuquerque, NM 87108).

The Association for Living Historical Farms and Agricultural Museums: membership organization; encourages research, exchange of ideas, and publication on historical agriculture, rural society, folklife, and historical interpretation. *Bulletin,* bimonthly newsletter (El Rancho de Las Golondrinas, Route 14, Box 214, Santa Fe, NM 87505).

Association for the Preservation of Civil War Sites: membership organization; protects endangered Civil War sites by purchasing property or negotiating protective easements; provides expertise on public policy issues and education on the history and documentation of the Civil War. *Hallowed Ground,* bimonthly (305 Charlotte Street, Fredericksburg, VA 22401).

Association of State Floodplain Managers: represents all government units and the private sector organizations responsible for floodplain management, flood hazards mitigation, flood preparedness, warning, and recovery, and the National Flood Insurance Program. Monthly newsletter and annual national directory (4233 West Beltline Highway, Madison, WI 53711).

Center for Compatible Economic Development: as a distinct unit of the Nature Conservancy, works with communities to develop businesses, products, and land uses that conserve ecosystems, enhance local economies, and achieve community goals (7 East Market Street, Leesburg, VA 22075).

Center for Marine Conservation: membership organization; concerned with endangered marine wildlife and its habitat; offers advice to organizations concerned with coastal wildlife sanctuaries. *Marine Conservation News,* quarterly; *Coastal Connection,* annually (1725 DeSales Street, N.W., Suite 500, Washington, DC 20036).

Center for the New West: membership organization; an independent, nonprofit, and nonpartisan institution for policy research, emphasizing trade, technology, and economic development issues. *Points West Chronicle,* quarterly (600 World Trade Center, 1625 Broadway, Denver, CO 80202).

Center for Rural Affairs: helps low-income people; concerned about the well-being of small, moderate-sized, and beginning farmers; particular focus on Nebraska and neighboring states. *Center for Rural Affairs,* monthly newsletter (P.O. Box 406, Walthill, NE 68067).

Citizens Clearinghouse for Hazardous Waste: membership organization; provides local leaders with technical and organizing assistance. *Everyone's Backyard,* quarterly newsletter; *Environmental Health Monthly,* newsletter (P.O. Box 6806, Falls Church, VA 22040).

Citizens Coal Council: federation of coal field citizen groups across the country working to protect people, homes, water, and communities from coal mining damage. *CCC Reporter,* quarterly (eastern office: 110 Maryland Avenue, N.E., Room 307, Washington, DC 20002; western office: 1705 South Pearl Street, Suite 5, Denver, CO 80210).

The Civil War Trust: membership organization; works to preserve the nation's most important Civil War sites through land acquisition; promotes the Civil War Discovery Trail and the Civil War Discovery System, an interactive, multimedia educational tool. *Landscape,* quarterly; *The Official Guidebook to the Civil War Discovery Trail,* semiannually (1225 Eye Street, N.W., Suite 401, Washington, DC 20005).

Clean Water Network: coalition of 550 organizations working to protect and strengthen clean water policies in the United States. *Status Report,* every six weeks (1350 New York Avenue, N.W., Suite 300, Washington, DC 20005).

Coast Alliance: strives to increase appreciation and awareness of our coastal lands through public education and outreach (215 Pennsylvania Avenue, S.E., Washington, DC 20003).

The Community Transportation Association of America: membership organization that serves transit agencies in rural areas and wherever elderly, disabled, or poor persons have inadequate access to transportation; offers information and technical assistance to community transportation agencies; *CTR,* monthly magazine (1440 New York Avenue, N.W., Suite 440, Washington, DC 20005).

The Conservation Fund: creates partnerships with the private sector, nonprofit organizations and public agencies to protect the nation's outdoor and historic heritage and pursues new opportunities to advance land and water conservation. *Common Ground,* free bimonthly newsletter; *Land Letter,* weekly newsletter for natural resources professionals (1800 North Kent Street, Suite 1120, Arlington, VA 22209).

Corporation for Enterprise Development: analyzes, designs, demonstrates, evaluates, and communicates economic development policy and practice; works with governments, foundations, and other organizations to promote economic opportunity for all, especially low-income communities (777 North Capitol Street, Suite 410, Washington, DC 20002).

The Countryside Institute/Glynwood Center: stimulates community stewardship through research, case studies, and on- and off-site training developed at the center's location in the Hudson River Valley. Sponsors the International Countryside Stewardship Exchange program (P.O. Box 157, Cold Spring, NY 10516).

Environmental Air Force: organization of volunteer pilots who donate flying time to conservation groups to inventory resources, monitor easements, and carry out various missions on behalf of the environment. Provides services on demand, at no charge, but requires that organizations using its services be members for an annual flat fee (22 Rittenhouse Road, Broomall, PA 19008).

The Environmental Law Institute: conducts research and prepares publications on environmental law; offers educational programs and advice on wetlands. *The Environmental Forum*, bimonthly; *The Environmental Law Reporter*, monthly; *National Wetlands Newsletter*, bimonthly (1616 P Street, N.W., Suite 200, Washington, DC 20036).

Environmental Policy Institute: works to influence public policy; engages in research and litigation; information clearinghouse; special areas of concern include groundwater protection, nuclear waste, and coastal resources. *Environmental Update*, quarterly (218 D Street, S.E., Washington, DC 20003).

The Foundation Center: service organization; good source of information on foundations, their patterns of giving, and their fields of interest; maintains offices and libraries open to the public in New York, Washington, D.C., San Francisco, and Cleveland and collections in nearly 150 cooperating libraries throughout the country; has a toll-free number (800-424-9836) for information on services and publications (1001 Connecticut Avenue, N.W., Suite 938, Washington, DC 20036).

The Groundwater Foundation: a national grassroots organization which promotes, educates, and provides technical assistance for community groundwater protection. *The Aquifer*, quarterly; *Infiltration*, quarterly (P.O. Box 22558, Lincoln, NE 68542).

Heartland Center for Leadership Development: helps local leadership respond to the challenges of the future, produces programs and publications on rural community survival, and provides training and technical assistance on strategic planning, organizational development, and leadership (941 O Street, Suite 920, Lincoln, NE 68508).

Housing Assistance Council: works to increase the availability of housing for low-income people in rural areas; administers revolving loan fund; provides technical assistance; undertakes research and training programs; publishes booklets on housing issues and programs. *HAC News*, biweekly newsletter (1025 Vermont Avenue, N.W., Suite 606, Washington, DC 20005).

Independent Sector: membership organization; encourages not-for-profit initiatives; works to influence federal policy on tax and lobbying issues relating to nonprofit organizations; issues publications on how to manage nonprofit organizations (1828 L Street, N.W., Washington, DC 20036).

Institute for Community Economics: membership organization for community land trusts; provides technical and financial assistance for development of affordable housing through community land trusts; provides legal and other information through publications. *Community Economics*, quarterly; *Update*, quarterly (57 School Street, Springfield, MA 01105).

Institute for Conservation Leadership: works to strengthen organizations, especially leaders thereof, that are working on behalf of the environment, by developing and conducting training programs, meetings, retreats, and conferences; also provides consulting and technical assistance. *The Network*, three times a year (6930 Carroll Avenue, Suite 420, Takoma Park, MD 20912).

International City/County Management Association: membership organization of primarily government administrators; provides technical assistance, training, and publications to enhance the quality of local government; serves as a clearinghouse of information on local government. *ICMA Newsletter*, biweekly; *Public Management*, monthly (777 North Capitol Street, N.E., Suite 500, Washington, DC 20002).

Izaak Walton League of America: membership organization; promotes citizen involvement in local environmental protection efforts; areas of concern include clean water, stream monitoring, carrying capacity, wildlife habitat, and conservation issues relating to hunting and outdoor ethics. *Outdoor America*, quarterly (707 Conservation Lane, Gaithersburg, MD 29878).

Land Trust Alliance: membership organization for land trusts and individuals; information clearinghouse; conducts educational programs, including a peer match program for land trust officials; coordinates policy development; provides technical information on tax aspects of estate planning and land conservation. Exchange, quarterly journal (1319 F Street, N.W., Suite 501, Washington, DC 20004).

Lighthawk: organization of volunteer pilots who donate flying time to conservation organizations to assess resources, monitor easements, transport politicians and speakers, and perform various missions on behalf of the environment. Asks its "conservation partners" to make donations to help defray the cost of fuel (P.O. Box 8163, Santa Fe, NM 87501).

Lincoln Institute of Land Policy: educational institution to study and teach land policy, including land economics and taxation. Sponsors seminars and programs and issues publications on land policy (113 Brattle Street, Cambridge, MA 02138-3400).

Mineral Policy Center: public interest organization working to prevent damage caused to U.S. land and water from irresponsible mineral development. Provides educational, technical, legal, and political strategy assistance. *Clementine,* journal published three times a year (1612 K Street, N.W., Suite 808, Washington, DC 20006).

National Alliance of Preservation Commissions: membership organization; provides information and education to members of preservation commissions and boards of architectural review. *Alliance Review,* quarterly (c/o School of Environmental Design, 609 Caldwell Hall, University of Georgia, Athens, GA 30602).

National Association for Interpretation: primarily volunteer organization that seeks to achieve and maintain excellence in the delivery of natural, cultural, and historical interpretive services. *Legacy,* bimonthly; *NAI News,* quarterly (P.O. Box 1892, Fort Collins, CO 80522).

National Association for the Preservation of Barns: membership organization to promote the restoration of barns and other farm buildings; seeks to establish a fund to receive donations for and to provide grants for barn restoration. Occasional newsletter (2943 Prairie du Chien Road NE, Iowa City, IA 52240).

National Association of Counties: membership organization; seeks to improve county government and represents the interests of counties at the national level; offers educational programs and technical assistance. *County News,* bimonthly (440 First Street, N.W., Washington, DC 20001).

National Association of Development Organizations: public interest group which promotes economic development in America's small metropolitan and rural areas. Members are regional development organizations whose staff provide professional assistance to local governments, businesses, and nonprofit organizations. *NADO News,* weekly newsletter (444 North Capitol Street, N.W., Suite 630, Washington, DC 20001).

National Association of Service and Conservation Corps: membership organization; provides assistance and information to youth corps programs. *NASCC News,* quarterly (666 11th Street, N.W., Suite 500, Washington, DC 20001).

National Association of Towns and Townships: membership organization; offers technical assistance, educational assistance, and public policy support to local government officials. *Washington Report,* monthly (1522 K Street, N.W., Suite 1010, Washington, DC 20005).

National Audubon Society: membership organization; carries out research, education, action and advocacy programs to protect wildlife and natural areas; ten regional offices and more than 500 chapters. *Audubon,* bimonthly magazine (700 Broadway, New York, NY 10003).

National Environmental Training Center for Small Communities: supports environmental educators in their efforts to improve the quality of drinking water, waste water, and solid waste services in small communities. *E-Train,* quarterly (P.O. Box 6064, Morgantown, WV 26506).

National Institute for Dispute Resolution: provides technical assistance, publications, and grants for dispute resolution and a focal point for practitioners, stakeholders, and institutions to discuss research and experience. *NIDR News,* bimonthly; *Dispute Resolution FORUM,* several times a year (1726 M Street, N.W., Suite 500, Washington, DC 20036).

National Network of Forest Practitioners: membership organization; provides a forum for rural community-based nongovernmental organizations striving to maintain the environmental integrity of forest land while enhancing its ability to provide income. *National Network of Forest Practitioners,* annual directory (c/o Forest Trust, P.O. Box 519, Santa Fe, NM 87504).

National Rural Housing Coalition: membership organization; advocates for affordable housing and basic community services for rural areas; coordinates a national network of rural housing advocates. *Legislative Update,* biweekly news memo; *FmHA Notes,* occasional (601 Pennsylvania Avenue, N.W., Washington, DC 20004).

National Scenic Byways Clearinghouse: information resource center on scenic byways; collects scenic byways studies, legislation, corridor management plans, and related information on scenic byways for public access (c/o American Automobile Association, 1440 New York Avenue, N.W., Washington, D.C. 20005).

National Storytelling Association: organization of educators, teachers, librarians, and storytellers dedicated to preserving, promoting, and educating the public about the art of storytelling and oral traditions. *Storytelling,* bimonthly magazine; *Inside Story,* bimonthly newsletter (P.O. Box 309, Jonesborough, TN 37659).

National Tour Association: membership organization for group-tour companies, tour suppliers, and tourist destinations. Facilitates contacts between tour operators and suppliers. *Courier,* monthly (546 East Main Street, Lexington, KY 40507).

National Trust for Historic Preservation: membership organization; encourages preservation of America's historical and cultural heritage; seven regional offices provide services to local organizations; National Main Street Center assists downtown revitalization programs; Rural Program promotes preservation in rural communities;

offers publications and educational programs. *Historic Preservation,* bimonthly magazine; *Preservation Forum,* quarterly journal for professionals and nonprofit organizations (1785 Massachusetts Avenue, N.W., Washington, DC 20036).

National Wildlife Federation: membership organization; conservation education programs, with a particular focus on wildlife; thirteen regional offices and chapters in every state. *National Wildlife,* monthly magazine; *Ranger Rick,* monthly magazine for children (1400 16th Street, N.W., Washington, DC 20036).

Natural Resources Defense Council: membership organization; monitors federal agencies and disseminates information to citizens; litigates and works to influence public policy; areas of concentration include air and water pollution, hazardous waste, coastal zones, and public land; publishes books and studies. *The Amicus Journal,* quarterly; *Newsline,* bimonthly newsletter (122 East 42nd Street, New York, NY 10168).

Natural Science for Youth Foundation: promotes environmental education programs; encourages establishment of nature centers; provides consulting services; *Directory of Natural Science Centers,* occasional (130 Azalea Drive, Roswell, GA 30075).

The Nature Conservancy: membership organization; encourages the preservation of natural diversity through the acquisition and protection of land that supports rare ecosystems and endangered species; has chapters in most states. *The Nature Conservancy News,* bimonthly magazine (1815 North Lynn Street, Arlington, VA 22209).

Partners for Livable Communities: membership organization; committed to improving communities' economic health and quality of life; library and clearinghouse of information on built and natural environment open to public; offers technical assistance to communities for a fee. *Livability,* quarterly newsletter (1429 21st Street, N.W., Washington, DC 20036).

Rails-to-Trails Conservancy: membership organization; devoted to converting abandoned railroad rights-of-way into trails for public use; advises on conversion process; assists in corridor acquisition. *Trailblazer,* quarterly newsletter (1400 16th Street, N.W., 3rd floor, Washington, DC 20036).

River Network: connects and provides information and technical assistance to grassroots river groups through its newsletter, publications, database of river information specialists, and hands-on support. *River Voices,* quarterly (P.O. Box 8787, Portland, OR 97207).

Rocky Mountain Institute: research and educational foundation that seeks to foster the efficient and sustainable use of natural resources. *RMI Newsletter,* three times a year; numerous other publications (1739 Snowmass Creek Road, Snowmass, CO 81654).

Rural Advancement Foundation International—USA: dedicated to the preservation of family farms and a sustainable system of agriculture. Works with a variety of farm, community, university, and governmental groups to provide practical assistance, market opportunities, and access to financial and technical resources. *RAFI Action,* newsletter three times a year (P.O. Box 655, Pittsboro, NC 27312).

Rural Coalition: alliance of almost 100 community-based organizations working to promote sustainable development in rural areas. Provides technical assistance to member groups and holds an annual assembly. Quarterly newsletter and annual report (110 Maryland Avenue, N.E., Washington, DC 20002).

Rural Local Initiatives Support Corporation: partnership initiative of foundations, the federal government, and the banking industry in support of rural community development corporations. Provides loans and grants in thirty-nine states to develop job-generating affordable housing and essential facilities and to provide training (1825 K Street, N.W., 11th Floor, Washington, DC 20006).

Scenic America: membership organization; works to preserve and enhance the scenic character of communities and countryside; promotes sign control; assists local organizations and units of government. *Viewpoints,* quarterly newsletter (21 Dupont Circle, N.W., Washington, DC 20036).

Sierra Club: membership organization; concerned with a broad array of environmental issues; educates on conservation; works on legislation and litigation; fifty-seven chapters active in local conservation issues. *Sierra,* bimonthly magazine (730 Polk Street, San Francisco, CA 94109).

Sierra Legal Defense Fund: provides legal representation at no charge for public interest groups, individuals, and other entities in lawsuits and administrative appeals to safeguard national forests, parks, wilderness areas, reduce air and water pollution, contain toxic materials, and preserve wildlife habitat (180 Montgomery Street, Suite 1400, San Francisco, CA 94104).

Society for American Archaeology: membership organization; promotes interest and research in the archeology of the American continents; discourages commercialism in the field of archeology. *American Antiquity,* quarterly journal; *bulletin,* bimonthly (900 Second Street, N.E., Suite 12, Washington, DC 20002).

Society for Range Management: membership organization; seeks to develop an understanding of range ecosystems and range-management principles; promotes public appreciation of range benefits; maintains roster of certified range managers. *Journal of Range Management,* bimonthly; *Rangelands,* bimonthly (2760 West 5th Avenue, Denver, CO 80204).

Society of American Foresters: membership organization; seeks to advance the practice of professional forestry and enhance public appreciation of forest resources; maintains roster of consulting foresters. *Journal of Forestry, monthly; Forest Science,* quarterly (5400 Grosvenor Lane, Bethesda, MD 20814).

Soil and Water Conservation Society: membership organization; concerned with wise use of land, soil, and water; educational programs. *Journal of Soil and Water Conservation,* bimonthly (7515 N.E. Ankeny Road, Ankeny, IA 50021).

Sonoran Institute: works nationwide with natural resource managers, landowners, conservation leaders, and local officials to create and implement projects that link sustainable development and natural resource protection (7290 East Broadway Boulevard, Suite M, Tuscon, AZ 85710).

Surface Transportation Policy Project: nationwide network of more than 150 organizations working to develop a national transportation system that better serves the economic, energy, environmental, and social interests of the nation. *Progress,* monthly newsletter; *Transfer,* weekly newsletter (1400 16th Street, N.W., Suite 300, Washington, DC 20036).

Terrene Institute: conducts research, producing publications, and fostering public-private partnerships to maintain a balanced environment. Focuses on water-quality issues, particularly toxic pollution, fisheries management, and nonpoint source pollution (1717 K Street, N.W., Suite 801, Washington, DC 20006).

Travel Industry Association of America: represents all facets of the tourism industry, developing policy on tourism issues and providing public education. Operates the Travel Data Center to provide up-to-date marketing and economic information on the U.S. travel industry. *The TIA Newsline,* monthly; *Contact USA,* annually (1100 New York Avenue, N.W., Suite 450, Washington, DC 20005).

The Trust for Public Land: acquires and arranges for the preservation of open space to serve the needs of people; assists local land trusts through its headquarters and regional and field offices. *TPL Updates,* occasional newsletter (116 New Montgomery Street, 4th floor, San Francisco, CA 94105).

The Urban Land Institute: membership organization; promotes improved land-development policy; conducts research and educational programs; publishes studies of use to planners, developers, and others involved in development. *Land Use Digest,* monthly; *Urban Land Magazine,* monthly (625 Indiana Avenue, NW, Suite 400, N.W., Washington, DC 20004).

The Wilderness Society: membership organization; primary focus on wilderness, wildlife, and public lands; involved in public education, public policy, and litigation; eight field offices. *Wilderness,* quarterly magazine (1400 Eye Street, N.W., Washington, DC 20005).

FEDERAL AGENCIES

Most of the following agencies have regional offices and many have state offices. The National Wildlife Federation's *Conservation Directory* (Suggested Reading, Chapter 7) lists most of the addresses. Many have local or county offices as well, listed in the U.S. Government pages in the telephone directory. Offices closer to home may be more responsive than headquarters.

Advisory Council on Historic Preservation: reviews the impact of proposed federal undertakings on properties listed in or eligible for listing in the National Register of Historic Places (1100 Pennsylvania Avenue, N.W., Washington, DC 20004).

American Folklife Center, Library of Congress: assists local governments, nonprofit organizations, and individuals in preserving and presenting American folklife; includes recorded and manuscript collections in the Archive of Folk Culture. *Folklife Center News,* quarterly (Washington, DC 20540).

Army Corps of Engineers: Issues permits for work in navigable waters in the United States, including wetlands; constructs flood control projects along rivers, lakes, and reservoirs; does shoreline protection work; and has an extensive recreation program (20 Massachusetts Avenue, N.W., Washington, DC 20314).

The Corporation for National Service: serves as the domestic Peace Corps by engaging citizens in full or part-time community service in education, public safety, human needs, and the environment in exchange for helping finance their higher education or repaying student loans (1201 New York Avenue, N.W., Washington, DC 20525).

Council on Environmental Quality: advises the President on environmental matters; oversees the implementation of the National Environmental Policy Act; prepares an annual report on the state of the environment (722 Jackson Place, N.W., Washington, DC 20006).

Department of Agriculture: contains Agricultural Stabilization and Conservation Service, Cooperative Extension Service, Forest Service, Rural Housing and Community Development Service, and Natural Resources Conservation Service (14th Street and Jefferson Drive, S.W., Washington, DC 20250).

Department of Housing and Urban Development, Office of Community Planning and Development: administers major federal community development, economic development, and housing rehabilitation programs (451 7th Street, S.W., Washington, DC 20410).

Department of the Interior: contains Bureau of Land Management, Bureau of Reclamation, U.S. Fish and Wildlife Service, U.S. Geological Survey, National Park Service, and Office of Surface Mining (18th and C Streets, N.W., Washington, DC 20240).

Department of Transportation: contains Federal Highway Administration (400 7th Street, S.W., Washington, DC 20590).

Environmental Protection Agency: undertakes federal environmental protection efforts, researches environmental problems, and administers governmental regulation programs; has ten regional offices (401 M Street, S.W., Washington, DC 20460).

Federal Emergency Management Agency: responds to any nationally declared emergency; administers the National Flood Insurance Program and the U.S. Fire Administration (500 C Street, S.W., Washington, DC 20472).

Federal Energy Regulatory Commission: regulates utilities, natural gas, oil and hydroelectric power (941 North Capitol Street, N.E., Washington, DC 20426).

Government Printing Office: issues most federal publications; makes subject bibliographies available on request (Washington, DC 20402).

National Endowment for the Arts: through its Design Program, awards grants for projects that promote excellence in architecture, landscape architecture, and community design; through its Folk Arts Program, awards grants for documenting folklife traditions (1100 Pennsylvania Avenue, N.W., Washington, DC 20506).

National Oceanic and Atmospheric Administration, Department of Commerce: administers coastal zone management program; strives to protect wetlands, water quality, beaches, wildlife, and uses of our coasts (14th Street and Constitution Avenue., N.W., Room 6013, Washington, DC 20230).

Department of Health and Human Services, Office of Community Services: administers Urban and Rural Community Economic Development Program, Rural Housing Program, and Community Facilities Development Program (330 C Street, S.W., Washington, DC 20201).

Tennessee Valley Authority: undertakes water projects, assists conservation efforts, supplies electricity, and develops resources in the Tennessee River watershed (400 West Summit Hill Drive, Knoxville, TN 37902).

Notes to Text

CHAPTER 1: RURAL CONCERNS

1. Texas Parks and Wildlife and the National Park Service, *Creating a Conservation and Recreation Legacy,* August 1994, p. 15.

2. *Beyond Sprawl: New Patterns of Growth to Fit the New California, Executive Summary.* Sponsored by Bank of America, the California Resources Agency, Greenbelt Alliance, and the Low Income Housing Fund, 1995, p. 8.

3. Kenneth M. Johnson and Calvin Beale, "The Rural Rebound: The Revival of Population Growth in Nonmetropolitan America" (paper prepared for the U.S. Department of Agriculture, Economic Research Service, 1995), p. 8.

4. "The Rich Are Different: They Can Afford Homes," *New York Times,* November 16, 1994.

5. "Nurturing New Jobs in a Land of Old Forests," *Washington Post,* February 27, 1995.

6. "Stewardship Exchange Sites," *Rural Pennsylvania,* January–February 1995.

7. Calvin Beale, U.S. Department of Agriculture, Economic Research Service, telephone conversation with Shelley Mastran, November 9, 1995.

8. U.S. Department of Agriculture, Economic Research Service, *Agricultural Resources and Environmental Indicators* (Washington, D.C.: USDA, December 1994), p. 47.

9. Ibid., p. 46.

10. Federal Interagency Flood Management Task Force, *Floodplain Management in the U.S.: An Assessment Report* (Washington, D.C.: FIFMTF, 1992), pp. I-2–I-3.

11. Frank McGilray, U.S. Fish and Wildlife Service, telephone conversation with author, November 1, 1995.

12. U.S. Department of Agriculture, Natural Resources Conservation Service, *Summary Report, National Resources Inventory* (Washington, D.C.: USDA, January 1995,) p. 4.

13. U.S. Department of Agriculture, Economic Research Service, *Foreign Agricultural Trade in the United States, Calendar Year 94 Supplement,* (Washington, D.C.: USDA, 1994), p. 30.

14. U.S. Department of Labor, Bureau of Labor Statistics, *Employment and Earnings* (Washington, D.C.: BLS, January 1994), p. 13.

15. U.S. Department of Agriculture, Economic Research Service, and U.S. Department of Commerce, Bureau of the Census, *Residents of Farms and Rural Areas: 1991* (Washington, D.C.: USDA and U.S. Department of Commerce, August 1993), p. 1.

16. U.S. Department of Agriculture, National Agricultural Statistics Service, *Farm and Land in Farms,* (Washington, D.C.: USDA, July 1995), p. 1.

17. Edward Thompson, Jr., *Winning Friends, Losing Ground: States and Local Communities Need a Federal Partner to Protect the Nation's Farmland* (Washington, D.C.: American Farmland Trust, 1995), p. 1.

18. U.S. Department of Agriculture, Natural Re-

sources Conservation Service, *Summary Report, 1992 National Resources Inventory* (Washington, D.C.: USDA, NRCS, January 1995), p. 5.

19. U.S. Department of Agriculture, Economic Research Service, *The New Generation of American Farmers: Farm Entry and Exit Prospects for the 1990s* (Washington, D. C.: USDA, October 1994), p. 5.

20. U.S. Forest Service, *Forest Resources of the United States, 1992,* General Technical Report RM-2334 (Washington, D.C.: USDA, 1993), p. 23.

21. Conservation Foundation, *State of the Environment: An Assessment at Mid-Decade* (Washington, D.C: CF, 1984), p. 172.

22. U.S. Department of the Interior, Fish and Wildlife Service, *1991 National Survey of Fishing, Hunting, and Wildlife Recreation* (Washington, D.C.: Government Printing Office, 1993).

23. "Outdoor Recreation in America—1995," annual survey conducted by the American Recreation Coalition, Washington, D.C.

24. Telephone conversation of Shelley Mastran with Roger Ulrich regarding unpublished manuscript by Russell Parsons, Louis Tassinary, and Roger Ulrich regarding the effects of roadside environments on drivers, December 1995.

25. Frederick Steiner to authors, December 20, 1994.

26. "National Survey on Recreation and the Environment, 1994–1995, Key Findings" (report on survey conducted for U.S. Forest Service, Bureau of Land Management, U.S. Army Corps of Engineers, and the National Park Service, October 25, 1995), Table 2.

27. American Association of State Highway and Transportation Officials, *A Policy on Geometric Design of Highways and Streets, 1990* (Washington, D.C.: AASHTO, 1990).

28. James P. Ludwig, Ecological Research Services, Bay City, Michigan, telephone conversation with author, February 1988.

29. Office of Surface Mining, Reclamation and Enforcement, Abandoned Mine Land Inventory System, September 30, 1995, from computerized data base.

30. Environmental Protection Agency, Office of Solid Waste, *Solving the Hazardous Waste Problem: EPA's RCRA Program,* (Washington, D.C., November 1986), p. 5.

31. Comprehensive Environmental Response, Compensation, and Liability Act (CERCLA) database, March 1995, EPA Hotline.

CHAPTER 2: ORGANIZING A RURAL CONSERVATION PROGRAM

1. Kim McAdams, "Public Survey Leads to New Trust," *Land Trusts' Exchange,* Summer 1983, p. 8.

2. Ibid.

3. Telephone conversation of Elizabeth Watson with Constance Chamberlin, August 1986.

4. Clare C. Swanger, "Preserving Taos: The Taos Land Trust," *Exchange* (journal of the Land Trust Alliance), vol. 12, no. 2, Spring 1993, p. 10; telephone conversation of Elizabeth Watson with Clare Swanger, February 15, 1996; and executive summary of the report, *Land Use, Conservation, and Development: A Survey of Landowner Attitudes in the Taos Area,* December 30, 1992, p. 4.

5. *The Corridor Management Plan for the Indiana National Road* (paper prepared for the Indiana National Road Association by the State of Indiana and the National Trust for Historic Preservation, 1995), p. 17.

6. Telephone conversation of Elizabeth Watson with Michele Byers, October 18, 1995.

7. Dianne Russell to Elizabeth Watson, October 5, 1995.

8. Telephone conversations of Rebecca Brown with Lanny Haldy, November 8 and 17, 1995.

9. Jane W. Schautz to Elizabeth Watson, August 21, 1986.

10. Interview by Elizabeth Watson with Brian Steen, Big Sur Land Trust, 1985.

11. Dianne Russell to Elizabeth Watson, October 5, 1995.

12. Telephone conversations of Elizabeth Watson with Tom Kerr, Wildlands Conservancy, December 28, 1995, and January 26, 1996.

13. David Startzell, "Volunteers as Trail Managers: The ATC Experience," *Pathways Across America: A Newsletter for National Scenic and Historic Trails,* Fall 1994, pp. 5, 9.

14. Speech by P. K. Pettus, former member of the Virginia Conservation Council, Washington, D.C., June 14, 1980.

15. Ibid.

16. Patricia Bidol, Lisa Bardwell, and Nancy Manring, eds., *Alternative Environmental Conflict Management Approaches: A Citizens' Manual* (Ann Arbor: Environmental Conflict Project, School of Natural Resources, University of Michigan, 1986), p. 13.

17. Information supplied by Rhonda G. Henderson, Rockingham County Department of Planning and Zoning, in letter of December 15, 1995.

18. Howard Bellman, Gail Bingham, Ronnie Brooks, Susan Carpenter, Peter Clark, and Robert Craig, "Environmental Conflict Resolution: Practitioners' Perspective of an Emerging Field," *Environmental Consensus* (newsletter of RESOLVE/Center for Environmental Conflict Resolution) Winter 1981, p. 1.

19. Such a procedure must not seem to substitute for the authority of elected and appointed officials, the danger of which was indicated by a successful state court challenge to the development guidance system in Hardin County, Kentucky, on this basis. "Some attorneys believe too much 'power' is granted to neighbors who have an of-

ficial part in the review process" (Forster Ndubisi, *Planning Implementation Tools and Techniques: A Resource Book for Local Governments* [Athens: University of Georgia, Institute of Community and Area Development, 1992], p. 212).

20. Caroline S. Tauxe, "Marginalizing Public Participation in Local Planning: An Ethnographic Account," *Journal of the American Planning Association*, vol. 61, no. 4, Autumn 1995, pp. 472, 477.

21. Clare C. Swanger, "Preserving Taos: The Taos Land Trust," *Exchange* (Journal of the Land Trust Alliance), vol. 12, no. 2, Spring 1993, p. 10; and telephone conversation of Elizabeth Watson with Clare Swanger, February 15, 1996.

22. Reeves Brown, "A Cowboy's Viewpoint: Stewardship from the Saddle," *Nonpoint Source News-Notes,* no. 33, November–December 1993, p. 11.

23. As suggested by Robert D. Putnam in "Bowling Alone," *Journal of Democracy,* vol. 6, no. 1, January 1995, pp. 65–77, and in his earlier work with Robert Leonardi and Raffaella Y. Nanetti, *Making Democracy Work: Civic Traditions in Modern Italy* (Princeton: Princeton University Press, 1993), it is such civic groups that form the foundation of a community's effectiveness and even its economic health.

24. Jack Thomas to Rebecca Brown, November 24, 1996, and conversation with Elizabeth Watson, September 6, 1996.

25. Ingerson, Alice E., ed., *Managing Land as Ecosystem and Economy* (Cambridge, Mass.: Lincoln Institute of Land Policy, 1995), p. 11.

26. Speech by James R. Pepper to the Federal Highway Administration, Boston, May 1993.

27. Leonard Ziokowski, Economic Development Council of Nartheastern Pennsylvania, by telephone conversation with Elizabeth Watson, December 8, 1995.

CHAPTER 3: ANALYZING THE RURAL COMMUNITY

1. Walter Cudnohufsky, "Dreaming the Future: Community Vision Planning," *Planning Commissioners Journal,* no. 11 (Summer 1993), p. 5.

2. Cheryl Doble and George McCulloch, *Managing Change: A Pilot Study in Rural Design and Planning* (n.p.: Tug Hill Commission, North Shore Design Project, n.d.), p. 13.

3. "Municipalities Create Vision for Future," *Pennsylvania Township News,* July 1995, p. 12.

CHAPTER 4: RURAL CONSERVATION THROUGH LOCAL GOVERNMENT

1. Telephone conversation of Elizabeth Watson with Randall Arendt, Natural Lands Trust, October 16, 1995.

2. Warren Zitzmann to author, October 1986.

3. From information supplied by Teresa Biddick, Collin County Open Space Manager (letter to Elizabeth Watson of September 6, 1995) and Roy Mann, Roy Mann Associates, Austin, Texas (letter of 31 August 1995).

4. Guilford Preservation Alliance, *Master Plan for Preservation and Scenic Conservation* (Guilford, Conn.: GPA, 1986 and 1995), and telephone conversation of Elizabeth Watson with Shirley Girioni, Guilford Preservation Alliance, November 22, 1995.

5. Robert E. Coughlin, *Zoning for Farming: A Guidebook for Pennsylvania Municipalities on How to Protect Valuable Agricultural Lands* (Harrisburg, Pennsylvania: Center for Rural Pennsylvania, n.d.), p. 72–75, and telephone conversation of Elizabeth Watson with Michelle Sofer, Peach Bottom Township, November 22, 1995.

6. Kenneth R. Harney, "Community Living: Look for Bike Paths, Not Golf Courses" ("The Nation's Housing" column), *Washington Post,* January 7, 1995.

7. Piedmont Environmental Council, "Fauquier Leads Virginia in Rural Protection," *PEC Newsreporter,* May 1986, pp. 1–3.

8. Christopher J. Duerksen, Erin Johnson, and Cheryl Fricke, *Colorado Growth Management Toolbox* (Denver: Colorado Division of Local Government, 1995), p. 38.

9. Kerry Hodges, ed., "Development Guidance System, Charles County, Maryland" in *Chesapeake Bay Communities, Making the Connection: A Catalog of Local Initiatives to Protect and Restore the Chesapeake Bay Watershed* (Annapolis, Md.: Environmental Protection Agency for the Chesapeake Bay Program, 1995), p. 14.

10. Conversation of Rebecca Brown with Tim Asher, Hardin County planner, December 15, 1995.

11. Conversation of Elizabeth Watson with Christopher J. Duerksen, Clarion Associates, August 30, 1996.

12. Conversation of Elizabeth Watson with Michael Clarke, Natural Lands Trust, January 2, 1996.

13. Conversation of Elizabeth Watson with Susan M. Smith, University of Tennessee (and supervisor of the project that led to writing of the manual cited as Hale 1994), August 30, 1996.

14. Barbarina Heyerdahl, "TDRs: An Innovative Approach to Growth Management," in *Balanced Growth: A Planning Guide for Local Government,* edited by John M. DeGrove (Washington, D.C.: International City-County Management Association, 1991), p. 64.

15. "The Hanalei Project," handout at conference "Preserving Hawaii's Traditional Landscapes," Honolulu, Hawaii, September 15–17, 1995; and Hanalei Project and Land and Community Associates, *Hanalei Design Guidelines Handbook* (Hanalei, Hawaii: The Hanalei Project, 1988).

16. Telephone conversations of Rebecca Brown with John C. Keene, Coughlin and Keene Associates, December 8, 1995, and Jon Mayes, Michigan Department of Natural

Resources Farmland Office, February 7, 1996.

17. Telephone conversation of Elizabeth Watson with Jim Benson, Minnesota Department of Revenue, Tax Research Division , February 7, 1996.

18. Telephone conversation of Elizabeth Watson with Freda Miller, Oregon Department of Fish and Wildlife, Habitat and Conservation Division, February 16, 1996.

19. "Tax Credits for Voluntary Conservation: Back to the Future," *GreenSense,* vol. 1, no. 3, Autumn 1995, p. 1.

20. Kat Imhoff to author, October 6, 1986.

21. Warren Zitzmann to author.

22. Rachel S. Cox, "For Small-Town Activists, Unity Spells Success," *Historic Preservation Forum News,* vol. 2, no. 2, January–February 1996, p. 4; and Andi Rierden, "Towns Just Saying 'No' to Federal Funds," *New York Times,* October 1, 1995.

CHAPTER 5: VOLUNTARY TECHNIQUES FOR PROTECTING PROPERTY

1. If the property is mortgaged at the time the owner wishes to put it under easement, the bank or other mortgage holder generally must agree to the arrangement, since it affects the holder's interest in the property.

2. At least forty-four states have passed legislation to govern the use of easements and to cure certain defects that often exist in their common law. Thus, the term "conservation easement" is a holdover from the past, when use of this technique was more likely to rely on common law as applied to easements. We have chosen to use "easement" in this text, but readers are cautioned that conservation restrictions under state law are the subject under discussion unless otherwise specified. On deed restrictions, anyone who delves into easements beyond this chapter is likely to encounter the term "covenant." Also known as a deed restriction, a covenant pertains to a restriction imposed on subsequent owners when title to a property is transferred, as opposed to an easement, which can be created without transfer of the title. An individual transferring a property to another owner can use a covenant instead of an easement to impose restrictions on the use and development of a property, but the covenant is usually unenforceable once the transferor dies. For organizations, covenants operate in the same fashion as easements (because organizations do not die) and are commonly used with limited development and revolving funds. Developers commonly use covenants to dictate certain conditions in subdivisions that may not be covered by zoning and subdivision regulations. Under state law, covenants typically lapse after a period of time, such as twenty years, unless recorded.

3. Program information provided by the American Farmland Trust, November 22, 1995; and Robin Pearson,

Michigan Department of Natural Resources, February 7, 1996.

4. Daniel P. O'Connell, "Securitizable Tax-Exempt Installment-Purchase Open-Space Financing Program" (private paper available from Evergreen Capital Advisors, Inc., 14 East 76th Street, Harvey Cedars, N.J. 08008-0306), and other materials presented at a conference of the Land Trust Alliance, Waterville Valley, New Hampshire, September 24, 1991; and conversation with O'Connell, January 27, 1996. Note that, unlike the California example of an installment sale cited in the case study on the Big Sur Land Trust, many local governments across the country, depending on state law, are able to undertake binding multiyear obligations. The interest paid by local governments is considered tax-exempt under the federal tax code, because it is interest paid by a municipality for a governmental purpose.

5. Telephone conversation of Elizabeth Watson with Marty Zeller, Conservation Partners, Denver, Colorado, January 26, 1996.

6. Telephone conversation of Elizabeth Watson with Michael Clarke, Natural Lands Trust, January 2 and 27, 1996.

7. Telephone conversation of Elizabeth Watson with Marty Zeller, Conservation Partners, Denver, Colorado, January 26, 1996.

8. Susan H. Duncan, "It Worked! The Story behind a Limited Partnership," *Exchange* (journal of the Land Trust Alliance), vol. 3, no. 4, Winter 1985.

9. Ira Stern, "The Rochester Creek Gorge: A New Land Trust's First Limited Development Project," *Exchange* (journal of the Land Trust Alliance), vol. 7, no. 4, Fall 1988, pp. 6–8.

10. Judith Evans, "Co-Housing, a Neighborly Thing to Do," *Washington Post,* January 27, 1996, Sec. E, pp. 1–4.

11. Telephone conversation of Elizabeth Watson with Marty Zeller, Conservation Partners, Denver, Colorado, January 26, 1996.

12. Colorado Heritage Area Partnership Project, "Heritage and Change in Colorado: U.S. Landscape Preservation and Heritage Area Programs," interim report of September 7, 1995, pp. 48–49 (available from CHAPP, 832 Emerson Street, Denver, Colo. 80218).

13. Telephone conversation of Elizabeth Watson with Randi S. Lemmon, former director of the Housatonic Valley Association, November 1986.

14. Telephone conversation of Elizabeth Watson with Tom Kerr, Wildlands Conservancy, December 28, 1995, and January 26, 1996.

15. Telephone conversation of Elizabeth Watson with G. Sage Lyons, Coastal Land Trust, December 28, 1995, and January 26, 1996.

16. For an excellent and more general discussion of this issue, see Michael G. Clarke, "Community Land Stew-

ardship: A Future Direction for Land Trusts," *Exchange* (journal of the Land Trust Alliance), vol. 11, no. 2, Spring 1992, pp. 1–9.

17. Timothy O. Traver, "Encouraging Open Space Planning, A Land Trust Helps Local Communities," *Exchange* (journal of the Land Trust Alliance), vol. 9, no. 1, Winter 1990, pp. 16–17.

18. Telephone conversation of Elizabeth Watson with Karen Edgecombe, general counsel to Plum Point Environmental Land Trust, January 3, 1996.

19. Jennie Gerard, Trust for Public Land, correspondence with Elizabeth Watson, July 1995.

20. Jon Roush, "Land Trusts and Property Rights," *Exchange* (journal of the Land Trust Alliance), vol. 11, no. 4, Fall 1992, p. 22.

CHAPTER 6: ECONOMIC DEVELOPMENT AND RURAL CONSERVATION

1. Nancy Lindroth, McCormick County Chamber of Commerce, to Shelley Mastran, April 6, 1995.

2. "This Chamber Means Commerce," promotional letter from Pontchatoula Chamber of Commerce, undated.

3. Donovan D. Rypkema, *The Economics of Historic Preservation* (Washington, D.C.: National Trust for Historic Preservation, 1994), p. 25.

4. Telephone conversation of Shelley Mastran with Jill Henderson, November 6, 1995.

5. Telephone conversation of Shelley Mastran with Bill Steiner, August 31, 1995.

6. Telephone conversation of Shelley Mastran with Craig Smith, September 19, 1995.

7. Data collected by the National Trust's Heritage Tourism Program, unpublished paper, 1994.

8. Telephone conversation of Shelley Mastran with Dr. Tom Lumsden, March 7, 1995.

9. Telephone conversation of Shelley Mastran with Barry Benepe, November 15, 1995.

10. "Farmers Turn to Lucrative Boutique Crops," *Washington Post*, November 24, 1990.

11. Patrick Long, Jo Clark, and Derek Liston, *Win, Lose or Draw?* (Washington, D.C.: Aspen Institute), p. 22.

12. Anita Lee, "Mississippi Stakes All on Riverboat Gambling," *Planning*, December 1993, p. 10.

13. "Casinos Deal Poor Mississippi County a Winning Hand," *Washington Post*, April 8, 1995.

14. Long, Clark, and Liston, *Win, Lose or Draw?* p. 51.

15. Robert Goodman, *Legalized Gambling as a Strategy for Economic Development* (Northampton, Mass.: United States Gambling Study, 1994), p. 51.

16. Mary Warren Miller, "Gambling Doesn't Pay in Historic Natchez," *Historic Preservation Forum*, Summer 1995, p. 45.

17. Mary Warren Miller, telephone conversation with Shelley Mastran, March 14, 1995.

18. Betty Ann Beierle, "Gambling Impacts," National Trust for Historic Preservation internal paper on the impacts of gambling in Black Hawk, 1994.

19. "Local Partners Invest Over $130 Million to Meet Heritage Corridor Goals Since 1984," *Canal Currents*, Spring 1993, p. 1.

CHAPTER 8: COMMUNITY EDUCATION AND SUPPORT

1. Cec Vogt, executive director of the Yakima River Greeway Foundation, to Shelley Mastran, August 1995.

2. Phoebe L. Hopkins, speech to the National Trust for Historic Preservation, Louisville, Kentucky, October 1982.

3. Stephen F. Christy, "Why Public Access?" in *Exchange* (journal of the Land Trust Alliance), vol. 8, no. 4, Fall 1989, p. 18.

4. A Yakima River Greenway Foundation board-member quoted in "A Brief Historical Synopsis of the Yakima River Regional Greenway" (undated), p. 4.

5. Telephone conversation of Samuel Stokes with Constance Chamberlin, June 1986.

CONCLUSION: PUTTING IT ALL TOGETHER

1. As quoted and analyzed in Charles McLaughlin, "Aldo Leopold's Land Ethic, 1887–1987," *Iowa Natural Heritage,* Winter 1987, p. 4.

Notes to Case Studies

2.1. Visits by Elizabeth Watson, 1980–84 and 1987–89; telephone conversations with Hilda S. Fisher, Phoebe L. Hopkins, Ann Orth (Berks County Conservancy), and Gilbert Malone, Esq. (township attorney for agricultural zoning), November–December 1995, January–February 1996. First quotation from Phoebe L. Hopkins from letter to Watson, October 1987; all other quotations from other conversations and correspondence with Watson. Updated information on agricultural security area provided by the Bureau of Farmland Protection, Pennsylvania Department of Agriculture, December 1995.

2.2. Adapted from Art Roche, "Heritage Trail," *Iowa Natural Heritage,* Fall 1986, pp. 7–9; Pat Nunnally, "Iowa's Heritage Trail," *American Land Forum,* March–April 1987, pp. 23–27; telephone conversations of Elizabeth Watson with Doug Cheever, 1988, and Rebecca Brown with Doug Cheever, November 1995. A more detailed telling of Dubuque's story is in Charles E. Little, *Greenways for America* (Baltimore: Johns Hopkins University Press, 1990).

2.3. Telephone conversations and correspondence of Elizabeth Watson with Mikki Sager, Page Crutcher, and Matt Sexton (The Conservation Fund), November 1995–February 1996; visit and interviews of Watson with J. D. Brickhouse, John Dorff (Eckerd Family Youth Alternatives, Inc.), Mavis Hill, Feather Phillips, and Sidney H. Shearin (Pettigrew State Park), January 18–19, 1996, and telephone conversations and correspondence with Brickhouse, Hill, and Phillips, February 1996. Tyrrell County's 1988 plan is entitled "Moving toward the Future Together: Tyrrell County and the Town of Columbia, A Guide for the Redevelopment and Revitalization of the Waterfront, Columbia, North Carolina"; quote from pp. 20–21. Tyrrell County's 1993 plan is entitled "Eco-Tourism in Tyrrell County: Opportunities, Constraints, and Ideas for Action."

2.4. Telephone conversations of Samuel Stokes with Frederic L. McLaughlin, 1986.

2.5. Adapted from Randi S. Lemmon, "Land Conservation via Mediation Planning," *Land Trusts' Exchange* (journal of the Land Trust Alliance), Summer 1985, pp. 8–9, and telephone conversation of John Meisel with Lynn Werner, October 1995.

3.1. Visits by Samuel Stokes, 1980–93; telephone conversations of Shelley Mastran with Dorothy Riester and Faith Knapp, 1995.

3.2. Conversations of Shelley Mastran with Bruce D. Jensen, Terri Myers, and Doris Voltin, 1995–96; correspondence of Mastran with Terri Myers, 1995; National Register nomination of Westphalia Rural Historic District.

3.3. Based in part on Terry Ryan LeVeque and James F. Palmer, *Cazenovia's Visual Resource* (Cazenovia, N.Y.: Town of Cazenovia, 1983); visits by Samuel Stokes, 1980–

85; conversation of Shelley Mastran with Dorothy Riester and Faith Knapp, 1995.

4.1. John Hart, *Farming on the Edge: Saving Family Farms in Marin County, California* (Berkeley: University of California Press, 1991); telephone conversation of Elizabeth Watson with Robert Berner, February 7, 1996; written materials provided by MALT, including its case statement, "Marin Farmland at Risk," December 1995. The statement that 54 percent of land trusts have protected farms comes from Land Trust Alliance, *National Directory of Conservation Land Trusts* (Washington, D.C.: LTA, 1995), p. vi.

4.2. Visit by Samuel Stokes, 1985; telephone conversation of Elizabeth Watson with Marlene Conaway, 1986; telephone conversations of John Meisel with Rupert Friday, November 1995; telephone conversation of Watson with Bill Powel, Carroll County Agricultural Land Preservation Program, September 6, 1996.

4.3. Telephone conversations and correspondence of Elizabeth Watson with James E. Miller, January–February 1996; telephone conversations with Marsha Oats (Hopkins and Associates), January 12, 1996; and with John Linn Hopkins (Hopkins and Associates), January 13, 1996.

5.1. Telephone conversations of John Meisel with Linda Mead and Jeff Marshall, November–December 1995 and January 1996; printed materials supplied by the Heritage Conservancy.

5.2. Visits by Elizabeth Watson and Samuel Stokes, 1984–85.

5.3. Visit by J. Timothy Keller, 1984.

5.4. Telephone conversations of Elizabeth Watson with William H. Schmidt, Vermont Land Trust, 1986.

5.5. Telephone conversation of Elizabeth Watson with Carolie Evans, 1986.

5.6. Telephone conversations of Elizabeth Watson with William H. Schmidt, 1986; William H. Schmidt, "Everyone Wins: More Saved than a Farm," *Journal for Constructive Change,* Spring 1984, pp. 23ff.; 1988 Vermont appeal letter; and telephone conversation of Rebecca Brown with Sherry Staples, Vermont Land Trust, November 22, 1995.

5.7. Visits by Elizabeth Watson, 1985–86; telephone conversations of Watson with Brian Steen, 1995, and Zad Leavy, 1996; brochures supplied by BSLT. Quotation in first paragraph from Wendy Grissim Brokaw, "Homegrown Preservation," *Monterey Life,* April 1982, p. 34.

6.1. Telephone conversations of Shelley Mastran with Connie Meek and Thom Guzman, 1995; "Bonaparte Cited for Ambition," *The Hawk Eye,* June 2, 1989, p. 1A; Michael T. Gunn, "Bonaparte, Iowa: Rebirth of a Small Town," *Main Street News,* no. 62, November 1990, pp. 1–4.

6.2. Telephone conversations of Shelley Mastran with Jimmy Neil Smith, Kimberly Sells, Sue Henley, and William E. Kennedy, all of Joneborough, Tennessee, 1995.

6.3. Telephone conversations of Shelley Mastran with Tina Lewis and Myles C. Rademan of Park City, Utah, and Lisbeth Henning, director of Utah Heritage Foundation, Salt Lake City, 1995.

6.4. Telephone conversations of Shelley Mastran with Mark S. Wolfe and Betty Ann Beierle, 1995; Patrick Long, Jo Clark, and Derek Liston, *Win, Lose, or Draw* (Washington, D.C.: Aspen Institute, 1994).

6.5. Visit by Shelley Mastran, 1993; telephone conversations of Shelley Mastran with James Davis and Mary Humstone, 1995.

7.1. Michael Staub, "We'll Never Quit It!" *Southern Exposure,* January-February, 1983, pp. 42–52 (Wilson quotation in third paragraph); telephone conversation of Shelley Mastran with Sheila Wilson, 1995 (quotation in seventh paragraph); telephone conversation of Samuel Stokes with Ben Drake, 1986 (quotation in last paragraph).

7.2. Telephone conversations of Samuel Stokes with Bill Thomas and Kathleen A. Blaha, 1985; telephone conversations of Shelley Mastran with Bill Thomas and Stuart Rabb, 1995.

7.3. Telephone conversations of Samuel Stokes with Mort Mather, 1985–87; telephone conversations of Shelley Mastran with Mort Mather and Vicki Adams, 1995.

7.4. Telephone conversations of Samuel Stokes with Gary Werner, 1985–87; telephone conversations and visit of Shelley Mastran with Gary Werner, 1995; conversation of Mastran with Kathy Bero, January 1996.

7.5. Telephone conversations of Shelley Mastran with Kathy Mitchell and Susan Van Wagoner, 1994–95; visit of Mastran with Kathy Mitchell, 1995; *Snickersville Turnpike: A Proposal for Restoration of a Rural Historic Road,* October 1994.

7.6. Telephone conversations of Shelley Mastran with DeWayne Anderson and Fred Delk, 1995.

8.1. Telephone conversations of Samuel Stokes with Marc Smiley, 1985–87; telephone conversations of Shelley Mastran with Cec Vogt, 1995.

8.2. Telephone conversations of Samuel Stokes with Barbara Stagg, 1985–87; telephone conversations of John Meisel with Barbara Stagg, November 1995; Benita J. Howell, "Heritage Tourism and Community Development: Lessons from Historic Rugby," *Tennessee's Business,* vol. 6, no. 1, 1995, pp. 37–44.

8.3. Visits of Genevieve P. Keller, J. Timothy Keller, and Samuel Stokes, 1980–87; telephone conversations of Shelley Mastran with Linda Cox, 1995.

Notes to Sidebars

1.1. Questions are from a speech by Alan Gussow; conveyed to authors by letter, May 6, 1986.

1.2. Real Estate Research Corporation, *The Costs of Sprawl.* (Washington, D.C.: Government Printing Office, 1974); American Farmland Trust, *Is Farmland Protection a Community Investment? How to Conduct a Cost of Community Services Study* (Northampton, Mass.: AFT, 1993). Culpeper study from Arthur B. Larson and Tamara A. Vance, "Fiscal Impacts of Residential Development in Culpeper County, Virginia," Warrenton, Va.: Piedmont Environmental Council, February 1988.

1.4. Information in part from Conservation Foundation, *State of the Environment 1982* (Washington, D.C.: CF, 1982), p. 109; EPA, "Memorandum from Acting Director, Office of Underground Storage Tanks," May 22, 1995.

2.1. Adapted from Preservation Pennsylvania, *Crisis Handbook: A Guide to Community Action* (Lancaster: Preservation Pennsylvania, n.d.).

2.6. Information in part from "Legal Considerations in Establishing a Historic Preservation Organization," (National Trust for Historic Preservation, *Information Series* no. 2114).

2.8. Information about the Silos and Smokestacks youth corps program comes from a telephone conversation by Shelley Mastran with Tom Gallaher, January 1996.

2.10. Adapted from *Crisis Handbook: A Guide to Community Action* (see note 2.1).

2.11. Lucy Moore, "The Democratic Art of Involving the Public," *Common Ground,* vol. 5, no. 5, July–August 1994, p. 2 (editorial).

2.12. Dennis Collins telephone conversation with Elizabeth Watson. Second quotation comes from Joan Flanagan, *The Successful Volunteer Organization: Getting Started and Getting Results in Nonprofit, Charitable, Grass Roots, and Community Groups* (Chicago, Ill.: Contemporary Books, 1981), pp. 271–72.

3.2. Information from Town of Cazenovia, N.Y., *Land Use Guide: A Report of the Cazenovia Community Resources Project* (Cazenovia: Town of Cazenovia, 1984), pp. 47–48.

3.7. *Code of Federal Regulations* (Washington, D.C.: Government Printing Office), vol. 36, pt. 60.

4.1. This list taken from unpublished manuscript. The questions have now been published in Randall Arendt, *Conservation Design for Subdivisions: A Practical Guide to Creating Open Space Networks* (Washington, D.C.: Island Press, 1996), p. 54.

4.5. Christopher J. Duerksen and Richard J. Roddewig, *Takings Law in Plain English* (Washington, D.C.: American Resources Information Network, 1994), esp. pp. 7, 23–26, and 41–43; Ann Louise Strong, Daniel R. Mandelker, and Eric Damian Kelly, "Property Rights and Takings," *Journal of the American Planning Association,* vol. 62, no. 1, pp. 5–16; Judith M. LaBelle, "Takings Law in Light of *Lucas v. South Carolina Coastal Council,*" *Pace Environmental Law Review,* vol. 10, no. 1, Fall 1992, pp. 73–84; Judith M. LaBelle, "The Legal Underpinnings of the Property Rights Movement," *Exchange* (journal of the Land Trust Alliance), vol. 13, no. 1, Winter 1994, pp. 4–6; and a telephone conversation with Judith M. LaBelle, the Countryside Institute, February 1996.

A recommended short discussion of the property rights "wise use" movement is Philip D. Brick, "Determined Opposition: The Wise Use Movement Challenges Environmentalism," *Environment,* vol. 37, no. 8, October 1995, pp. 17–30, 36–42. Other citations on property rights may be found in Suggested Reading for Chapter 1. The remark by the zoning administrator is from a telephone conversation of Elizabeth Watson with Jason Cherry, September 1987. Quotes of W. Tayloe Murphy, Jr., are taken from a speech to the Virginia chapter of the American Society of Landscape Architects, April 1995. For a discussion of the public trust doctrine grounded in a review of "public rights in ecological integrity," see Jerry Mitchell, "Ecological Integrity as a Public Right," *Planning and Law Division Newsletter* (of American Planning Association), April 1994, pp. 1, 5–7. Humbach sets forth his thesis in "Law and a New Land Ethic," *Exchange* (journal of the Land Trust Alliance), vol. 9, no. 4, Fall 1990, pp. 13–15, 24; the quote is from p. 15.

4.8. Adapted from Herbert H. Smith, *The Citizen's Guide to Zoning* (Chicago: American Planning Association, 1993), pp. 148–49.

4.9. Kelleann Foster, "Activating Ordinances: A Multimedia Prototype Aids Community Planning," *Landscape Architecture,* vol. 85, no. 10, October 1995, p. 34, and communication with Elizabeth Watson, September 4, 1996.

4.14. Information from National Park Service (NPS) and National Conference of State Historic Preservation Officers (prep. Carole Zellie; ed. Richard L. Kronick), *Preserving Your Community's Heritage through the Certified Local Government Program* (Washington. D.C.: U.S. Department of the Interior, NPS, 1995).

4.16. First quotation from Judith Getzels and Charles Thurow, eds., *Rural and Small Town Planning* (Chicago: American Planning Association, undated), p. 55. Description of Delta County, Michigan, ordinance is from John C. Maurer (Society of American Foresters, Working Group on Land-Use Planning and Design), "Land Use Planning," *Journal of American Forestry,* vol. 80, September 1982, pp. 579–602. Information on mining can be found in William J. Curry III and Cyril A. Fox, Jr., *A Role for Local Governments in Controlling Strip Mining Activities* (Pittsburgh: Western Pennsylvania Conservancy, 1978). The description of the Massachusetts River Protection Act and local programs is found in Joan Channing Kimball, *Riverways Community Guide: Strategies for Drafting and Passing Local River Protection Bylaws* (Boston: Massachusetts Riverways Program, Department of Fisheries, Wildlife and Environmental Law Enforcement, 1993). The description of the Rockingham County, Virginia, ordinance includes information supplied by Rhonda G. Henderson, Department of Planning and Zoning (letter of December 15, 1995) and Harold W. Roller, Virginia Cooperative Extension (letter of December 19, 1995).

5.3. Valley Conservation Council brochure on ripar-

ian easements; "Riparian Easement Placed on Middle River Tract," *Vision* (newsletter of the Valley Conservation Council), vol. 4, no. 3, Summer 1993, pp. 1–2; and telephone conversation of Rebecca Brown with Faye Cooper, Valley Conservation Council, December 1995.

5.4. Telephone conversation of Elizabeth Watson with Tom Duffus, January 1996.

5.5. Telephone conversations of John Meisel with Dawn Darbey, Nantucket Land Bank Commission, December 1995; Joseph Rosenblum, "Land Banking," National Council for Urban Economic Development Information Service, ed. Juyne K. Linger, report no. 15, June 1978.

5.6. Guidelines reprinted with permission from a policy statement of the San Juan Preservation Trust.

5.7. New Hampshire Charitable Fund information from Melinda Marble, *Social Investment and Community Foundations* (Washington, D.C.: Council on Foundations, 1988), p. 19. Sudbury Valley example from Piton Foundation, with Frances Brody and John Weiser, *Program-Related Investment Primer,* rev. ed. (Washington, D.C.: Council on Foundations, 1993), p. 63, and telephone conversation of Elizabeth Watson with Stephen T. Johnson, Sudbury Valley Trustees, January 26, 1996. Tennessee Gorge example from Graham Hawks, "Capitalizing on a Big Project," *Exchange* (journal of the Land Trust Alliance), vol. 9, no. 1, Winter 1990, p. 7 [reprinted from *The Tennessee Conservationist*]; and conversation of Shelley Mastran with Jim Brown, Tennessee River Gorge Trust, January 22, 1996. Evans Ranch example from conversations and visit of Elizabeth Watson with Marty Zeller, then of Colorado Open Lands, 1985, and updated in conversation with Zeller, January 26, 1995. Overall guidance for this sidebar was provided by Elizabeth Morton, November and December 1995, researcher with the Project on Social Investing, Massachusetts Institute of Technology.

5.8. Telephone conversation of Elizabeth Watson with Luther Propst, Sonoran Institute, December 1995; correspondence from Propst of January 3, 1996; and printed materials supplied by the institute. Southern Utah example from "Small Tracts," *Common Ground,* vol. 6, no. 6, September–October 1995, p. 4.

5.9. "IRAs and CRTs: A Superb Tax Saving Idea!," by Robin K. Jepsen, and "Charity Begins at Home," both in *Big Sur Land Trust News,* Summer–Fall 1995, p. 2; conversation and correspondence with Zad Leavy, general counsel to the Big Sur Land Trust, January–February 1996.

5.10. Institute for Community Economics, *Profiles of Community Land Trusts* (Springfield, Mass.: ICE, January 1993), pp. 15–20; telephone conversations of Elizabeth Watson with Wendy Scott, Wisconsin Farmland Conservancy, September 6 and 9, 1996; telephone conversation of Watson with Tom Quinn, Wisconsin Farmland Conservancy, September 9, 1996, and correspondence of September 12, 1996.

5.11. Joel Russell, "The Opportunities and Risks of Developer Easements," *Exchange* (journal of the Land Trust Alliance), vol. 12, no. 1, Winter 1993, pp. 7, 8. The quote from Tom Saunders is from a telephone conversation with John Meisel, January 1996. The planning issue raised by Saunders is addressed in a recent publication by Randall Arendt, *Conservation Design for Subdivisions: A Practical Guide to Creating Open Space Networks* (Washington, D.C.: Island Press, 1996).

5.12. Portions of this list were adapted with the permission and assistance of Mark C. Ackelson, Iowa Natural Heritage Foundation, from his speech in Monterey, Calif., February 1987.

6.4. University of Minnesota, Minnesota Extension Service Tourism Center, *A Training Guide for Rural Tourism Development* (St. Paul: Distribution Center, U of M), "Appearance," pp. 4–5.

6.5. National Main Street Center, *Miracle on Main Street* (Washington, D.C.: National Trust for Historic Preservation, n.d.).

6.6. Heritage Tourism Program, National Trust for Historic Preservation, *Getting Started: How to Succeed in Heritage Tourism* (Washington, D.C.: NTHP, n.d.).

6.8. Sarah L. Richardson, *Colorado Community Tourism Action Guide,* 1991; reprinted in University of Minnesota, *Training Guide* (see note 6.4).

7.5. Adapted in part from Phyllis Myers, "The Myers Index," *GreenSense: Financing Parks and Conservation,* vol. 1, no. 3, Autumn 1995, pp. 3–4.

8.2. Adapted from Jack E. Boucher, *Suggestions for Producing Publishable Photographs* (Washington, D.C.: Preservation Press, 1978).

8.3. Richard Beamish, *Getting the Word Out in the Fight to Save the Earth,* (Baltimore: Johns Hopkins University Press, 1995), pp. 27–28.

8.4. With thanks to Pat Munoz, "Starting a Major Donor Program," *River Network's River Fundraising Alert,* vol. 2, no. 1, Spring 1995, p. 2.

Conclusion. The inspiration for this list came from a number of sources. Special thanks are due to the following: Michael G. Clarke of the Natural Lands Trust, especially for his article "Community Land Stewardship: A Future Direction for Land Trusts," *Exchange* (journal of the Land Trust Alliance), vol. 11, no. 2, Spring 1992, pp. 1–9; and Randall Arendt, especially for sharing his manuscript for *Conservation Design for Subdivisions: A Practical Guide to Creating Open Space Networks* (Washington, D.C.: Island Press, 1996). Michael Clarke and Judith M. LaBelle, Esq., of the Countryside Institute and Glynwood Center, Cold Spring, New York, provided stimulating discussion of these points with Elizabeth Watson.

References and Suggested Reading

There are numerous publications on the topics discussed in this book. We have chosen to list here those that are of greatest interest to conservation leaders working at the local level. For the most part, we have chosen publications that are focused specifically on the subjects treated in the book. In most cases, we have listed only one of an author's publications, either the most recent or an introductory version.

Several organizations and publishers—the American Planning Association, the Lincoln Institute of Land Policy, the Land Trust Alliance, the National Trust for Historic Preservation, the Johns Hopkins University Press, and Island Press, for instance—publish works of interest to conservationists. We suggest you write to them for a current listing.

Publications by nonprofit organizations and government agencies may be ordered from those organizations. Their addresses will be found either as part of the entry or in Sources of Assistance in Appendix 2.

CHAPTER 1: RURAL CONCERNS

Alexander, Susan. 1993. *Clean Water in Your Watershed: A Citizen's Guide to Watershed Protection.* Washington, D.C.: Terrene Institute. 90 pp.

A practical guide to water source protection with worksheets and a list of agencies to contact. Shows how to identify problems and the tools to solve them.

American Farmland Trust (AFT). 1986. *Density-Related Public Costs.* Washington, D.C.: AFT. 44 pp.

Sets forth a methodology for analysis of the fiscal impacts of growth on local government revenues and costs, using Loudoun County, Virginia, as a model.

———. 1990. *Saving the Farm: A Handbook for Conserving Agricultural Land.* Washington, D.C.: AFT. 150 pp.

Comprehensive notebook on farmland conservation programs and zoning techniques to save agricultural land. Featuring model policies and programs from California, the book is applicable across the country.

———. 1992. *Does Farmland Protection Pay? The Cost of Community Services in Three Massachusetts Towns.* Lancaster, Mass.: Massachusetts Department of Food and Agriculture. 38 pp.

Reports the results of cost of services (COS) studies in three Massachusetts towns, showing that residential development costs more in services than it pays in taxes; whereas, privately owned farm and open land, although raising less gross income than developed land, costs little in services and produces, therefore, a tax-base surplus.

———. 1993. *Is Farmland Protection a Community Investment? How to Do a Cost of Community Services Study.* Northampton, Mass.: AFT. 24 pp.

Provides a step-by-step methodology for local communities to use in conducting a cost of community service study. Includes sample tables for displaying the data collected.

Beatley, Timothy, David J. Brower, and Anna K. Schwab. 1994. *An Introduction to Coastal Zone Management.* Covelo, Calif.: Island Press. 200 pp.

A comprehensive introduction to coastal zone management which reviews current federal, state, and local programs. Focuses on ecology, population trends, and policy issues.

Brick, Philip D., and R. McGreggor Cawley, eds. 1996. *A Wolf in the Garden: The Land Rights Movement and the New Environmental Debate.* Lanham, Md.: Rowman Littlefield. 323 pp.

Collection of essays by commentators on property rights, incorporating a wide range of opinion. Closing essay attempts to reconcile differing points of view through an emphasis on the importance of place.

Carlson, Daniel, Lisa Wormser, and Cy Ulberg. 1995. *At Road's End: Transportation and Land Use Choices for Communities.* Covelo, Calif.: Island Press. 288 pp.

A guide to transportation planning which takes into account multiple ways of providing mobility and enhanced transportation corridors.

Council on Environmental Quality (CEQ). *Environmental Quality.* Washington, D.C.: CEQ, annual publication.

Assesses the state of the environment and summarizes recent federal environmental legislation and regulations. Highlights different topics each year.

Deetz, James. 1977. *In Small Things Forgotten.* Garden City, N.Y.: Anchor Press. 184 pp.

A brief and readable introduction to the archeology of early American life. Introductory chapter explains what archeology is and how it works to provide understanding of past cultures. Illustrates how archeological evidence—construction materials, utensils, grave markers, and the like—reveals the life of early Americans. An excellent introduction to archeology for the layperson.

Diamond, Henry L., and Patrick F. Noonan. 1996. *Land Use in America.* Washington, D.C.: Island Press. 340 pp.

Follow-up to an examination of the status of local, state, and federal land use policy since William Reilly's *The Use of Land* (1972). Concludes that, in spite of considerable federal environmental legislation, little has changed to rationalize land use policy. Offers a ten-point agenda for the future. Includes essays contributed by other leading environmentalists.

Duerksen, Christopher J., and Richard J. Roddewig. 1994. *Takings Law in Plain English.* Washington, D.C.: American Resources Information Network. 45 pp.

Straightforward primer for the layperson on takings law and how it has been applied. Provides a history of court interpretations of the law and examples of its use. Contains a useful section on real estate economics and takings, as well as a practical guide to responding to the takings issue at the local level.

Dwight, Pamela, ed. 1993. *Landmark Yellow Pages.* Washington, D.C.: Preservation Press. 395 pp.

Encyclopedia of information about historic preservation. Includes discussions of preservation issues, from adaptive use to local preservation ordinances to education; lists preservation contractors and consultants by specialty; and provides names and addresses of public and nonprofit preservation agencies and organizations.

Environmental Law Institute. *National Wetlands Newsletter.* Washington, D.C. Bimonthly publication.

Discusses wetland issues; describes federal, state, and local legislation; summarizes litigation; and reviews publications on wetlands.

Flink, Charles A., and Robert M. Searns, edited by Loring LaB. Schwarz, 1993. *Greenways: A Guide to Planning, Design, and Development.* Washington, D.C.: Island Press. 375 pp.

Contains information on the myriad practicalities of developing greenways.

Hart, John. 1991. *Farming on the Edge: Saving Family Farms in Marin County, California.* Berkeley: University of California Press. 174 pp.

Well-illustrated story of how Marin County, California, preserved family farming. Describes the various techniques used to keep agriculture strong against powerful development pressures. Features profiles of local citizens and activists, providing a real-life perspective.

Henry, Susan L. 1993. *Protecting Archeological Sites on Private Lands.* Washington, D.C.: U.S. Department of the Interior, National Park Service. 133 pp.

Provides informative and easy-to-read discussion of both regulatory and nonregulatory strategies to protect archeological sites on private lands. Includes sections on how to obtain archeological expertise, working with developers, and sources of financial assistance.

Hiss, Tony. 1990. *The Experience of Place.* New York: Alfred A. Knopf. 233 pp.

An introduction to cultural geography for the layperson. Advocates looking at the natural and built environments with a fresh eye. Discusses both cities and the countryside with an emphasis on integration, regionalism, and comprehensive planning.

Housing Assistance Council (HAC). 1994. *Taking Stock of Rural Poverty and Housing for the 1990s.* Washington, D.C.: HAC. 190 pp.

Describes trends in poverty, housing, public assistance, and employment. Includes census data and case studies for selected communities.

Hylton, Thomas. 1995. *Save Our Land, Save Our Towns.* Harrisburg, Pa.: RB Books. 127 pp.

Well-written and beautifully illustrated discussion of patterns of growth in Pennsylvania. Argues against sprawl and for traditional town development. Offers "Ten Rules for a Quality Community."

Jackson, John Brinckerhoff. 1994. *A Sense of Place, A Sense of Time.* New Haven: Yale University Press. 212 pp.

Essays about the author's efforts to understand and define the contemporary American landscape, focusing largely on the role of the road in the landscape. The essays also deal with mobile homes, churches, trees, parks, gardens, the southwestern pueblo dwellings, and the idea of working at home.

————. 1984. *Discovering the Vernacular Landscape.* New Haven: Yale University Press. 165 pp.

A provocative series of essays by the founder of *Landscape* magazine which explore various aspects of the everyday landscape in America, from mobile homes to parks to country towns. Jackson attempts to foster an understanding and appreciation of the more commonplace aspects of the landscape.

Kemmis, Daniel. 1990. *Community and the Politics of Place.* Norman: University of Oklahoma Press. 150 pp.

A series of highly readable, linked essays concerned with the revitalization of "community." Identifies elements that can serve to revive the language of community and public life. Incorporates important observations on life in the rural West but is applicable everywhere.

Kuntzler, James Howard. 1993. *The Geography of Nowhere.* New York: Simon and Schuster. 303 pp.

Critique of contemporary landscape created by automobile dependence: highway-oriented strip centers, shopping malls, and residential suburbs. Advocates neotraditional town planning, clustered development, and land preservation.

Lapping, Mark B., Thomas L. Daniels, and John W. Keller. 1989. *Rural Planning and Development in the United States.* New York: Guilford Press. 342 pp.

Explores the role of agriculture, forestry, recreation, fisheries, and mining in rural development. Focuses on the conservation of natural areas, the operation of land markets, and the role of environmental law in planning and development.

Lee, Antoinette J. 1992. *Past Meets Future.* Washington, D.C.: Preservation Press. 288 pp.

A comprehensive series of essays on the historic preservation movement: past, present, and future. Discusses the accomplishments of historic preservation and the challenges ahead.

Legator, Marvin, and Sabrina Strawn, eds. 1993. *Chemical Alert!: A Community Action Handbook.* Austin: University of Texas Press. 238 pp.

Practical guide for communities in how to join together to fight health threats from toxic substances. Explains how to gather information, identify health hazards, and build a data base on health hazards. Also offers suggestions on how to organize the community and design questionnaires.

Little, Charles, E. 1990. *Greenways for America.* Baltimore: Johns Hopkins University Press. 288 pp.

A comprehensive account of the greenways movement. Inspirational stories describe dozens of greenway projects, both public and private, that have improved environmental quality, invigorated local economies, and preserved outdoor space.

Maddex, Diane, ed. 1985. *All about Old Buildings: The Whole Preservation Catalog.* Washington, D.C.: National Trust for Historic Preservation. 433 pp.

A comprehensive and heavily illustrated sourcebook on historic preservation and architectural history. Contains lists of organizations, numerous quotations, extensive bibliographies, and definitions. Out of print, but there is no substitute; it is available in libraries, and copies can still be found in some specialty bookstores.

McComas, Steve. 1994. *Lake Smarts: The First Lake Maintenance Handbook—A Do-It-Yourself Guide to Solving Lake Problems.* Washington, D.C.: Terrene Institute. 228 pp.

Contains easy and affordable projects to help clean up and maintain lakes and ponds.

Meinig, D. W., ed. 1979. *The Interpretation of Ordinary Landscapes: Geographical Essays.* New York: Oxford University Press. 255 pp.

Nine provocative essays on exploring the American landscape by several of the foremost researchers of human geography and landscape history.

National Audubon Society. 1989–90. *Audubon Wildlife Report*. San Diego: Academic Press. 585 pp.

Describes the status of certain endangered species and gives information on federal and state programs to protect wildlife. This edition features the U.S. Army Corps of Engineers.

National Trust for Historic Preservation (NTHP). Information Series. Washington, D.C.: NTHP.

The following titles in this series are of particular interest: *Basic Preservation Procedures* (no. 2148), *Archeology and Historic Preservation* (no. 2186), *Using Old Fram Buildings* (no. 2146), and *Preserving Historic Bridges* (no. 2136).

Platt, Rutherford H. 1996. *Land Use and Society: Geography, Law, and Public Policy*. Washington, D.C.: Island Press. 507 pp.

Offers a well-written, geographer's perspective into a complex recounting of urban and environmental issues and the evolution of current land use policy—local, state, regional, and federal. An excellent reference that includes especially useful chapters on property rights and basic constitutional concerns in planning.

President's Council on Sustainable Development. 1996. *Sustainable America: A New Consensus for Prosperity, Opportunity, and a Healthy Environment for the Future*. Washington, D.C.: U.S. Government Printing Office. 186 pp.

The final report of the first three years of this presidential council, setting ten national goals toward sustainable development and providing indicators of progress toward each goal. Chapters develop themes related to reforming the current system of environmental management, increasing citizen awareness, strengthening communities, improving natural resources stewardship, addressing population growth, and working internationally to support sustainable development policies.

Rivers, Trails, and Conservation Assistance, National Park Service. 1995. *The Economic Benefits of Protecting Rivers, Trails, and Greenway Corridors*. 4th ed. 164 pp.

Compiles various data on the impact on property values of protecting open-space recreational and ecological corridors, as well as the expenditures in and public costs and benefits of greenways. Offers a variety of methods for communities to use in calculating and explaining the benefits of greenways.

Ryan, Karen-Lee, ed. 1993. *Trails for the Twenty-First Century: Planning, Design, and Management Manual for Multi-Use Trails*. Washington, D.C.: Island Press. 213 pp.

Sponsored by the Rails-to-Trails Conservancy, this hand-

book explores the many practicalities of developing trails.

Salant, Priscilla, and Anita J. Waller. 1995. *Guide to Rural Data*. Covelo, Calif.: Island Press. 160 pp.

Explains how to find and obtain the most current information on rural America both in printed form and electronically. Shows how data can be used to analyze social and economic change.

Sampson, R. Neil, and Dwight Hair, eds. 1990. *Natural Resources for the Twenty-first Century*. Washington, D.C.: Island Press. 349 pp.

A collection of papers presented at a conference on "Natural Resources for the Twenty-first Century" held in 1988. Part 1 assesses the current condition of renewable natural resources and on identifying factors most influential in leading to its current condition. Topics include climate, cropland, forests, rangelands, wetlands, water resources, wildlife, fisheries, and outdoor recreation. Part 2 focuses on making intelligent choices for sustaining natural resources in the future.

Small Town Institute. *Small Town*. Ellensburg, Wash. Bimonthly publication. (P.O. Box 517, Ellensburg, WA 98926.)

Covers a wide range of topics of interest to rural leaders "concerned with finding new solutions to the problems facing small towns and countryside communities."

Smardon, Richard C., James F. Palmer, and John P. Felleman, eds. 1986. *Foundations for Visual Project Analysis*. New York: John Wiley and Sons. 374 pp.

Traces history of landscape appreciation, describes the techniques for analyzing the landscape, discusses methodologies for assessing the scenic impact of new developments, and reviews laws governing scenery protection.

U.S. Department of Agriculture, Economic Research Service (ERS). 1994. *Agricultural Resources and Environmental Indicators*. Washington, D.C.: ERS. 205 pp.

Comprehensive look at land use, soil quality, water use and quality, nutrients, pesticides, crop rotation, and conservation reserve and wetlands programs. Provides data on a range of indicators, presented through maps, tables, and graphs.

CHAPTER 2: ORGANIZING A RURAL CONSERVATION PROGRAM

The literature on organizational and leadership development and dispute resolution is extensive. To stay current as it develops, watch the work of the American Planning Association, the Institute for Conservation Leadership, the Cooperative Extension Service, the Land Trust

Alliance, the National Center for Nonprofit Boards, National Institute for Dispute Resolution, the National Trust for Historic Preservation, and the River Network. All have publications that focus on improving the effectiveness of local organizations and governments and thus publish and provide training and technical assistance on subjects discussed in Chapter 2.

American Association of University Women (AAUW). 1989. *The Leader Handbook: Tested AAUW Tools and Techniques for Effective Leadership.* Washington, D.C.: AAUW. 199 pp. (2401 Virginia Avenue, N.W., Washington, DC 20037.)

Provides suggestions and skill-building exercises to help leaders learn how to plan activities, set goals, delegate authority, solve problems, and work in coalitions.

Ames, Steven, ed. 1993 *A Guide to Community Visioning.* Chicago: Planners Press. 35 pp.

This manual, developed by the Oregon chapter of the American Planning Association, suggests a four-step process: describing the community and its values, creating a trend statement, writing a community vision, and developing action agendas and priorities. Includes case studies and ideas for using graphics to stimulate the process.

Bredouw, Pam, and Robin McClelland. 1991. *A "Bottom Up" Primer: A Guide to Citizen Participation.* Olympia, Wash.: State of Washington, Department of Community Development, Growth Management Division. 23 pp. (Ninth and Columbia, Mail Stop: GH-51, P.O. Box 48300, Olympia, WA 98504.)

Short and simple, but filled with ideas for encouraging citizen participation, especially a clever list of "tools from A to Z" (advertisements to zip codes) for encouraging the collecting and sharing of information. Includes tips on forming and chairing committees and a good discussion of the role of a facilitator.

———. 1991. *Towards Managing Growth in Washington: A Guide to Community Visioning.* Olympia, Wash.: State of Washington, Department of Community Development, Growth Management Division. 31 pp. (Ninth and Columbia, Mail Stop: GH-51, P.O. Box 48300, Olympia, WA 98504.)

A useful short description of the visioning process, including detailed forms and worksheets, two sample questionnaires, and very brief sample statements for vision, goals, and work programs, and related planning commission policies.

Center for Democracy and Citizenship. 1995. *Reinventing Citizenship: The Practice of Public Work.* Minneapolis, Minn.: Minnesota Extension Service and Hubert H. Humphrey Institute of Public Affairs, University of Minnesota. 76 pp. Document no. BU-6586-S. (Center for

Democracy and Citizenship, Humphrey Institute, 301 19th Avenue South, Minneaplis, MN 55455.)

More conceptual than a handbook, this brief document reflects on the role of citizenship in the changing American society and on different approaches to problem solving. While the process of organizing as discussed here is simple guidance, the discussion of evaluation is excellent. The short bibliography offers an especially wide variety of readings.

Creighton, James L. 1992. *Involving Citizens in Community Decision Making: A Guidebook.* 2nd ed. Washington, D.C.: Program for Community Problem Solving. (915 15th Street, N.W., Suite 600, Washington, DC 20005.)

Provides detailed guidance on creating a citizen participation plan, as well as hints for using a wide array of such techniques as polling and the use of neutral third parties.

Fisher, Roger, William Ury, and Bruce Patton. 1991. *Getting to Yes: Negotiating Agreement without Giving In.* 2nd ed. Boston: Houghton Mifflin. 200 pp.

Discusses a method of "principled negotiation" which includes focusing on interests rather than positions and inventing options for mutual gain. Pointing a different direction from the classic "hard bargaining" familiar to realtors and attorneys, this handbook is recommended as companion reading to any other publications on dispute resolution.

Fulton, William. 1988. *Reaching Consensus in Land-Use Negotiations.* Chicago: American Planning Association. Planning Advisory Service Report no. 417. 13 pp.

Articulates a common set of principles for three types of negotiation: mediation, collaborative decision making, and design-based negotiation. Contains useful examples.

Gil, Efraim, Enid Lucchesi, Gilbert Tauber, and Dudley Onderdonk. 1983. *Working with Consultants.* Chicago: American Planning Association. 33 pp.

Describes how to recruit, evaluate, and contract for consulting services and how to manage a consulting project. Although written from the point of view of a public agency, it is also useful for nonprofit organizations.

Hester, Randolph T., Jr. 1990. *Community Design Primer.* Mendocino, Calif.: Ridge Times Press. 116 pp. (Community Design Primer, 2707 Mathews Street, Berkeley, CA 94702.)

Contains fifteen exercises for identifying community design concerns, encouraging public participation, and supporting community change. An excellent basic text for grassroots activists.

Jones, Sandra L. 1994. *Campaign Tips for Conservation Activists*. Ashland, N.H.: Jones Consulting. 50 pp. (4 Riverside Drive, Ashland, NH 03217.)

Although source is specific to the author's experience in New Hampshire, activists everywhere will appreciate the sage advice here. Offers many questions by way of helping the reader to analyze what is involved in environmental issue campaigns.

Kahn, Si. 1991. *Organizing: A Guide for Grassroots Leaders*. Rev. ed. Silver Spring, Md.: National Association of Social Workers. 345 pp. (NASW, 750 First Street, N.E., Suite 700, Washington, DC 20002.)

Written for organizers by a well-known union organizer, this is a thoughtful and sympathetic book, filled with practical tips and encouragement.

Kemmis, Daniel. 1990. *Community and the Politics of Place*. (See entry under Chapter 1.)

Especially for this chapter, see the chapters entitled "Stalemate" and "Barn Raising" on—among other issues—the shortcomings of public hearings, and "The Art of the Possible" on consensus and collaboration in decision making and the civic virtues of "neighborliness."

Klein, Richard D. 1990. *Everyone Wins! A Citizen's Guide to Development*. Chicago: Planners Press. 143 pp.

This lively handbook contains blunt advice, effective strategies, and a positive outlook for dealing with development proposals in anyone's neighborhood. Step-by-step methods for developing tactics and an overall strategy should be of value to any community-organizing effort, including approaches for enlisting decision makers and mobilizing public support. Useful introductory information on twenty specific development issues, from archeology to schools to zoning.

Land Trust Alliance (LTA). 1990. *Starting a Land Trust: A Guide to Forming a Land Conservation Organization*. Washington, D.C.: LTA. 175 pp.

A practical handbook for anyone starting a land trust, and a primer for new board members. Includes a discussion of land protection tools and financing.

———. 1993. *The Standards and Practices Guidebook: An Operating Manual for Land Trusts*. Washington, D.C.: LTA. 564 pp.

As the land trust field has grown, so has the movement's sense of responsibility in providing a code of conduct; this hefty manual about every aspect of land trust operations is the result. Although written for land trusts, it is useful for any nonprofit, with sixty sample documents.

A fifteen-page booklet simply listing the standards and practices is also available from LTA.

———. Various dates. *Infopaks*. Washington, D.C.: LTA.

Useful compilations of documents, book excerpts, and periodical literature; includes "Lobbying and Political Campaigns: Advancing Your Cause within Nonprofit Guidelines."

Mantell, Michael A., Stephen F. Harper, and Luther Propst. 1990. *Creating Successful Communities: A Guidebook to Growth Management Strategies*. And, *Resource Guide for Creating Successful Communities*. Washington, D.C.: Island Press. Guidebook: 232 pp. Resource guide: 208 pp.

The guidebook for *Creating Successful Communities* organizes much of its material on planning, voluntary land conservation, legal considerations, and state and federal programs by subject: agricultural land, rivers and wetlands, historic and cultural resources, aesthetic resources, and open space resources. All chapters contain multiple profiles of communities whose work is exemplary. The companion resource guide includes chapters on starting and managing a nonprofit corporation and developing an effective local program; reproduces local ordinances dealing with the same resource list, actual articles of incorporation for two organizations, and easements.

Moore, Allen B. and James A. Feldt. 1993. *Facilitating Community and Decision-making Groups*. Melbourne, Fla.: Krieger Publishing. 168 pp.

Provides understanding about the dynamics of and practical suggestions for conducting community meetings.

Mulford, Charles L., and Gerald E. Klonglan. Undated. *Creating Coordination among Organizations*. Ames: Iowa State University Extension. 26 pp.

Aimed largely at cooperation among local governments, this booklet can help organizations of all kinds analyze their reasons for cooperation and their chances for success. Includes a list of barriers to coordination.

National Center for Nonprofit Boards (NCNB). Various dates. *Nonprofit Governance Series* and *Board Bookshelf*. Washington, D.C.: NCNB.

The governance series offers booklets on responsibilities of nonprofit boards, role of the chief executive and the chair, the board's role in fund raising and strategic planning, effective meetings and retreats, and much more. The "bookshelf" is a discounted purchase of all publications available from NCNB.

National Trust for Historic Preservation (NTHP). Information Series. Washington, D.C.: NTHP.

A number of the booklets in this series treat organizational development; although many titles may seem specific to historic preservation groups, they apply equally well to other kinds of organizations: *Cultural and Ethnic Diversity in Historic Preservation* (no. 2165), *Investing in Volunteers: A Guide to Effective Volunteer Management* (no. 2137), *Legal Considerations in Establishing a Historic Preservation Organization* (no. 2114), *Membership Development: A Guide for Nonprofit Preservation Organizations* (no. 2149), *Organizing for Change* (no. 2167), *Organizing Volunteers for Preservation Projects* (no. 2109), *Rescuing Historic Resources: How to Respond to a Preservation Emergency* (no. 2151), *A Self-Assessment Guide for Community Preservation Organizations* (no. 2145), *Steering Nonprofits: Advice for Boards and Staff* (no. 2154), *Strategic Planning for Nonprofit Organizations* (no. 2166), and *Using Professional Consultants in Preservation* (no. 2126).

O'Connell, Brian, and Ann Brown O'Connell. 1989. *Volunteers in Action*. New York: Foundation Center. 346 pp.

Essential reading for those who both lead and participate in volunteer activities. Identifies areas of service, discusses volunteer motivations, and provides cases of volunteers in action.

O'Connell, Brian. 1993. *The Board Member's Book: Making a Difference in Voluntary Organizations*. 2nd ed. New York: Foundation Center. 198 pp.

An invaluable handbook useful not only to the board members of nonprofit organizations but also to anyone involved in managing or organizing a cooperative effort, governmental as well as nonprofit. Discussions of the qualities of leaders, strategic planning, working with committees, fund raising, budgeting, and evaluation demystify these concerns in a warm, no-nonsense style. Includes an extensive list of references.

Ricard, Virginia B. 1993. *Developing Intercultural Communication Skills*. Melbourne, Fla.: Krieger Publishing. 184 pp.

Even if learning to communicate with others with different cultural backgrounds is not a top priority, the information in this book can improve anyone's communications skills. Six areas common to all cultures are highlighted: valuing, observing, listening, thinking, speaking, and gesturing.

Susskind, Lawrence, and Jeffrey Cruikshank. 1987. *Breaking the Impasse: Consensual Approaches to Resolving Public Disputes*. New York: Basic Books. 276 pp.

Discusses both unassisted negotiation and mediation, in an appealing how-to-do-it style; highly recommended for both those new to the subject and those with experience.

Thomas, Ronald L., Mary C. Means, and Margaret A. Grieve. 1988. *Taking Charge: How Communities Are Planning Their Futures*. Washington, D.C.: International City Management Association. 86 pp.

Sections entitled "Planning for Success," "Taking the Lead," "Creating a Vision vs. Producing a Plan," "Building Consensus," and "Managing for Outcomes" are written in punchy, no-nonsense language and always focus on building greater public support throughout the planning process.

CHAPTER 3: ANALYZING THE RURAL COMMUNITY

Bartis, Peter. 1990. *Folklife and Fieldwork: A Layman's Introduction to Field Techniques*. Washington, D.C.: American Folklife Center. 36 pp.

Introduction to folklife, the American Folklife Center, and techniques for documenting and presenting folk heritage. Explains what information to collect, how to interview and document, how to create a folklife archive, and how to develop programs for the public.

Buchanan, Terry. 1983. *Photographing Historic Buildings*. London: Her Majesty's Stationery Office. 108 pp. (Preservation Resource Group, Inc.: P.O. Box 1768, Rockville, MD 20849.)

Covers the techniques for both exterior and interior photographs.

Copps, David H. 1995. *Views from the Road: A Community Guide for Assessing Rural Historic Landscapes*. Washington, D.C.: Island Press. 182 pp.

A guide for communities in assessing historic landscapes viewed from rural roads. Presents a methodology for evaluating visual experiences from the road, inventorying features, and analyzing the results. Includes case studies on the Red Hills region of Georgia and Florida and the Bluegrass region of Kentucky.

Courtney, Elizabeth. 1991. *Vermont's Scenic Landscapes: A Guide for Growth and Protection*. Montpelier: Vermont Agency of Natural Resources. 80 pp. (Vermont Agency of Natural Resources, Planning Division, 103 South Main Street, Waterbury, VT 05671.)

Beautifully illustrated discussion of Vermont's landscape and how it should be protected. Sections on evaluating scenic landscapes and designing compatible development are applicable to any area of the United States.

Doble, Cheryl, and George McCulloch. Undated. *Managing Change: A Pilot Study in Rural Design and Planning*. Watertown, N.Y.: New York State Tug Hill Commission. 58 pp.

Reports on a project to enable communities along the northern shore of Oneida Lake in upstate New York to develop a vision of their future that protected community assets, met community needs, and accommodated new growth. The project delineated "character areas" and undertook a variety of exercises to identify and address design issues.

Harker, Donald F., and Elizabeth Unger Natter. 1994. *Where We Live: A Citizen's Guide to Conducting a Community Environmental Inventory*. Washington, D.C.: Island Press. 336 pp.

A workbook to help citizens organize, find information about their environment, and protect their communities from environmental threats. Contains information on examining local resource issues and facilities, with addresses of state agencies. Although it fails to include historic, scenic, or agricultural resources in the inventorying suggested, it gives extensive information on how to deal with such local environmental protection issues as toxins and water quality.

Marsh, William M. 1978. *Environmental Analysis: For Land Use and Site Planning*. New York: McGraw-Hill. 292 pp.

An excellent description of the techniques for inventorying and mapping natural resources. Specific information on slope, soils, drainage, vegetation, and floodplains.

———. 1991. *Landscape Planning: Environmental Applications*. New York: John Wiley and Sons. 340 pp.

Brings the fields of physical geography, planning, and landscape architecture together in an effort to address current environmental problems and issues. The result is an effective integration among land planning, land science, and landscape design. Topics include: landscape form and function, topography, soils, groundwater, flood hazards, shoreline processes, wetlands, and vegetation.

McAlester, Virginia, and Lee McAlester. 1984. *A Field Guide to American Houses*. Mount Vernon, N.Y.: Knopf. 525 pp. (12th ed., 1995.)

A comprehensive handbook on architectural styles. There are numerous regional and state guides as well. The State Historic Preservation Office can advise which one is best for a particular state.

McClelland, Linda Flint., J. Timothy Keller, Genevieve P. Keller, and Robert Z. Melnick. Undated. *Guidelines for Evaluating and Documenting Rural Historic Landscapes*. National Register Bulletin no. 30. Washington, D.C.: U.S. Department of the Interior, National Park Service. 33 pp.

Discusses the eleven characteristics of a rural historic landscape. Explains how to identify rural historic resources and evaluate their significance for nominations to the National Register.

McHarg, Ian L. 1969. *Design with Nature*. Garden City, N.Y.: Doubleday. 198 pp.

A pioneering work of essays and case studies that stresses the need for environmental design in harmony with the natural conditions of an area. Explains environmental inventories and the use of maps to analyze the suitability of land for development.

National Trust for Historic Preservation (NTHP). Information Series. *Introduction to Photographing Historic Properties* (no. 2142). Washington, D.C.: NTHP.

Noss, Reed F., and Allen Y. Cooperrider. 1994. *Saving Nature's Legacy: Protecting and Restoring Biodiversity*. Covelo, Calif.: Island Press. 380 pp.

A thorough introduction to the issues of land management and conservation biodiversity in the United States. Begins with the groundwork for conservation biodiversity and then presents a framework for future management.

Sargent, Frederic O., Paul Lusk, Jose Rivera, and Maria Varela. 1991. *Rural Environmental Planning for Sustainable Communities*. Washington, D.C.: Island Press. 250 pp.

A comprehensive look at rural environmental planning to determine, develop, and implement creative plans for balancing economic development and environmental protection in small communities and rural areas. Includes techniques for preserving natural, cultural, and agricultural resources and presents case studies of rural environmental plans from communities throughout the United States.

Smardon, Richard C., James F. Palmer, and John P. Felleman, eds. 1986. *Foundations for Visual Project Analysis*. (See entry under Chapter 1.)

Smith, Daniel S., and Paul C. Hellmund, eds. 1993. *Ecology of Greenways: Design and Function of Linear Conservation Areas*. Minneapolis: University of Minnesota Press. 222 pp.

An introduction to the ecological functions of nature corridors and how they are designed. Advises on how to minimize the negative effects of recreational greenways on natural systems.

Steiner, Frederick R., James R. Pease, and Robert E. Coughlin, eds. 1994. *A Decade with LESA: The Evolution of Land Evaluation and Site Assessment*. Ankeny, Iowa: Soil and Water Conservation Society. 300 pp.

An overview of farmland protection, the background and status of LESA, a survey and evaluation of LESA systems and models, the political context of LESA. Includes case studies and a discussion of the linkage between LESA and GIS. For an application of LESA to local government, see "State and Local LESA Systems" and "Linking LESA Systems into Local Land-Use Planning."

Steiner, Frederick R. *The Living Landscape: An Ecological Approach to Landscape Planning*. 1991. New York : McGraw-Hill. 356 pp.

A text on ecological planning. Outlines the traditional planning framework and suggests a new approach that links planning to human interaction with the environment.

Town of Cazenovia, N.Y. 1984. *Land Use Guide: A Report of the Cazenovia Community Resources Project*. Cazenovia, N.Y.: Town of Cazenovia. 87 pp. (7 Albany St., Cazenovia, NY 13035.)

Good example of one rural community's analysis of its resources and recommendations for their protection.

U.S. Department of the Interior, National Park Service. 1994. *Guidelines for Evaluating and Documenting Traditional Cultural Properties*. National Register Bulletin 38. Washington, D.C.: U.S. Government Printing Office. 22 pp.

A guide for recognizing and documenting traditional cultural properties—places whose significance derives from their role in communities' beliefs, customs, and practices. Explains how to determine if properties are eligible for the National Register. Leads the reader step-by-step through procedures for determining eligibility for the National Register and discusses documentation.

————. 1985. *Guidelines for Local Surveys: A Basis for Preservation Planning*. National Register Bulletin 24. Washington, D.C.: U.S. Government Printing Office. 112 pp.

Wiggins, Lyna L., and Steven P. French. 1991. *GIS: Assessing Your Needs and Choosing a System*. Chicago: Planners Press, PAS Report Number 433. 26 pp.

Good introduction to GIS and helpful handbook for deciding what kind of GIS fits a particular situation or community analysis. Explains the first step in implementing a GIS: how to conduct a users' needs assessment.

Woods, Mike D., and Gerald Hall. 1990. *A Guide for Local Community Survey Efforts*. Stillwater: Oklahoma State University Cooperative Extension. 14 pp.

Basic guide to collecting and analyzing a wide range of community information. An appendix includes six different sample surveys.

CHAPTER 4: LAND-AND-PROTECTION TECHNIQUES THAT LOCAL GOVERNMENTS CAN USE

The American Planning Association is an excellent source of a wide variety of information, including its Planning Advisory Service. The APA's publications, often written for professional and urban audiences and too numerous to list completely here, are nonetheless valuable resources. Of special note is APA's long-term program to formulate a new generation of model land development codes for enactment by states (and by extension, municipalities).

The literature of planning, growth management, and environmental issues related to growth is vast. Included in this chapter's list are some of the more useful texts for community activists. Many state agencies or organizations are developing guides to growth management, which we encourage you to consult for specific information on your state.

An excellent way to stay up to date in this field is to read the periodicals of the American Planning Association, including its magazine *Planning,* and the newsletter of the Small Town and Rural Planning Division, and *GreenSense* (Trust for Public Land, on innovative financing for land protection); *Farmland Preservation Report* (independently published; order from 900 LaGrange Road, Street, Md. 21154); *Land Lines* (Lincoln Institute on Land Policy); *Nonpoint Source News-Notes* (Terrene Institute); *Preservation Law Reporter* (National Trust for Historic Preservation); and *Small Town* (Small Town Institute).

Arendt, Randall G. 1996. *Conservation Design for Subdivisions: A Practical Guide to Creating Open Space Networks*. Washington, D.C.: Island Press. 184 pp.

Arendt's simple approach for any given property is to locate house sites, not first but last—*after* special features on the property are identified, roads (and trails) are laid out, and property lines drawn (see Figures 4.5–4.14). Includes model ordinances.

Arendt, Randall, with Elizabeth A. Brabec, Harry L. Dodson, Christine Reid, and Robert D. Yaro. 1994. *Rural by Design: Maintaining Small Town Character*. Chicago: Planners Press. 441 pp. (Available from the American Planning Association.)

Includes striking color graphics that have changed the way many people conceive development alternatives. Provides information on design of town centers and commercial development, affordable housing, street design for rural subdivisions, scenic roads, sewage disposal, and open space. Discusses the economics of preserving open space and agriculture, and regional contexts for growth management. Twenty-two case examples. Appendixes include ordinances and neotraditional design standards. Extensive bibliography.

American Farmland Trust. 1986. *Density-Related Public Costs*. (See entry under Chapter 1.)

American Planning Association (APA). *Planning Advisory Service Reports*. Chicago: APA.

These well-researched "memos" can be invaluable. Newer issues may be the first place to turn. (Numbers indicate chronological order; those after 394 date after May 1986). A sampling of titles: *Aesthetics and Land-Use Controls: Beyond Ecology and Economics* (no. 399), *Capital Improvements Programs: Linking Budgeting and Planning* (no. 442), *The Planning Commission: Its Composition and Function, 1987* (no. 400), *Planning, Growth, and Public Facilities: A Primer for Local Officials* (no. 447), *Preparing a Historic Preservation Ordinance* (no. 374), *Preparing a Historic Preservation Plan* (no. 450), *Preparing a Landscaping Ordinance* (no. 431), *Preserving Rural Character* (no. 429), *Protecting Nontidal Wetlands* (nos. 412–13), *Regulating Mobile Homes* (no. 360), *Reinventing the Village* (no. 430), *Saving Face: How Corporate Franchise Design Can Respect Community Identity* (no. 452), *State and Local Regulations for Reducing Agricultural Erosion* (no. 386), *The Transportation/Land Use Connection: A Framework for Practical Policy* (nos. 448–49), and *Tree Conservation Ordinances: Land-use Regulations Go Green* (no. 446).

Callies, David L., ed. 1996. *Takings: Land Development and Regulatory Takings after* Dolan *and* Lucas. Chicago: American Bar Association. (750 N. Lake Shore Drive, Chicago, IL. 60611.)

A compendium of articles by a variety of experts, writing on such topics as regulatory takings, investment-backed expectations, partial takings, and substantive due process. Includes articles on the impacts of changes in "takings law" on planning and open space preservation. A good reference for those who need this level of detail.

Carlson, Christine, and Steven Durrant. 1985. *The Farm Landscape of Whatcom County: Managing Change through Design*. San Francisco: Trust for Public Land. 38 pp. (Order from: Department of Landscape Architec-

ture, Box 355734, University of Washington, Seattle, WA 98195.)

Extensively illustrated with photographs, this brief set of design guidelines for dairy farms is one result of a visual resources project conducted by a local group with outside assistance. The first of its kind, it recognizes the economic realities of prefabricated agricultural structures from loafing sheds to silos.

Coughlin, Robert E. Undated. *Zoning for Farming: A Guidebook for Pennsylvania Municipalities on How to Protect Valuable Agricultural Lands*. Harrisburg, Pa.: Center for Rural Pennsylvania. 76 pp. (212 Locust Street, Suite 604, Harrisburg, PA 17101.)

Although focused on Pennsylvania, this small handbook is an excellent general resource on agricultural zoning and related programs. Discusses the elements of an effective farmland protection program and how to integrate them and provides invaluable general guidelines for formulating an ordinance.

Craighead, Paula, ed. 1991. *The Hidden Design in Land Use Ordinances: Assessing the Visual Impact of Dimensions Used for Town Planning in Maine Landscapes*. Portland, Maine: New England Studies Program, University of Southern Maine. 72 pp. (Available from American Planning Association.)

Designed to help community members and decision makers "become more comfortable with the visual reality of zoning . . . [and] how their land use laws will affect the 'look' of the town as it grows and develops." Although written for Maine communities, it is useful everywhere. Heavily illustrated.

Daniels, Thomas L., and Deborah Bowers. 1997. *Holding Our Ground: The Protection of America's Farms and Farmland*. Washington, D.C.: Island Press.

Discusses agricultural zoning, development rights, urban growth boundaries, land trusts, and personal planning for transfer or inheritance of the farm.

Daniels, Thomas L., John W. Keller, and Mark B. Lapping. 1995. *The Small Town Planning Handbook*. 2nd ed. Chicago: Planners Press. 305 pp.

Written for rural counties and small towns by practitioners steeped in local and rural planning. Discusses preparation of a "miniplan" (structured like a comprehensive plan but less detailed) and putting the plan into action. The sections on conducting a community survey prior to planning and on making economic development happen afterward are particularly strong.

DeGrove, John M., ed. 1991. *Balanced Growth: A Planning Guide for Local Government*. Washington, D.C.:

International City County Management Association. 163 pp.

Collection of papers and articles describing techniques for growth management. Especially strong on the philosophical, political, and other considerations underlying growth management and fiscal options to pay for capital improvements. Contains a number of useful checklists.

Doble, Cheryl, and George McCulloch. Undated. *Managing Change: A Pilot Study in Rural Design and Planning.* (See entry under Chapter 3.)

Duerksen, Christopher J., and Richard J. Roddewig. 1994. *Takings Law in Plain English.* 2nd ed. (See entry under Chapter 1.)

Einsweiler, Robert C., and Deborah A. Miness. 1992. *Managing Community Growth and Change.* Washington, D.C.: U.S. Department of Commerce, Economic Development Administration. U.S. Government Printing Office, no. 1994-386-552/03413 through 03416. Vol. 1 (03413): *Managing Growth and Change in Urban, Suburban, and Rural Settings.* 133 pp. Vol. 2 (03414): *Bibliography of Academic and Professional Literature on Growth and Growth Management.* 170 pp. Vol. 3 (03415, by Elizabeth E. Templin): *Bibliography of Educational Materials on Growth Management for Local Officials.* 89 pp. Vol. 4 (03416, by Jane Hetland Stevenson): *Directory of Federal Data Sources and Overview of State Data Needs and Activities in Growth Management.* (Order from Lincoln Institute on Land Policy.)

Volume 1 explores different frameworks for understanding growth management (political, real estate, fiscal, legal) and discusses urbanization in agricultural and forest areas, traffic, fiscal stress, shortage of affordable housing, water pollution, destruction of wildlife habitats, reduction in open space, reduction in public access to beaches and shores, degradation of the quality of life, and loss of community character. Includes nine case studies. Volume 2 covers growth management literature—nearly 600 entries—including a bibliography of bibliographies. Volume 3 focuses on simpler texts, videos, and slide shows on a wide variety of subjects.

Fisher, Roger, William Ury, and Bruce Patton. 1991. *Getting to Yes: Negotiating Agreement without Giving In.* 2nd ed. (See entry under Chapter 2.)

Ford, Kristina, with James Lopach and Dennis O'Donnell. 1990. *Planning Small Town America.* Chicago: Planners Press. 179 pp.

Sheds a different light on the idea that sprawl development rarely pays for itself, by showing how communities now coping with such development should analyze their "committed" lands and their fiscal impacts and create tax and regulatory incentives for encouraging infill.

Gottsegen, Amanda. 1992. *Planning for the Transfer of Development Rights: A Handbook for New Jersey Municipalities.* Mt. Holly, N.J.: Burlington County Board of Chosen Freeholders. 181 pp. (Burlington County Land Use Office, 49 Rancocas Road, Mt. Holly, NJ 08060.)

A clear, thorough, and well-organized discussion of transfer of development rights, not limited in application to New Jersey. Includes a discussion of the relationship of TDR to other farmland preservation techniques and to state-level policies and regulations, plus a case study of Chesterfield Township's program and copy of the Burlington County ordinance.

Hale, Kendall. 1994. *Land Use Guidance System Handbook.* Cullowhee, N.C.: Western North Carolina Tomorrow. 48 pp. (Order from WNCT, P.O. Box 222, Cullowhee, NC 28733.)

This brief handbook includes hefty appendices reproducing sample forms, plus diagrams and text for use in public slide shows. It thoroughly describes the review of development under an alternative to zoning based on an ordinance adopted in 1989 by Bedford County, Virginia. It contains almost enough information to craft an ordinance, but readers may wish to conduct further research on developing the point system, which is merely illustrated here.

Hamilton, Neil D. 1992. *A Livestock Producer's Legal Guide to Nuisance, Land Use Control, and Environmental Law.* Des Moines, Iowa: Drake University Agricultural Law Center. 174 pp. (Drake University Agricultural Law Center, Des Moines, IA 50311.)

Filled with information on right-to-farm laws (the appendix covers all fifty states, with helpful addresses) as well as land use controls and environmental laws; although addressed to the livestock producer, other farmers and nonfarmers as well will find the information useful. Includes many short examples.

Hart, John. 1991. *Farming on the Edge: Saving Family Farms in Marin County, California.* (See entry under Chapter 1.)

Hester, Randolph T., Jr. 1990. *Community Design Primer.* Mendocino, Calif.: Ridge Times Press. (See entry under Chapter 2.)

Hiemstra, Hal, and Nancy Bushwick Malloy, eds. 1989. *Plowing the Urban Fringe: An Assessment of Alternative Approaches to Farmland Preservation.* Ft. Lauderdale, Fla.: Florida Atlantic University, Florida International University, Joint Center for Environmental and Urban Problems. Monograph no. 88-2.

Covers various approaches to agricultural preservation in Wisconsin, California, Oregon, Illinois, New York, New Jersey, Montgomery County, Maryland (the TDR program), and Suffolk County, New York.

Hiss, Tony. 1990. *The Experience of Place.* (See entry under Chapter 1.)

Hylton, Thomas. 1995. *Save Our Land, Save Our Towns.* (See entry under Chapter 1.)

Kass, Stephen L., Judith M. LaBelle, and David A. Hansell. 1992. *Rehabilitating Older and Historic Buildings: Law Taxation Strategies.* 2nd ed. New York: John Wiley and Sons. 587 pp.

Covers the entirety of preservation law, from federal tax incentives to local regulations. Extensive appendices include all the basic laws and regulations.

Katz, Peter, ed. 1994. *The New Urbanism: Toward an Architecture of Community.* New York: McGraw-Hill. 245 pp.

The most complete documentation of the range of designs and developments in what has also been called "neotraditional" development. Heavily illustrated with useful short essays. While it does not resolve the issue of how to use this new form of development—as infill in metropolitan areas, or as a way of shaping growth extending deep into the countryside—it does illustrate the possibilities.

Land Trust Alliance (LTA). Various dates. *Infopaks.* Washington, D.C.: LTA.

Useful compilations of documents, book excerpts, and periodical literature; series includes "Land Use Planning."

Lang, J. Christopher, and Kate Stout. 1996. *Building with Nantucket in Mind: Guidelines for Protecting the Historic Architecture and Landscape of Nantucket Island.* Rev. ed. Nantucket, Mass.: Nantucket Historic District Commission. 184 pp. (3 South Beach Street, Nantucket, MA 02554.)

Extensively illustrated guidelines demonstrate a sensitivity to both scenic and architectural qualities of a historic landscape. Useful beyond Nantucket's own shores.

Lapping, Mark B., Thomas L. Daniels, and John W. Keller. 1989. *Rural Planning and Development in the United States.* (See entry under Chapter 1.)

Little, Charles E. 1990. *Greenways for America.* (See entry under Chapter 1.)

Maguire, Meg (Maguire/Reeder, Ltd.). 1993. Video. *Looking at Change Before It Occurs.* Washington, D.C.: Design Arts Program, National Endowment for the Arts. (Order from Design Access, c/o National Building Museum, 401 F Street, N.W., Washington, DC 20001.)

Shows how several techniques for computerized visual simulation can help decision makers assess and shape change, and points out how such techniques can be abused. Includes a pamphlet on technologies and institutions featured. Ideal for educating lay planners and citizens.

Malme, Jane. 1993. *Preferential Property Tax Treatment of Land.* Cambridge, Mass.: Lincoln Institute of Land Policy. 46 pp.

Covers the details of preferential tax treatment for agricultural, recreational, and open space lands. Includes a summary table characterizing individual state laws.

Mandelker, Daniel R., and William R. Ewald. 1988. *Street Graphics and the Law.* Rev. ed. Chicago: Planners Press. 207 pp.

Discusses the legal basis for the regulation of signs and how to design appropriate street signs for businesses. Includes an annotated model ordinance and extensive illustrations.

Mantell, Michael A., Stephen F. Harper, and Luther Propst. 1990. *Creating Successful Communities: A Guidebook to Growth Management Strategies.* (See entry under Chapter 2.)

National Park Service (NPS) and National Conference of State Historic Preservation Officers (prepared by Carole Zellie; Richard L. Kronick, ed.). 1995. *Preserving Your Community's Heritage thorugh the Certified Local Government Program.* Washington, D.C.: U.S. Department of the Interior, NPS. 17 pp. (Order from a State Historic Preservation Officer or from CLG Coordinator, NPS, P.O. Box 37127, Stop 2255, Washington, DC 20013.)

This well-illustrated, idea-filled booklet reviews the myriad activities of local historic preservation programs large and small.

National Trust for Historic Preservation. Information Series. Washington, D.C.: NTHP.

Several titles in this series are of interest, including *BARN AGAIN! A Guide to Rehabilitation of Older Farm Buildings* (no. 2BAR), *Basic Preservation Procedures* (no. 2I48), *Design Review in Historic Districts* (no. 2I85), *Maintaining Community Character: How to Establish a Local Historic District* (no. 2I58), *Procedural Due Process in Plain English: A Guide for Preser-*

vation Commissions (no. 2PRO), *Safety, Building Codes and Historic Preservation* (no. 2I57), and *Using Old Farm Buildings* (no. 2I46).

Ndubisi, Forster. 1992. *Planning Implementation Tools and Techniques: A Resource Book for Local Governments.* Athens, Ga.: Institute of Community and Area Development (ICAD), University of Georgia. 224 pp. (ICAD, University of Georgia, Athens, GA 30602.)

Contains descriptions of traditional regulatory tools, fiscal tools, "performance, rating, and impact systems," and resource-oriented tools (environmental, aesthetic, historic). Written for public officials, with smaller communities in mind, it avoids the complexities of in-depth works on individual tools but makes useful comparisons among them.

Nelessen, Anton Clarence. 1994. *Visions for a New American Dream: Principles, Process, and an Ordinance to Plan and Design Small Communities.* Chicago: Planners Press. 374 pp.

Provides guidelines for planning and designing small communities, including hamlets, villages, and neighborhoods. Discusses the principles of community design, explains how to analyze patterns of past settlement, and presents methods for developing a vision of future communities, including the visual preference survey and workshops using hands-on models. Uses ten design principles, such as "pedestrianism," open spaces, and streetscapes, to explain small-community design. Includes a model ordinance.

Northeast Regional Office of the National Trust for Historic Preservation. 1991. *Saving Place: A Guide and Report Card for Protecting Community Character.* Boston: National Trust. 50 pp. (Order no. 2107. Companion publication, *Place Notes;* order no. 2IPN.)

Written for residents of rural communities, describes in simple terms more than fifty planning tools and techniques for addressing planning and preservation issues.

Peterson, Pat, and Roger Sternberg. 1990. *A Citizen's Guide to Conserving Land and Creating Affordable Housing.* Burlington, Vt.: Burlington Community Land Trust. 36 pp. (P.O. Box 523, Burlington, VT 05402.)

A short but useful discussion of planning and land use as it relates to providing affordable housing, suggesting "creative land development" (a version of clustering) and community land trust action as part of a community's approach. Includes useful short chapters such as "Identifying Community Needs and the Resources to Meet Them" and "Strategies for Local Control," plus case studies, all drawn from Vermont but useful generally.

Platt, Rutherford H. 1996. *Land Use and Society: Geography, Law, and Public Policy.* (See entry under Chapter 1.)

Porter, Douglas R., and David A. Salvesen, eds. 1995. *Collaborative Planning for Wetlands and Wildlife.* Washington, D.C.: Island Press. 352 pp.

Discusses approaches to effective "area-wide, collaborative planning" and includes case studies demonstrating "how different communities have creatively reconciled the often competing goals of development and environmental protection" (p. 5).

Sargent, Frederick O., et al. 1991. *Rural Environmental Planning for Sustainable Communities.* Washington, D.C.: Island Press. 254 pp.

Handbook for rural planning commissions and citizens. Among topics covered are agricultural planning, protecting lake and river basins and other natural areas, and recreational planning, as well as planning for aesthetics and growth control. Includes chapters on public surveys, inventorying, and social and economic impacts of rural planning.

Scheer, Brenda Case, and Wolfgang F. E. Preiser, eds. 1994. *Design Review: Challenging Urban Aesthetic Control.* New York: Chapman and Hall. 219 pp.

Anyone who plans to embark on design review would do well to review the current state of affairs as described in this book. At once a critique and a resource, the introduction alone is worth the price of the book. Although this book is preoccupied with urban areas, its ideas apply to design review in any setting.

Schiffman, Irving. 1989. *Alternative Techniques for Managing Growth.* Berkeley: Institute of Governmental Studies (IGS), University of California at Berkeley. 135 pp. (IGS, 102 Moses Hall, University of California, Berkeley, CA 94720.)

Describes twenty-six land-use management techniques, from agricultural buffers to zero lot line housing, listing potential benefits and limitations, interrelationships with other techniques, and references. Especially valuable for its short descriptions of how to streamline land use review regulations, as well as for its discussions of capital-improvement programming, fiscal-impact analysis, and urban-area boundary designation.

Smardon, Richard C., and James P. Karp. 1993. *The Legal Landscape: Guidelines for Regulating Environmental and Aesthetic Quality.* New York: Van Nostrand Reinhold. 287 pp.

Gives examples of highly professional and objective approaches to the protection of scenic resources. Discusses the basics of law, community planning, and aesthetics; federal and state aesthetic regulation; and litigation and aesthetics in practice, complete with case studies, case law citations, references at the end of every chapter, and the status of aesthetics in each of the fifty states. Covers such topics as zoning, historic preservation, design review, outdoor advertising, wilderness preservation, surface mining, timber harvesting, and facility siting.

Smardon, Richard C., James F. Palmer, and John P. Felleman, eds. 1986. *Foundations for Visual Project Analysis.* (See entry under Chapter 1.)

Smith, Herbert H. 1979. *The Citizen's Guide to Planning.* Rev. ed. Chicago: Planners Press. 198 pp.

Covers the duties of the planning commission, the comprehensive plan, planning through the capital budget and community improvements, the relationship of planning to zoning, and citizen action.

———. 1993. *The Citizen's Guide to Zoning.* 3rd ed. Chicago: Planners Press. 267 pp.

A concise manual explaining the philosophy, constitutionality, and administration of zoning. Reviews the role of citizens, explains the variance procedure, and briefly examines emerging techniques.

Solnit, Albert. 1987. *The Job of the Planning Commissioner.* Chicago: Planners Press. 198 pp.

A readable introduction to planning and zoning intended for citizens serving on planning boards in California. Contains useful ideas for board members elsewhere on such subjects as board ethics, environmental considerations, and group dynamics.

Southern Environmental Law Center (SELC). 1987. *Visual Pollution and Sign Control: A Legal Handbook on Billboard Control.* Charlottesville, Va.: SELC. 36 pp. (Order from Scenic America.)

A how-to manual for obtaining a strong local ordinance for sign control, including recommended provisions. Also discusses federal and state controls and issues in local and constitutional law.

Steiner, Frederick R. 1991. *The Living Landscape: An Ecological Approach to Landscape Planning.* (See entry under Chapter 3.)

Steiner, Frederick R., James R. Pease, and Robert E. Coughlin, eds. 1994. *A Decade with LESA: The Evolution of Land Evaluation and Site Assessment.* (See entry under Chapter 3.)

Thomas, Ronald L., Mary C. Means, and Margaret A. Grieve. 1988. *Taking Charge: How Communities Are Planning Their Futures.* (See entry under Chapter 2.)

CHAPTER 5: VOLUNTARY TECHNIQUES FOR PROTECTING PROPERTY

The dominant source of information on voluntary land conservation is the Land Trust Alliance. An excellent way to stay up to date in this field is to read the following periodicals: *Exchange* (Land Trust Alliance), *GreenSense* (Trust for Public Land, on innovative financing), and *Common Ground* (Conservation Fund).

Adirondack Land Trust (ALT). 1988. *Developing a Land Conservation Strategy: A Handbook for Land Trusts.* Rev. ed. Keene Valley, N.Y.: ALT. 38 pp. (Box 65, Keene Valley, NY 12943.)

Offers criteria for land conservation projects and a simple discussion of inventorying and mapping natural and scenic resources; covers ways to narrow the focus through geographic and ownership considerations, critical resources, or themes such as corridors or valleys. A popular and necessary part of any land trust's library.

Arthur Andersen and Co. 1995. *Tax Economics of Charitable Giving.* Self-published by Arthur Andersen and Co. 230 pp. (Order from Land Trust Alliance.)

Covers federal tax law, including planned-giving techniques for fund raising, what constitutes a charitable gift, voluntary land conservation techniques, and more.

Diehl, Janet, and Thomas S. Barrett. 1988. *The Conservation Easement Handbook: Managing Land Conservation and Historic Preservation Easement Programs.* Alexandria, Va. (Washington, D.C.): Land Trust Exchange and Trust for Public Land. 269 pp. (Order from Land Trust Alliance.)

Gathers the best of theory and practice in conducting an easement program, including developing criteria, drafting an easement, gathering base-line data, monitoring observance of restrictions, and ensuring perpetuity. Includes a model easement, updated in 1996 and available separately. A brochure on easements is also available from the Land Trust Alliance, along with a video, *For the Common Good: Preserving Private Lands with Conservation Easements.*

Endicott, Eve, ed. 1993. *Land Conservation through Public/Private Partnerships.* Washington, D.C.: Island Press. 364 pp.

A thoughtful examination of the decades-old practice of public-private partnerships, which has become widespread in the 1990s. Describes national programs and state and local aspects of such partnerships and the myriad funding arrangements that have grown up around them.

Fisher, Roger, William Ury, and Roger Patton. 1991. *Getting to Yes: Negotiating Agreement without Giving In.* (See entry under Chapter 2.)

Hart, John. 1991. *Farming on the Edge: Saving Family Farms in Marin County, California.* (See entry under Chapter 1.)

Institute for Community Economics (ICE). January 1993. *Profiles of Community Land Trusts.* Springfield, Mass.: ICE. 56 pp.

Briefly updates the 1982 *Community Land Trust Handbook*—available from ICE in tandem with this booklet—with new examples of community land trusts, drawn from ICE's journal *Community Economics.* Profiles seven rural and seven urban organizations. An excellent introduction to the concept of community land trusts.

Land Trust Alliance (LTA). 1990. *Appraising Easements: Guidelines for Valuation of Historic Preservation and Land Conservation Easements.* 2nd ed. Washington, D.C.: Land Trust Alliance and National Trust for Historic Preservation. 82 pp.

Written by experts knowledgeable about both easements and appraisal, to provide basic guidance on appraisal procedures for organizations, appraisers, and advisors to property owners.

————. 1990. *Starting a Land Trust : A Guide to Forming a Land Conservation Organization.* (See entry under Chapter 2; also available are a brochure and video introducing land trusts, *Land Trusts in America: Guardians of the Future.*)

————. 1993. *Conservation Options: A Landowner's Guide.* Washington, D.C.: LTA. 55 pp.

Short, clear explanations of conservation tools available to property owners, including examples and at-a-glance charts. A brochure on the same topic is also available.

————. 1993. *The Standards and Practices Guidebook: An Operating Manual for Land Trusts.* (See entry under Chapter 2.)

————. 1995. *National Directory of Conservation Land Trusts.* Washington, D.C.: LTA. 238 pp.

Lists 1,095 organizations by state and provides a profile of land trusts that summarizes the scope of their activities. Updated periodically.

————. Various dates. *Infopaks.* Washington, D.C.: LTA.

Useful compilations of documents, book excerpts, and periodical literature; series includes "Managing Conservation Easements," "Land Use Planning," and "Greenways: An Introduction."

Lind, Brenda. 1991. *The Conservation Easement Stewardship Guide: Designing, Monitoring, and Enforcing Easements.* Washington, D.C.: Land Trust Alliance, 1991. 107 pp.

A basic handbook on selecting and drafting "monitorable and enforceable" easements, obtaining baseline documentation of the property under easement, monitoring the condition of the property over time, relations with owners and the community, enforcement, funding, and such special circumstances as amendment, condemnation, and backup assistance from partner organizations.

Little, Charles E. 1990. *Greenways for America.* (See entry under Chapter 1.)

Mantell, Michael A., Stephen F. Harper, and Luther Propst. 1990. *Creating Successful Communities: A Guidebook to Growth Management Strategies.* And, *Resource Guide for Creating Successful Communities.* (See entry under Chapter 2.)

Meder-Montgomery, Marilyn. 1984. *Preservation Easements: A Legal Mechanism for Protecting Cultural Resources.* Denver: Colorado Historical Society. 165 pp. (Colorado Historical Society, Colorado State Museum, 1300 Broadway, Denver, CO 80203.)

A thorough discussion of easement program concerns, preservation or otherwise, with appendixes going well beyond the usual reproduction of legislation and easement documents to include, for example, reproductions of an easement inspection report form and an analysis of long-term inspection costs. A section on program considerations for the Colorado Historical Foundation is a model for other organizations.

National Trust for Historic Preservation (NHTP). Information Series. Washington, D.C.: NTHP.

The following titles in this series are of particular interest: *Appraising Historic Properties* (no. 2187), *Establishing an Easement Program to Protect Historic, Scenic and Natural Resources* (no. 2125), and *Preservation Revolving Funds* (no. 2178).

Peterson, Pat, and Roger Sternberg. 1990. *A Citizen's Guide to Conserving Land and Creating Affordable Housing.* (See entry under Chapter 4.)

Piton Foundation, with Frances Brody and John Weiser. 1993. *Program-Related Investment Primer.* Rev. ed. Washington, D.C.: Council on Foundations. (1828 L Street, N.W., Suite 300, Washington, DC 20036.)

A general text to consult on ways that foundations can use their capital—in addition to their investment income—to provide financing for income-producing projects proposed by nonprofit organizations.

Small, Stephen J. 1990. *The Federal Tax Law of Conservation Easements* 3rd ed. (with supplements, 1986–1988, 1988–1995). Washington, D.C.: Land Trust Alliance. 437 pp. plus 1995 supplement.

The definitive guide for attorneys, including an invaluable interpretation of the Internal Revenue Service's regulations governing gifts of conservation easements and copies of all relevant documents.

———. *Preserving Family Lands: Essential Tax Strategies for the Landowner.* Rev. 2nd ed. Boston, Mass.: Landowner Planning Center (LPC). 99 pp. (LPC, P.O. Box 4508, Boston, MA 02101.)

An easy-to-read handbook about land-saving options; valuable for attorneys and land trust board members new to the process. A video of a 1993 teleconference led by the author, *Your Family Land: Legacy or Memory?*, is available from the Land Trust Alliance.

Trust for Public Land. 1995. *Doing Deals: A Guide to Buying Land for Conservation.* Washington, D.C.: Land Trust Alliance (LTA) and Trust for Public Land. 175 pp. (Order from LTA.)

Details nearly every aspect of a land purchase project except tax considerations. It walks the reader through considerations for the organization; assembling important information about the land, the owner, the community, and public agencies that might become involved; negotiating the "deal" itself; taking steps to assure that title, appraisal, environmental assessment, and surveying are done well; and financing the project. Includes examples and useful checklists.

Wright, John B. 1993. *Rocky Mountain Divide: Selling and Saving the West.* Austin: University of Texas Press. 272 pp.

Well-written and insightful discussion of land conservation in Colorado and Utah—which transcends its regional limits in its examination of what shapes people's attitudes toward land, development, and conservation. The author views land trusts as vital to the future of conservation in the West.

CHAPTER 6: RURAL CONSERVATION AND ECONOMIC DEVELOPMENT

There is a substantial body of literature on the subject of economic development, much of it theoretical, but increasingly practical as well. Listed here are selected books that pertain directly to the kinds of economic development this chapter focuses on: particularly heritage tourism and downtown revitalization.

Beaumont, Constance E. 1994. *How Superstore Sprawl Can Harm Communities—and What Citizens Can Do About It.* Washington, D.C.: National Trust for Historic Preservation. 120 pp.

Discusses the impacts of superstore sprawl and presents various legal, organizational and media strategies for combatting it. Includes several success stories of communities dealing with superstore development, as well as models for how superstore development compatible with conservation and historic preservation can occur.

Cole, Barbara A., and Philip B. Herr. 1992. *High Stakes Decision-Making: Understanding the Choices Your Community Can Make.* Washington, D.C.: National Trust for Historic Preservation. 61 pp.

Workbook about the choices communities must consider when turning to gambling as a way to improve their economies and save their historic buildings. Helpful in identifying and prioritizing planning steps that should be taken to direct and guide the growth that is inevitable in gaming communities.

Flora, Jan L., James J. Chriss, Eddie Gale, Gary P. Green, Frederick E. Schmidt, and Cornelia Flora. 1991. *From the Grassroots: Profiles of 103 Rural Self-Development Projects.* U.S. Department of Agriculture, Economic Research Service, Agriculture and Rural Economy Division. Staff report no. 9123. 109 pp.

Provides useful information to community leaders and development professionals about the phenomenon of "self-development," or reliance on a community's own financial and organizational resources to initiate projects generating jobs or income. Contains profiles of self-development projects, arranged by category. Categories include community-based development, local business/industrial development, and tourism/historic development.

Galston, William A., and Karen J. Baehler. *Rural Development in the United States.* 1995. Corvelo, Calif.: Island Press. 353 pp.

Comprehensive and well-written overview of rural development in the 1990s. Discusses the theoretical framework of development and analyzes rural development by sector: natural resources, manufacturing, service, tourism, the elderly, high technology, and telecommunications.

Goodman, Robert. 1994. *Legalized Gambling as a Strategy for Economic Development.* Northampton, Mass.: United States Gambling Study. 222 pp. (245 Main Street, Northampton, MA 01060.)

A comprehensive study assessing the economic, social, and legal consequences that occur when governments and communities use gambling as a way to improve their economies.

Ingerson, Alice E. *Managing Land as Ecosystem and Economy.* 1995. Cambridge, Mass: Lincoln Institute of Land Policy. 36 pp.

Argues for managing land simultaneously as an ecosystem and an economic resource. Suggests financial incentives for conservation and ways of valuing ecosystems.

National Trust for Historic Preservation. Information Series. Washington, D.C.: NTHP

The following in this series are of particular interest: *Getting Started in Heritage Tourism*; *Heritage Tourism: Partnerships and Responsibilities* (no. 2142); *From Visitors to Volunteers: Organizing a Historic Homes Tour* (no. 2150); and *Regional Heritage Areas: Approaches to Sustainable Development* (no. 2188).

President's Council on Sustainable Development. 1996. *Sustainable America: A New Consensus for Prosperity, Opportunity, and a Healthy Environment for the Future.* (See entry under Chapter 1.)

Rypkema, Donovan D. 1994. *The Economics of Historic Preservation: A Community Leader's Guide.* Washington, D.C.: National Trust for Historic Preservation. 131 pp.

A convincing primer for preservation activists and decision makers which presents a series of arguments for the economic benefits of historic preservation, including downtown revitalization and heritage tourism.

Smith, Kennedy, Kate Juncas, Bill Parrish, and Suzanne G. Dane. 1991. *Revitalizing Downtown.* Washington, D.C.: National Main Street Center. 200 pp.

Comprehensive, step-by-step book on downtown revitalization. Includes launching an effective organization, developing a dynamic promotion, building on downtown assets through design, and expanding business through economic restructuring. Not specifically focused on small towns, but useful for any downtown revitalization effort.

Spitzer, Theodore Morrow and Hilary Baum. 1995. *Public Markets and Community Revitalization.* Washington, D.C.: Urban Land Institute and the Project for Public Spaces. 120 pp.

Comprehensive book on the history, benefits, and development of public markets, including farmers' markets. Provides practical information on management, feasibility, business plans, and operations. Includes seven case studies illustrating various aspects of public market development.

University of Minnesota, Minnesota Extension Service Tourism Center. 1991. *A Training Guide for Rural Tourism Development.* 276 pp. (Distribution Center, Minnesota Extension Service, University of Minnesota, Coffey Hall, Room 3, 1420 Eckles Avenue, St. Paul, MN 55108.)

Easy-to-use notebook contains teaching materials designed for community groups working to develop and expand their economic base through tourism.

Western Rural Development Center (WRDC). 1994. *Community Tourism Assessment Handbook.* 60 pp. (WRDC, Oregon State University, Corvallis, OR 97331.)

A manual to guide communities through a process that determines their actual tourism potential. Process involves weighing the social, economic, and environmental costs as well as the benefits of tourism to determine if tourism development is a strategy worth pursuing.

CHAPTER 7: HELP FROM THE OUTSIDE

In addition to the following publications, there are many booklets and brochures published by federal agencies on the programs and laws they administer. They are too numerous and change too frequently to list here. You should, however, contact the agencies that interest you to obtain those publications currently available.

Bass, Ronald, and Albert Herson. 1993. *Mastering NEPA: A Step-by-Step Approach.* Point Arena, Calif.: Solano Press. 233 pp.

A simplified, user-friendly handbook on how to work with the National Environmental Policy Act. Contains background on the purpose of NEPA and how and when to prepare an environmental impact statement. Also identifies points where citizens and local governments can insert themselves usefully into the NEPA process.

Beatley, Timothy, David J. Brower, and Anna K. Schwab. 1994. *An Introduction to Coastal Zone Management.* (See entry under Chapter 1.)

Bolling, David M. 1994. *How to Save a River.* Washington, D.C.: Island Press. 266 pp.

An excellent book that explains how citizen groups can build the organizational strength, political power, and campaign strategy to protect rivers that are threatened by development. Step-by-step chapters cover everything from getting organized and building public support to "getting it done."

Burke, David G., Erik J. Meyers, Ralph W. Tiner, Jr., and Hazel Groman. 1988. *Protecting Nontidal Wetlands.* Chicago: Planners Press. PAS report number 412/413. 76 pp.

A complete guide to understanding nontidal wetlands and the regulations that protect them. Includes an overview of the definition and classification of wetlands as well as chapters on federal, state, and local regulatory programs. Also included is a model ordinance for nontidal wetland protection.

Carlson, Daniel, Lisa Wormser, and Cy Ulberg. 1995. *At Road's End: Transportation and Land Use Choices for Communities.* (See entry under Chapter 1.)

Chan, I Mei, ed. 1995. *Building on the Past, Traveling to the Future.* Washington, D.C.: Federal Highway Administration and National Trust for Historic Preservation. 79 pp. (Order from National Trust for Historic Preservation.)

Provides profiles of historic preservation projects funded by the transportation enhancements provision of the Intermodal Surface Transportation Efficiency Act of 1991, explaining the application process, project requirements, and project selection. Ten detailed case studies of funded projects, as well as sixteen smaller case studies, are included.

Civil War Sites Advisory Commission. 1993. *Civil War Sites Advisory Commission Report on the Nation's Civil War Battlefields.* Washington, D.C.: National Park Service. 64 pp.

Well-illustrated report on the status of America's Civil War battlefields. Inventories the battlefield sites in terms of size, ownership, geographic distribution, and level of protection. Discusses methods of battlefield protection and makes recommendations to the Congress and Secretary of the Interior on future battlefield protection.

Conservation Law Foundation (CLF). 1995. *Take Back Your Streets: How to Protect Communities from Asphalt and Traffic.* Boston: CLF. 53 pp.

Well-illustrated, practical guide to minimizing the negative impacts of transportation improvements to community life. Explains how to keep informed about federal and state transportation projects, legal recourses available, and "traffic calming" measures that can be applied.

Cylinder, Paul D., Kenneth M. Bogdan, Ellyn Miller Davis, and Albert I. Herson. 1995. *Wetlands Regulation: A Complete Guide to Federal and California Programs.* Point Arena, Calif.: Solano Press Books. 363 pp.

A reference on wetland regulation and the related issues. Shows the relationship between the federal regulatory system and California's.

Endicott, Eve, ed. 1993. *Land Conservation through Public-Private Partnerships.* Washington, D.C.: Island Press. 364 pp.

Thoughtful examination of public-private partnerships, which have become widespread in the 1990s. Describes national programs and state and local aspects of such partnerships, as well as the myriad funding arrangements that have been developed around them.

Environmental Law Institute. *National Wetlands Newsletter.* (See entry under Chapter 1.)

Environmental Protection Agency. 1993. *Everything You Wanted to Know About Environmental Regulations . . . But Were Afraid to Ask.* Washington, D.C.: U.S. Government Printing Office. 85 pp.

Explains in clear language the federal laws and regulations pertaining to water (nonpoint source pollution, wellhead protection, wetlands), hazardous and solid waste, air quality, and other pollutants.

———. 1993. *The Plain English Guide to the Clean Air Act.* Washington, D.C.: U.S. Government Printing Office. 28 pp.

Straightforward and well-illustrated primer on the 1990 amendments to the Clean Air Act. Covers pollutants, mobile sources, acid rain, the ozone layer, and nonattainment areas.

Federal Highway Administration. 1996. *A Community Guide to Planning and Managing a Scenic Byway.* Washington, D.C.: Federal Highway Administration.

Practical guide for communities in designating scenic byways and developing corridor management plans. Discusses how to inventory and evaluate the resources of the corridor, build a coalition of byway interests, and develop management strategies for the corridor.

Firestone, David B., and Frank C. Reed. 1993. *Environmental Law for Non-Lawyers.* 2nd ed. South Royalton, Vt.: SoRo Press. 316 pp.

Describes key federal laws, typical state and local laws, and the legal remedies available to citizens.

Flink, Charles A., and Robert M. Searns. 1993. *Greenways: A Guide to Planning, Design, and Development.* Washington, D.C.: Island Press. 320 pp.

Information on how to develop a greenway plan, including physical development, organizing the community, partnerships, and ecological design principles.

Government Services Administration and the Executive Office of the President. *Catalog of Federal Domestic Assistance.* Washington, D.C.: U.S. Government Printing Office. Annual publication.

Provides detailed information on all federal government assistance programs. For each program, gives categories of available assistance and specifies eligibility, application procedures, and evaluation criteria. Gives the dollar amount spent through the program for the most recent fiscal year.

Harker, Donald F., and Elizabeth Unger Natter. 1994. *Where We Live: A Citizen's Guide to Conducting a Community Environmental Inventory.* (See entry under Chapter 3.)

John, DeWitt. 1994. *Civic Environmentalism: Alternatives to Regulation in States and Communities.* Washington, D.C.: CQ Press (a division of Congressional Quarterly, Inc.). 347 pp.

Explores the potential for a new style of decentralized, "bottom-up" environmental politics and policy at the state and local levels to address the prevention of pollution, management of ecosystems, and the reduction of nonpoint pollution. Suggests that states and localities consider education, technical assistance, economic incentives, and subsidies.

Kennedy, Frances H., and Douglas R. Porter. 1994. *Dollar$ and Sense of Battlefield Preservation.* Washington, D.C.: Preservation Press. 99 pp.

Handbook for community leaders providing arguments for the economic benefits of battlefield preservation and explaining how to develop a battlefield preservation plan. Includes a glossary of tools for protecting battlefields and a comprehensive list of organizations and references to contact.

Myers, Phyllis. 1992. *Lessons from the States: Strengthening Land Conservation Programs through Grants to Nonprofit Land Trusts.* Washington, D.C.: Land Trust Alliance. 71 pp.

A valuable report discussing case studies and model approaches to state-funded public-private partnerships for land conservation.

National Audubon Society. 1989–90. *Audubon Wildlife Report.* (See entry under Chapter 1.)

National Trust for Historic Preservation. Information Series. Washington, D.C.: NTHP.

The following titles in this series are of particular interest: *A Guide to Tax-Advantaged Rehabilitation* (no. 2189) and *The Protection of America's Scenic Byways* (no. 2168).

National Wildlife Federation. *Conservation Directory.* Washington, D.C.: NWF. Annual publication.

Lists private organizations and government agencies at the national and state levels that are concerned with natural resource use and management. Briefly describes each organization and names its key officials.

Platt, Rutherford H. 1996. *Land Use and Society: Geography, Law, and Public Policy.* (See entry under Chapter 1.)

Ryan, Karen-Lee, and Julie A. Winterich. 1993. *Secrets of Successful Rail-Trails.* Washington, D.C.: Rails-to-Trails Conservancy. 192 pp.

A comprehensive, step-by-step guide on how to create successful rail-trails.

Schulman, Neil. 1993. *Protecting Instream Flows: A Resource Guide for River Guardians.* Portland, Ore.: River Network Publications. 90 pp.

An explanation of water law and river protection tools and strategies. Includes case studies, model programs, flow assessement methods, and a state-by-state list of advocacy group and agency contacts.

Slavitt, Lesley. 1993. *Preserving and Revitalizing Older Communities: Sources of Federal Assistance.* Washington, D.C.: National Park Service, Preservation Assistance Division. 146 pp.

Describes a variety of federal assistance programs that can play a role in historic preservation. Included are programs that support small business, job training, and community facilities, in addition to those that finance the repair and rehabilitation of historic structures.

Wallin, Phillip, and Rita Haberman. 1992. *People Protecting Rivers: A Collection of Lessons from Grassroots Activists.* Portland, Ore.: River Network Publications, 72 pp.

Presents case studies of river protection efforts on the Charles River (Massachusettts), Clark River (Montana and Idaho), Gauley River (West Virginia), Sacramento River (California) and Upper Mississippi River (Minnesota).

Zorack, John L. 1990. *The Lobbying Handbook.* Washington, D.C.: Professional Lobbying and Consulting Center. 1118 pp.

Comprehensive lobbying guide, providing information on the basics of lobbying, lobbying strategies, how to gain access to Congress, how to get political mileage from fund-raising events, and pitfalls to avoid. Explains in depth how Congress works.

CHAPTER 8: COMMUNITY EDUCATION

Adler, Elizabeth. 1993. *Everyone's Guide to Successful Publications.* Berkeley, Calif.: Peachpit Press. 412 pp.

Thorough, start-to-finish guide to producing powerful brochures, newsletters, flyers, and business communications. Contains planning lists and checklists.

Arthur Andersen and Co. 1995. *Tax Economics of Charitable Giving.* (See entry under Chapter 5.)

Beamish, Richard. 1995. *Getting the Word Out in the Fight to Save the Earth*. Baltimore: Johns Hopkins University Press. 181 pp.

A well-illustrated, easy-to-read book of advice for nonprofit citizen groups. Gives instructions and examples of how groups can raise funds, pressure government officials, use the news media, and affect public policy to protect their communities and the environment.

Buchanan, Terry. 1983. *Photographing Historic Buildings*. (See entry under Chapter 3.)

Environmental Data Research Institute (EDRI). 1996. *Environmental Grantmaking Foundations*. Rochester, N.Y.: EDRI. 800 pp. (1655 Elmwood Avenue, Suite 225, Rochester, NY 14620.)

Carries entries of independent, community, and company-sponsored foundations that have given environmental grants, including members of the Environmental Grantmakers Association. Fully indexed and impressively detailed. Although it may not have the most up-to-the-minute information for sources to target, it should reduce time and travel costs to the nearest Foundation Center library.

Firstenberg, Paul B. 1986. *Managing for Profit in the Nonprofit World*. New York: Foundation Center. 253 pp.

Proposes specific strategies to improve a nonprofit organization's financial condition by creating income-producing programs, maximizing returns on endowments, and making innovative approaches to traditional funding sources.

Flanagan, Joan. 1982. *The Grass Roots Fundraising Book: How to Raise Money in Your Community*. Chicago: Contemporary Books. 336 pp.

Filled with ideas about benefit events, both small and large, plus tips on planning a fund-raising calendar and fund raising through coporations, deferred giving, and direct mail. Does not include discussion of raising funds from foundations and government agencies. A classic.

———. 1993. *Successful Fundraising: A Complete Handbook for Volunteers and Professionals*. Chicago: Contemporary Books. 302 pp.

Outlines the opportunities and strategies used by nonprofit groups, communities, and private organizations for successful fund raising. Covers everything from basic fund raising to memberships, pledges, gifts, corporate contributions, and grants.

Grassroots Fundraising Journal. Berkeley, Calif. Bimonthly publication. (P.O. Box 11607, Berkeley, CA 94712.)

Written specifically for small nonprofit organizations, this publication contains how-to articles on raising money from sources other than foundations and government. Articles cover such subjects as building membership, asking individuals for money, attracting large gifts, and using direct mail.

Johnson, Kenny, and Linda Walsh. 1991. *River Wealth*. Portland, Ore.: River Network Publications. 41 pp.

A guidebook to help river conservationists share their fund-raising experiences and knowledge. Contains ideas on how to raise financial support for river protection.

Johnson, Kenny, Shauna Whidden, and Linda Walsh. 1992. *River Wise*. Portland, Ore.: River Network Publications. 33 pp.

A guidebook to help river conservationists share their experiences and knowledge about community education and involvement. Contains helpful advice on how to educate people about the values of rivers.

Land Trust Alliance (LTA). Various dates. *Infopaks*. Washington, D.C.: LTA.

Useful compilations of documents, book excerpts, and periodical literature; series includes "Fundraising Essentials for Land Trusts."

National Trust for Historic Preservation. Information Series. Washington, D.C.: NTHP.

The following titles in this series are of particular interest: *Heritage Education: A Community-School Partnership* (no. 2173), *Share Your Success: Fund-Raising Ideas* (no. 2180), and *Building Support Through Public Relations: A Guide for Nonprofit Preservation Organizations* (no. 2163).

Parrella, Deborah. 1995. *Project Seasons*. Shelburne, Vt.: Shelburne Farms. 318 pp. (Stewardship Institute, Shelburne Farms, Shelburne, VT 05482.)

A classroom teacher's aid to environmental learning exercises for children in kindergarten through sixth grade in the Northeast.

Piton Foundation, with Frances Brody and John Weiser. 1993. Rev. ed. *Program-Related Investment Primer*. (See entry under Chapter 5.)

Reiss, Alvin H. *Don't Just Applaud—Send Money!* 1995. New York: Theatre Communications Group (TCG). 200 pp. (TCG, 355 Lexington Avenue, New York, NY 10017.)

Presents the most successful strategies for funding and marketing the arts, but useful for conservation organizations as well. Covers fund-raising events, outrageous promotions, business support, and the tourist trade.

Steckel, Richard, with Robin Simons and Peter Lengsfelder. 1989. *Filthy Rich and Other Nonprofit Fantasies: Changing the Way Nonprofits Do Business in the '90s.* Berkeley, Calif.: Ten Speed Press. 223 pp.

Irreverent, filled with ideas and examples, and fun to read, this book is a terrific handbook on entrepreneurial ventures and corporate partnerships. Includes a brief systematic approach to creating a vision and assessing the organization's assets and market, and an offer by the authors to critique the organization's plan in a worksheet provided at the back of the book.

Figure Credits

Title page: USDA photo, Jonathan Wright

Map of case study sites: Prepared by Omni Graphics from data supplied by the authors.

1.1 George F. Thompson

1.2 Economic Research Service, USDA. Source: Bureau of the Census.

1.3, 1.4 USDA—Natural Resources Conservation Service, Erwin W. Cole

1.5, 1.6 Samuel N. Stokes

1.7 Baldwin Productions, for the National Trust for Historic Preservation

1.8 Constance Beaumont

1.9 Historic Harrisville

1.10 Utah Power and Light Company

1.11 Historic American Engineering Record, Jack E. Boucher

1.12 George F. Thompson

1.13 Samuel N. Stokes and Land and Community Associates

1.14 U.S. Department of Agriculture, Natural Resources Conservation Service (NRCS), Tim McCabe

1.15 USDA, NRCS, Tim McCabe

1.16 USDA, NRCS, Austin A. Ledbetter

1.17 Shelley S. Mastran

1.18 Massachusetts Audubon Society, reprinted by permission

1.19 USDA, NRCS, Tim McCabe

1.20 USDA, NRCS, Merly B. Brunsvoid

1.21 USDA, NRCS

1.22 USDA, NRCS, Gene Alexander

1.23 USDA, NRCS, Erwin W. Cole

1.24 USDA, NRCS, Gene Alexander

1.25 Shelley S. Mastran

1.26 USDA, NRCS, Byron Schumaker

1.27 USDA, NRCS, Tim McCabe

1.28 USDA

1.29 Garrett E. Crow, *New England's Rare, Threatened, and Endangered Plants* (Washington, D.C.: U.S. Government Printing Office, 1982), p. 2

1.30 Smithsonian Institution, Alice Tangerini

1.31 Johnson, Nestor, Mortier and Rodriguez, Architects, P.C.; Victor Johnson, photographer

1.32 William H. Tishler

1.33 Samuel N. Stokes

1.34 USDA, NRCS

1.35 A. Elizabeth Watson

1.36 Jefferson Patterson Park and Museum, Robert K. Evans

1.37 American Folklife Center, Michael Crummett

1.38 Mary M. Humstone

1.39 George F. Thompson

1.40 USDA, NRCS, R. Neil Sampson

1.41 Copyright Catherine C. Harned

2.1 USDA, Fred White

2.2 American Folklife Center, Carl Fleischhauer

2.3, 2.4 Phoebe L. Hopkins

2.5 Courtesy of the Oley Valley Community Fair

2.6., 2.7 Phoebe L. Hopkins

2.8 William G. Moffat

2.9 Map reprinted from Constance K. Chamberlin, *Waterford: The Challenge* (Waterford, Va.: Waterford Foundation, 1980), p. 8.

2.10 Air Photographics, Inc.

2.11 Heritage Trail, Tom Jirsa

2.12 Frances S. Voliva

2.13 Page Crutcher, courtesy of The Conservation Fund

2.14 A. Elizabeth Watson

2.15 Max Liverman, courtesty of Pocosin Arts

2.16 Yakima River Greenway Foundation, Marc Smiley

2.17 Reprinted by permission from Land and Community Associates, *A Conservation Handbook for Amana Villages* (Charlottesville, Va.: Amana Heritage Society, Iowa Division of Historic Preservation, and LCA, 1978)

2.18 Michigan Department of Transportation and the Federal Highway Administration, *Final Supplement to the Final Environmental Impact Statement for I-69, Charlotte to Lansing, Eaton County,* August 11, 1983, p. 7.

2.19 E. Garrett Brinton

3.1 Mary M. Humstone

3.2 Samuel N. Stokes

3.3 Reprinted by permission from Eleanor C. Chard, ed., *Cazenovia: The Story of an Upland Community* (Cazenovia, N.Y.: Cazenovia Preservation Foundation, 1977), opp. p. 4

3.4, 3.5 Samuel N. Stokes

3.6 Cazenovia Community Resources Project and State University of New York at Syracuse. Adapted by Land and Community Associates.

3.7 U.S. Geological Survey

3.8 Land and Community Associates

3.9 Cazenovia Community Resources Project and State University of New York at Syracuse. Adapted by Land and Community Associates.

3.10 USDA, Soil Conservation Service, *Soil Survey of Madison County, New York* (Washington, D.C.: Government Printing Office, 1981), sheet 22

3.11 USDA, NRCS, Tim McCabe

3.12 USDA, Agricultural Stabilization and Conservation Service

3.13 Reprinted by permission from William M. Marsh, *Environmental Planning and Analysis: For Land Use and Site Planning* (New York: McGraw-Hill, 1978), p. 111

3.14 Stuart D. Klipper

3.15 Reprinted by permission from Frederick Steiner, *Ecological Planning for Farmland Preservation* (Chicago: American Planning Association, 1981), p. 42

3.16.A Teresa Lee Myers

3.16.B *The Rosebud News,* Rosebud, Texas

3.16.C Teresa Lee Myers

3.16.D David Moore

3.16.E–G Teresa Lee Myers

3.16.H David Moore

3.16.I–K Teresa Lee Myers

3.17 Land and Community Associates

3.18 American Folklife Center, Michael Crummett

3.19 Reprinted from Bureau of Land Management, *Visual Resource Management* (Washington, D.C.: U.S. Government Printing Office, 1980), p. 19

3.20 Courtesy of the *Cazenovia Republican*

3.21, 3.22 Cazenovia Community Resources Project and State University of New York at Syracuse. Adapted by Land and Community Associates

3.23 Land and Community Associates

3.24 Allen R. Lewis and Nicholas Colas

4.1 Brenda M. Manske

4.2 Windham Regional Planning and Development Commission and Town of Weston

4.3 USDA, NRCS, Doug Wilson

4.4 USDA, NRCS, Hilton D. Taylor

4.5–4.14 Randall Arendt, Natural Lands Trust. Reprinted by permission of Island Press.

4.15 George F. Thompson

4.16 Phil Grout

4.17 Joe Getty, Historical Society of Carroll County

4.18–4.23 Land and Community Associates and Samuel N. Stokes

4.24–4.51 Dan Marriott. (4.24–31, 4.34–35, 4.38–41, and 4.44–51 are based on drawings for the first edition by Land and Community Associates; 4.32 & .33 and 4.36 & .37 are adapted from the Historic District Design Guidelines of Birmingham Township, Chester County, Pennsylvania, p. A12706.)

4.52, 4.53 Mary Anna Okin

4.54, 4.55 Ed McMahon

4.56 Edgar T. Crisler, Jr.

4.57 Charles H. P. Duell

4.58 Samuel N. Stokes

5.1 Mary M. Humstone

5.2 Heritage Conservancy, Bucks County, Pennsylvania

5.3, 5.4 Samuel N. Stokes

5.5 Maryland Historical Trust, Michael Bourne

5.6 J. Timothy Keller

5.7 Robert Myhr

5.8 Copyright William Webb

5.9 Copyright Morley Baer

5.10, 5.11 Copyright William Webb

5.12 Martin Zeller

5.13 National Trust for Historic Preservation, *Preservation News,* November 1987, p. 19. Reprinted by permission of Preservation North Carolina.

6.1 Shelley S. Mastran
6.2 Gaines Jontz. Reprinted courtesy of the South Carolina Downtown Development Association
6.3, 6.4 National Trust for Historic Preservation Library Collection, University of Maryland at College Park
6.5–6.8 Shelley S. Mastran
6.9 National Storytelling Association
6.10 Sarah E. Polster
6.11 Copyright Simon Benepe
6.12 Matthew F. Smith
6.13 Shelley S. Mastran
6.14 Julian W. Adams, Historic Natchez Foundation
6.15 Shelley S. Mastran
6.16 Dana R. Vaillancourt
6.17, 6.18 Tennessee Overhill Experience
6.19 Copyright Jim McElholm, Single Source, Inc. Reprinted by permission.
6.20 Tennessee Overhill Experience
6.21 Edward Ranney, Canal Corridor Association
6.22 Tracks Across Wyoming
6.23 Mary M. Humstone
7.1 Michigan Department of Natural Resources
7.2, 7.3 *The Asheville Citizen*, Kathy Scruggs
7.4 Mike Towne
7.5 Mary M. Humstone
7.6, 7.7 Photograph by Steve Croy. Drawing by Tess Feltes. Reprinted from Garrett E. Crow, *New England's Rare, Threatened, and Endangered Plants* (Washington, D.C.: Government Printing Office, 1982), p. 7.
7.8 National Park Service
7.9 Reprinted from L. H. Everts, *The Official Atlas of Kansas, 1887*. Courtesy of the Kansas State Historical Society.

7.10 Historic American Buildings Survey, Bruce MacKnight
7.11 Copyright Joseph W. A. Whitehorne. Reprinted courtesy of The Conservation Fund.
7.12 Charles F. Floyd
7.13 Shelley S. Mastran
7.14 Rick Buettner, courtesy of the Northern Virginia Regional Park Authority
7.15–7.17 Gary Werner
7.18 Shelley S. Mastran
7.19, 7.20 USDA, NRCS, Tim McCabe
8.1 Yakima River Greenway Foundation
8.2 *Yakima Herald Republic*, Tim Toth
8.3 Reprinted by permission of the *Cazenovia Republican*
8.4 The Yadkin/Pee Dee Lakes Project
8.5 USDA, NRCS, Erwin W. Cole
8.6 Dorothy W. Riester
8.7 USDA, NRCS, Don R. Phillips
8.8 Historical Society of Carroll County
8.9, 8.10 Reprinted by permission from Stewardship Institute, *Project Seasons* (Shelburne, Vt.: Shelburne Farms, 1995).
8.11 Jerome M. Johnson
8.12 Drawing by Hanque Macaari, with the permission of William H. Tishler
8.13 Little Traverse Conservancy
8.14, 8.15 Courtesy of Historic Rugby
8.16 A. Elizabeth Watson
8.17 Waterford Foundation, Judy Patterson
8.18 Waterford Foundation, A. Rose
Conclusion: Samuel N. Stokes

Index

Boldface page numbers refer to definitions or principal entries.

International Countryside Stewardship Exchange, **331**, 393
Interns, 85, **92**, 360
Interpretation, 272–73; examples of, 84, 277, 297, 298. *See also* Education
Inventorying: community concerns, needs, and values, 7–8, 69–70; for easements, 226; and environmental review, 197–98; examples of, 63–65, 115–20, 140–41; for notification programs, 216; tourism resources, 269–70, 274. *See also* Mapping; Photography; *and Contents, Chapter 3*
Iowa, 7, 75–77, 86, 92–93, 260–62, 361
Irrigation, 23–25
ISTEA. See Intermodal Surface Transportation Efficiency Act
Izaak Walton League, 308, **393**

John Singleton Mosby Heritage Area, 291–92
Jonesborough, Tenn., 276–78
Junkyards, 49, 170

Kansas, 270
Katy Trail State Park, Mo., 274
Kent County, Mich., 337
Kentucky, 166, 187, 209, 309–10, 341, 344
Kinsley, Michael, 259
Kosciusko, Miss., 258

Lackawanna Valley Heritage Area (Pa.), 297
Lake Forest Open Lands Association (Ill.), 370
Land banking, 229
Land development codes, 176
Land Evaluation and Site Assessment (LESA), **156–57**, 186–87, 190
Landfills, **54–55**, 64, 67–68, 78, 208, 343
Landmarks. *See* National Historic Landmarks; National Natural Landmarks
Land ownership, inventorying, 152–54
Landsat photographs, 126
Landscapes. *See* Cultural landscapes; Scenic resources
Land Trust Alliance, 247, 303, 315, **393**
Land trusts, 214–15, 246–47; examples of, 171–73, 218–19, 221–24, 232, 242–46, 350; and nature centers, 366. *See also Contents, Chapter 5*

Land use: inventorying, 152–54; suitability analysis, 154–57, 187. *See also* Cultural landscapes; Growth management; Land use regulations; Zoning
Land use regulations: administration of, 212; for air pollution, 208; for communications towers, 208–9; combining zoning and subdivision controls, 176; as contrasted with voluntary techniques, 214–15, 224; drafting and tailoring, 211–12; for erosion and storm-water runoff, 176; flexible, 176–89; for floodplain management, 316; for forests, 208; for hazardous waste sites, 208; for mining, 208; for noise pollution, 208; for power lines, 208–9; to protect rivers, 209; for signs, 209; by states, 304–6; for water pollution, 209; for wildlife, 209. *See also* Design review; Subdivision regulations; Zoning
La Plata Open Space Conservancy (Colo.), 336
Large-lot zoning, **171**, 171–73; relationship to agricultural zoning, 173; and clustering, 184
Laudholm Trust (Me.), 318–19
LBJ Heartland (Tex.), 291, 297
Leadership, 87, **88–89**; and collaboration, 75; and tourism, 270; training, 344, 361, 393
Lease-purchase agreements, 234
Leases for conservation, 182, **221**, 243, 248, 322, 368; for preservation, 260, 261
Legislation, federal, 302–3. *See also specific federal laws and Contents, Chapter 7*
Legislation, state, 302–3; enabling, 160; takings, 20, 168
Leopold, Aldo, 386
LESA. *See* Land Evaluation and Site Assessment
LeVeque, Terry, 118–19, 148
Lexington, Ky., 166
Life estate, **235–36**, 245
Lighthawk (organization), 127, **393–94**
Limited development, 173, 232, **236–40**
Limited partnerships, 239
Lincoln Institute of Land Policy, 212, **394**
Lindsborg, Kans., 270
Litigation, 99–101, 121, 168–69; examples of, 98–99, 309–10
Little Traverse Conservancy (Mich.), 368

Living history programs, 364–66
Loans: from foundations, 238–39, 249; guarantees of, 232, 238; from local government, 249–51, 374; to property owners, 87, 201, 221, 288
Lobbying, 95, 101, **303–4**, 336
Loudoun County, Va., 12, 204, 206, 338–40, 376–78
Louisiana, 260

McCormick, S.C., 259–60
Mailing lists, using, 357–58
Maine, 305, 318–19
Main Street Program of the National Trust for Historic Preservation, **266**, 345
Main Street revitalization, 15, 48, 266, 267, 269, 345; appearance and design in, 263–64; basics of, 258–60; examples of, 201, 260–62, 276, 278; limitations to, 264; as social focus of the community, 262–63
Mammoth Cave RC&D (Ky.), 344
Management agreement, 221, 226, 228
Manassas National Battlefield Park (Va.), 328
Manteo, N.C., 152
Mapping, 122–24; base map for, 124; in Cazenovia, N.Y., 121; composite and synthesis, 155–57; by computer (*see* Geographic Information System); for a plan, 162; and resource analysis, 154–57; and subdivision regulations, 176; for tours, 272, 298; and zoning, 170. *See also* Inventorying; *Contents, Chapter 3*
Marin County, Calif., 171–73
Maryland, 187, 305, 315; Calvert County, 82, 249–51, 378; Carroll County, 183–86, 363; easements in, 227, 229–30; Forest Conservation Act of, 252; TDR in, 189
Maryland Agricultural Land Foundation, 185–86
Maryland Environmental Trust, 227, 252
Maryland Historical Trust, 227
Massachusetts, 17, 152, 209, 214, 294; Blackstone River Valley National Heritage Corridor, 56, 107, 291; housing in, 360; Nantucket, 199, 229; wetlands protection in, 316
Master plan. *See* Planning
Mediation, 101–2
Meetings of organizations, 78, 105

Library of Congress Cataloging-in-Publication Data

Stokes, Samuel N., 1940–
   Saving America's countryside : a guide to rural conservation / Samuel N.
Stokes, A. Elizabeth Watson, and Shelley S. Mastran : with contributions by
Genevieve P. Keller and J. Timothy Keller : for the National Trust for Historic Preservation. — 2nd ed.
     p.   cm.
Includes bibliographical references and index.
   ISBN 0-8018-5547-0 (alk. paper). — ISBN 0-8018-5548-9 (pbk. : alk.
paper)
   1. Historic sites—United States—Conservation and restoration. 2. Landscape protection—United States.   3. Conservation of natural resources—
United States.   4. United States—Rural conditions. I. Watson, A. Elizabeth.   II. Mastran, Shelley Smith.   III. National Trust for Historic Preservation in the United States.   IV. Title.
E159.S76   1997
363.6'9'0973—dc21   96-45398   CIP